Addressing Offending Behaviour

Addressing Offending Behaviour
Context, practice and values

Edited by

Simon Green, Elizabeth Lancaster and Simon Feasey

WILLAN
PUBLISHING

Published by

Willan Publishing
Culmcott House
Mill Street, Uffculme
Cullompton, Devon
EX15 3AT, UK
Tel: +44(0)1884 840337
Fax: +44(0)1884 840251
e-mail: info@willanpublishing.co.uk
website: www.willanpublishing.co.uk

Published simultaneously in the USA and Canada by

Willan Publishing
c/o ISBS, 920 NE 58th Ave, Suite 300,
Portland, Oregon 97213-3786, USA
Tel: +001(0)503 287 3093
Fax: +001(0)503 280 8832
e-mail: info@isbs.com
website: www.isbs.com

First published 2008

ISBN   978-1-84392-243-8 paperback
       978-1-84392-244-5 hardback

British Library Cataloguing-in-Publication Data

A catalogue record for this book is available from the British Library.

Project managed by Deer Park Productions, Tavistock, Devon
Typeset by GCS, Leighton Buzzard, Bedfordshire
Printed and bound by T.J. International Ltd, Padstow, Cornwall

Contents

Acknowledgements

The production of this book has been lengthy and sometimes difficult. This is the first time the three of us have attempted to put together an edited collection and with hindsight we probably didn't pick a particularly straightforward project to start with. The fact that it has now reached print is testament to the help, advice and understanding of a wide range of people. We would like to thank a few of them here.

Thanks go to Gerry Johnstone, Yvonne Jewkes and Paul Senior for their helpful commentary on the original book proposal and for their ongoing advice and support. It is also important to note that from the day we contacted Brian Willan with the idea for this text, he, and the rest of his team, have always been approachable, helpful and understanding. Our thanks must also go to Steve Cosgrove and Phil Clare at the Yorkshire and Humberside Probation Consortium who have been resolute in their support for this text and in their oversight of the Diploma in Probation Studies in our region. We would also like to thank all of the contributors to this text. We think this collection has turned out better than we could have ever hoped for and we have been privileged to work with you all.

At Hull thanks must also go to Peter Young for his cleverness and leadership (in that order) and to Helen Johnston for always listening (or pretending to) and always knowing what to say. Thanks also to Louise Sturgeon-Adams, Richard Barnes, Matthew Happold, Mike McCahill, Clive Norris, Anthea Hucklesby, Clive Coleman, Norman Davidson and Keith Bottomley for making Hull (past and present) an unpretentious, intellectually stimulating and most of all friendly place to work and study. At Bradford thanks go to all those involved in teaching on the Diploma in Probation Studies, particularly the teaching 'team' of Pauline Ashworth, Clare Beckett, Jeannie Lumb and Cheryl Shackleton. Adrian James (now of the University of Sheffield) deserves credit for bringing the DipPS to Bradford in the first place and in so doing changing the course of several people's professional lives. At Sheffield Hallam thanks are owed to friends and colleagues within the Criminology and Community Justice Subject Group (too numerous to mention by name!), co-conspirators who have contributed to the delivery of the Diploma in Probation Studies and members of the Hallam Centre for Community Justice.

And last, but by no means least, we would like to thank our families. The list of things for which we need to thank them would go on forever and would still not do them justice. So just thank you.

Simon Green, Elizabeth Lancaster and Simon Feasey

Notes on the contributors

Pauline Ashworth has recently taken up appointment as a teaching fellow in social work at the University of York. She previously taught criminal justice and social work at the University of Bradford, and still tutors in criminal justice for the Open University. She spent many years as a probation service officer and probation officer in court and field teams in a range of settings. She specialises in practice teaching and learning, offering training in communication skills and methods of intervention. A key interest is in the link between theories/methods and practice, and how the former can shape and enhance the latter.

Clare Beckett lectures in Social Policy at the University of Bradford. She is Programme Leader for the BA Honours Community Justice and for the MA Diversity and Social Policy. She is author of *Margaret Thatcher* (Haus Publishing, 2006) and joint author of *Bevan* (Haus Publishing, 2005). She has jointly edited *Negotiating Boundaries – Identities, Sexualities, Diversities* (Cambridge Scholars Press, 2007). Her current research interests interrogate the processes of supervision in a diverse world, focusing on probation supervision.

Julian Buchanan is Professor of Criminal and Community Justice at Glyndŵr University where he established the Social Inclusion Research Unit, and has over 25 years experience in the drugs field as a practitioner, lecturer and researcher. His research interests include problem drug use, drug policy and practice, social exclusion, criminal justice and marginalised people. He has published in a wide range of journals, is on the editorial board of the *Open Addiction Journal*, *Probation Journal* and *British Journal of Community Justice*, and is Specialist Assessor for the *International Journal of Drug Policy*.

Rob Canton is Professor in Community and Criminal Justice at De Montfort University, Leicester. He worked in the Probation Service for many years in a number of different practice and training roles. His particular research interests include mental disorder and offending, most aspects of probation, the ethics of penal practice and international exchanges of knowledge and practice. He has been extensively involved in recent years in work to help other countries to develop their practices in supervising offenders, especially Ukraine and Russia. He has also contributed to probation development in Turkey and Romania.

Bankole Cole is Lecturer in Criminology and Director of the Centre for Criminology and Criminal Justice at the University of Hull. His research areas include comparative policing and criminal justice, race and diversity issues in criminal justice, community engagement and accountability mechanisms in the local delivery of criminal justice. His most recent publication is *Globalisation, Citizenship and the War on Terror*, co-edited with M. Mullard (Edward Elgar, 2007).

Simon Feasey is Principal Lecturer in Criminal Justice at Sheffield Hallam University and Deputy Director of the Hallam Centre for Community Justice. Prior to embarking on an academic career Simon had worked for the Probation Service for a number of years, experiencing a broad range of roles, and in the 1990s was involved in the development of 'What Works' within probation practice. His current research interests are located within resettlement, community safety and prolific and priority offenders. He also delivers teaching and training to criminal justice practitioners and undergraduate and postgraduate students.

Anthony Goodman was a probation officer for 15 years before moving to Middlesex University where he trained probation officers when this was based in social work. His doctoral thesis was on the changing nature of probation practice and he has continued to research and write in this area. He has been an external examiner on a probation training degree programme for the past four years.

Hannah Goodman Chong is a research fellow with the Community and Criminal Justice Division of De Montfort University. She is interested in researching and writing about the needs of victims of crime. She has previously worked as a research fellow with the Centre for Social Action at De Montfort University, as a probation service officer for the resettlement team in Leicester and as project development worker for the Victims and Witnesses Action Group which was a priority group of the Leicester Crime and Disorder Reduction Partnership.

Simon Green is Lecturer in Criminology and Community Justice at the University of Hull. He is involved in the training of probation officers across Yorkshire and Humberside and has an interest in the relationship between social theory and evolving forms of community punishment. Other research interests include victims, restorative justice, community and sociological theory.

Yvonne Jewkes is Professor of Criminology at the University of Leicester. She has published many books on the media and crime, cybercrime and imprisonment including, most recently, *Prisons and Punishment 3-Volume Set* (Sage, 2008), *Handbook on Prisons* (Willan, 2007), *Crime Online* (Willan, 2007) and, with Jamie Bennett, *Dictionary of Prisons and Punishment* (Willan, 2008). She is co-editor of *Crime, Media, Culture: An International Journal*, and series editor of the Sage *Key Approaches to Criminology* series. Her current research interests include Internet access in prisons and the architecture of incarceration.

Elizabeth Lancaster studied trade union history for her PhD and worked as a welfare rights adviser, probation officer and Senior Lecturer in Social Work at the University of Bradford. As Director of the Diploma in Probation Studies she was involved in managing and teaching on the Diploma until 2005. She has published articles on working with the perpetrators of sexual crime and on values in the criminal justice system. Although no longer working in academia full time, she tutors for the Open University.

Amanda Loumansky is a senior lecturer in the Business School at Middlesex University where she teaches Child Law and the English Legal System. Amanda has published in the field of ethics and has recently completed research in the United States on behalf of the British Academy.

Trish McCulloch is a lecturer in Social Work at the University of Dundee. Prior to becoming an academic in 2003, Trish worked as a social worker in youth and adult justice settings. Research interests and publications have addressed various aspects of criminal justice including the social context of offending and desistance and the role of community in responding to crime.

Fergus McNeill is Deputy Head (Research) in the Glasgow School of Social Work, and a Network Leader in the Scottish Centre for Crime and Justice Research at the University of Glasgow. He previously worked in residential drug rehabilitation and as a criminal justice social worker. His research interests and publications have addressed sentencing, community penalties and youth justice. Latterly his work has focused on the policy and practice implications of research evidence about the process of desistance from offending. His first book, *Reducing Reoffending: Social Work and Community Justice in Scotland* (co-authored with Bill Whyte), was published by Willan in 2007.

Iolo Madoc-Jones is subject leader in the Social Care subject area at Glyndŵr University. He practised as a probation officer and senior probation officer for 15 years before joining the University of Wales and currently teaches on the BA social work and BA therapeutic childcare programmes, specialising in theory and practice-related issues. He is presently completing his PhD which focuses on the experiences of linguistic minorities in the criminal justice system in the UK. He has published widely on the issues of justice and language in journals such as *The British Journal of Social Work*, *The Howard Journal* and *Children and Family Social Work*.

Mike Nash is Reader in Criminology and Head of Department at the Institute of Criminal Justice Studies, University of Portsmouth. He has written extensively on public protection and criminal justice policy. He works closely with a range of local and national public protection agencies. His latest book (with Andy Williams) entitled the *Anatomy of Serious Further Offending* was published by Oxford University Press in 2008.

Dave Phillips is a senior lecturer and course leader for the BA (Hons) Community Justice (Probation Studies) at Sheffield Hallam University. He has 20 years' experience working as a probation officer, specialising in work with high-risk offenders. This is an area that he has investigated further in his current role. He is particularly concerned with developing training for offender managers who deal increasingly with risk assessment and management.

Alyson Rees currently teaches on the MA in Social Work at Cardiff University. She was a probation officer for 17 years and has run many groups for offenders, and more latterly has worked for the NSPCC in a domestic violence unit, running groups for the perpetrators of domestic violence. Alyson's current research interests are around domestic violence, fostering and child neglect.

Mark Rivett is Senior Lecturer in the School for Policy Studies, Bristol University and a family therapist in South Wales. He is a qualified social worker and family therapist and is current editor of the *Journal for Family Therapy*. Most recently he managed an NSPCC domestic violence project in Cardiff which worked with abusive men, their partners and also children who had witnessed domestic violence. His publications cover therapeutic approaches to work with abusive men and to children who witness domestic violence. He has also published books on family therapy and working with men.

Mark Sambrook is a probation officer who has worked for Humberside Probation Trust in a variety of roles since 1990. Currently he is a facilitator, treatment manager and regional trainer for the Integrated Domestic Abuse Programme. This role involves working within two long-standing areas of interest. Specifically, these are enabling and supporting staff to develop as reflective and critical thinkers and practitioners, and working with men who have offended, concentrating on issues of belief systems and masculinity.

Paul Senior is Director of the Hallam Centre for Community Justice at Sheffield Hallam University and Visiting Professor at the University of Wales, NEWI. Paul has a professional background in probation and has been involved in professional education, consultancy and research for 25 years. Between 1995 and 2001 he also worked as an organisational development consultant working on projects with the Home Office, the Community Justice National Training Organisation, CCETSW and other national organisations. He has published widely on resettlement, probation practice and criminal justice policy-making. His latest publication is *Understanding Modernisation in Criminal Justice* (Open University Press, 2007) with Chris Crowther-Dowey and Matt Long.

Anna Souhami is Lecturer in Criminology at the School of Law, Edinburgh University. Her main research interests lie in the sociology of criminal justice professions and policy. Her current research explores the emergent system for the governance of youth crime in England and Wales. Her previous research in youth justice examined the radical restructuring of youth justice services in England and Wales under the Crime and Disorder Act 1998 and its effects on youth justice professionals' sense of occupational identity and culture. She is the author of *Transforming Youth Justice: Occupational Identity and Cultural Change* (Willan, 2007).

Louise Sturgeon-Adams is Lecturer in Community Justice at the Centre for Criminology and Criminal Justice, University of Hull. She is qualified as a probation officer and has worked as a counsellor for people with drug and alcohol problems. She is experienced in a range of qualitative research methodologies and is currently undertaking research into the culture of cannabis cultivation. She has a developing interest in the ways in which practitioners within the criminal justice system manage the competing demands of various aspects of working with offenders.

Chris Tallant is a senior probation officer for Humberside Probation Trust and is currently involved in the training and development of trainee probation officers and probation services officers. Through his work as a probation officer, practice teacher and practice development assessor he has maintained a long-term interest in the connections between theory and practice and the importance of staff developing as good reflective practitioners. His ongoing interests include the management of offenders and the impact of diversity in the workplace.

Martin Wasik is Professor of Criminal Justice at Keele University. From 1999 to 2007 he was chairman of the Sentencing Advisory Panel, for which work he was appointed CBE in 2008. Martin also sits part-time as a Crown Court judge, practising on the Midland Circuit.

Brian Williams was Professor of Community Justice and Victimology at De Montfort University in Leicester. His main research interests were services for victims of crime, restorative justice, community justice and criminological research ethics. He previously worked at Keele, Sheffield and Teeside universities, and as a probation officer. He was an Executive Committee member of the British Society of Criminology and chair of its Professional and Ethics Committees. His most recent book was *Victims of Crime and Community Justice* (Jessica Kingsley, 2005). Brian died in a motor accident in March 2007.

List of abbreviations

ACE	Assessment, Case management and Evaluation
ACMD	Advisory Council on the Misuse of Drugs
ACOP	Association of Chief Officers of Probation
ASPIRE	Assess, Sentence Plan, Implement, Review, Evaluate
ASRO	addressing substance-related offending
AUR	automatic unconditional release
BASW	British Association of Social Workers
BME	black and minority ethnic
CAFCASS	Children and Family Court Advisory Support Service
CALM	controlling anger and learning to manage it
CBT	cognitive-behavioural therapy
CCA	common client assessment tool
CDRP	Crime and Disorder Reduction Partnership
CDVP	community domestic violence programme
CHI	Commission for Health Improvement
CJA	Criminal Justice Act
CJSW	Criminal Justice Social Work [Development Centre]
CNI	Criminogenic Needs Inventory (New Zealand)
CPO	chief probation officer/community punishment order
CPRO	community punishment and rehabilitation order
CRO	community rehabilitation order
CSA	Child Support Agency
CSAP	Correctional Services Accreditation Panel
C-SOGP	community – sex offender group programme
CSP	community safety partnership
DAIP	Domestic Abuse Intervention Program (Duluth, USA)
DID	drink impaired driver
DIP	Drugs Intervention Programme
DoH	Department of Health
DSPD	dangerous and severe personality disorder
DTTO	drug treatment and testing order
EM	electronic monitoring
ETE	education, training and employment,
HDC	home detention curfew
HMIP	Her Majesty's Inspectorate of Probation

IDAP	Integrated Domestic Abuse Programme
IDVA	independent domestic violence advocate
IPP	imprisonment for public protection
JPPAP	Joint Prisons and Probation Accreditation Panel
JRF	Joseph Rowntree Foundation
LEDS	Life Events and Difficulties Schedule
LSI-R	Level of Service Inventory – Revised
MaCRN	Maori Culture Related Needs Assessment (New Zealand)
MAPPA	multi-agency public protection arrangements
MAPPP	multi-agency public protection panel
MARAC	Multi-Agency Risk Assessment Conference
MI	motivational interviewing
MSC	Multicultural Counselling Competences
MUD	moral underclass discourse
NAPO	National Association of Probation Officers
NOMIS	National Offender Management Information System
NOMS	National Offender Management System
NPM	New Public Management
NPS	National Probation Service
N-SOGP	Northumbria – sex offender group programme
OASys	Offender Assessment System
OGRS	Offender Group Reconviction Score
OMIC	Offender Management Inspection Criteria
OMM	Offender Management Model
OSAP	offender substance abuse programme
PCEP (YJ)	Professional Certificate in Effective Practice (Youth Justice)
PI	programme identity
PPO	prolific and other priority offender scheme
PRISM	personal reduction in substance misuse
PSA	public service agreement
PSM	pro-social modelling
PSR	pre-sentence report
R&R	Reasoning and Rehabilitation
RAPt	Rehabilitation for Addicted Prisoners Trust
RED	redistributionist discourse
RoH	risk of harm
SDVC	Specialist Domestic Violence Court
SEU	Social Exclusion Unit
SGC	Sentencing Guidelines Council
SID	social integrationist discourse
SIR	Statistical Information on Recidivism
SMART	specific, measurable, achievable, relevant, timed
SMARTA	specific, measurable, achievable, relevant, time-bound, anti-discriminatory
SLOP	Statement of Local Objectives and Priorities
SNOP	Statement of National Objectives and Priorities
SOO	sex offender order

SPJ	structured professional judgment
STOP	Straight Thinking on Probation
TFBAO	Think First Black and Asian Offender Programme
TI	treatment integrity
TV-SOGP	Thames Valley – sex offender group programme
WSU	women's safety unit
VAC	voluntary after-care
VCS	voluntary and community sector
VLO	victim liaison officer
YJB	Youth Justice Board
YJCEA	Youth Justice and Criminal Evidence Act 1999
YOI	young offender institution
YOT	youth offending team

Introduction

Simon Green, Elizabeth Lancaster and Simon Feasey

Our primary motivation for editing a collection of this sort was to begin redressing what we saw as a serious deficit in the literature. Emerging from our collective experience of working with offenders and training criminal justice practitioners we have often been frustrated by the lack of coherent literature which brings together theoretical and practical debates about how work with offenders is carried out. This text aims to bridge this gap, combining wider theoretical and contextual debates with more practice-orientated concerns. Our objective is that this book should become a critical reference text for practitioners, researchers and academics interested in addressing offending behaviour.

Further, in contrast to many other texts, this book is not specifically about 'probation work' but about 'work with offenders', and consequently draws on generic issues of practice that are applicable to both the voluntary and community sectors as well as the statutory. In a climate of increasing cooperation between academic teaching and criminal justice training (for example, the establishment of the 'Skills for Justice' organisation) this text aims to become essential reading for a new generation of more skills-based, employment-orientated undergraduate programmes and for those training and working in the criminal justice sector.

The motivations for embarking on this project are twofold: one, to share the combined experience of those of us teaching and working in this field; and two, to inject a more critical appreciation of current policy and practice into the criminal justice training arena. This book is designed to provide an up-to-date discussion of the types of work that are typically undertaken with offenders. While there are many good texts about probation or probation-related issues on the market they tend to be about specific areas of interest such as the 'What Works' debate or the findings from a particular study. This text is substantially different from these as it is concerned with providing the first account in some time of the different ways in which offenders are helped to change their behaviour.

This text focuses on bridging academic and practitioner concerns and integrates theory within a discussion of offender management. Therefore the bulk of the chapters (particularly in Part 2) discuss the actual forms of work undertaken, the skills required and the types of assessment tools and intervention strategies used. This is matched by a consideration of the theoretical and conceptual underpinnings of practice along with its limitations and possible dangers. Hence this book is distinguished from others in two ways: firstly, through a clear focus on the actual practice of working with offenders; and secondly, through a very real attempt to span both intellectual and practical considerations. This will broaden the appeal of the text making it relevant to academics, students, researchers, practitioners and trainee practitioners interested in addressing offending behaviour. With this broad base in mind we offer a text that provides a synthesis of academic and practitioner concerns.

All contributors have considered, where possible, the following themes:

- the current legislative framework and policy debate;
- the relevant skills and techniques employed by practitioners when working with offenders;
- the broader theoretical and conceptual issues that provide an understanding of how and why certain interventions are used with offenders;
- a critical consideration of the limitations and potential dangers of current practice;
- some discussion questions or topics that can be used by students, trainees and practitioners to consider the critical issues;
- selected further reading at the end of each chapter.

We hope this meshing of themes has provided a hybrid study that details both the practical and intellectual issues in working with offenders.

Contributors have been drawn from those in academic posts who have direct experience of working with offenders or strong research and/or teaching portfolios in the particular area of their chapter. Part 2 also includes senior practitioners, some with an established track record of publishing. While some of these will be less well known in academic circles they will be recognised names within practitioner circles.

The book is split into three sections with the second section containing the majority of the chapters. Part 1 provides a contextual framework for working with offenders, Part 2 the key skills and interventions and Part 3 looks at the treatment of minority and vulnerable offender populations.

The first part of the book discusses the context for working with offenders. Wasik details the changing legal framework for working with offenders, Nash notes the broad policy context, the 'managerialist'initiatives which shape criminal justice policy being in evidence across most of the public sector, while Goodman considers the 'What Works' agendaand its impact on practice. Jewkes concludes this part by offering an analysis of the social construction offenders which informs both the legal framework and the broad policies which structure day-to-day practice with offenders.

We have divided the middle section of the volume into two parts, the first dealing with generic issues, the second looking at specialised areas of working with offenders. Generic issues cover both individual practice considerations and the broader themes/influences on practice. Individual practice considerations include Tallant, Sambrook and Green's exploration of different types of engagement skills, highlighting a tension between managing offender needs and managing organisational needs. Ashworth explores an often overlooked element of practice, the written word, and considers the skills required to produce accurate, relevant, useful and understandable records, suggesting that these skills are often downplayed, paradoxically, given the reliance on written forms of communication throughout the whole criminal justice system. Sturgeon-Adams offers guidance for practitioners in how to evaluate their own practice. Evaluation is not something to be left to 'the academics' but is an intrinsic part of effective practice and she approaches the subject from a perspective of practitioner empowerment. Madoc-Jones challenges the current cognitive-behavioural orthodoxy by applying different models of intervention to a recurring case example, discussing how a model of intervention might be applied differently depending on the theoretical lens through which it is viewed.

The broader themes and influences on practice incorporate Loumansky, Goodman and Feasey's consideration of the impact of the enforcement culture on practice and the move away from practitioner discretion, with practitioners becoming more risk averse in the process. Phillips' discussion of practice in a risk-based penology calls for a shift in emphasis from the instrument of assessment to the process of assessment, and a rebalancing of the system towards a consideration of individual desistance factors and a return to proportionality and rigorous cooperation between agencies. The importance of individual desistance factors is echoed by McCulloch and McNeill who note that desistance literature, which pursues a broader agenda than that provided by the 'what works' literature, has as yet had little impact on policy and practice, arguing that interventions should pay greater heed to the community, social and personal context in which offenders live and change.

Cooperation between agencies is the core of Souhami's chapter in which she explores multi-agency and inter-agency working in the youth justice sector before drawing conclusions for the whole criminal justice sector, suggesting that as multi-agency working becomes more deeply embedded it risks eroding the diversity at its core.

The second part of the middle section focuses on specialist areas of practice though much of what is written here has relevance in the generic context also. A trio of chapters – on dangerous offenders, substance misuse and mentally disordered offenders – discuss interweaving themes. Nash describes dangerous offenders as the issue that has driven the criminal justice agenda for a decade or more, illustrating how the perception of and response to dangerousness 'has had significant knock-on effects in the criminal justice system for other less serious and more common offenders' and suggesting that 'defensible' decision-making is giving way to 'defensive' decision-making and catching some offenders in an 'upwardly punitive spiral'. This theme is continued by Canton who considers policy to be distorted by an overemphasis on the risk posed by mentally disturbed people. He suggests there needs to be an appreciation of social influences on mental distress, a theme mirrored by Buchanan who concludes there is little chance of reintegration of those who have problems with substance misuse without looking at deep-seated underlying psychosocial and structural problems. This has some resonance with Senior's view that successful resettlement following prison requires needs-based support. Lack of staff skills, lack of coordination and communication between agencies together with a focus on the most risky lead to the most needy being overlooked.

Two chapters consider group work – the first looks at accredited programmes generally and the second at groups as the vehicle for intervention with domestic violence perpetrators. Feasey revisits the importance of process issues in undertaking group work noting that the experience of being in an accredited programme is dynamic and driven by interactions between group members. Rivett and Rees explore the context of work with victims and perpetrators of domestic violence and the predominant approaches, observing that a consensus has developed around intervention with such offenders though the evidence of effectiveness is still uncertain.

Williams and Goodman Chong review the current legislative and policy framework in respect of victims, and the skills and techniques required by practitioners picking up on the worrying theme that consideration of the needs of offenders is seen to be at the expense of the needs of victims.

Contributors in the final part all express some dissatisfaction with the values base of the criminal justice system. Lancaster notes the similarity in the values statements of key organisations in the criminal justice system, particularly in the need to 'respect' service users. She argues that values discussions take place at different conceptual levels and that there should be a recognition of these different levels in order to foster a holistic approach to 'values talk' in the criminal justice system. Beckett and Cole respectively acknowledge the theoretical debates and the attempts to incorporate gender and minority ethnic awareness into policy and practice. Both conclude that much remains to be done. Beckett suggests that the criminal justice system still uses traditional reactions to work differentially with women and that current models of offender management employ a generic 'gender blind' approach. Cole argues that while significant changes are taking place in the criminal justice system in order to address ethnic diversity, criminal justice interventions are not yet responding adequately to 'race' issues, suggesting that a starting point should be the recognition of racism as a criminogenic risk factor. Green concludes this section, and the volume, by writing about the most overlooked category of offenders – 'poor people' – who also form the majority. He argues that the welfare and redistribution values which recognised poverty, and hence 'poor people', have been replaced by a new set of moral values about personal and civic responsibility, in which poverty as an issue is lost. He proposes the extension into the community of the incentives and earned privileges scheme of the prison setting and suggests that this would fit well with other community justice initiatives.

As editors, we had a view of what the book would look like as a whole, and proposed areas of discussion and synopses of each chapter for our contributors. Each contributor, of course, has added their personal emphasis and developed their chapters in particular ways, but out of this individuality a certain commonality has emerged. Thus a number of contributors have argued for the need to be mindful of the social influences when addressing offending; others have developed arguments around diversity and difference with a caution about the 'one size fits all' approach to intervention and offender management; a third strand suggests caution about the evidence base of accepted methods of intervention. These common areas of discussion have helped give the book a cohesion for which the editors are hugely grateful.

Finally, it is our solemn duty to record the untimely death of two of our contributors. John Whitfield died in the early stages of preparing this book and the chapter on multi-agency working was consequently undertaken by Anna Souhami. Brian Williams died as we were preparing the text for publication. His co-author, Hannah Goodman Chong, has chosen not to amend the sections of the chapter prepared by Brian and we have consequently included these in their unrevised form. Condolences are sincerely offered to all those affected by these deaths.

Part I

Context

Chapter 1

The legal framework

Martin Wasik

A brief history

The origins of dealing with offenders in the community in an attempt to assist in their rehabilitation goes back to the latter part of the nineteenth century, when voluntary societies appointed police court missionaries to help with the reformation of drunkards and others who appeared before the inner-city courts. The Probation of Offenders Act 1907 put this practice on a statutory footing, and enabled courts to make probation orders in a manner quite similar to that which existed until the end of the twentieth century. Probation was regarded as a form of diversion from the criminal courts. It was imposed 'instead of sentencing', and required the offender's consent. The probation order was for many years effectively the only community sentence available to the courts. It gradually became more flexible in content, offering a range of requirements tailored to the needs of the offender which could be written into the order by the court. Local probation services began to offer attendance at 'day centres', accommodation at a probation hostel or various activities and programmes which could be described to the court in a social inquiry report and be made part of the order to be served. Treatment for a mental condition could be ordered as part of a 'psychiatric probation order'. Attendance centres for young offenders were created by statute in 1948, but the community service order was the next major change, introduced as an experiment in 1972 and made generally available in 1975 (Advisory Council on the Penal System 1970).

Community service, another order to which the offender had to consent, involved the performance of between 40 and 240 hours' work (as specified by the court) in the community. The order was overseen and managed by the probation service, but work on site was carried out alongside community volunteers. Community service rapidly gained general acceptance, perhaps because it had elements to appeal to all penal perspectives. It was punitive, requiring the offender to perform physical tasks for the benefit of the community. It was rehabilitative, with the prospect (at least) that the positive values of the volunteers might rub off on the offender. Community service was also the first tangible move in the sentencing system towards reparation, but indirectly through repayment to the community rather than directly to the victim of the offence. A limited mix of probation and community service was also developed, known as a combination order. At this time community-based disposals were usually referred to as 'intermediate sanctions' or 'alternatives to custody', but it was never clear whether community service was an alternative to custody, an alternative to probation or a little of both. Was it part of, or distinct from, the sentencing tariff occupied by discharges, fines and custody? Should a smaller number of hours of community service be equivalent to other non-custodial penalties and a larger number of hours be seen as alternatives to custody? If so, what was the 'conversion scale' between numbers of hours of community service and weeks or months in prison? The development of community service stirred an important debate over the rationale of community sentences generally (Pease 1978; Ashworth 1983: 385–407). The debate was overtaken by wider legislative change.

The Criminal Justice Act 1991

The Criminal Justice Act 1991, based on a 1990 White Paper (Home Office 1990), for the first time set out in statute a general sentencing framework (Wasik and Taylor 1994; Easton and Piper 2005). Central to the Act was the principle of proportionality – that each upward move in the scale of available sentences, from discharge, to fine, through community sentence to custody, had to be justified on the basis of the seriousness of the offence. The Act declared that an offence always had to be 'serious enough' to justify a community sentence, or be 'so serious' that only custody could be justified. It was based on proportionality (or 'desert') principles, but it allowed the courts to incapacitate high-risk violent and sexual offenders by the introduction of 'longer-than-commensurate' and 'extended' prison sentences. Community sentences were significantly reworked in the Act, with a rejection of the 'alternatives to custody' model. They were now, instead, to be regarded as restrictions on liberty, capable of being graded in terms of their relative severity (Wasik and von Hirsch 1988). This change reflected the decline in the rehabilitative model, which had held sway in the middle decades of the twentieth century, and the resurgence of 'desert' which had begun in the United States in the 1970s and was becoming influential worldwide (von Hirsch 1976). This did not mean that rehabilitative efforts in community sentences were to be abandoned – it meant that the duration of the order and the requirements it imposed on the offender must be kept in proportion with the seriousness of the crime(s) committed. The rhetoric of desert also chimed well with policy-makers, who wanted to see a fall in the prison population but were faced with resistance from sentencers and the public over community measures which were seen as 'soft'. It was thought that rebranding these measures as restrictions on liberty might help to convert some of the doubters, but more recent surveys show that the problems endure (Coulsfield 2004; Linklater 2004). After the 1991 Act there was now no question that community service fitted within the sentencing tariff and was to be regarded as a form of punishment. Probation also became, for the first time, a sentence in its own right. The Act also introduced the curfew order, which could be enforced by electronic tagging. The curfew was the first community sentence designed to be punitive and restrictive of liberty, with no rehabilitative pretensions at all.

Some of the intended effects of the 1991 Act were watered down in the Criminal Justice Act 1993, but these reverses did not affect community sentences. A White Paper published in 1995, however, returned to the theme that community penalties were insufficiently tough, the public and sentencers lacked confidence in them and they were not enforced rigorously enough (Home Office 1995). The Crime (Sentences) Act 1997 abolished the requirement that the offender must consent to probation and to community service. As the technology became more reliable there was an exponential growth in the use of electronic tagging to enforce not just curfew orders (Nellis 2004), but to monitor bail conditions and home detention curfew on early release from custody (Dodgeson *et al.* 2001). Tagging could now be combined with other elements in a community sentence. The drug treatment and testing order (DTTO) was introduced in 1998. This innovative community sentence could be imposed for a period of between six months and three years, with offenders required to undergo treatment for drug dependency and to submit themselves for testing at regular intervals (Turnbull *et al.* 2000; Hough *et al.* 2003). The Court of Appeal issued guidance on the proper use of the DTTO in *Attorney-General's Reference (No. 64 of 2003)* [2004] 2 Cr App R (S) 105. It stated that judges should pass sentences which had a realistic prospect of reducing drug addiction whenever it was possible sensibly to do so, but clear evidence was necessary that the offender was determined to free himself from drugs. A DTTO would be more likely to be imposed in the case of an acquisitive offence carried out to obtain money for drugs and could be appropriate even where the offender had a bad offending record, but a DTTO would rarely be suitable for serious offences involving violence or threats of violence with a weapon. The DTTO had the further element that the sentencer imposing the order could oversee its management, requiring the offender to return monthly to court for progress reviews (McKittrick and Rex 2003; Robinson and Dignan 2004). In 2000 the names of several of the community sentences were changed in a further attempt to make them sound more rigorous. 'Community service' became 'community punishment' and 'probation' became 'community rehabilitation', a change criticised as unnecessary and confusing (Faulkner 2001).

From the 1990s onwards sentencing became an ever more volatile and politicised area of public policy (Wasik 2004). 'Populist punitiveness' over sentencing was, and still is, fuelled by the media and by politicians (Bottoms 1995), but research demonstrates consistently that when members of the public are properly informed of the facts of a case and educated as to the sentencing alternatives available, they will propose a sentence comparable to, or more lenient than, the sentence which would be selected by a criminal court (see Hough and Roberts 2002; Halliday 2001: App. 5). The traditional discretion of the courts in sentencing matters was coming under pressure from Parliament. The White Paper in 1990 declared that 'sentencing principles and sentencing practice were matters of legitimate concern to the government' (Home Office 1990). While it was generally accepted that it was for Parliament to set the agenda in penal policy, but for judges and magistrates to make individual sentencing decisions, there was disagreement over the 'middle ground' in sentencing. General principles of sentencing, aggravating and mitigating factors, guidelines and starting points had all been gradually developed over the latter decades of the twentieth century by the Court of Appeal, with little or no intervention from government. That all changed in the 1991 Act with the new legislative framework. There was much opposition to the Act from judges and magistrates, with the Lord Chief Justice of the day describing it as a 'straitjacket' on judicial decision-making, and insisting that what was needed instead of legislative restrictions was 'the widest range of possible measures, and the broadest discretion to deploy them' (Taylor 1993). Parliament pressed on, however, bolting onto the sentencing framework various special rules such as minimum sentences in the Crime (Sentences) Act 1997 for domestic burglary, drug trafficking and (in the Criminal Justice Act 2003 and the Violent Crime Reduction Act 2006) firearms offences. The Court of Appeal responded by reinstating flexibility wherever it could (see *Cunningham* (1993) 14 Cr App R (S) 444 on the general provisions of the 1991 Act), and by emphasising judicial discretion to avoid legislative prescription where 'exceptional circumstances' existed (see *McInerney* [2003] 2 Cr App R (S) 240 on the three-strikes rule for domestic burglary and *Offen* (No. 2) [2001] Cr App R (S) 44 on automatic life sentence provisions, repealed by the 2003 Act).

The Criminal Justice Act 2003

The Criminal Justice Act 2003 (CJA 2003) is now the key statute, certainly as far as offenders aged 18 and over are concerned (Ashworth 2005: ch. 10; Taylor, Wasik and Leng 2004: ch. 12) The Act was, in the main, the product of the Halliday Review (Halliday 2001), as subsequently endorsed by the government (Home Office 2002). The Act recasts community provisions once again. Replacing the earlier range of community sentences, there is now a single community order, within which one or more of 12 possible requirements may be specified by the court. These requirements, with some minor differences, reflect the former community sentences, but the terminology has changed again, so that (for example) 'community service', which became 'community punishment' in 2000, is now a 'community order with an unpaid work requirement'. Halliday's criticism of the old community sentences was that they had grown up piecemeal, and should be simplified and made more understandable to the community, sentencers and offenders (Halliday 2001: para. 6.2, though see Rex 2002). The new order is used for offenders aged 18 and over in the Crown Court and in magistrates' courts for offences committed on or after 4 April 2005 (the relevant commencement date). A different community sentencing regime, with a range of different orders, continues for young offenders under 16. A third scheme exists for 16- and 17-year-old offenders, who have not been brought within the 2003 Act provisions and still fall to be dealt with under the old community sentences. Initially this situation was for an interim period only (until April 2007), but it has now been extended by Parliament until April 2009 (SI 2007/391).

The new scheme adopts the 1991 Act criteria in providing that a court must not pass a community order on an offender unless it is of the opinion that the offence (or combination of the offence and one or more offences associated with it) was serious enough to warrant such a sentence (CJA 2003, s.148(1)). This is the 'community sentence threshold' of offence seriousness, below which a different option, such as a fine or a conditional discharge, should be used. Just because an offence is 'serious enough' to justify a community order does not mean that such a sentence is inevitable. If appropriate, a fine or conditional discharge can still be used instead. The Criminal Justice and Immigration Act 2008 made the community order unavailable for offences which do not carry imprisonment as a penalty, a change designed to restrict the availability of more intensive (and expensive) community measures on serious offences (Home Office 2006b).The phrase 'associated with' in s.148(1) means that the court must weigh up any other offences for which the offender is being sentenced at the same time, and any further offences which the offender admits and has asked the court to take into consideration. If the offence is 'so serious that neither a fine alone nor a community sentence can be justified' then a custodial sentence will normally be imposed (CJA 2003, s.152(2)). This is the 'custodial sentence threshold'. It is clear from the statute (CJA 2003, s.166(2)) and from case-law (*Cox* [1993] 1 WLR 188), however, that even if an offence crosses the custody threshold, mitigating features relating to the offender, together with a timely guilty plea (see SGC 2007) can mean that the sentencer may suspend the period in custody or impose a community order instead.

Community Order Requirements

Every community order under the 2003 Act contains a general duty on the offender to keep in touch with the responsible officer (who will be a probation officer if the offender is aged 18 or over) and must notify that officer of any change of address. A community order may contain one or more of 12 requirements. These are now set out in turn, together with some key features of each requirement. These descriptions are drawn from the Probation Bench Handbook (National Offender Management Service 2007), an excellent authoritative source of information for sentencers. The Handbook should be consulted for full details of the requirements and for further information. The effectiveness of these various requirements is considered in depth in other chapters in this book but see also Harper and Chitty (2005) for a thorough review of a number of specific programmes.

(i) *Unpaid work requirement*

- Main purposes: punishment, reparation and rehabilitation.
- Expressed in hours between 40 and 300.
- The court must be satisfied that the offender is suitable to perform work.
- The requirement must be completed within one year.
- A small amount of basic skills learning can be incorporated within the requirement, to take place while carrying out the work.
- If a significant amount of skills learning is necessary, an activity requirement might be included in the order as well.

(ii) *Activity requirement*

- Main purposes: rehabilitation and reparation.
- Expressed in days but details of the actual period and content of each attendance will be given in the order.
- The requirement involves the offender attending a specified place, such as a community rehabilitation centre, to take part in activities such as debt counselling or financial management; employment, training and education; mediation; mentoring.

(iii) *Programme requirement*

- Main purpose: rehabilitation.
- Normally expressed in terms of the number of sessions (e.g. two sessions of three hours a week for 11 weeks).
- Cannot be included in an order unless recommended in a pre-sentence report (PSR).
- A programme requirement will normally be combined with a supervision requirement to provide additional support.
- The programme must be accredited by the Correctional Services Accreditation Panel (CSAP).
- Exceptionally, multiple programme requirements can be made by inserting a separate requirement for each programme into the order, e.g. a general offending behaviour programme, followed by an offence-specific programme.
- Programmes fall into five categories – general offending, violent offending, sex offending, substance misuse and domestic violence.

- The National Probation Service currently offers the following programmes, though not all programmes are available in all areas of the
  country:
  1 enhanced thinking skills
  2 think first
  3 one to one
  4 the women's programme
  5 aggression replacement training
  6 controlling anger and learning to manage it (CALM)
  7 community – sex offender group-work programme (C-SOGP)
  8 Thames Valley – sex offender group-work programme (TV-SOGP)
  9 Northumbria – sex offender group programme (N-SOGP)
  10 drink impaired drivers (DIDs)
  11 addressing substance-related offending (ASRO)
  12 offender substance abuse programme (OSAP)
  13 personal reduction in substance misuse (PRISM)
  14 community domestic violence programme (CDVP)
  15 integrated domestic abuse programme (IDAP)
  16 internet sex offender programme.

(iv) *Prohibited activity requirement*

- Main purposes: punishment and protection.
- Expressed as refraining from a specified activity on a day or days, or
  during a period for up to 36 months.
- The court must consult the probation service before making the
  requirement.
- A prohibited activity requirement might be used in relation to drink-
  related offending linked to pubs in general; prohibition from association
  with named individual(s); stalking or sex offending – prohibition from
  approaching or communicating with victim and/or family members
  without prior approval; sex offender – prohibition from taking work or any
  other organised activity which will involve a person under the relevant
  age; sex offender – prohibition from approaching or communicating with
  any child under the relevant age without prior approval; sex offender –
  prohibition from residing or staying in the same household as any child
  under the relevant age.
- Where appropriate a prohibited activity can be used with a supervision
  requirement to support and reinforce desired changes in behaviour.

(v) *Curfew requirement*

- Main purposes: punishment and protection.
- Expressed in hours between two and 12 in any one day, and limited to
  operate within six months of the order being made.
- Requirement must normally be electronically monitored.

- A single requirement of an electronically monitored curfew can be used as a simple punishment.
- Curfews can also be considered alongside a long unpaid work requirement in cases with a low level of offending-related need and risk of harm but where the seriousness level is high, or as part of a complex package of interventions with high levels of offending-related need and/or risk of harm where the seriousness level is very high.

(vi) *Exclusion requirement*

- Main purposes: punishment and protection.
- Expressed as exclusion from a place or area for a specified period of up to two years; the exclusion may be limited to particular specified periods.
- A report is advisable in cases where significant risk of harm is identified.
- An exclusion requirement might be used in drink-related, public order or violent offences associated with particular public houses or areas of town; stalking – exclusion from area of victim's home or workplace; sex offender excluded from named swimming pool, leisure centre, playground or from a specified radius of named schools; persistent shop theft – exclusion from a named store or shopping area; domestic violence cases – exclusion from the victim's home and environs.
- The court should normally impose electronic monitoring.
- Where appropriate an exclusion requirement can be used with a supervision requirement to support and reinforce desired changes in behaviour.

(vii) *Residence requirement*

- Main purposes: rehabilitation and protection.
- Expressed in months or years up to 36 months.
- Residence can be at approved premises or at a private address.
- Residence in a hostel or institution must be proposed by the probation service and will normally be accompanied by a supervision requirement to ensure support and contact.
- A residence requirement should be distinguished from a curfew requirement.

(viii) *Mental health treatment requirement*

- Main purpose: rehabilitation.
- Expressed in months or years between six and 36 months.
- The court must be satisfied on the evidence of a doctor that the mental condition of the offender is such as requires and may be susceptible to treatment, but does not warrant the making of a hospital order or guardianship order, and that treatment has been or can be arranged.

- The offender must be willing to comply with the requirement.
- A supervision requirement will normally be proposed to provide additional support, unless the treatment is to be residential in which case supervision would not normally be necessary and the role of the responsible officer would be limited to that of case manager; a separate residence requirement is not necessary.

(ix) *Drug rehabilitation requirement*

- Main purpose: rehabilitation.
- Expressed in months or years between six and 36 months.
- The court cannot impose a DRR unless the probation service has recommended it.
- The court must also be satisfied that the offender is dependent on or has a propensity to misuse drugs that this is susceptible to treatment and that treatment has been or can be arranged.
- The offender must be willing to comply with the requirement.
- Drug rehabilitation includes testing, but sentencers may wish to consider whether an accredited substance misuse programme should be undertaken through a separate programme requirement.
- Progress reviews by the court are mandatory for requirements of over 12 months and optional for those under 12 months.
- Court of Appeal guidance on DTTOs (set out above) is applicable here.

(x) *Alcohol treatment requirement*

- Main purpose: rehabilitation.
- Expressed in months or years between six and 36 months.
- The court must be satisfied that the offender is dependent on alcohol, requires and may be susceptible to treatment, and treatment has been or can be arranged.
- The offender must be willing to comply with the requirement.
- Where attendance on an accredited substance misuse programme or the drink impaired drivers programme is necessary, this would be specified in a separate programme requirement.

(xi) *Supervision requirement*

- Main purpose: rehabilitation.
- Expressed in months or years between six and 36 months and, if included in an order, is always the same length as the order.
- There should be a clear expectation between the court and the offender about what work is to be undertaken and what this will involve.
- The Probation Service will indicate the initial frequency of contact.
- Typically supervision can involve contact to undertake work to promote personal and behavioural change; monitor and review patterns of behaviour

and personal activity; undertake work to increase motivation and provide practical support to increase compliance with other requirements; deliver pre- and post-programme work for accredited programmes; support and reinforce learning being undertaken as part of a programme or activity requirement; deliver individual counselling; form and maintain working alliances to support the offender through other requirements in the order; model pro-social behaviour.

- Normally the contact would be individual but these activities can be carried out in small groups if appropriate.

(xii) *Attendance centre requirement (if offender is aged under 25)*

- Main purpose: punishment.
- Expressed in hours between 12 and 36, with a maximum of three hours per attendance and one attendance per day.
- A centre must be available and accessible to the offender.
- If an attendance requirement is the only requirement then the responsible officer will be the officer in charge of the centre.

In addition to the specific points mentioned, a number of general provisions apply whatever the requirement or requirements inserted by the court. The requirement or requirements must be such as in the opinion of the court is or taken together are, the most suitable for the offender, and the restrictions on liberty imposed by the order must be such as in the opinion of the court are commensurate with the seriousness of the offence (or offences) committed (CJA 2003, s.148(2)). There is an obvious tension between these two criteria, a difficulty which was also to be found in the earlier law (Rex 1988, and see further below). Where more than one requirement is inserted into the community order, the court should consider whether they are compatible with each other (CJA 2003, s.177(6)). Whenever the court makes a community order imposing a curfew requirement or an exclusion requirement, the court *must* normally also impose an electronic monitoring requirement, and *may* do so in respect of any of the other requirements (s.177(3) and (4)).

The agreement of the offender to the requirement is *not* necessary except where mental health treatment or drug or alcohol rehabilitation is involved. In every case the community order should specify the area in which the offender will live throughout the order, and the court must ensure that, so far as possible, the order will avoid conflict with the offender's religious beliefs, conflict with the requirements of any other order to which he may be subject, and avoids interference with the times (if any) at which the offender attends work, school or other educational establishment. The order must specify a date, not more than three years from the date of the making of the order, by which all the requirements must have been completed or fully complied with (s.177(5)), but there are some other rules for particular requirements which are more specific than this. All the hours under an unpaid work requirement should normally be completed within 12 months, for example. Details of the order and its requirements will be written down and copies given to the offender, the responsible officer and to certain other persons who will be affected by the order. There are further detailed provisions in the Act relating to each of the requirements, but these are not covered in this chapter.

Guidance on the community order

The practical operation of the community order is only partly laid down in the statute. Additional guidance is provided by the Sentencing Guidelines Council (SGC), and by national standards applicable to the National Probation Service (now part of the National Offender Management Service – NOMS). The SGC was set up by the Criminal Justice Act 2003, and issues sentencing guidelines to which all courts must have regard (CJA 2003, s.172). It issued guidelines on the new community order at the end of 2004. The guidelines state that when deciding which requirements to include the court has to consider both the degree of restriction on liberty which is involved and the suitability of the requirement(s) for the offender, but that the first consideration for the court should be proportionality ahead of suitability (SGC 2004: para. 1.1.13). This shows that the principle of proportionality, or 'desert', remains central to achieving consistency in community sentencing (compare Wasik and von Hirsch 1988, an article which argues for this approach, with Morris and Tonry 1990, which prefers much greater interchangeability among community measures). Desert is a limiting principle on the onerousness of community sentence length and requirements.

The SGC then goes on to provide that the community order should be divided into three sentencing ranges (as was suggested in Halliday 2001: para. 6.8) to reflect cases of low, medium and high degrees of seriousness. The low range is for cases which only just cross the community sentence threshold, and for persistent petty offenders whose offences only merit a community sentence by virtue of failing to respond to the previous imposition of fines. Here, one requirement will normally be appropriate, such as short period of unpaid work (40–80 hours), or a curfew, or a prohibited activity requirement, or an exclusion requirement if no electronic monitoring is necessary. The high range is for cases falling just short of custody, or where the offence crosses the custody threshold but the personal mitigation is such that a community sentence can be passed instead. More intensive sentences which combine two or more requirements are appropriate here. Suitable requirements might include unpaid work of 150–300 hours, an activity requirement up to the maximum of 60 days, an exclusion order for up to the maximum of 12 months, and/or a curfew order of up to 12 hours a day for 4–6 months. The middle range caters for those cases which fall in between, where suitable requirements might include 80–150 hours of community work, an activity requirement in the middle range (20–30 days), a curfew requirement in the middle range (up to 12 hours for 2–3 months, for example), an exclusion requirement lasting for six months and/ or a prohibited activity requirement. It is important to note that the three sentencing ranges are not intended to be prescriptive, and should remain flexible enough to take account of offender suitability, his or her ability to comply and the varying availability of particular requirements in the local area (SGC 2004: para. 1.1.14).

In many cases the PSR (or other appropriate report) provided by the National Probation Service will be crucial in helping the sentencer to decide whether a community sentence is appropriate and, if so, which requirement or combination of requirements will be the most suitable for the offender. Offending behaviour programmes are accredited by the Home Office and regulated in accordance with national standards. There has been very substantial government investment in research, evaluation and programme accreditation by the Correctional Services Accreditation Panel. Accreditation is based upon available empirical evidence that the particular programme has been designed in a manner consistent with what is likely to be effective in reducing reoffending. The PSR will also make considerable use of risk prediction tools, especially OASys (Offender Assessment System), which allows the report writer to present a balanced view of the likelihood of reconviction, the relative degree of risk of future harm and the factors which must be addressed (such as drug misuse) if the offender's criminality is to be addressed. Not all programmes are available in every area. The sentencing court should be advised as to local availability and should clearly specify the name of the relevant programme when making the community order.

The normal expectation is that the court will order a report whenever a community sentence is a likely outcome, although the SGC suggests that the court may consider dispensing with a report if the offence falls within the low range of seriousness and the sentencer has just a single requirement in mind (SGC 2004: para. 1.1.17). The government is consulting again on this matter, from the point of view of better targeting of probation resources (Home Office 2006b). The SGC guidelines state that, wherever possible, sentencers should indicate their provisional thinking on which of the three sentencing ranges is relevant and the purpose(s) of sentencing that the package of requirements is intended to fulfil (SGC 2004: para. 1.1.16). While this proposal is sensible and has been welcomed by the probation service, it does not appear to have worked well in practice. The main difficulty is that a series of Court of Appeal decisions, going back to *Gillam* (1980) 2 Cr App R (S) 267, say that an indication of sentence which raises a legitimate expectation on the part of the offender will be binding on the judge (or a different judge dealing with the matter later on) if the report is positive. The tradition has been for courts to avoid this restriction by stating that 'all options are open' when asking for a report.

As we have seen, under the framework of the 2003 Act there is just one community order rather than a number of separate community sentences.

This does not, of course, mean that an offender who has received a community order in the past cannot receive another one. Further community orders, perhaps with different requirements, may well be appropriate for the repeat offender. The SGC guidelines say that whenever an offender is ordered to serve a community order the court record should show clearly which requirements have been imposed. Any future sentencer, whether dealing with breach or a future offence, should have full information about the requirements that were inserted into a previous community order, whether that sentence was a low-, medium- or high-level order, and the offender's response. This will enable the later court to consider the merits of imposing the same or different requirements as part of another community order (SGC 2004: para. 1.1.36).

Research on the use and impact of the community order shows that, for the most part, courts have been using it in a manner consistent with the legislative intent and the guidelines (Centre for Crime and Justice Studies 2007). Probation officers appear to be reasonably satisfied with the new arrangements, which they regard as more flexible than the earlier scheme. The number of requirements used in the community order is again in line with expectations, although the researchers note that in a few cases orders are defined as low seriousness but have as many as three requirements. More generally, there is imbalance in the use of different requirements. While the unpaid work requirement is very popular with sentencers, half of the 12 requirements available under the Act are rarely used. There is some variation across probation areas with regard to the number and type of requirements used.

Breach, revocation and amendment of a community order

If the offender fails, without reasonable cause, to comply with one or more of the requirements in a community order, the responsible officer can either give a warning or initiate breach proceedings. If the offender fails to comply for a second time within a 12-month period, the responsible officer must initiate breach proceedings. When the matter comes before the court, the court must either increase the severity of the sentence (such as by imposing new requirements, or increasing the number of hours of unpaid work, or lengthening the supervision or operational period of the sentence) or revoke the order and resentence for the original offence (CJA 2003: sch. 8, paras 5–6). A differently structured community sentence could be imposed on resentencing. While Parliament changed the law in the 2003 Act to require an additional penalty as a consequence of breach, the government is now considering whether offender managers should have power, within a framework set by the court on sentence, to vary the punishment depending on their behaviour, without having to go back to court (Home Office 2006a, 2006b).

The court must always take account of the circumstances of the breach (CJA 2003: sch. 8, para. 9(2)), and make allowance for any portion of requirements which the offender has successfully completed before the breach. The SGC says that, in considering which course to adopt when sentencing for breach, the court's primary objective is to ensure that the requirements are completed. Custody should be a last resort, to be reserved for cases where deliberate and repeated breach where all reasonable efforts to ensure that the offender complies have failed (SGC 2004: para. 1.1.45). If the offender commits a further offence during the period of a community order this is not technically a breach, but will be dealt with alongside sentencing for the new offence by revocation of the community order and resentencing. Again, when deciding what sentence to impose after revocation, the court should take into account the extent to which the offender complied with the order before committing the further offence.

Sometimes the terms of a community order can be varied following application to the court. This might occur if the offender's circumstances change, so that it is no longer possible for him to comply with one of the requirements. An order can also be brought to an end early if the offender has made exceptionally good progress.

Custodial sentence supervision

Sentences of under 12 months

Leaving aside special measures for dangerous offenders (considered further below) the standard custodial sentences are imprisonment for offenders aged 21 and over and detention in a young offender institution for offenders aged 18, 19 or 20. If a court imposes a custodial sentence of less than 12 months under current law the offender will be released at the half-way point of the sentence. For many, the release date will in fact be earlier, as a result of operation of the home detention curfew (HDC) scheme. On release there is no supervision or opportunity for placement on a programme to address offending behaviour. Short sentences such as this have been the subject of much criticism from reformers, who argue that there is insufficient time to undertake any meaningful work with offenders during the custodial part of the sentence and after release there is no provision for supervision or opportunity for placement on a rehabilitative programme. (See, in particular, the critical comments of Lord Woolf in *McInerney* [2003] 2 Cr App R (S) 240, at pp. 254–9). Reconviction rates after short sentences are very high, giving the effect of a short sentence revolving door.

The Criminal Justice Act 2003 contains provisions which, if ever brought into force, will change the regime of short sentences. The new sentence of 'custody plus', as proposed by in the Halliday Report (Halliday 2001) was scheduled for introduction in autumn 2006 as part of a package of increasing magistrates' courts' sentencing powers from six months to 12 months, but implementation has been deferred indefinitely. The custody plus sentence of between 28 and 51 weeks would comprise a term in custody of between two and 13 weeks (to be set by the court) plus a licence period of at least 26 weeks. So for any sentence of custody plus the licence period will always be proportionately longer than the custodial part – at least 2:1 and at its extreme as much as 24:1 (i.e. two weeks in custody and 49 weeks on licence). The offender would then be subject to supervision until the end of the sentence. The court would specify one or more requirements to be complied with during that supervision period, chosen from the list of requirements for the community order (set out above) save that requirements (vii) to (x) could not be included. Draft SGC Guidelines on custody plus state that, although the period of time spent in custody under a custody plus sentence will often be shorter than is the case now, custody plus is potentially more onerous because of the presence of licence requirements which will last to the very end of the sentence (SGC 2006: para. 22).

Sentences of 12 months and over

For custodial sentences of at least 12 months but below four years, before the 2003 Act an adult offender would be released from custody at the half-way point of sentence and then would be supervised under licence until the three-quarter point of sentence. For some, the actual release date will be earlier as a result of release on HDC. If the sentence was for four years or more an adult offender would be eligible for release from the halfway point of sentence and, if not released before, would automatically be released at the two-thirds point of the sentence. Whatever the exact time of release, the offender would be supervised to the three-quarter point of sentence unless a violent offence or a sexual offence had been committed and the court had ordered that supervision should continue for a longer period of time. These arrangements have been changed by the 2003 Act, with effect from 4 April 2005 and they apply to offenders sentenced for offences committed on or after that date.

Assuming that the offender is not given an indeterminate (life) sentence or otherwise caught by the 'dangerous offender' provisions of the Act (see below), the offender will now be released from custody at the half-way point of the sentence, but will then be on licence until the very end of the sentence. The requirements to be inserted into the licence are not (in general) a matter for the sentencing court, but will be set by the executive authorities shortly before the offender is released. The SGC guidelines indicate that these requirements 'are expected to be more demanding and involve a greater restriction on liberty than current licence conditions' (SGC 2004: para. 2.1.5). Breach of a requirement will result in the offender being returned to custody following executive recall. Although licence requirements in sentences of 12 months or more are not generally a matter for the court, there is provision in the Act for the sentencing court to indicate what requirement or requirements it thinks might be appropriate. Any such indication is not binding on the authorities. The thinking here is that, especially in the case of long sentences, it will rarely be possible for a sentencer to predict the most appropriate licence requirements, and this is better done by the authorities shortly before release. A court might suggest, however, that the offender should complete a programme directed at drug misuse, anger management or improving literacy skills and could recommend that this should be considered as a licence requirement if not undertaken and completed in custody.

Suspended sentences

One of the effects of the Criminal Justice Act 1991 was to marginalise the power to suspend a prison sentence and to make it available in 'exceptional circumstances' only. The new form of suspended sentence created by the Criminal Justice Act 2003 is quite different, and has proved to be popular with sentencers. The new suspended sentence (originally termed 'custody minus' in the Halliday proposals) applies where the court imposes a sentence of imprisonment or detention in a young offender institution of not less than 14 days but up to 12 months. It is available for offenders aged 18 and over. The court may suspend that sentence for a specified period between six months and two years. During that 'operational period' the court can impose one or more requirements for the offender to undertake in the community. The requirement or requirements must last for a period of not less than six months and not more than two years (CJA 2003, s.189(3)) unless an unpaid work requirement is imposed in which case the period must be 12 months. Obviously, the period during which the requirement(s) operate (known as the 'supervision period') cannot last longer than the operational period of the suspended sentence. The menu of available requirements is identical to those for the new community order, set out above. In addition there is always the condition that the offender must keep in touch with the responsible officer (CJA 2003, s.220). If the offender fails to comply with a requirement during the supervision period, or commits any further offence, the suspended sentence can be activated in full, or in part, or the terms of the supervision can be made more onerous. There is a presumption that the suspended sentence will be activated and that the activated term will run consecutively to any custodial sentence imposed for a further offence. The 2003 Act also provides that a court imposing a suspended sentence may require that the offender attends court for periodic review hearings (ss.191–192), in a manner similar to the drug rehabilitation requirement described above.

There are a number of similarities between the new suspended sentence and a community order, especially the identical menu of requirements. The main difference of principle is that a suspended sentence can only be imposed where the offence is so serious that it merits custody of up to 12 months, while an offence meriting a community order will generally fall below that threshold. In practice, however, personal mitigation and a timely guilty plea may rescue an offender from an immediate custodial sentence (CJA 2003, s.166(2)) and then the choice between suspending the sentence or passing a community order will be a fine one. When comparing the suspended sentence with a community order the SGC guidelines suggest that, since the suspended sentence is in itself a punishment and deterrent, the number and onerousness of the requirements to be inserted into a suspended sentence should normally be less than would be appropriate for a community order. It says that a court wishing to impose onerous or intensive requirements (such as a drug rehabilitation requirement) on an offender might review its decision to suspend sentence and consider whether a community order might be more appropriate (SGC 2004: para. 2.2.14). Of course requirements imposed under a community order may take effect for up to 36 months, while the operational period of a suspended sentence can be 24 months at most and will often be shorter. Finally, as we have seen, a suspended sentence can be made subject to periodic reviews, while a community order cannot unless it contains a drug rehabilitation requirement.

Research on the operation of the suspended sentence indicates that it has proved popular with sentencers. There is little evidence that the introduction of the suspended sentence has diverted large numbers of offenders away from immediate custody, and there may well have been some 'net-widening' with suspended sentences being imposed on offenders who would formerly have received a community disposal (CCJS 2007). Also, it appears that sentencers are typically imposing more requirements in a suspended sentence than in a community order. This is not consistent with the SGC guidelines and may lead to a high level of breach.

Dangerous offenders

The Criminal Justice Act 2003 provides a range of new sentences which are applicable if an offender has been convicted of one of a list of 'specified offences' in the Act, and the court considers that there is a 'significant risk of serious harm arising from the commission by the offender of further specified offences' in the future. These sentences, of imprisonment (or detention) for public protection (IPP), and the extended sentence, may only be imposed by the Crown Court, but a magistrates' court may commit an offender to the Crown Court with a view to such a sentence being passed. In the case of an IPP the court will set a minimum term which must expire before the Parole Board can consider releasing the offender and, after release, the offender will be on licence for at least ten years. If the sentence is an extended sentence the court will specify a custodial period and an extension period (during which the offender will be on licence). The extension period can be for up to five years in the case of a specified violent offence, or up to eight years in the case of a specified sexual offence. The list of specified offences is very broad. It includes, for example, assault occasioning actual bodily harm where, perhaps, there will be many offenders who do not represent a significant risk of serious harm. This is a matter for the sentencing court in all cases, but where a specified offence has been committed and there is a previous specified offence on the offender's criminal record, the statute originally created a presumption that the new sentences will be appropriate. The Court of Appeal issued guidance for sentencers in *Lang* [2006] 2 Cr App R (S) 6 on the imposition of these sentences. The Court stressed that a wide variety of information about the offender would need to be considered prior to imposing such a sentence, and the court would rely on the PSR prepared in accordance with the appropriate guidance (National Probation Service 2005), details of the offender's previous offending and, where appropriate, a psychiatric report. The probation service will carry out a full OASys assessment on all offenders under consideration for one of these sentences, will identify the person or persons at risk from the offender, and assess the level of that risk and the nature and seriousness of the potential impact (National Probation Service 2005).

The tight drafting of these provisions meant that these sentences were imposed in a substantial number of cases. Home Office figures show that they were being imposed by the courts at the rate of about 100 per month. The offences for which they were most frequently imposed were (in descending order) robbery, wounding with intent, arson, rape or attempted rape and attempted murder. It is robbery sentencing which predominates, and this is reflected in a large number of decisions of the Court of Appeal which dealt with appeals in such cases. The average length of the minimum term set by the courts, across the range, was around 30 months (equivalent, of course, to a fixed-term sentence of five years assuming release from the IPP at the first opportunity). In reality, many offenders sentenced under these provisions will spend much longer in custody before being released by the Parole Board. The Criminal Justice and Immigration Act 2008 has amended the law so as to restrict the use of IPP to cases in which a minimum term of at least two years is appropriate. The statutory presumption of dangerousness, mentioned above, has been repealed. The intended effect of these changes is to reduce significantly the number of offenders who qualify in future for an IPP or an extended sentence.

Before recommending release on licence the Parole Board must consider whether the safety of the public would be placed at unacceptable risk by release (see Hood and Shute 2000). The Board will be informed by a further report prepared by the probation service containing information on risk management and resettlement. The Board will take into account, among other factors, whether the offender has shown a willingness to address his offending behaviour by taking part in programmes or activities in prison designed to address his risk, and whether the offender is likely to comply with the conditions of his licence and the requirements of supervision. The licence period is designed primarily to provide protection for the public. The 2003 Act, extending provisions in earlier law, require the probation, police and prison services to establish multi-agency public protection arrangements (MAPPA) for the assessment and management of violent and sexual offenders. The MAPPA framework identifies three separate risk levels for offender management. Those offenders who pose the highest risk of causing serious harm are referred to a multi-agency public protection panel (MAPPP) where their cases are scrutinised regularly. Offenders will be managed under MAPPA if they fall within one of three categories as defined in the Criminal Justice Act 2003 – registered sex offenders, violent and other sex offenders who have committed a specified offence and have received a prison sentence of more than 12 months, and other offenders who, although they do not fall into either of the first two categories, are considered to represent some risk of causing serious harm.

Discussion questions

1 To what extent has the revised sentencing framework in the Criminal Justice Act 2003 been designed to address different forms of offending behaviour?
2 How far do the guidelines developed by the Sentencing Guidelines Council assist the courts in selecting appropriate sentences and sentence requirements?
3 Why has the courts' use of (a) the suspended sentence and (b) the dangerous offender sentencing provisions outstripped government expectations? What are the implications of that (over-)use?

Further reading

Bottoms, A., Rex, S. and Robinson, G. (eds) (2004) *Alternatives to Prison: Options for an Insecure Society*. Cullompton: Willan. A wide-ranging collection of essays on management of various categories of offenders.
Harper, G. and Chitty, C. (eds) (2005) *The Impact of Corrections on Reoffending: A Review of 'What Works'*, Home Office Research Study No. 291. London: Home Office. The title says it: this is currently the most comprehensive and authoritative review of 'what works'.
Maguire, M., Morgan, R. and Reiner, R. (eds) (2007) *Oxford Handbook of Criminology*, 4th edn. Oxford Oxford University Press. The fullest treatment available of theory, research, policy and current debates.

References

Advisory Council on the Penal System (1970) *Non-Custodial and Semi-Custodial Penalties*. London: HMSO.
Ashworth, A. (1983) *Sentencing and Penal Policy*. London: Weidenfield & Nicolson.
Ashworth, A. (2005) *Sentencing and Criminal Justice*. Cambridge: Cambridge University Press.
Bottoms, A. (1995) 'The philosophy and politics of punishment and sentencing', in C.M.V. Clarkson and R. Morgan (eds), *The Politics of Sentencing Reform*. Oxford: Clarendon Press, pp. 17–49.

Centre for Crime and Justice Studies (2007) *The Use and Impact of the Community Order and the Suspended Sentence Order*. London: CCJS.

Coulsfield, Lord (2004) *Crime, Courts and Confidence: Report of an Independent Inquiry into Alternatives to Prison*. London: Esmée Fairbairn Foundation.

Dodgeson, K., Goodwin, P., Howard, P., Llewellyn-Thomas, S., Mortimer, E., Russell, N. and Weiner, M. (2001) *Electronic Monitoring of Released Prisoners: An Evaluation of the Home Office Detention Curfew Scheme*. Home Office Research Study No. 222. London: Home Office.

Easton, S. and Piper, C. (2005) *Sentencing and Punishment: The Quest for Justice*. Oxford: Oxford University Press.

Faulkner, D. (2001) *Crime, State and Citizen*. Winchester: Waterside Press.

Halliday, J. (2001) *Making Punishments Work: Review of the Sentencing Framework for England and Wales*. London: Home Office.

Harper, G. and Chitty, C. (eds) (2005) *The Impact of Corrections on Reoffending: A review of 'What Works'*, Home Office Research Study No. 291. London: Home Office.

Home Office (1990) *Crime, Justice and Protecting the Public*, Cm 965. London: HMSO.

Home Office (1995) *Strengthening Punishment in the Community*, Cm 2780. London: HMSO.

Home Office (2002) *Justice for All*, Cm 5563. London: Stationery Office.

Home Office (2006a) *Rebalancing the Criminal Justice System*. London: CJS.

Home Office (2006b) *Making Sentencing Clearer*. London: CJS.

Hood, R. and Shute, S. (2000) *The Parole System at Work: A Study of Risk-based Decision-making*, Home Office Research Study No. 202. London: Home Office

Hough, M. and Roberts, J. (2002) *Changing Attitudes to Punishment: Public Opinion, Crime and Justice*. Cullompton: Willan.

Hough, M., Clancy, A., McSweeney, T. and Turnbull, T. (2003) *The Impact of Drug Treatment and Testing Orders on Offending: Two-year Reconviction Results*, Home Office Research Study Findings No. 184. London: Home Office.

Linklater, Baroness (2004) *Rethinking Crime and Punishment: The Report*. London: Esmée Fairbairn Foundation.

McKittrick, N. and Rex, S. (2003) 'Sentence management: a new role for the judiciary?', in M. Tonry (ed.) *Confronting Crime: Crime Control Policy Under New Labour*. Cullompton: Willan, pp. 140–55.

Morris, N. and Tonry, M. (1990) *Between Prison and Probation*. Oxford: Oxford University Press.

National Probation Service (2005) *Guide for Sentences of Public Protection*. London: National Probation Directorate.

National Probation Service (2007) *Probation Bench Handbook*, 2nd edn. London: National Offender Management Service.

Nellis, M. (2004) 'Electronic monitoring and the community supervision of offenders', in A. Bottoms, S. Rex and G. Robinson (eds) *Alternatives to Prison: Options for an Insecure Society*. Cullompton: Willan, pp. 224–47.

Pease, K. (1978) 'Community service and the tariff', *Criminal Law Review*, 269–77.

Rex, S. (1998) 'Applying desert principles to community sentences: lessons from two Criminal Justice Acts', *Criminal Law Review*, 381–91.

Rex, S. (2002) 'Reinventing community penalties: the role of communication', in S. Rex and M. Tonry (eds) *Reform and Punishment: The Future of Sentencing*. Cullompton: Willan, pp. 138–57.

Robinson, G. and Dignan, J. (2004) 'Sentence Management', in A. Bottoms, S. Rex and G. Robinson (eds) *Alternatives to Prison: Options for an Insecure Society*. Cullompton: Willan, pp. 313–40.

Sentencing Guidelines Council (2004) *New Sentences: Criminal Justice Act 2003: Guideline*. London: SGC.

Sentencing Guidelines Council (2006) *Custodial Sentences of Less than 12 Months: Criminal Justice Act 2003: Consultation Guideline*. London: SGC.

Sentencing Guidelines Council (2007) *Reduction in Sentence for a Guilty Plea: Revised Guideline*. London: SGC.

Taylor, Lord Chief Justice (1993) 'Text of an Address to the Annual Conference of the Society at Gleneagles on 21st March 1993', *Journal of the Law Society of Scotland*, 129–31.

Taylor, R., Wasik, M. and Leng, R. (2004) *Blackstone's Guide to the Criminal Justice Act 2003*. Oxford: Oxford University Press.

Turnbull, P., McSweeney, T., Webster, R., Edmunds, M. and Hough, M. (2000) *Drug Treatment and Testing Orders: Final Evaluation Report*. London: Home Office.

Von Hirsch, A. (1976) *Doing Justice: The Choice of Punishments*. New York: Hill & Wang.

Wasik, M. (2004) 'Going round in circles? Reflections on fifty years of change in sentencing', *Criminal Law Review*, 253–65.

Wasik, M. and Taylor, R. (1994) *Blackstone's Guide to the Criminal Justice Act 1991*, 2nd edn. London: Blackstone Press.

Wasik, M. and von Hirsch, A. (1988) 'Non-custodial penalties and the principles of desert', *Criminal Law Review*, 555–72.

Chapter 2

The policy context

Mike Nash

Introduction

With the election of the 'new' Labour government in 1997, criminal justice agencies, along with the rest of the public sector, were to experience a sustained period of modernisation through a process of new public management (NPM) or 'managerialism'. Inefficient and outdated practices and processes were to be abolished and in their place a modernisation project would sweep in reforms based upon the best of private sector initiatives. However, McLaughlin *et al.* (2001) argue that the process went further than this and actually represented '... a fundamental assault on the professional cultures and discourses and power relations embedded in the public sector' (p. 303). Yet alongside this cherishing of market principles and apparent threat to traditional service values, there appeared to be a stance that at least offered some form of hope to Labour traditionalists and many working in the criminal justice organisations at the time. This was Tony Blair's celebrated 'tough on crime, tough on the causes of crime'. In these few words he had repositioned the Labour Party, enabling it to tackle the Conservatives head-on in their favoured law and order area (and eventually to electorally defeat them) while suggesting that a constructive rehabilitationist position would not disappear from the agenda. In their historic third term it is beyond dispute that a revolution has occurred, but has it delivered the improved effectiveness demanded by the Prime Minister? In the spring and summer of 2006 a huge media campaign took aim at the government across almost all aspects of its criminal justice organisations and programmes. The results were accusations of 'policy making on the hoof' (*BBC News*, 20 June 2006) and a resurgence of populist policymaking unseen since the days of Michael Howard as Conservative Home Secretary. This chapter will review the evolution of criminal justice policy under Blair in an attempt to determine the success or otherwise of what has been a massive change process.

A familiar backcloth?

Prior to the 1997 electoral victory for Labour, the party made a great deal of the failure of Conservative law and order policies. These failures were connected to a growing fear of crime as revealed by a succession of British Crime Surveys, rises in the prison population, urban social unrest (especially among young people) and concerns with the release and whereabouts of predatory paedophiles to name but a few. A decade on has the situation improved? During the summer of 2006 the media had given saturation coverage for weeks to a number of criminal justice 'scandals'. These were in many ways little different to those of the mid-1990s or earlier. The Home Office itself had come in for particularly scathing criticism, costing then Home Secretary Charles Clarke his job. Of particular concern had been the 'losses' of prisoners upon release from custody (those whose whereabouts were unknown but should have been subject to licence supervision). Among these were a number of very serious offenders including those convicted of murder and rape. Much of the media interest had been fuelled by high-profile murders committed by people who had been released 'early' from their prison sentences, including a life sentence. Inquiries by the Chief Inspector of Probation (HMIP 2006a, 2006b) revealed a number of flaws in the release process. The inquiry reports made much more public the previously secretive considerations of probation and prison staff and the Parole Board. With this opening-up of the process came much greater public approbation for those involved and a questioning of their judgments based, it must be said, more upon media distortion than real evidence. One result of the media glare has been a reported additional caution in crucial risk assessment decisions. One immediate impact has been fewer people released on parole and on life licence. From April to September 2006, out of 901 requests for lifer release only 106 were granted, the ratio typically being 1 in 5 previously (*BBC News*, 6 November 2006). In its 2005–6 annual report, the chairman of the Parole Board Sir Duncan Nichol stated, 'we will be absolutely sure before we release' (Parole Board 2006). However, the problems did not stop with prisoner release arrangements. A leading feature of Labour's revolution had been the use of technology and although successful in some respects – CCTV for example – newspaper reports revealed problems with other aspects ('more than 1,500 offenders rip off their tags', *BBC News*, 26 May 2006). An apparent lack of enforcement of community penalties (a mainstay of the probation revolution), a major increase in newly created offences and increased sentence lengths somewhat remarkably coincided with a surge in the prison population – now regularly exceeding 80,000. In an almost exact echo of the late 1980s calls were made to find ways of lowering the prison population to avoid a prisons' crisis, just at a time when other criminal justice measures were increasing it exponentially. Add to this a public panic over knife crime and increasingly gun crime related to gang violence and it seems as if nothing has changed. So has the revolution failed or is it the case that such crises are inevitable whatever system of governance is in place?

Seeds of the revolution

As noted above, Labour's plans for criminal justice were part and parcel of major public sector reform. The 'labour' part of their political philosophy (commitment to the public sector) was to be rebranded to appeal to middle England in an attempt to win over disgruntled Conservative supporters. The public sector would be retained, but reformed to ensure better services, a more efficient use of resources and much greater public accountability. The basis of this revolution would be the adoption of private sector principles and methods. Thus although Labour traditionalists might have balked at the programme of reform, it did at least suggest a positive future for a public sector that had appeared increasingly under threat from Conservative policies. However, what had begun as a Conservative reform process became one of transformation under Blair. The essential principles of the conservative reforms (applied across the public sector) were to be: efficiency gains to end public sector lack of competitiveness, financial control to reduce the public sector borrowing requirement and thus facilitate tax cuts, and ideological developments aimed at breaking the dependency culture and introducing competition to the state machine (Massey and Pyper 2005: 46).

In essence the public sector was to be reined in and its focus to become outward looking (on customers or service users) rather than itself. Performance measurement and audit would become key components of everyday public sector life, backed by a range of public sector agreements introduced by then Chancellor Gordon Brown in the Comprehensive Spending Review of 1998. As they have developed these agreements have included a number of shared, cross-cutting targets underlining the government's intention to join up its provision much more than previously. The focus upon end-users means that organisations have to be clear about their outputs and targets, leading to the acronym 'SMART' entering the lexicon (Specific, Measurable, Achievable, Relevant and Timed). By 2003 there were over 400 key performance targets (Massey and Pyper 2005: 145) with no sign of their reducing in number or scope. Practitioners of course might argue that public service is not the same as business and that targets and outputs are varied and at times in opposition to each other. For example, if one considers the notion of a customer, who is the customer of the prison service? Many might argue that it is the prisoners themselves. They should have decent living conditions, good facilities for education, training, visits and exercise and the opportunity to put their offending behaviour behind them. This of course requires considerable expenditure on resources, physical and human. Yet other targets or policies – say to increase crime detection, or lengthen the punishments for particular crimes, or newly criminalise certain behaviours, or restrict early release arrangements – may all increase the numbers going into or remaining in prison thus immediately threatening another target relating to prisoner well-being and rehabilitation. The customer of the prison service may therefore be the courts who supply the prisoners or the public who may demand that more people are incarcerated. This is different to a manufacturer producing an electrical item that may be improved to become cheaper or more saleable as a result of invention and innovation. The aim remains the same – to sell to the customer. In many areas of criminal justice this market philosophy simply does not apply.

Criminal justice policy in many contexts

Criminal justice agencies have therefore to operate in the new world of public sector management (see, for example, Horton and Farnham 1999; Massey and Pyper 2005; Savage and Atkinson 2001). This chapter cannot possibly review the scale and impact of new public management (NPM) but these texts should offer a sound introduction to what has been an all-consuming process. NPM has become something of a New Labour mantra and its effect has been very well described by Parsons (2000):

> NPM is the nearest we have come in this country, for a few hundred years at least, to a kind of state religion. To question or deny its essential doctrines is to place oneself beyond the pale. To shout as it parades past that it is stark naked – that the emperor has no clothes – is to risk being bundled away or injected with a tranquilliser or sent to a gulag. (Cited in Massey and Pyper 2005: 149)

Public sector managers therefore need constantly to focus upon cutting costs, on ensuring that central policies and guidelines are adhered to and complied with, that their organisation is ever ready for the next inspection and that its customer focus is always ready to adapt to the next political directive. Can the criminal justice sector easily fit into this model? The answer of course depends upon one's moral and philosophical view concerning how criminal justice processes should be administered. Consider the possible tension in the following example. The Crown Prosecution Service is asked to process cases more quickly and at lower cost. To do this it needs to avoid delays and repeat hearings. This could mean encouraging a greater number of guilty pleas by 'negotiating' over the charges or reducing the number of occasions the defence can request adjournments to prepare its case. Either of these methods might speed the flow of cases through the courts and make their targets appear more impressive. But what is the effect? Defendants may be encouraged to plead guilty to charges they are not actually guilty of or accept a lower quality of legal advice. If the rights of defendants are to be taken seriously then measures such as these are unlikely to gain favour. But, in an era when offender rights may be less prominent and a crime control ethos in the ascendancy, there may be a greater acceptance of those rights being abrogated (Home Office 2006c).

Criminal justice policy therefore cannot simply be run on market principles. It is a highly politicised area and one that attracts huge media interest. No matter how carefully planned targets may be, they can be knocked off course in an instant and replaced with another which is viewed as more pressing by the government. For example the 1991 Criminal Justice Act (a Conservative measure) was widely held as being concerned with reducing the size of the prison population (and therefore cost). Despite being wrapped in quite punitive clothes there was a clear intent to punish more offenders in the community and within 12 months of its enactment the prison population had reduced from 48,000 to 42,000. However, the murder of schoolboy James Bulger by two teenagers in 1993 contributed to a moral panic over youth crime and 'soft' sentencing (with special antipathy reserved for repeat cautioning of young offenders) that saw a raft of new measures introduced in the 1993 Criminal Justice Act – measures which effectively led to a rapid rise in prison numbers. Due to the political battle between the emerging (Labour) and old (Conservative) parties of law and order a sharp reversal of policy was undertaken. Then Home Secretary Michael Howard announced the following indicating that prison numbers would again have to rise:

I do not flinch from that. We shall no longer judge the success of our system of justice by a fall in our prison population ... Let us be clear. Prison works. It ensures that we are protected from murderers, muggers and rapists – and it makes many who are tempted to commit crime think twice. (Newburn 2003: 204)

Thus a carefully thought-out strategy, which placed the Probation Service at the forefront of delivering a new-style punishment in the community, was overturned at a stroke. Huge amounts of consultation and training had gone into the implementation of the 1991 Act, and one (very tragic) case was to reverse the policy. Notice also how Howard was able to conflate the problem into the most serious (and least numerous) of offenders when inevitably it is those lower on the seriousness scale that suffer most from a general increase in punitiveness.

Law and order policy, as an integral part of public sector policy in general, therefore became less of a clash of differing ideologies and more of an escalation of the same agenda. In other words Labour and Conservative politicians occupied the same ground, with each side equally keen to reach the summit. Neither side therefore acted as a brake on the other's ambitions, it was more a case of outdoing each other in the punitive stakes. In their quest to win the middle ground of British politics both major parties have adopted a range of measures that have progressively increased the prison population (now seen as a positive achievement) at the expense of a humane or reformist approach to offenders (now seen as an unnecessary political objective). If for a moment we fast-forward to 2006, then Prime Minster Blair made his intentions very clear, and at the same time appeared to damn many of his own reforms by association. The issues raised earlier in this chapter led to a seminal speech by Tony Blair with the apocalyptic title 'Our Nation's Future' (PM's Office, 23 June 2006) – a speech that would outline his vision of rebalancing the criminal justice system in favour of the victim. In making much of the new world in which we live (fixed order of community has gone, different employment patterns, absence of deference, more women in work, more prosperity and more opportunities for crime), he appeared to reject much of the basis of the traditional British legal system. As Blair stated, 'So we end up fighting 21st-century problems with 19th-century solutions.' He implied that the legal establishment – of which he was a member – were completely out of touch with the reality of inner-city life, for example. There may of course be elements of truth in this claim but in other respects the Blair agenda has undone much of this local knowledge and replaced it with top-down central directives (see, for example, Wargent 2002, on the local governance of probation). Despite massive reforms of policing, the CPS and the court services, the Prime Minister reported a detection rate falling from 47 per cent in 1951 to 26 per cent in 2004/5. Conviction rates over the same period fell from 96 per cent to 74 per cent. These figures cannot simply be put down to a 'changed world' or even a lack of understanding. It must also reflect performance, at least some of which has deteriorated under the modernisation programme launched by his government in 1997 and the Conservatives since 1979. Tony Blair has, however, shifted the argument from performance to a certain extent and refocused it on rights and balance within the criminal justice system. What was once regarded as a rightful concern for human rights is now regarded as a system balanced in favour of the offender. As Blair indicated, 'It's no use saying that in theory there should be no conflict between the traditional protections for the suspect and the rights of the law-abiding majority because, as a result of the changing nature of crime and society, there is, in practice, such a conflict ...'

Blair made much of judging the effectiveness of criminal justice policy by reference to the 'reality of the street and the community'. This would, he felt, require a 'wholesale reform' and made mention of the new National Offender Management Service (NOMS) as being crucial, but already it seems needing to change. This view is encapsulated in his thoughts on sentencing reform:

> It is the culture of political and legal decision-making that has to change, to take account of the way the world has changed. It is not this or that judicial decision, this or that law. It is a complete change of mindset, an avowed, articulated determination to make protection of the law-abiding public the priority and to measure that not by the theory of the textbook but by the reality of the street and community in which real people live real lives.

For practitioners who have worked in the criminal justice field for the past 15 years, it must have been difficult to imagine what any other reform could mean. However, once again it appears as if responding to a series of high-profile cases would trigger significant change. The government announced on 29 March 2007 that the functions of the Home Office would be split. In future the police service would remain in the Home Office but with greater emphasis on national security. The remaining functions would be joined with the Department for Constitutional Affairs in a new Ministry of Justice, including courts, prisons and probation. It will be interesting to see if the hard-nosed ends of policing functions being removed from the traditionally 'helping' services will lead to a rediscovery of some of their traditional functions. This space is certainly worth watching.

A policy case example

In many respects, the history of the Probation Service over the past 15 years or so perfectly demonstrates the ebb and flow of criminal justice policy. As mentioned earlier, the rising tide of populist punitiveness in the 1980s threatened its very existence and its survival since is testimony not only to its ability to reinvent and transform itself, but also to how shifting ideologies can impact upon criminal justice agencies. The 1991 Criminal Justice Act, as we noted above, offered threats and opportunities, but we should look just before this to identify the beginnings of significant probation change.

A useful starting point would be the Statement of National Objectives and Priorities (SNOP) set for the Probation Service (Home Office 1984). This national setting of priorities required local probation areas to respond with their own list (Statement of Local Objectives and Priorities – SLOP) and really triggered the process of increasing central control over a previously largely autonomous service. However, it was to be a philosophical twist to the notion of punishment and custody that would really signal a major transformation of probation. In 1988 a Home Office Green Paper, *Punishment, Custody and Community*, followed by the White Paper, *Crime, Justice and Protecting the Public* (Home Office 1990), revealed a reinvention of Conservative views on punishment. As ever, an attempt to lower the cost of the public purse to make room for tax cuts probably lay behind a change that may not have sat easily with many party stalwarts. The new notion was that, in essence, prison didn't work and was a 'good way of making bad people worse'. It bred a dependency culture and was not the appropriate punishment for less serious offenders. Therefore disposals in the community would be beefed up to improve credibility and prison would be reserved for the most serious (mostly sexual and violent) offenders. Community sentences would be rebranded as constituting a restriction on liberty and would be a punishment rather than an *alternative* to it, the philosophy upon which the Probation Service had been founded. Probation officers would therefore become supervisors of punishment in the community, with emerging minimum national standards for supervision (Home Office 1990). Community disposals would therefore represent a restriction of liberty and it was this change in penal philosophy that would underpin the 1991 Criminal Justice Act. (For a review of the changes throughout this period refer to Brownlee 1998; Worrall 1997; Newburn 2003). From the mid-1980s to the early 1990s therefore, the Probation Service faced a good deal of external pressure to change and found itself increasingly under central direction. The change did represent a fundamental cultural shift for many but should not be viewed as coming only from the outside. In 1988 the Association of Chief Officers of Probation (ACOP) had released a document entitled *More Demanding than Prison*. As much as anything this may have been a position statement to fend off government threats to use other agencies if probation was not prepared to follow through with reform.

Thus the notionally liberal aims of the 1991 CJA (to reduce the use of custody and increase the use of community penalties) was in fact an illiberal measure for probation in that it shifted it towards becoming a punishing organisation. The penal philosophy emerging in this period has been described as 'bifurcation' (Bottoms 1977) and perhaps more aptly 'punitive bifurcation' (Cavadino and Dignan 1992) – a twin-track approach which saw tough sentences for serious offenders and easier, community-based penalties for less serious offences. For probation officers it appeared as if their professional survival depended upon a major culture shift. Obviously for many of those trained under a social work philosophy, this would not be easy. Recognising this, the government launched a review of probation training in 1994, and in 1995 suggested ending the higher education monopoly. Decisions were put on ice, however, until the new Home Secretary, Jack Straw, announced the Diploma in Probation Studies in 1997, becoming a fusion of higher education and vocational study (NVQ). Thus it can be seen that during the 1980s and into the 1990s probation policy was effectively shifted from the local to the centre, with the establishment of national standards, cash limits to budgets and a rethinking of the notion of punishment in the community. The establishment of a new training regime would ensure that new entrants would be more suited to the philosophical revolution that was underway.

However, as we have noted throughout this chapter, each new phase of the revolution appeared never to go quite far enough. In 1995 a Green Paper, *Strengthening Punishment in the Community* (Home Office 1995), was launched in effect to convince the public that community punishments really were sufficiently rigorous to combat crime. Therefore the toughening up of the 1991 CJA was already regarded as ineffective, and remember at this point that the battle for the law and order hearts and minds was well and truly enjoined by Conservative and Labour politicians. As we know, Labour emerged victorious in 1997 and quickly established its own reformist agenda, the 'What Works' philosophy. This entailed making increasing use of evidence-led interventions supported by research into their effectiveness. Informed largely by developments in Canada, the Home Office launched its Correctional Policy Framework in 1999. It signalled a programmatic approach to working with offenders, thus offering some hope for a revival of the rehabilitationist spirit, but in a more proscribed form, for example: 'usually, they will be characterised by a sequence of activities designed to achieve clearly defined objectives based on a theoretical model or empirical evidence' (Home Office 1999). The programme rapidly unfolded and became what Raynor (2002: 182) described as 'the largest initiative in evidence-based corrections to be undertaken anywhere in the world'. Significantly – and a precursor of things to come – a panel was established to accredit effective programmes, and it was to be a joint enterprise between Prison and Probation Services (the Joint Prisons and Probation Accreditation Panel – JPPAP).

To smooth the path of this interventions development, what appeared to be the final managerial reform was introduced. Discussions had already been undertaken in respect of unifying the Prison and Probation Services into a single agency (Home Office 1998), but this had been shelved, at least for the time being. Instead, in 2001, the National Probation Service was created out of the Criminal Justice and Court Services Act 2000. In a largely uncontested manner, the traditional 54 local probation areas, each led by their own committee, were reorganised into 42 areas, to be coterminous with police and CPS areas – a good example of the newly emerging joined-up philosophy. There was briefly talk of strike action by the National Association of Probation Officers and there has been a longer-term fight over the independence of probation boards (Wargent 2002). The new service would be 100 per cent Home Office funded and chief officers would become civil servants. The service's traditional role in family work was removed and a new organisation, the Children and Family Court Advisory Service (CAFCASS) was established. This was a further signal that probation was becoming firmly entrenched in the crime control field.

However, as noted in the previous paragraph, these developments only *appeared* to be the final phase of the revolution. In March 2003 Patrick Carter was asked to review the correctional services in England and Wales. His eventual report in December 2003 (Carter 2003 and Home Office 2004) led to recommendations for the 'end-to-end' management of offenders (throughout the term of their sentence, in custody and outside). The review spoke of 'seamless' sentences and the oversight of the case by an offender manager at every stage. The new organisation would employ over 70,000 staff with a budget in excess of £4.3 billion. A national offender manager would oversee the work of ten regional managers who would eventually have responsibility for the Prison and Probation Service budgets in their areas. The Carter review recommended four major areas: tough and rigorous sentences, a new role for the judiciary, a new approach to managing offenders and improving contestability and competition in the corrections sector. It is interesting to note the words concerning the judiciary – 'judges and magistrates need to continue to be able to make entirely independent sentencing decisions' – in the light of ministerial comments on sentences in the 2006 'scandals' commented on earlier in this chapter. NOMS has been viewed as a new dawn for the way in which offenders are dealt with, as former Home Secretary David Blunkett proclaimed in his speech announcing the changes:

> This is a once-in-a-generation opportunity to transform the way we manage offenders, to make sure they pay back the community they have harmed, to reduce re-offending and to cut crime. As I said two years ago in my speech to the Prison Service Conference, I am not interested in reform for reform's sake but in breaking patterns of crime and creating a virtuous circle of prevention, detection, punishment and rehabilitation through a reformed police service and through a modernised criminal justice system and prison and probation services.

Thus reform and modernisation were the way forward and would be the way to further protect the public. Yet by the time NOMS was launched in 2004 we had already had at least 15 years of significant change. It really did feel like a permanent revolution. The Probation Service can therefore be viewed as a good barometer for the changes in penal policy and philosophy that have unfolded during the past 15 years or so. During this period it has been forcibly moved away from its befriending role. It now finds itself ever more closely entwined with the prison service, quite aside from it becoming a close bedfellow of the police service in its public protection role (police services now also designate constables as 'offender managers' in public protection cases). It has for many become a punishing service but remains the only one likely to work closely with offenders and *their families*, in the *community*. This crucial role is, however, increasingly at risk as a result of the bureaucratic centralising tendencies noted earlier.

The tension of modern criminal justice policy

Following his election to office, Prime Minister Tony Blair had made much of his local and community-based polices. In many respects he was right to be proud of his government's achievements with a series of improvements to local housing, leisure, health and environmental facilities. Yet that progress had occurred in parallel with a resurgence of central control, a real top-down philosophy. What appears to be an obsession with setting central targets and performance measurement has led to a compliance culture across the public sector. This is unfortunately frequently at odds with the notion of public service still held on to by many staff. The media furore unleashed in the spring of 2006 quite clearly suggested that the revolution had not worked. Despite knowing that certain measurables, such as the risk of being a victim of domestic burglary halving since 1995 (Home Office 2005), the government appears as if it will allow its long-term success to be derailed by short-term, unusual and frequently unpreventable incidents of the kind reported earlier in this chapter.

Criminal justice policy therefore suffers from the problem of rarely being left alone long enough to deliver its objectives. Perhaps the obvious bottom line for all involved is to reduce the incidence of crime in our communities. This is a laudable aim and, to a certain extent, is achievable. If we accept that crime cannot be eliminated then measures can be taken to reduce the extent of crime and perhaps to target resources at those we know are most likely to victimise the most vulnerable. Standing outside the populist arguments for a moment, it would become evident that to work towards the goal of crime reduction a variety of approaches would be needed, with some more suited than the next to particular problem behaviours. Thus better car security will reduce the volume of car theft. More effective home security will lower burglary rates. Higher standards of street lighting may reduce incidents of anti-social behaviour and personal attacks on the public – in other words basic crime prevention measures can and do work. Equally, offenders once caught may require a variety of interventions to help them desist from future crime. For some that intervention will have to be custody, not only to mark the seriousness of their crime but also to further protect the public. For such people it remains important that custody continues to strive to provide a positive experience. We know that prison can brutalise its inmates and this will not help them to return to the community as a law-abiding individual. For others it may well be appropriate to deal with them in the community. However, it is here that we can see the rhetoric of populism most significantly impacting upon well thought-out measures. Since the notion of punishment in the community was discovered in the late 1980s the rehabilitative agenda has taken something of a back seat. We have seen the reconstruction of the Probation Service into a punishing agency, or as Paul Boateng, a minister at the Home Office, said, 'We are a law enforcement agency. That is what we are. That is what we do' (Newburn 2003: 156). This tough talk exactly epitomises the determination to eliminate anything supposedly 'soft' from the criminal justice system but this in itself is based upon a false premise. The assumption is that probation officers and others only have the offender's interests at heart and are not interested in protecting the wider community. This is a strange notion. Why would a probation officer or youth justice worker want to spend time with people who may well have committed very nasty crimes and could be difficult and unpleasant people? They do it on the basis of trying to help the offender not to do it again. This is a form of crime prevention. It may work and it may not, just as having strong security on a car may work but may not if the offender is skilled or brazen. For some offenders, befriending or focused programmes may help reduce incidents of future crime. They may not. Or they may work later having failed earlier because the time was not right. None of this should be surprising when dealing with individuals, especially troubled and difficult individuals. Yet these interventions are increasingly regarded as a let-off, or as upholding offender rights at the expense of the public. In the case of young offenders, Muncie comments that what might once have been regarded as indicators of the need for welfare support are now read as possible precursors for criminality (2006: 781). 'Helping' interventions are thus reshaped as punishment, or as a restriction of liberty. Worse, those that should be aimed at enabling offenders to give something back to the community (the old community service orders) are increasingly talked about as becoming a highly visible demonstration of an offender's wrongdoing – a public shaming rebranded as 'payback'. This is another example of the US seepage into British criminal justice philosophy.

Conclusion

It is therefore seemingly impossible to divorce criminal justice policy from its populist influences. Constructive long-term measures are developed and, if left alone, can yield positive results (excellent examples might be restorative justice conferences for young offenders and circles of trust for serious sex offenders). Yet, the minute something goes wrong with these developments – and, importantly, this becomes public knowledge – they can be abandoned by government and rubbished by decision-makers. According to Loader (2006) this has not always been the case. In charting the history of what he terms the 'Platonic Guardians', he describes the influence of the liberal elite in criminal justice policymaking until its demise from the mid-1990s. He makes the point that they and their worldview even survived a good deal of the Thatcher years, such was their hold within the Home Office and among influential criminologists. Yet at this time the seeds of change were beginning to sprout. In quoting one senior Home Office civil servant, he noted that Thatcher had moved onto hallowed territory when commenting publicly on specific penalties and sentences, 'in a way that her predecessors wouldn't have dreamed of doing … there was a very strict understanding … that ministers [didn't] comment on what judges did or didn't do' (Loader 2006: 574). Consider this against the outright attack on the tariff set in a paedophile's life sentence tariff by then Home Secretary John Reid and the Prime Minister. Despite this only being a minimum tariff, and despite the judge indicating that the offender would spend many years in prison and may never be released, his tariff was misconstrued constantly in the media as a 'sentence' – a situation insufficiently corrected by the politicians. One must assume this is because the politicians would have been regarded as too soft had they appeared in any way to justify the tariff set by the judge (see BBC Online, 15 June 2006).

Loader describes the decline of the liberal influence in penal policymaking as a result of the winning out of a 'culture of intolerance', a political culture '… dominated by actors preoccupied with being seen to react immediately and resolutely to mass-mediated, emotionally charged and urgently pressed public concerns about crime and disorder' (Loader 2006: 581). He contrasts this culture of intolerance with what one of his respondents describes as a 'culture of deliberation'. He argues that the heat needs to be taken out of crime otherwise they play with 'passions that cannot easily be regulated … expectations that are not easily sated and … create spirals of outrage …' (Loader 2006: 583). As he concludes, 'These … are the all too probable and perilous consequences of political actors choosing to ride a tiger they can neither tame, nor easily dismount.'

Respected academics such as Loader contributed to the thinking behind Blair's 'Our Nation's Future' speech referred to earlier, but one has to question if he listened at all. On 16 July 2006 *The Observer* reported that the Home Office would 'target babies and toddlers under 2 in the war on anti-social behaviour'. This referred to a plan to use nurses and health visitors to work with dysfunctional families who do not ask for help and later experience problems with anti-social children. Thus ever earlier intervention is justified as a pre-emptive strike and, as a consequence, failure to 'take advantage' of this may result in stiffer penalties later on (Blair 1997, in Muncie 2006: 782). These measures would accompany further restrictions on parole release and the ending of the one-third sentencing discount for dangerous offenders. The tough response to a relatively small number of disastrous cases was unfolding and, according to the same report, police figures would soon reveal a surge in robbery and violent offences across the country (Doward *et al.* 2006), furthering demands for the government to respond in an even tougher fashion. This chapter had intended to conclude with Loader's words but perhaps it can be left to Martin Narey, formerly Director of the Prison Service, to say how far, or how little, criminal justice policy has moved in the last two decades:

> It takes guts for politicians to recognise that for some people, prison isn't the appropriate place. The only Home Secretary brave enough to point out the reality that prison is an ineffective way of dealing with petty offenders was Douglas Hurd when he was working for Margaret Thatcher for God's sake. (*The Observer*, 16 July 2006)

Discussion questions

1 Is there an inevitability about the increasingly punitive direction of criminal justice policy?
2 Can you think of any ways in which law and order issues can become depoliticised?
3 What transformed the Labour Party into the champions of Conservative law and order values?

Further reading

Dunbar, I. and Langdon, A. (1998) *Tough Justice: Sentencing and Penal Policies in the 1990s*. London: Blackstone Press. An excellent overview of policy and political developments at the end of the Conservative government and the emergence of 'New' Labour.

Mathews, R. and Young, J. (eds) (2003) *The New Politics of Crime and Punishment*. Cullompton: Willan. A critical account of a wide range of policy initiatives under the Labour government in the late 1900s and early twenty-first century.

Tonry, M. (2004) *Punishment and Politics: Evidence and Emulation in the Making of English Crime Control Policy*. Cullompton: Willan. Another critique of recent Labour policies, with an emphasis on alternatives and concerns over the wholesale importation of American ideas.

References

ACOP (1988) *More Demanding Than Prison*. Wakefield: ACOP.

BBC News Online (2006) 'No. 10 denies sentencing panic', 15 June, at: http://news.bbc.co.uk/1/hi/uk_politics/5083686.stm (last accessed 4 June 2008).

Bottoms, A.E. (1977) 'Reflections on the renaissance of dangerousness', *Howard Journal*, 16: 70–96.

Brownlee, I. (1998) *Community Punishment: A Critical Introduction*. Harlow: Longman.

Carter, P. (2003) *Managing Offenders: Reducing Crime. A New Approach*. London: Strategy Unit.

Cavadino, M. and Dignan, J. (1992) *The Penal System: An Introduction*. London: Sage.

Doward, J., Hinsliff, G., Beach, A. and Temko, N. (2006) 'Fresh blow to Reid as violent crime rises', *The Observer*, 16 July 2006.

Home Office (1984) *Probation Service in England and Wales: Statement of National Objectives and Priorities*. London: Home Office.

Home Office (1988) *Punishment, Custody and the Community*, Cm 424. London: HMSO.

Home Office (1990) *Crime, Justice and Protecting the Public*, Cm 965. London: HMSO.

Home Office (1995) *Strengthening Punishment in the Community*. London: HMSO.

Home Office (1998) *Joining Forces to Protect the Public. Prisons–Probation: A Consultation Document*. London: Home Office.

Home Office (1999) *The Correctional Policy Framework: Effective Execution of the Sentences of the Courts so as to Reduce Reoffending and Protect the Public*. London: Home Office.

Home Office (2004) *Reducing Crime – Changing Lives*. London: Home Office.

Home Office (2005) *Crime Statistics for England and Wales*. London: Home Office.

HMIP (2006a) *An Independent Review of a Serious Further Offence Case: Damien Hanson & Elliot White*. London: Home Office.

HMIP (2006b) *Anthony Rice: An Independent Review of a Serious Further Offence Case*. London: Home Office.

Home Office (2006c) *Rebalancing the Criminal Justice System in Favour of the Law-abiding Majority. Cutting Crime, Reducing Reoffending and Protecting the Public.* London: Home Office.

Horton, S. and Farnham, D. (1999) *Public Management in Britain.* Basingstoke: Macmillan.

Loader, I. (2006) 'Fall of the "Platonic Guardians". Liberalism, criminology and political responses to crime in England and Wales', *British Journal of Criminology,* 46: 561–86.

McLaughlin, E., Muncie, J. and Hughes, G. (2001) 'The permanent revolution: New Labour, new public management and the modernization of criminal justice', *Criminal Justice,* 1 (3): 301–18.

Massey, A. and Pyper, R. (2005) *Public Management and Modernisation in Britain.* Basingstoke: Palgrave Macmillan.

Muncie, J. (2006) 'Governing young people: coherence and contradiction in contemporary youth justice', *Critical Social Policy,* 26 (4): 770–93.

Newburn, T. (2003) *Crime and Criminal Justice Policy,* 2nd edn. Harlow: Pearson Education.

Parole Board for England and Wales (2006) *Annual Report and Accounts, 2005–6.* London: Parole Board.

Raynor, P. (2002) 'What Works: have we moved on?', in D. Ward, J. Scott and M. Lacey (eds) *Probation: Working for Justice.* Oxford: Oxford University Press.

Savage, S.P. and Atkinson, R. (2001) *Pubic Policy Under Blair.* Basingstoke: Palgrave.

Wargent, M. (2002) 'The new governance of probation', *Howard Journal,* 41 (2): 182–200.

Worrall, A. (1997) *Punishment in the Community: The Future of Criminal Justice.* Harlow: Longman.

Chapter 3

The evidence base

Anthony Goodman

Introduction

The practice of working with offenders has evolved over many years, from an approach of rescuing the fallen, to what has most recently become known as 'what works' and 'effective practice'. This chapter will briefly consider the impact of these changes and the evaluations of practice that have been made over time. This evaluation will focus on probation practice, as throughout its long history the probation service, latterly as the National Probation Service and now as part of the National Offender Management Service (NOMS), has been the key organisation in terms of offering sustained intervention to reduce offending. It will be argued that the evidence base for much of what has gone on is complex and contentious. In the long-term the service will need to rediscover some of the good practice initiatives that have been lost. This is particularly true with respect to anti-discriminatory practice issues. The need for training for probation professionals is not in doubt. Working with common sense or nous is no substitute for having an underpinning set of theories or rationale for good practice and this is considered in relation to effective practice.

The effectiveness of NOMS is in the public arena and the headlines do not read in a positive manner for probation. Alan Travis writing in *The Guardian*, on their front page (23 October 2007) revealed figures, just released by the Ministry of Justice, which disclosed that 83 high-risk offenders released from prison in the previous year had been charged with a further serious offence such as murder or rape. The figure for the previous year was 61. Of these 83 cases, 12 had been from the 1,249 offenders in the highest category of risk, known as the 'critical few'. These offenders would have received the highest level of supervision and surveillance from probation and the police. By a simple arithmetical deduction a further 71 cases were of a lower (but not the lowest) perceived level of risk. Even though the Probation Service supervised annually almost 15,500 offenders in the medium- and high-level risk categories, over 1,700 have been returned to prison as being in breach of their licence conditions. The system is not failsafe. The reliance on actuarial notions of risk and computer-generated scoring was not protecting the public in a way hoped for by its advocates.

To understand what has happened to probation practice it is helpful to examine changes to such practice over time. This chapter will consider the historical context of developing practice before examining what is known as 'what works'. Finally, the role that effective practice initiatives have taken and the implications for what might happen in the future are considered. The resurgence of a more person-focused approach that implies that the offender should be more than a passive recipient of cognitive-behavioural treatment is an interesting development. It will not be a cheap option. In the vanguard of increased reoffending (as mentioned above), despite ongoing supervision, the chapter will conclude on whether the blueprint for a future Probation Service that has become process driven is in serious danger of losing its credibility. Yet again, the Probation Service is at a crossroads and its future is unclear.

The early period of working with offenders

In the nineteenth century both male and female police court missionaries were employed by the Church of England Temperance Society to support offenders who had taken a pledge to desist from offending. The Act which established the Probation Service was the 1907 Probation of Offenders Act and was heralded as an Act that would empty the prisons, though it did not have this result. The probation order was not a sentence in its own right but was a recognisance entered into, at court, by the offender. The Samuel Committee of 1909 recommended 'that in future legislation the term 'probation' should be applied only to release under supervision, and not to binding over without supervision or dismissal' (Bochel 1976: 147).

Denney (1998) commented that the 1907 Probation of Offenders Act did not see probation taking on a central role within the criminal justice system. However, May (1991) observes that the first part of the twentieth century was a period of change when probation became an 'expert' within the criminal justice system. This echoes the work of McWilliams who in a quartet of essays (1983, 1985, 1986, 1987) traced the history of the Probation Service from its evangelical roots and the desire to 'rescue' the fallen through the golden age of the 'treatment' model to a 'managerialist' model.

In the prisons, the origins of prison welfare can be traced back to 1936, when the National Discharged Prisoners' Aid Society appointed its first welfare officer to undertake prison visiting in regional prisons. In the same year a full-time prison welfare officer was appointed to Wakefield regional training prison (Appleyard 1971: 107). An important point on the relationship between the public and private sectors at this time was that the Police Court Missions and the Discharged Prisoners Aid Societies:

Submitted to a considerable degree of state regulation, in return for which the state provided them both with funding and with a new kind of power over their clients, backed with the threat of imprisonment ... [or] with being compelled to report to the police. (Ryan and Ward 1989: 89)

The consequence of this was the service becoming more scientifically based under the auspices of the Home Office.

The middle period of working with offenders

In 1958 Radzinowicz produced a report called *The Results of Probation* which gave a very positive outcome for probation supervision. For first offenders it stated the rate of success was 76.8 per cent and 89.2 per cent for males and females respectively and 64.1 per cent and 79.1 per cent for boy and girl juveniles. For all offenders it revealed an 81.2 per cent success (non-reoffending) rate for adults and 65.7 per cent for juveniles. For those with one previous conviction the figures were 67.3 per cent and 55.3 per cent, and for two or more previous convictions the figures were 51.5 per cent and 42.1 per cent (1958: 5–7). Probation appeared to work less well after a period of imprisonment, but almost as well if given again after a first order had been completed.

In 1962 (reprinted 1966) the *Report of the Departmental Committee on the Probation Service* started by giving their brief as 'examin[ing] all aspects of the probation service'. Probation was described as:

The submission of an offender while at liberty to a specified period of supervision by a social caseworker who is an officer of the court: during this period the offender remains liable, if not of good conduct, to be dealt with by the court. (Home Office 1962: 2)

The idea of the offender's consent was acknowledged to be 'conditional' as other sanctions were likely to be 'less congenial'. The report did not question the value of 'casework' with offenders; indeed it stated that: 'Rare sensitivity may be needed in establishing and developing' this relationship. The probation officer was described as a 'professional caseworker' and probation practice was located as a specialised field within social work. In an acknowledgment that the background of the offender may well include social disadvantage, it continued:

Failings, anxieties and problems are the outcome of diverse causes which may be understood and altered. There may, in the first place, be scope for altering external influences by helping the individual to change his home or economic circumstances, his habits or companions. Here, although the need may sometimes be for direct material assistance,

> the caseworker's aim will be to encourage people to help themselves rather than be helped; to co-operate rather than obey. (Ibid.: 24–5)

Literature written before and during the 1960s focused on the social work (psychological) needs of offenders, e.g. King (1969), Foren and Bailey (1968). The latter authors, in making a distinction between the formal authority of the probation officer and their personal authority, noted that whichever was more marked, 'the aim must always be to strengthen the client's ego' (ibid.: 94).

The move from untrained voluntary organisations to the Probation Service was replayed when the Probation Service took over work with ex-prisoners from the Discharged Prisoners' Aid Societies in 1966. The Home Office report *Penal Practice in a Changing Society* produced in 1959 and reprinted in 1966 commented: 'It is a disquieting feature of our society that, in the years since the war, rising standards in material prosperity, education and social welfare have brought no decrease in the high rate of crime reached during the war' (1966: 1). The report acknowledged that since the Gladstone report of 1895 deterrence through fear had not worked. The first report of the Home Office Research Unit *Persistent Criminals* published in 1963 focused on the problem of what to do with offenders who had repeatedly served prison sentences (Hammond and Chayen 1963). These were typically men sentenced to preventative detention under the 1908 and 1948 Acts. This allowed the courts to impose very long terms in prison on offenders aged over 30 years who had been convicted of an offence which could receive a sentence of two years or more, who had three or more previous convictions since the age of 17, and who had had a least two experiences of imprisonment. In 1965 a short Home Office paper was published entitled *The Adult Offender* which started with a quotation from Sir Alexander Paterson: that 'You cannot train men for freedom in conditions of captivity.' It acknowledged that some offenders were dangerous but many were 'disturbed, unstable and immature' (1965: 3). It commented that: 'Long periods in prison may punish, or possibly deter them. But do them no good – certainly do not fit them for re-entry into society. Every additional year of prison progressively unfits them' (ibid.: 3).The report was preparing the ground for the introduction of parole in the 1967 Act. By this stage 28 Discharged Prisoners' Aid Societies out of 36 had passed their after-care responsibilities over to the Probation Service. The voluntary organisations were meeting together to plan for the future (and in the event became the National Association for the Care and Resettlement of Offenders (NACRO)). The use of volunteers was still heavily promoted. In 1966 the Home Office published *Residential Provision for Homeless Discharged Offenders*. This report regarded the provision of discharged prisoner hostels as essential, for those with different types of need, including alcoholics. Interestingly it added under the heading 'Education of the public' that 'a real attempt must be made to gain the sympathy of the community as a whole for the special problems and difficulties of the offender' (1966: 23).

From the pessimism of 'nothing works' to 'what works'

There has been a continuing debate about the changing nature of the service in the literature for decades and two key contributions will be mentioned briefly here: Martinson, and Bottoms and McWilliams. Martinson (1974) was famous for his assertion that 'nothing works' in reducing offending. His commissioned research was originally repressed and he had to go to court to get it published. Hence its impact became even more powerful, as was his language. He wrote:

> Even if we can't 'treat' offenders so as to make them do better, a great many of the programmes designed to rehabilitate them at least did not make them do *worse* ... *the implication is clear: that if we can't do more for (and to) offenders, at least we can safely do less.* (1974: 48, italics in original)

Five years later Martinson issued a retraction of this view:

> On the basis of the evidence in our current study, I withdraw this conclusion. I have often said that treatment added to the networks of criminal justice is 'impotent', and I withdraw this characterisation as well. I protested at the slogan used by the media to sum up what I said – 'nothing works'. The press has no time for scientific quibbling and got to the heart of the matter better than I did. (1979: 254)

Bottoms and McWilliams (1979) discussed a 'non-treatment paradigm' whereby offenders would report to see their probation officer but 'treatment' would be optional. They pointed out that the 1907 Probation of Offenders Act had not just been about supporting offenders. The list of duties contained in this Act started:

> ... to visit or receive reports from the person under supervision at such reasonable intervals as may be specified in the probation order or, subject thereto, as the probation may see fit (s.4(a)). (Cited in Bottoms and McWilliams 1979: 175)

Thus in 1907, surveillance and supervision were already on the probation agenda. It was the 1948 Criminal Justice Act which highlighted the treatment ethos with 'advise, assist and befriend' and accelerated the trend towards a 'treatment model' of intervention with offenders. The publication of a 'non-treatment paradigm' therefore sent shock waves through the Probation Service as it questioned the 'treatment' model and substituted a 'help' model instead, though an earlier report by the Butterworth Committee (Home Office 1962) had stated the need to 'protect society' and 'ensure the good conduct' of the probationer.

A further contribution is worthy of note for its early recording of themes which were to dominate the literature in subsequent years. Haxby (1978) discussed the possibility of a correctional service and detailed how the management structure within the probation service grew between 1966 and 1974 when middle managers increased fourfold. He linked this and other events to 'encroachments upon the autonomy of the probation officer' (ibid.: 36) as new statutory tasks were imposed on the service, such as parole (introduced in the Criminal Justice Act 1967) and the supervision of young people from detention centres and Borstals.

The Home Office and working with offenders: from indifference to 'hands-on'

The Home Office largely did not prioritise the work of the service until 1984 when it published its 'Statement of National Objectives and Priorities' (SNOP) (Home Office 1984). As May pointed out: 'Nowhere was the attempt to control local variations more clear than in the 1984 SNOP for the probation services in England and Wales' (1995: 872). According to SNOP the ethos of probation was to service the needs of the court, which became the client rather than the offender. SNOP charged the 55 probation services with the priority of working with offenders in the community and downgrading work with prisoners and community work.

Lloyd (1986) analysed the initial individual services' responses to SNOP, in their 'Statements of Local Objectives and Priorities' (SLOPs). This provided three 'main points of conflict' between central government/Home Office and local service managements, namely: 'the autonomy of probation officers; the control implications of taking on more serious offenders on probation and the need to respond to human plight' (Lloyd 1986: 72). The reaction of the Home Office response in subsequent White, Green, Blue and Peppermint (coloured) Papers was to threaten probation management with outside direct entrants and the implementation of 'cash limits' to the services to force through the proposed changes.

This period was one where the standing of professionals was challenged as clinicians and practitioners lost their power to management professionals. Furthermore, the welfare professionals lost their status as the notion of 'just deserts' gained credence and there was a drift towards a punitive tendency and a backlash against liberalism (Garland 2000). This was manifested in a lack of interest from the Home Office in the resettlement of prisoners. Rutherford, in a set of interesting conversations with chief probation officers, highlighted the opposition of senior probation management to the prioritising of SNOP:

> We publicly stated that the Home Office had completely got it wrong, that their lack of investment in decent through-care made after-care

very much more difficult ... we continued to build up specialist through-care. (CPO in Rutherford 1993: 108)

In November 1988, the *Parole system in England and Wales: Report of the Review Committee* was published, chaired by Lord Carlisle. It reviewed the 'history and philosophy of parole and remission' and concluded that actual sentences needed to be linked closer to the sentence passed by the judge and parole would be abolished for sentences less than four years when the offender would be released at the mid-point. Offenders serving less than one year would not receive compulsory probation after-care supervision, but sentences of more than one year would include time on compulsory licence. It rejected the use of electronic tagging for those released from custody and wanted 'a more consistent approach to the supervision by the probation service of prisoners released on licence' (Carlisle 1988: 93).

The following year two reports were published by the Audit Commission and the National Audit Office. It is worth looking in a little depth at these as they are further evidence of how pressure was applied to the Probation Service to change its mode of operation. What is also interesting is how opinion is passed off as uncontested fact. Firstly, the title of the Audit Commission report is interesting in its own right: *The Probation Service: Promoting Value for Money*. Would many probation officers working at the time recognise the assertion that:

> Increasingly, doubts were cast on the effectiveness of social casework, and the wisdom of maintaining the 'individual practitioner' model. These doubts led to a loss of confidence within the Probation Service and to more strenuous efforts to assess the effectiveness of the service's traditional methods of working. (Audit Commission 1989: 16)

The report's comment on the SNOP document was that overall it had 'had a profound effect' (ibid.: 52). What was also needed was improved management and for the service to demonstrate that it was systematically effective. This would require performance indicators, financial management information systems and clarified lines of accountability if it was to deliver value for money. It described probation as being at a 'watershed'. Its conclusions were that probation faced a great opportunity; however, it required greater targeting of its activities and needed to be more effective, with clearer lines of accountability. The final *unsubstantiated* point made is worth quoting in full:

> Assessing the economy, efficiency and effectiveness of the Probation Service is not easy. There is some persuasive general evidence which points to the conclusion that the net effect of probation activity is to push offenders 'up-tariff' into more serious and costly sentences, rather than to divert them away from custody. It is also evident that there is

> a damaging lack of confidence among decision makers elsewhere in the criminal justice system. (Ibid.: 68)

This sounds in a bizarre way a call for dynamic non-intervention! The report of the National Audit Office (1989) was also concerned with improving the efficiency and effectiveness of the Probation Service. Following on from SNOP it was critical of the level of measurable objectives in the probation services and the effect of local probation discretion on priorities. The two reports dovetailed together and the implication was clear: services had to change and the Home Office had to manage this change and the work of the service. The old regime of probation had to go. What is concerning from these two reports is how profound their implications were and what limited evidence they were based on.

In 1990 the Green Paper *Supervision and Punishment in the Community* set out ways in which the courts' and the public's confidence could be strengthened in community penalties, including making existing penalties tougher. Also that year the White Paper *Crime, Justice and Protecting the Public* looked at how this could be implemented, requiring probation services to set out their implementation plans, including intensive probation programmes.

All the proposals in the reports were included in the 1991 Criminal Justice Act, which had a twofold impact on the criminal justice system. Offenders were to be sentenced in a manner commensurate with the seriousness of the crime – the notion of 'just deserts' – and probation became a community sentence in its own right and did not require the agreement of the offender. All offenders sentenced to 12 months or more in prison would have a period of time on release on licence to the Probation Service. Thus offenders who had previously been seen as poor candidates for parole, e.g. sex and other violent offenders, who received long sentences but then disappeared on discharge, would now go on to probation caseloads.

The other major innovation was the imposition of *National Standards for the Supervision of Offenders in the Community*, first published in 1992. This version acknowledged that '[S]upervision is challenging and skilful, requiring professional social work in the field of criminal justice'. The second version three years later saw the aim of the standards as '[S]trengthening the supervision of offenders in the community, providing punishment and a disciplined programme for offenders, building on the skill and experience of practitioners and service managers'. The latest incarnation of National Standards 2005, which replaces the 2002 version, continues this punitive trajectory. This last set of standards states that priority should be given to the punitive and restrictive elements of the sentence and only then that the rehabilitative requirements can be started. There is no evidence that punishment works and the standards have successively downplayed the notion of rehabilitation. It is hard to evaluate how they add to the protection of the public as probation is not a 24-hour, seven days per week surveillance operation and was never intended to be so, whether the offender wears an electronic tag or not.

The growth of evidence based practice

The first What Works conference took place in 1991 and the Home Office published a survey of research on this and cognitive-behavioural methods of intervention by Vennard *et al.* in 1997. On the positive side, replacing the emphasis on national standards and value for money by 'What Works' meant a movement away from key performance indicators to outcomes (see Merrington and Stanley 2000).

In 1995 the then Conservative Home Secretary, Michael Howard, ended the requirement that probation officers needed to have probation training and this situation endured until Labour was elected in 1997 when they introduced a new probation qualification, not to be based in social work departments. In the same year (1995) James McGuire published *What Works: Reducing Reoffending*, McGuire being an important figure in the effective practice movement as we will see.

In 1998 Underdown published *Strategies for Effective Supervision*, which was a blueprint for producing pathfinder projects for supervision. The introduction to this report by the then HM Chief Inspector of Probation Graham Smith was described as '[T]he most important foreword I have ever written.' In evangelical terms he continued that the evidence within the report enabled the service to 'have a beginning understanding of what makes ... programmes [that performed better than custody] so successful. The movement to achieve this is known as What Works.' Tucked away in Chapter 4 entitled 'Management Enquiries' was the unwelcome comment:

> Ross and Ross note that, in reviewing published and unpublished material over the past 30 years, most evaluated programmes were found to be unsuccessful in preventing reoffending. The relevant outcome message for managers and policy makers is the highly conditional one: 'some service programmes are working with at least some offenders under some circumstances'. (Underwood 1998: 36)

This cautionary note did not stop the drive towards compulsory programmes as the intervention of choice. However, the 'Introduction of structured programmes requires substantial training provision, well integrated into the overall implementation' (Underwood 1998: 136). What was also interesting was that in the early stages these programmes were predominantly being delivered by qualified probation officers – 46 per cent of all programme staff, outnumbering unqualified probation services officers by the ratio of 2:1 (ibid.: 137). Thus the deliverers had a fully trained background and detailed knowledge and skills of offender management.

In the same year, the Probation Inspectorate published Chapman and Hough's *Evidence Based Practice*, in the foreword of which Graham Smith commented: 'It is vital that managers and practitioners make good use of the sound advice and practical assistance this Guide provides.' The Guide is interesting in that it includes brief discussions of some criminological theories such as: biology and genetics; subcultural theories, differential association and social control; drift and neutralisation labelling and symbolic interactionism; and rational choice, cognitive and behavioural approaches – but not individual/sociological positivist theories that might imply that problems arising from childhood and/or inequalities might offer some insights into offending behaviour (Chapman and Hough 1998). In one section motivational interviewing and the problem of working with relapse are mentioned, methods employed by 'traditional' probation over many years. Acknowledgment is made that the style of the practitioner's intervention and the 'quality of the relationship with the individual' (ibid.: 58) are critical to bringing about change and overcoming resistance. This is as close as the Guide gets to acknowledging interventions other than the cognitive model. A further publication from the Probation Inspectorate was in 2000 by James McGuire entitled *Cognitive-Behavioural Approaches*. This was very much a working introduction to cognitive methods of intervention with an emphasis on theory and practice.

Since this time there has been a growth in the cognitive-behavioural model and a retreat from considering continuity with offenders as important. Prison through-care has virtually disappeared as offenders are risk assessed and managed. However, this lack of continuity of contact and reliance on actuarially produced risk scales has the potential to put the public at risk. It relies on probation staff being able to make informed assessments on offenders they may barely know, without the time to speak to staff in prison who may have formed an opinion on the offender. The lack of joined-up working, ironically a mantra of New Labour, puts the public at greater risk than 'old-fashioned' probation practice based much more on 'clinical' judgment. In this respect recent research described below makes some worrying points.

Fitzgibbon and Green carried out a small-scale study of eOASys to explore the accuracy and effectiveness of this assessment tool and whether in particular it improved the situation of mentally vulnerable offenders. The findings were that full risk assessments were not carried out; indeed significant factors like harassment, obsessional behaviours, previous suicide attempts, psychiatric treatment, domestic violence and being a rape victim were not followed through in the eOASys assessment. Indeed '[t]he majority of the sample had little supplementary information to reinforce or expand on the "tick boxes"' (Fitzgibbon and Green 2006: 38). They added:

> This was unfortunate as some of the most detailed casework in the files pre-dated the introduction of eOASys and perhaps should have been included for a more complete assessment. (Ibid.: 39)

In their conclusion, citing a number of sources to make a case that the risk assessment tool could lead to 'risk averse' judgments, they comment that often: 'assessments were inaccurate and defensive due to lack of experience and exploration of the case files' (ibid.: 43). These findings were replicated to an extent in an exploration of hate attitudes in eOASys assessments by Goodman and Loumansky (2006), which found that there was little or no comment on this in the files and that not all questions on the form were answered. Thus the notion of informed assessment leading to treatment has the potential to be built on a dodgy foundation. The blame for this must be put on the Home Office rather than individual probation staff who were capable of undertaking assessment of risk but perhaps less able to superficially move this onto a form that requires a tick-box mentality. A reduction of professional knowledge and skills too far?

Offender management staff as professionals or operatives?

This notion of back to the future or how innovation in probation management has resulted in an inferior service to offenders and consequently making the public less safe is manifested in the publication *The NOMS Offender Management Model* (Home Office 2006, version 2), which acknowledged that in the terminology that pervaded the 'correctional services' in the 1990s few organisations could explain what was meant by this. The introduction stated that the same mistake should not be made with 'Offender Management'. The nub now was an end-to-end supervision of offenders whether in custody or in the community. The report states that the operational role of offender manager contains the statutory role and authority as defined in sections 197 and 198 of the Criminal Justice Act 2003. The 'responsible officer' has a duty to:

• Make arrangements in connection with the requirements of the sentence;
• Promote the offender's compliance; and
• Take enforcement action as required. (Home Office 2006: 20)

The report shows the influence of management consultants rather than those with a grip on the reality of working with offenders. The use of flow charts on how to work with offenders and acronyms like ASPIRE, which stands for Assess, Sentence Plan, Implement, Review, Evaluate, indicates to this author at least that it has been written for untrained operatives. Talk to the offender and work with them on their problems is not really neatly subsumed within the injunction:

> The assessment process starts by gathering information, from different sources, including from the offender him/herself, and including from other assessments completed by other service providers. A view then has to be formed about what this all means set in the context of the objectives of the organisation. This second component of assessment – forming a view – is important. Dealing safely and effectively with offenders can rarely, if ever, be reduced to a simple set of 'if – then'

decision rules based upon information alone. It may be necessary to adjust the objectives in a case, as a result of what emerges from the assessment. (Ibid.: 21)

This paragraph renders the offender into a passive role, not one that could be construed as having a stake in what programme is being planned for them. In short the document reads like a tool kit for untrained staff who have not had a professional grounding in the complexities of working with real people with personal difficulties.

Barkley and Collett (2000), when discussing the need to work on 'being tough on the causes of crime' as well as 'crime' per se, examine the housing needs of ex-offenders. They do not minimise the responsibility to make the offender responsible for their actions but they express concern that the need to deal with essential practical problems has been left behind. In this respect they cite findings of a retrospective study of the McGuire offending programme by Roberts *et al.*:

Offenders whose main problem was housing or accommodation were significantly less likely to complete the programme than offenders without that main problem. (Barkley and Collett 2000: 239)

They concluded that probation staff should continue to exert their traditional concern for homeless offenders. This approach would meet with the approval of both Stephen Farrall and Shad Maruna. Farrall (2002) in his research found that desistance was linked to overcoming practical problems like housing and family formation, which in turn was linked to aspects like employment. It was the social context in which the probationer lived that was important, particularly employment and relationships (see McCulloch and McNeil, this volume). These findings sound suspiciously like the work that was undertaken by probation staff before the brave new world of the National Probation Service and NOMS. Maruna (2001) examined personal narratives of offenders and argued that it was how these were constructed that offered the potential to stop recidivism. The obstacles to going straight were not delusions but were a consequence of their poor education, opportunities, etc. His comment that a 'desisting ex-offender reaches back into early experiences to find and re-establish an "old me" in order to desist' (ibid.: 89) would suggest that more traditional methods of intervention, including motivational interviewing, might be more successful than cognitive-behavioural approaches, especially if linked to practical support.

Harper and Chitty (2005) in their executive summary to the Home Office Research Study 291 review of 'What Works' highlighted the changes in criminal justice policy over time, namely that the climate had become more punitive and the use of custody had increased. The use of community sentences also increased while the use of fines decreased. Into this changing scenario has been imposed the 'What Works' agenda, mostly imported from the United States and Canada and it is difficult to generalise from there to this country. They also acknowledged that the research design had been weak in the studies, rarely achieving the standard of a randomised control trial.

In terms of factors associated with offending there was no evidence that a lack of basic skills was a predictor of offending, although a lack basic skills could be linked to school experiences, social exclusion, etc. Drawing on studies from the United States they were dismissive of the concept of social capital being associated with crime. They were more persuaded of the importance of family support and social networks. They usefully produced a table of results from a variety of programmes, including the type of intervention, the key findings, sample sizes and critical comments. Some of these findings might surprise the reader who might think that all programmes benefit the offender rather more than those who did not receive this intervention. On the positive side, many of the sex offender treatment programmes cited in Harper and Chitty (2005) have significantly lower reconviction rates. For example, Allam (1998) showed a rate of 8.1 per cent lower than a control group 1–3 year follow-up; however, the comparison group was described as weakly matched. Dobash et al. (1996) had a significantly lower rate in frequency of violence for domestic violence offenders (again a weakly matched control group). Hollin *et al.* (2004) evaluated a number of programmes: Enhanced Thinking Skills, Reasoning and Rehabilitation (R&R), Think First, One2One, Addressing Substance Related Offending Probation. The key findings were: 'Significantly higher reconviction rates of 12 percentage points for offenders with a programme order compared to a similar group without programme orders after 18 months. Significantly lower rates for completers and higher rates for non-completers' (Harper and Chitty 2005: xiv). Thus like the proverbial curate's egg the results are good in parts. Offenders who do well and complete the programme do better; if they do not complete the programme they do worse.

Perhaps the best known programme is the STOP programme evaluated by Raynor and Vanstone, based on R&R. This programme was evaluated using a group of community-sentenced offenders compared to a prison-sentenced group. After one year the community-treated group had a lower reconviction rate, but after two years there was no significant difference. According to Rex (2001) the emphasis on cognitive aspects in work with offenders led to 'environmental' factors being neglected. Indeed, she commented that Raynor and Vanstone had conceded that this had been neglected in their study. Raynor and Vanstone (2001) commented that the STOP programme had pre-dated the Home Office initiatives and that it had been driven by curiosity that 'allows organisations to learn' (ibid.: 201). They expressed anxiety about the consequences of the formation of a centralised national service, which has indeed come to pass.

Other studies mentioned by Harper and Chitty (2005) showed positive and negative effects. Steele and Van Arendsen (2001) for Think First Probation had a higher reconviction rate after one year for a treatment group of adult men and women compared to another group serving a community sentence. Stewart-Ong *et al.* (2003) showed that adult males on a community-based pre-accredited Think First Probation programme had a 24 percentage point (significantly) higher rate of reconviction compared to adult males sentenced to custody without a programme. Sugg (2000) found that a treatment group given Aggression Replacement Training had a lower rate (9.2 per cent) than a non-treatment group with similar community penalties. Again those who completed the programme did best. All the above groups had the comment that the comparison groups were weakly matched, apart from Hollin *et al.* where the comparison groups were unmatched. This shows the complexity of giving uncritical approval for the accredited programme approach.

Wilkinson (2005) re-evaluated the R&R programme, which he stated was 'predicated on the notion that many repeat offenders reoffend because of deficits in their social intelligence' (ibid.: 71). Palmer (2003) offers some evidence that moral reasoning is more limited among offenders, particularly younger ones. Wilkinson was critical that evaluations did not include non-starters and drop-outs from the programme. The explanation that dropouts had not had the 'full dose' would not be accepted in clinical trials. He concluded that R&R had still to demonstrate its effectiveness. It is disappointing that the effectiveness of programmes is unproven when the 'What Works' movement has become an important weapon in the armoury of probation. Perhaps we should exercise caution in uncritically accepting what works in absolute terms of success or failure. In the same light, it is unfortunate that all that went before has been rejected in terms of effectiveness. The words of Pawson and Tilley (1997) in the final chapter of their book *Realistic Evaluation* are relevant here:

> Our baseline argument throughout has been not that programs are 'things' that may (or may not) 'work'; rather they contain certain ideas which work for certain subjects in certain situations. (Ibid.: 215)

The decision to implement 'existing, largely overseas, research findings as a template for success' has been questioned as misguided by Ellis and Winstone (2002). They continue:

> [T]he Home Office is, in effect, taking a large gamble on the outcome of the international research findings, but with no guarantee of success in the English and Welsh context ... the interim evidence suggests that the odds on failure are shortening. (Ibid.: 352)

Conclusion

It could be argued that what has happened to the implementation of 'What Works' is that there has been a division into two camps of those for the change and those against it. On the 'for' side are writers like Underdown, Raynor and Roberts. The latter perspective, including Farrall and Maruna who argue for the importance of social capital, is neatly encapsulated by one of the chief protagonists:

> Overall, and in spite of the rhetoric, the foundations of What Works cannot be said to be neat, evidence based, carefully considered and well planned. Instead we are faced with a messy, uncoordinated, coincidental set of factors that lie behind this highly significant initiative. (Mair 2004: 21)

This gladiatorial approach to work with offenders might be seen as too simplistic in describing the current debates. The middle ground might be achieved in the contribution of Ros Burnett (2004), a former probation officer. While she was scathing about the variation of practice that she encountered in her colleagues, she expressed concern that in the attempt to 'toughen its image' the positive aspects of the old regime might be lost. While perhaps she is seen as a proponent of 'What Works' she does not dismiss the importance of one-to-one work with offenders, as effective practice initiatives 'do not yet provide all the answers' (ibid.: 185).

The Offender Management Bill published on 22 November 2006 proposed to abolish Probation Boards and create Probation Trusts. This became the Offender Management Act in July 2007, with some of the more contentious parts not being implemented immediately. Civil servants referred to this as a 'light touch'. Thus it is not clear when and how competitive tendering would be introduced and how 'effectiveness' will be determined. The work of the Probation Service faces the prospect of being opened up to voluntary and private competition, rather than partnership. The danger with competitive tendering and the need for probation areas to drive down costs is that training of staff will become superficial and Fordist. However, there is no evidence that production-line control of offenders has any virtue, and is likely to make the public less safe. The offender manager might be keeping the offender in their sights, but may not actually know the offender as they are assigned to different programmes and controls. We are in danger of losing the holistic approach, namely actually spending time getting to know the offender and then essentially using this knowledge to work effectively with them.

Discussion questions

1 How can an examination of the history of working with offenders help us to consider contemporary issues of good practice?
2 What has been the impact of 'National Standards for the Supervision of Offenders in the Community' on the treatment of offenders?

3 What has been the impact of the 'What Works' initiative on the way that offenders are supervised?

Further reading

Burnett, R. and Roberts C. (eds) (2004) *What Works in Probation and Youth Justice.* Cullompton: Willan. This edited book is written from a positive perspective towards the 'What Works' movement – indeed it is dedicated to the late Sir Graham Smith, Chief Probation Officer and Chief Inspector of Probation who was a strong advocate of the new approach. Interestingly, Burnett does have a sympathy for traditional one-to-one work.

Cherry, S. (2005) *Transforming Behaviour. Pro-social Modelling in Practice.* Cullompton: Willan. Cherry continues the work of Trotter and explores the use of authority and empathic relationships. It reintroduces much of what has been forgotten in working with offenders, that they are not clones, but that rather a therapeutic relationship can bring about change in behaviour and outlook.

McGuire, J. (ed.) (1995) *What Works: Reducing Offending.* Chichester: Wiley. This edited book has a number of interesting chapters that helped launch the 'What Works' movement in England and Wales, in particular the chapters by Lipsey on meta-analysis and the review of what works by McGuire and Priestley with their statement of the six key principles for effective programmes.

Mair, G. (ed.) (2004) *What Matters in Probation.* Cullompton: Willan. In the other corner steps forward George Mair who is sceptical about 'What Works'. His chapter title on the origins of 'What Works' includes the phrase: 'a house built on sand?' Other chapters attack the omission of gender and diversity issues etc. in what works.

Trotter, C. (1999) *Working with Involuntary Clients.* London: Sage. Trotter dares to use the 'client' word, abolished by the Home Office to describe offenders. This book is very clear on the relationship between supervisor and offender and on what works and what doesn't work with offenders.

References

Appleyard, G. (1971) 'Prison welfare?', *Howard Journal of Penology*, XIII (2): 106–13.

Audit Commission (1989) *The Probation Service: Promoting Value for Money.* London: HMSO.

Barkley, D. and Collett, S. (2000) 'Back to the future: housing and support for offenders', *Probation Journal*, 47 (4): 235–42.

Biestek, F. (1963) *The Casework Relationship.* London: George Allen & Unwin.

Bochel, B. (1976) *Probation and After-Care: Its Development in England and Wales.* Edinburgh: Scottish Academic Press.

Bottoms, A. and McWilliams, W. (1979) 'A non-treatment paradigm for probation practice', *British Journal of Social Work*, 9 (2): 159–202.

Burnett, R. (2004) 'One-to-one ways of promoting desistence: in search of an evidence base', in R. Burnett and C. Roberts (eds), *What Works in Probation and Youth Justice. Developing Evidence Based Practice.* Cullompton: Willan.

Carlisle Committee (1988) *The Parole System of England and Wales: Report of the Review Committee*, Cm 532. London: HMSO.

Chapman, T. and Hough, M. (1998) *Evidence-Based Practice: A Guide to Effective Practice*. London: HM Inspectorate of Probation.

Denney, D. (1998) *Social Policy and Social Work*. Oxford: Clarendon Press.

Ellis, T. and Winstone, J. (2002) 'The policy impact of a survey of programme evaluations in England and Wales', in J. McGuire (ed.), *Offender Rehabilitation and Treatment. Effective Programmes and Policies to Reduce Re-offending.* Chichester: John Wiley & Sons.

Farrall, S. (2002) *Rethinking What Works with Offenders*. Cullompton: Willan.

Fitzgibbon, W. and Green, R. (2006) 'Mentally disordered offenders: challenges in using the OASys risk assessment tool', *British Journal of Community Justice*, 4 (2): 35–45.

Folkard, M., Smith, D. and Smith, D. (1974) *Intensive Matched Probation and After-Care Treatment (IMPACT)*, Vol. 1, Home Office Research Study 24. London: HMSO.

Foren, R. and Bailey, R. (1968) *Authority in Social Casework*. Oxford: Pergamon Press.

Garland, D. (2000) 'The culture of high crime societies: some preconditions of recent "law and order" policies', *British Journal of Criminology*, 40 (3): 347–75.

Goodman, A. and Loumansky, A (2006) 'Report on Hate Crime for a Probation Area'. Unpublished.

Hammond, W. and Chayen, E. (1963) *Persistent Criminals*, Home Office Research Unit Report No. 5. London: HMSO.

Harper, G. and Chitty, C. (2005) *The Impact of Corrections on Reoffending: A Review of What Works*, Home Office Research Study 291. London: Home Office.

Haxby, D. (1978) *Probation: A Changing Service*. London: Constable.

Holmes, T. (1900) *Pictures and Problems from London Police Courts*. London: Thomas Nelson & Sons.

Home Office (1959, reprinted 1966) *Penal Practice in a Changing Society*, Cmnd 645. London: HMSO.

Home Office (March 1962) *Report of the Departmental Committee on the Probation Service*, Cmnd 1650. London: HMSO.

Home Office (December 1965) *The Adult Offender*, Cmnd 2852. London: HMSO.

Home Office (1966) *Residential Provision for Homeless Discharged Offenders: Report of the Working Party on the Place of Voluntary Service in After-Care.* London: HMSO.

Home Office (1984) *Probation Service in England and Wales. Statement of National Objectives and Priorities*. London: HMSO.

Home Office (1990a) *Crime, Justice and Protecting the Public*, Cm 965. London: Home Office.

Home Office (1990b) *Supervision and Punishment in the Community: A Framework for Action*, Cm 966. London: Home Office.

Home Office (1992, 2002, 2005) *National Standards for the Supervision of Offenders in the Community*. London: Home Office.

Home Office (May 2006) *The NOMS Offender Management Model*, version 2. London: Home Office.

Jarvis, F.V. (1972) *Advise, Assist and Befriend. A History of the Probation and After-Care Service*. London: National Association of Probation Officers.

King, J. (1969) *The Probation and After-Care Service.* London: Butterworths.

Lloyd, C. (1986) *Response to SNOP*. Cambridge: University of Cambridge, Institute of Criminology.

McGuire, J. (1995) *What Works: Reducing Reoffending*. Chichester: John Wiley & Sons.

McGuire, J. (2000) *Cognitive-Behavioural Approaches. An Introduction to Theory and Research*. London: Home Office, HM Inspectorate of Probation.

McWilliams, B. (1983) 'The Mission to the English Police Courts 1876–1936', *Howard Journal of Criminal Justice*, 22: 129–47.

McWilliams, B. (1985) 'The Mission transformed: professionalization of probation between the wars', *Howard Journal of Criminal Justice*, 24 (4): 257–74.

McWilliams, B. (1986) 'The English probation system and the diagnostic ideal', *Howard Journal of Criminal Justice*, 25 (4): 241–60.

McWilliams, B. (1987) 'Probation, pragmatism and policy', *Howard Journal of Criminal Justice*, 26 (2): 97–121.

Mair, G. (2004) 'The origins of what works in England and Wales: a house built on sand?, in G. Mair (ed.), *What Matters in Probation*. Cullompton: Willan.

Martinson, R. (1974) 'What Works? – Questions and answers about prison reform', *The Public Interest*, 35: 22–54.

Martinson, R. (1979) 'New findings, new views: a note of caution regarding sentencing reform', *Hofstra Law Review*, (7) 2: 243–58.

Maruna, S. (2001) *Making Good*. Washington, DC: American Psychological Association.

May, T. (1991) *Probation: Politics, Policy and Practice*. Milton Keynes: Open University Press.

May, T. (1995) 'Probation and community sanctions', in M. Maguire, R. Morgan and R. Reiner (eds), *The Oxford Handbook in Criminology*. Oxford: Clarendon Press.

Merrington, S. and Stanley, S. (2000) 'Reflections: doubts about the What Works initiative', *Probation Journal*, 47 (4): 272–5.

National Audit Office (17 May 1989) *Home Office: Control and Management of Probation Services in England and Wales*. Report by the Comptroller and Auditor General. London: HMSO.

Palmer, E. (2003) *Offending Behaviour: Moral Reasoning, Criminal Conduct and the Rehabilitation of Offenders*. Cullompton: Willan.

Pawson, R. and Tilley, N. (1997) *Realistic Evaluation*. London: Sage.

Radzinowicz, L. (1958) *The Results of Probation. A Report of the Cambridge Department of Criminal Science*. London: Macmillan.

Raynor, P. and Vanstone, M. (2001) '"Straight thinking on probation": evidence-based practice and the culture of curiosity', in G. Bernfield, D. Farrington and A. Leschied (eds), *Offender Rehabilitation in Practice*. Chichester: John Wiley & Sons.

Rex, S. (2001) 'Beyond cognitive-behaviouralism? reflections on the effectiveness literature', in A. Bottoms, L. Gelsthorpe and S. Rex (eds), *Community Penalties: Challenges and Changes*. Cullompton: Willan.

Rutherford, A. (1993) *Criminal Justice and the Pursuit of Decency*. Oxford: Oxford University Press.

Ryan, M. and Ward, T. (1989) *Privatisation and the Penal System*. Milton Keynes: Open University Press.

Travis, A. (2007) 'Increase in serious crime by offenders on parole', *The Guardian*, 23 October.

Underdown, A. (1998) *Strategies for Effective Offender Supervision*. HM Inspectorate of Probation. London: Home Office.

Wilkinson, J. (2005) 'Evaluating evidence for the effectiveness of the reasoning and rehabilitation programme', *Howard Journal of Criminal Justice*, 44 (1): 70–85.

Chapter 4

Offending media: the social construction of offenders, victims and the Probation Service

Yvonne Jewkes

Introduction

This is a time of unprecedented concern about crime, an age in which narratives of offending and victimisation are cyclically rehearsed by the popular media. One of the most prevalent messages – imparted with various degrees of subtlety across much of the UK's contemporary media, but with particular vigour in the conservative press – is that people commit crimes because 'they' are not like 'us'. An understanding of 'otherness' helps to explain why identities are often characterised by polarisation and by the discursive marking of inclusion and exclusion within oppositional classificatory systems: 'insiders' and 'outsiders', 'us' and 'them', victims and offenders, black and white, hardworking and 'dole-scrounging', 'normal' and 'deviant'. Drawing on perspectives from media theory and criminology this chapter will analyse the social construction of offenders and victims using press reports of crimes committed by individuals released early from custody. Focusing on five 'mega-cases' (Soothill *et al.* 2002; Peelo 2006), which are but a small sample of the available news stories on the same theme, the chapter aims to illustrate how media representations of exceptional offences construct the 'outsider' status of perpetrators as unequivocal and incontestable while encouraging audience identification with victims and victimhood.

The chapter will also discuss the processes by which people who are employed in occupations that involve working with 'outsiders' can themselves become marginalised and demonised. As social workers, immigration officers, psychiatrists, probation officers and armed police officers have all discovered, professions which operate on the terrain of political conflict frequently find themselves subjected to negative and damaging media coverage with long-term consequences for the morale of those who work within them (Aldridge 1999). The case studies that will be referred to throughout the chapter are uniformly critical of the professions that process and manage offenders through the criminal justice system, especially those who work in the probation service.

Five 'mega-cases' and the news values that underpin them

For many years probation was not considered especially newsworthy; indeed one commentator describes the profession as 'stubbornly lacking in news value' (Aldridge 1999). That all changed in 2005 and 2006 when a number of high-profile, salaciously reported murder cases in London and elsewhere in England propelled the Probation Service into an unwelcome spotlight. The headlines were succinct and uncompromising in their apportioning of blame:

> Probation Service allowed banker's killers into London (*Sunday Times*, 18 December 2005)

> Offenders on probation carry out 10,000 crimes a month (*Telegraph*, 15 May 2006)

> On licence to kill (*The Times*, 7 November 2006)

The main themes that connected the reported offences were that they were perpetrated against 'innocent' victims by individuals who were under the supervision of the Probation Service. Among these offences were several that received what might be regarded as a 'normal' level of coverage. For example, in November 2006 Mark Goldstraw was sentenced to life imprisonment for killing his 16-year-old ex-girlfriend, her ten-year-old sister, her brother aged seven and her stepfather, by setting fire to their home while they slept. Goldstraw, 31, had been released on parole in 2004 after serving a seven-year prison sentence for the manslaughter of a previous girlfriend. Eight months earlier Yusuf Bouhaddaou was sentenced to life imprisonment for the murder of teacher Robert Symons at his home in Chiswick, West London, having been released on licence five weeks earlier.[1]

However, five cases which contained the same basic elements – the murders of 'innocent' victims by individuals on probation – arguably became 'mega-cases' (Peelo 2006). Shocking us more than an illegal killing normally would do, mega-cases are unusual events that particularly offend society, are repeatedly reported (in some cases, over several years), serve as a point of reference to help the audience interpret later killings and are reported in such a way that the victims are turned into 'public property' (Peelo 2006). It is these elements that combine to give certain homicide cases shared symbolic meaning, locating the reader or viewer in the position of 'mediated witness' and stirring a level of social disturbance that transcends the routine reporting of serious crimes (Peelo 2006). In brief, these five mega-cases were as follows:

1 In September 2003 Marian Bates was murdered by armed raiders in her jewellery shop in Nottingham while trying to protect her daughter. This incident and the long-running trial that followed it first brought the

problem of offenders committing serious crimes while on probation to widespread attention. The offenders included a teenager who was under supervision following his release from a young offender institution (YOI) 20 days earlier. Peter Williams had reportedly breached his curfew order numerous times and removed his electronic tag. Following sentencing in March 2005, it was reported that the private monitoring company Premier had failed to inform his youth offending team (YOT) that the electronic tag had been removed until it was too late, and that Williams' case manager was 'inexperienced' and had no formal qualifications in youth work, social work or probation. Officials admitted there had been an 'error of judgment' in not revoking Williams' licence earlier and said they had changed their procedures following the case (*Telegraph*, 23 March 2005). Although the offence itself took place before the period under discussion, the story retained its newsworthiness with 473 mentions in UK newspapers between the date of the murder (30 September 2003) and the end of 2004, and 413 mentions in 2005 and 2006 (http://www.lexisnexis.com).

2 City banker John Monckton was murdered at his home in Chelsea when his wife opened the front door to two men posing as postal workers in November 2004. At the time of the murder Damien Hanson was on licence having been released from custody halfway through a 12-year sentence for attempted murder and Elliott White was on bail awaiting a court appearance on drugs charges. This case accounted for more stories than any of the other mega-cases among them, 100 mentions in *The Times* and *Sunday Times*, 90 in the *Mail* and *Mail On Sunday*, and 41 in *The Guardian*. Extensive coverage was given to systemic errors, including the claim that Hanson was released despite being assessed as 91 per cent likely to reoffend, and that the probation office to which he was supposed to report was in an area of London that he was excluded from entering according to the terms of his parole. Following the trial in December 2005, the Chief Inspector of Probation concluded that there was a 'collective failure' in the supervision of Hanson and White which amounted to 'the exact opposite of effective offender managing' (*BBC News online*, 20 March 2006). Four probation officers were suspended, though none were named.

3 Sixteen-year-old Mary-Ann Leneghan and her 18-year-old friend were sexually assaulted, tortured and left for dead in a park in Reading by a gang of six men in May 2005. While the older girl survived being shot in the head, Mary-Ann died from multiple stab wounds. At their trial in April 2006 it was reported that four of the gang, the youngest of whom was 18, were on probation at the time of the murder. Following the case, then Home Secretary Charles Clarke announced that it was vital for the Probation Service that 'lessons are learned' from Mary-Ann's murder. The case increased the impetus for the government's review of the service in 2006, and ultimately added to the pressure on Clarke to resign from his

post when – following news that around a thousand foreign nationals released from prison had not been deported and were 'missing' – he was forced to admit that the Home Office had experienced seven years of systemic failures.

4 Anthony Rice murdered Naomi Bryant in her home in Winchester in August 2005, nine months after being released from prison on licence from a life sentence. Following this case the Chief Inspector of Probation was quoted in the press as saying that prison and parole officials were side-tracked by considering Rice's human rights above their duties to the public, and that there were 'substantial deficiencies' in the supervision of Rice by Hampshire probation officers (*Sun Online*, accessed 7 December 2006). New training procedures were introduced. Rice was sentenced to life in October 2006.

5 Lawyer Tom ap Rhys Pryce was murdered near his home in Kensal Green, London, in January 2006. His killers, Donnel Carty, 19, and Delano Brown, 18, first mugged him as he left a tube station near his home and then stabbed him three times before leaving him to die yards from his house. The pair were sentenced to life imprisonment in November 2006. While the murder and trial resulted in fewer stories in the UK press than some of the other mega-cases (38 mentions in *The Telegraph* compared to 81 stories about the Monckton case, and 39 in *The Times* compared to 42 references in that newspaper to the murder of Mary-Ann Leneghan) the event is notable for the particularly emotive quality of the reporting (see below).

When considering why these five cases were highly newsworthy, it is useful to analyse the 'news values' underpinning them (see Jewkes 2004, for a fuller analysis). Like all crime news the cases outlined above are negative in essence, and meet the required threshold of public interest because they concern violent crimes in which 'innocent' victims have had their lives cut tragically short by offenders being processed by an ineffective and lenient justice system. They can thus be reported in a simplified manner, which not only privileges brevity, clarity and unambiguity in its presentation, but encourages the reader or viewer to suspend their skills of critical interpretation and respond in unanimous accord which, in cases like those described above, usually amounts to moral indignation and censure. The stories also conform to the news value proximity which has both spatial and cultural dynamics. Spatial proximity refers to the geographical 'nearness' of an event (all the events occurred in London or other cities proximate to major news-gathering centres), while cultural proximity refers to the 'relevance' of an event to an audience (the victims, while diverse in terms of their socio-economic status, are uniformly presented as ordinary people, just like you or I). Three of the stories concern high-status victims, professionals whose ambition and work ethic is compared favourably to the greedy motivations of the offenders. Two of the stories have a sexual element which is one of the most salient news values, especially in the popular press, who seek to increase their circulation figures by titillating their readership. Paradoxically, the stories collectively contain an element of 'newness' or novelty (that the Probation Service in England and Wales is culpable for some of the worst crimes committed in recent years), but are at the same time presented as predictable outcomes of a society that has raised a generation of feckless youth and supports a criminal justice system which has become soft on crime. The fact that four of the offences were carried out by young men is also significant. Young people are frequently used as a kind of social barometer with which to test the health of society more generally. Children and adolescents represent the future and if they engage in deviant behaviour it is often viewed as symptomatic of a society that is declining ever further into a moral morass. For the media, then, deviant youth – like those implicated in four of the crimes under discussion – is used as a shorthand ascription for a range of gloomy and fatalistic predictions about spiralling levels of crime and amoral behaviour in society at large.

Two further news values that shape these stories and explain the heavy coverage of them – risk and individualisation – are interlinked. For Reiner (2001) individualism is a consequence of the increasing tendency to view society as being obsessed with 'risk' and all its attendant notions, including risk assessment, risk management and risk avoidance. Despite the fact that the vast majority of serious offences are committed by people known to the victim, the media give prominence to cases like the five outlined in a manner and frequency that perpetuate a picture of serious crime as random, meaningless, unpredictable and ready to strike anyone at any time. Each of the offenders in the cases under discussion are described in terms such as 'loner', 'animal' and 'violent thug', all qualities which allude to the offender's lack of normative social ties (Blackman and Walkerdine 2001). While evidence shows that most of the people in contact with the Probation Service are excluded from the full range of goods and services associated with citizenship (Smith and Stewart 1998; SEU 2002), their experiences of marginalisation and deprivation are underplayed by the media who continue to discuss individual moral responsibility as if it exists in a vacuum, somehow detached from the circumstances in which people find themselves (Drakeford and Vanstone 1996). Many commentators argue that offenders are not different people, but people in much more desperate circumstances than most, who have resorted to more desperate measures (see, for example, Arnold and Jordan 1996; Smith and Stewart 1998). Yet the motives of the offenders in our mega-cases are uniformly described in terms of greed and pleasure (and, again, as if these drives were at odds with prevailing social norms). Of course the media themselves do not operate in a vacuum, and it might justifiably be argued that the rhetoric of 'offending behaviour' that permeates the current penal policy climate detaches individuals from societal norms, ignores the social and personal contexts which make offending intelligible and stresses stigmatisation and marginalisation rather than inclusion and integration (Smith and Stewart 1998). But it is the media who circulate such ideas, giving them currency and perhaps even causing young men to behave according to expectations: 'The deeply offensive image of young criminals as hyenas is a self-fulfilling prophesy: given no other role, that is what they will become' (Arnold and Jordan 1996: 41).

Victims, on the other hand, are usually located within the contexts of their family and immediate community. In mega-cases, the media go further and construct victims as symbolic members of a wider community. We come to know them through the tragic circumstances that befall them; they 'belong' to all of us. According to Peelo the outrage that mega-cases stir in an audience is a mixture of three ingredients: the ordinariness of life invaded by brutal events, the worthiness of the life lost and the perceived innocence or vulnerability of the victim. To take each of these in turn, one of the reasons that mega-cases illicit such strong feelings of emotional identification is that they 'defamiliarise' what we know and present it back to us in unsettling ways: 'the shock to society of a killing is greater according to its invasion into homely cosiness' (Peelo 2006: 164). It is unsurprising, then, that all the mega-cases are presented by the media as examples that defamiliarise the familiar, moments when the brutal invades the ordinary. The fact that the murders of John Monckton, Tom ap Rhys Pryce and Naomi Bryant occurred in or just outside their homes, and that of Marian Bates took place in the business she had owned for 30 years, engenders disgust and dismay precisely because of the routine, domestic ordinariness that these settings convey. The 'worthiness' and 'vulnerability' of the victims might have proved problematic for the media given that none of the victims fall into the superficial categories of 'idealised victim' usually employed by the media.[2] In the cases of lawyer Tom ap Rhys Pryce and banker John Monckton, both of whom occupied positions at the higher end of the socio-economic scale, 'worthiness' is conveyed via discourses of success, wealth and achievement which is compared favourably to the motivations of their killers. For example, John Monckton is described in *The Times* (18 December 2005) as a 'devout Roman Catholic' who was targeted by a psychopath whose motive was to 'gain the trappings of wealth', while Tom ap Rhys Pryce is referred to as 'a gifted chorister as well as a first-class Cambridge graduate' who was the random victim of 'a ruthless gang of robbers whose only interest in his world of hard work and ambition was in getting their hands on as many of his valuables as possible' (*Telegraph*, 28 November 2006). The lawyer's 'ordinariness' is underlined throughout the press coverage of the case via discourses that portray him as a loving partner who was making wedding plans with his fiancée, a 'thoroughly decent, sincere and down-to-earth' colleague, and a 'loyal and attentive' son. Victims of serious crime are always considered more newsworthy if their relatives and close friends are willing to make themselves part of the story and audiences are encouraged to engage with criminal events as 'human interest' stories by identifying with the emotions of those who have been most directly hurt by the event (Peelo 2006). Although much reference is made in the press to John Monckton's career, salary and house (variously valued in the popular media between £3 million and £5 million) this is balanced by references to, and testimonials from, his family, friends and colleagues. Marian Bates is also constructed as a professional person, loving partner and good parent, while Naomi Bryant – who might have posed problems for the media insofar as she was a 40-year-old single mother who had met Anthony Rice a few days earlier and had visited several pubs with him before taking him home where he attacked her – is nevertheless portrayed as an ideal mother and devoted daughter whose own mother won the right to a full inquest into the incident. Mary-Ann Leneghan arguably presented the most significant dilemma for the media as she was about as far from an 'ideal' victim as it is possible for a 16-year-old girl to be. A student who had regularly bunked off school and had no job, Mary-Ann was described in court as having 'fallen into bad company'. She and her older friend 'certainly were not the sort of girls who would have been found tucked up in bed at 10 o'clock at night' according to the prosecuting lawyer and faithfully reported in the *Daily Mail* (14 January 2006). The *Mail* story goes on to say that 'with the naivety of youth they found the drug scene attractive and exciting' and that Mary-Ann was 'particularly friendly' with the gang-leader who subsequently tortured and murdered her, Adrian Thomas. This narrative possibly accounts for the fact that the case appeared just twice in the *Daily Mail* – a newspaper that champions the human-interest story. By way of comparison the disappearance of middle-class, high-achieving teenager Milly Dowler in 2002 appeared in the *Mail* on 92 occasions. Other newspapers, however, located Mary-Ann firmly within a familial context and reproduced a statement from Mary-Ann's relatives saying that she was 'a wonderful girl who was greatly loved by her friends and family' (*The Guardian*, 20 March 2006).

The media's inclination to deal in binary oppositions – good versus evil, folk heroes and folk devils, black against white, guilty or innocent, 'normal' as opposed to 'sick', 'deviant' or 'dangerous' – results in a simplistic portrayal of offenders as evil monsters with no hope of rehabilitation and victims as saintly figures who happened to be in the wrong place at the wrong time. Semiotic cues such as references to the 'chance collision between two starkly different cultures [which] left Mr ap Rhys Pryce bleeding to death on a damp pavement' (*Telegraph*, 28 November 2006) and the 'vicious thug' who killed John Monckton being dubbed 'Omen', '666' and 'Devil's Child' (*Sunday Times*, 18 December 2006) add up to a mediated vision of crime in which shades of grey are absent and a complex reality is substituted for a simple, incontestable, bite-sized message. The popular media communicate in stereotypes as a kind of shorthand, making it easier for readers to know when to 'hiss and boo as the villain appears and when to identify with the good and worthy' (Peelo 2006: 163). But in addition to the villain/perpetrator and hero/victim roles, there is an 'additional cast of players'. To the three ingredients already discussed, then, we can add a fourth element that heightens a sense of social disruption and moral outrage: someone (or something) that is clearly identified as being to blame.

Blunders, blame and professional 'failure'

One important consequence of the media's obsession with dangerousness and their perpetuation of the notion that we are all potential victims of random brutality is that the professions which assess and manage risk can be made scapegoats when things go wrong. This is, in itself, not a new phenomenon. Two decades ago the deaths of three children who were in the care of local authorities brought hostile media reporting and caused those working in social services departments to become preoccupied with their 'media image' (Aldridge 1999). Accused of not intervening sufficiently in cases where youngsters were known to be at risk, the media later did a U-turn while simultaneously increasing their invective when suspicions of sexual abuse within families in Cleveland (1987), Rochdale (1990) and the Orkney Isles (1991) resulted in the censure of social services for intervening too much (Aldridge 1999). The headlines and editorials that accompanied all these cases bear striking similarities to those used in the more recent stories about offenders on probation. 'Row over who was to blame' (*Daily Telegraph*), 'Probe reveals basic blunders' (*Daily Express*) and 'Our deadly blunders' (*Sun*) all appeared on 26 July 1985 following the death of toddler Tyra Henry at the hands of her father. Twenty-one years later headlines included 'Killer "should not have been out"' (*BBC News online*, 10 May 2006), 'Blunder led to murder' (*Sun Online*, accessed 7 December 2006) and 'Another deadly blunder' (*Inside Time*, June 2006).

The similarity between the interpretive frame used in coverage of the social work cases of the mid-1980s and that employed in the reporting of the probation cases two decades later should not be understood wholly in terms of lazy journalism. The death of a child in care and the random murder of an individual at the hands of a dangerous offender elicit similar levels of collective shock and anxiety, but if professional failure was the sole driver of newsworthiness, condemnatory press treatment might be anticipated every time an 'innocent' victim comes to harm (Aldridge 1999). The reason why these professions were targeted at particular points in time, then, goes beyond news values and the status of the victim. In both the social work and probation cases, the over-reliance on references to blame, blunders and professional incompetence is crucially linked to the prevailing political climate.

The scandals that befell social services departments in the 1980s coincided with the period when Margaret Thatcher's government was waging a war against Labour-led local authorities. The media's delight in endlessly recycling stories concerning 'loony lefties' and 'reds under the bed' masked Thatcher's more serious goal which was to cut local government spending in order to reduce direct taxation (Aldridge 1999). The ridiculing of local government policies targeting issues around gender, sexual orientation and, especially, race (given that the overtly racist reporting of mugging and the inner-city riots of the previous decade was still fresh in people's minds) caused 'political correctness' to be regarded as a pejorative term. The three most high-profile incidents of children being killed by their parents while in the care of social services occurred in left-wing London boroughs where 'race' was a politically sensitive issue, and two of the victims, Jasmine Beckford and Tyra Henry, were African Caribbean. According to Aldridge (1999: 93), these factors heightened the stories' news value and resulted in a racialisation of the cases with headlines ranging from the pseudo-analytical 'Are black power politics costing the lives of children?' (*Daily Express*, 27 July 1985) to the crude 'Animal gets life' (*Sun*, 26 July 1985).

While crimes committed by offenders on licence have happened ever since the system was introduced, the press seized upon the cases that occurred in 2005 and 2006 as if they were a frightening new strain of crime in the manner of the mugging panic in the 1970s (Hall *et al.* 1978). The symbolic power of the offences was further enhanced by the wider debates they generated concerning gun crime, knives, gang culture, drugs and even rap music. In both eras, notions of potential 'dangerousness' came to be applied indiscriminately to whole sections of society. In this oversimplified worldview of popular journalism, there is an inference that young men – especially those of African Caribbean descent – are responsible for a disproportionate number of crimes. On occasions this conclusion is more blatantly communicated:

> British society has created successive generations of inner-city youths without any sense of morality or respect for authority. Immersed in street gangs, obsessed with drugs and violent rap music, they live by the code of the gun and the knife … The family has broken down in Britain, with more than 40 per cent of marriages ending in divorce and almost 50 per cent of children born out of wedlock. This is particularly the case in some African Caribbean communities, leading to a disturbing prevalence of criminality among youths deprived of wise mentors. (*Daily Express*, 30 November 2006)

At the same time, victims of serious crime who are black or Asian are under-reported. For example, the ap Rhys Price case received 5,525 words in the national press, whereas the murder on the same day in the same city of Asian cement merchant Balbir Matharu received only 1,385 words (*The Guardian*, 27 January 2006, cited in Greer 2007).

We live in a society where political process and media discourse are indistinguishable and mutually constitutive. The popular media generally favour discourses of deterrence and repression and, on the whole, their concentration on serious, random, atypical offences legitimates their support for more police, more prisons and a tougher criminal justice system. More than this, however, the media's willingness to tap into racist discourses in their reporting of the social work cases in the 1980s illustrated how discourses of otherness and dangerousness can be mobilised to legitimate the reconstruction of local government and social policy (Aldridge 1999). Was a similar process being undertaken in relation to the reconstruction of the Probation Service and criminal justice policy in 2006? And is the current focus on hapless victims of serious crime who have been let down by institutions and individuals who should have protected them merely a political smokescreen, deflecting attention from other serious social problems? Sensationalised media reporting perpetuates a sense of a stratified, deeply divided and mutually hostile population which politicians play up in order to galvanise the support of an anxious and fearful public. Might it be arguable, then, that the media hysteria over offenders 'on licence to kill' was largely a distraction to 'soften up' the Probation Service and encourage public support for government proposals to radically reform probation in England and Wales?

Reforming probation: the political context

The recent history of the Probation Service is complex and can only be discussed in the briefest detail here. Following a long period of near invisibility, probation came under political scrutiny from 1988 when the Conservative government shifted its rhetoric from 'clients' to 'offenders' and sought to increase the profile of the service in local communities (Aldridge 1999). The Michael Howard era was seen as watershed when, as Home Secretary, Howard uncoupled the Probation Service from social work, criticised and then dismantled its training practices and promised to recruit more former soldiers and police officers in order to 'dilute its "liberal do-gooding ethos"' (*The Guardian*, 27 June 1994, cited in Aldridge 1999: 97). Opposition to the government's plans was voiced by both the Association of Chief Officers of Probation (ACOP) and the National Association of Probation Officers (NAPO) but their campaigns received little support – or even coverage – in the national media. In 2000 the service was centralised, becoming the National Probation Service for England and Wales and four years later it became accountable to the National Offender Management Service (NOMS). Charles Clarke was planning further restructuring and centralisation of the service when he was forced to resign in April 2006. In November 2006, the very month that media reporting of failures in the Probation Service reached its zenith, new Home Secretary John Reid unveiled more plans for radical reform. These included proposals to introduce 'contestability'; that is, the contracting-out of some parts of the service to private and voluntary organisations. While the privatisation of probation is not a particularly surprising move from a government that has pursued a policy of contestability in the Prison Service (despite opposition from their own backbenchers and from the probation union NAPO), it is difficult to separate Reid's announcement from his other public statements at around the same time which made clear that he blamed the Probation Service for the spate of murders by individuals under their supervision. The inference was that the introduction of contestability was their punishment for not doing their job properly.

At the same time, the Prison Service and parole system have undergone major changes in the last decade, not least because of the sheer scale of numbers they must now deal with. The prison population in England and Wales has grown from just under 10,000 prisoners in 1940 to over 84,000 prisoners in 2008. The last 15 years have seen the number of prisoners in English and Welsh prisons double in size, rising from just over 40,000 prisoners in 1993 (Home Office 2006; cf. Butler 2007). Prison has been described as a 'sophisticated sausage machine' (Caird 1974: 9), and it is not surprising that the more people are stuffed in at one end, the more problems and pressures are created at the other. One consequence of the population crisis is that the Parole Board no longer has sufficient resources to conduct face-to-face interviews with all offenders who apply for parole. While the most serious offenders are still interviewed, many of the individuals described in this chapter were originally sentenced for non-violent or less serious crimes than those they went on to commit when released and were therefore processed via a paper-based assessment procedure. In 2002 the government introduced OASys, an electronic risk assessment tool. Active in only 12 of the 42 probation areas of England and Wales by the end of 2006, the system has been condemned by NAPO as having the primary purpose of producing data for the Home Office rather than analysing the behaviour of offenders. The multi-agency public protection panels (MAPPP) introduced in 2001 have also been found wanting, given that the offences that are the focus of this chapter were carried out by individuals who were either under MAPPP supervision, or who should have been according to independent reports following the cases. In the case of Naomi Bryant, the local MAPPP in Hampshire was reportedly 'distracted' by Anthony Rice's human rights, and allowed him to attend a pub quiz where he met his victim (see http://inspectorates.homeoffice.gov.uk/hmiprobation).

Another aspect of the evolution of offender management worth mentioning briefly in this context is the dominance of psychology and psychiatric discourses within sentence management. In prisons the notion of rehabilitation has been undermined by a risk assessment approach. Education and training – which arguably give offenders not only workplace skills but also aspirations to better themselves – have been squeezed in favour of offending behaviour courses which purport to change established patterns of behaviour. The combined effect of these two initiatives – depersonalising the parole system and requiring offenders to undertake courses on anger management, victim empathy, enhanced thinking and the like – have, in the words of one ex-offender, marked the end of 'authentic relationships between prisoners and staff' (James 2006: unpaginated). In their coverage of the five 'mega-cases' several newspapers reported that the offenders in question had 'played the system', a belief endorsed by the

Chief Executive of the Parole Board who observed in relation to Damian Hanson who murdered John Monckton that 'the Hanson in the [parole] report and the Hanson in the trial were like two different people ... He is a vicious thug who played the system' (*The Times*, 18 December 2005). *The Times* further reports that Hanson built up an image as a model prisoner, attending courses in anger management and behaviour modification, and volunteering for work with under-privileged children, all of which resulted in a favourable parole dossier.

The consequences for the probation system of this new approach to measuring an offender's 'progress' through their sentence is underlined by Erwin James:

> [T]he probation system has to supervise people that nobody in prison has ever really got to know. Under-resourced and overstretched ... probation officers also have no hope of getting to know the people they are supposed to be supervising, beyond what the parole dossier, based largely on the person's 'progress' in prison, tells them. Where once they were akin to an official friend, offering support, advice and encouragement, now they are primarily a policing agency, responsible for 'enforcement' – a politically influenced development that has led to a new cynicism ... [The offenders] knew that all they had to do was to turn up and make sure their boxes were ticked. (James 2006: unpaginated)

While the blame for these institutional failings to adequately protect the public might reasonably be laid at the door of the government who introduced them, former Home Secretary John Reid consistently denied that his government should be held responsible, and responded to the murder cases by announcing a review of the systems that process offenders. His overhaul of the Probation Service – and the timing of the announcement in November 2006 – were particularly controversial for three reasons. First, he revealed proposals to privatise up to a third of Probation Service work during a speech delivered inside Wormwood Scrubs prison. Focusing on areas of underperformance and failure within probation, Reid addressed his speech to an audience that included prisoners, thus undermining the very people who will be supervising those individuals when they are released into the community. Second, he placed six local probation areas into 'capability reviews' because their performance was 'poor or mediocre' in national performance tables. Third, he simultaneously launched an inquiry into bail hostels following the broadcast of a BBC *Panorama* programme which claimed that paedophiles were not being adequately monitored after their release from prison. His haste in linking the programme's findings to his proposals for reform underline the 'populist punitive' stance that has characterised recent governments' policies on crime and crime control.

Reid's bullish stance on probation was predictable. In part, his proposals bore the legacy of the last twenty years of political desire to transform the service into a more 'macho' operation, including former Labour Home Secretary (now Minister of Justice) Jack Straw's call to turn it into a 'corrections service' (Aldridge 1999: 99). At the same time, Reid may have been seeking to publicly distance himself from Charles Clarke's confession that the Home Office had made mistakes due to seven years of systemic failures. But above all, he isolated himself and his office from any charges of blame while appearing to offer strong leadership. The consequences for the Probation Service may be long-lasting. Harry Fletcher, Assistant General Secretary of NAPO, is reported as saying that the London Probation Service had been in 'financial chaos' and was experiencing a recruitment freeze at the time of the Monckton murder (*BBC News online*, 20 March 2006). However, the problems of understaffing, low staff morale and poor staff retention have received a fraction of the coverage of individual and institutional failures or the Home Secretary's plans for reform. Social workers' belief that negative press reporting about their profession in the 1980s was 'real in its consequences' (Aldridge 1999: 90) is equally true of the Probation Service since 2006.

Conclusion

Representations of crime, deviance and control illustrate the extent to which the popular media serve as one of the primary sites of social inclusion and exclusion in late modernity. Through a process of alienation and demonisation they establish the 'otherness' of those who deviate and (re)assert the innocence and normality, not only of the victims of serious offending, but of all of us (Blackman and Walkerdine 2001).

The inference that people commit crimes because 'they' are not like 'us' is circulated in multifarious ways by the popular media. By examining a small sample of cases that bear certain similarities we have seen how sensationalised and stylised dialogue and familiar authorial techniques contribute to the construction of public narratives about serious offences committed by individuals on licence from prison and their repercussions for those who work in probation. In analysing the media's reporting of five 'mega-cases' reported in 2005 and 2006 I hope to have demonstrated how the media's presentation of offenders as 'others' and their crimes as senseless and random not only stimulate public sentiments of revulsion and repugnance but also reinforce populist ideas about punishment and allow politicians to apportion blame and make radical changes to criminal justice in order to be seen to be acting tough on crime. While not unique, the five 'mega' stories discussed not only serve to elevate the perceived deviance of a whole category of individuals but also infer that these offences are symptomatic of a wider problem of moral decline and decrepitude in a society in which the professionals charged with protecting the public can no longer be trusted to do so.

Discussion questions

1 How might the construction of offender 'otherness' affect criminal justice practitioners' own perspectives of their 'clients'?
2 Is it either possible or desirable to work with offenders in ways which are not influenced by media representations?
3 How would you characterise the relationship between the media, public perceptions and the professional esteem, status and morale of those who work with offenders?

Further reading

Davis, P., Francis, P. and Greer, C. (2007) *Victims, Crime and Society.* London: Sage. A recent contribution to the 'victims' literature which includes a chapter on 'News media, victims and crime' by Chris Greer.

Jewkes, Y. (2004) *Media and Crime.* London: Sage (a second, revised edition will be published in 2009). Provides a full analysis of the relationship between media, crime and criminal justice, including discussions of news values and constructions of victims and offenders.

Jewkes, Y. (2004) 'Media representations of criminal justice', in J. Muncie and D. Wilson (eds), *Student Handbook of Criminal Justice and Criminology.* London: Cavendish. Looks at how the media shape public perceptions of the police, courts and prisons.

Mason, P. (ed.) (2003) *Criminal Visions: Media Representations of Crime and Justice.* Cullompton: Willan. A useful edited collection covering a diverse range of subjects relating to crime and crime control.

Peelo, M. (2006) 'Framing homicide narratives in newspapers: mediated witness and the construction of virtual victimhood', *Crime, Media, Culture: An International Journal,* 2 (2): 159–75. Provides a more detailed analysis of 'mega-cases'.

Notes

1 Another high-profile case that was reported in the period under analysis was the trial of two young black men accused and subsequently convicted of murdering Damilola Taylor in Peckham in 2000. While a long-running story that conformed to many cardinal news values, it is judged not to be a 'mega-case' in the context of crimes committed by individuals on probation because the fact that the offenders were under supervision at the time of the offence was less central to the story than other elements.

2 In the hierarchy of 'ideal(ised)' victimhood, young, female, white, middle-class, 'respectable' and conventionally attractive victims are most likely to receive prominent news coverage. Hence the disappearances of Madeleine McCann, Sarah Payne, Milly Dowler and the 'Soham girls', Holly Wells and Jessica Chapman, were all eminently more newsworthy stories than they would have been if the victim was male, or working class, or was of African Caribbean or Asian descent, or a truant or persistent runaway, or had been in care, or had drug problems, or was a prostitute – or any combination of these factors (Jewkes 2004).

References

Aldridge, M. (1999) 'Poor relations: state social work and the press in the UK', in B. Franklin (ed.), *Social Policy, the Media and Misrepresentation*. London: Routledge.

Arnold, J. and Jordan, B. (1996) 'Poverty', in M. Drakeford and M. Vanstone (eds), *Beyond Offending Behaviour*. Aldershot: Arena.

Blackman, L. and Walkerdine, V. (2001) *Mass Hysteria: Critical Psychology and Media Studies*. Basingstoke: Palgrave.

Butler, M. (2007) 'Prison population', in Y. Jewkes and J. Bennett (eds), *Dictionary of Prisons and Punishment*. Cullompton: Willan.

Caird, R. (1974) *A Good and Useful Life: Imprisonment in Britain Today*. London: Hart-Davis.

Drakeford, M. and Vanstone, M. (eds) (1996) *Beyond Offending Behaviour*. Aldershot: Arena.

Greer, C. (2007) 'News media, victims and crime', in P. Davis, P. Francis and C. Greer (eds), *Victims, Crime and Society*. London: Sage.

Hall, S., Critcher, C., Jefferson, T., Clarke, J. and Roberts, B. (eds) (1978) *Policing the Crisis: Mugging, the State and Law and Order*. London: Macmillan.

Home Office (2006) 'Population in custody', at www.homeoffice.gov.uk/rds/.

James, E. (2006) 'Ticking the wrong boxes', at http://commentisfree.guardian.co.uk/erwin_james/2006/03/ticking_the_wrong_boxes.html.

Jewkes, Y. (2004) *Media and Crime*. London: Sage.

Peelo, M. (2006) 'Framing homicide narratives in newspapers: mediated witness and the construction of virtual victimhood', *Crime, Media, Culture: An International Journal*, 2 (2): 159–75

Reiner, R. (2001) 'The rise of virtual vigilantism: crime reporting since World War II', *Criminal Justice Matters*, Spring, 43.

Smith, D. and Stewart, J. (1998) 'Probation and social exclusion', in C. Jones Finer and M. Nellis (eds), *Crime and Social Exclusion*. Oxford: Blackwell.

Social Exclusion Unit (2002) *Reducing Re-Offending by Ex-Prisoners*. London: Social Exclusion Unit.

Soothill, K., Peelo, M., Francis, B., Pearson, J. and Ackerley, E. (2002) 'Homicide and the media: identifying top cases in The Times', *Howard Journal of Criminal Justice*, 41 (5): 401–21.

Part 2

Practice: Generic Skills

Chapter 5

Engagement skills: best practice or effective practice?

Chris Tallant, Mark Sambrook, Simon Green

Introduction

This chapter will seek to explore the different engagement skills that are utilised when working with offenders and the practical problems involved in such work. It will be argued that while the opportunity still exists to do constructive work with offenders, there is a tension between managing offender needs and managing organisational needs. The prevailing climate in the criminal justice sector would suggest that organisational needs now dominate, yet there are some signs that a shift back towards offender-centred engagement is both desirable and compatible with the effective practice mantra (Burnett and McNeill 2005). In order to show some of the fundamental ways in which practitioners engage with offenders we will explore some of the engagement models of practice including motivational interviewing techniques, pro-social modelling and the cycle of change.

Engaging offenders: the current context

Kadushin and Kadushin (1997) state that a practitioner who is likely to develop a positive relationship with an offender needs to be respectful, interested, caring, concerned, supportive, patient and understanding. In recent times the direction of policy appears to have been at variance with this perspective, with an emphasis on confronting offending behaviour, restrictive and punitive interventions and risk management. However, we may also be seeing a resurgence of interest in the practitioner–offender relationship. For instance, the recently published offender management model (Home Office 2006) suggests that:

> Correctional work is at its most effective when offenders are involved in their own assessment, engaged as 'active collaborators' in deciding and implementing their own plan, and come to see themselves as being able to control their own futures, rather than being the victim

of circumstances. This is called 'agency'. Core correctional practice describes the staff behaviours which are most highly associated with securing the high level of engagement and collaboration necessary to help offenders achieve a sense of 'agency'. (Home Office 2006: 39)

Further, this document refers to a range of rehabilitative and restorative interventions as a means to enable punishment, help, change and control. This newly proposed offender management model argues that punishment should be at a minimum, while most offenders will require help. At the higher risk levels some offenders will require a combination of change and help while a small number, the 'dangerous and prolific', will require a system of control. Words such as support, coaching and motivation are returning within the framework of end-to-end offender management.

This offender management model lies at the heart of the National Offender Management Service's (NOMS) strategy for developing an integrated approach to reducing reoffending. Within this model the Prison Service, Probation Service, approved premises and partner agencies will work together to provide end-to-end management of an offender's sentence (Home Office 2005a, 2006). This model entails the bifurcation of work with offenders. On the one hand, there will be offender managers, responsible for the oversight of an offender's sentence (though they will work with high-risk offenders), while on the other hand there will be interventions practitioners, responsible for doing specific work with offenders. Within this context an intervention is therefore defined as: 'those activities and resources selected by an offender manager to deliver specific sentence requirements or address specific criminogenic or public protection needs' (Home Office 2006: 30). Engagement skills are thus an essential component in the repertoire of any one who has responsibility for addressing offending behaviour. Given that the growth of NOMS also includes the commissioning of offender interventions work from non-statutory agencies in the private, voluntary and community sectors, engagement skills will need to form a core component of a wide range of agencies who will be competing for contracts with NOMS.

Different professionals within the criminal justice system clearly have different functions. The first point of contact for an offender within the criminal justice system is usually the police whose primary role is to investigate the alleged crime by gathering the evidence and interviewing the suspect. It then becomes the Crown Prosecutions Service's role to decide whether there is a case to answer. If a decision is made to prosecute the case goes to trial at which stage other agencies in the criminal justice system such as the Probation Service and mental health, drug and victim services become involved (for a good overview of this process see Ashworth and Redmayne 2005). Each of these may have a different role in terms of their relationship with the offender, and each agency will provide a different service, yet what all these agencies and their practitioners have in common is the human interaction with either a defendant or an offender (depending on stage). So regardless of the agency, the practitioner has to have a set of principles which both guides and drives their practice. This chapter is concerned to explore the underlying principles that inform how practitioners can best engage with involuntary clients (Trotter 2006) such as offenders so that they can take an active part in changing their lives.

Engaging offenders:[1] the principles of best practice

One of the fundamental goals to successful engagement is presented by Kadushin and Kadushin (1997) who suggest that it is essential for interviewers to see offenders as they are and not how they wish them to be. This enables achievable, agreed goals to be decided between the practitioner and the offender, thus empowering and engaging the offender to work to their own targets rather than have external targets imposed upon them. For example, the public protection agenda or some of the effective practice principles place organisational constraints upon practitioners which could limit their capacity to take the time and understanding to properly engage offenders.

Good engagement is about understanding that the starting point is discovering what the offender's view of their reality is:

> The practitioner is not moralistic, cold, aloof, derogatory, or disapproving. The non-judgemental attitude is one that suggests that the interviewer is not concerned with praise or blame but solely with understanding. The accepting practitioner seeks to explain the individual's behaviour rather than to determine the worth of such behaviour. (Kadushin and Kadushin 1997: 104)

This does not mean agreeing or condoning the offender's frame of reference but it does mean granting their perspective validity. In working to change behaviour an important point to remember is that while consideration should be given to the offender's behaviour being the result of 'faulty thinking' the practitioner should not necessarily begin from that aspect as it could bias the assessment process.

Much of the current practice within the criminal justice system is founded on the 'what works' philosophy (McGuire 1995; Underdown 2001; Mair 2004). This approach is based on meta-research findings about which ways of working are considered to be successful in addressing and reducing offending behaviour (for example, see Gendreau and Ross 1979; Gendreau et al. 1996). This research suggests that any intervention should address the underlying problems and needs of the offender. There is a need to work with the offender to identify the social and personal factors which contribute to their offending behaviour and then assist them to tackle their problems. Intervention is not likely to be successful unless it is related to the daily struggles that people are facing. In the main these are considered to be relationship difficulties, drug and alcohol use, finances and aggression (Home Office 2005b). Using proven models concentrating on these factors can lead to effective work.

The NOMS end-to-end case management model involves there being an offender manager with responsibility for overseeing an offender's progress over the duration of their sentence. This does not mean that all the work is done by the offender manager, specialist interventions officers and partnership agencies are also involved, each working to provide the appropriate intervention for the level of risk presented by the offender. In order for this process to be effective clarification of role by all participants should be a factor which continues throughout the duration of the work with the offender. This entails more than merely explaining your role but constantly exploring the purpose of your time together. This is particularly important in times of crisis where relapse can occur or in cases of non-compliance where decisions have to be made about taking an order back to court.

Clarification of role is particularly crucial in the criminal justice system, where there is an increasing emphasis on collaborative working partnerships involving statutory, voluntary, charitable and private organisations. In the case study later in this chapter various agencies are involved including prison officers, community- and prison-based drugs practitioners, electronic tagging providers, probation officers in community teams and hostel practitioners. Within this case study it becomes apparent that clarification and exploration of roles is vital not just in terms of interactions between practitioner and offender, but in also in interactions between practitioners.

Trotter (2006) suggests that role-related issues that should be discussed with clients include:

- the dual role of the practitioner (care and control);
- what is negotiable and what is not negotiable;
- how the practitioner's authority might be used;
- the offender's expectations of the practitioner;
- confidentiality;
- who has right to information;
- the nature of the professional relationship;
- the theoretical approach the practitioner takes to the work.

In helping individuals to understand the nature of the dual role of the practitioner discussion will often focus on negotiable and non-negotiable aspects of the intervention process. Clarity of likely consequences for non-compliance is important, as is clarity about legal requirements. Another part of the ongoing engagement process is showing the individual appropriate ways to deal with problematic situations. Effective engagement is thus reliant on mutual understanding between the offender and the practitioner. Without this understanding the nature of the relationship becomes ambiguous and suspicions and distrust begin to cloud such work.

In the case study to follow, Sebastian receives money but does not pay his rent, choosing instead to use the money to buy drugs. After a conversation between the practitioner and the hostel manager an interview took place with Sebastian to discuss the issue of repayment of the unpaid rent owing to the hostel. This was a clear breach of hostel rules and licence conditions, constituting grounds for recall. However, the practitioner used the session to explore what was negotiable and not negotiable. That the money must be paid back in full was agreed by all parties. Discussion then moved on to negotiable aspects of the process which involved the amounts and timescale of the repayments.

An important point for the practitioner was that the offender understood whether non-negotiable requirements are based on a legal mandate, organisational expectations or the individual practitioner's expectations. The practitioner should also help the offender to understand the role of other practitioners within the process, their organisation's policies and how the offender can productively participate in the process. Effective work with offenders involves exploring what they expect from the intervention and clarifying any misconceptions. For instance, issues of confidentiality between partnership agencies could require clarification.

Key skills in the engagement process

Pro-social modelling

Alongside these important role clarifications is the practice of pro-social modelling. Pro-social modelling is based on the principle that the offender will learn positive attitudes and behaviours from the example the practitioner sets and the ways in which the practitioner responds to both pro- and anti-social attitudes (Trotter 2006). Pro-social modelling is summarised by Trotter (2006: 89) as being intended to:

- identify positive or pro-social comments or behaviours as they occur in their interactions with clients;
- reward those comments and behaviours wherever possible, most often by the use of praise;
- model pro-social expressions and actions; and
- challenge anti-social or pro-criminal comments or behaviours.

In essence pro-social modelling is aimed at praising the desired attitudes and behaviour and challenging the undesired attitudes and behaviour. This is supplemented by the practitioner also behaving in a pro-social manner (i.e. turning up on time to appointments, treating the offender with respect). While this might seen as a rather simplistic and superficial technique Trotter (2006) argues that it is remarkable how few practitioners adopt this approach. Trotter (2006) asserts that although this approach is itself does not directly address the underlying problems that often lead to offending (e.g. poverty, drug abuse, unemployment) pro-social modelling is a constructive approach to engaging offenders and achieving change.

Several key documents in the Probation Service assert the importance of this practice for engaging offenders and encouraging change (Chapman and Hough 1998; Home Office 2006). Trotter (2006) states that both his own and other research into pro-social modelling (Andrews *et al.* 1979, Andrews and Bonta 2003) demonstrates its effectiveness at achieving changes among the offending population, concluding that when practitioners use pro-social modelling offenders are imprisoned at half the rate compared to those practitioners who did not use pro-social modelling. Chapman and Hough (1998) reinforce this message:

> Research indicates that pro-social modelling results in higher levels of compliance with supervision programmes as well as lower reoffending rates. It is important that the probation officer explicitly identifies with the offender the pieces of behaviour to be learned and practised. The approach emphasises the importance of demonstrating respect for individuals, by being punctual, reliable, courteous, friendly, honest and open. (Chapman and Hough 1998: 16)

Pro-social modelling is thus seen as a core ingredient within the Probation Service and one of the lynchpins of evidence-based practice and effective offender engagement. Using pro-social techniques can also be a helpful way of avoiding the pitfalls of either sympathising or colluding with the offender's justifications for their anti-social or criminal behaviour. Pro-social modelling can therefore also help clarify roles for both the offender and the practitioner.

Continuing to build on Trotter's (2006) guidelines for role clarification it may also be that offenders have an interest in the particular approach a practitioner uses. In clarifying their role practitioners should be open to talk about the ideas and theories that structure their work and provide opportunities for offenders to ask questions. One of the primary reasons for working with offenders is to effect behavioural change. However, in the criminal justice context the individual is usually not a voluntary participant and is therefore often uncommitted to changing their behaviour. In order to get offenders to engage with this process of change, proven techniques are used to help achieve the desired motivation from offenders to change. One such approach is motivational interviewing (Miller and Rollnick 2002).

Motivational interviewing

The essence of motivational interviewing can be boiled down to three core components (for a discussion of motivational interviewing in relation to substance misuse see Buchanan, this volume). The first of these is collaboration, which entails exploring the issues with offenders rather than imposing an agenda upon them. For this process to be effective collaboration must be approached in a supportive rather than argumentative fashion (Clark *et al.* 2006). Without this offenders may comply by attendance but behaviour change will not occur unless the practitioner builds a respectful relationship. The second component is evocation. Clarke *et al.* (2006) take the view that:

> We have always relied heavily on 'telling', educating and reasoning. However, this approach has more to do with eliciting and 'pulling out' from the offender rather than installing or 'putting in'. When working for behaviour change, we set aside the traditional probation role of the dominating expert who tells the submissive recipient how to change. We want the offender in an active-speaking role, rather than a passive-listening role. (Clark *et al.* 2006: 38)

Finally, Clarke *et al.* (2006) discuss autonomy. Change is more likely to occur if the offender thinks they are in charge of their behaviour and that the changes they make are as a result of their own choices. Further, they are more likely to continue with new, more pro-social behaviours, if they believe they are making changes for their own good reasons.

A key aspect of motivational interviewing is that the practitioner expresses empathy; this involves not only understanding the offender's point of view, but as McMurran (2002) notes, also looking at the process of change from the offender's perspective. It is important within this process to recognise that resistance to change is a natural part of the change process and is not necessarily reason for concern. However, the practitioner needs to acquire the ability to respond to this, not with a confrontational style but with one which involves reflective listening and other strategies that strive to challenge while working with, or 'rolling with', resistance. According to Miller and Rollnick (2002), resistance is at the heart of motivational interviewing:

> Resistance is often the life of the play. It is the twist that adds drama and excitement to the plot. Viewing resistance as a perverse character flaw is a sad mistake. Resistance lies at the very heart of human change. It arises from the motives and struggles of the actors. It foreshadows certain ends to which the play may or may not lead. The true art of a counselor is tested in the recognition and handling of resistance. (Miller and Rollnick 2002: 109–10)

Resistance can also be understood as a sign of 'dissonance' within the change process. Dissonance occurs when the offender begins to feel left behind or unhappy with the pace of the interview. In these circumstances it is important for the practitioner to double back over the themes already covered so that the offender has the opportunity to regain their sense of place and progress. Miller and Rollnick (2002) go on to remind practitioners that whether there is change or resistance 'talk' this will be specific to a particular change; the offender may want to change some traits but not others, for example to stop using heroin but continue using amphetamines (see Miller and Rollnick 2002: chapters 5 and 8). As such, dissonance needs to be understood and approached, not as a general attitude, but one that is linked to a particular behaviour or habit.

Other important features to look out for in the motivational interview include discrepancy and self-efficacy. Discrepancy is generally the gap between the present status and a desired goal. Discrepancy is therefore the difference between the offender's attitude and goals (Miller and Rollnick 2002). Building a positive and collaborative relationship by the use of empathy can lead to a situation where an offender's values can be explored with them. This will then enable the offender to recognise when behaviour comes into conflict with their own deeply held values. Miller and Rollnick (2002) ague that under these circumstances it is usually the behaviour that changes.

For example, the offender called Sebastian in the case study below has a young son and wishes to be a good father to him. Yet he also has a heroin addiction. In this instance an interview with Sebastian would focus on the discrepancy between Sebastian's desire to be a good father and his ongoing heroin addiction. The hope is that Sebastian will realise the two are incompatible and become motivated to address his addiction so that he can be a good father to his son. Ultimately, when this stage is reached offenders should be voicing the arguments for change themselves.

Finally, self-efficacy is about both the offender and the practitioner's confidence in their ability to reach the desired change or outcome. This is crucial because if either does not believe in their ability to complete the change process then it will not happen. Miller and Rollnick (2002) argue that the practitioner's positive or negative perspective on the likelihood of change can become a self-fulfilling prophecy that either supports or undermines the offender's own confidence. Self-efficacy is the belief that change is achievable. Without an offender believing in their capacity for improvement the process is doomed. The role of the practitioner is not to tell the offender 'I will change you', but 'If you wish, I can help you change' (Miller and Rollnick 2002: 41). This process also involves amplifying strengths rather than focusing on repairing weaknesses and fixing flaws (Clarke et al. 2006).

Cycle of change

One of the core tools for helping to think about an offender's process of change is the cycle of change (Prochaska and Di Clemente 1982). McGuire (2000) states that even when offenders accept the potential benefits of change, they will not necessarily be ready or willing to do so. Some offenders are not interested in making changes and others may well be resistant to it. The cycle of change is a useful way of engaging with offenders about the process of change. It was developed from the study of addictive behaviours and is valuable for making assessments and decisions about appropriate forms of intervention with an offender (for a discussion[2] of the cycle of change in relation to substance misuse see Buchanan, this volume).

Prochaska and Di Clemente's (1982) cycle of change is based on six stages which have been used to address a range of problem behaviours (see Figure 5.1).

Before change begins there is a pre-contemplation stage where the individual has no intention of changing their behaviour. Many individuals in this stage are unaware of their problems. The pre-contemplation stage is often characterised as reluctance, rebelliousness, resignation and rationalising (or techniques of neutralisation in the Sykes and Matza (1957) sense). Input at this stage needs to be in the form of coaxing, encouraging, informing and

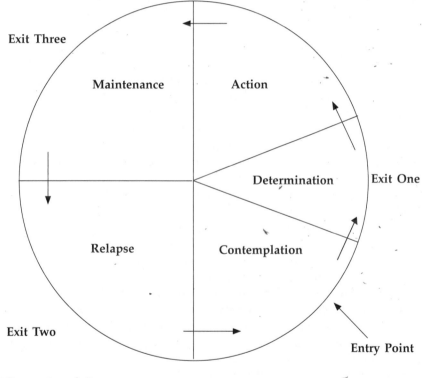

Pre-contemplation

Exit One: Choosing not to change
Exit Two: Giving up on trying
Exit Three: Stable, successful change

Figure 5.1 The cycle of change
Source: Prochaska and Di Clemente's (1982) 'Cycle of Change', adapted from McGuire (2000: 70).

advising rather than mounting 'high-intensity' programmes or increasing confrontation. This is because any attempt to put unmotivated offenders onto programmes is most likely to lead to the offender ignoring the process. According to Miller and Rollnick (2002) the offender must first be engaged and then personally motivated before programme work can be effectively delivered:

> Clinicians often believe that more education, more intense treatment, or more confrontation will necessarily produce more change. Nowhere is this less true than with precontemplators. More intensity will often produce fewer results with this group. (Miller and Rollnick 2002: 208)

Contemplation is the stage at which the offender becomes aware that a problem exists and is seriously thinking about change though they may not be ready to make a full commitment. Determination is the stage which combines intention and the development of a plan of action. The offender is preparing to change in the near future and may have learned from past attempts when thinking about how to achieve change. Hence, at this stage, offenders are intending to take action and it is the role of the practitioner to help the offender develop an achievable and realistic approach to change. Action is the stage in which individuals modify their behaviour, experiences or environment in order to overcome their problems. Action involves the most overt behavioural changes and requires considerable commitment of time and energy. Active listening and affirmation for what has been accomplished are important at this time. However, if the offender does not have adequate self-efficacy (see earlier discussion) they are not likely to achieve long-term success. Maintenance is the stage in which people work to prevent relapse and consolidate the gains attained during action. For addictive behaviours this stage extends from six months to an indeterminate period past the initial action. Relapse is seen as a step back rather than an utter failure and can be as a result of dropping one's guard or 'just testing'. Eroded self-efficacy can also contribute to the decision to relapse. Motivational interviewing after relapse can help the individual to renew or recommence the journey through the early stages once again.

The keys skills discussed above are drawn from probation, social work and addictions practice. They are by no means specific to offenders or the criminal justice system and have been applied in a range of different fields to address a range of different unwanted attitudes and behaviours. Neither are these skills an exhaustive list of the range of engagement techniques that can be drawn upon to help address offending behaviour. Yet they do constitute the core of current probation thinking about how to engage offenders in changing their attitudes and behaviour. The intention has been to outline these core skills and suggest further reading (see end of chapter also) to help develop a more critical appreciation of them. Describing these key skills is all well and good, but does little to prepare you for the messy reality of applying these skills in practice. Hence, we are next going to draw upon an actual example where things do not go according to plan and work with an offender rapidly deteriorates after a very positive start.

Lessons from the field: a case study of Sebastian[3]

Sebastian is a 30-year-old male who has been a heroin user for several years and has recently moved into the area. He has family and a young son living in another part of the country. He is not allowed contact with his son. He had previously been sentenced[1] to custody for 2.5 years for varying offences of dishonesty. He had recently undertaken a RAPt (Rehabilitation for Addicted Prisoners Trust) programme while in custody.[4] Upon release a condition of his licence was to live in a rehabilitation hostel (voluntary sector) and complete the remainder of the RAPt course. His sentence plan, which was drawn up between his offender manager and the hostel, involved maintaining abstinence from drugs and alcohol (he had not had a problem with alcohol but the rules of the hostel stated that residents could not use either). Alongside this Sebastian was expected to eventually find accommodation for himself and seek educational and/or employment opportunities. As Sebastian had only recently moved into the area, the offender manager assigned to Sebastian's case had not had contact with Sebastian before his arrival at the hostel.

The initial assessment with Sebastian involved the offender manager using a risk and need assessment tool to inform a sentence plan. This process draws upon motivational interviewing techniques to help ascertain how the offender can become motivated to change and maintain change. The offender manager and Sebastian then consider where Sebastian is on the cycle of change and develop a SMARTA[5] action plan. Other agencies involved include a national employment charity, a community drugs agency and the key worker at the hostel.

Sebastian has moved into the area to make a fresh start for himself so there were already some positive signs that Sebastian was motivated to change. His cycle of change suggested he was already in the action phase regarding his drug use and working towards getting qualifications so he could get a job. However, in other areas he was still in the determination phase of the cycle, in particular finding his own housing and rebuilding his relationship with his family.

To start with, Sebastian engaged well with the remainder of his RAPt programme and his offender manager, regularly attending appointments and receiving good feedback from the key worker at the hostel. The plan was working well because Sebastian was committed to change, had support from a fellow resident at the hostel and had made particularly good progress by enrolling on a computer course and attending basic skills classes. Sebastian was also able to reflect on his past behaviour and come to the opinion that it was both unacceptable and incompatible with his long-term aspirations of being a good father and providing a good role model to his son. He also had also enlisted the help of a specialist housing provider based in a local community drugs agency. In his supervision sessions Sebastian would bring in detailed and very positive feedback from his key worker in the hostel and his offender manager reinforced this progress by using appropriate praise and support (pro-social modelling).

Things continue positively for about six months. Sebastian completed his basic skills training, had registered for local housing and was waiting to start college. He had also had several successful family visits which had spurred him on further. At random drug and alcohol tests he had continually produced negative results. Then, out of the blue, Sebastian arrives at the probation office one morning and tells his offender manager that he has been evicted from the hostel over the weekend for testing positive for alcohol, though not for drugs. Sebastian had then been asked to leave the hostel with almost immediate effect. This not only placed him in breach of the conditions of his licence it also heightened his risk of reoffending.

Following his eviction stop-gap accommodation was found for Sebastian in a probation hostel but over the next few weeks Sebastian returned to heavy drug use and ended up stealing his hostel rent money and subsequently finding himself in debt. His attitude towards re-engagement with drug rehabilitation programme was both negative and dismissive.

The first, and perhaps most obvious, lesson to emerge from Sebastian's story is the problem of contradictory and competing approaches by different organisations. In this instance the offender manager and the community drug agency are broadly using the same practice model (motivational) while the hostel philosophy is one of total abstinence with no room for manoeuvre (zero tolerance). Hence, if there are incompatible practice models there is a real danger that this will lead to tensions and confusions for both offenders and practitioners. In Sebastian's case the decision to evict him effectively put him in breach of his licence conditions (to reside) and technically meant he could be recalled to prison. The lead agency in terms of 'enforcement' (probation) and the lead agency in terms of 'treatment' (RAPt) are therefore working to different models and as a result Sebastian could easily end up back in prison for having had an alcoholic drink which was entirely unrelated to his conviction. In terms of the cycle of change this raises issues about how agencies manage relapse. In this example, a motivational style would see relapse as part of the cycle of change and seek to work with the offender to overcome the relapse and move forward towards change once more.

These types of tensions are not peculiar to partnership work and can just as easily occur within an organisation. In the case of Sebastian, the offender manager may have the difficult job of navigating between the motivational ethos which would encourage continued support and collaboration with Sebastian and the pressure to begin breach proceedings which may have led Sebastian straight back to prison. These pressures are not abstract or without consequences for either practitioner or offender. For example, Sebastian was angry and upset because he believed he had failed, but also felt very let down by the hostel. The offender manager found himself in conflict with the hostel staff who wanted Sebastian removed and his line manager who wanted Sebastian recalled. So even within organisations there are tensions which can pull in different directions and work against each other to the potential detriment of the offender and therefore society (in terms of the risk of reoffending).

It is this tension which prompted the question in the title of this chapter. Is best practice the same thing as effective practice? At one level it would seem that effective practice is primarily governed by the 'what works' agenda (Underdown 1998) and the wider evidence-based practice criteria (Chapman and Hough 1998). Both of these emphasise a range of measurable and therefore auditable outcomes which focus upon procedural and organisational activity (for more details see Merrington and Stanley 2007). While this is entirely appropriate for the modern probation service these measures of effectiveness seem to pay scant attention to the engagement dimension under discussion here. As stated in the introduction to this chapter Burnett and McNeill (2005) have argued that this imbalance needs to be addressed to take account of the practitioner-offender relationship. Given that the engagement skills outlined above are empirically proven techniques it does not seem that this rebalancing is at odds with the wider goals of effective practice, but could in fact promote them still further. As Merrington and Stanley (2007) comment:

> It appears, therefore, that measuring the effectiveness of the case management involves at least two dimensions: the effectiveness of the case management process/organisation and the effectiveness of the casework relationship. (Merrington and Stanley 2007: 447)

This is a very encouraging signal that the importance of engaging with offenders is being acknowledged as a key dimension in addressing offending behaviour. Merrington and Stanley (2007) are not alone in this assertion, and the Home Office (2006) also seems to be increasingly convinced of the benefits of engagement. Drawing on the meta-analysis of Dowden and Andrews (2004) the NOMS offender management model outlines the five core elements of correctional practice:

- the firm, fair and clear use of authority;
- modelling pro-social and anti-criminal attitudes, cognitions and behaviours;

- teaching concrete problem-solving skills;
- using community resources (brokerage);
- forming and working through warm, open and enthusiastic relationships.
(Dowden and Rock 2004, taken from Home Office 2006: 39)

The importance placed on pro-social modelling and the nature of the practitioner–offender relationship is clear in this list and strongly suggests that engagement is a vital ingredient in tackling offending behaviour. This was never truer than in the case of Sebastian. In this case, a failure to acknowledge the motivational framework in which he had been working would probably have led Sebastian back to prison. Fortunately (and without wishing to sound at all sanctimonious!), the offender manager in this instance worked with Sebastian to help him overcome his relapse and move back towards changing his behaviour. This process relied heavily on an open, honest and critical dialogue where Sebastian began to reflect on his earlier relapse and with the help of the offender manager set new goals for himself. The primary motivation for Sebastian was to be a good father and it was this focus which became the benchmark for all of Sebastian's subsequent goals and activity. Eventually Sebastian graduated from the RAPt programme moved into the independent housing sector and began to forge new relationships with his family.

The practitioner's role in engagement terms is not to judge people. Their role is to search for understanding with offenders about their choices while avoiding either condemnation or collusion with them. This can only be done by reflecting on decisions and choices that have been made, the reasons for those decisions and the impact these decisions have on other people. In Sebastian's case this involved prompting him with questions designed to help him think about his relapse and how it affected him and others. This enabled an honest and critical dialogue to develop where Sebastian was able to recognise some of the poor decisions he had made, in particular, getting high on drugs so that he could block out the guilt and shame of 'failing' himself and his family by losing his hostel place. Sebastian was also able to see the contradiction between his behaviour and his longer-term goals of being a good father. This led to him to revisit earlier thoughts about what good fathers do, what characteristics they have and how Sebastian might go about identifying specific steps to help him become a good father himself, even if the long-term goal was many years hence.

Conclusion: reconciling engagement with effective practice

Why engagement skills have spent some time in the hinterland of effective practice is unclear but can perhaps be linked to the ideological shift in probation work over the last couple of decades (see the chapters by Nash and Goodman in this text) where the emphasis on treatment has been overtaken by an emphasis on enforcement, risk management and public protection. Garland's (1996) social commentary on the ways in which the state has responded to high crime rates can also help to shed some light on this imbalance. Garland (1996) argues that the state seeks to adapt to its apparent inability to reduce crime in contemporary society. One of these adaptations is to change the targets or priorities of the state apparatus to ones that can be internally measured and achieved, rather than targets directed at wider individual and societal improvements which are much harder to either measure or control. This amounts to an effective shifting of the goalposts: the aim is no longer to rehabilitate offenders or reduce crime, but to ensure the correct forms are filled in by the correct deadlines and that the right number and sorts of offenders get put on this or that accredited programme. This discussion also resonates with the new penology (Feeley and Simon 1992) which emphasises the shift from transformative goals of rehabilitation to a focus on the management of different risk groups. These insightful commentaries resonate very strongly with recent changes in how work with offenders is conducted. How well a practitioner engages with an offender is difficult to quantify and hard to gauge. Engagement therefore resists crude measurement and arguably goes against the prevailing audit and management ethos that has risen to ascendency in recent years.

Yet perhaps the pendulum is beginning to swing back towards engagement. The recent acknowledgement of the importance of the offender–practitioner relationship discussed above is encouraging and it would therefore seem an apposite time to consider how the engagement process might be more fully incorporated into addressing offending behaviour. This would clearly need to fit within the current political and policy climate so the list below attempts to apply the 'what works' principles to the engagement process:

- a collaborative and consistent approach by all workers and partnership agencies;
- good and effective communication between partnership agencies;
- development of a plan of working which engages with offenders in a way which facilitates the key factors in pro-social modelling while taking into account the dual role of care and control;
- establishment of the links between breach proceedings and the quality of engagement with offenders;
- creation of time and space for engagement to occur;
- education, training and supervision which focuses on engagement skills;
- ongoing assessment and measurement of the engagement process.

Enshrining these principles within the organisational context of working with offenders builds on the growing acknowledgment that engagement forms a central plank of effective practice. The example of Sebastian places engagement at odds with effective practice and the potential negative consequences are clear for all to see. The mistake has been to place engagement skills and work outside of the effective practice arena. Best practice and effective practice are therefore not necessarily in conflict over engagement: they should be united in an ongoing effort to improve how offending behaviour is addressed.

Discussion questions

1 How far are the core engagement skills outlined in this chapter able to address offending behaviour?
2 There is often a tension between the needs of the organisation and the needs of the offender. How might this tension be best managed?
3 The media, politicians and apparently the public are becoming more and more punitive. The values of offender engagement do not easily fit with this punitive mentality. Is engagement therefore out of kilter with contemporary attitudes and if so should it not be consigned to history?

Further reading

Home Office (2006) *NOMS Offender Management Model*. London: HMSO. One of the key documents in recent years. This text provides a thorough overview of how the Probation Service will be working in the next few years. While there are still many unanswered questions about the future direction and organisation of the Probation Service this document provides a very useful reference point for beginning to understand the organisational complexities of the current Probation Service.

Kadushin, A. and Kadushin, G. (1997) *The Social Work Interview: A Guide for Human Services Professionals*, 4th edn. Chichester: Columbia. This is the definitive text on how to go about interviewing people. The key tactics and skills for interviewing offenders are largely contained within its covers and it is hard to imagine how anyone working with offenders could get by without this text.

Miller, W.R. and Rollnick, S. (2002) *Motivational Interviewing: Preparing People for Change*, 2nd edn. London: Guilford Press. This is a clear, thorough and well organised book that outlines the key elements of motivational interviewing – the ideal companion for Kadushin and Kadushin's (1997) work.

Morgan, R. and Gelsthorpe, L. (eds) (2007) *Handbook of Probation*. Cullompton: Willan. This book is a comprehensive and detailed edited collection that contains twenty chapters by some of the leading authorities in the field. Although this book is probation orientated most of the chapters contain important debates and developments that are relevant to both the community and voluntary sector.

Trotter, C. (2006) *Working with Involuntary Clients – A Guide to Practice*, 2nd edn. London: Sage. This is a key text for anyone working with offenders. Trotter outlines some of the fundamental processes that lead to effective engagement with involuntary clients. Trotter's clear writing style and his critical commentary provide a very good basis for developing practice.

Notes

1 For a number of reasons we have chosen to use the word 'offender' to describe the people we work with. We did experiment with service-user and client but felt that they were currently out of vogue in terms of preferred language and possibly confusing in terms of context setting.

2 In some versions the pre-contemplation phase is outside of the cycle, hence the cycle itself is often only made up of five stages: contemplation, determination, action, maintenance and relapse.

3 The name and key details of this case have been altered for reasons of confidentiality.

4 RAPt is an accredited 12-step programme based on total abstinence from drugs and alcohol. The standardised programme has three stages of intervention – assessment, primary treatment and after-care.

5 SMARTA is an acronym for: Specific; Measurable, Achievable, Realistic, Time-bound and Anti-discriminatory. These are the guiding principles for setting appropriate targets.

References

Andrews, D.A. and Bonta, J. (2003) *The Psychology of Criminal Conduct*. Cincinnati, OH: Anderson.

Andrews, D.A., Keissling, J.J., Russell, R.J. and Grant, B.A. (1979) *Volunteers and the One-to-One Supervision of Adult Probationers*. Toronto: Ontario Ministry of Correctional Services.

Ashworth, A. and Redmayne, M. (2005) *The Criminal Process*, 3rd edn. Oxford: Oxford University Press.

Burnett, R. and McNeill, F. (2005) 'The place of the officer-offender relationship in assisting offenders to desist from crime', *Probation Journal*, 52 (3): 221–242.

Chapman, T. and Hough, M. (1998) *A Guide to Effective Practice: Evidence Based Practice*, ed. Jane Furness, Her Majesty's Inspectorate of Probation. London: Home Office.

Clarke M.D., Walters S., Gingerich R. and Metzler M. (2006) 'Importance, confidence and readiness for change: motivational interviewing for probation and parole', *Perspectives* (American Probation and Parole Association), 30 (2): 36–45.

Dowden, C. and Andrews, D.A. (2004) 'The importance of staff practice in delivering effective correctional treatment: a meta-analytic review of core correctional practices', *International Journal of Offender Therapy and Comparative Criminology*, 48 (2): 203–214.

Feeley, M. and Simon, J. (1992) 'The new penology: notes on the emerging strategy of corrections and its implications', *Criminology*, 30 (4): 452–74.

Garland, D. (1996) 'The limits of the sovereign state: strategies of crime control in contemporary society', *British Journal of Criminology*, 36 (4): 445–71.

Gendreau, P. and Ross, R. (1979) 'Effective correctional treatment: bibliotherapy for cynics', *Crime and Delinquency*, 25: 463–89.

Gendreau, P., Goggin, C. and Little, T. (1996) 'A meta-analysis of the predictors of adult offender recidivism: what works!', *Criminology*, 34: 575–607.

Home Office (2005a) *Yorkshire and Humberside Regional Reducing Offending Action Plan, November 2005 – April 2007*. London: Home Office, National Offender Management Service.

Home Office (2005b) *The National Reducing Reoffending Delivery Plan*: London: Home Office, National Offender Management Service.

Home Office (2006) *NOMS Offender Management Model*. London: HMSO.

Kadushin A. and Kadushin G. (1997) *The Social Work Interview: A Guide for Human services professionals*, 4th edn. Chichester: Columbia.

McGuire, J. (1995) *What Works: Reducing Offending, Guidelines from Research and Practice*. Chichester: John Wiley & Son.

McGuire, J. (2000) *Cognitive-Behavioural Approaches: An Introduction to Theory and Research*, ed. Jane Furness, Her Majesty's Inspectorate of Probation. London: Home Office.

McMurran, M. (2002) 'Motivation to change: selection criterion or treatment need?' in M. McMurran ed. *Motivating Offenders to Change: A Guide to Enhancing Engagement in Therapy*. New York: John Wiley & Sons.

Mair, G. (2004) *What Matters in Probation?* Cullompton: Willan.

Merrington, S. and Stanley, S. (2007) 'Effectiveness: who counts what?' in R. Morgan and L. Gelsthorpe (eds) *Handbook of Probation*. Cullompton: Willan.

Miller W.R. and Rollnick S. (2002) *Motivational Interviewing: Preparing People for Change*, 2nd edn. London: Guilford Press.

Prochaska, J.O. and Di Clemente, C.C. (1982) 'Transtheoretical therapy: toward a more integrative model of change', *Psychotherapy: Theory, Research and Practice*, 19: 276–88.

Sykes, G. and Matza, D. (1957) 'Techniques of neutralisation', *American Sociological Review*, 22.

Trotter, C. (1996) 'The impact of different supervision practices in community corrections', *Australian and New Zealand Journal of Criminology*, 29 (1): 29–46.

Trotter C. (2006) *Working with Involuntary Clients – A Guide to Practice*, 2nd edn. London: Sage.

Underdown, A. (1998) *Strategies for Effective Offender Supervision*. London: Her Majesty's Inspectorate of Probation.

Underdown, A. (2001) 'Making "What Works" work: challenges in the delivery of community penalties', in A. Bottoms, L. Gelsthorpe and S. Rex (eds), *Community Penalties: Change and Challenges*. Cullompton: Willan.

Chapter 6

Written communication

Pauline Ashworth

Introduction

The criminal justice system could not function without the written word, yet
it is something that is usually taken for granted in the hustle and bustle of
dealing with and processing offenders through the complex procedural maze
that currently exists. Papers, reports, records, memos, letters, pro formas
– formal and informal – circulate constantly throughout the system helping
to keep the flow of information and ideas, judgments and assessments,
moving. These documents take on a 'life of their own' – once they have
left the hands of the writer – and, as such, what they contain is subject to
interpretation and re-interpretation depending on the purpose, expectations,
beliefs, values or demands of those who read them. Katie Prince, writing
about social work records, notes:

> Social work records constitute a complex web of communicated words
> and meaning, first spoken, then interpreted and lastly converted into
> written language to be read and re-interpreted at various times, by
> various others. (Prince 1996: ix)

The written word is extremely powerful, nowhere more so than in the
criminal justice system, which places a premium on written forms of communication. Doel and Shardlow (1998: 108) refer to the 'procedures, *politics
and power* of the written record' (emphasis added). As such the written
word is critically important, not only because the system would grind to a
halt without it, but also because written assessments, reports and records
wield such influence in the decisions that are made about offenders' lives
and treatment.

Despite the centrality of written communication, it is very much taken
for granted, if often bemoaned, by practitioners. Yet writing is not an
adjunct to the work of the criminal justice system; it is integral as we
cannot communicate fully without committing our thoughts to 'paper'.
While different roles will demand different types or forms of written work,

few people who work within the criminal justice system 'escape' the task of writing things down for others to read. It has been estimated (Prince 1996: ix) that writing records alone can take up to one-fifth of a professional social worker's time. It is not inconceivable that a similar figure applies to practitioners in the criminal justice system. Often it can be seen as a tedious chore or, perhaps at best, a secondary aspect of the 'real' work. Thompson (2002) comments: 'It is not uncommon for people workers to complain that too much time is spent on "paper work", and not enough on actually working with *people*' (p. 108, italics in original). Although understandable given the inexorable rise in 'paperwork', this is a dangerous belief as it could mean that what is written is not given the attention it demands. Dutton and Kohli (in Vass 1996) note that 'boredom or un-interest in the task may produce a reluctance to put pen to paper.' (p. 67) But being able to communicate effectively in writing is a vital part of what we do, an essential skill.

The range of documents, reports, records, assessments – paper and electronic – produced within the criminal justice system is vast. In addition, there are all the memos and notes we make for ourselves during interviews, phone calls or conferences that reflect our interpretation of what we are hearing and witnessing. As well as being determined by the purpose of the interview or discussion, what we choose to write down will be affected by the degree of concentration we bring to the task, the interest we have in what is being said, our pre-conceptions, values and beliefs, as well as by a range of other personal and situational factors. Nothing can prevent these 'orientation' factors from intruding; the question is how far they are allowed to distort or prejudice what we write.

In this chapter, we will consider the implications of the subjective nature of writing and of what might be called the 'Chinese whisper effect' of producing written reports, records and so on, and passing them on. Are we confident that what we have written down reflects reality? How do we know that those who read it subsequently understand what we write? Is it possible to ensure that the integrity of what we have written is upheld? In examining these questions, we will see that there are no definitive rules or set formulae; writing is, almost by definition, a subjective activity depending on a range of different influences, factors and styles.

Over the past decade or so, increasing emphasis has been placed upon *standardising* practice, including what is written. This tendency may lead us to ignore or overlook the *subjective* nature of what we write and the degree of *discretion*, *selectivity* and *professional judgment* required to produce it. Thus we need to be acutely aware of the ways in which discretion and subjectivity will affect what we write – and also how it is received. Our readers will bring to the report or record their own biases, expectations and preconceptions. While, as noted above, there are no definitive rules or formulae to help overcome the potential biases, what we can highlight is a series of questions or factors to think about when putting thoughts and observations in writing, factors which will influence the interpretation and understanding of what is written and which it is important to reflect on when considering what to write and how to write it.

A number of key questions need to be asked in order to analyse how we are to set about the task outlined above:

- What is a 'document' for – what is its purpose?
- Who is the 'audience' – who will be reading it?
- What is our orientation to the task?
- How do the above shape or influence what is written?

What follows will examine these questions to see how we can sharpen and focus what we write to suit our purpose and enhance the quality and integrity of what we write and communicate to others.

Form and purpose

The existence of many different forms of written communication within the criminal justice system suggests that we will adopt different styles to suit not only the particular purpose but also the context and medium. For example, scribbling a note while balancing a phone against one's ear will produce something different from constructing a court report or completing an assessment form or supervision plan in conjunction with an offender. In the former, we do not have the time to think about the exact wording or examine what we are writing for different meanings. Nor do most of us possess shorthand to enable us to record such conversations verbatim. What we produce will be a product of selectivity, our concentration, listening skills, preconceptions and even how we feel or what we know about the person on the other end of the line. While this may be evident in this informal context, it is also true that what we write formally can be the result of selectivity, preconceptions, prejudice, sentiment and our particular purpose.

It is worth reflecting on the range of purposes that give rise to written documents. In the criminal justice context, for example, we write things down for a number of reasons:

- to record information, decisions, assessments;
- to communicate information, decisions, assessments;
- to request information, decisions;
- to respond to requests for information, decisions;
- to influence decisions;
- to shape or invite responses;
- to justify actions or decisions;
- to demonstrate accountability;
- to provide evidence of work done;
- as a way of working with an offender to encourage self-reflection or involvement in problem-solving.

These different purposes will be influenced in different ways by such things as deadlines and the speed required to produce the document, or our awareness of the audience whether it be external (e.g. court) or internal (colleagues), or our understanding of the relevance of data protection and confidentiality in relation to the document – who is going to have access to it? This latter influence has changed significantly in recent decades with the introduction of various pieces of data protection legislation, but there are still occasions when we can assume a degree of privacy about what we write, especially in terms of offender access.

Before leaving the question of purpose, it is important to note that many documents will combine two or more of the reasons listed above to make the rationale more complex. For instance, in writing a report for court, our purpose is to communicate information about the offender, indicate our assessment of his or her relative risk *and* influence or guide the decision about sentencing. The last objective, while perhaps not overtly done, will almost inevitably shape our decision about what we write – and perhaps what we leave out – in the information/assessment part of the report.

Recordkeeping can have many different uses or purposes. These have been outlined – in relation to social work, but nonetheless relevant to the criminal justice context – in a British Association of Social Workers (BASW) report as: management control; continuity, self-justification, legal record, work support, supervision and teaching, information storage, personal evaluation, planning, research, financial control, agency evaluation, personal identity (BASW 1983, cited in Doel and Shardlow 1998: 108) Given such a range of purposes, it is perhaps not surprising that they can sometimes conflict; for instance, the need for self-justification (for some piece of intervention) might lead to conflict with the need for a legal record as the former *could* lead to deliberate censoring or selecting out some aspects of what occurred. Similarly, awareness of management scrutiny, financial control and evaluation could affect the degree to which we make the case for funding for a particular piece of work.

Another example might be contained in the record we create of our contacts with an offender. Here, as well as fulfilling the purpose of recording the facts of what occurred, we are giving ourselves an aide-memoire of what we observed and what we experienced during the contact; we are also providing a historical record of what occurred for colleagues who might pick up the case in our absence or at a later date. Interwoven in this record will be our thoughts, impressions, feelings, ideas about the encounter and the offender. These can be conscious and deliberate, but sometimes they will be hidden or implied, not clearly acknowledged because of the way in which they are written down. How does the inclusion of personal impressions and thoughts affect our purpose – to communicate information (facts)? Clearly it will have an effect; the question is whether it is positive that is, constructive.

Doel and Shardlow (1998) suggest that 'with each piece of recording, (we) need to ask (ourselves) what the specific purposes are (as) … being clear about the purpose of making a written record helps to decide what needs to go in it' (p. 108). To illustrate the significance of this, it would be helpful to give some examples. At the same time, we can now turn to a consideration of the wider implications of writing things down.

Written language

Communication is made up of both verbal and non-verbal components. As well as the actual words we use and the way(s) in which we structure them into sentences, when speaking we rely heavily on non-verbal elements such as facial expression, gestures, movements and even how we position ourselves in relation to the person we are talking with. Further, we will use different emphasis, intonation, pauses and so on to convey how we wish what we are saying to be understood. It has been estimated that up to 80 per cent of all communication consists of these non-verbal elements.

The question, for our purposes, is: how do we communicate fully when we cannot rely on such non-verbal cues to guide our audience? What happens to what we are saying when we cannot use different tones, hand gestures, eye movements to convey our meaning – i.e. when we are communicating in writing? The reader cannot *see* how we position ourselves, nor do they witness the emphasis we place on particular words or phrases by punching the air or slapping the table. They don't hear the dramatic pauses we use to indicate that what we are about to say is important. So how *do* we communicate in writing?

Use of language

We do it in several ways, ways that are perhaps less obvious or immediate than when we speak, but which are nonetheless powerful. Our reliance on language alone – as opposed to gesture and intonation – means that we must invest in the words we use all the meaning we wish to convey. This is perfectly acceptable as long as we make it clear that what we are doing is expressing a personal viewpoint or interpretation of the facts we are presenting. *Some* of the tactics we can use, however, are not unbiased. Thus we might use 'steering' words such as 'obviously' to emphasise and draw attention to a point or a conclusion we want our audience to reach; such apparently innocuous directing words can disguise the fact that something is not necessarily obvious, or that we have not fully made the case we are arguing, but we want the reader to think we have. Another 'ploy' might be to repeat an idea or a statement using different words to make sure the reader has got the point or to convince them that it is a point worth taking note of.

More problematic are the subtle shifts in language usage which convey information not only about factual, directly observed and observable phenomena, but also about the way in which those 'facts' should be interpreted. One of the more insidious of these shifts is the growing tendency to use adjectives as nouns. For instance, rather than writing that 'John's ability to care for himself is inadequate', we might find the over-simplification of 'John is an inadequate'. Even the former phrasing is problematic as it gives no substance to the assertion; there is no evidence cited to justify such a conclusion which merely presents the statement as fact. Far worse, though, is the generalised and dismissive description of John as 'an inadequate' with its implications of hopelessness and utter dependence. This linguistic shift from adjective to noun gives the point a spurious factual weight that leaves the reader in no doubt about John's capabilities.

Other examples of this tendency to cloak judgment or personal opinion in the language of 'fact' include phrases and ways of describing people that have become standardised and even clichéd in written documents. The following are some examples taken from actual records and reports (adapted from Doel and Shardlow 1998):

- Jean is aggressive and self-centred
- Frank presents in a hostile manner
- Derek is very manipulative
- Julie indulges in promiscuous behaviour
- Peter is testing the boundaries
- Sally laughs and dresses inappropriately
- Steve is a difficult problem case
- Doreen is needy and dependent

Before considering what might be 'wrong' with such ways of depicting offenders in reports or records, it is interesting to reflect on how the people so depicted might describe themselves. Thus:

- Jean – *I know how to ask for what I want*
- Frank – *I don't like what you want me to do*
- Derek – *I know how to play the system*
- Julie – *I have a lot of sexual partners*
- Peter – *I have a lot of sexual partners*
- Sally – *You don't have my taste in jokes and clothes*
- Steve – *You don't know what to do with me*
- Doreen – *I wish I could do more for myself*

There are several points to make here. First is the crucial *distinction between fact and judgment*, or between fact and supposition. Often we are called upon to make a judgment about what we witness, as it is part of our professional role to make such judgments. We are invited to give our professional opinion on a range of issues relating to offender assessment, response and management. This is as it should be. The problem arises when judgments become judgmental. A lack of clarity about the distinction can lead to the subtle intrusion of prejudice, personal values and beliefs about how others should live their lives. The description of Steve as 'a difficult problem case' might lead us – and others – to *expect* problems every time we encounter him, or to assume that this aspect of his behaviour in one situation governs all his behaviour. And, of course, it begs the question – what do we mean by 'difficult' or 'problem'? for whom and in whose terms? Similarly, describing Julie as 'indulging in promiscuous behaviour' suggests that the author finds such behaviour distasteful, the use of the word 'indulge' implying some kind of selfishness and licentiousness that is disapproved of. Further, given the way in which Peter's sexual activity is described as 'testing the boundaries', we might reasonably infer gender discrimination or stereotyping.

All of the above examples are in some way judgmental or prejudiced; despite their reliance on commonly used and generally accepted phrases, they nonetheless contain elements of personal judgement. For instance, the description of Derek as 'very manipulative' might reflect more about how we feel in relation to him – i.e. manipulated – than about Derek's behaviour. It is worth noting that we are all 'manipulative' to some degree as it is only through some form of manipulation (some might call it 'persuasion') that we can get many of our needs met.

It is an extremely useful – and sometimes sobering – exercise to reflect on what we have written and how it might have been expressed had it been written by the person involved. In this way, we can become more aware of any tendency we might have developed toward personal judgment or to impose meaning, to try to steer the reader to our personal viewpoint or assessment of an offender or a situation.

A second point relates to the *presentation* of fact and opinion. None of the above statements includes an acknowledgment of the fact that they are judgments – which should be based on factual evidence. It is only with the inclusion of the evidence from which such conclusions have been drawn that the reader is able to make an informed assessment of the situation or person referred to. For example, to render the statement 'Jean is aggressive and self-centred' non-judgmental, it would be necessary to include some examples of the behaviour that have given rise to such a conclusion. Even then, it would only be possible to infer that *in this or that situation* Jean's behaviour was *perceived* as aggressive and self-centred. It may be that in other situations, with other people, where Jean does not feel intimidated or misunderstood, her behaviour is quite different. Some attempt to contextualise Jean's behaviour needs to be made.

Thompson (2002: 117) suggests that opinions should be introduced by such phrases as 'I believe …' or 'In my opinion …' Such qualifications are necessary not only to avoid the temptation to translate personal experiences or judgments into 'facts', but also to alert the readers to the nature of what is coming and to allow them to assess the conclusion reached for themselves. Moreover, rather than offering a simple, sweeping conclusion such as

'Mr Hughes is a violent man' – or even 'I believe Mr Hughes is a violent man' – it is better and more accurate to state the 'precise facts' that have led to that conclusion – i.e. 'Mr Hughes has three convictions for grievous bodily harm'. This leaves it open for the reader to draw conclusions, but more importantly, it allows for further questions about the circumstances behind the convictions. The bald statement, 'Mr Hughes is a violent man' does not encourage further examination – it is stated as a given fact.

Selectivity

The above is closely linked to a point touched on earlier about *selectivity*. As Doel and Shardlow (1998) note: 'Every statement is selective, no matter how factual it is' (p. 110). We could add that every *observation* that we make is the product of selection; in an interview, for example, we choose what we focus our attention on based on a range of conscious and unconscious factors including the purpose of the interview, previous knowledge of the offender, previous experience of similar situations and offenders as well as more personal, subjective factors relating to how we are feeling on the particular day or towards the particular individual. Awareness of this can help us to avoid asserting opinion as fact or moving from particular, context-bound instances to generalised statements. It might also contribute to anti-discriminatory practice (see below).

Another point relating to *selectivity* refers to the increasing demand to be brief and to the point. Gone are the days when it was possible – and encouraged – for extensive and detailed records to be kept with lengthy assessments based on observations and interviews. We should not necessarily pine for those days as they could give rise to some rambling and incomprehensible musings. However, the demand for brevity and speed means that we are always looking for ways to reduce the amount of time spent and the number of words we write. This can lead us to the prejudicial shorthand whereby adjectives are used as all-encompassing nouns. As noted earlier, a particularly insidious example of this is where someone is described as 'an inadequate'.

The demand for brevity can also lead us to reliance on jargon and acronyms which might not be common usage among our readers. The implications of this become stronger when we think about offender access to records, but it is also a consideration when thinking about other readers who may not be familiar with 'in-house' abbreviations. The effect of jargon and acronyms can be to create a form of in-group/out-group dynamic whereby those not in the know can feel excluded, perhaps afraid to ask for clarification because of the apparent expectation that they *ought to know*. This can be especially problematic for someone trying to join the group – a new employee or colleague, for instance – but also for offenders who are perhaps already struggling to grasp what is going on. How many readers know instantly what OASys signifies (Offender Assessment System: used by prisons and probation to assess risk of reoffending and risk of harm); or CSA (which depending on context can mean either Child Support Agency or be an abbreviation for child sexual abuse).

Again, it is accepted that a certain amount of abbreviation is unavoidable, but awareness of the effect of using it is necessary if we are to communicate effectively with others.

Another problem with this drive for brevity is that it can often result in a form of laziness. We develop over time some phrases and ways of structuring our reports and records that, when first used, were innovative and accurate. We are pleased with them, and find they are well received. The temptation then is to use them again – and again – in apparently similar circumstances. However, it may be that while they were relevant and accurate when first devised, they lose their direct applicability as well as their meaning after many repetitions. We can therefore fail to think clearly about the person or the situation we are writing about, and think only in terms of our well-worn phrases and descriptions.

This tendency occurs not only with individuals but also within agencies and teams. Doel and Shardlow (1998), writing for students, note:

> Frameworks for recording vary from agency to agency, but students will be used to their own professional language to colour these frameworks. It is important that students question the meaning and the impact of phrases which have become routine and commonplace, and begin to identify new phrases which might be in danger of becoming over-used, no matter how worthy their intentions. (p. 109)

Presentation

Closely linked to the use of language is the way in which we present what we have written, especially its *clarity*. Thompson (2002) notes, rightly, that '… (e)ffective communication depends to a large extent on clarity' (p. 116). There is a temptation, especially in formal reports, to seek to 'make an impression' by using technical language or jargon, long sentences or sophisticated turns of phrase. The basic rule must be that what you write must be clearly understandable. Generally speaking, court reports, for example, are read quickly and anything that is not immediately clear may well be ignored; if this lack of clarity affects the whole report, it may have the effect of irritating or alienating the reader who might then be inclined to dismiss it wholesale. This is not just a problem for the writer but also could have serious consequences for the subject of the report, the offender. The aim should be to keep what you write *simple* – without of course being simplistic. Some things are complex by their very nature, but this is not to say you must complicate them further by obscure language and sentence construction.

An important factor contributing to clarity – and one that in this writer's view is sadly losing importance in much of what is written these days – is *grammar*. Poor grammar, punctuation and spelling can seriously mar a report or record. Anecdotal evidence suggests that a report containing grammatical or spelling errors tends to be taken less seriously than one where the grammar and spelling are correct. Apart from anything else, these factors influence the ease with which something can be read, and anything that makes reading difficult will automatically prejudice the reader against it – perhaps understandably given the amount of reading that is required. Further, and perhaps even more damaging, poor grammar and spelling mistakes can also be taken to imply that the work behind the report was similarly sloppy and careless. As Thompson (2002) says: 'Poor presentation can therefore undermine what is, in other respects, high-quality work' (p. 117). For this reason alone, it is important that attention is paid to the 'basics'.

Secondly, the tendency to use over-formalized or technical language can have an effect on our communication with offenders. It can create confusion and alienation as the offender can be made to feel inadequate or even stupid because they cannot understand what we are saying. Given the increasing access offenders now have to what is written about them, we need to pay attention to the words we use in records and reports as well as in the letters and e-mails we might write. Pamela Trevithick (2000) cites a piece of research that highlights this problem clearly. While it relates to social workers' recording, I think the point is a general one. In 1991 a project group of the Social Services Inspectorate circulated a questionnaire, which contained a list of words and phrases frequently used within social services, asking service users what they meant to them. The following are some examples of the responses:

- *voluntary agencies* – people with no experience, volunteers;
- *encompass* – a way of finding direction;
- *agencies* – second-hand clothes shops;
- *maintain* – mixed up with 'maintenance' – money paid for children in divorce settlements;
- *networks* – no one knew this word;
- *sensitive* – tender and sore;
- *criteria* – most did not know this word;
- *advocacy* – some thought this meant that if they did not agree with the assessment, they would be penalised;
- *function* – wedding party, funeral;
- *common* – cheap and nasty.

These responses may appear humorous to someone 'in the know', but they were genuinely made and we should take the implications seriously. Of course, this is not to say that these words and phrases should not be used, but it is important to remind ourselves that not everyone understands some of the terms we commonly (*sic*) use. We need, as Thompson says, to question the meaning of the words we use, particularly *written* words which, as we noted at the beginning, stand alone and cannot rely on the non-verbal elaboration of the spoken word.

Open and shared records

Nowadays, offenders have access to much of what is written about them in files or reports. Various pieces of legislation have ensured that clients of most public agencies can request to see files and documents relating to them. Initially the Data Protection Act of 1984 gave people the right to see information held about them on computer. At the time, this did not greatly affect the work of most agencies working with offenders as most of the information was still paper-based at that time. Access to all files, however, was granted a few years later.

When first introduced in 1987, the Access to Personal Files Act was met with a degree of cynicism and resistance by practitioners, as those responsible for keeping the files were required to come to terms with the implications for recording practice. For a while, the Probation Service kept separate records, one that the offender could have access to and another, with confidential 'third-party' information, that was restricted. However, the right to see their records was not widely known or publicised to offenders. Nor, indeed, was the existence of the 'third-party files'. Now the National Probation Service website directly informs offenders of their right to see records kept on them 'except where there is good reason for you not to'. The reasons cited include the possibility of harm being caused or the investigation of a crime being impeded. Access would also be denied if it would 'break an agreement with somebody else outside the probation service to keep information confidential, such as a psychiatrist or a victim of your crime'.

Here is not the place to go into detail about the rights, wrongs and wider ramifications of data protection, but it is useful to consider the implications for what is written of the fact that most records are now accessible to the people they are written about. All that has been said above about clarity and avoidance of unnecessary jargon is clearly important here. It also highlights the crucial importance of the distinction between professional judgment and judgmental statements. It is a good general rule that you should not write anything that you cannot substantiate – and preferably the evidence substantiating the statements you make should be included, as it is unlikely that you will always be on hand to explain what you have written. This point applies to other written documents, perhaps most especially to the reports which are sent to court and which, as noted at the very beginning of this chapter, take on a life of their own as they are subject to interpretation and reinterpretation by solicitors, magistrates, judges and court officers.

Of course, there is still the possibility that what you have written will not be understood or accepted by the person to whom it refers. One possible way round this problem is to undertake *shared recording* whereby the offender or subject of the record takes an active part in the process of writing the record. This was experimented with in research undertaken by Katie Prince at the University of East London and reported on in 1996 in her book entitled *Boring Records?* She set out to examine the effect of 'client participation in the process of recording'. Among the many interesting findings she discovered was the fact that both clients *and* social workers felt a strong mixture of 'anger, fear, cynicism, confusion and anxiety' when confronted with the issue of keeping records. While the source of these feelings was different, it was clear that, on both sides of the 'divide', there were strong misgivings about the very concept of keeping a record. Clients felt mistrustful of what was being written about them; social workers felt unsure about what they were writing.

Initially, involving clients in the process of recording was met with scepticism and some trepidation, but for those who embraced the idea, it proved to be liberating and served as a useful tool in developing the working relationship. While I am not advocating that this practice should be generally adopted as it would tend to be especially time-consuming and might in some way hamper the professional judgments we are required to make – indeed one of the service users involved in the experiment commented that shared recording would result in compromise to create something that was 'bland' and ultimately meaningless – in some cases and situations it could be possible to share what is being written in order to give the offender the opportunity to comment on the accuracy of what is being said about him or her, and to check understanding of what has occurred on both sides.

Whatever the advantages and disadvantages of *shared* records, the professional, 'good practice' positives of *open* records should be clear by now. Offenders can challenge misrepresentations and inaccuracies; better working relationships can be established based on a greater degree of openness and trust; the need to distinguish between fact and professional opinion is highlighted; clarity and simplicity are encouraged; personal bias and unsubstantiated and prejudicial speculations are discouraged. Awareness of the need to pay attention to these things should have a positive effect on everything that is written about others.

Anti-discriminatory practice

Much of what has already been said is of direct relevance to anti-discriminatory working. It was noted at the beginning of this chapter that the written word is extremely powerful – the oft-cited injunction not to believe everything one reads is popular precisely because there is a strong tendency *towards* belief in the written word. As such, it can be used to discriminate against and oppress others. Further, once in writing, what began as speculation or suggestion can take on the aura of fact. It is therefore incumbent on the writer to take responsibility for what they write.

Closely linked to the issue of anti-discrimination is the question of confidentiality. Many of the social work clients in Prince's research, touched on earlier, while appreciating the necessity for some form of record, also commented on how they 'felt disadvantaged by record keeping ... [regarding] it as a price to be paid for help with their children' (Prince 1996: xi). Part of the sense of disadvantage came from knowing that others would have access to what was written. The issue of confidentiality is therefore, as Thompson (2002) notes, 'both very important and very complex' (p. 114).

Different agencies will have different policies and approaches to the subject, but it is possible to generalise some key points. First, confidentiality is to the agency not to the individual; any work done with an offender can be communicated and shared within the agency and, in the case of reports, with other agencies in the wider criminal justice system. It follows therefore that any records or assessments or reports *belong to the agency* not the individual offender *or the worker*. It is dishonest and misleading to allow someone to believe that 'secrets' can be kept. Secondly, confidentiality cannot be maintained where a criminal offence or risk of harm is disclosed. Failure to make this clear can have long-term damaging effects on working relationships with offenders.

Audience

This brings us to the question posed at the start relating to the *audience*. Awareness of who will be reading what we have written can have both positive and negative effects, some of which have already been mentioned but it is worth reiterating them here. Some of the documents produced within the criminal justice system have specific, almost targeted, audiences. For instance, court reports are directed at helping the magistrate or judge come to a decision about sentencing. Others will have sight of the report, notably the defendant and his or her solicitor, but the focus in the writer's mind is the sentencer. As such, the style, structure and content of the report will be aimed at a single purpose, which should make it simpler to focus.

Difficulties arise when there is more than one primary audience and more than one purpose. Records, for instance, are kept for a number of reasons including accountability, as a working aide-memoire, to communicate with colleagues about progress with a particular case, as a working tool to be shared with offenders and so on. Accountability to one's organisation and to the offender with whom one is working can sometimes seem to conflict; this is particularly so where the worker has not been clear about his or her professional role and sees their primary task as developing a 'friendly relationship' with the offender in order to encourage engagement. We are straying into the area of professional role here, but it is worth noting that lack of clarity about this can lead to confusion about what to record and how to record it.

Computerised communication and recording

It is not possible to write a chapter on written communication without some reference to the increased use of computer technology to record and communicate within the system. Dutton and Kohli (in Vass 1996) note how the 'growing use of technology ... [makes] ... information more immediately accessible and therefore more immediately part of ... practice' (p. 71).

The fact that information contained in records is now 'more *immediately part of practice*' should make us aware of the growing audience for what we write. Nowadays, other colleagues and related agencies have more direct access to records that in the past were 'ours', and the ease of access will make them more inclined to draw on them. We need to be aware of this, and of the responsibility we have for ensuring that what is held 'on file' is accurate, clear, relevant and usable.

The reference to *immediate accessibility* is important as it highlights the fact that information is now available *on demand* and it is therefore critical that it is accurate and clear. It also reflects the *expectation* that information will be accessible quickly which means that it should be *produced* quickly. Records need to be kept up to date. Further, given the ease with which computer records can be produced, and the growing tendency in the modern world to rely on text messaging and rapidly written e-mails – devoid of non-verbal cues to assist interpretation – it is even more vital that attention is paid in official records and reports to what we are writing and how it is written, where what might be called 'text-speak' is not appropriate.

Most of what has already been said applies to this different medium but it is worth noting the particular issues relating to the use of computers. Nowadays, it is rare that reports will be handwritten and passed to secretarial staff for typing which eliminates the problems caused by illegibility, but it also means that there is often no one to question the sense of what is written before it is submitted. Clearly a greater onus is placed on the writer to ensure accuracy, grammatical correctness and fluidity.

With regard to recording, the introduction of computers has gone alongside the emergence of standardisation and pro forma-based records. Trevithick (2000) refers to how in recent years 'more structured, systematized forms of recording have been encouraged' (p. 169). There are several good reasons for this, including ordering information, facilitating communication and checking validity. However, too much reliance on standardisation can affect the quality or value of what is produced in relation to a particular offender. All the more reason to pay close attention to developing skills in recording accurately and sufficiently comprehensively to make what is written meaningful.

Conclusion

In this chapter I have tried to highlight some of the questions and issues that need to be addressed when thinking about written communication. The skills required in order to produce accurate, relevant, useful and understandable reports and records are often downplayed but they are critically important in the work that is done with offenders. The reliance on written forms of communication is a central thread running through the whole criminal justice system. Close attention needs to be paid to the quality of what is produced to ensure that the quality of the actual work that is done is both enhanced and recognised.

Discussion questions

1 Take a piece of writing (an extract from a report, a case record, for example) that you have done about an offender with whom you are working/have worked. Imagine you are the offender and rewrite what you have written from his or her point of view. What is different about the two pieces of writing? Why do you think that is?
2 Think about initiating a discussion within your team (or student group) about policy – and practice – on open/shared records. How do people stand on the issue? How far does practice differ among colleagues? What are the implications, if any?
3 When observing a colleague interviewing an offender, take notes as if you were undertaking the interview yourself (or reverse the roles if you are doing the interview). Afterwards, compare what you have written – note what you have chosen to record, the words used, the impressions noted. What similarities and differences are there? What implications or conclusions can you draw about your approach to note-taking?

Further reading

Fairclough, N. (1989) *Language and Power*. London: Longman Part of the Longman 'Language in Social Life' series, this book is for those interested in the power of language to shape and construct our social relationships and reality. It focuses on the processes whereby power is conveyed and maintained – and how language is a key element in that process. Readers are challenged to become aware of the power of the language they use and are guided to develop ways of resisting its potentially oppressive practice.

Hopkins, G. (1998) *Plain English for Social Services: A Guide to Better Communication*. Lyme Regis: Russell House. A very useful, practical and accessible guide to the use of plain language. The author draws on clear practice-based examples developed in training courses.

Hopkins, G. (1998) *The Write Stuff: A Guide to Effective Writing in Social Care and Related Services*. Lyme Regis: Russell House. Companion to *Plain English ...*, this book focuses specifically on the written word. It is an excellent practice-based guide, demonstrating how to communicate effectively without the use of jargon, complex sentence construction and overly formal language.

Thompson, N. (2003) *Communication and Language: A Handbook of Theory and Practice.* Basingstoke: Palgrave Macmillan. Drawing on theories relating to communication and language explored in Part 1, Part 2 of this book examines the practical implications of such theoretical understanding. In particular, it addresses ways of making communication effective, writing clearly (including the use of electronic methods), communication systems and the organisational culture that governs communication – all of which highlight the problems created by the failure to communicate. Useful suggestions for further reading are offered.

References

Doel, M. and Shardlow, S. (1998) *The New Social Work Practice: Exercises and Activities for Training and Developing Social Workers.* Aldershot: Ashgate.

Dutton, J. and Kohli, R. (1996) 'The core skills of social work', in A.A. Vass (ed.), *Social Work Competences: Core Knowledge, Values and Skills.* London: Sage.

Prince, K. (1996) *Boring Records? Communication, Speech and Writing in Social Work.* London: Jessica Kingsley.

Thompson, N. (2002) *People Skills*, 2nd edn. Basingstoke: Palgrave Macmillan.

Trevithick, P. (2000) *Social Work Skills: A Practice Handbook.* Buckingham: Open University Press.

Website

http://www.probation/homeoffice.gov.uk

Chapter 7

Evaluating practice

Louise Sturgeon-Adams

The centrality of the notion of evidence-based practice, based upon the principles of the 'what works' debate, is embedded within the Probation Service (see, for example, Harper and Chitty 2005). This debate, and the research upon which it is based, has been concerned, on the whole, with large-scale evaluations of programme efficacy and aggregate results, where outcome measures have focused primarily on rates of reoffending. This research has been of major importance in the adoption of the cognitive-behavioural model as the main approach to working with offenders, especially within the group setting. The advantages and disadvantages of the adoption of such a model have been discussed elsewhere (for example, Smith 2004; Mair 2000) and it is not within the scope of this chapter to undertake such a review. However, it is the author's experience, in teaching methods of research and evaluation to professionals over a number of years, that this has left practitioners with the impression that evaluation is something that is undertaken by others, and does not fall within their remit or area of expertise.

The overall aim of this chapter is to provide a basic understanding of the importance of evaluating practice when undertaking individual work with offenders. Furthermore, it aims to provide guidance for practitioners about how to attempt to evaluate their own practice and incorporate subsequent learning into their ongoing work as an aspect of continuing professional development. Throughout the chapter, reference will be made to those aspects of evaluation which are seen as problematic for practitioners, and which act as barriers in terms of undertaking evaluation. One of the significant problems with evaluation is that it can be seen by practitioners as nothing more than a test of their personal competence against which they will be judged by their employer, under the umbrella of the concept of accountability; it can therefore be experienced as a process that is personally threatening, which can result in a level of resistance. This notion of experiencing evaluation as threatening can be exacerbated by the view that it is seen as the preserve of academic researchers who are deemed to be 'experts' in the area. The focus of this chapter is to contribute to the debate surrounding effective practice by approaching it from a perspective of practitioner empowerment; it is therefore intended as an accessible resource, where evaluation is viewed as emanating from the realm of learning, rather than simply from the realm of demonstrating 'success'. The emphasis of the chapter will be to focus on the notion that evaluation can and should be seen as an intrinsic element of effective practice, in that it can be one of the key learning tools for practitioners that can serve to strengthen ongoing work with offenders and act as a tool to aid reflective practice. Furthermore, it will be seen as a tool by which practitioners are able to reconcile organisational demands with accountability to those with whom they undertake work. It is hoped that this chapter will serve to demystify the process in order that practitioners are able to proceed with a degree of confidence. Throughout this chapter, reference will be made to work with offenders subject to probation supervision, as this is the arena in which the author's experience lies. However, the concept of evaluation as discussed here can be applied to work with offenders in any organisational setting.

In order to contextualise the debate, the chapter will provide an introduction to approaches to evaluation and their place within a wider debate about empirical evidence and the approaches that have been employed historically. This will include a discussion of the philosophical underpinnings of evaluation, but only in as far as it is necessary in order to make sense of the concept of evaluation. This will be followed by an overview of approaches to practitioner evaluation and how these can be incorporated into the work that is already carried out and the information (evidence) that is already gathered within the current framework for offender supervision. There is a view among practitioners that evaluation is extremely time-consuming and resource-intensive and can therefore only add to the pressures of their already difficult role. Parallels will be drawn, therefore, between the ongoing process of assessment as employed currently within the context of undertaking individual work with offenders and the importance of gathering relevant, good-quality evidence on which to base evaluation. It is hoped that such an approach should serve to make the evaluative process more accessible to a practitioner audience. The realist effectiveness cycle and application of single case design will be highlighted as being particularly relevant for individual work with offenders and a guide for undertaking evaluation will be outlined. The discussion will turn, briefly, to the ethical considerations that have an impact upon evaluative work within the probation context, for example the notion of informed consent. It is hoped that the chapter will provide a critical introduction to evaluation of practice and provide practitioners with sufficient skills and knowledge to apply the basic principles to their own work.

Evaluation in context

In order to understand the evaluative process, an acknowledgment needs to be made of the fact that there are philosophical underpinnings to our endeavours which shape the ways in which behaviour is understood. This means that all evaluative (and, indeed, research) activity is underscored by a desire to gather knowledge about the social world. This chapter is not concerned with the detail of philosophical debates surrounding such an endeavour, but it is important to acknowledge that evaluative activity necessarily involves us in questions of philosophy and social theory which influence the ways in which such evaluation is understood and constructed. This notion can be problematic for practitioners as it can seem as though they need to be concerned with debates which simply complicate and mystify the process which, for them, needs to be concerned with a pragmatic approach to working with offenders. However, the importance of evaluation as a concept is intrinsically linked with our ideas about establishing an understanding of the social world and the processes within it (not least of which is an understanding of human behaviour), as these ideas significantly influence the approach taken to evaluation, the methods it employs and, indeed, how useful it is deemed to be. All research is based upon some kind of understanding of the social world, with its own inherent beliefs and assumptions, whether or not these are articulated. The ways in which the resulting knowledge should be viewed and understood depends, therefore, upon the perspective from which it comes. This is no different from the way in which we construct our understanding of the world on an everyday basis. As May (1997) states, 'Values, prejudices and prior beliefs affect the way we all think about an event, person or subject' (1997: 2). These ways of understanding, however, can prove problematic for practitioners, especially in the current climate and with the wholesale adoption of the 'what works' approach, being based, as it is, in a positivist model which assumes that 'the social sciences can and should proceed on the model of the natural sciences, and the closer they can get to this model the better ... they will be' (Smith 2004: 39).

Positivism has been, in various guises, the dominant means of understanding the social world, with its origins in 'pure' science, and herein lies a problem for practitioners. Positivism holds that the social world can be studied in the same way as the natural world and that behaviour can be explained and predicted, within this perspective, by objective investigation, whereby the researcher retains detachment from the subjects and produces a set of 'laws' which are then used to predict the behaviour of the population as a whole. It is concerned with cause and effect in the social world, which proponents believe it is possible to gain knowledge of. Theories are tested against facts. Facts are obtained by the meticulous collection and analysis of data. In summary, positivism holds that 'there is a world out there that we can record and we can analyse independently of people's interpretation of it' (May 1997: 11). This perspective, however, is neither possible nor desirable for practitioners 'because of the inevitable unpredictability of human life, which means that the logic of theory of the natural sciences is necessarily different from that of theories in the natural sciences' (Smith 2004: 40).

Adoption of the positivist model can act as a huge disincentive when encouraging practitioners to undertake evaluation, as it can lead to the belief that they need to adopt a 'scientific' model in which they feel, quite rightly, that they are lacking in skills. Furthermore, most of their work is undertaken with relatively small groups of offenders, or indeed individuals, where such 'scientific' models cannot be applied. It is hoped, therefore, that this chapter can serve to encourage practitioners to explore interpretivist models of evaluation which can be applied to single cases. In contrast to positivists, interpretivists argue that we cannot understand the social world as we might understand the natural world, that we cannot observe it as this will not give us understanding of it. This is because people have consciousness and therefore deal in the currency of ideas and interact with the social world, giving meaning to it. This means that the social world is different from the natural world and is summarised as follows:

> Rules exist in social action through which we understand each other. Rules, of course, are often broken and also subject to different interpretations. For that reason, we cannot predict human behaviour. People are constantly engaged in the process of interpretation and it is this which we would seek to understand. (May 1997: 2)

The perspectives outlined above have traditionally been divided into two opposing camps in which positivism aims to produce facts and laws about the social world and interpretivism aims to understand meanings within the social world. It has been argued by many (see, for example, Smith in Mair 2004) that positivism, and its search for facts, leads directly to the use of quantitative methods (i.e. experimental, statistical, verifiable) and that the interpretive position requires the application of qualitative methods (i.e. interviews, case studies). This division has been mirrored by the view that practitioners should undertake qualitative research and academic researchers should carry out quantitative 'scientific' research. We can see, therefore, that academic arguments regarding the value of social science research as opposed to scientific research are mirrored within the supposed practitioner/ academic divide. For the purposes of evaluation, it is important to recognise that these divisions are unhelpful and that evaluative methods should be chosen for their appropriateness to the task in hand. Furthermore, there needs to be an acknowledgment, at this stage, that quantitative measures are able to tell us 'what' has happened, but they are not able to tell us 'why'. When undertaking evaluative work with offenders, it is clearly as important to know why certain outcomes have resulted from interventions in order to inform future practice.

Having touched upon the theoretical underpinnings of evaluation it is necessary to look at any differences there may be between research and evaluation. This is a distinction that is particularly unhelpful to practitioners as it emphasises a division between academic researchers as 'experts' and practitioners who necessarily focus on the 'real world'. The distinction between the two groups is helpful to neither when, in practice, the boundaries are blurred and the terms can be used interchangeably, and it is certainly true that the same methods can be applied to both activities. Research is seen by some as asking 'relatively broad questions about, for example, the origins and generation of social problems' (Lishman 1999: 2), while evaluation can be seen as a more practice-orientated approach in that the results are aimed at improving future practice. A very useful definition is provided by Lishman who states that 'Evaluation examines our effectiveness and can help us to improve it, can increase our accountability to users and clients, develops our knowledge and identifies gaps in knowledge, and helps us develop new models of practice and service delivery' (Lishman 1999: 101).

Lishman also draws a distinction between evaluation *about* practice and evaluation *of* practice. Both types of evaluation are crucial to a concept of effective practice, in terms of employing the methods that are thought to have effects with clients, and as a part of a commitment to accountability to clients. Effective practitioners need to be able to review research findings and to undertake evaluation with their own clients. It is also argued (Vanstone 1999) that, within the criminal justice system, the gap between research and practice needs to be closed and therefore requires 'the involvement of practitioners who behave not only as effective helpers but as social scientists' (p. 230).

In terms of evaluation that is specific to probation practice, Merrington and Hine (2001) are quite clear that research 'is generally seen as an academic exercise designed to produce knowledge, which may be useful in a variety of contexts, but not necessarily linked to any organisational or strategic objective' (p. 2–5), whereas evaluation, in terms of the what works (effective practice) initiative is defined as 'finding out whether the programme is achieving its objectives' (Chapman and Hough 1998, cited in Merrington and Hine 2001: 2–1). The many definitions that are available are encompassed within the following: 'Evaluation is presented as a form of applied social research, the primary purpose of which is not to discover new knowledge, as is the case with basic research, but to study the effectiveness with which existing knowledge is used to inform and guide practical action' (Clarke 1999: 2).

Contemporary perspectives on evaluation

Clarke (1999) holds that there are two main types of evaluation: formative and summative, where formative evaluation is 'done to provide feedback to people who are trying to improve something' (Scriven 1980, in Clarke 1999: 7) and summative evaluation, aims 'to determine the overall effectiveness or impact of a programme or project' (Clarke 1999: 8). Clarke summarises the two as in Table 7.1.

Although the distinction between the two types of evaluation is useful, it simply identifies two ends of a continuum and therefore fails to acknowledge the possible complexities of evaluation in practice. A useful review of perspectives on evaluation of practice is provided by Kazi (2000). This article provides an extremely useful link between the practice of evaluation and the theoretical underpinnings as outlined previously. It outlines the development of social science debates and identifies the extreme positions of the realists at one end of a continuum and the non-realists at the other end. These positions correspond with those outlined above in which (a) the realists view reality as existing independently, as 'knowable' and which therefore points towards methodologies which concentrate on reliability and validity testing, and (b) the non-realists who hold that there is no such thing as reality existing outside of mental constructs and who therefore concentrate on meanings and perspectives and choose methodologies accordingly.

Table 7.1 Formative and summative evaluation

	Formative	Summative
Target audience	Programme managers/practitioners	Policymakers, funders, the public
Focus of data collection	Clarification of goals, nature of implementation, identifying outcomes	Implementation issues, outcome measures
Role of evaluator	Interactive	Independent
Methodology	Quantitative and qualitative (emphasis on the latter)	Emphasis on quantitative
Frequency of data collection	Continuous monitoring	Limited
Reporting procedures	Informal via discussion groups and meetings	Formal reports
Frequency of reporting	Throughout period of observation/study	On completion of evaluation

Within this theoretical framework, Kazi (2000) provides a classification of the main contemporary perspectives on evaluation of practice. These are summarised briefly below:

- *Empirical practice* – emphasis on evidence-based outcomes, single case evaluation and randomised controlled trials.

- *Pragmatism* – emphasis on mixed methods, places the needs of practice first.

- *Interpretivist approaches including critical theory, feminist evaluation and social constructionism* – politically orientated, empowering, emancipatory, concentrates on meanings within narratives.

- *Post-positivist approaches such as scientific realism* – incorporates all three perspectives outlined above to determine 'why a programme works, for whom and in what circumstances' (Kazi 2000: 764).

Divisions such as those described above can be useful when encouraging practitioners to develop evaluative approaches to their own work. However, such categories can serve as yet another means by which practitioners feel deskilled, which in turn can make them less likely to want to incorporate evaluative methods into their own practice. In order to address this problem, an approach to evaluation has been developed of which 'the main purpose is the development and improvement of the models of practice' (Kazi 2003: 30) and which is based upon the realist effectiveness cycle which, it is said, 'enables a dialectical relationship between this model and the realities of practice, which enables the refinement and development of this model based on the realities of practice' (Kazi 2003: 30).

Planning and undertaking evaluation

Having touched briefly on the philosophical underpinnings of evaluation, it is now possible to discuss how practitioners can utilise this knowledge in terms of its application. It has been said that: 'An evaluation is a study which has a distinctive purpose; it is not a new or different strategy. The purpose of an evaluation is to assess the effects and effectiveness of something, typically some innovation or intervention: policy, practice or service' (Robson 1993: 170).

Throughout the exercise of undertaking an evaluation it is important for practitioners to remember that the main purpose is 'an attempt to assess the worth or value of some innovation or intervention, some service or approach' (Robson 1993: 171) and it is important that they remain focused on the task in order to do the best for each client. Ultimately, this process is not directly about meeting organisational goals – it is about assisting offenders to make changes which reduce the likelihood that they will reoffend. Meeting organisational goals can then be one of the important outcomes of the process. It is also crucial for practitioners to remember that evaluation in the 'real world' can be a messy business – people do not necessarily behave in ways that allow them to fit neatly into an evaluative model. It is important not to be sidetracked by this as it is part of the learning process and is as valuable for practitioners as is a process that goes exactly according to plan.

In undertaking the process of evaluation, it is crucial for practitioners to begin to have confidence in their own abilities and build the necessary skills. They need to be aware that they are not being tested for competence per se, and that they are not being asked to demonstrate the perfect intervention; rather they are being asked to demonstrate the ability to plan and carry out an evaluation and understand the findings. The focus of practitioner evaluation should remain within the realm of learning, rather than within the realm of demonstrating 'success' (which is clearly a concept that is open to interpretation) – it is the process of learning that is crucial, so that practitioners are able to give themselves the opportunity to develop the necessary skills and feel confident to incorporate them into their own practice. It should be acknowledged that practitioners will have a desire to demonstrate 'effective' work (and that they will, as individuals, define this in a variety of ways).

The focus of evaluation

Evaluation has a relatively clear purpose within probation practice. In its narrowest terms this concentrates on 'finding out whether the programme is achieving its objectives' (Chapman and Hough 1998: 9) where programme can be taken to mean 'any initiative designed to bring about specific objectives' and 'can be understood as meaning any planned piece of work with offenders, whether that is delivered within a group setting or one-to-one' (Merrington and Hine 2001: 2–1).

As is stated by Merrington and Hine (2001), an investigation of effectiveness, in terms of probation practice, can easily convert from 'Does the intervention achieve its intended objectives?' to 'Does the intervention reduce reconviction rates?' and therefore lead to a very narrow understanding of effectiveness. It is important 'to have some understanding of the context of the outcome and of why that particular outcome occurred' (Merrington and Hine 2001: 2–2). In other words, the particular context and details of any individual case are important for understanding the outcomes.

Therefore evaluation of practice needs to focus as much on process as it does on outcomes in order for us to understand how and why interventions may have a positive effect. However, as practitioners in this field are only too aware, many offenders experience a myriad of problems and issues which are seen to contribute to their patterns of offending. This becomes crucial to setting goals, which is discussed further on.

What practitioners are being asked to do in undertaking evaluations of their own practice has been entitled the 'scientist-practitioner' model in which each client 'is viewed at one and the same time as a consumer of a service and a focus for research'. Practitioners are required to facilitate change, but without evaluating their activity 'we cannot be sure that it is appropriate nor can we collect data that will lead to any overall improvement in practice' (McGuire 2000: 93). Futhermore, it can be said that 'attempting to identify correctly what are a person's real problems, and then selecting a way of working that will be of assistance' (McGuire 2000: 93) are part of the research and evaluative process.

The process of evaluation

It has already been stated that one of the difficulties with evaluating practice is to enable practitioners to feel comfortable and skilled with the process. One of the most important concepts for practitioners to understand, therefore, is that, while they may not be aware of it, *they already undertake evaluation* as part of their practice. What they do not do is make this explicit. They need to be aware, therefore, that although the terminology of evaluation is unfamiliar, *the process is not.* Bloom (1999) has stated that:

> the fundamental evaluation step is first taken when professionals learn to define clearly the client's problems, target the issues of highest priority, use specific interventions known to be useful in resolving these kind of problems or challenges, and then proceed to monitor how the problems change (and the other strengths do not change) during and after the service programme. Good problem-solving practice intrinsically involves good evaluation procedures (Bloom 1999: 198)

The process of undertaking an evaluation remains the same, whatever the subject of inquiry, and follows several basic steps (Merrington and Hine 2001):

1 Clarify the objectives of the evaluation
2 Design the evaluation
3 Collect the data
4 Analyse the data
5 Report findings. (Merrington and Hine 2001)

These steps are explored in more detail below and should provide the necessary level of understanding for practitioners to develop a model of evaluation which parallels the work they undertake with clients. Following these steps will allow the practitioner to make the evaluative aspects of the work they undertake explicit.

Clarify the objectives of the evaluation

This is the most important stage, as this will provide the framework for the evaluation as a whole and it is based upon contextualising the piece of practice (usually an intervention) that is to be evaluated. This is where the practitioner begins to clarify the evaluation, as well as clarifying and justifying the intervention to be used. The practitioner can utilise a set of questions which will assist in planning the evaluation. These questions should be applied, obviously, within the context of positive change. Merrington and Hine (2001) summarise these questions as follows:

- What is already known about this practice?
- What is the theory that underpins this practice?
- What are the objectives of the practice?
- What do we want to know from this evaluation?

The practitioner therefore needs to plan the following:

1 Specify the aims and objectives of the piece of practice or intervention to be evaluated.
2 Specify the aims and objectives of the evaluation.
3 Contextualise the practice in terms of its theoretical basis and in terms of what is already known about it.

This process, in effect, allows the practitioner to develop a working hypothesis which will focus upon the area of desired change (which could be behavioural or attitudinal) and make explicit how that desired change is to be encouraged in terms of the chosen intervention. It can be seen, therefore, that beginning to think about evaluation at this stage should enable the practitioner to be absolutely specific about the choices they make in terms of the proposed intervention and the theoretical basis which supports such a choice.

Some areas of work can lend themselves more obviously to models of evaluation than others, using a case-study or single-system design. One obvious example would be working with a client in order to reduce consumption of alcohol/drug use over a period of time. A continuous or intermittent measure of consumption/use could be taken over several weeks while working with the client using motivational interviewing within the cycle of change model (see Tallant *et al.*, this volume). This usage could then be analysed for any changes in consumption over the period of the intervention and conclusions drawn about that particular case. However, it is important that practitioners do not fall into the trap of attempting to measure particular areas of behaviour simply because they seem more easily measurable. It is possible to evaluate any intervention that is undertaken with an offender – the key to undertaking a clear and useful evaluation is to be specific about the area of desired change. Merrington and Hine

(2001) provide a list of examples of possible areas of focus for the evaluation:

- re-offending attitude change;
- behaviour change;
- skill/knowledge change;
- problem reduction;
- changes in social circumstances;
- attendance/completion.

The crucial first stage of the evaluation is for the practitioner to recognise that the process of planning for an evaluation corresponds with the process of undertaking an assessment of the offender's situation at the start of contact. Therefore evaluative methods can be applied to any 'case', i.e. work with an offender. In undertaking an assessment, the practitioner will undertake a process of identifying significant issues. This will clearly cover a variety of areas of possible intervention, including many of the dynamic factors affecting offending behaviour. Throughout the process of assessment, the practitioner will arrive at conclusions about the most significant areas of concern, based upon risk and/or need (depending to a certain extent upon organisational context and previous assessments). Judgments will then be made about the nature of desired change and how best to work with this in terms of an intervention. This has been summarised by Merrington and Hine (2001) who state that: 'There are clear parallels between the process of probation casework and outcome evaluation. One emphasises setting aims, selecting measures, intervention, and re-assessment. The other emphasises setting aims, selecting measures, intervention, measurement and analysis' (Merrington and Hine 2001: 6–1). The key to successful evaluation is that practitioners recognise the parallel processes that are taking place and utilise the information accordingly.

If practitioners adopt the realist effectiveness cycle (Kazi 2003) they can tie the evaluation to a process of reflection and learning which 'links the models of intervention with the circumstances in which evaluation takes place' (Kazi 2003: 28). The effectiveness cycle begins with the stage of identifying theory and models of intervention and service provision in which 'theoretical constructs may be based on what is known about the particular areas of work' (Kazi 2003: 28). Stage two consists of hypotheses which identify the desired outcomes of an intervention and the process that may impinge upon this. Stage three identifies the data to be collected and stage four identifies the specifics of the actual intervention. It is said that the 'realist effectiveness cycle enables a dialectical relationship between this model and the realities of practice, which enables the refinement and development of this model based on the realities of practice' (Kazi 2003: 30). Use of this cycle enables a practitioner to 'make judgements about the merit and worth of practice' but 'the main purpose is the development and improvement of the models of practice' (Kazi 2003: 30).

Design the evaluation

As has been stated above, the process of evaluation can and should be integrated with the work that is being undertaken with the offender. Evaluation can therefore be built into any work that is planned at the outset using the basic stages outlined below:

1 *Assessment* – this will generally take place at the first contact with the offender, for example when writing a pre-sentence report for the courts.

2 *Definition of problems* – the range of problems that have contributed to the offending behaviour will be identified. These may range from homelessness to lack of social skills to drug/alcohol problems.

3 *Prioritisation of problems* – it is necessary to identify those problems which have the most significant impact on offending behaviour. These will relate to the possible areas of desired change as outlined above.

4 *Selection of interventions to address problems* – when problems have been prioritised, appropriate interventions will be chosen in an attempt to address the problems of highest priority. These interventions will be based upon models of effective practice, identified by previous research.

5 *Selection of measurement tools* – these can be quantitative, perhaps utilising ratings scales which are applicable to particular issues, and/or qualitative, which will be focused on gaining an understanding of the context in which change is (or is not) taking place, usually from interviews/assessments with the offender. This stage therefore addresses the identification of outcomes and the processes which affect these outcomes.

6 *Pre-intervention measurement* – a level of measurement is required before the intervention takes place; this will usually be quantitative and qualitative.

7 *Intervention* – the intervention itself is carried out.

8 *Post-intervention measurement* – a level of measurement is then required following the intervention.

Throughout the process of planning the intervention, the practitioner will have the following questions in mind:

- What is to be measured?
- What is the most appropriate way of measuring this?
- What kind of data will be collected?
- Are there pre-existing data that can be used to inform the process?

It should be clear from the steps outlined above that the practitioner is not required, in fact, to undertake anything that they do not already undertake

– it is simply that the language is different and certain aspects of the work are made explicit. They might argue that they do not, in the normal course of events, 'measure' the outcomes of their work. However, this is clearly not the case, given that practitioners continually ask themselves whether or not their interventions are 'working'. What they are being asked to do, within the evaluative framework, is to make these judgments explicit and based on recorded data, rather than presented as a rather more nebulous concept.

At the planning stage the practitioner will be required to consider any ethical issues that are raised by undertaking such an evaluation and it may be that they may raise ethical objections to undertaking evaluative work. The key consideration will be about informed consent and whether or not to discuss the evaluative process with the client (who may now be viewed as a research 'subject', given that such a discussion can have consequences for the outcome of the intervention). It is crucial, at this stage, for the practitioner to remember that they are evaluating their own work, i.e. their choice and conduct of an intervention. If their evaluation is truly integrated into the work that they are undertaking, and is viewed as a crucial part of assessing their own effectiveness, the main purpose is that it should support and act as a learning tool for undertaking work with the offender. This is not the same as using the offender as a subject in a research project, where informed consent should always be sought. The fact is that practitioners make ongoing judgments about their effectiveness with offenders in any case. The fact that these judgments are planned at the outset and clearly stated does not change the nature of the work that is undertaken routinely, it simply makes the outcomes measurable and specific.

Collect the data

As has been stated above, in order to make judgments regarding the effectiveness of an intervention, data needs to be collected before an intervention and after the intervention. The most useful way to view this process is by looking at it as an ongoing process of assessment, whereby the practitioner is stating (in detail) the nature of the situation before the intervention takes place, carrying out the intervention, and then making an assessment of the situation again at that point. Alongside such measurements, data need to be collected regarding the context in which the intervention takes place, in terms of both the static and dynamic factors which may influence the outcomes.

Analyse the data

Analysis of the data can be summarised as an assessment of whether or not the objectives have been met and the factors that have influenced any change that has taken place. The practitioner may find it useful at this point to ask a number of questions that will enable this assessment to be made:

1 What do the data reveal about any changes that have taken place?
2 Are the changes for better or worse?
3 Have these changes occurred in conjunction with the intervention?
4 What do the data tell me about the particular area of practice, i.e. was the intervention as useful as I thought it would be?
5 Did it work as I thought it would?
6 What are the possible reasons for this?
7 Are the results as I expected?
8 Is the problem/issue worse or better since the intervention?
9 Have some things improved while others have not changed or become bigger issues?
10 Have there been other things happening for the client that may have affected the outcome of the intervention (e.g. significant life events/new partner/new job/particular crisis) that may have affected the client for better or for worse?
11 How confident am I that change can be attributed to the intervention?
12 Were there any problems/issues with the evaluation strategy itself that may have affected the results?
13 Were there any problems with the intervention or my use of it that could have affected the results?

At this stage of the analysis, the practitioner will need to refer back to the objectives that were set in the planning stage:

– about the intervention; and

– about what the evaluation expected to find.

14 How far have the objectives that were set been met?

In developing answers to these questions, the practitioner will be addressing the four stages of the effectiveness cycle: the theory, the assessment, the intervention and the outcomes. All of this information will feed back into the starting theoretical position and allow an assessment to be made regarding the effectiveness of this intervention in these circumstances for this individual.

Example – a case study

The case study outlined below describes the first three weeks of an intervention with an offender. One of the key points to keep in mind when planning an evaluation is that it can take place over any time period and, to be fully integrated into practice, it must be ongoing, so that an assessment of 'success' can be made at any point in time.

Introduction

M is a female offender who was convicted of shoplifting. She was sentenced to a community order with a supervision condition. M had a long-standing issue with alcohol, stating that she drank in order to cope with panic attacks. However, once she had consumed alcohol she would act irresponsibly and steal (usually alcohol) from shops. She was assessed as being at high risk of reoffending if she did not begin to tackle her levels of alcohol consumption, but was assessed as unsuitable for group-work for her alcohol problem due to her high levels of anxiety, especially in social situations. The following objectives were therefore identified:

Objectives of the intervention
1 To monitor levels of anxiety in order to obtain an accurate picture.
2 To introduce and practice relaxation techniques, aiming at reducing levels of anxiety.
3 To monitor levels of alcohol consumption, aiming to raise awareness of the consequences of increased consumption.

Intervention
A solution-focused approach was adopted within a cognitive-behavioural model. The outcome measures identified as follows.

Outcome measures
1 Anxiety levels – to be scored using a diary.
2 Anxiety levels – thoughts and feelings to be explored by means of commentary in the diary.
3 Relaxation technique – effects to be scored using diary.
4 Relaxation technique – thoughts and feelings to be explored by means of diary.
5 Alcohol consumption – to be scored using diary.
6 Alcohol consumption – thoughts and feelings to be explored by means of a diary.

The intervention

M clearly expressed the view that she felt her main problem was one of anxiety rather than alcohol, which she felt she used to cope with her fears. It was therefore agreed that to focus on the anxiety as the central issue would be appropriate. For the first week, M was asked to keep a detailed diary in which she recorded her level of anxiety at various points during the day (on a scale of one to ten). This provided a picture of changes in her levels of anxiety over one week. She was also asked to record what she was doing, her thoughts and her feelings at these points. In this first meeting, M was told that the main purpose of this diary was to get a detailed picture of her levels of anxiety. The first quantitative measure for the evaluation was therefore the scores from the self-evaluation of anxiety. The qualitative data was from the notes about thoughts and feelings which were recorded with the scores and provided the detailed information required in order to understand the raw scores. The second quantitative measure was units of alcohol consumed and this was, again, supplemented by qualitative data regarding thoughts and feelings about what was taking place at that point in time.

The scores from the diary were charted and discussed with M during supervision and it became clear to her that her anxiety rose considerably when a social interaction was about to take place, and this was at the point when her desire to consume alcohol rose.

It was also clear that her levels of 'background' anxiety were also high. It was then suggested that M begin to think about learning relaxation techniques as a way of trying to reduce her general levels of anxiety. The officer then introduced the idea of a breathing technique, which M was asked to practise daily for the following week. She was asked to record the points at which she practised the technique and to score and provide commentary on each occasion.

Results

Week 1
Levels of anxiety reduced considerably directly after the first supervision session, but then rose again throughout the rest of the week. This pattern was mirrored by alcohol consumption. M did not at all drink for three days, but then consumed 12 units on each of the following three days. Her qualitative commentary reported that, following the first session, she had felt good knowing that somebody was prepared to take her panic attacks seriously, but that it had been hard to maintain this positive view throughout the week.

Week 2
Once again, anxiety levels were reduced following the supervision session. M practised the breathing technique intermittently, but found it a challenge to do this consistently. However, she reported that she felt the breathing technique was helping a little (and her anxiety scores were lower, once again, for the first half of the week). In terms of alcohol, she had managed to abstain until the day before supervision, when she had drunk 10 units. She had been out shopping and had experienced a severe panic attack in a shop. When she came home she consumed the alcohol due to feeling very depressed and increasingly anxious about her situation.

Week 3
The incident the day before supervision clearly showed that M was still experiencing enormous problems with anxiety. Part of the commentary in her diary revealed that she was now experiencing feelings of failure about her attempts to reduce her levels of anxiety, which was serving to increase her levels of anxiety.

At this point, the intervention was reassessed. It had become clear, from the quantitative and qualitative data, that supporting the client was having a positive effect on her anxiety, but that the approach taken with the intervention was not as helpful as had been anticipated. However, what was also clear was that M had been able to make the decision to remain at home when she had drunk alcohol, given that she was now aware that to go out could result in a very poor outcome.

In terms of the objectives, the following had been achieved:

1 A pattern of levels of anxiety and corresponding thoughts and feelings was emerging.
2 Relaxation techniques had proved less useful than was hoped in controlling levels of anxiety.
3 Awareness of the consequences of drinking alcohol had been raised.

The application of evaluative methods had therefore been used to assess the problems at the beginning of contact; to monitor changes in behaviour during the intervention; to assess which parts of the intervention were useful and the reasons for that; and to establish whether or not it was appropriate to change the intervention given the information gathered. It is possible to see, therefore, that evaluative methods such as those described above will, when applied correctly, assist and not hinder the process of change.

Conclusion

It is hoped that this chapter has provided sufficient contextual information for practitioners to develop an understanding of the significance and importance of evaluative work in developing effective approaches to working with offenders. It is hoped also that the discussion provided will assist practitioners with understanding the context and process of evaluation and therefore go some way to enabling them to experiment with such methods, thereby gaining confidence and skills in this area. Throughout the chapter, the author has attempted to focus on those areas which present significant challenges for practitioners and it is hoped that a number of these concerns have been addressed in the attempt to apply what has traditionally been seen as the preserve of academic researchers to practice as it is experienced every day by those who undertake this difficult and challenging work. In addition, it is hoped that this chapter will encourage practitioners to deconstruct the work that they undertake in order that they may begin to view evaluation as one aspect of the work that they carry out routinely, and that what is required of them is a slight shift in perspective, where they make explicit those areas of work that are implicit, rather than the adoption of a different way of working.

Discussion questions

1 How can practitioners make best use of the information that they routinely gather in order to inform the evaluative process?
2 How can practitioners incorporate evaluation into everyday practice?
3 What is the intrinsic value of evaluation as an aspect of professional development?

Further reading

Kazi, M.A.F. (2003) *Realist Evaluation in Practice: Health and Social Work.* London: Sage. This text outlines and explains the development of the realist effectiveness cycle and provides case studies which explore, in some detail, the application of this approach to a variety of settings. The main strength of this text is its willingness to engage with the complexities of the 'real world' and demonstrate the ways in which these complexities are a crucial aspect of the evaluative process.

Rubin, A. and Babbie, E. (2001) *Research Methods for Social Work,* 4th edn. London: Thomson Learning. This text explores the single case design in detail. The strength of this text lies in its approach to data collection and its emphasis on the importance of a combination of quantitative and qualitative data collection and analysis. It emphasises the fact that certain quantitative measurements can be gathered and plotted on a timeline, as part of the evaluation, but it also discusses how, throughout an evaluative period, it is also crucial to maintain a continuous dialogue with the client. The dialogue is, in fact, the more important element of the evaluation, because it is in the dialogue (in other words, the qualitative data) that the reasons for any change (either positive or negative) can be explored.

Smith, D. (2004) 'The uses and abuses of positivism' in G. Mair (ed.), *What Matters in Probation.* Cullompton: Willan. This chapter should be regarded as essential background reading for any practitioner embarking on the process of evaluation. It redresses the balance between the reality of working with clients (and undertaking evaluation) and the implicit assumption within the 'what works' approach that evaluation of working with real people can, and indeed should, be focused around a 'scientific', positivist model. The notion of positivism is unpacked and explored in such a way as to clarify the argument for practitioners.

References

Bloom, M. (1999) 'Single-system evaluation', in I. Shaw, and J. Lishman (eds), *Evaluation and Social Work Practice.* London: Sage.

Chapman, T. and Hough, M. (1998) *A Guide to Effective Practice: Evidence Based Practice,* (ed.) Jane Furness, Her Majesty's Inspectorate of Probation. London: Home Office.

Clarke, A. (1999) *Evaluation Research: An Introduction to Principles, Methods and Practice.* London: Sage.

Harper, G. and Chitty, C. (eds) (2005) *The Impact of Corrections on Re-offending: A Review of 'What Works',* Home Office Research Study No. 291. London: Home Office.

Kazi, M.A.F. (2000) 'Contemporary perspectives in the evaluation of practice', *British Journal of Social Work*, 30: 755–68.

Kazi, M.A.F. (2003) *Realist Evaluation in Practice: Health and Social Work*. London: Sage.

Lishman, J. (1999) 'Introduction', in I. Shaw, and J. Lishman (eds), *Evaluation and Social Work Practice*. London: Sage.

McGuire, J. (2000) *Cognitive-Behavioural Approaches: An Introduction to Theory and Research*. London: Home Office.

Mair, G. (2000) 'Creditable accreditation?', *Probation Journal*, 47 (4): 268–71.

May, T. (1997) *Social Research, Issues, Methods and Process*. Buckingham: Open University Press.

Merrington, S. and Hine, J. (2001) *A Handbook for Evaluating Probation Work with Offenders*. London: Home Office.

Robson, C. (1993) *Real World Research*. Oxford: Blackwell.

Rubin, A. and Babbie, E. (2001) *Research Methods for Social Work*, 4th edn. London: Thomson Learning.

Smith, D. (2004) 'The uses and abuses of positivism', in G. Mair (ed.) *What Matters in Probation*. Cullompton: Willan.

Vanstone, M. (1999) 'Behavioural and cognitive interventions', in I. Shaw and J. Lishman (eds), *Evaluation and Social Work Practice*. London: Sage.

Chapter 8

Models of intervention

Iolo Madoc-Jones

Introduction

This chapter explores models of intervention that can be used to address offending behaviour. There are a several reasons for including a chapter on this topic, the first of these being that a number of authors have linked conceptual clarity on the part of those working with problem behaviour with effective practice (Rees 1978; Corby 1982; Mayer and Timms 1970; Schlichter and Horan 1981; Johnson 1981; Vennard 1997; Harper and Chitty 2004). These writers have typically been critical of those who adopt vague eclectic approaches to their work. By using models practitioners can better order, describe and understand events (Howe 1990). Clear models can also enable service users to better understand interventions. According to Ivanoff *et al.* (1994) a client has the right to understand the model that guides a practitioner's actions. By having models of intervention explained to them, clients might be better engaged in the change process and the impact of an intervention might be extended beyond the interview setting.

Secondly, while some research has suggested that some programmes adopting a cognitive behavioural model of intervention can be successful in reducing offending behaviour (Izzo and Ross 1990; Gendreau and Andrews 1990; McGuire 1995; Rex 2002), other research has suggested that very few criminal justice staff are familiar with the cognitive-behavioural model of change (Oldfield 1998; HMIP 2002, 2003). One reason for this might be that recently a wider range of people have come to play a role in addressing offending behaviour and for many of these untrained staff the cognitive-behavioural model of intervention is new (Kemshall *et al.* 2004). For others the space for critical reflection about the model might be limited. Gorman (2001), for example, suggests that exploring and questioning the cognitive behavioural model of intervention has been considered tantamount to an act of heresy in the Probation Service over the last few years. Whatever the cause, lack of familiarity with the cognitive model of intervention could have a detrimental impact upon the efficacy of practice.

Thirdly, and to the contrary, a number of publications have recently questioned whether the cognitive-behavioural model of intervention is the most effective in reducing offending behaviour (Mair 2000; Merrington and Stanley 2000; Worrall 2000; Gorman 2001; Oldfield 2002). Contemporary research, for example has not unequivocally shown that Home Office-sponsored accredited cognitive-behavioural programmes routinely produce reductions in reoffending (Vennard 1997; Mair 2004; Harper and Chitty 2004). What this creates is the need for other models of intervention to be understood because they might also have a contribution to make to reducing offending behaviour.

Finally, over time most professional groups develop a working model for practice (Thompson 1995; McNeil 2001). Informal or 'working', in the sense of not being academically recorded, such models are built up over time and are often culturally transmitted to new recruits. They are inevitably eclectic, being influenced by the approaches to practice that hold sway within any profession over the years (McNeil 2000, 2001). Exploring competing models of interventions can assist in the processes of clarifying and making sense of working models and help practitioners to avoid the trap of operating to eclectic approaches which are vague or based on common-sense assumptions which might be discriminatory.

For these reasons this chapter explores models of intervention for addressing offending behaviour. The chapter begins by considering how a model for intervention differs from a theory for intervention. Some of the theoretical positions that exist and that can underpin a model of intervention are then outlined. Next, the models of intervention that are used most widely in contemporary criminal justice practice with offenders are explored. The models considered are the cognitive-behavioural, task-centred, solution-based, person-centred and psychoanalytic models. In addition to these models, however, the radical model is also considered. This is because of the illuminating contrast this model offers to the other more conventional approaches to addressing offending behaviour. In exploring models the common format is adopted of first outlining the principles of the model and then considering the theoretical context which has shaped practice using the model. Following on from this some of the key issues related to the use of the model in the criminal justice system are explored, and the application of the model is illustrated using a recurrent case example. To conclude, the issue of how a model for intervention might be applied differently depending on the theoretical lens though which it is viewed is revisited. This sets the context for an understanding of how models might relate to each other and why a model of intervention might come in and out of fashion over time.

At various times the term offender or client will be used to describe the recipient of intervention. The rationale for using one over the other will be the precedent set for describing service recipients from within the particular model.

Models and theories

A model of intervention should be distinguished from a theory for intervention. According to Thompson (1995) a model describes a set of interrelationships but does not necessarily explain them. This is where theory comes in to offer a framework for understanding a model. Howe (1990) argues that in the field of interventions, all models have generally been underpinned and associated with particular theories about the nature of social reality and the nature of society.

According to Gergen (1999) two main positions exist in relation to the nature of social reality. These are the realist and the relativist positions. Realists believe that there are hard facts about social life and that these hard facts exist independently of people's subjective perceptions about them. For them there are rules to social life and all behaviour, including offending behaviour, can be understood in terms of these rules. As a result, people's own subjective ideas about why they behave the way they do are of little concern. Interventions based on this theoretical position focus on the person as an object, and on understanding the rules of social life to objectively diagnose problems and then to apply the correct treatment.

Relativists on the other hand reject the suggestion that there are hard facts about social life. They argue that the social world cannot be studied objectively in the same way as the natural world because humans act on the basis of their subjective ideas about what is going on. People's own ideas about why they behave the way they do is therefore of central concern to relativists. Interventions based on this theoretical position focus on the person as a subject, and on understanding the way people make sense of their worlds and then act.

According to Howe (1990) there are two theoretical positions on the nature of society. The consensus view is that society is most usefully examined as a well-ordered, stable and fair phenomenon. From this perspective whatever social problems exist, do not do so because of the way society is organised. As a result, interventions based on this theoretical position would focus on the individual as the source of problem behaviour. The conflict view on the other hand is that society is a fragmented, conflict-ridden entity. From this perspective social problems exist as a result of the unequal distribution of power in society. Interventions based on this theoretical position would therefore focus on society as a source of problem behaviours.

Different theories about the nature of social reality and the nature of society can give rise to very different interpretations of a model. This is an issue to which this chapter will return. However, for the time being it is sufficient to note as Howe (1990) does that most models of interventions have traditionally been associated with particular theoretical positions on the nature of social reality and society. These traditional associations make it possible to begin the process of examining models of intervention in a meaningful way.

The Case Study
Paul is the youngest of three children, now an adult aged 21. He has four convictions for theft, one for possession of heroin and has recently been convicted of an offence of robbery. One morning he punched a milkman to the ground and stole his money. Paul's mother and father split up when he was 10. His father died when he was 12. Paul did not do well in school and has no qualifications but he is literate. He is currently unemployed and lives with his mother. He says that his problems are that he cannot find a job, drinks too heavily and cannot stop using heroin.

Cognitive-behavioural models

Cognitive-behavioural models draw, with differing emphases, on the insights that derive from the behavioural and the cognitive schools of psychology.

Behaviourism starts from the premise that behaviours are learnt. One of the ways in which this happens was outlined by Skinner and called the process of operant conditioning (1938). He argued that all behaviours are subject either to reinforcement or punishment. Behaviours which are reinforced will tend to be repeated and become established while those which are punished will tend to be extinguished.

A behaviour can be reinforced in a positive or negative way. A behaviour is positively reinforced when it leads to a rewarding consequence and it is negatively reinforced when it avoids an aversive consequence. In this way a violent act, for example, might be positively reinforced if it leads to the acquisition of goods. Conversely a violent act might be negatively reinforced if it removes a perceived threat.

A behaviour can also be punished in a positive or negative way. A behaviour is positively punished when it leads to an aversive consequence and it is negatively punished when the behaviour leads to the withdrawal of something that was pleasurable. In this way an act of violence might be positively punished if it leads to pain or discomfort. Conversely a violent act might be negatively punished if it leads to an offender being ejected from their home on a cold night.

Other ways in which behaviours are learnt have been proposed by Bandura (1977) and Sutherland (1947). Bandura (1977) proposed that new behaviours are acquired, reinforced or extinguished at a distance – by observation of how others behave and what the consequences of that behaviour are to them. Sutherland (1947) proposed that behaviour is not only learnt when a behaviour and its consequences are directly observed but when an individual is exposed to people who hold favourable definitions towards a behaviour.

Approaches to addressing problem behaviours which draw on behavioural models are very straightforward in that the aim is to extinguish an undesirable behaviour (by adding punishments or removing reinforcers) and replace it with a desirable behaviour (by adding reinforcement or eradicating punishments). Behaviour modification of this kind is familiar to most parents with small children; it has also been used in hostels through the development of token economies wherein some behaviours are rewarded with tokens which can then be cashed in at the end of a specified period for a desirable reward. Approaches to practice which derive from both Bandura's and Sutherland's propositions are those which involve exposing offenders to pro-social environments and pro-social modelling.

By the 1960s many writers had begun to criticise behavioural accounts of learning for being incomplete. It was argued that they failed to consider that human beings had minds and that they might do more than simply react to their environments. Models therefore arose which gave cognition a more central role in explaining behaviour. Cognitive psychology focused on exploring the way individuals think (cognitive processes) (Ross and Fabiano 1985) or the thoughts that they have (cognitive products) (Beck 1976; Ellis and Greinger 1977; Yochelson and Samenow 1976). In the mid-1970s a number of authors published works that combined, with different emphasis, the ideas from the behavioural and cognitive traditions of psychology (Mahoney 1974; Goldfried and Merbaum 1973; Meichenbaum 1985). In general practitioners who adopt cognitive-behavioural models tend to consider a behaviour not as an event but as a process which begins with a stimulus that engenders thoughts and feelings, leading to actions which have either reinforcement or punishment consequences.

As Blackburn (1995) states, however, the cognitive-behavioural model lacks a unitary theoretical framework, and reflects an uneasy alliance of disparate philosophies. This is because 'cognition' or cognitive ability can be interpreted as just another biological or environmentally determined capacity (Ellis and Greinger 1977; Ross and Fabiano 1985), or as 'free will' in action. There are interpretations of the cognitive behavioural model therefore which cast the person as either an object or a subject. In the former case the interventions that follow focus on an offender's external environment or their genetically or environmentally determined cognitive skills levels. In the latter case, however, what offenders think, rather than how they think, is much more of a central concern (Yochelson and Samenow 1976).

Either way, the cognitive behavioural model has been criticised for promoting an approach to practice that fails to recognise or address the wider structural, cultural or discursive factors that might give rise to offending behaviour. Milner and O'Byrne (1998) point out that even when a practitioner using the cognitive behavioural model accepts that social conditions have a part to play in offending behaviour, they are normally only concerned with a person's immediate environment. Equally when there is a focus on an offender's thoughts, the concern is with the thoughts of the individual in isolation from the society they inhabit.

Key issues

Cognitive behavioural approaches represent the mainstay of current rehabilitative practices in the statutory UK criminal justice context. Numerous studies suggest that cognitive behavioural approaches have been effective in reducing reoffending (Izzo and Ross 1990; Gendreau and Andrews 1990; McGuire 1995; Rex 2002).

According to Kendall (2004) a particular interpretation of the cognitive-behavioural model has come to dominate practice in the statutory criminal justice context of England and Wales. One principle underpinning what she calls correctional cognitive behaviourism is that crime is considered to arise primarily from the cognitive choices individuals 'freely' make. The way that social environments and social exclusion may limit the behavioural options available to people is downplayed. Correctional cognitive behaviourism on the other hand also focuses on cognitive deficits. In doing so it straddles theoretical positions and moves from a theory of crime as a specific behavioural event to criminality as an inherent tendency. Hence as well as embracing the ideas of free will, the correctional cognitive behavioural model also embraces the deficit notion that those who offend are ill or different from 'normal' people. The offender is then pathologised and words such as 'treatment' are embraced to describe the process of intervention. Integral to this notion of treatment is a 'doctor–patient' relationship and a power imbalance in terms of expertise and knowledge between the receiver and the giver of treatment. Objections to this are that such an approach underestimates the prevalence of criminal behaviour, and that the resulting therapeutic process accords a low priority to what offenders themselves have to say about why they offend and what might help.

Case example: cognitive-behavioural practice

Paul's probation officer identifies that Paul evidences deficits in his cognitive skills. As a result he arranges for Paul to attend the Think First programme which attempts to develop participants' critical reasoning, empathic, lateral thinking and decision-making skills. At the same time the probation officer gives Paul homework to do – he is required to gather evidence, to discuss at the next supervision session, to justify his belief that he 'will never stop using heroin' and that his crime and drug taking 'is not that bad'. The probation officer hopes that Paul will realise that his thoughts and beliefs are not accurate and will exchange these maladaptive thoughts for those that make it less likely he will reoffend.

Task-centred models of intervention

The task-centred model was first articulated by Reid and Epstein (1972) and is a variant of brief therapy which Eckert (1993) defines as 'any psychological intervention intended to produce change as quickly as possible' (in O'Connell 1998: 2).

The task-centred model is largely pragmatic in nature, being focused on the completion of tasks that will directly help the client with their problems. Hence the approach is often termed 'problem-solving'. In the task-centred model insight into how and why a problem arose is not considered to be important. On the basis of the belief that the best way to achieve results is to take action (Milner and O'Byrne 1998), what is considered important is that specific, measurable, achievable, realistic and time-limited (SMART) objectives are set for the future and then acted upon.

Doel and Marsh (1992) suggest that problem identification is a key stage in task-centred practice. They suggest intervention should begin with a list being compiled that includes all the client's problems. Next the worker and client should identify whether there are any common themes and what priorities should be set for action. Following on from this, the worker and the client should focus on one or two problems and set goals in relation to them. Task-centred practice usually leads to the creation of a contract between the worker and the client, setting out in very clear SMART terms tasks to be completed between intervention sessions. The tasks are designed to lead the client incrementally towards the goal that has been identified.

Milner and O'Byrne (1998) identify a number of possible tasks that a client might perform. Among them are exploratory tasks that involve actions which lead to further examination of the problem, e.g. keeping a diary, interventive tasks that involve actions which go some way to solving a problem, e.g. going to the job centre, and reversal tasks which involve doing the opposite of what the person has been doing, e.g. going out socialising instead of staying in. A key element to these tasks is that they are positive, that is they involve doing something rather than not doing something. Within intervention sessions the focus is primarily upon quantifying progress toward goals, reviewing progress, discussing obstacles to change and what the client has learnt from undertaking new behaviours.

According to Milner and O'Byrne (1998) and O'Connell (1998) in traditional task-centred practice clients are considered to be free agents, essentially capable of making meaningful decisions about how they behave. In task-centred practice therefore what clients would have to say about why they offend is critical and as a result they have typically defined their own problems and set their own individual and SMART goals for the future. As a result the objective doctor-patient hierarchy associated with the worker–client relationship in correctional cognitive behaviourism is often replaced with a collaborative egalitarian and reflective relationship.

While on the face of it there would appear to be no reason why the task-centred model could not embrace the notion that problem behaviours stem from problem environments, and hence be used to design plans that seek to challenge inequality and oppression, the model has primarily been used by those who locate problem behaviour at the level of the individual and how they see and respond to the circumstances they face (Milner and O'Byrne 1998).

The emphasis within the task-centred model on problems and the choices people make in relation to them lays it open to charges of having a negative focus and ignoring social context. However, this is countered by supporters of the method who argue that it is the problem rather than the person that is usually the client and a client may chose to focus on whatever problems they want (Doel 1998). As a result it is argued the model presents as being less susceptible than cognitive-behavioural approaches to charges of pathologising offenders or of being oppressive to groups whose offending is related to social exclusion.

Key issues

Research exists which suggests that working with client goals is more likely to lead to positive outcomes than working to goals set by workers (Trotter 1999). In the statutory context, however, Trotter (1999) has noted that workers often deal with involuntary clients whose motivation for change, level of insight into problems and commitment to a therapeutic relationship is low. In such instances getting clients interested in setting their own goals, let alone allowing them to define these goals by themselves, is problematic. Nontheless the task-centred model has been successfully used in the criminal justice context (Trotter 1999; Andrews *et al.* 1979; Rubin 1985; Kurtz and Linnemann 2006). At these times the model has had to be combined with motivational interviewing techniques to encourage engagement in the change process.

Case example: task-centred practice

In an interview Paul and the worker identify the problems he faces. Exploring these problems in more detail they agree that drinking is an obstacle to him dealing with his other problems and should be a key focus for work. Paul believes that membership of an AA group might help as he thinks controlled drinking to be beyond him, but he says he is too shy and paranoid to attend such a group by himself.

Aim – Paul to bring his drinking under more control.

Objective 1 – Paul to begin attending AA on a weekly basis.

Process:
- *Week 2* – Paul will be met at his home by an AA volunteer. They will both go to an AA meeting and then they will return to his home.
- *Week 3* – Paul will be met at his home by the volunteer. They will both go to an AA meeting. Paul will return home on his own.
- *Week 4* – Paul will meet his volunteer at the AA meeting and return home on his own.
- *Week 5* – Paul will meet his volunteer at the AA meeting. They will not sit together. Paul will return home on his own.
- *Week 6* – Paul will go to the AA meeting and return home on his own. When he gets back he will be met by his volunteer.
- *Week 7* – Paul will go to the AA meeting and return on his own.

According to Kurtz and Linnemann (2006) most of the literature indicates that beyond a certain level the length of supervision or contact between a worker and a client has little influence on the future criminality of the client. Similarly Reid and Shyne (1969) identified that interventions that were allowed to run on and on were no more or less effective than those that were cut short. The 'brief' nature of task-centred approaches may therefore have much to offer in terms of efficiencies to agencies involved in the criminal justice system.

Solution-based models of intervention

The solution-based model was popularised by de Shazer (1984, 1985) and Berg (1991, 1992, 1994) from the 1980s onwards and is usually considered to invert the focus of the task-centred model while maintaining many of its features. Instead of focusing on problems the solution based model of intervention focuses on solutions.

The solution-based model eschews problem talk and begins from the premise that whatever problems or difficulties a person faces, there are likely to have been times when they did not exist or were more manageable. The solution-based approach is to concentrate on these exceptional times, and therefore those occasions when the person had clearly found their own solutions to their problems. The aim is then to amplify, sustain and develop the person's own unnoticed strengths and resources (Lee *et al.* 2003). Because of this, it is an approach to practice often described as strengths-based.

Solution-based models embrace a systems perspective. A person is therefore considered to be part of a system that involves interrelated and connected parts. Change in one part of a system is thought to be capable of leading to change in another. Because of this, there is no assumption that any solution has to neatly fit a problem in a linear fashion. Hence if finding employment, for example, had worked in the past as a solution to domestic violence, it would be a legitimate goal for the client to set for themselves.

Identifying and clarifying appropriate goals are key tasks for the worker in solution-based approaches. Various techniques are used to help clients identify goals as a prelude to setting SMART objectives for the future. The first of these involves the use of scaled questions wherein individuals are required to design a scale from zero to ten, with ten representing their particular problem being absent or manageable, and zero their problem at its worst. A client is then invited to identify where they sit on the scale at present and consider what would need to happen for them to move up the scale to the next point and nearer their desired end state. The purpose of scaled questioning is to break the change process down into easier and more manageable steps and to encourage an individual in the change process with small successes.

Miracle questions are also used to identify goals and solutions. A miracle question would resemble the following: 'Suppose tonight, while you were

> **Case example: solution-based practice**
> Using a solution-based model, a drug worker engages with Paul who identifies that in the future he would like to be working full-time as a chef. In a session that eschews problem talk, the worker asks Paul the miracle question: 'Suppose that you wake up tomorrow morning and found you did have a full-time job as a chef what would you notice that was different?' Paul identifies that he would have more qualifications for being a chef on his bedroom wall, he would be heroin free, he would be associating with people who also work and do not offend. Next Paul and the worker set out on a scale, weighted towards solutions, with the above scenario representing ten on the scale and the reverse – having no job or qualifications, using heroin every day, being with friends who offend and don't work – at zero. The worker and Paul identify that in relation to this scale at present Paul is at four – a situation where he uses heroin regularly (but not everyday) has no qualifications and only rarely spends time with other people who work and do not offend. The worker invites Paul to identify what would be necessary to move from four on the scale to five, and Paul identifies getting more friends who don't use heroin as his priority. Accordingly Paul and the worker devise a SMART plan to put this into effect.

asleep, a miracle happened (or a fairy godmother came) and the problem was ended, how would you know? Or what would be different, or what would spouse/parent see? What would you be doing?' The response to such a question can highlight solutions to the problem which can then be considered for implementation.

As in the case of the task-centred model, the client is centre stage and considered to be acting intentionally at all times. As was the case with the task-centred model there is no reason why the solution-based model could not be used to promote social change (Milner and O'Byrne 1998). However, the model has rarely been used for such purposes, and has been primarily used to focus on the individual and the way they are dealing with their social circumstances.

Key issues

Research exists which positively evaluates the effectiveness of strengths-based practices with offenders (Clark 1997; Van Wormer 1999; George *et al.* 1990; Early and Linnea 2000). In the criminal justice context, solution-based models have been used in respect of domestic violence (Sirles *et al.* 1993; O'Hanlon and Hudson 1992) and sexual abuse (Dolan 1991).

While the popularity of solution-based models is growing (O'Connell and Palmer 2003), most published accounts of solution-based approaches refer to practice in the voluntary sector of United States of America. There is a dearth of publications regarding solution-based approaches in the statutory criminal justice context and in the United Kingdom. One reason for this in the UK might be that the solution-based model places the client's views centre stage, deliberately avoids problem talk and does not assume that a solution has to neatly 'fit' the problem. This might be problematic in the statutory UK context where offence focused work has come to be considered an integral and necessary part of rehabilitative practices. Equally because the solution-based approach focuses on strengths, it might, in a punitive cultural climate, be considered too much of a soft option. The common belief that offenders should be punished and that they experience guilt when reflecting on their past behaviour, would undoubtedly give greater legitimacy to approaches that directly focus on past offending behaviour.

Person-centred models of intervention

Person-centred models are based on the positive view that a person who is fully in touch with their inner self would be pro-social in their attitudes and behaviours. The goals of a worker using this model are to establish a warm and genuine relationship with a client so that the client can be freed up to discuss, explore, develop and realise their inner self (Rogers 1992). The person-centred worker attempts to tune into the client and then to reflect back to them what they are saying, so that the client develops and sharpens their understanding and appreciation of themselves (Rogers 1992). The way the worker does this is through the exercise of unconditional positive regard and empathy.

Unconditional positive regard is important because only in the presence of such regard will a person be truly free to explore their perceptions. Empathy is important because it allows the worker to tune into the client so that the worker comes to reflect the client's perceptions, allowing the client and worker to work together to explore perceptions and feelings in more depth (Rogers 1992). Rogers describes empathy as:

> Entering the private perceptual world of the other and becoming thoroughly at home in it, being sensitive, moment by moment, to the changing felt meanings which flow in this other person, to fear, rage or tenderness or confusion or whatever s/he is experiencing. It means temporarily living in the other's life, moving about in it delicately without making judgments. (1980: 142–3)

Rogers is often considered to be one of the founding fathers of the person-centred model. He was of the view that human beings are intentional social beings who strive towards realisation, that is to making sense of themselves and the world around them (1961). Traditional person-centred approaches say very little about the nature of society. Person-centred workers typically locate the source of difficulties within the person rather than society, and seek change at the level of the person.

Key issues

In one respect the goals of person-centred approaches are ambitious. It is a holistic approach which seeks to work with people to deal with existential matters. On the other hand, however, the goals are quite small in that developing an empathic relationship, and an understanding of the other person's perspective are considered to be positive ends in themselves (Thompson 1992). One consequence of this, however, is that person-centred practices defy easy quantification and measurement. This might well represent a considerable problem in light of the significance of performance management and target setting in the statutory and non-statutory criminal justice context.

The approach taken by person-centred workers is usually described as non-directive and exploratory. The worker does not tell the client what to do. As was the case with solution-based approaches, that this means the focus is not directly on offending behaviour would be problematic in the contemporary statutory criminal justice context. It might also lay the model open to the same accusations of being soft on offenders as the solution-based model.

The approach is based on reflective exchanges between the therapist and client. A typical offender's experiences of education and life may mean, however, that they lack familiarity with reflective thinking and non-directive exchanges. Relationship building is at the heart of the approach, but in the statutory criminal justice context the notion that a relationship of trust, understanding and unconditional positive regard can be developed when contact is statutorily mandated and the worker is duty bound to report significant disclosures or breaches is problematic.

Burnett and McNeil (2005) also argue that, while for decades the casework relationship has been at the heart of statutory criminal justice interventions, recently the emphasis on accredited group-work programmes and case management has reduced the opportunities for workers to develop a meaningful relationship with clients. This may however be considered less of an issue in the non-statutory setting and especially in residential facilities where staff might still experience extended and prolonged contact with offenders.

Rogers (1961) argued that empathy and unconditional positive regard were sufficient conditions for effective change to take place. More recently, however, these qualities have been considered the starting point for effective practice. Vennard (1997), for example, found that 45 per cent of the variance in outcomes between intervention programmes could be attributed to whether the workers involved expressed empathy and positive regard for their clients.

Case example: person-centred practice

In a series of sessions focused on Paul, the worker and Paul develop a therapeutic relationship, which leads to Paul opening up about his life and his feelings. In person-centred terms this is an end in itself. In one session he explores his hopes, fears and aspirations about life:

Paul: I don't know how I ended up in this situation really and how it's going to end up.
Worker: You feel concerned about the future.
Paul: Yes, if I don't change things soon I'm afraid I'll end up dead or in jail for a very long time.
Worker: Change is something you think is important but which seems to scare you.
Paul: Yes, that's right, I mean I don't know any other life and I'm sure I'd just mess it all up and end up back where I started.
Worker: Fear of failing is stopping you from starting then?
Paul: Yes that's right I suppose but if I don't do something then that's bad too.
Worker: You seem worried about the path you're on but at the same time scared to try another path. That sounds like quite a difficult position to be in.
Paul: It is, but I guess it's also true that doing something is no worse than doing nothing isn't it?
Worker: That would seem to be true from what you've said.
Paul: I could try.

Psychoanalytical models of intervention

Psychoanalysis was outlined by Freud who proposed that people had personalities which were made up of three separate systems interacting with each other called the id, the ego and the superego. The id is the instinctual part of personality and it resides in the unconscious. The main goal of the id is to satisfy basic impulses as immediately as possible. The superego reflects the internalisation of society's rules. The main goal of the superego is to maintain the very highest standards of behaviour. The ego is the part of the personality that develops as a person experiences reality. It is the rational, reasoning part of personality and the part that tries to find ways of satisfying both the id and the superego. In simple terms, the ego is the umpire in the middle, balancing the demands of the id with the demands of the superego. For example, the ego must strike a balance between the id which might tell someone who sees a small amount of money on the floor to just 'Take it', and the superego which might say 'You should not steal and must return the money to its owner'. Freud argued that if a balance is not struck that satisfies both the id and the superego, then tension and disturbance would be created. To manage this tension an individual might deploy defence mechanisms which might lead them, for example, to deny their feelings or repress them into their unconscious.

Freud proposed that an inner balance would only be struck if adults as children had successfully negotiated five stages of psychosexual development. The details of these stages are not important here but Freud called them the oral, anal, phallic, latent and genital phases. It is with the introduction of psychosexual concepts that many people begin to struggle with Freud's ideas. Essentially he proposed that the sex drive was one of the more powerful of the id drives and that satisfying this drive in an acceptable way was the key to healthy development.

The intervention based on Freud's ideas is called psychodynamic or psychoanalytic therapy, and it is a form of intervention that encourages a client to revisit the stages of development and explore their unconscious inner selves and conflicts. As the client talks, it is expected that problems will reveal themselves from the unconscious either in repetitive patterns of behaviour, in dreams, the words the client uses, the subjects they avoid, the way the client relates to the worker or in slips of the tongue (Freudian slips). As the client explores past events significant relationships from the past are recreated in the dynamic between the therapist and client in the present. This gives rise to the possibility of revisiting traumatic relationships or incidences and successfully negotiating them in the present.

Freud's ideas are immensely complicated and it would not be possible to do justice to them here. While many people find some of his ideas unpalatable, according to Payne (1995) they have been influential in establishing a whole range of psychotherapeutic approaches. At the heart of most psychotherapeutic approaches are the beliefs that that actions arise from thought processes, that people have unconscious motivations, that past disturbances cause present difficulties and that talking about problems can lead to insight and change.

Psychodynamic approaches attribute problem behaviours to problem environments in a client's past. Because of this the client is generally seen as a passive victim of their life and an object of assessment and intervention. Traditionally the model for intervention has had very little to say about society, the focus of intervention is the individual client and the concern is with how they might be helped to accommodate themselves to their world.

Key issues

Psychodynamic models of working were used extensively in the criminal justice system of the USA and UK at the time when the What Works? research was suggesting intervention programmes with offenders, in general, did not work. Psychoanalytical and psychotherapeutic practices therefore fell considerably out of favour over the ensuing two decades.

However, it is worth noting that Martinson, the author who originally published research which was widely quoted as suggesting that 'nothing works', actually withdrew his conclusion some years later commenting on the potential effectiveness of a range of intervention models and mediums including individual and group psychotherapeutic approaches.

> Startling results are found again and again in our study for programmes as diverse as individual psychotherapy, group counselling, intensive supervision and 'individual' aid, advice, counselling. (1979: 254).

Psychodynamic and psychotherapeutic approaches share the ambitions of person-centred models in seeking to address fundamental concerns at the heart of a person's being. Because of this, however, they can still be accused of targeting what has become known as non-criminogenic as opposed to criminogenic needs. Non-criminogenic needs are those needs which, it has been argued, are not in themselves likely to cause future criminality, e.g. anxiety and low self-esteem.

In the contemporary climate, a problematic feature of Freudian-based psychoanalysis is that practice is prolonged. Typically, counselling from a Freudian perspective involves long-term treatment with the therapist and client meeting a number of times a week. Its practicality is therefore particularly questionable, for example, in a custodial setting or in the context of large caseloads of offenders to be managed.

Case study: psychoanalytic practice

In lengthy counselling sessions with his worker, Paul uncovers from his unconscious details about his abusive experiences as a child at the hands of his birth father. Over a period of years the worker helps Paul to contextualise and verbalise his experiences, to transfer some of his feelings on to the therapist and work through them. Paul learns that he is angry at his father and especially for the fact that he died when Paul was only 12. Paul learns that he has internalised a sense of himself as being worthless, and it is this which prompts him to act self destructively. Paul feels that as the youngest child, he was ignored and that despite the abuse his mother doted on his father. Paul comes to understand that much of his violent behaviour is associated with his desire to be more like his father in order to have a better relationship with his mother and be more important to her.

Radical models of intervention

Instead of focusing on individuals as the source of problems, radical models focus on society and seek to reduce offending behaviour by changing the nature and structure of society. The key to radical models is that intervention moves beyond the idea of psychological deficit to having an emphasis on collective working to achieve societal change.

Radical models emphasise empowering practices. Empowerment literally means 'becoming powerful' and while it has become something of a buzzword, and often means different things to different people, to radical practitioners it is an approach to practice 'concerned with how people may gain collective control over their lives, so as to achieve their interests as a group' (Thomas and Pierson 1995: 134). For Gutierrez (1990) empowerment involves actions which increase the self-efficacy of service recipients and develop self and group consciousness concerning the effects of power and oppression. For her, empowering practices help service recipients appreciate how political and social structures contribute to personal or group powerlessness and problems. Because individuals are always less powerful than groups, empowering practice tend to focus on collectives, and seeks to network and link individuals in similar situations together. As collectives they might then engage in direct action to change local and national service provision.

Radical models can be very varied. As long as an approach defines its aims in terms of raising awareness about the impact of power, it would warrant the broad title of being a radical model of intervention. Conceived in this way, there is no reason why any of the models discussed thus far could not be adapted for radical ends. Having said this, depending on whether the model conceived of human behaviour as under voluntary or external control, the goals of radical practice might differ. In the case of models embracing the notion of behaviour as being under voluntary control, increased consciousness of the effects of power and oppression might be considered a goal in itself. In the case of models embracing the notion of behaviour as conforming to objective laws, consciousness-raising might simply represent a beginning step on the road to more direct collective action.

Key issues

Radical models are often considered to be 'political' in nature but to assert this only in the case of radical practices is to ignore the political nature of all interventions. As Worsley (1977) points out, 'The position of being uninvolved is of course itself a position. It tacitly entails letting things go on as they are' (p. 72) (in Thompson 1992: 15).

Psychologically-based approaches can also be described as political. Rose (1996), for example, has commented extensively upon the 'psy-complex', the term given to the ideological function of psychological knowledge, theory or practice in the regulation and maintenance of society. By failing to address how social conditions give rise to offending behaviour it might be argued that the correctional cognitive-behavioural, or traditional task-centred models are political. By not challenging the existing order they might be accused of being supportive of the prevailing liberal political climate, capitalist orthodoxy and the unequal distribution of power in society.

Whether there is scope for radical models to inform contemporary statutory criminal justice practice, however, seems doubtful. Such an approach would have to be maintained against a backdrop of accusations of political correctness and, by focusing on social structure not individual responsibility, of being soft on offenders (Stepney 2005). While as recently as 2000 McNeil found that many criminal justice staff stressed the significance of social factors in the lives and behaviour of offenders, Kendall (2004) and Stepney (2005) suggest the pre-eminence of neo-liberal philosophies emphasising choice and responsibility, and the corresponding promotion of supervisory practices which are offence-focused, reduces the opportunity for statutory staff to engage with radical models of intervention. While radical practice has always been more commonly associated with the non-statutory and voluntary sector, the advent of the mixed economy of welfare and the increasing reliance of the non-statutory sector on statutory funding may impact upon the continued ability of agencies in these sectors to remain sufficiently independent to engage in radical practice.

The concern within radical models to move beyond individual psychology foregrounds the preoccupations within most models of intervention with the personal psychology of offenders as opposed to the structures of society and with the individual in isolation from their social and economic contexts. In some cultures the rights of the individual are not emphasised and the duties that arise from being part of a family or social group are more important. Radical models are not necessarily more sensitive to such issues of diversity. However, by foregrounding issues of power they present as models that offer a more embedded challenge to routine ways of approaching people and the difficulties they face.

Case study: radical practice

Paul's worker recognises Paul's status as a black working-class man who, in a time of high employment, has been pushed to the margins of society. The worker does not suggest to Paul that his problems are all of his own making, or arise from inner drives or cognitive deficits; rather the worker engages with Paul to help him recognise how there are powerful groups in society who protect their own interests and reduce the opportunities available to others. The worker puts Paul in touch with other young black men who are experiencing difficulties and together they develop their understanding of how issues of race, class and gender influence their lives. They work as a group with the worker to bring their concerns to the attention of the local authority and they seek funding for a mentoring project with young black men, and challenge employers who fail to create work opportunities for those with criminal records.

Reviewing models for practice

Several models of intervention have been considered in this chapter. These models were associated with particular perspectives on the nature of social reality and of society. While this approach made it possible to make a start on understanding the models in question, it had the side effect of presenting models in a vary static way. In fact models of intervention are very fluid constructions. This is because, depending on the theoretical lens through which they are viewed, they can be interpreted in many different ways and support many different practices.

For example, it has already been mentioned that the cognitive behavioural model could be interpreted so as to embrace a conceptualisation of the person as either object or subject. As a result the model can support a range of interventions – those focused on an offender's social environment, on their cognitive skills or on their thoughts and beliefs. The correctional cognitive-behavioural model on the other hand straddles this dichotomy and embraces what might be termed a compatibilist position of the person as both object and subject.

In these two interpretations of the cognitive-behavioural model the individual person or their immediate environment is the target for intervention. However, other interpretations of the cognitive behavioural model exist which are underpinned by a critical theoretical framework (Ulman 1990). Such interpretations foreground the way the ideology underpinning the unequal distribution of power in society creates the environmental conditions which might support offending behaviour. An example of such an approach might be a domestic violence perpetrator's programme which, while adopting a cognitive behavioural model, recognises how the ideology of patriarchy impacts upon people's environment and cognitions.

The cognitive behavioural model is not alone in being open to a range of interpretations depending on the theoretical lens through which it is viewed. While the task-centred and solution-based models were associated with the relativist argument that people are intentional in their actions, and the consensus view that society is essentially fair and just, it would be possible to apply both models within a realist framework or a conflict view of society. While Doel and Marsh (1992) argue that forcing clients under threat to engage with the task-centred model would be against the spirit of the model, task-centred 'treatment' plans could be drawn up for offenders to follow. Equally the model could be used with individual offenders, groups of offenders or high crime communities to challenge existing social arrangements.

Similar reworking of the person-centred and psychotherapeutic models have taken place. Attempts have been made to locate both models within a more critical theoretical framework to recognise the role of power and its impact on the person (Proctor *et al.* 2006).

Just as models traditionally associated with the consensus view of society can be reinterpreted to embrace a view of society as in conflict, radical models, with their focus on empowerment, consciousness-raising and collective action, can be reinterpreted to embrace a more modified consensual view of society. It might be argued that such a reinterpretation of the radical model would involve it becoming colonised and domesticated in the service of the status quo. Then describing what is left as a 'radical' model of intervention becomes something of a semantic problem. However, collectives have been formed, especially in the non-statutory contexts, to empower service users to make claims for services. These collectives seek small-scale changes and reform of the system rather than revolutionary changes in society. As Morley states, empowerment or radical practice can often be pursued without challenging or even 'without necessarily acknowledging that a major cause of powerlessness is social and economic inequality' (1995: 35).

If a model of intervention allows of a different interpretation depending on the theoretical lens through which it is viewed, it follows that so long as the underlying theoretical assumptions remain the same, different models of intervention might be meaningfully combined by practitioners. While eclecticism in practice has been subject to some criticism (Rees 1978; Corby 1982; Mayer and Timms 1970; Schlichter and Horan 1981; Johnson 1981; Vennard 1997), the primary target of this criticism has been vague eclecticism as opposed to eclecticism per se.

Fashions and trends in models of intervention

Having discussed models of intervention and how they might be interpreted and combined effectively, what remains to be considered is how a particular model of intervention might come to be favoured over others at any particular point in time.

The intellectual traditions of liberalism, conservatism, Marxism and social reformism have exerted an important social and political influence over the centuries. Much like models of interventions, these traditions contain influential assumptions about human nature and the nature of society. These traditions should not be confused with political parties of similar names. Political regimes and parties often distort these traditions or invoke a mixture of different ones at different times in their history. However, the fact they do this highlights that at different times different assumptions about human nature and society are to the fore. Models of interventions can either accord with the social and political mood of the time or not. In this way models of intervention can fall in or out of favour or become reinterpreted over time (McWilliams 1987).

The post-Second World War period, for example, was characterised by optimism over the ability of the state to create a better society for all. As a result of this mood of optimism the welfare state and the NHS were established in the UK. An integral part of this optimism was the belief in the ability of science to offer real answers to some of society's problems. During this time models of interventions which seemed to offer a science for practice came to the fore. Behavioural and psychotherapeutic approaches primarily drew on realism and the notion that behaviour could be understood and changed in a planned, systematic and scientific way.

The 1960s and 1970s on the other hand were decades when there was a general challenge to traditional orthodoxies within society. Civil rights movements sprang up across the Western world in an effort to address and challenge racial and gender discrimination. The scientific certainty of the modern period gave way over these two decades to uncertainty and eventually within the field of interventions to increased interest in radical models of interventions. These interventions appeared to offer a real challenge to the existing, and seemingly oppressive, traditional structures of society.

Since the turn to the right and to conservative/liberal thinking from the late 1980s onwards, models of intervention that focus on choice and freedom have come to greater prominence. The current popularity of the compatibilist correctional cognitive-behavioural model may owe as much to its resonance with the 'tough on crime, tough on the causes of crime' mantra of New Labour and to its managerial concerns than to research which suggests that it is a model of intervention which is effective in reducing offending behaviour.

Conclusion

In the non-statutory context, staff are more likely to be in contact with offenders in informal settings and to be less subject to the managerial pressures that require them to adopt particular models of intervention. As a result various models of intervention are likely to guide work with offending behaviour in these contexts. Such therapeutic freedom of expression is not without its problems, however. As stated, numerous authors have identified a tendency for deregulated practice in social care contexts to become unhelpfully vague and eclectic (Rees 1978; Corby 1982; Mayer and Timms 1970; Schlichter and Horan 1981).

In statutory criminal justice practice, however, a particular cognitive behavioural model of intervention underpinned by a specific theoretical framework has been championed. Offenders are primarily considered to offend because they have cognitive skills deficits which lead to faulty thinking. The proper intervention from this perspective looks to develop an offender's cognitive capacities and critical thinking skills in particular. While such championing of a model and theory may address many of the problems that arise from rampant eclecticism, this one-size-fits all approach to statutory intervention has been subject to some considerable criticism (Mair 2004; Smith 2004; Kendall 2004). This criticism arises as a result of research which suggests that cognitive behavioural interventions have not been as effective as first thought (Mair 2000; Merrington and Stanley 2000; Worrall 2000; Gorman 2001; Oldfield 2002). Equally however it arises from concern over whether there is still scope for reflective and critical practice to take place and for adapting and developing interventions to meet the diverse experiences and needs of individuals who come into contact with the criminal justice system.

This chapter has sought to make a contribution to developing a more critical appreciation of models of intervention. Six models were considered along with the theoretical perspectives that could inform how the models might be interpreted and combined. As omnipresent as cognitive behavioural approaches are in the statutory context, it has been highlighted that models of intervention are likely to continue to come in and out of fashion or be reinterpreted as the social and political climate changes.

Discussion questions

1 To what extent does having a model for intervention (with all its traditional theoretical assumptions) make obsolete or subvert the process of assessment?
2 What scope is there for criminal justice practitioners to embrace the radical model of intervention?
3 What theoretical assumptions about the nature of social reality and the nature of society underpin and guide your own approach to practice?

Further reading

Cognitive behaviourism

Hollin, C. (1992) *Cognitive-Behavioural Interventions with Young Offenders*. Boston, MA: Allyn and Bacon.
McGuire, J. (2000) *Cognitive-Behavioural Approaches – An introduction to theory and research*. Edited by Jane Furniss, HMI Probation.
Available free to download at http://inspectorates.homeoffice.gov.uk/hmiprobation/docs/cogbeh1.pdf (last accessed 17 August 2006)
Sheldon, B. (2005) *Cognitive-Behavioural Therapy*. London: Routledge.
Sheldon's book comprehensively explores the theoretical underpinnings and practical applications of cognitive-behavioural approaches in an accessible way, while McGuire explores how the model may be applied to examine offending behaviour in criminal justice contexts.

Task centred practice

Doel, M. (1998) 'Task-centred work', in R. Adams, L. Dominelli and M. Payne (eds), *Social Work: Themes, Issues and Critical Debates*. Oxford: Open University Press.

Reid, W. and Epstein, L. (1972) *Task-centred casework*. New York: Columbia University Press.

Reid and Epstein's early book on task-centred practice describes the model in readable detail and includes a useful chapter on shaping client tasks while Doel applies it to social work context in the UK.

Solution-focused practice

Kurtz, D. and Linnemann, T. (2006) Improving Probation Through Client Strengths: Evaluating Strengths based Treatments for At Risk Youth. *Western Criminology Review*, 7 (1): 9–19.

O'Connell, B. (1998) *Solution Focussed Therapy*. London: Sage.

O'Connell, B. and Palmer, S. (eds) (2003) *Handbook of Solution-Focused Therapy*. London: Sage.

O'Connell and Palmer's book comprises 15 chapters and describes the application of SFT by specialists in a variety of different UK contexts, while O'Connell's early work sets out the theoretical premise of the approach and Kurtz and Linnemann explore its efficacy with young people.

Person-centred practice

Mearns, D. and Thorne, B. (1988) *Person-centred Counselling in Action*. London: Sage.

Mearns, D. and Thorne, B. (2000) *Person-Centred Therapy Today*. London: Sage.

Tudor, K. and Worrall, M. (2006) *Person Centred Therapy: A Clinical Philosophy*. London: Routledge.

Mearns and Thorne follow and describe the person-centred approach one step at a time in a series of case studies, while Tudor and Worral examine more of the roots of person-centred thinking in existential and phenomenological philosophy.

Psychotherapeutic/psychoanalytic practice

Bateman, A. and Holmes, J. (1995) *Introduction to Psychoanalysis: Contemporary Theory and Practice*. London: Routledge.

Jacobs, M. (2004) *Psychodynamic Counselling in Action*. London: Sage.

Jacob's book is an accessible and readable account of what remains a theoretically complex approach to practice, while Bateman and Holmes' book is for the more ambitious reader keen to develop their understanding.

Radical practice

Adams, R., Dominelli, L. and Payne, M (2002) *Critical Practice in Social Work*. Basingstoke: Palgrave. A range of useful and authoritative articles on this area can be accessed at: http://www.radical.org.uk/barefoot/.

Lagan, M. (1998) 'Radical social work', in R. Adams, L. Dominelli and M. Payne (eds), *Social work: Themes, Issues and Critical Debates*. Basingstoke: Palgrave.

Adams *et al.* and Lagan usefully explore the history and contemporary application of the radical and critical traditions, while articles on the Barefoot social worker site by experienced practitioners provide food for thought by bringing a radical perspective to bear on contemporary social problems.

Compilations

Adams, R., Dominelli, L. and Payne, M. (eds) (1998) *Social Work: Themes, Issues and Critical Debates*. Basingstoke: Palgrave.

Howe, D. (1990) *An Introduction to Social Work Theory*. Aldershot: Gower.

Milner, J. and O'Byrne, P. (1998) *Assessment in Social Work*. Basingstoke: Palgrave.

Payne, M. (1995) *Modern Social Work Theory: A Critical Introduction*. Basingstoke: Macmillan.

Milner and O'Byrne explore how models of intervention might inform and be used in the assessment process while Adams *et al.* explore models in broader contexts. However, Howe's book continues to provide the most clear theoretical framework for relating one model of practice to another.

References

Andrews, D.A., Keissling, J.J., Russell, R.J. and Grant, B.A. (1979) *Volunteers and the One-to-One Supervision of Adult Offenders*. Toronto: Ontario Ministry of Correctional Services.

Bandura, A. (1977) *Social Learning Theory*. New York: General Learning Press.

Beck, A.T. (1976) *Cognitive Therapy and the Emotional Disorders*. New York: International Universities Press.

Berg, I.K. (1991) *Family Preservation – A Brief Therapy Workbook*. London: Brief Therapy Press.

Berg, I.K. (1992) *Working with the Problem Drinker: A Solution-Focused Approach*. New York: W.W. Norton.

Berg, I.K. (1994) *Family-Based Services: A Solution-Focused Approach*. New York: W.W. Norton.

Blackburn, R. (1995) *The Psychology of Criminal Conduct*. London: Routledge.

Burnett, R. and McNeil, F. (2005) 'The place of the officer–offender relationship in assisting offenders to desist from crime', *Probation Journal*, 52 (3): 221–42.

Clark, M. (1997) 'Strengths-based practice: a new paradigm', *Corrections Today*, 59: 200–2.

Corby, B. (1982) 'Theory and practice in long-term social work', *British Journal of Social Work*, 12 (6): 619–38.

de Shazer, S. (1984) 'The death of resistance', *Family Process*, 23: 11–17.

de Shazer, S. (1985) *Key to Solutions in Brief Therapy*. New York: W.W. Norton.

Doel, M. (1998) 'Task-centred work', in R. Adams, L. Dominelli and M. Payne (eds), *Social Work: Themes, Issues and Critical Debates*. Oxford: Open University Press.

Doel, M. and Marsh, P. (1992) *Task-Centred Social Work*. Aldershot: Ashgate.

Dolan, Y.M. (1991) *Resolving Sexual Abuse: Solution-Focused Therapy and Ericksonian Hypnosis for Adult Survivors*. New York: Norton.

Dryden, W. (1995) *Brief Rational Emotive Behaviour Therapy*. Chichester: John Wiley & Sons.

Early, T.J. and Linnea, F.G. (2000) 'Valuing families: social work practice with families from a strengths perspective', *Social Work*, 45: 118–33.

Eckert, P. (1993) 'Acceleration of change: catalysts in brief therapy', *Clinical Psychological Review*, 13: 241–53.

Ellis, A. and Greinger, R. (1977) *Handbook of Rational Emotive Therapy*. New York: Springer Verlag.

Gendreau, P. (1996) 'Offender rehabilitation, what we know and what needs to be done', *Criminal Justice and Behaviour*, 23: 144–61.

Gendreau, P. and Andrews, D.A. (1990) 'Tertiary prevention: what the meta-analysis of the offender treatment literature tells us about what works', *Canadian Journal of Criminology*, 32: 173–4.

George, E., Iveson, C. and Ratner, H. (1990) *Problem to Solution: Brief Therapy with Individuals and Families*. London: Brief Therapy Press.

Gergen, K.J. (1999) *An Invitation to Social Construction*. London: Sage.

Goldfried, M.R. and Merbaum, M. (1973) *Behaviour Change Through Self-Control*. New York: Holt, Rinehart & Winston.

Gorman, K. (2001) 'Cognitive behaviourism and the Holy Grail: the quest for a universal means of managing offender risk', *Probation Journal*, 48 (1): 3–9.

Gutierrez, L. (1990) 'Working with women of colour: an empowerment perspective', *Social Work*, 35 (2): 149–53.

Harper, G. and Chitty, C. (2004) *The Impact of Corrections on Re-offending: A Review of 'What Works'*, Home Office Research Study 291. Available free to download from: http://www.homeoffice.gov.uk/rds.

HMIP (2002) *Audit of Accredited Programmes: North Wales Area of the National Probation Service*. London: HMIP.

HMIP (2003) *Audit of Accredited Programmes: Essex Area of the National Probation Service*. London: HMIP.

Howe, D. (1990) *An Introduction to Social Work Theory*. Aldershot: Gower.

Ivanoff, A., Blythe, B. and Tripodi, T. (1994) *Involuntary Clients in Social Work Practice*. New York: Aldine de Gruyter.

Izzo, R. and Ross, R.R. (1990) 'Meta-analysis of rehabilitation programmes for juvenile delinquents: a brief report', *Criminal Justice and Behaviour*, 17: 34–8.

Johnson, V.S. (1981) 'Staff drift: a problem in treatment integrity', *Criminal Justice and Behaviour*, 8: 223–32.

Kemshall, H., Holt, P., Bailey, R. and Boswell, G. (2004) 'Beyond programmes: organisational and cultural issues in the implementation of what works', in G. Mair (ed.), *What Matters in Probation*. Cullompton: Willan.

Kendall, K. (2004) 'Dangerous thinking: a critical history of correctional cognitive behaviourism', in G. Mair (ed.), *What Matters in Probation*. Cullompton: Willan.

Kriesberg, S. (1992) *Transforming Power: Domination, Empowerment and Education*. New York: State University of New York.

Kurtz, D. and Linnemann, T. (2006) 'Improving probation through client strengths: evaluating strengths based treatments for at risk youth', *Western Criminology Review*, 7 (1): 9–19.

Lee, M.Y., Sebold, J. and Uken, A. (2003) *Solution-Focused Treatment of Domestic Violence Offenders: Accountability for Change*. Oxford: Oxford University Press.

McGuire, J. (1995) *What Works: Reducing Reoffending*. Chichester: John Wiley & Sons.

McNeill, F. (2000) 'Making criminology work: theory and practice in local context', *Probation Journal*, 47 (2): 108–18.

McNeill, F. (2001) 'Developing effectiveness: frontline perspectives', *Social Work Education*, 20 (6): 670–87.

McWilliams, W. (1987) 'Probation, pragmatism and policy', *Howard Journal of Criminal Justice*, 26 (2): 97–121.

Mahoney, M.J. (1974) *Cognition and Behaviour Modification*. Cambridge, MA: Ballinger.

Mair, G. (2000) 'Credible accreditation?', *Probation Journal*, 47: 268–71.

Mair, G. (2004) 'Introduction: what works and what matters', in G. Mair (ed.), *What Matters in Probation*. Cullompton: Willan.

Martinson, R. (1979) 'New findings, new views: a note of caution regarding sentencing reform', *Hofstra Law Review*, 7: 243–58.

Mayer, J. and Timms, N. (1970) *The Client Speaks*. London. Routledge & Kegan Paul.

Meichenbaum, D. (1985) *Stress Inoculation Training*. New York: Pergamon Press.

Merrington, S. and Stanley, S. (2000) 'Doubts about the what works initiative', *Probation Journal*, 47: 272–5.

Milner, J. and O'Byrne, P. (1998) *Assessment in Social Work*. Basingstoke: Palgrave.

Morley, L. (1995) 'Theorising empowerment in the UK public services', *Empowerment in Organisations*, 3 (3): 35–41.

O'Connell, B. (1998) *Solution-Focused Therapy*. London: Sage.

O'Connell, B. and Palmer, S. (eds) (2003) *Handbook of Solution-Focused Therapy*. London: Sage.

O'Hanlon, B. and Hudson, P. (1992) *Stop Blaming, Start Loving! A Solution-Oriented Approach to Improving Your Relationship*. New York: Norton.

Oldfield, M. (1998) 'Case management: developing theory and practice', *Vista*, 4 (1): 21–36.

Oldfield, M. (2002) 'What works and the conjunctural politics of probation: effectiveness, managerialism and neo-liberalism', *British Journal of Community Justice*, 1 (1): 79–88.

Payne, M. (1995) *Modern Social Work Theory: A Critical Introduction*. Basingstoke. Macmillan.

Proctor, G., Cooper, M., Sanders, P and Malcolm, B. (2006) *Politicizing the Person-Centred Approach: An Agenda for Social Change*. Ross-on-Wye: PCCS Books.

Rees, S. (1978) *Social Work Face to Face*. London: Edward Arnold.

Reid, W. and Epstein, L. (1972) *Task-Centred Casework*. New York: Columbia University Press.

Reid, W.J. and Shyne, A. (1969) *Brief and Extended Casework*. New York: Columbia University Press.

Rex, S. (2002) 'Beyond cognitive behaviourism? Reflections on the effectiveness literature', in A. Bottoms, L. Gelsthorpe and S. Rex (eds), *Community Penalties: Change and Challenges*. Cullompton: Willan.

Rogers, C.R. (1961) *On Becoming a Person*. Boston: Houghton Mifflin.

Rogers, C.R. (1980) *A Way of Being*. Boston: Houghton Mifflin

Rogers, C.R. (1992) 'The necessary and sufficient conditions of therapeutic personality change', *Journal of Consulting and Clinical Psychology*, 60: 827–32.

Rose, D. (1996) *Inventing Ourselves: Psychology, Power and Personhood*. Cambridge: Cambridge University Press.

Ross, R. and Fabiano, E. (1985) *Time to Think: A Cognitive Model of Delinquency Prevention and Offender Rehabilitation*. Ottawa: Air Training and Publications.

Rubin, A. (1985) 'Practice effectiveness: more grounds for optimism', *Social Work*, 30: 469–76.

Schlichter, K.J. and Horan, J.J. (1981) 'Effects of stress inoculation on the anger and aggression management skills of institutionalised juvenile delinquents', *Cognitive Therapy and Research*, 5: 359–67.

Sirles, E., Lipchik, E. and Kowalski, K. (1993) 'A consumer's perspective on domestic violence interventions', *Journal of Family Violence*, 8 (3): 267–76.

Skinner, B.F. (1938) *The Behavior of Organisms*. New York: Appleton-Century-Crofts.

Stepney, P. (2005) 'Mission impossible? Critical practice in social work', *British Journal of Social Work*, advanced access, published 18 November. Available at: http://bjsw.oxfordjournals.org/cgi/reprint/bch388v1.pdf.

Sutherland, E. (1947) *Principles of Criminology*. Philadelphia: J.B. Lippincott.

Thomas, M. and Pierson, J. (1995) *Dictionary of Social Work*. London: Collins.

Thompson, N. (1992) *Existentialism and Social Work*. Aldershot: Avebury.

Thompson, N. (1995) *Theory and Practice in Health and Social Welfare*. Buckingham: Open University Press.

Trotter, C. (1999) *Working with Involuntary Clients*. London: Sage.

Ulman, J. (1990) 'Toward a synthesis of Marx and Skinner', *Behavior and Social Issues*, 1 (1): 57–70.

Van Wormer, K. (1999) 'The strengths perspective: a paradigm for correctional counselling', *Federal Probation*, 63 (1): 51–8.

Vennard, J. (1997) 'Evaluating the effectiveness of community programmes with service users', *Vista*, May: 15–26.

Worrall, A. (2000) 'What works at one arm point? A study of the transportation of a penal concept', *Probation Journal*, 47 (4): 243–9.

Worsley, P. (ed.) (1977) *Introduction to Sociology*. Harmondsworth: Penguin.

Yochelson, S. and Samenow, S.E. (1976) *The Criminal Personality*, Vol. 1. Northvale, NJ: Aronson.

Chapter 9

Desistance-focused approaches

Trish McCulloch and Fergus McNeill

Introduction

The pursuit of effectiveness in the treatment and management of offenders has been one of the few observed continuities throughout the history of penal policy and practice. Over the last two decades this pursuit has centred on the question of 'what works in reducing reoffending?' – a perhaps inevitable consequence of spiralling prison numbers and costs, politically unacceptable reoffending rates, emerging transatlantic research evidence and, perhaps most notably, an increasingly politicised public policy arena. More recently, it might be argued that the agenda has moved on somewhat, currently turning on the question of 'what works in offender management?' While it needs to be acknowledged that the rise of 'offender management' as a bold new headline for probation services has resulted, yet again, in a significant shift in emphasis – i.e. towards the creation of 'new and improved' structural arrangements and increasingly standardised technologies of control – there is much evidence to suggest that the increasingly elusive goal of reducing reoffending remains central to current concerns (Blunkett 2004; Carter 2004; Home Office 2004, 2005).

Conversely, despite well documented developments in our knowledge and understanding of 'what works?' in reducing reoffending, not to mention well-resourced practice initiatives in this area, research, policy and practice continue to highlight that our knowledge, and success, in this area remains embryonic. Moreover, an increasing number of recent studies point to the limitations of the 'what works?' research evidence, resulting in renewed academic, political and professional attention to the broader factors and processes which may be associated with decisions to persist in and desist from crime.

Criminal careers research has long been considered relevant to understanding the particular factors associated with the onset, escalation and persistence of criminal behaviour. However, it is only recently that the related research around desistance – that is ceasing and refraining from offending – has come to be recognised as having something to contribute to contemporary debates about offender management and crime reduction (Farrall 2002; McNeill 2006; Maruna 2001; Rex 1999). By focusing on *when*, *how* and *why* change occurs and is sustained, the desistance literature pursues a broader agenda than that provided by the 'what works?' research. Consequently, it supports an approach to crime reduction which recognises the complex personal, interpersonal and social contexts of criminal careers and their termination. The relevance of this broader agenda to developing our understanding of 'what works?' is now well endorsed at an academic level and, as Farrall and Bowling (1999) observe, is considered 'crucial for the development of effective crime prevention and criminal justice practices' (p. 253). Nonetheless, the muted impact that desistance research has had on policy and practice to date is both surprising and problematic, not least because knowledge about the process of desistance is clearly critical to our ability to influence and support that process.

This chapter will identify and discuss the theoretical perspectives associated with desistance theory and will examine recent research findings in this area. Consideration will be given to the implications of this emerging research discourse for working with people who offend, with particular attention given to the role of social context in supporting desistance. Having identified a theoretical rationale for 'why' workers should attend to the social context of offenders' lives and offending choices in supporting desistance, attention will be given in closing to 'how' probation can more effectively support change in this area.

Traditional theories of desistance

Most reviews of the literature on desistance note that research in this area tends to fall within three broad theoretical perspectives, that is: maturational reform theory, social bonds theory and narrative approaches (Maruna 2000; Farrall 2002; McNeill 2003).

Maturational reform theory is the oldest and most influential explanation of desistance and is based on the now well evidenced correlations between age and criminal behaviour (Glueck and Glueck 1940; Farrington 1997). While this theory provides some general indication of 'when' desistance is likely to occur, as critics observe, research in this area has generally failed to unpack the meaning of age and as such does little to increase our understanding of 'how' and 'why' this change takes place (Maruna 2000). More recent studies suggest that chronological age has little or no inherent meaning in and of itself. Rather, the term 'age' is seen to index a range of different biological, social and experiential variables. This is supported by a recent Scottish study which explored desistance and persistence among three groups of young people aged 14–15 (the peak age for recruitment into offending for boys), 18–19 (the peak age of offending) and 22–25 (the age by which many would be expected to grow out of crime) (McIvor *et al.* 2000). While the researchers identified some significant age-related differences, the study also points to significant gender, attitudinal and narrative differences *within* the age groups. For example, the young women in the sample tended to offer moral as opposed to utilitarian rationales for stopping offending and were more likely to emphasise the importance of relational aspects of the process. Additionally, some young women linked their decisions to desist to the assumption of parental responsibilities whereas, in general, young men focused more on personal choice and agency. These findings alert us to the fact that while age remains a significant factor in explaining persistence and desistance patterns, those wider variables (i.e. gender, life transitions, etc.) which interact and are associated with particular ages and stages would appear to be equally significant.

Social bonds theory is the second influential theory within the desistance literature and highlights the correlation between desistance and a number of social and personal variables. Essentially, social bonds theory suggests that varying ties to family, relationships, employment or educational processes in early adulthood explain changes in criminality. Certainly a number of research studies now exist which indicate that desistance is associated with positive change in one or more of the above areas, a finding which, among other things, has legitimised a renewed attention to the social context of persistence and desistance decisions. However, as Maruna (1999) observes, these correlations are by no means apparent in all of the research studies. Graham and Bowling's (1995) study of young people aged 14–25 found that while social transitions like leaving home and forming a new family unit were highly correlated with desistance for females, no such correlation was found for males of the same age. Further, Uggen's (1996) research found that the relationship between desistance and finding employment was age dependent and was most consistent for persons aged over 27 years (Maruna 1999). There remains some debate as to what these differences tell us. Graham and Bowling (1995), for example, speculate that the formation of social ties and life transitions 'only provide opportunities for change to occur; its realisation is mediated by individual contingencies' (p. 35). More recent studies suggest, however, that the differences may be due to the fact that males need longer to mature and/or grasp opportunities for change (Flood-Page *et al.* 2000; Farrall 2002). Clearly, though our understanding is still evolving in this area, the complex and inconclusive nature of the findings alerts us to the fact that the relationship between the formation of social ties and desistance is by no means straightforward but rather is one which, as Sampson and Laub (1997) observe, has 'strings attached'.

Narrative approaches, informed largely by qualitative research, provide yet another perspective and suggest that individual desistance occurs as a result of subjective changes in the person's sense of self and identity – reflected, for example, in changing motivations, greater concern for others and more consideration for the future. Maruna's work (1997, 1999 2000, 2001), itself building on earlier work by Burnett (1992), has been particularly illuminating in this area and has done much to foreground the value of 'offender' perspectives in understanding desistance or the process of 'going straight'. In an important recent study, Maruna (2001) explored the subjective dimensions of change by comparing the narrative 'scripts' of 20 persisters and 30 desisters who shared similar criminogenic traits and backgrounds and who lived in similarly criminogenic environments. In particular, the study highlighted the significance of the 'stories' or 'scripts' which individuals constructed and utilised to explain their persistence or desistance trajectories (past, present and future) and, perhaps more importantly, the roles that individual actors assigned themselves within these scripts. While recognising the uniqueness of individual stories, Maruna identifies two core scripts as emerging from persisters and desisters, that of the 'condemnation script' and the 'redemption script' respectively. In the condemnation script the active offender typically occupies the role of the 'condemned victim', one who, perceiving their life script as having been written for them some time ago, generally considers themselves to be 'doomed to deviance'. By contrast, the accounts of the desisters revealed a different narrative in which the individual actor, normally with the support of a significant other, assumes the role of change agent and is no longer merely the object of outside forces:

> The redemption script begins by establishing the goodness and conventionality of the narrator – a victim who gets involved with crime and drugs to achieve some sort of power over otherwise bleak circumstances. This deviance eventually becomes its own trap, however, as the narrator becomes ensnared in the vicious cycle of crime and imprisonment. Yet, with the help of some outside force, someone who 'believed in' the ex-offender, the narrator is able to accomplish what he or she was 'always meant to do'. Newly empowered, he or she now seeks to 'give something back' to society as a display of gratitude. (p. 87)

Such findings foreground the significance of the subjective narratives and identities which persisters and desisters (often with the help of others) actively construct for themselves. While not negating the significance of these findings in developing our understanding of desistance, critiques of narrative theory again point to the failure of this single perspective to attend to the question of 'why' and 'how' individual narratives change.

Towards an integrative theory of desistance

The three broad perspectives discussed above provide useful insights into the particular factors associated with desistance though, as Farrall and Bowling (1999) observe, each of them considered in isolation fails to offer much assistance to practitioners in developing interventions to support desistance. Moreover, as has been highlighted, more recent studies suggest that no one perspective can fully explain decisions to desist and increasingly point to the interplay between the three perspectives (Farrall and Bowling 1999; Maruna 2000; Farrall 2002; Maruna *et al.* 2004; Bottoms *et al.* 2004). In the most recent, and perhaps most significant study of probation and desistance, Farrall (2002) observes that desistance is related to what he terms 'objective' changes in the offender's life (i.e. maturation, the gaining of employment or a significant relationship) and the offender's 'subjective' assessment of the relevance or value of these changes:

> ... the desistance literature has pointed to a range of factors associated with the ending of active involvement in offending. Most of these factors are related to acquiring 'something' (most commonly employment, a life partner or a family) which the desister values in some way and which initiates a re-evaluation of his or her own life. (p. 11)

Similarly, Bottoms *et al.* (2004), in considering the various factors that might be involved in the process of desistance, call for an 'interactive theoretical framework ... that gives proper weight to both structure and agency, in continuous interaction' (p. 372). It would seem then that desistance resides somewhere in the interfaces between developing personal maturity, changing social bonds associated with certain life transitions, and the individual subjective narrative constructions which offenders build around these key events and changes. It is not just the events and changes that matter; it is what these events and changes *mean* to the people involved. This more integrative theory of desistance – and the growing academic and professional interest allied to it – is both timely and promising. At the most basic level it offers a constructive path through a familiar, though increasingly futile, agency/structure debate, towards a more integrated and individualised understanding of how structure and agency interact and engage within the complex process of desistance. More broadly, it provides a much needed baseline for developing our conceptual and practice knowledge in this area, legitimising renewed attention to key variables and processes all too easily overlooked in a penal climate increasingly preoccupied with standardised technologies of correction and control.

The precise implications of this research discourse for developing interventions capable of supporting the complex process of desistance are broad and yet to be fully explored, far less understood (Bottoms *et al.* 2004). Nonetheless, a small number of research studies have begun to explore the role that probation may play in supporting desistance (for example Rex 1999; Farrall 2002; McCulloch 2005). In one study of 'assisted desistance', Rex (1999) explored the experiences of 60 probationers. She found that those who attributed changes in their behaviour to probation supervision described it as active and participatory. Probationers' commitment to desist appeared to be generated by personal and professional commitment shown by their probation officers, whose reasonableness, fairness and encouragement seemed to engender a sense of personal loyalty and accountability. Probationers interpreted advice about their behaviours and underlying problems as evidence of concern for them as people, and 'were motivated by what they saw as a display of interest in their well-being' (Rex 1999). Such evidence resonates with other arguments about the pivotal role that relationship plays in effective interventions (Barry 2000; Burnett 2004; Burnett and McNeill 2005; McNeill *et al.* 2005). However, the worker-client relationship is neither the only nor the most important resource in promoting desistance. Related studies of young people in trouble suggest that their own resources and social networks are often better at resolving their difficulties than professional staff (Hill 1999) – a finding which is echoed (and developed) by a growing number of probation studies, most notably Farrall's (2002) exploration of the progress or lack of progress towards desistance achieved by a group of 199 probationers (see also Haines 1990; Braithwaite 1999; McCulloch 2005). Reflecting something of a renaissance in attention to the social context of criminal careers and their termination, each of these studies suggest that, in addition to addressing individual decision making, motivation and reasoning skills, interventions concerned to support the complex process of desistance should pay greater heed to the community, social and personal contexts in which persistence and desistance takes place. Necessarily, this requires a 'decentring' of the offending subject and his or her perceived deficits in favour of recognition of the broader social contexts and conditions required to support change. Farrall (2002), drawing on his own research findings, puts this point more directly and identifies the need to now 'conceptualise probation intervention as being aimed at altering some aspects of an individual's social and personal circumstances' (p. 214).

Moving the agenda forward: from 'what' to 'how'

While there is much evidence to suggest that the above messages may need to be restated in the current climate – not least recent research findings which suggest a reluctance among 'offence-focused' probation staff to directly address family-related obstacles, social and environmental factors, or other 'underlying issues' (Maguire *et al.* 1998; Farrall 2002; Dowden and Andrews 2004) – there is a danger in ending our inquiry here. Less than straightforward findings emerging from both the effectiveness and the desistance literatures indicate that there is a great deal more to designing effective interventions and programmes than knowing 'what' to target. Indeed, as Palmer (1995) observed over a decade ago, at least as much attention needs now to be given to 'how' particular areas or obstacles are targeted. Moreover, Maruna (2000) suggests that most practitioners are well aware that if their clients could find rewarding careers or develop satisfying relationships they would likely 'go straight' (p. 12). If this remains the case, then the more pressing question, suggests Maruna (2000), is 'how' can probation interventions help individuals to achieve these social goals?

Recalling probation's long-standing concern with – and contribution to – the achievement of social justice (Smith and Vanstone 2002), it is of some surprise that there are relatively few studies which attend in any direct way to the efficacy or otherwise of methods used to support individuals or groups to develop their social networks and achieve social change. Indeed, of the limited studies which do speak to this area, most tend to conclude by acknowledging the limitations of existing knowledge and the need for further research (for example, Davies 1974; Palmer 1995; Farrall 2002; McCulloch 2005).

The effectiveness research is particularly limited in its direction as to 'how' workers should tackle the social context of offending behaviour; though the research does highlight 'generally' effective methods of intervention (i.e. cognitive, behavioural, skills orientated and multi-modal programmes (Losel 1995)). Summarising these findings, Lipsey (1995) suggests that 'it is much better to target behaviour for change and approach it in a relatively structured, concrete fashion, than to target psychological process for change and approach it using variations in traditional counselling and casework technique' (p. 74). Dowden and Andrews' (2004) review of effective 'core correctional practices' builds on these 'general' messages and provides, according to the authors, 'strong preliminary evidence' (p. 203) regarding the effectiveness of the following five core practice skills:

- effective use of authority;
- anti-criminal modelling and reinforcement;
- problem-solving;
- effective use of community resources;
- quality of interpersonal resources.

To date, the above messages appear to have been either lost in translation or hi-jacked by programmes focusing on offending behaviour, attitudes or reasoning skills (Dowden and Andrews 2004). However, there is nothing to suggest that these 'general' findings are not as relevant to tackling offenders' social needs as they are to tackling attitudinal and cognitive needs.

The desistance literature, noted for its broader attention to 'when, how, and why' change occurs, is a little more forthcoming in this area. Attending directly to the question of 'how' probation interventions can help individuals to achieve their social goals, Maruna (2000) suggests that the task is to get the person to the point where they are 'employable' and 'marriageable' and in this respect identifies a need to better understand how to encourage 'cognitive changes' within the individual. In a similar vein, but in relation to the reintegration of ex-prisoners to society, Maruna and LeBel (2003) make a convincing case for a shift towards 'strengths-based' (rather than needs-based or risk-based) narratives and approaches. Others point to the importance of the 'relational' element of supervision and, in particular, to the process of ensuring probationers feel valued and are actively engaged in the change process (Pitts 1999; Trotter 1999). As noted, Rex's (1999) research endorses this message, though it also indicates that most probationers valued 'guidance' and 'advice' on how they might resolve social and personal problems rather than direct practical assistance. In contrast, Farrall's (2002) research questions the efficacy of what he terms purely 'talking' approaches to obstacle resolution and suggests that more by the way of 'direct action' is required to maximise the impact of probation supervision. For Farrall (2002), this requires a step back from the exclusive focus on cognitive behavioural work which he notes is geared solely towards increasing probationers' 'human capital' – towards the development of interventions capable of also building probationers' 'social capital' – i.e. sustainable opportunities for change, for example around education, training, employment and accommodation.

While then the effectiveness literature and, more notably, the desistance literature provide some insight into 'how' interventions can assist offenders to achieve and sustain change in their social contexts, it is fair to say that our understanding and knowledge in this area remains very much in its infancy. In an attempt to move this discussion forward we turn in this final section to the findings of a small-scale research study which, drawing on worker and probationer perspectives, sought to address this question directly.

Exploring the 'how' of social change – worker and probationer perspectives

Conducted by one of the authors, the study in question evolved from the author's (then a criminal justice social worker) experience-based conviction about the relevance of social context in supporting and sustaining desistance, coupled with a growing awareness of the limited success of probation interventions in supporting change in this area. As one active offender frankly put it: 'those that want to help you cannie help you'.[1] In addition, then, to gaining an insight into the level and nature of attention given to social context in contemporary probation practice, the study was principally concerned to better understand how workers could more effectively assist probationers to achieve and sustain change in their social circumstances. The study was conducted in a Scottish criminal justice social work agency in 2004 and involved 12, in-depth, semi-structured interviews with social workers and their probationers. The study set out to address the following three interrelated questions:

1 What attention is given to probationers' social problems within contemporary probation supervision?
2 What methods are used to address probationers' social problems?
3 What methods do workers and probationers identify as most useful in supporting change in probationers' social problems?

Though our focus here relates primarily to the latter two research questions in light of concerns raised within recent literature regarding the diminishing attention being given to probationers' social context, it is worth noting that one of the surprising findings to emerge from the study was that, within the cases examined, considerable attention was given to addressing probationers' social problems as a means of reducing further offending. Moreover, participants' – both workers and probationers – apparent ease and cogent rationale for integrating these at times polarised objectives was encouraging and might suggest that the often cited tension between 'welfare' and 'offence-focused' approaches is less difficult for workers and probationers to reconcile than it is for the wider academic and political community.[2]

Methods used to address probationers' social problems

The study found that the methods used to address probationers' social problems generally concur with the findings from wider probation research which identify the use of talking methods, referrals to other agencies and direct help as the most common methods used to address probationers' problems (Rex 1998; Farrall 2002). More particular to this study, participants highlighted the involvement of family members and being visited at home as methods also employed to address social problems. More generally, the study presented a relatively positive picture of the quality of local practice in addressing social problems and suggested that workers were approaching work in this area in a way which was broadly consistent with recent research messages (i.e. participants relayed what appeared to be an overarching task-centred or problem-solving approach to tackling social problems, the use of multiple methods to address single problem areas and, the matching of methods with the characteristics or 'learning style' of the probationer). However, the more troubling finding to emerge from the study was that, despite this fact, though in common with the findings of previous studies (Farrall 2002; McIvor and Barry 1998; Rex 1998), most workers reported limited success in enabling probationers to overcome their problems. Further, where 'improvements' were achieved, in common with Farrall's (2002) findings, most attributed improvements to a combination of the work done within probation and the wider normative processes going on in the probationer's life. As one probationer described in recounting the many and interrelated processes which impacted on his ability to address his social problems and, in turn, offending behaviour:

> It was just kenning [knowing] about all your stuff, all like in the one room, rather than just waking up in the morning and going what's happening. Kenning about everything and sort of like that's when I realised. Then wi' being on probation you have to be of good behaviour too so I was sort of like being alright and then once I got the job that was it. I've got a new job now too. That one was only temporary but the one I'm at now is permanent.

[How did you get the new job? (Researcher)]

My dad, like cos fae I got probation and I was trying to calm down, with stopping going out, not getting charged, getting a job. I think it sort of showed my dad tae I was able to dae it like, so he got [me] an application for his work and then I got a job.

On the one hand this illustration usefully underscores that probation cannot enable probationers to address their social problems in isolation – a finding which, in turn, highlights the need for workers to become more attuned to the normative processes which can and do facilitate change in this area and more adept at influencing and supporting these processes towards the resolution of social problems. However, noting recent research which suggests that probationers' failure to achieve and sustain behaviour change may be linked to the failure of traditional and recent interventions to enable probationers to overcome 'day-to-day' problems (Farrall 2002; Raynor and Vanstone 1997), probation's limited success in this area cannot be overlooked and (again) foregrounds the need to better understand the particular methods and processes which can assist probationers to overcome their personal and social problems and achieve desistance.

Most helpful methods in addressing social problems

A common theme in probationer accounts of what was most helpful in assisting them to address their social problems was the value of being listened to, closely followed by talking about social problems and receiving advice and guidance. The provision of advice and guidance is now well recognised as a useful method in helping probationers to resolve a range of problems (McIvor and Barry 1998; Rex 1998), though the value of talking and, more significantly, listening to probationers is less well documented. The findings from this study suggest that listening to probationers is not only *as* important as providing advice and guidance but is integral in assisting probationers to take on board advice given. As one probationer explains:

Until [Worker 1] came on the scene I didnae hae anyone to confide in … so I was just hitting the tins or hitting the bottle. She's different. She'll sit down and she'll listen to [me] … ken she doesnae try and hurry [me] up or anything, she'll just sit there until I'm finished and then she'll say, right, is there anything else you want to talk about? If I say yes then she'll let [me] carry on and if I say no I'll say, right, is there anything you want to speak to me about. If she says yes, I'll say, I'm ready to listen.

This message sits well with aforementioned probation research which emphasises the importance of the relational element of supervision and of probationers being valued and respected if they are to engage in the process of change (Rex 1999; Trotter 1999). However, it is a message which sits notably less comfortably with the current correctional-managerial paradigm driving penal policy and practice developments. For now, it remains unclear how these tensions are to be resolved in the current landscape though the findings from this and other studies suggest that if politicians, managers and practitioners are committed to enabling probationers to overcome the problems and obstacles which lie in the way of desistance then these less fashionable or politically palatable messages need to be heard and more routinely embedded into the rhetoric, policy and practice of probation.

The process of 'talking about' problems also emerged as a more crucial and complex process in addressing social problems than is often recognised. For example, in common with Rex's (1998) probationers, probationers in this study indicated that talking about their problems often involved a process of problem clarification and identification, a process considered central in enabling probationers to understand their problems and in turn address them. Talking about problems was also frequently used to refer to dialogue which incorporated the provision of advice and guidance, the development of thinking skills and practical problem-solving. As one worker elaborates:

> We just talk … talk through, play through scenarios, in terms of when he gets approached by these people, how he could deal with the situation so he doesn't get into trouble; like identifying ways of coping with that and withdrawing. A lot of it is to do with developing his thinking skills and the way he deals with difficult situations, confrontational situations and just showing him how he can cope with that.

In addition then to underlining the range of processes denoted by the term 'talking about' problems, the above account highlights what appeared to be a very natural, and at times unconscious, ability among workers to effectively combine more traditional talking methods with more directive methods of intervention (i.e. cognitive training and concrete problem-solving). In light of more recent studies which have questioned the efficacy of talking methods in supporting change these findings are worth noting and suggest that talking to probationers about their problems can be a more complex, structured and useful process than is often assumed. More specifically, the considerable emphasis placed by probationers on gaining a thorough understanding of their problems *in order to* address them suggests that greater attention needs to be given to the process of assessment *within* probation supervision, a process which the wider findings of the study suggest needs to be participatory, individualised and contextualised. Further, the value placed by participants on dialogue which incorporated direct attempts to develop probationers' thinking skills (cognitive training) and ability to resolve real problems (concrete problem-solving) suggests a need for workers to more routinely integrate traditional talking methods with more structured and directive methods of addressing problems.

Also included within participant accounts of what was 'most helpful' was the involvement of family members (cited as a useful method of intervention by almost half of the study's participants). While this could be seen to reflect the age and life stage of the probationers involved in this study,[3] the value placed by participants on the involvement of family members seemed to reflect either a recognition that efforts to address social problems were most effective when workers worked alongside, and in one case mobilised, the support of family members, or a conviction that efforts would have been more effective had significant family members been involved. This finding sits well with wider research studies which stress the importance of probationers' personal and community networks in addressing social problems (Braithwaite 1999; Haines 1990; Maruna 2001). However, the limited and more often than not chance use of this method – at least in the cases examined – suggests that workers are still some way from routinely utilising what Smith and Vanstone (2002) refer to as 'the naturally occurring guardians' (p. 824) within probationers' lives. This perhaps forgotten 'method' of addressing social problems would appear to be ripe for recovery in contemporary probation practice, leading some to highlight the need for more active collaboration between probation, significant others and local community agencies (Rex 2001). More fundamentally, however, it will require more active collaboration between workers and probationers themselves towards identifying the network of family members, friends and community agencies which can be mobilised to help probationers address the social problems which lie in the way of desistance. Again, this highlights the importance of workers engaging in participatory, individualised and contextualised assessments that focus as much on the needs and problems underlying a probationer's offending behaviour as they do on the natural supports and networks which can be utilised to address these problems. Naturally, once workers and probationers have identified the potential pro-social networks which surround probationers, the challenge will be to strengthen, support and mobilise those networks – a process which, as Farrall (2002) observes, will involve 'the probationer's social circumstances and relationships with others [becoming] ... both the *object* of the intervention and the *medium* through which ... change can be achieved' (p. 214).

Finally, in light of recent studies which suggest that more in the way of 'direct help' (i.e. providing probationers with training/employment contacts – or indeed 'real jobs', preparing probationers for interviews, providing relationship counselling, etc.) is needed to assist probationers to overcome their problems (Farrall 2002), one of the surprising findings to emerge from the study was that none of the participants identified direct help among their discussion of most helpful methods. Rather, in common with the probationers in Rex's (1998) study, probationers reported that they didn't expect probation to 'resolve' their problems for them but wanted advice and guidance as to how they themselves could do that, coupled with encouragement and support as they engaged in that process. Although it is possible that probationers' views on this issue were constrained by their current experience of probation, the impression gained from conducting the research was that probationers had a sufficiently informed, critical and realistic view of what they expected from probation – more so, it might be argued, than can at times be said for policy-makers, academics and practitioners. However, this is not to suggest that probationers did not value 'direct help' in resolving social problems, the study merely indicated that probationers did not expect or need that help to come directly from probation workers. As one probationer put it:

> I think [more direct help] would help for the likes of us but I don't think it's a job for the probation officers themselves, like I think they've got enough on their plate without having to find jobs for people ... I think that's up to the job centre and that.

In slight contrast then to Farrall's (2002) vision of a Probation Service which works to directly resolve probationers' social problems – i.e. by 'creating jobs locally for their caseloads' or providing the counselling necessary to restore broken relationships (p. 221) – the findings from this study suggest that it is perhaps more desirable, as well as more realistic and inclusive, for probation to direct its efforts towards developing the individual and community partnerships needed to enable probationers to achieve these goals themselves. However, even this more modest vision of probation presents a considerable challenge for current policy and practice. As has been argued, at a practice level it will require a more participatory, contextualised and solution-focused approach to probation assessment, a more active commitment to working collaboratively with the individuals and resources within probationers' communities (which will inevitably require workers spending more time in these communities) and a more explicit attention to motivating, supporting and enabling probationers to do the same. In addition, any success on the part of probation services to work more collaboratively and effectively with probationers, those around them and community resources will be wholly dependent on those resources being in place.

As others have already noted, this is a challenge which reaches beyond the realms of probation and penal policy (Chapman 1995; Farrall 2002; Rex 2001) and will require targeted, integrated and evaluated action on the part of government to ensure that resources exist within communities which are both accessible to individuals and capable of enabling them to overcome their problems and realise their potential. Moreover, the wider challenge lies not only in resourcing communities to foster and support desistance in practical ways, it lies in working actively to *persuade* communities (and society more generally) that making such efforts is necessary for both moral and pragmatic reasons. If, therefore, criminal justice and social work agencies are to work effectively to support desistance, they will need to revisit and revive earlier concerns with the role of community development in crime prevention (Gilling 1995; McNeill 2000) and to engage more effectively with more contemporary debates about public attitudes to offenders, to punishment and to reintegration (Maruna and King 2004).

Conclusion

This chapter has sought to provide an overview of the theory base associated with the desistance literature, giving attention to the particular factors understood to impact on and support the complex process of desistance. There now exists a growing body of evidence which indicates that in addition to addressing individual decision-making, motivation and reasoning skills, interventions concerned to support the complex process of desistance should pay greater heed to the community, social and personal contexts in which offenders live and change – a perspective which has done much to legitimise renewed attention to core variables and processes all to easily overlooked in the present 'get tough' penal landscape. However, as has been argued, until recently there appears to have been a tendency for debate and discussion in this area to become somewhat stuck on the 'what' of intervention, with little direction provided for practitioners as to 'how' particular areas, obstacles or problems are most effectively targeted and overcome. The small-scale research study drawn upon in this chapter provides some insight into how workers might more effectively assist probationers to overcome the personal and social problems which lie in the way of desistance though the preliminary and generalised nature of these findings highlight the need to now develop our curiosity, knowledge and skill in this area. At the very least, we can be confident that the process of developing our knowledge and skill in supporting desistance will require us to attend more keenly to the wealth of experience, knowledge, and expertise which resides within those persisters and would-be desisters we seek to assist and work alongside.

Discussion questions

1 What can we learn from the desistance literature regarding 'what' we should be focusing on in our efforts to support individuals to achieve and sustain desistance from crime?
2 What does existing research and our practice experience have to tell us about 'how' workers can support individuals to overcome the personal and social problems which lie in the way of desistance?
3 What are the opportunities for, and obstacles to, the development of desistance-focused practice within your own professional practice, your organisation and the wider socio-political climate?

Further reading

Farrall, S. and Calverley, A. (2006) *Understanding Desistance from Crime: Theoretical Directions in Resettlement and Rehabilitation*. Berkshire: Open University Press. A comprehensive introduction and overview of the desistance research literature, drawing on detailed interviews with both persisters and desisters.

McNeill, F. (2006) 'A desistance paradigm for offender management', *Criminology and Criminal Justice*, 6 (1): 37–60. In the context of a review of earlier paradigms for probation practice, this paper explores the theoretical, empirical and moral arguments for an alternative and novel paradigm based largely on desistance research.

Maruna, S. (2001) *Making Good*. Washington DC: American Psychological Association. Drawing on offenders' own stories, Maruna offers a fascinating and accessible analysis of the lived realities of repeat offenders who, against all the odds, have managed to 'make good' and desist from offending.

Notes

1 Of course it is worth considering this perspective in the light of Maruna's (2001) aforementioned work on the narrative scripts constructed by persisters and desisters.

2 Though welcome, the above finding needs to be treated with caution on two counts. Firstly, the finding reflects the perspectives of a small sample group and is not entirely congruent with the findings of other Scottish or UK studies. Secondly, the finding emerges from a time and place when the delivery and content of probation supervision is subject to considerable scrutiny and change, reflecting the ongoing influence of the effectiveness research on Scottish probation practice alongside wider political concerns to reform and, it might be argued, 'rebrand' Scottish criminal justice social work services (McNeill and Whyte 2007).

3 All of the probationers interviewed were aged between 17 and 35. This decision was based on methodology considerations identified by previous studies which suggest that probationers within this age range are more likely to be experiencing a number of salient life changes and social circumstances which relate to decisions to persist in or desist from offending.

References

Barry, M. (2000) 'The mentor/monitor debate in criminal justice: what works for offenders', *British Journal of Social Work*, 30 (5): 575–95.

Blunkett, D. (2004) *Reducing Crime – Changing Lives: The Government's Plans for Transforming the Management of Offenders*. London: Home Office.

Bottoms, A., Shapland, J., Costello, A., Holmes, D. and Muir, G. (2004) 'Towards desistance: theoretical underpinnings for an empirical study', *Howard Journal of Criminal Justice*, 43: 368–389.

Braithwaite, J. (1999) 'Restorative justice: assessing optimistic and pessimistic accounts', in M. Tonry, (ed.), *Crime and Justice: A Review of Research*. Chicago: University of Chicago Press.

Burnett, R. (1992) *The Dynamics of Recidivism.* Oxford: University of Oxford Centre for Criminological Research.

Burnett, R. (2004) 'One-to-one ways of promoting desistance: In search of an evidence base', in R. Burnett and C. Roberts (eds), *What Works in Probation and Youth Justice.* Cullompton: Willan.

Burnett, R. and McNeill, F. (2005) 'The place of the officer–offender relationship in assisting offenders to desist from crime', *Probation Journal,* 52 (3): 247–68.

Carter, P. (2004) *Correctional Services Review: Managing Offenders, Reducing Crime – A New Approach.* London: Strategy Unit.

Chapman, T. (1995) 'Creating a culture of change: a case study of a car crime project in Belfast', in J. McGuire (1995) *What Works: Reducing Re-offending.* Chichester: Wiley.

Davies, M. (1974) *Social Work in the Environment.* London: HMSO.

Dowden, C. and Andrews, D. A. (2004) 'The importance of staff practice in delivering effective correctional treatment: a meta-analytic review of core correctional practice', *International Journal of Offender Therapy and Comparative Criminology,* 48: 203–14.

Farrall, S. (2002) *Rethinking What Works with Offenders: Probation, Social Context and Desistance from Crime.* Cullompton: Willan.

Farrall, S. and Bowling, B. (1999) 'Structuration, human development and desistance from crime', *British Journal of Criminology,* 17: 252–67.

Farrington, D.P. (1997) 'Human development and criminal careers', in M. Maguire, R. Morgan, and R. Reiner (eds), *The Oxford Handbook of Criminology,* 2nd edn. Oxford: Oxford University Press.

Flood-Page, C. Campbell, S., Harrington, V. and Miller, J. (2000) *Youth Crime: Findings from the 1998/1999 Youth Lifestyles Survey,* Home Office Research Study No. 209. London: Home Office.

Gilling, D. (1995) 'The challenge of crime prevention', *Probation Journal,* 42 (1): 31–34.

Glueck, S. and Glueck, E. (1940) *Juvenile Delinquents Grown Up.* New York: Commonwealth Fund.

Graham, J. and Bowling, B. (1995) *Young People and Crime,* Home Office Research Study No. 145. London: Home Office.

Haines, K. (1990) *After-Care Services for Released Prisoners: A Review of the Literature.* Cambridge: University of Cambridge.

Hill, M. (1999) 'What's the problem? Who can help? The perspectives of children and young people on their well-being and on helping professionals', *Journal of Social Work Practice,* 13 (2): 135–45.

Home Office (2004) *Reducing Crime, Changing Lives.* London: Home Office.

Home Office (2005) *Restructuring Probation to Reduce Re-offending.* London: Home Office.

Lipsey, M. (1995) 'What do we learn from 400 research studies on the effectiveness of treatment with juvenile delinquents?', in J. McGuire (ed.), *What Works: Reducing Re-offending.* Chichester: Wiley.

Losel, M.W. (1995) 'The efficacy of correctional treatment: a review and synthesis of meta-evaluations', in J. McGuire (ed.), *What Works: Reducing Re-offending.* Chichester: Wiley.

McCulloch, T. (2005) 'Probation, social context and desistance: retracing the relationship', *Probation Journal,* 52: 8–22.

McIvor, G. and Barry, M. (1998) *Social Work and Criminal Justice: Volume 6 Probation*. Edinburgh: Scottish Office Central Research Unit.

McIvor, G., Jamieson, J. and Murray, C. (2000) 'Study examines gender differences in desistance from crime', *Offender Programs Report*, 4 (1): 5–9.

McNeill, F. (2000) 'Community development in criminal justice: probation work and crime prevention', *Irish Social Worker*, 18 (2–4): 14–18.

McNeill, F. (2002) *Beyond 'What Works': How and Why do People Stop Offending?*, CJSW Briefing Paper 5. Edinburgh: Criminal Justice Social Work Development Centre.

McNeill, F. (2003) 'Desistance-focused probation practice', in W.H. Chui and M. Nellis (eds), *Moving Probation Forward: Evidence, arguments and practice* (pp. 146–62). Harlow: Pearson Education.

McNeill, F. (2006) 'A desistance paradigm for offender management', *Criminology and Criminal Justice*, 6 (1): 37–60.

McNeill, F. and Whyte, B. (2007) *Reducing Reoffending: Social Work and Community Justice in Scotland*. Cullompton: Willan.

McNeill, F., Batchelor, S., Burnett, R. and Knox, J. (2005) *21st Century Social Work. Reducing Re-offending: Key Practice Skills*. Edinburgh: Scottish Executive.

Maguire, M., Raynor, P., Vanstone, M. and Kynchy, J. (1998) *Voluntary After-Care*, HORS 73. London: Home Office.

Maruna, S. (1997) 'Going straight: desistance from crime and self-narratives of reform', *Narrative Study of Lives*, 5: 59–93.

Maruna, S. (1999) 'Desistance and development: The psychosocial process of "going straight"', in M. Brogden (ed.), *British Society of Criminology Conference Selected Proceedings*, 2: 1–35.

Maruna, S. (2000) 'Desistance from crime and offender rehabilitation: a tale of two research literatures', *Offender Programs Report*, 4: 1–13.

Maruna, S. (2001) *Making Good*. Washington DC: American Psychological Association.

Maruna, S. and King, A. (2004) 'Public opinion and community penalties', in A. Bottoms, S. Rex, and G. Robinson, (eds), *Alternatives to Prison: Options for an Insecure Society*. Cullompton: Willan.

Maruna, S. and LeBel, T. (2003) 'Welcome home? Examining the "re-entry court" concept from a strengths-based perspective', *Western Criminology Review*, 4 (2): 91–107.

Maruna, S., Porter, L. and Carvalho, I. (2004) 'The Liverpool desistance study and probation practice: opening the dialogue', *Probation Journal*, 51: 221–32.

Palmer, T. (1995) 'Programmatic and non-programmatic aspects of successful intervention: new directions for research', *Crime and Delinquency*, 41: 100–31.

Pitts, J. (1999) *Working with Young Offenders*, 2nd edn. London: Macmillan Press.

Raynor, P. and Vanstone, M. (1997) *Straight Thinking on Probation (STOP): The Mid-Glamorgan Experiment*, Probation Studies Unit Report No. 4. Oxford: University of Oxford Centre for Criminological Research.

Rex, S. (1998) 'Perceptions of Probation in a Context of "just deserts"'. PhD thesis, University of Cambridge.

Rex, S. (1999) 'Desistance from offending: experiences of probation', *Howard Journal*, 38: 366–83.

Rex, S. (2001) 'Beyond cognitive-behaviouralism? Reflections on the effectiveness literature', in A. Bottoms, L. Gelsthorpe, and S. Rex (eds), *Community Penalties: Change and Challenges*. Cullompton: Willan.

Sampson, R.J. and Laub, J.H. (1997) 'A life-course theory of cumulative disadvantage and the stability of delinquency', in T. Thornberry (ed.), *Developmental Theories of Crime and Delinquency*. London: Transaction.

Smith, D. and Vanstone, M. (2002) 'Probation and social justice', *British Journal of Social Work*, 32: 815–30.

Trotter, C. (1999) *Working with Involuntary Clients: A Guide to Practice*. London: Sage.

Uggen, C. (1996) 'Age, employment and the duration structure of recidivism: estimating the "true effect" of work on crime', unpublished paper presented at the 1996 American Sociological Association conference, New York, cited in Maruna, S. (1999) 'Desistance and development: the psychosocial process of "Going Straight."', in M. Brogden (ed.), *British Society of Criminology Conference Selected Proceedings*, 2: 1–35.

Chapter 10

Beyond the risk agenda

Dave Phillips

Introduction

Risk assessment and management have come to dominate the thinking of all criminal justice agencies and may be a reflection of living in a 'risk society'. The rise of risk – and there can be uncertainty about the meaning of the term – has been gradual but it is now centre stage. There are consequences in this for politicians, organisations, practitioners and offenders. There are also consequences in terms of public expectation, cost-effective use of resources, scientific assessment tools, bias and ethical considerations within a risk-based criminal justice system. These aspects of risk frame and dominate debates within the criminal justice system.

There are other narratives within this discourse that should be heard and that widen the debate to re-emphasise and rebalance it to include various forms of community interventions (Bottoms *et al.* 2004). Currently practitioners may feel isolated and disempowered (Farrow 2004). The debate needs to be widened in order to assist practitioners to manage risk with less anxiety. Practitioners may also be able to work towards this through working more closely with professionals in other agencies by encouraging closer cooperation and understanding. Such considerations may open up the debate from risk assessment into a wider field of interventions to redress balance, increase effectiveness and re-establish professional discretion. For offenders and public safety it may move the debate towards the acquisition of social capital and helping offenders to be considered as active participants. These issues provide the themes of this chapter. I shall begin by considering the idea of a 'risk society'.

Risk society and the political consequences of public expectation

It may help to contextualise the debate by examining the concept of a 'risk society'. Beck characterised risk as something that was unseen and global.

He identified contemporary society as a 'risk society' (in Kemshall 2003). The rapid development of technology and information exchange has fuelled public anxiety and it is possible to know what is happening on the other side of the world within seconds, as with the attacks on the World Trade Center and the Pentagon on 11 September 2001 and the catastrophic Asian tsunami in 2004, for example. Indeed, public debate is generally articulated in terms of anxieties about 'global warming', 'the war on terror' and so on. Related to these growing anxieties and concerns is a desire among politicians and civil servants to appear to be in control of events.

Public expectations are high. It becomes clear that the Home Office, and in particular the criminal justice system, as viewed by the public, press and media, has a remit that goes beyond the arrest of criminals, their prosecution, sentencing, punishment and rehabilitation, to something much wider. The system must control immigration, keep track of 'failed asylum seekers', absconders from open prisons and anti-social behaviour, together with the assessment, management and supervision of high-risk offenders. The consequences of these increased expectations within the criminal justice system have been profound for organisations, politicians, practitioners and offenders. I intend to examine these, beginning with political consequences. It is fair to say that these can be dramatic.

Charles Clarke, shortly before he resigned as Home Secretary in May 2006, stated: 'Keeping the public safe is the first duty of the criminal justice system' (Home Office 2006: Foreword). His resignation was related to the perceived under-performance and consequent failure of the Home Office in protecting the public from harm and dealing with issues of asylum and immigration. Both concerns were viewed as interchangeable in the popular press (*Daily Mail*, '100 freed early to rape and murder', 17 April 2006 and *passim*). Recent reports on high-profile cases, such as Climbié 2003, Monckton 2006 and Rice 2006 (CHI 2003: HMIP 2006a, 2006b), were seen as confirmation that everything is out of control (Fraser 2006; Jewkes, this volume). Viewing any news bulletin in any medium will bring a rich harvest of criminal incidents fuelling anxiety about the risk involved in daily life. Coupled with this, in the public mind, is the perceived rise in violent crime and the inability of the criminal justice system to cope adequately. 'This is despite massive increases in legislation, risk centred penology, the expansion of policing, multi-agency work and measures designed to control anti-social behaviour' (Hayles 2006).

In one sense, then, Charles Clarke's statement can be viewed as a hostage to fortune. As Kemshall says, 'Perhaps the very actions of the government have inadvertently increased these levels of concern and anxiety' (Kemshall and Maguire 2003: 103). When things go wrong a resignation is demanded, inspectors' reports are produced, gaps in the system are identified and new measures suggested.

Resources follow risk – the consequences of a business model for organisations

Organisations are required to reorganise themselves around the concept of risk as a way of managing limited resources. This is the second set of consequences that I wish to consider. The imperatives of public protection have driven criminal justice agencies towards directing their limited resources to those individuals who are perceived as most 'risky'. If these offenders could be controlled, contained and excluded, then fewer incidents of a serious nature would occur and politicians would receive the credit, or at least avoid blame. The Police Service in England and Wales, for example, uses the National Intelligence Model (NIM 2000) that has three stated objectives: 'to provide strategic direction, make tactical resourcing decisions about operational policing, and the management of risk'. It describes itself as being primarily a 'business model for use in allocating resources' (National Intelligence Model, http://www.police.uk/nim2/, 25 July 2006), the objective being to assist the police in targeting their resources appropriately and to aid tactical deployment. In this it has parallels with the National Offender Management Service (NOMS) model and with ASSET which will be discussed later.

All concern themselves with different levels of operational working and partnerships, and risk has different meanings depending on the organisational context. However, one common factor is to direct scarce resources to the areas of highest risk. Such contemporary penology is dominated by economic expediency. As we shall see, this can have profound effects and impact on 'best practice'. The Probation Service provides an example of how these concerns can change both the nature of the organisation and the role of practitioners within it. One piece of legislation, the 1991 Criminal Justice Act, changed the role of the probation officer within the legislative framework (Bottoms et al. 2004). It placed risk 'at the heart of the sentencing and parole decisions' (Kemshall 2002: 102). Probation officers were no longer the 'social workers' of the courts and no longer advised, assisted and befriended. Clients became offenders (Chui and Nellis 2003; Bottoms et al. 2004). The language of community interventions was changed and the way in which practitioners were required to consider their role changed with it.

By 1999, the Home Office was using the calculation of risk to direct 'more intensive rehabilitative programmes at offenders who are more likely to offend on the basis of statistical tables derived from an analysis between prior history and subsequent rates of conviction in large samples of offenders' (Bottoms et al. 2004: 7–8). So the principle of risk as a determinant of the level of input was articulated and activated. Risk assessment was said to be both 'sound' and 'considered, aiming to reduce reoffending and assist reintegration' (PC 10/2005, and PC 15/2006). A number of authors (Bottoms et al. 2004; Kemshall and Maguire 2003) have commented on the ways in which the drive to achieve government targets and key performance indicators has resulted in subsuming best practice beneath organisational and strategic needs.

The prominence of the risk principle and the way in which it may become subverted by targets have a number of consequences. We have seen how it is a major determinant in the allocation of resources. Additionally, once this determinant has been established, organisations begin to change their structure to fit this model. The role of practitioners within organisations then changes.

The Probation Service may serve as an example of this since it has experienced intense changes, from reorganisation into a National Probation Service (NPS 2001), followed by a further transformation into yet another structure, the National Offender Management Service (NOMS 2006) involving both the Probation and Prison Services.

The purpose of the reorganisation is 'to provide the overarching framework within which change and improvement projects can be located' (Home Office 2005, Public Protection Framework, version 1). Developments in information technology have strongly assisted in driving this forward. The National Offender Management Information System (NOMIS), launched by the Home Office, is an integrated IT system designed to ensure that information follows the offender throughout the 'seamless sentence', bringing both the custodial and community parts of a sentence into closer cooperation and coordination. Although this is a prison and probation service imperative, it will affect organisations across the sector including mental health provision and voluntary organisations.

Consequences for practitioners

I now want to turn my attention to the ways in which the centrality of risk assessment has also changed the role and occupational description of many practitioners. Where risk becomes central to policy, there is a demand for organisations to focus on a model with risk at its centre. This, in turn, pushes organisations to search for 'scientific' assessment tools. This causes great anxiety, since assessment tools, appearing to be scientific, seem to impose certainty on an uncertain world. The argument then runs that, if the tools are scientific and the organisations 'fit for purpose', then any mistake is the fault of the practitioner, rather than of the organisation or the assessment tool (Kemshall 1998a). Where accuracy cannot be guaranteed, the key to decisions in terms of public accountability is what Kemshall terms 'defensibility' (Kemshall 1998a). However, this may not be proof against public panic in a risk society. It should be remembered that risk assessments as used by the insurance industry, based on a system of actuarial and clinical features, deal with 'probability' and on balance are correct, allowing them to make a financial profit. Assessments are not infallible. In the public sector, where error results not in financial loss but in physical injury, rising public expectations and anxiety mean that any decision may become indefensible, particularly in the light of a further serious offence. The goal posts are being changed.

Many workers have experienced the three o'clock in the morning dread awakening when they rehearse the details of the most risky and worrying high-risk case. They may ask themselves whether they have done all that they could and should. This anxiety can outweigh all other considerations and is a cause of stress. Moore demonstrates how 'in the tricky or nightmare case everyone's rights seem to be infringed, no clear benefits appear to be gained and the professional becomes further beset by that occupational hazard, Repetitive Doubt Syndrome (RDS)' (Moore 1996: 3). The underlying cause of RDS may be located in the anxieties that professional workers experience around the assessment of risk, the meanings and interpretations given to the term, the assessment process and its subsequent management.

Having explained some of the consequences for politicians, organisations and practitioners, I now want to examine the possible effects on offenders. The consequence of a risk-based system has the potential to exclude and discriminate against certain categories and groups (Garland 2001; Kemshall 2003).

Consequences for offenders

Certain offenders may receive differential treatment because of gender, ethnicity, mental health, lifestyle and the type of offence that they have committed: exclusion and marginalisation may follow (Garland 2001). Race and gender need careful consideration and, in addition, some crimes bring with them general public disgust and anger. I shall begin with women offenders and then explore the possible impact of assessment on other groups such as black offenders, travellers, those diagnosed with mental illness and, finally, the category of sex offenders.

Firstly, there may be discrimination because of sex and gender. Sentencing studies provide evidence for both greater leniency and greater severity towards women. This may depend on whether the woman appears to conform to a stereotype of passivity and contrition or seems assertive and unrepentant (Hudson 2002; Beckett, this volume): the former deserves help and the latter punishment. If race is added to this dimension, then the effects may be greater. This may in turn influence the assessment of risk and dangerousness. It is important to ask what this means in terms of a risk assessment. Women 'attract disproportionate sentencing not because they are seen as being as risky as high risk men, but because risk assessments show them to be riskier than other women' (Kemshall 2002: 108).

McIvor et al. (2004) conclude that crime desistance is different for women. Their research into 276 young men and women found that many women were keen to be viewed as desisting, even though they acknowledged recent offending. The authors attribute this to the existence of socially disapproving attitudes to female offending. 'Women are judged, not on the basis of the criminal act itself but in accordance with their family, sexual and interpersonal relationships' (McIvor *et al.* 2004: 195).

Secondly, there may be discrimination because of race and ethnicity. Bhui points out that any assessment tool that is universally applied has the potential to be universally discriminating (Bhui 1999). He also points out factors that may impede the application of a full risk assessment, such as a lack of trust between a white probation officer and a black offender and frequently changing government imperatives and directives. Black offenders with mental health problems in the criminal justice system may be perceived as dangerous because of factors that are unrelated to their offending (Bhui 1999). Counteracting this bias requires a sophisticated use of assessment tools.

Since the bombings in the London Underground on 7 July 2005 a further dimension to assessment has been added. Hudson and Bramhall discuss the 'alchemy of race' in which there is 'a construction of Pakistani/Muslim as a criminalised other ... leading to unintended, but demonstrable, criminal justice disadvantage for this group' (Hudson and Bramhall 2005: 737).

Thirdly, discrimination and bias may result from stereotypes around different 'lifestyles'. Irish travellers, for example, are often overlooked as an ethnic minority. There are particular problems related to issues such as domestic violence, health, social welfare and educational difficulties which may be construed negatively (Power 2003; Cullen 2005). Bowling and Phillips have pointed out that the fact of an offender being remanded in custody may increase the perception of the risk that he poses because of the lack of fixed accommodation, employment and possibly poor physical appearance (Bowling and Phillips 2002).

Fourthly, certain behaviours may give rise to discrimination. For individuals diagnosed as experiencing mental illness, 'the criminal justice route remains a gateway to mental health provision' (Bottoms *et al.* 2004: 346), rather than directly through the health service. It has also been observed that mentally ill offenders 'may not have different criminogenic needs from other offenders but they may have more of them' (Bottoms *et al.* 2004: 351). Bottoms has also shown that black offenders are disproportionately diagnosed as experiencing mental illness.

Finally, the type of offence may be subject to such general disapproval and disgust that it may lead to disproportionate punishment and risk assessment. Perpetrators of sexual crimes, predominantly male, are most likely to be the recipients of 'repetitive retribution' (Kemshall and Maguire 2003: 111). With continuing (2008) debates about the introduction of a British equivalent of Megan's Law, it is likely that sex offenders will become subject to surveillance and retribution. Yet effective work in this area, as Cowburn points out, 'requires workers to develop a critical awareness of themselves and how they contribute to the construction of male forms of life and language games' (Cowburn 2006: 173). The management of sex offenders and their perceived risk reveals a lack of public trust in agencies to assess and manage that risk. Each fresh incident ratchets up the scale of intervention and control, seeking again to make certain what is uncertain. Each incident erodes community satisfaction with practitioners and seeks a policy that excludes and punishes perpetrators (Kemshall and Maguire 2003: 102).

This list is not exhaustive but may serve to illustrate the dangers of misrepresentation and distortion of data. In addition to the innate bias of the criminal justice system against certain groups, there is also the question of individual practitioner bias. I want to consider this next.

The bias of the practitioner

Practitioner bias may manifest itself in a number of ways (Moore 1996; Kemshall 1996, 2003; Strachan and Tallant 1997). It may take the form of over identification between practitioner and offender (*attribution bias*) which can lead to unreal optimism (Kemshall 1997). Discrete events may be perceived as having a causal link (*illusory correlations*). Greater importance may be attributed to some events than to others (*selectivity bias*). The interpretation of how the individual has reacted in a previous similar situation may result in *confirmation bias*. The adage that 'past behaviour is the best predictor of future behaviour' may influence the practitioner's perceptions of that behaviour (Bhui 1995). The main point to emphasise is that, while reducing inconsistency of assessment, actuarially based risk tools may increase the likelihood of consistently discriminatory assessments (Kemshall 1997). Strachan and Tallant (1997) also emphasise the need for practitioners to avoid anecdotal evidence and develop an awareness of their own stereotypes and assumptions. It is important that reflective practitioners have examined their own prejudices and subjective assumptions and the impact this may have on risk assessment. It is proposed that such assessments are subject to inspection, monitoring and research (Hudson and Bramhall 2005).

Every care must be taken to ensure, as far as is possible, that decisions are reached using the most accurate, comprehensive and balanced information. Meetings where this information is exchanged should be based on a shared knowledge of differing risk assessment tools and the purpose for which they were created and on balancing human rights, including the right to privacy, with the right of the public to be protected. This places practitioners, in whatever organisation they operate, in an important and powerful position. Practitioners have been eloquently warned that 'the precarious ethical position held by decision-makers is invaluable in restoring a due sense of humility and a willingness to tolerate doubt' (Moore 1996: 3).

Finally in this section I want to bring together both discriminatory issues and those of practitioner bias to consider the ethical implications of risk assessment.

Ethical considerations

We have seen how risk-based penology has the capacity to reform and reinforce excluded groups. The designation of 'high risk' or 'dangerous offender' in itself is 'a condemnatory label' (Hudson and Bramhall 2006: 738). Sometimes even the label prevents individuals benefiting from human rights legislation. 'Offenders who lack opportunity, in employment for example, can have these "needs" re-inscribed as risks requiring additional surveillance, enforcement, and treatment. Correction, rather than social justice, is promoted' (Kemshall and McGuire 2003: 346). There is a tradition not only of exclusion but also of categorising individuals, especially those who offend, as weak individuals who make bad moral choices, are both undeserving and demanding and can therefore be excluded from society. The undeserving can be blamed as much for the circumstances in which they live as for choices that they make (Hudson 2002, 2003).

Statistical information may be itself a reflection of discriminatory practices and this raises questions about fairness and proportionality (Bhui 1999; Robinson and Dignan 2004). The sentence passed by the court should be proportionate to the seriousness of the offence but, as Kemshall points out, risk can replace 'fairness and proportionality and ... where punishment follows risk, there may also be disproportionate and discriminatory sentencing' (Kemshall 2002: 108). However, it is possible, as we have seen, that individuals may be sentenced or denied access to resources or release into the community because of their lifestyle or ethnicity, factors that may have no connection with the offence.

The tendency to exclude, discriminate and impose perpetual retribution can lead to a system where rehabilitation is difficult. The USA may provide an example of where this can lead (Nellis 2002). In some states, actions against convicted prisoners are draconian, offender reintegration has deteriorated and recidivism rates increased. Prisoners lose property and civil rights, accumulate debt and are unsupported after release (Richards and Jones 2004). Uggen asks whether reintegration is possible when ex-offenders, these 'less than average citizens are denied full citizenship rights and retain the stigma of the convicted?' (Uggen 2004: 294). This is important since, if risk designation can exclude and discriminate, then part of the rebalancing may be connected with the promotion of inclusion, active citizenship by the offenders and participation in the process of risk assessment.

Risk has become central to the criminal justice system, and this places conflicting demands on practitioners, pressuring them to be infallible in terms of risk assessment and management while simultaneously guarding against bias and stereotyping, and protecting human rights. Inspectorate Reports (Climbié: CHI 2003; Monckton: HMIP 2006a; Rice: HMIP 2006b) suggest that too great an emphasis was placed on the human rights of individual offenders to the detriment of risk assessment. It is, indeed, a difficult balance to maintain and requires great professional skill on the part of practitioners. Assessment tools are designed as universal instruments intended to bring consistency and accuracy to the process of risk assessment. They are congruent with a changing political agenda that attempts to measure risk in an ordered and manageable way (Robinson 2003; Kemshall 2003). Since I have referred to assessment tools and their importance, the time has come to consider these.

Risk assessment tools

A number of risk assessment tools are used by the Probation, Prison and Police Services, drug agencies, special hospitals and others. For practitioners in the criminal justice system and beyond, who operate in the 'swampy lowlands' of everyday practice as identified by Schön (in Thompson 2006: 53), risk assessment and management tools might seem to provide the 'Holy Grail' of public protection. These tools impose a structure on assessment and organise the way in which information is collected. They also decide what information is relevant and the importance of that relevance.

However, this confidence may be misplaced, and there are a number of factors that all practitioners across the criminal justice system might consider. I am going to take as an example the Offender Assessment System (OASys) tool that was developed from earlier systems dating back to the Bales scores of the 1930s. It is one of the most sophisticated, evidence- and research-based assessment tools and it may stand as a model for other similar tools. The questions asked here may be asked of others.

In 1996, statistics provided the basis for the Offender Group Reconviction Score (OGRS) for the Probation Service. Risk was defined both as the risk of reoffending and risk of harm to the public. This contributed to the rise of assessment tools designed to quantify and assess the level of risk. These imperatives were also assisted by the increasing sophistication of information technology (Loader and Sparks 2002; Robinson 2003). The Assessment, Case Management and Evaluation tool (ACE 1996) was a precursor of OASys, launched by the Home Office in 1999. OASys is described as a third-generation assessment tool bringing together static factors, such as offending history, and dynamic factors, such as attitudes, that can be used to identify criminogenic needs (Kemshall 2002).

This system is 'located firmly in the "What Works" agenda and in research, extensively North American' (Mohammed 2002: 1). On this point an interesting study by Hamley (2003), applying Multicultural Counselling Competences (MSC) to the OASys assessment tool, identified OASys as a 'fairly ethnocentric assessment tool' (ibid.: 2) and asked whether any standard tool 'could adequately assess the multiplicity of needs and risk factors of the British offending population' (ibid.: 5). She emphasises the restricted research base of OASys (a short timespan and overwhelmingly white British males) and its bias towards white Western methods of intervention. It mostly assesses needs in ways that are culturally-bound, omitting areas of life that may not be as important to mainstream British culture but are vital to others.

A degree of critical scepticism is welcome. Robinson and Dignan (2004) explore the ambivalence that practitioners feel towards assessment systems and stress the need to question the integrity of such tools and to remain critical. On the one hand, it is argued, professionals feel deskilled, but, on the other, such instruments do rely on the professional integrity and competence of the assessor.

It should be remembered that risk assessment is a process, not a task. OASys is a lengthy document and acts as a guide to some important factors. What is essential is that workers remember this and overcome the temptation to skip certain sections. Risk, for example, is located a long way into the document. This does not indicate that it is not important – indeed, it may be claimed as one of the most important sections of the document. A professional will be critically aware of this and not be tempted to skip over this section.

There are examples from other agencies. In youth justice the Asset document was developed by Oxford University in 1999 for use by Youth Offending Teams (YOTs) across the country. It contains extensive sections on risk assessments that must form part of the 'Intervention Plan'. Additionally, Asset includes 'protective factors' that are perceived as reducing risk. This is something that is not prominent in the OAsys tool.

Drug agencies have been impelled to devise their own risk assessment procedures. In one striking example, the drug agencies within a particular county area have devised a single common client assessment tool (CCA 2004) that is used by drug treatment programmes in that area, the only exception being a community drugs team that deals with complex cases that uses a more complex tool. This CCA draws together as much information as possible, including existing orders to which the individual may be subject, the amount of drug and alcohol use, related health issues, history of drug use, personal history, childcare and employment issues, accommodation and, finally, a risk assessment. This is based on a number of criteria that include issues around self-harm and harm to others, childcare, violence (including domestic abuse), self-neglect and offending behaviour. These are tick boxes but there is provision for an intervention plan that articulates risk management, if applicable.

Special hospitals, such as Rampton, have used a number of psychological and mental health-based assessment tools that include sections on risk. The one in use (2006) is based on a psychological assessment tool to create a system based on the use of structured clinical judgment for making risk decisions. The format for structuring judgments there is based on the HCR-20 tool for assessing risk (Webster *et al.* 1997). In addition to specific assessment tools, there are general principles that inform the debate around best practice for risk assessment and management (Moore 1996; Titterton 2005).

Assessment tools are used in a variety of different settings and for a variety of different purposes. A child protection meeting, for example, may have the safety and well-being of a child as the issues of paramount importance. A multi-agency public protection panel (MAPPP) meeting will consider a number of issues including the risk that the offender poses to former or future victims. A drug agency or a health service organisation, with links with the criminal justice system, may have differing objectives and different understandings of the meaning and interpretation of risk. The definitions and tools used to measure them may have different criteria, be based on different models and the meetings in which they are used may involve organisations with different agendas and objectives. I now want to consider how risk is managed and this depends largely, I believe, on partnerships, working across boundaries and cooperation.

Working in partnership for increased mutual understanding

Ideas requiring closer cooperation between different parts of the criminal justice system have now been incorporated into the Criminal Justice Act 2003, blurring the divisions between custody and community penalties by the provision of custody plus (although this provision may not be activated in the near future), custody minus, intermittent custody and new generic sentences (see Wasik 2001). Many of these new organisational and legislative changes derive their energy and direction from managing issues surrounding risk.

One of the key recommendations of the Monckton Report was the concept of 'working together'. It identified the 'discontinuity of offender management' (Home Office 2006: 5) as a significant problem, emphasising the importance of professionalism in addressing it. There is 'a paramount need for workers to be clear about their own responsibilities within the process and that employers identify clear responsibilities rather than tasks and expect them to take the initiative, make decisions and act on them' (ibid.: 2). The report into the death of Victoria Climbié identifies similar key themes including the need for 'referral and communication between different agencies together with prompt and effective assessment investigations' (CHI 2003).

It is possible that many practitioners, at all levels in the criminal justice system, may have a limited understanding of how parts of the criminal justice system assess and manage risk as they tend to work alone instead of sharing the management of risk. Training for new employees does not seem to include work experience elsewhere. This is unfortunate, since one way in which practitioners can reduce their anxiety is through cooperation and understanding through working more closely with other practitioners. The Probation Service may serve as an example and I intend to look at two aspects of this: firstly, to show why partnerships are important and, secondly, to examine the aspects that need to be considered for effective working.

A Home Office paper (July 2006) advocates increasing the involvement of partners from the voluntary and community sectors with work previously carried out solely by the Probation Service. Inter-agency working and partnerships will require coordination and mutual comprehension of roles. Assessment tools will become increasingly important if offenders are not to be lost in the 'holes' within the network of organisations (Home Office 2006). Youth offending teams and the former drug treatment and testing order teams are models of multidisciplinary teams within agencies. Benefits don't just appear magically from such multidisciplinary teams. Attention needs to be paid to how different organisational cultures are reconciled within multi-agency teams to improve function and efficiency.

There needs to be greater awareness of the process of offender management, especially in the case of contestability for the new Probation/ Prison Service (NOMS). It is possible that effectiveness may decline in direct proportion to the increase in the number of agencies involved in offender management, particularly if practitioners only have experience of working in one agency. An offender manager may not possess the detailed knowledge necessary to manage effectively different inputs by different agencies. The legislation requiring increasing cooperation between different organisations, through Multi-Agency Public Protection Panels (MAPPPs) for example, has gradually drawn other agencies into this agenda. A multi-agency agenda demonstrates that risk does not exist in isolation. It is insufficient to rely on the information possessed by only one organisation, always bearing in mind the reservations about the 'panoptical society' (Hudson 2001).

The current legislation (2003) has encouraged the bringing together of risk assessment, using e-OASys, in terms of the 'possibility of area to area exchange of data and also exchange of data with the prison system' (NPS 2003: 193). Sections 325 to 327 of the 2003 Criminal Justice Act reinforce the statutory duties on the Police and Probation Services to assess and manage risk. Commonly identified factors, such as gender, ethnicity, mental health, lifestyle and type of offence, will result in further work and possibly a referral to MAPPPs (Kemshall 2002). These panels deal with the highest-risk cases and present one of the most powerful forums in which agencies come together to share information. They formalise and legalise the informal meetings that have always taken place.

Kemshall argues that MAPPPs are a 'closed professional system', resulting in little challenge from the subject or victim, leading to assessments based on opinion and conjecture rather than fact (Kemshall 2002: 107). The 2003 Act draws in other organisations by extending the duty to assess and manage risk to the Prison Service and other named bodies such as local housing authorities, health authorities, employment services, the Benefits Agency and youth offending teams. These organisations have gradually been brought into the risk agenda.

It is important to consider whether practitioners working within this 'closed system' understand the purpose and nature of evidence. There appears to be no commonality of training for participating individuals. It also seems to be true that both offender and victim are passive recipients of this process. We have seen that there are biases against certain groups, that practitioners may compound these and add a few more of their own and that, in addition, the offender is viewed as a passive and excluded individual. Parole Boards at which the offender is invited to attend might provide a model. It seems important to widen the debate from the 'closed professional system' to include an agenda that features the idea of the community and desistance theory to make the offender a more active participant in the process. I want, therefore, to consider ways in which these organisations, politicians, practitioners and perhaps offenders might enlarge and rebalance the debate, by looking at ideas of community, desistance and social capital.

Widening the debate

There are a number of narratives within the discourse of risk that are worthy of consideration, including the growing volume of discussion around the concept of community, desistance theory and the acquisition of social capital. Risk assessment must be dynamic, directly linked to actions and lead to desistance. Involving the wider community 'would require the Probation Service, for example, to broaden its remit from individualised risk to community risk management' (Kemshall 2002: 109). Commentators have touched on the problems inherent in this approach, suggesting that the definitions of community are difficult and variable and those communities that are already stretched and vulnerable may support an agenda of punishment and exclusion (Kemshall 2002; Tonry 2003; Loader and Sparks 2002). This question could be opened out to ask 'What makes people safer in the community?'

It is possible that the idea of community has more validity if seen in the context of emerging desistance theory and research and the idea of social capital (McCulloch and McNeill, this volume). Desistance research is much less well developed than the study of recidivism (Burnett and Maruna 2004). A recent review concluded that there is 'considerable conceptual discord with respect to the measurement of desistance' (Bushway et al. 2004: 88). So the ideas around social capital need exploration, definition and refinement. They also need to be seen to fit in with the current risk agenda and to assist the debate to move on.

The idea of social capital is a significant one in desistance theory. The principle is that the more an individual has to lose, the greater are the constraints against reoffending. So if risk assessment is important, then ideas around desistance should also be. It is important to redress the balance of the debate. Indeed, commentators (Maruna and Immarigeon 2004; Farrall 2002) emphasise the 'relational' nature of social capital. Practitioners may use social capital by shifting from offending behaviour towards desistance behaviour. One of the most important consequences of this principle is that social capital reverses the idea of the offender as 'a relatively passive figure' (Burnett 2004: 153) and emphasises the 'value of the practitioner/offender relationship in contributing to positive therapeutic outcomes' (Burnett 2004: 173–4). This may in turn also involve a dialogue about the 'offender as citizen' (Gregory 2006: 63). The debate therefore becomes wider and asks practitioners and policy makers to look beyond the risk agenda. 'Offenders can be and are changed not only by manipulating threat but also by increasing their legitimate opportunities. It is poor science and poor public policy to ignore this fact' (Maruna and Immarigeon 2004: ix).

Conclusion

This chapter does not advocate the abandonment of risk assessment as a method of allocating resources. The public is entitled to expect proper supervision of dangerous offenders. There is, perhaps, a need to rebalance the system towards a consideration of individual desistance factors, a return to proportionality and rigorous cooperation between agencies, particularly in using risk assessment tools and preparing practitioners to engage with differing interagency agendas and cultures. Opportunities for learning about the principles of risk assessment across agency boundaries could be provided by implementing exchanges between organisations.

As public concern about risk increases, governments, through the agency of the criminal justice system in particular, fail to meet the growing expectations. Specific serious offences are translated into general systemic failure. Concerns about working with a risk-based penology centre around the fear of incorrect designations of the level of risk and failure to review this in the light of changing circumstances. In this drive towards safety, proportionality, human rights, bias against particular groups and cultural awareness may be lost. Assessment tools need to be applied by reflective practitioners with a clear and powerful ethical belief system.

In summary, this chapter has sought to examine how working in a 'risk society' has placed increased responsibilities on the criminal justice system and widened its remit, calling on practitioners to produce certainty out of uncertainty and clarity out of the chaos of human lives. Scientific tools can help but cannot produce certainty. There is a danger that the focus on risk across the spectrum excludes or marginalises other important perspectives and silences voices that need to be heard. We need to restore balance by shifting emphasis from the instrument of assessment to the process of assessment by professional and critically reflective practitioners in public protection.

An examination of risk raises a number of important issues that need to be addressed by criminal justice agencies as a whole and not just the individual practitioner, although the issues may not be the same for both. How will agencies in general deal with the way in which political aspirations and public perceptions affect them in theory and in practice?

Will adherence to the current business model and assessment tools create more effective services? Both the organisation and the critical practitioner need to ask questions about social capital. What is meant by it? How may it help with not only the management of risk but ultimately with desistance from offending? In turn, this may lead to a re-evaluation of the importance of the therapeutic relationship between practitioner and offender, and to questions about how such a relationship is defined and its impact evaluated. Part of that relationship may raise questions about the balancing of human rights of both offender and victim.

Discussion questions

1 What ethical imperatives need to be considered when intervening in offenders' lives?
2 How do practitioners cooperate effectively and ensure that they are aware of the different agendas and meanings within organisations?
3 What is effective in working with offenders and does this take practitioners beyond the risk agenda?

Further reading

Gorman, K. *et al.* (2006) *Constructive Work with Offenders*. London: Jessica Kingsley. The editors, of this book, together with their co-contributors, are experienced practitioners, academics and writers. The book is a guide to constructive work with offenders, together with issues and dilemmas raised by current thinking.

Hudson, B. (2003) *Justice in the Risk Society*. London: Sage. This book is a useful guide to the elevation of risk to its place of prominence in the criminal justice system and explores the ethical and legal questions that arise.

Kemshall, H. (2003) *Understanding Risk in Criminal Justice*. Maidenhead: Open University Press. Hazel Kemshall has written many books and articles around the concept of risk and is a leading authority on the subject. This book synthesises ideas around risk assessment tools together with ethical and practical issues.

Moore, B. (1996) *Risk Assessment: A Practitioner's Guide to Predicting Harmful Behaviour*. London: Whiting & Birch. The author deals in a very practical way with the issues that surround sound risk assessments across a number of settings. There are general principles to be followed and plenty of practice examples: a very sound book with which to begin.

References

Bhui, S. (1999) 'Race, racism and risk assessment: linking theory to practice with black mentally disordered offenders', *Probation Journal*, 46 (3): 171–81.

Bottoms, A., Rex, S. and Robinson, G. (eds) (2004) *Alternatives to Prison: Options for an Insecure Society*. Cullompton: Willan.

Bowling, B. and Phillips, C. (2002) 'Racism, ethnicity, crime and criminal justice', in M. Maguire, R. Morgan and R. Rainer (eds), *Oxford Handbook of Criminology*. Oxford: Oxford University Press.

Burnett, R. (2004) 'One-to-one ways of promoting desistence: In search of an Evidence Base', in R. Burnett and C. Roberts (eds) *What Works in Probation and Youth Justice: Developing Evidence-based Practice*. Cullompton: Willan.

Burnett, R. and Maruna, S. (2004) 'So "prison works". Does it? The criminal careers of 130 men released from prison under Home Secretary, Michael Howard', *Howard Journal*, 43 (4): 390–404.

Bushway, S.D., Brame, R. and Paternoster, R. (2004) 'Connecting recidivism: measuring changes in criminality over the lifespan', in S. Maruna and R. Immarigeon (eds), *After Crime and Punishment: Pathways to Offender Reintegration*. Cullompton: Willan.

Chui, W.H. and Nellis, M. (eds) (2003) *Moving Probation Forward: Evidence, Arguments and Practice*. Harlow: Longman.

Commission for Health Improvement (CHI) (2003) *Victoria Climbié Inquiry Report. Key Findings of the Self Audits of NHS Organisations, Social Services Departments and Police Forces*. Available online at: http://www.chi.nhs.uk (last accessed 1 August 2006).

Cowburn, M. (2006) 'Constructive work with male sex offenders: male forms of life, language games and change', in K. Gorman *et al.* (eds), *Constructive Works with Offenders*. London: Jessica Kingsley.

Cullen, E. (2005) Review of *Room to Roam: England's Irish Travellers*, by Calm Power, published by Action Group for Irish Youth, in *Probation Journal*, 52 (1). See online: http://www.irish.org.uk (last accessed 1 August 2006).

Daily Mail (2006) '100 freed early to rape and murder', *Daily Mail*, 17 April.

Dominelli, L. (2006) 'Dangerous constructions: black offenders in the criminal justice system', in K. Gorman *et al.* (eds), *Constructive Work with Offenders*. London: Jessica Kingsley.

Eadie, T. and Winwin Sein, S. (2005/6) 'When the going gets tough, will the tough get going: retaining staff through challenging times', *Vista*, 10 (3): 171–8.

Farrall, S. (2002) *Rethinking What Works with Offenders: Probation, Social Context and Desistance from Crime*. Cullompton: Willan.

Farrow, K. (2004) 'Still committed after all these years? Morale in the modern-day probation service', *Probation Journal*, 51 (3): 206–20.

Fraser, D. (2006) *A Land Fit for Criminals: An Insider's View of Crime, Punishment and Justice in the UK*. Lewes: Book Guild.

Garland, D. (2001) *The Culture of Crime Control: Crime and Social Order in Contemporary Society*. Oxford: Oxford University Press.

Gorman, K., Gregory, M., Hayles, M. and Parton, N. (eds) (2006) *Constructive Work with Offenders*. London: Jessica Kingsley.

Gregory, M. (2006) 'The offender as citizen: socially inclusive strategies for working with offenders within the community', in K. Gorman *et al.* (eds), *Constructive Work with Offenders*. London: Jessica Kingsley.

Hamley, I.M. (2003) 'The Offender Assessment System and Multi Cultural Probation Practice: An Evaluation'. Unpublished BA dissertation, University of Birmingham.

Hayles, M. (2006) 'Constructing safety: a collaborative approach to managing risk and building responsibility', in K. Gorman *et al.* (eds), *Constructive Work with Offenders*. London: Jessica Kingsley.

Her Majesty's Inspectorate of Probation (HMIP) (2006a) *An Independent Review of a Serious Further Offence Case: Damien Hanson and Elliot White*. London: HMIP.

Her Majesty's Inspectorate of Probation (HMIP) (2006b) *An Independent Review of a Serious Further Offence Case: Anthony Rice*. London: HMIP.

Home Office (2005) *Public Protection Framework: Risk of Harm and MAPPA Thresholds*. London: NPD.

Home Office (2006) *Rebalancing the Criminal Justice System in Favour of the Law-Abiding Majority: Cutting Crime, Reducing Reoffending and Protecting the Public*. London: Home Office.

Hudson, B. (2001) 'Punishment, rights and difference: defending justice in the risk society', in K. Stenson and R.R. Sullivan (eds), *Crime, Risk and Justice: The Politics of Crime Control in Liberal Democracies*. Cullompton: Willan.

Hudson, B. (2002) 'Punishment and control', in M. Maguire, R. Morgan and R. Rainer (eds), *Oxford Handbook of Criminology*. Oxford: Oxford University Press, pp. 233–63.

Hudson, B. (2003) *Justice in the Risk Society*. London: Sage.

Hudson, B. and Bramhall, G. (2005) 'Assessing the "Other": constructions of "Asianness" in risk assessments by probation officers', *British Journal of Criminology*, 45: 721–74.

Kemshall, H. (1995) Risk in probation practice: the hazards and dangers of supervision', *Probation Journal*, 42 (2): 67–72.

Kemshall, H. (1996) *Reviewing Risk: A Review of Research on the Assessment and Management of Risk and Dangerousness: Implications for Policy and Practice in the Probation Service*. London: Home Office.

Kemshall, H. (1997) 'Offender risk and probation practice', in H. Kemshall and J. Pritchard (eds), *Good Practice in Risk Assessment and Risk Management*. Vols. 1 and 2. London: Jessica Kingsley.

Kemshall, H. (1998a) 'Defensible decisions for risk or "it's the doers wot get the blame"', *Probation Journal*, 45 (2): 67–72.

Kemshall, H. (1998b) *Risk in Probation Practice*. Aldershot: Ashgate.

Kemshall, H. (2001) 'Researching risk in the probation service', in C.J. Finer and G.L. Hundt (eds), *The Business of Research: Issues of Policy and Practice*. Oxford: Blackwell.

Kemshall, H. (2002) 'Risk, public protection and justice', in D. Ward, J. Scott and M. Lacey (eds), *Probation: Working for Justice*. Oxford: Oxford University Press.

Kemshall, H. (2003) *Understanding Risk in Criminal Justice*. Maidenhead: Open University Press.

Kemshall, H. and Maguire, M. (2003) 'Sex offenders, risk penality and the problem of disclosure', in A. Matravers (ed.), *Sex Offenders in the Community: Managing and Reducing the Risks*. Cullompton: Willan.

Loader, I. and Sparks, R. (2002) 'Contemporary landscapes of crime order, and control, governance risk and globalisation', in M. Maguire, R. Morgan and R. Rainer (eds), *Oxford Handbook of Criminology*. Oxford: Oxford University Press.

McIvor, G., Murray, C. and Jamieson, J. (2004) 'Desistance from crime: is it different for women and girls?', in S. Maruna and R. Immarigeon (eds), *After Crime and Punishment: Pathways to Integration*. Cullompton: Willan.

Mann, S. (project manager) *et al.* (2002) *Offender Assessment System (OASys)*. London: Home Office.

Maruna, S. and Immarigeon, R. (eds) (2004) *After Crime and Punishment: Pathways to Offender Reintegration*. Cullompton: Willan.

Mohammed, N. and NPD (2002) *National Probation Service Briefing Document: Introduction to OASys*. London: NPD.

Moore, B. (1996) *Risk Assessment: A Practitioner's Guide to Predicting Harmful Behaviour*. London: Whiting & Birch.

National Intelligence Model – see: http://www.police.uk/nim2/ (accessed 25 June 2006).

Nellis, M. (2002) 'Community justice, time and the new national probation service', *Howard Journal of Criminal Justice*, 41: 59–86.

Nottinghamshire Drug Agencies (2004) *Common Client Assessment Tool*. Nottingham: Nottinghamshire Drug Agencies.

NPS (August 2003) *National Probation Service Bulletin*, issue 14. Available at: http://probation.homeoffice.gov.uk/files/pdf/NPD_Bulletin_14.pdf.

PC10/2005, *Public Protection Framework: Risk of Harm and MAPPA Thresholds*. London: Home Office.

PC15/2006, *Independent Review of Serious Offence Case*. London: Home Office.

Power, C. (2003) 'Irish travellers: ethnicity, racism and pre-sentence reports', *Probation Journal*, 50 (3): 252–76.

Richards, S.C. and Jones, R.S. (2004) 'Beating the perpetual incarceration machine: overcoming structural impediments to re-entry', in S. Maruna and R. Immarigeon (eds), *After Crime and Punishment: Pathways to Integration*. Cullompton: Willan.

Robinson, G. (2003) 'Risk and risk assessment', in W.H. Chui and M. Nellis (eds), *Moving Probation Forward: Evidence, Arguments and Practice*. Harlow: Longman.

Robinson, G. and Dignan, J. (2004) 'Sentence management', in A. Bottoms, S. Rex, and G. Robinson (eds), *Alternatives to Prison: Options for an Insecure Society*. Cullompton: Willan.

Singer, L. (2004) *Reassurance Policing: An Evaluation of the Local Management of Community Safety*, Home Office Research Study No. 288. London: Home Office.

Strachan, R. and Tallant, C. (1997) 'Improving judgement and appreciating bias within the risk assessment process', in H. Kemshall and J. Pritchard (eds), *Good Practice in Risk Assessment and Risk Management 2: Protection, Rights and Responsibilities*. London: Jessica Kingsley.

Thompson, N. (2006) *Promoting Workplace Learning*: Bristol: BASW/Policy Press.

Titterton, M. (2005) *Risk and Risk Taking in Health and Social Welfare*. London: Jessica Kingsley.

Tomlinson, K. (2003), *Effective Interagency Working: A Review of the Literature and Examples from Practice*, Local Government Research Report No. 40. Slough: National Foundation for Educational Research (NFER).

Tonry, M. (ed.) (2003) *Confronting Crime: Crime Control Policy under New Labour*. Cullompton: Willan.

Uggen, C., Manza, J. and Behrens, A. (2004) 'Less than average citizen: stigma, role transition and the civic reintegration of convicted felons', in S. Maruna and R. Immarigeon (eds), *After Crime and Punishment: Pathways to Offender Reintegration*. Cullompton: Willan.

Walklate, S. (2004) *Gender, Crime and Criminal Justice*, 2nd edn. Cullompton: Willan.

Wasik, M. (2001) *Emmins on Sentencing*, 4th edn. London: Blackstone Press.

Webster, C.D., Douglas, K.S., Eaves, D. and Hart, S.D. (1997) *HCR-20: Assessing Risk for Violence (version 2)*. Burnaby, BC: Mental Health Law and Policy Institute, Simon Fraser University.

Chapter 11

Enforcement and compliance

*Amanda Loumansky, Anthony Goodman
and Simon Feasey*

Introduction

This chapter will plot the development of the enforcement and performance
culture within criminal justice with a particular emphasis on the Probation
Service. However, a broader perspective will be considered in debating how
this impacts on decision-making and case management within multi-agency
approaches to working with offenders. This has been neatly summarised by
Garland:

> In the new framework rehabilitation is viewed as a means of managing
> risk, not a welfarist end in itself. If a treatment programme does not
> work, one can revert to other, more effective means, such as close
> supervision or custody. The contemporary emphasis on rigorous
> 'breach' procedures ... serves precisely this function. (2001: 176)

Background

This chapter is being written at a curious time in terms of criminal justice
practice. When New Labour was elected in 1997 they continued with the
Conservative White Paper that had been published just before the general
election in that year, passing the Crime Sentences Act 1997 that led to
mandatory life sentences for some serious repeat offences. Probation training
was resuscitated under New Labour (it had ceased in 1995), although not
to be based within social work. The Conservatives' attempts to toughen up
the Probation Service moved on seamlessly with Jack Straw, the Labour
Home Secretary, implementing a third version of National Standards for
the Supervision of Offenders that was even tougher than those that had
endured before (National Standards are discussed later in this chapter).
However, there was a consequence to this toughening up of sentences and
probation supervision in that the prison population grew steadily until
in January 2007 the Home Secretary was forced to write to judges asking

them not to send offenders to prison unless they really felt that they had to.

The irony was that the *Daily Mail* was then able to display a headline 'Don't jail any more criminals' (24 January 2007) with the message above: 'In a desperate day for justice, with all jails full, the Lord Chancellor, Attorney General and Home Secretary issue plea to judges ...' Thus right (of centre) thinking citizens were reminded that the government had failed to build more prisons to warehouse these felons. In *The Guardian*, on the same day, the story was relegated to a single column on page 4 under the less dramatic headline: 'Reid urges courts to send fewer people to jail'. In this commentary the statistic was given that the prison numbers had gone through the 80,000 barrier with 500 being held in emergency police cells. It would appear that getting tough on crime is good publicity as long as the policy doesn't backfire on the policy makers.

With the prison population an enduring concern for the Home Office, any discussion of National Standards and enforcement within offender management must take account of the divergent criminal justice priorities associated with rehabilitation, punishment and public protection. The tensions and contradictions inherent within criminal justice processes are similarly played out within the enforcement and compliance culture. It is only with the development of a sound understanding of the legislative framework, an awareness of the current National Standards and associated implementation guidance, and clarity regarding the extent to which professional decision-making is bound by the appropriate use of discretion that practitioners can begin to manage these tensions effectively.

The potentially devastating impact of a failure in the supervision of offenders by the Probation Service has been highlighted by a number of high-profile serious offences taking place (see Jewkes, this volume). On 6 December 2006 *The Guardian* newspaper reported that 'Criminals under the supervision of the probation service have been convicted of nearly 100 murders and more than 500 other serious violent and sexual offences, including rape, over the last two years'. Harry Fletcher of NAPO, the probation union, responded in the same article that '... the level and nature of the reoffending was not surprising given the previous convictions and backgrounds of those on probation.' According to Hudson:

> Criminal justice is about risk management in the sense that though risks might not be able to be eliminated, they can be kept within reasonable levels, and can be reduced where they can be anticipated. This essentially means that risks must be balanced: the risk to the public of being victimised must be balanced against the risk to offenders (actual and potential) of underserved restriction of liberty or other form of deprivation. We are all of us, obviously, both potential victims and potential offenders at risk therefore both of undeserved burdens of punishment and at risk of harm by our fellows. (Hudson 2004: 46)

Much of the current debate has on the one hand focused on the perceived failure of the Probation Service to keep its house in order – and on the other the removal of discretion when even relatively minor breaches occur. This chapter will explore the practice issues that arise when an offender fails to comply with the requirements of a statutory order. Ashworth (2004), writing about the Criminal Justice Act 2003, contended that 'many current policies are not supported either by principle or by evidence of effectiveness'. He catalogued a number of criminal justice acts on the statute since the millennium and examined the need to safeguard human rights when the government proclaimed that all changes were designed to rebalance the system in favour of the victim. Citing evidence that more and longer custodial sentences have a marginal deterrent effect Ashworth pointed out that the crime rate was dropping before the rate of imprisonment began to rise sharply. In short: '[T]he notion of "rebalancing" the system in favour of victims [is used by the government] in order to justify changes that are unlikely to benefit victims, and which are problematic on other grounds' (Ashworth 2004).

The introduction of National Standards – a brief context

The climate of enforcement and National Standards that currently prevails within offender management can be traced back legally to the passing of the Criminal Justice Act 1991. Prior to that the regulation of the probation order had been located within a relatively loose legal context as indicated by the Power of Criminal Courts Act 1973, section 2(6), which stated that an offender should:

> keep in touch with the probation officer responsible for his or her supervision in accordance with such instructions as s/he may from time to time be given by that officer and should notify him or her of any change of address.

Although it was the case that the Home Office had introduced National Standards for Community Service in 1989, maintaining contact with offenders on probation orders reflected the lack of specificity and detail surrounding enforcement and breach, and was still generally determined by the traditional culture of 'advise, assist and befriend' in a legal context within which the probation order was not located as a punishment of the court. However, within a rapidly changing penal environment which witnessed a shift from welfare to justice principles within sentencing and the primacy of 'just deserts' as a sentencing rationale, the Criminal Justice Act 1991 introduced the probation order as a legitimate punishment of the court. As a mechanism for developing a more punitive and rigorous framework for community supervision the Act also introduced the facility for the Secretary of State to regulate the supervision of offenders and the functions of probation officers. Section 15(1) states:

The Secretary of State may make rules for regulating:

(a) the supervision of offenders who are subject to probation orders;
(b) the arrangements to be made under Schedule 3 to the 1973 Act for persons who are subject to community service orders to perform work under those orders and the performance by such persons of such work;
(c) the monitoring of the whereabouts of persons who are subject to curfew orders;
(d) without prejudice to the generality of paragraphs (a) to (c) above, the functions of the responsible officers of such persons as are mentioned in those paragraphs.

(CJA 1991: 15(1))

Thus the legal framework for National Standards was born and the first version emerged in 1992. They intended to articulate a set of requirements that offenders were expected to conform to and that probation officers were required to enforce, with the clear intention that failures of offenders to comply would result in breach action and a return to court. However, the development of an enforcement culture within the Probation Service was resisted by the service at all levels and for many practitioners and managers the impact initially was relatively marginal. Traditional welfare approaches to engaging with offenders were well embedded and there was overt hostility to the attempt to develop a law enforcement ethos within probation practice. Consequently National Standards maintained a relatively low profile in terms of service priorities at a both practice and management level.

In order to address this early resistance to the implementation of the standards the Her Majesty's Inspectorate of Probation (HMIP) at the Home Office undertook a number of Quality and Effectiveness reports throughout the 1990s which revealed the relative failure of the Probation Service to implement National Standards. By 1998 the service was subject to substantial criticism from the Chief Inspector and the Home Affairs Select Committee on Alternatives to Custody. The Home Affairs Committee Report examined community sentences in 1998 and commented:

Strict enforcement of community sentences is vital if they are to represent a credible alternative to prison and retain the confidence of sentencers and the public. If community sentences are to be credible they must be enforced stringently. It is therefore entirely unacceptable that local probation services are, on average, taking breach action in accordance with the National Standards relating to probation orders in barely a quarter of cases ... Consideration should be given to reworking the funding formula for local services to provide an incentive for services to meet this target. (Home Affairs Committee Third Report 1998, para. 87: xxvi)

The report emphasised the fact that probation services were failing to comply with National Standards 'in barely a quarter of cases'. There was a threat that probation funds should be contingent on probation officers fulfilling National Standards requirements.

In response to these criticisms the Association of Chief Officers of Probation (ACOP) developed an action plan in 1999 which resulted in a series of ACOP audits undertaken by the Criminal Policy Research Unit at the South Bank University. The creation of the National Probation Service in 2001 provided the opportunity to set targets in relation to the enforcement of National Standards and the first strategic statement emerging form the newly formed Probation Directorate included 'Enforcement' as Stretch Objective number five:

The confidence of ministers and the public in the NPS is critically dependent on the extent to which staff are enforcing the terms and conditions of statutory orders and licences. This goes to the heart of proper punishment and the rule of law by upholding the authority of the courts and Parole Board in their sentencing and early release decisions. (Home Office 2001)

A cash-linked Key Performance Indicator to meet National Standards in 90 per cent of cases was instrumental in ensuring a rapid and sustained improvement in the audited figures so that by 2004 most probation areas were achieving the required standard. A second strategic document from that year, *Bold Steps*, was able to refer to recent research undertaken by MORI with magistrates which included an assessment of their confidence with the Probation Service's approach to enforcement:

Prior to the national service, we know that many magistrates had little confidence about probation's part in this process as practice varied hugely across England and Wales. However, the increase in public and sentencer confidence has generated a certainty of action. Practice is now consistently high across the service. A recent national survey of magistrates shows that eight out of ten respondents agree that the probation service is effective at enforcing community sentences. (Home Office 2004)

There have been a number of revisions to National Standards since 1992 which have generally resulted in a tighter and enhanced punitive enforcement culture which has been associated with a more rapid return of offenders to court for breach, the imposition of greater penalties as a consequence of breach action and the reduction in the extent to which probation officers are able to exercise their professional discretion when making decisions around enforcement.

National Standards 1992 stated: 'No two offenders are identical. It is essential that supervision takes adequate account of the individual needs and circumstances of each person' (NS 1992: 3). They also commented: 'Supervision is *challenging and skilful* requiring *professional social work in the field of criminal justice*' (NS 1992: 1). The use of italics is in the original document. Since then, revised and substantially different versions of the standards have been published in 1995, 2000, 2002, 2005 and most recently in 2007. The changes have reflected the shift of the Probation Service toward a greater law enforcement culture; an opening statement from the 2000 version states: 'WE ARE A LAW ENFORCEMENT AGENCY. It's what we are. It's what we do' (Paul Boateng, Minister for Prisons and Probation: NS 2000).

More recently the standards have been significantly amended to take account of the restructuring of the delivery of services in accordance with the National Offender Management Model and in particular the introduction of the tiering of offenders by risk. Within this context, expectations of offenders and offender managers are differentiated according to the level of risk that individual offenders present to the public. Within the timeframe of 15 years probation practice has therefore shifted from that in which the nature of the relationship between an offender and supervisor was largely defined by an individual negotiation dependent on the competing demands of the therapeutic relationship and the statutory requirements of an order to a culture of practice which incorporates a closely prescribed set of requirements within which punishment and enforcement are prioritised and which are reported on within a highly managed audit process. Inevitably this has impacted on the nature of the relationship between offenders and supervisors and raises a series of key practice issues that need debating and resolving.

Enforcement and effective practice

Probably the single most important debate with regard to the development of the enforcement culture is its relationship with that other underpinning paradigm relevant to the development of the modern Probation Service and NOMS: What Works? While there is good evidence that the effective implementation of stringent National Standards has resulted in greater confidence by sentencers in the capabilities of the Probation Service, is there also a body of evidence that the enforcement initiatives have impacted positively on the rehabilitative agenda which is also a key part of the NOMS mission statement? Working with offenders has always required supervisors to achieve a careful balance between the care and control functions implicit within their professional role and there are concerns that the development of National Standards over the last decade has tilted this balance too far in the direction of punishment and control and that this is potentially at the cost of undermining the opportunities for reform and rehabilitation and, ultimately, reducing reconviction rates. The debate is complex but worth pursuing.

A useful starting point is some of the research published in relation to the efficacy of effective enforcement within what was previously called community service (now known as 'unpaid work'). Research published by Gill McIvor found that stricter approaches to managing attendance improved compliance within community service schemes in Scotland and that clear communication about enforcement helped to develop a more positive approach to compliance (McIvor 1995). From a policy development perspective, these findings were timely given the recent implementation of the first version of National Standards following the 1991 Criminal Justice Act. There was also an obvious and clear association with some of the underpinning principles of pro-social modelling that was also developing greater currency during the 1990s. Reinforcing pro-social behaviours such as compliance and challenging anti-social responses within a negotiated relationship where expectations about contact and compliance are both explicitly stated and consistently maintained provides a professional rationale for a culture of practice in which consistent enforcement can potentially be seen as part of a therapeutic engagement (Trotter 2006).

In 2001 the Home Office published findings that suggested a link between effective enforcement and a reduction in reconviction rates: 'Where appropriate enforcement action was taken, offenders had a lower than predicted reconviction rate. Where not all enforcement action was taken, offenders had a higher than predicted reconviction rate' (May and Wadwell 2001). This was, however, a small-scale study and an additional finding concluded that enforcement action was more likely to be taken against offenders with a lower likelihood of reconviction. It is also important to maintain a distinction between enforcement and breach action; appropriate enforcement may or may not lead to breach proceedings depending on how an offender responds to the process. However, there was emerging evidence that the development of stricter National Standards was resulting in the implementation of more rapid breach sanctions which in turn served to undermine the possible rehabilitative impact of the supervision process. In 2000 the *Probation Journal* published an article that raised concerns about the potential impact of the breach culture on the effectiveness of accredited programmes. Research into programme effectiveness had clearly demonstrated that those offenders who started a programme and failed to complete were at a raised level of risk of reconviction, greater than those who had completed and also greater than those who had a comparable profile but did not undertake the programme (Hedderman and Hearnden 2000). It was therefore recognised that increasing compliance with and completion of programmes was potentially a prerequisite for impacting on risk of reconviction. However, the more rigorous and stringent National Standards were at risk of undermining the opportunities for increasing completion rates: 'Yet each revision of National Standards has been directed at reducing the number of failures an offender is permitted and increasing the chances of an order being terminated' (Hedderman and Hearnden 2000). Concerns about the propensity for immediate breach were reinforced by a Home Office on-line report published in 2003 which investigated the impact of differential breach rates across probation areas. When comparisons were drawn between 'high' and 'low' breach rate probation areas, very little difference was found in terms of actual reconviction rates. The overall reconviction rate for breached offenders remained high: 'Over three-quarters of offenders breached at court were reconvicted within two years. This group was more likely to be reconvicted than those who completed their orders successfully or had orders terminated early for good behaviour' (Hearnden and Millie 2003). There were also some indications that those who were initially breached but who continued to be supervised by the Probation Service, became compliant and consequently avoided breach action, were reconvicted at a lower rate. The authors' final conclusion was indicative of a shift in thinking within the enforcement arena: 'One option may be to explore ways of rewarding good attendance and of addressing noncompliance without recourse to breach action' (Hearnden and Millie 2003).

This theme was picked up by a Home Office that was also acutely concerned with the ever rising prison population and the increasing severity of sentencing within the courts. As a consequence Probation Circular 43/2004 *Managing Compliance and Enforcement of Community Penalties* was published and was intended to reframe the enforcement debate within a framework of compliance and order completion:

> The NPD has an overall compliance target of 70% for 2004/05 and an interim target of 65% by December 2004 has been agreed with the Prime Minister's Delivery Unit. Enforcement of unacceptable absences must still be pursued robustly but attention also needs to be given to reducing the number of offenders who need enforcement action. (PC 43/2004)

The circular detailed approaches that might mitigate against early returns to court and the imposition of custodial sentences. These included close consultations with managers over issues of acceptable/unacceptable absence, the continuation of supervison after the initiation of breach and a number of strategies designed to promote greater compliance, including:

- use of appointment cards;
- working to reduce the barriers to attendance as part of the management of the order;
- scheduling appointments to occur at a set time each week or to fit in with other essential commitments such as work, Community Drug Team appointments, etc.;

- providing bus fares or transporting offenders;
- using technology such as e-mail/texting appointment reminders, use of alarm system on mobile phones, reminder phone calls;
- reminder letters, home visiting, issuing diaries/weekly diary sheets;
- in appropriate cases officers/compliance officers visiting on day of failure to attend;
- ensuring the offender is engaged in the supervision plan – establishing what he/she needs to do to reduce *their* reoffending to achieve *their* goals;
- use of volunteers and mentors to support attendance.

(PC 43/2004)

The use of discretion

One of the more contested debates within any discussion of the application of National Standards is the extent to which individual offender managers are legitimately able to exercise a degree of professional discretion within their decision-making. Clearly National Standards were introduced partly to ensure consistency and fairness within the delivery of services to offenders and to ensure that offenders had a clear and common understanding of what was expected of them during a period of supervision and what the consequences would be of failing to achieve this. However, the use of discretion within probation and criminal justice practice generally is well established and reflects the need to respond to unique situations and circumstances in a manner that reflects the specific nuances of the case. Particular offenders have distinct needs and these might impact on how an offender manager makes decision about resource allocation, types of intervention and who does what, when and how. In order to develop a service that properly respects the diversity of the offender population, offender managers need to be sensitive to the divergent needs, concerns, cultures and contexts of individual offender experience.

How this actually translates into clearly prescribed parameters for the application of professional discretion within enforcement is, however, somewhat unclear. It is useful to return to an early probation circular that discussed this issue:

> In supervising offenders, probation staff will need to continue to use their professional discretion and judgement taking into account all the circumstances of the case. The Standards should be applied using the service's knowledge of an offender, the risks posed and the offender's response to supervision to date. (PC 24/2000)

The circular indicated that discretion should be applied on a case-by-case basis and that any decision made should be recorded on the case file. The area of practice that has most commonly required the exercise of discretion has been that of the classification of acceptable and unacceptable absence. When an offender fails to keep a required appointment he or she may offer an explanation of this failure and at that point the offender manager is required to decide whether the explanation is of sufficient credibility to justify an acceptable absence. Clearly this is a significant judgment as an unacceptable absence has consequences of a warning or breach. PC 24/2000 provided some guidance on the issue of acceptability:

> All absences should be regarded as unacceptable unless proved otherwise. Acceptable absences would include:
>
> - medical appointments notified in advance with appointment cards shown for verification;
> - unscheduled work commitments that can be verified;
> - job interviews that can be verified;
> - proven appointments with other agencies such as DSS.
>
> Unacceptable absences would include:
>
> - absence where no verification of reason is produced;
> - turning up too late for programmed activity without verified reason.
>
> (PC 24/2000)

Verification and providing proof were identified as key elements of an acceptable absence. Recently National Standards 2007 have been published along with some guidance on implementation. There is little detail in terms of this key issue of acceptable absence beyond:

> The Offender Manager forms a view about the reasonableness or otherwise of any excuse provided by an offender for any apparent failure to comply. Judgements as to reasonableness take account of the nature of the failure, the circumstances of it and the circumstances of the offender. (NS 2007)

This perhaps suggests a greater opportunity to draw on professional decision-making provided it is undertaken with proper consideration for the demands of risk management and public protection. However, as a counterbalance to this there is a comment in the introductory comment which states:

> NOMS recognises that there are infinite combinations of sentence, offender characteristics and circumstances. It expects these standards will be met in all but exceptional individual circumstances, and that any decision to depart from them in any case *will be endorsed, with reasons, by the relevant line manager* (emphasis in original) on the individual offender case record. (NS 2007)

In addition to classifications of absence type, the other key area in which offender managers might exercise a degree of discretion is within the overall sequencing of the various interventions that form a part of the community sentence and plan. Given the nature of the sentencing framework prescribed by the Criminal Justice Act 2003, it is quite possible for an offender to receive a community sentence which has a complex range of separate interventions designed to punish, change, help and control. It is the role of the offender manager to ensure that these interventions are delivered in a timely fashion that will ensure that objectives and outcomes are achieved. 'Interventions and activities should be sequenced as necessary in order to secure maximum compliance and co-operation, and to maximise the effectiveness of each' (NS 2007). Further detail is provided within the Offender Management Model Section 9:

> Which interventions are selected and drawn down for each offender will depend in part on the requirements of the sentence and in part on the assessment of the offender ... In the main, punitive interventions, which will form part of the structure of the sentence itself, will need to be implemented immediately, or almost immediately, after commencement. In one shape or form, they will normally span the whole sentence. So, imprisonment, hostel placements and curfews take effect immediately; unpaid work, intermittent custody and Attendance Centre attendance take effect after a short arrangements delay. If the punitive elements in the sentence are not effected briskly, the credibility of NOMS – and all of its other objectives – are put at risk. (OMM 2005)

It is therefore apparent that within the application of National Standards there is a particular emphasis on compliance and enforcement which requires offender managers to balance sometimes competing demands of rehabilitation, punishment and public protection. In order to achieve this, practitioners need to have a sound understanding of where their professional discretion lies and how this can be utilised in a fashion that ensures accountability and avoids discrimination. A useful reminder of key priorities is found in National Standards 2007 which states that the achievement of the aims of the service should be undertaken:

> with due regard to the human rights, dignity and safety of offenders, victims and partners, and that services will be respectful and responsive to the diverse needs and circumstances encountered in correctional work. The mix of aims varies from case to case, but *managing the risk of harm posed by offenders and protection of the public is always paramount.* (NS 2007, emphasis added)

Making enforcement decisions that raise the risk to the public are fraught with potential dangers. In 2003 PC Gerald Walker was killed by David

Parfitt who had recently been released on a home detention curfew with drug testing requirements attached. In the subsequent inquiry Professor Rod Morgan commented that the case had been poorly managed by the Probation Service and that failures to comply and positive drug tests had not been appropriately enforced. If the proper action had been taken Parfitt would not have been at liberty to commit the murder of PC Walker:

> I find that Parfitt's PO was applying, in contravention of the criteria set out in Probation Circular 132/2001, her own judgement of what compliance and drug use it was reasonable to expect of Parfitt, given his well-established dependence, prior to his imprisonment, on both heroin and crack cocaine. (Morgan 2004)

On this occasion 'her own judgement' had disastrous unintended consequences and the inquiry reminds practitioners of the need to prioritise public protection, to ensure a sound knowledge and understanding of the National Standards and service criteria that apply to their area of practice and to apply professional discretion in a manner that guarantees the purposes of supervison as reflected by the expectations of NOMs, the Home Office, the courts and the general public.

Learning from American exceptionalism: punitivism and the case of electronic monitoring

Criminal justice policy in the UK has a habit of following the American model rather than its European contemporaries. The prison population is incredibly high in the USA and the danger is that Britain will solidify its position as the highest user of custody in Western Europe. Indeed the Justice Secretary Jack Straw recently announced that three 'super-prisons' are to be built as part of a building and modernisation programme that would add 10,500 places by 2014, bringing the total up to 96,000 (*BBC News*, 5 December 2007).

One significant feature that has pervaded the UK criminal justice system is the pilgrimage to the USA to learn how they deal with problems within the criminal justice system. The irony here is of course that homicide figures are much worse than in this country and the US has the highest level of incarceration in the world (Jones and Newburn 2007). This exponential growth in incarceration in the USA began in the 1980s and was accompanied by the ratcheting up of punitive community sanctions, including 'intensive supervision, home confinement, with or without electronic monitoring (EM), day reporting centres, and boot camps' (Padgett *et al.* 2006: 62). This growth in the punitive apparatus was accompanied by the dissolution of rehabilitation:

> Probation and parole agencies have de-emphasised the social work ethos that used to dominate their work and instead present themselves as providers of inexpensive, community-based punishments, oriented towards monitoring of offenders and the management of risk. Sentencing has changed, particularly in the USA, from being a discretionary art of individualised dispositions to a much more rigid and mechanical application of penalty guidelines and mandatory sentences. (Garland 2001: 18)

Jones and Newburn 'catalogue the emergence of a strong private corrections industry in the UK' (2007: 2) as well as American slogans such as 'three strikes and you're out', 'honesty in sentencing' and 'zero tolerance policing'. These have resulted in a 'generalised shift toward a more punitive culture of control' (ibid.: 3).

An interesting area in the punitive approach to offenders is in the growth of electronic monitoring in the UK and the role of key civil servants. In a chapter entitled 'Privatising punishment', Jones and Newburn highlight the role of Hugh Marriage, Deputy Head of the Probation Unit in the Home Office. In their interview with Marriage firstly they reveal his view of the Probation Service:

> In Hugh Marriage's own words, he wanted to 'challenge the culture in the UK', particularly 'the old style unreformed probation service, the sacred cows that's existed in this country since I think probably the mid-sixties and I regard as a complete bane of my professional life. They're nice people but they're completely ineffective'. (Ibid.: 57)

Instead Marriage describes arranging for UK staff to fly out to the USA to see how they organised electronic monitoring in order to sell it in this country. To politicians and magistrates it was sold as a punitive endeavour and to NAPO (the probation officers' union) it was portrayed as a means of reducing the prison population and for its rehabilitational aspects.

Padgett et al. take this latter approach in their article 'Under surveillance' (2006) commenting that 'Greater technological control capacities need not always result in more control' (ibid.: 86). They argue that research on electronic monitoring in Florida's state-wide home confinement programme showed that it was effective for serious offenders and this led them to question whether this was '"bad news" for the leading theoretical interpretations for penal reform ...' (ibid.: 85).

To counter this in a 'reaction essay' Lilly (2006) argued that Padgett et al.'s research on EM did not engage in the larger picture within which EM is situated, namely that it is part of surveillance technology, which was not so evident during its development. Its use has become a political rather than evidenced-based decision, it is part of what he described as the 'corrections commercial complex' and the vendors of EM 'are more interested in profit than rehabilitation or reintegration of criminals into the community' (ibid.: 93).

Nellis (2006), in a second reaction essay to Padgett *et al.*, while conceding that EM adds an element of control that probation supervision cannot provide, commented that EM on its own has no rationale for having a rehabilitational effect. Describing their research as 'muddled', he differentiated between EM on its own and EM 'in conjunction with rehabilitative programmes' (ibid.: 105). Padgett *et al.* argued that the ethics of EM should be sidelined until the effectiveness of this approach was established, but Nellis is uncomfortable with this. He argued that 'what works' and 'what's right' should not be easily separated. This debate on the importance of an ethical approach to outcomes is important as increased levels of punishment and surveillance are incorporated into the UK. There is an important debate to be had as the Probation Service is stripped of its ability to engage with offenders and is substituted with simplistic punishment outcomes. A further complication is the changing relationship between the Probation Service and the voluntary and private sector – both 'not-for-profit' and profit-making concerns. O'Malley (2004) analyses this and highlights the straitjacket that many organisations find themselves in as they fight for contracts and are then evaluated in terms of outputs rather than outcomes. The 'risk-oriented rational choice model' was displacing 'socially oriented and explanatory criminology' and programmes were to be based on cost-effectiveness and geared towards consumer protection (O'Malley 2001).

Voluntary sector organisations are also subject to number crunching as if they were in the statutory sector. This can be described as the 'audit explosion'. However, 'managerial rationalism' can be undermined by 'popular punitivism' and this led Hudson to argue for a 'jurisprudence of rights', essential, she believed, if justice was to survive in a risk society (Hudson 2001). Stenson (2001) has described the retreat from liberalism and the fact that many offenders are from the poorer sections of society, an inconvenient factor that risk-oriented solutions can ignore.

Joan Petersilia has written extensively on prison rehabilitation in the USA. In discussing how the ethos of parole has changed, she commented:

> Newly hired parole officers often embrace the surveillance versus the rehabilitation model of parole, along with the quasi-policing role that parole has taken on in some locales … Parole agents began to carry concealed firearms in the 1980's. Firearms are now provided in most jurisdictions and represent a major investment of training resources, agent time and administrative oversight. The programming innovations likewise represent a theme of control and supervision rather than service and assistance. (2003: 90)

Over 30 years ago the US Supreme Court considered whether a petitioner's rights to due process under the 14th Amendment applied to the parole system. In the case of *Morrisey* v. *Brewer* 408 US 47 (1972) Morrisey had pleaded guilty to fraud and was given a seven-year sentence. He was released from the Iowa State Penitentiary just over a year later. Seven months after that his parole officer submitted a report to the Iowa Board of Parole which directly led to the revocation of the parole. As a result of this Morrisey was returned to prison. The judge clarified the role of parole and pointed out that it could only take place where the individual abides by the conditions set. Before deciding the due process question, the Supreme Court examined the role of parole. The court made clear the fact that for parole to be successful the individual who was released early from prison had to 'substantially' abide by a set of rules until the end of his sentence. It was the role of the parole officer to provide guidance and assistance; however, an element of coercion existed with the threat of withdrawal of parole always available.

Conclusion

This chapter has considered the changing culture of community sentence supervision, including the impact of National Standards. This has resulted in enforcement being treated more seriously and changes in how far supervising staff are willing and able to use discretion in their contact with offenders. It has not argued that there was a 'golden age' when the balance between supervision and enforcement was appropriate. However, there has been a strong swing of the pendulum away from probation officer discretion towards targeted levels of compliance, backed by financial sanction, if staff do not comply. In addition, high-profile cases when discretion has 'backfired' on the case manager make it less likely that staff will want to expose themselves to public scrutiny in higher-risk cases. When staff are overstretched and feel stressed they are likely to fall back to fulfilling procedural requirements and become 'risk averse'.

At the time of writing it has been announced that there will be a large increase in prison building; however, the extra 10,500 places will be quickly filled if sentencers continue with their upward trajectory in sentencing offenders to custody and breach rates continue to rise. There is a difficult balancing act required for offenders to receive appropriate court orders and for professionals to be able to supervise them without 'technical' breaches resulting in offenders ending up in prison. If we are living in a less tolerant society the trick has to be for offenders to be able to pay back for their criminal behaviour without making the sanctions difficult to comply with, given that many offenders lead fairly chaotic lives.

The American experience of embracing a punitive response rather than engaging with the offender has led to a burgeoning prison population and the United Kingdom is in danger of replicating this over here. The USA has a strong, influential and private corrections industry and many of these corporations are now established in the United Kingdom. Privatising punishment may play well with the popular press but will do little to protect the public as money is diverted into building and maintaining the custodial estate at the expense of the smaller community supervisory one. The use of electronic monitoring as a means of reducing the prison population may seem attractive, but again if the public is to be protected it is not a cheap panacea at the expense of a suitably trained and professional workforce. While technological advances may have a place in a modern criminal justice system, there remains the interface between the offender and the public. The organisation which fills this space – the Probation Service, NOMS or whatever it may be re-badged as – will require staff who can recognise when offenders need positive role modelling, are under stress and/or require skilled intervention. Surveillance is an expensive commodity and even offenders deemed to be part of the 'critical few' who are managed at the highest level of risk under multi-agency public protection arrangements, need more than some form of tracking arrangement in order to protect the public. Whether probation will retain anything of its former identity or it will become totally fixated with enforcement is a key question. To protect the public it will need a workforce that is sufficiently resourced and with appropriate knowledge, values and skills. The issue is how can this message be transmitted to the public when probation has never been strong at building a public persona?

Discussion questions

1 Have the changes from a social work to an enforcement model resulted in the public becoming safer?
2 Should the United Kingdom follow the American model of high levels of incarceration?
3 Should case managers be allowed any discretion in how they supervise court orders?

Further reading

Burney, E. (2005) *Making People Behave*. Cullompton: Willan. This book charts the changes that have been taking place in England to try and enforce good behaviour. It is a useful reminder that society has become formally less tolerant towards incivilities.

Johnson, R. (2005) 'Brave new prisons: the growing social isolation of modern penal institutions', in A. Liebling and S. Maruna (eds), *The Effects of Imprisonment*. Cullompton: Willan. This chapter discusses American prisons and serves as a useful reminder of punitive approaches to criminal justice, particularly imprisonment. The discussion of 'tough technology' has a resonance with notions of enforcement and compliance.

McNeill, F. and Whyte, B. (2007) *Reducing Reoffending: Social Work and Community Justice in Scotland*. Cullompton: Willan. This book critically describes the development of work with offenders in Scotland where adherence to a social work model retains influence on practice. Research is cited that highlights the importance of relationship and the interesting question is how far will the criminal justice system there retain its differences to England and Wales?

Mair, G. and Canton, R. (2007) 'Sentencing, community penalties and the role of the probation service', in L. Gelsthorpe and R. Morgan (eds), *Handbook of Probation*. Cullompton: Willan. This chapter comments that community penalties are being used for less serious offenders while conditions have become ever more rigidly enforced. It concludes with some interesting comments on the re-emergence of the concept of relationship between offender and supervisor.

Nellis, M. (2005) 'Dim prospects: humanistic values and the fate of community justice', in J. Winstone and F. Pakes (eds), *Community Justice: Issues for Probation and Criminal Justice*. Cullompton: Willan. Nellis examines the concept of community justice and the 'new punitiveness' in England and Wales in relation to humanistic-rehabilitative discourse. He points out the dangers of 'soulless managerialism' and the dangers of liberalism being discredited.

References

Ashworth, A. (2004) 'Criminal Justice Act 2003: Part 2: Criminal Justice Reform – Principles, Human Rights and Public Protection', *Criminal Law Review*, July, 516–32.

Garland, D. (2001) *The Culture of Control: Crime and Social Order in Contemporary Society*. Oxford: Oxford University Press.

Hearnden, I. and Millie, A. (2003) *Investigating Links between Probation Enforcement and Reconviction*, Home Office On-line Report 41/03.

Hedderman, C. and Hearnden, I. (2000) 'The missing link: effective enforcement and effective supervision', *Probation Journal*, 47 (2): 126–8.

HM Inspectorate of Probation (2006a) *Putting Risk of Harm in Context*. London: Home Office.

HM Inspectorate of Probation (2006b) *An Independent Review of a Serious Further Offence Case: Anthony Rice*. London: Home Office.

Home Affairs Committee (28 July 1998) *Alternatives to Prison Sentences*, Third Report, Volumes I and II. London: Stationery Office.

Home Office (1995, 2000, 2002, 2005, 2007) *National Standards*. London: Home Office.

Home Office (2001) *New Choreography – A Strategic Framework 2001–4*. London: Home Office.

Home Office (2004) *Bold Steps – NPS Business Plan 2004–5*. London: Home Office.

Home Office (2005) *NOMS Offender Management Model 2005*. London: Home Office.

Hudson, B. (2001) 'Punishment, rights and difference: defending justice in the risk society', in K. Stenson and R. Sullivan (eds), *Crime, Risk and Justice*. Cullompton: Willan, pp. 144–72.

Hudson, B. (2004) *Justice in the Risk Society*. London: Sage.

Jones, T. and Newburn, T. (2007) *Policy Transfer and Criminal Justice: Exploring US Influence over British Crime Control Policy*. Maidenhead: Open University Press.

Lilly, J.R. (2006) 'Reaction essay: issues beyond EM reports', *Criminology and Public Policy*, 5 (1): 93–102.

McIvor, J. (1995) *Working with Offenders*. London: Jessica Kingsley.

May, C. and Wadwell, J. (2001) *Enforcing Community Penalties: The Relationship between Enforcement and Reconviction*, Home Office Findings No. 155. London: Home Office.

Morgan, R. (2004) *Report by HM Chief Inspector of Probation into the Death of Police Constable Gerald Walker*. London: Home Office.

Nellis, M. (2006) 'Surveillance, rehabilitation and electronic monitoring: getting the issues clear', *Criminology and Public Policy*, 5 (1): 103–8.

O'Malley, P. (2001) 'Policing crime risks in the neo-liberal era', in K. Stenson and R. Sullivan (eds), *Crime, Risk and Justice*. Cullompton: Willan, pp. 89–103.

O'Malley, P. (2004) *Risk, Uncertainty and Government*. London: Glasshouse Press.

Padgett, K., Bales, W. and Blomberg, T. (2006) 'Under surveillance: an empirical test of the effectiveness and consequences of electronic monitoring', *Criminology and Public Policy*, 5 (1): 61–92.

Petersilia, J. (2003) *When Prisoners Come Home: Parole and Prisoner Re-entry*. Oxford: Oxford University Press.

Probation Circular 24/2000: *Guidance on Enforcement of Orders*. London: Home Office.

Probation Circular 43/2004: *Managing Compliance and Enforcement of Community Penalties*. London: Home Office.

Stenson, K. (2001) 'The new politics of crime control', in K. Stenson and R. Sullivan (eds), *Crime, Risk and Justice*. Cullompton: Willan, pp. 15–28.

The Guardian, Letter Page, 19 and 25 April 2004.

Trotter, C. (2006) *Working with Involuntary Clients – A Guide to Practice*, 2nd edn. London: Sage.

Chapter 12

Multi-agency practice: experiences in the youth justice system

Anna Souhami

Multi-agency practice in the criminal justice system

Over the last two decades, the criminal justice system has seen a dramatic expansion in multi-agency practice. Since the mid-1980s, the advantages of a partnership approach to crime prevention have been espoused not only by policy-makers but also by practitioners: indeed local developments initiated by agencies and practitioners over the last twenty years have been highly influential in shaping subsequent policy.[1] The emerging consensus about the benefits of multi-agency practice culminated in the Crime and Disorder Act in 1998, which made partnership work in crime prevention a statutory duty in England and Wales. The Act required local authorities, police forces, probation committees and health authorities to work together to address crime and disorder, and to consult community groups and the voluntary sector. For the first time, therefore, multi-agency work became a part of normal practice and policy – something that had been advocated by the influential Morgan Report nearly a decade earlier (Home Office 1991).

However, it is in the youth justice system where multi-agency practice is arguably most fully developed. Under the Crime and Disorder Act, both the management and delivery of youth offending services became a multi-agency responsibility. The formation of youth offending teams (YOTs) was the cornerstone of this approach. YOTs replaced the specialist teams of social workers in local authority social services 'youth justice' or 'juvenile justice' teams. They are 'stand-alone' teams, not belonging to any one department or agency, but consist of representatives from all the core agencies that work with young offenders – social workers, probation officers, police officers, and education and health authority staff – and provide scope to involve practitioners from other agencies or organisations, such as the Prison Service, local authority youth services or voluntary organisations. These staff can be seconded to the YOT, or employed directly in the YOT by the local authority. They are managed directly by a YOT manager, who can be appointed from any of the core partner agencies, and managed locally by multi-agency 'steering groups' and chief executives' departments. They are accountable nationally to the Youth Justice Board (YJB) which was also established by the Act, and which aimed to consolidate the central supervision of youth justice services which had previously been spread across several government departments. As well as being multi-agency units in themselves, YOTs work in partnership with a range of services including those across the statutory, voluntary and corporate sectors, and are linked into wider crime and disorder strategies and other multi-agency initiatives. They therefore exemplify both 'multi-agency' working, where agencies come together to address a particular problem, and 'inter-agency' working, where there is a degree of 'melding' of relations between agencies, usually resulting in new structures and forms of working (Crawford 1994, 1997).

This chapter explores the implications of experiences in the youth justice system for multi-agency strategies in addressing offending behaviour. Why has 'joined up' working come into prominence in the field of criminal justice? What are its perceived advantages? What does multi-agency work involve? And what are the potential obstacles to effective multi-agency practice?

In exploring these questions, the chapter draws on an ethnographic study of the development of a YOT in a Midlands town, which followed the transition of a social services youth justice team into a multi-agency organisation as practitioners attempted to develop new multi-agency roles and practice (Souhami 2007). This was therefore a period in which core questions about the nature and purpose of multi-agency work were at issue, and when its problems and possibilities were brought into focus.

Multi-agency practice and offending behaviour

The expansion of multi-agency strategies to address offending behaviour has developed alongside a series of shifts in thinking about crime and its management.

Firstly, towards the end of the 1980s a strategy for organising work with offenders emerged which was unconnected to traditional 'welfare' or 'justice' approaches which had previously preoccupied the criminal justice system. In line with a shift towards the 'new public management' (Hood 1991), a 'corporatist' strategy (e.g. Pratt 1989) was concerned not with transformative or moral goals, such as rehabilitation or treatment, but with managing the offending population as efficiently and effectively as possible (for example, see Feeley and Simon 1992).

This approach was underpinned by a re-emerging optimism in the possibilities of the criminal justice system as a site for intervention. An orthodoxy had developed in previous decades that the criminal justice system was not only unable to prevent reoffending (e.g. Martinson 1974), but had the potential to reinforce patterns of offending through the establishment of delinquent identities, thus doing more harm than good. However, by the end of the 1980s, increasing attention was being paid to the 'what works' agenda, which emphasised the importance of evidence and outcomes in criminal justice interventions. Evaluative research appeared to show that, if directed appropriately, some forms of intervention could be successful in reducing offending behaviour for some people (Muncie 2004; Goodman, this volume).

In this context, the identification of 'risk' factors became central to directing policy and practice. Intervention could be targeted to where it was likely to have the most impact. In the arena of youth justice, for example, the Crime and Disorder Act refocused the delivery of youth justice services towards selected 'risk conditions' associated with offending such as poor parenting, chaotic family life, truancy and school exclusion, and associating with delinquent peers (Home Office 1997).

Alongside these developments it became acknowledged that it was more effective – and cheaper – to address offending at an early stage. Parts of the criminal justice system therefore became gradually realigned towards the prevention of offending and reoffending and this came to take precedence over the goals of 'cure' or containment that had preoccupied the previous decades. Thus the 1998 Crime and Disorder Act established 'preventing offending by children and young persons' as the principal aim of the youth justice system, in which the aim was to address offending by 'nipping it in the bud' (Home Office 1997). This, however, was a particular interpretation of crime prevention, characterised by a 'robust interventionism' (Pitts 2001: 169) in which it is assumed that prevention can be achieved by targeting young people thought likely to offend and by drawing them into the system at an early stage. Indeed, not to intervene is considered harmful, and as allowing '[young people] to go on wrecking their own lives as well as disrupting their families and communities' (Home Office 1997).

Finally, there was a shift in thinking about the nature of offending behaviour itself. A consensus emerged that crime is a complex phenomenon with multiple causes and effects. In other words, people who offend will present multiple problems, which may be connected to a range of factors related to, for example, their family, social, economic, health or education needs. For these reasons, crime cannot be dealt with by one agency alone. Instead, an effective approach to addressing offending behaviour requires the input of a variety of agencies.

In this way, the growth in multi-agency work has developed in a climate in which work with offending behaviour is seen to require efficiency and effectiveness, a proactive 'problem-solving' approach and the involvement of a range of agencies. In this context, multi-agency work can be seen to have a number of significant benefits.

The benefits of multi-agency work

A holistic service

First, multi-agency strategies appear effective. Because they draw together representatives from all the relevant agencies, multi-agency teams are well placed both to identify the range of needs experienced by their service users and provide a holistic service to address them. For example, if YOT workers find that a young person has particular needs outside their immediate field of expertise, there are practitioners immediately on hand who can provide advice or input. Similarly, because they can pool information and expertise, multi-agency teams are able to identify those considered to be most at risk of offending and attempt to prevent them from doing so. Given the increasing emphasis on pre-emptive targeting of children and young people thought to be at 'high risk' of involvement in offending, this is considered to be a particularly important benefit of YOTs (Youth Justice Board 2004a).

Efficiency

Second, multi-agency work appears efficient. By consolidating the diverse expertise and resources of staff from different agencies into a single structure multi-agency work can allow for a better coordinated and more efficient use of resources – whether funding, expertise, effort or information. In particular, it can remove obstructions to cooperation between agencies, allowing practitioners to make faster and easier referrals and providing quicker and easier access to information held by different agencies. In other words, as Burnett (2005) puts it, staff can effectively become 'brokers' for their home agency, allowing the team direct access into local services which may have previously been unresponsive.

A common approach

Further, multi-agency practice attempts to bring about a consistent and coherent approach to offending behaviour. By co-opting various professional and interest groups into a collective whole with consistent aims and objectives, the capacity for conflict and disruption between these agencies is reduced (Pratt 1989), removing further obstructions to effective and efficient practice. For example, the Audit Commission (1996) found that before the formation of YOTs, the agencies who worked with young offenders had different views about what they were trying to achieve. The resulting tensions and inconsistencies were inefficient, with agencies working at different purposes and sometimes inadvertently obstructing each others' work. The development of inter-agency teams was explicitly intended to consolidate these different working styles into a 'common approach to youth justice work' (Home Office 1997) with an overarching aim that agencies could work towards. In other words, multi-agency work is an attempt to 'design out' conflict (Pitts 2000: 9) in the youth justice system and allow for its smooth running.

Innovation

The formation of multi-agency teams can also bring about more active, innovative services. By enabling staff to work outside their traditional structures and practices, multi-agency practice allows for the development of new ways of working, providing an environment where creativity is encouraged (Burnett and Appleton 2004; Souhami 2007). The establishment of multi-agency structures may also create new possibilities for funding which provide for the development of innovative programmes.

Status

Finally, a multi-agency structure can also raise the status of its services in the local authority. The 'stand-alone', inter-agency structure of YOTs was designed explicitly with this purpose in mind (Youth Justice Board 2004a). By removing them from the ownership of any one department or agency, it was envisaged that youth offending would be accepted as the corporate responsibility of the local authority and all statutory partners. Their local governance by multi-agency management boards and chief executives' departments aimed to encourage all partner agencies to participate fully in both the establishment and operation of YOTs, through the management of YOT performance and through the provision of staffing, funding and services. Further, YOT managers were intentionally positioned outside the structures of partner agencies to prevent them being 'buried' within the management of any local agency. In this way, it was envisaged YOT managers would be able to have a greater status at the local level and thus more influence on the wider local authority agenda. A recent (2003) survey by the YJB indicates that, given the variety of local arrangements in place, the governance structure of YOTs has not always developed in this manner. However, where it has, YOTs appear to have been more prominent within the delivery of the crime and disorder agendas (Youth Justice Board 2004a).

Working in a multi-agency team

Multi-agency practice has therefore come to be seen as having a number of important advantages in addressing offending behaviour. However, it also raises a number of challenges for practitioners. Drawing on the experiences of staff in the developing Midlands YOT, the following pages consider some of the implications of multi-agency work for practitioners' professional skills and identity. What does it mean to work in a 'multi-agency' way?

A central question in the development of multi-agency practice is the extent to which staff retain a distinct identity as specialist practitioners, and how far they take on new, shared responsibilities defined by the partnership.

While multi-agency work aims to bring together a diverse range of specialist skills, resources and services, the development of some work that is common to all practitioners is perhaps inevitable. As staff are brought together to address a common problem with shared objectives, they are to some extent required to put aside their usual roles and become involved in new, shared ways of working and thinking. As a result, professional boundaries inevitably become blurred. This is particularly apparent in the kind of 'inter-agency' relations required of working in a YOT, where staff from different professional backgrounds work alongside each other in the same offices, doing similar work. In fact, official guidance makes it clear that the development of shared work is encouraged: while some degree of specialist input can be maintained, 'in principle' any team member can undertake any function, such as writing pre-sentence reports and supervising offenders (Home Office *et al.* 1998).

For many specialist staff in the Midlands YOT, the chance to transcend their usual role was an important attraction of inter-agency work. A probation officer said he felt he had become 'complacent' in his previous role and wanted the 'personal challenge' afforded by being able to 'take on extras'; a police officer said that the opportunity to take on new activities was the sole reason for him applying to the YOT: 'I said originally, if they wanted a straight police officer, then maybe I'm not your man. But if they wanted a police officer with other interests, then I would be interested.' Yet the experiences of these staff indicate that the combination of specialist and generic practice raises a number of difficulties for multi-agency workers.

Developing a multi-agency role

Firstly, it appears that finding an appropriate balance between the specialist and 'generic' elements of their role is vital both for multi-agency workers' job satisfaction and their sense of team membership. For example, education and health staff in the Midlands YOT felt they were spending more time in general casework than specialist interventions. As a result, they felt their professional expertise and experience had been made redundant and described feeling devalued, undermined and deskilled. Moreover, they felt they were not only losing their own professional identity but were replacing it with that of another profession: they were 'becoming social workers'. This was a cause of considerable resentment. As the education officer put it, 'If I'd wanted to be a social worker on the YOT, I would have trained as one, wouldn't I?' Yet the research also showed that some degree of shared work is essential for practitioners' sense of inclusion. For example, staff were initially unsure about how to involve police officers in the generic work of the Midlands YOT: they were prevented by law from acting as appropriate adults; was it appropriate for them to take on a caseload or write court reports? As a result, police staff described feeling marginalised, 'snubbed' and 'fobbed off'. It also resulted in an uneven workload: health, probation and education staff were overwhelmed with work while police staff had relatively little to do.

Yet while the balance between specialist input and new, shared tasks appears to be crucial for the cohesion of multi-agency teams and thus their effective functioning, it is also difficult to negotiate. In particular, it can be complicated by pressures inherent in multi-agency work.

Specialist services and multi-agency pressures

Experiences in the youth justice system suggest that multi-agency teams can inadvertently create pressures which undermine the ability of staff to provide a specialist service. Firstly, as staff become distanced from their parent agency they can find it difficult to maintain specialist training and supervision. This is particularly problematic for those staff employed in multi-agency teams on a full-time, long-term basis who are unlikely to have a line manager with appropriate expertise within the team. Secondly, because of the workloads experienced within teams staff can feel under pressure to take on generic or administrative duties such as undertaking court duty, writing court reports and taking on casework rather than working within their areas of expertise (Youth Justice Board 2004b). In the Midlands YOT, for example, education and health staff felt that they were being asked to spend more time in this kind of work than they were in specialist interventions. Again, this was considerably resented. As the education officer put it, 'It detracts from what I'm here for, doesn't it?'

Transferring skills

Further, practitioners' specialist skills cannot always be easily transferred to the multi-agency team. Even where the nature of the specialist input appears relatively straightforward, the new context may demand fundamental changes in the way practitioners approach their work. For example, official guidance suggested that the role of health staff on a YOT could include conducting assessments for mental health issues or drug and alcohol misuse, providing interventions and facilitating access to resources where young people had particular needs (Home Office et al. 1998), and this was very similar to the way the role was envisaged in the Midlands YOT. Yet while these were tasks in which the newly appointed health officer was highly experienced, performing them in a YOT required important departures from her previous practice. In particular, the focus on offending behaviour and the compulsory nature of the interventions required a significant shift in thinking. As she said, 'It's trying to get in my head it's a completely different way of working. In my previous line you accepted that clients offended but it really wasn't that much of an interest to us. If somebody didn't turn up that's OK, it was up to them, it was really very much their choice.' Other staff had not previously worked with children and young people before and found that they were, as a probation officer put it, 'totally different clients' which required critical shifts in the approach and scope of their work. One probation officer explained, 'probation is getting more and more to do with enforcement, specifically looking at offending behaviour. They [YOT workers] focus on other things. Offending behaviour is possibly not even on the list.'

Qualification

In addition, the development of new practice that the setting may demand puts at issue questions of qualification. Although practitioners may have extensive experience in their home agency, they may be new to the kind of work required in the multi-agency organisation. Indeed, in the context of youth justice where the recruitment of a diverse workforce is encouraged, it is likely that some new staff will not have professional qualifications in work with young and vulnerable children.

If practitioners' roles are closely determined according to specialism, questions of qualification might not be as acute. But if there is some development of generic roles, how do agency-specific qualifications transfer? For example, it might be quite appropriate for a health officer in a YOT to provide assessments or interventions for young people with mental health or substance misuse needs and so on. But are they qualified to be a general case worker or to write pre-sentence reports?

This issue became of crucial importance in the Midlands YOT. Practitioners from partner agencies who were tasked with generic work of this kind said they felt inexperienced and unprepared to undertake to do the work now required of them. As an education officer explained, this had serious implications: 'I've just done a PSR on my own ... I don't think it's right that I should be doing it. Certainly not without more training ... I think it's a very grave thing, it's somebody's justice, it's somebody's liberty.' It also made for an anxious and unhappy working life: 'I feel totally out of my depth on a few of my cases who've got real social work needs. I'm just sort of trying my best.'

In the field of youth justice, the YJB has attempted to address these issues by developing a new national qualifications framework aimed at ensuring that all staff within YOTs (including volunteers) are trained and skilled in 'effective practice' with young people who offend. Most significant among the new generic qualifications is the Professional Certificate in Effective Practice (Youth Justice), which is aimed at all youth justice staff and is designed to be the core professional qualification in youth justice (Fulwood and Powell 2004). This appears to have been attractive to practitioners: the YJB recently announced that it had reached its target that 80 per cent of youth justice practitioners had achieved or were engaged in the PCEP (YJ) or equivalent. Indeed, YOT staff report that the potential for training and career progression that it offers seems to increase the quality and range of applicants to new YOT posts. However, these developments raise further questions about the nature of expertise in multi-agency work. Are the specialist skills of different partner agencies becoming replaced by a new form of multi-agency expertise? This is discussed further below.

Representing an agency on team

Further, the question of what it means to represent an agency in a multi-agency team is not always straightforward. As outlined above, practitioners' contributions are often envisaged as transcending the professional skills they bring with them. Indeed, some staff – such as police staff – are often unable to carry out their core tasks at all. How, then, should staff understand their role as a 'representative' of their parent agency?

This question is further complicated by the fact that many practitioners who participate in multi-agency partnerships are often atypical of those in their profession (e.g. Crawford and Jones 1995; Sampson *et al.* 1988). Because multi-agency work to some extent separates its members from their parent agency, particularly where it operates outside traditional organisational structures, roles and practices (Crawford 1994, 1997), it may be more likely to appeal to those who feel able to detach themselves from their culture, work and colleagues. This is particularly likely to be the case where partnership work is felt to conflict with core aspects of organisational life. For example, Crawford and Jones (1995) found that in the climate of 'old-fashioned machismo' (Reiner 2000: 97) in the police service in which action, excitement and a punitive approach to offenders is prized, inter-agency work which does not have these characteristics is often regarded pejoratively as 'social work' rather than 'real police work' and therefore as 'women's work'. This is perhaps particularly at issue in the field of youth justice. Joining a YOT not only demands a long-term severance from traditional police work, but involves taking on work recently 'owned' by social workers, traditionally welfarist in approach and differently gendered. It is therefore likely that some sense of disconnection from the dominant ethos of the police is necessary for police staff to be able to take up a position on a YOT. In the Midlands YOT, for example, both (male) police officers said that they felt uncomfortable and out of place in the police service and saw this as an integral part of their move to the YOT. As one of them explained, 'I have nothing in common with younger police officers. They're different animals … I don't get on well with police officers generally.'

In this way, a central dilemma in multi-agency work is that the representatives of parent agencies are likely to be unrepresentative of those who work in them. This has several implications for practice. Firstly, it suggests that the relationship between inter-agency workers and their colleagues in the parent agencies should not be taken for granted (Crawford and Jones 1995), and this may have implications for the ability of multi-agency staff to act as 'brokers' for their parent agency. But secondly, it raises questions about what multi-agency work means in this context. If staff cannot easily perform a specialist service, and if they are unrepresentative of an agency ethos or culture, in what way do they represent their parent agency?

In fact, it appears that the unrepresentativeness of multi-agency staff paradoxically may be important for effective multi-agency work. As

Crawford and Jones (1995) argue, the ability for front-line workers to 'get on' with their colleagues is crucial for developing interpersonal trust relationships, which in turn is essential for partnerships to function effectively. In particular, where cultural conflicts are expected, the ability for staff not to be seen as 'one of the opposition' (as a police officer in the YOT put it) is essential for inter-agency relations. This was acknowledged by a police officer in the Midlands YOT, who felt it was his difference to the dominant, macho culture of the police service that made him an effective YOT member: 'I feel that I blend in quite well with organisations, I'm not a prickly individual, I'm looking for the positive issues. I think many officers coming into the job [as a YOT member] will be too aggressive for the group … certainly their more in your face sort of attitude.'

Obstacles to multi-agency practice

Many of the difficulties experienced in multi-agency work concern the relationships between agencies. Indeed, conflicts between agencies can be argued to be integral to the nature of multi-agency work itself as it attempts to consolidate diverse approaches and resources into a shared form of service delivery. The following pages explore three particular areas of difficulty and the challenges that these raise for multi-agency staff.

Information exchange

Facilitating the sharing of information between collaborating agencies is a central strand of the rationale for multi-agency work. Because crime has multiple causes and effects, individual agencies are unlikely to be aware of all the information they need to address offending behaviour: information exchange is therefore required for effective practice.

In the restructuring of the youth justice system the importance placed on information exchange was reinforced by new powers under the Crime and Disorder Act which gave local authorities, police authorities, health authorities and others the capacity to share information where it is 'necessary or expedient' to comply with their statutory duty to work together to prevent offending (CDA, s. 115). So, for example, a YOT might request police records of contacts with the child or their family, information from education authorities on school attendance and behaviour, and so on (Home Office *et al.* 1998). However, the key mechanism of information exchange is within the partnership itself. Because of their close working relationships multi-agency staff can share information quickly and informally – particularly if they are working in the same offices. Indeed, the ability to bypass the formal and often bureaucratic systems of communication between agencies is often considered the central strength of multi-agency work. As one practitioner in the Midlands YOT put it, 'sometimes we can make half a dozen phone calls trying to get to a particular person, now I feel as though we've got direct access into that service ... we've got link people in the building' (see also, for example, Burnett 2005; Sampson et al. 1988).

However, while informal working practices undoubtedly allow for more fluid and effective communication between agencies, they are also unaccountable. As such they allow for unacceptable practices, including breaches of confidentiality. Further, they can cause tensions between workers from different agencies. Practitioners may have a different understanding of confidentiality and of its appropriate application and relevance in specific contexts. Health workers in particular have difficulty in sharing what they perceive to be confidential information about a service user. For the police, however, 'intelligence gathering' is now one of the most important parts of their role.

Recognising that such concerns can be a barrier to information exchange, the YJB has issued guidance setting out the legislative framework in which it takes place and for the development of information protocols to which all statutory partners and organisations commissioned to provide services are expected to sign up (Youth Justice Board 2005). However, while it is crucial to clarify agency expectations about these issues, notions of confidentiality and its application are open to differences in interpretation which may not be easily captured by formal protocols. For this reason, experiences in the Midlands YOT suggest that questions of information exchange may continue to be a focus for tensions between agencies. For example, some social workers explained that despite their official obligations to do so, they tended not to act on information about offences that might came to light during supervision so that they would not destroy the young person's trust and compromise the development of a constructive relationship. It was assumed that this tacit practice could not continue with the introduction of police staff on the team. One social worker said: 'I can't imagine a police officer turning a blind eye like we do.' In other words, social work staff felt that police staff would have no qualms in acting on any offence that came to light. This had implications for information exchange, as another social worker explained: 'If I know about [service-user's] drug use I can minimise it and change his pattern of offending. Now I'll have to tell him to shut his mouth. The whole philosophy has changed.' In other words, information sharing became the focus of deeper concerns about multi-agency work, in particular questions of conflict in the power and culture of partner agencies.

Power and conflict in multi-agency work

The power relations between agencies are a central feature of multi-agency work. Because of deep-rooted, structural differences between agencies, such as their access to resources and their claims to expertise and status, it is argued that conflict is inevitable: indeed, conflict is always present, even when there seems to be consensus and cooperation (e.g. Crawford and Jones 1995; Gilling 1994; Pearson et al. 1992; Sampson et al. 1988). The police are usually seen as the dominant agency in partnership work, particularly in contrast to the traditionally low-status social services (Thomas 1986). However, power differentials between agencies are not static and indeed in the early stages of the development of YOTs these positions seemed to be reversed: youth justice remained a sphere dominated by social work staff and practice and one in which the expertise of police staff was seen to have little currency or status.

Structural differences between agencies can have a powerful impact on relations within a partnership. More powerful agencies set the agenda, dominate decision-making and may even pull out of the partnership when it suits their own strategic interests (see, for example, Sampson *et al*. 1988; Pearson *et al*. 1992; Crawford and Jones 1995). Power may not always exercised in an overt way, but through a lack of action which leaves the dominant power relations unaltered. For example, for a considerable period in the formation of the Midlands YOT decisions were not taken and formal processes such as taking minutes in meetings or recording supervision sessions were abandoned, thereby maintaining the status quo.

In particular, power relations are manifested in a differential ability to define – whether in relation to the objectives of the partnership, the nature of the problems to be addressed or the courses of action considered legitimate. Questions of definition are particularly at issue in multi-agency crime prevention as the nature of the work tends to be highly elastic. There is therefore considerable scope for flexibility in the definition of the aims of partnerships and the roles of staff within them, and therefore for the exercise of power. This was acknowledged by one social worker in the Midlands YOT: 'I know we're all equal members, but it's quite a big proportion of the team, isn't it, social work, we're a big body, so we'll have a lot of control over what happens I should imagine.' For example, the differential power to define was particularly apparent in the early stages of the formation of the Midlands YOT when roles were fluid and uncertain. The team at that time was dominated by former youth justice social workers who considered the newly arrived multi-agency practitioners 'a bolt-on team' who would supplement their existing work. This power differential excluded any other definitions of practitioners' roles. As one social worker acknowledged, 'I'm quite aware I'm talking from my perspective all the time, you see, about how they can help me do my job, not the other way round.'

The importance of the differential exercise of power is that it ultimately leads to conflicts between agencies that undermines multi-agency working. However, as Crawford (1994) points out, it is often assumed that conflicts between agencies are pathological and destructive. For this reason multi-agency partnerships may be unwilling to accept that it exists and ignore it as long as the appearance of consensus can be maintained. Yet as the power relations between agencies makes conflict inevitable, if it is not addressed overtly it will instead be dealt with in informal, invisible and unaccountable ways. In other words, the denial of conflict 'leaves differential power relations unchallenged, unregulated and unrestrained' (Crawford 1994: 338).

Instead, in the context of multi-agency partnerships, conflict may in fact be desirable and productive. The crucial challenge for multi-agency staff, he argues, is therefore to negotiate conflict in a 'socially constructive manner' (*ibid*) which recognises and addresses the power differentials inherent between them.

Cultural conflicts

Finally, conflicts in the cultures of different agencies are a particular issue in multi-agency work, and one which has often been seen to impact on the implementation of multi-agency strategies (for example, Crawford 1994, 1997; Crawford and Jones 1995; Gilling 1994; Pearson *et al.* 1992; Sampson *et al.* 1988). It is argued that such conflicts are inevitable: because of their different traditions, cultures and working assumptions, staff are likely to have different conceptions of the problems at hand and thus a different understanding of the appropriate approach to them (Crawford and Jones 1995). Indeed, a central strand of the rationale for the formation of multi-agency YOTs was that they would help to consolidate such differences of approach in the youth justice system, thus implicitly acknowledging that conflict between youth justice agencies both exists and is built into the structure of YOTs.

The implication is that conflicts in the cultures of different agencies, whether real or perceived, may undermine working relationships and thus be a barrier to multi-agency practice. In particular, conflicts are often expected between practitioners from the police and social work or probation, who 'represent, at least symbolically, important polar interests within the system of crime control and the criminal justice process' (Crawford 1997: 97). Similarly, former youth justice social workers in the Midlands YOT were concerned that the police had a punitive and inflexible working culture which was incompatible with their 'welfarist' approach. As one social worker put it, 'Having a police officer sitting alongside you is unusual because it always been a them and us situation in the past.' Or as another social worker said, 'The police have always seen social workers as in league with the service user. Social workers have always seen the police as bastards who are locking them up.' How then could functional working relationships develop?

However, experiences in the Midlands YOT indicate that inter-agency conflicts may be more complex than accounts of opposing occupational agendas suggest. Firstly, even if different agencies have competing ideas about the aims of and approach to working with offenders, these may not be not straightforwardly understood or played out among their representatives. In other words, conflicts in working cultures will not necessarily be directly translated into conflicts between multi-agency staff. In fact, given that multi-agency work is likely to appeal in particular to those who feel unrepresentative of their home agency, multi-agency workers' attitudes to their occupational culture is likely to be particularly complex. In the Midlands YOT, for example, a police officer explained that he had 'nothing in common' with the dominant culture in the police. Instead, he described his approach to work with young people in strikingly similar terms to many social work staff: he aimed to raise young people's confidence and self-esteem, 'give them a pride in being part of a community' and develop their skills. This approach to addressing offending behaviour arguably had less in common with the macho, action-oriented dominant ethos of policing than with the welfarist ethos of social work.

Secondly, multi-agency work can illuminate not just the differences between the culture and approach of different agencies, but the similarities, complexity and confusion among them as well. The need to develop new forms of multi-agency practice outside the routines and conventions of their home agency requires practitioners to engage with fundamental questions about the aims and scope of their work. What does it mean to address offending behaviour? What practices should be adopted? And what is the underlying ethos that shapes them? For example, the establishment of group work with young offenders was the first piece of multi-agency practice developed in the Midlands YOT. Their formation raised a series of practical questions about the way they were run: should young people be breached for non-attendance, or should the groups be voluntary? Should staff provide transport to the sessions or should young people make their own way there? Underlying these issues were core questions about the nature and purpose of the work of the team, including the degree to which young people should be considered responsible for their actions, how far the work of the team should be considered 'punishment', and so on. It became clear that there was no clear position within each agency about these issues. Instead, disagreement and diversity was widespread among practitioners from all agencies. As the education officer said, 'everybody within our group, and we're multi-agency group-workers, we all disagreed on what we should do ... There's a lot of different philosophies out there about what the team is, punitive approaches, and welfare approaches ... I think it's individual.' These dilemmas would of course always have been inherent in the work of the team. However, the departure from the previous conventions of participating agencies with the development of multi-agency practice brought them into focus.

In other words, the notion of clear conflicts between agencies may in fact mask a more complex picture. However, the realisation that, instead of being divided by clear occupational agendas, staff from different agencies are united in confusion and ambiguity can be deeply unsettling. In the Midlands YOT it was experienced as the partnership collapsing: in the context of such diversity and uncertainty, what did team membership mean? But as some have suggested (e.g. Sampson *et al.* 1988) the acknowledgment of shared uncertainties can also be an important basis on which to start building a common approach to addressing offending behaviour.

This, however, raises a different dilemma. It can be argued that inter-agency conflict is a necessary and important part of relations between agencies. For example, Pitts argues that the negotiation of the conflicts

221

between the different ethical, legal and administrative responsibilities of the various youth justice agencies is an essential feature of the youth justice system, which 'exists precisely to provide a site upon which conflict can be enacted': it is 'a place where the competing claims of rules and needs, guilt and suffering, justice and welfare can be confronted' (2000: 8). Should, then, a common approach to offending behaviour be something to which inter-agency partnerships should aspire?

Conclusion: future challenges – towards a multi-agency profession?

In recent decades multi-agency practice has come to represent a new orthodoxy in criminal justice initiatives. The ability of multi-agency teams to identify a diverse range of needs and address them through a coherent, consistent and holistic service chimes with a criminal justice climate which both recognises the complex and multi-faceted nature of offending behaviour and demands proactive, efficient strategies to address it.

While multi-agency strategies have proliferated across the criminal justice system, the challenges they represent for the practitioners within them are considerable. Staff joining a multi-agency team may find themselves in a context in which they are required to alter fundamentally their approaches to work or even abandon them altogether. They must negotiate the balance between generic and specialist input, between maintaining links with their home agency and coping with a multi-agency workload, and between retaining a specialist expertise and identity without feeling marginalised from the core activities of the organisation. And they are confronted with tensions inherent to the structural and cultural differences between participating agencies.

Yet despite the difficulties and tensions it creates, experiences in the youth justice system where multi-agency practice is most firmly entrenched suggest that it also brings considerable rewards. Multi-agency work is often described as innovative, active and exciting. Long-serving staff report a significant and positive cultural change in services in a relatively short time. Multi-agency YOT work appears to have become seen by practitioners in a range of agencies as a long-term career rather than a short-term secondment: the YJB and YOTs report an increasing proportion of staff permanently employed as YOT workers or in 'technical' secondments whereby staff are unlikely to return to their parent agency.

However, the apparent success and sustainability of multi-agency work in the youth justice system suggests a further challenge for the future of multi-agency practice. As multi-agency work becomes more deeply embedded and more professionalised it risks eroding the diversity at its core. An increasing proportion of permanent staff in multi-agency teams obstructs the refreshing of specialist skills and services that secondment provides – and which is considered the 'lifeblood' of multi-agency work (Youth Justice Board 2007). Further, the development of a permanent, multi-agency workforce raises the possibility of the emergence of a new form of multi-agency profession, with its own knowledge base, training, values and skills (see Goldson 2000). In the field of youth justice this appears to have been actively encouraged by the development of the qualification framework for youth justice which promotes a particular form of 'effective practice' as the common skill base across the youth justice workforce. In other words, the distinct contributions of partner agencies risk becoming assimilated into a new form of inter-agency expertise. In this way, a challenge for the future of multi-agency practice in the criminal justice system is to ensure its success does not paradoxically undermine its fundamental purpose.

Discussion questions

1 Is multi-agency practice an effective means of addressing offending behaviour?
2 By drawing together diverse professions into a partnership with shared objectives, multi-agency practice attempts to reduce conflict between agencies. Is this always a desirable goal?
3 Multi-agency workers face a tension between retaining a distinct identity as specialist practitioners and taking on new responsibilities shared by the partnership. How can this tension be managed?

Further reading

Bateman, T. and Pitts, J. (2005) *The RHP Companion to Youth Justice*. Lyme Regis: Russell House. An accessible, practice-focused collection covering a wide range of key areas of youth justice work, including a clear and concise chapter about multi-agency work.

Burnett, R. and Appleton, C. (2004) *Joined-Up Youth Justice: Tackling Crime in Partnership*. Lyme Regis: Russell House. This is a clearly written account of the practical strategies and problems involved in establishing a multi-agency youth offending team. While it is about a youth justice initiative, the issues it describes would be useful for anyone working in multi-agency partnerships.

Home Office (1991) *Safer Communities: The Local Delivery of Crime Prevention through the Partnership Approach* (Morgan Report), Standing Conference on Crime Prevention. London: Home Office. This document has been hugely influential in the development of partnership work in the criminal justice system. It reviews the advantages of multi-agency work and explores the ways in which it could be made normal business for local authorities. Although the report's recommendations were not acted upon by the then Conservative government, they are the basis for the reforms later implemented under the Crime and Disorder Act 1998.

Hughes, G., McLaughlin, E. and Muncie, J. (eds) (2002) *Crime Prevention and Community Safety: New Directions*. London: Sage. A collection of 16 chapters on key debates about community safety, including multi-agency partnership. Particularly useful are the chapters by Coretta Phillips on the experience of three partnerships established under the Crime and Disorder Act and by Gordon Hughes on the theoretical debates about partnership working.

Note

1 For example, locally constituted multi-agency diversion panels such as the Northamptonshire Juvenile Liaison Bureau were commended by the Audit Commission as a model of multi-agency working (Audit Commission 1996), and may have influenced some features of the YOTs established by the Crime and Disorder Act. However, as discussed later in the chapter, YOTs were to deliver a very different service: they were not created to divert young people from the formal criminal justice system, but rather to enable more formal intervention.

References

Audit Commission (1996) *Misspent Youth*. London: Audit Commission.

Burnett, R. (2005) 'Youth offending teams', in T. Bateman and J. Pitts (eds), *The RHP Companion to Youth Justice*. Lyne Regis: Russell House.

Burnett, R. and Appleton, C. (2004) 'Joined up services to tackle youth crime: a case-study in England', *British Journal of Criminology*, 44 (1): 34–55.

Crawford, A. (1994) 'The partnership approach: corporatism at the local level?', *Social and Legal Studies*, 3 (4): 497–519.

Crawford, A. (1997) *The Local Governance of Crime: Appeals to Community and Partnerships*. Oxford: Clarendon Press.

Crawford, A. and Jones, M. (1995) 'Inter-agency co-operation and community-based crime prevention: some reflections on the work of Pearson and colleagues', *British Journal of Criminology*, 35 (1): 17–33.

Feeley, M. and Simon, J. (1992) 'The new penology', *Criminology*, 30 (4): 452–74.

Fulwood, C. and Powell, H. (2004) 'Towards effective practice in the youth justice system', in R. Burnett and C. Roberts (eds), *What Works in Probation and Youth Justice: Developing Evidence-Based Practice*. Cullompton: Willan.

Gilling, D.J. (1994) 'Multi-agency crime prevention: some barriers to collaboration', *Howard Journal*, 33 (3): 246–57.

Goldson, B. (2000) '"Children in need" or "young offenders"? Hardening ideology, organizational change and new challenges for social work with children in trouble', *Child and Family Social Work*, 5: 255–65.

Home Office (1991) *Safer Communities: The Local Delivery of Crime Prevention through the Partnership Approach* (Morgan Report), Standing Conference on Crime Prevention. London: Home Office.

Home Office (1997) *No More Excuses: A New Approach to Tackling Youth Crime in England and Wales*. London: HMSO.

Home Office, Department of Heath, Welsh Office and Department for Education and Employment (1998) *Establishing Youth Offending Teams*. London: HMSO.

Hood, C. (1991) 'A public management for all seasons?', *Public Administration*, 69 (1): 3–19.

Martinson, R. (1974) 'What works? Questions and answers about prison reform', *Public Interest*, 35: 22–54.

Muncie, J. (2002) 'A new deal for youth? Early intervention and correctionalism', in G. Hughes, E. McLaughlin and J. Muncie (eds), *Crime Prevention and Community Safety: New Directions*. London: Sage.

Muncie, J. (2004) *Youth and Crime*, 2nd edn. London: Sage.

Pearson, G., Blagg, H., Smith, D., Sampson, A. and Stubbs, P. (1992) 'Crime, community and conflict: the multi-agency approach', in D. Downes (ed.), *Unravelling Criminal Justice*. London: Macmillan, pp. 46–72.

Pitts, J. (2000) 'The new youth justice and the politics of electoral anxiety', in B. Goldson (ed.), *The New Youth Justice*. Lyme Regis: Russell House.

Pitts, J. (2001) 'The new correctionalism: young people, youth justice and New Labour', in R. Matthews and J. Pitts, *Crime, Disorder and Community Safety*. London: Routledge.

Pratt, J. (1989) 'Corporatism: the third model of juvenile justice', *British Journal of Criminology*, 29 (3): 236–54.

Reiner, R. (2000) *The Politics of the Police*, 3rd edn. Oxford: Oxford University Press.

Sampson, A., Stubbs, D., Smith, D., Pearson, G. and Blagg, H. (1988) 'Crime, localities and the multi-agency approach', *British Journal of Criminology*, 28 (4): 473–93.

Souhami, A. (2007) *Transforming Youth Justice: Occupational Identity and Cultural Change*. Cullompton: Willan.

Thomas, T. (1986) *The Police and Social Workers*. Aldershot: Gower.

Youth Justice Board (2004a) *Sustaining the Success: Extending the Guidance Establishing Youth Offending Teams*. London: Youth Justice Board.

Youth Justice Board (2004b) *The Provision of Health, Education and Substance Misuse Workers in Youth Offending Teams and the Health/Education Needs of Young People Supervised by Youth Offending Teams*. London: Youth Justice Board.

Youth Justice Board (2005) *Guidance for Youth Offending Teams on Information Sharing*. London: Youth Justice Board.

Youth Justice Board (2007) *Strands and Structures of the Workforce*. Online at: http://www.yjb.gov.uk/engb/practitioners/WorkforceDevelopment/WorkforceStrategies/StrandsandStructureoftheWorkforce.

Part 3

Practice: Specialist Skills

Chapter 13

Working with dangerous offenders

Mike Nash

Introduction

It is difficult to think of an issue that has driven the criminal justice agenda more than that of dangerous offenders over the past decade or so. Emanating from concerns over the release from custody of predatory paedophiles in the mid-1990s through to popular associations between serious crime and mental illness in the dangerous and severe personality disorder (DSPD) debate and the commission of further serious offences by those released from custody, dangerousness continues to be a major political driver. Because of strong media and therefore public interest, it also becomes a very significant aspect of everyday criminal justice practice, leading to the introduction of new policies and legislation at a bewildering pace. Thus the perception of and response to dangerousness has significant knock-on effects within the criminal justice process for other less serious and by definition more common offenders. This chapter will explore the development and impact of this agenda with particular reference to the working context of probation and police staff. It will argue that the *responses* to dangerousness have had a significant impact upon its perception and have, in effect, redefined and worsened the problem.

Scene setting

It is easy to place the beginnings of recent western punitive criminal justice agendas in the election of new right governments (Reagan and Thatcher) in the USA and the UK. It would be equally easy to date the targeting of dangerous offenders from this period, but probably much more appropriate to site it in the *demise* of these regimes. Many of the measures that presently govern our dealings with potentially dangerous offenders are associated with policy developments under Democratic governments in America and New Labour governments in the UK. Indeed, the degree of 'change' within these political groupings, particularly in the UK, has been extremely significant.

For our purposes in the UK, it was to be the political battle between Tony Blair as then leader of the Opposition and former Home Secretary Michael Howard that would set in place the dangerousness agenda and determine themes that have both persisted and been expanded upon since the early 1990s.

As noted above, the late 1980s and early 1990s are perhaps the most recent periods that have served to shape the current dangerousness agenda. A series of cases highlighted by the media, fuelling a public reaction and thus provoking a political response, have significantly influenced dangerous offender policy and legislation. In the field of dangerousness it is often the spectacular that leads to change just as, at the time of writing, the largest robbery in UK history of £40 million (*The Guardian*, 23 February 2006) will undoubtedly lead to wholesale changes in the storage and transport of large sums of cash. Similarly, a spate of serious knife attacks, many resulting in murder, has previously led to a knife amnesty in England and Wales, a change to the law in Scotland and undoubtedly further legislative change in the offing; especially with an apparent surge in knife-related murders in 2007–8. If not exactly policymaking on the hoof, this does appear to be reactive rather than a carefully considered process. However, before considering the impact of a few of these cases, a slightly longer step back into history is appropriate.

Earlier dangerousness debates

The 1970s marked what has been dubbed the 'first dangerousness debate', which essentially arose from the abolition of the death penalty permanently in 1969 (although it was to take until 1999 and the adoption of the European Convention on Human Rights to finally abolish it for five wartime military offences). The concern at the beginning of the 1970s therefore focused on what to do with offenders who would otherwise have been hanged and who would likely be returned to the community at some point in the future. The debate triggered a number of government committees and commissions and a flurry of academic writing (see, for example, Bottoms 1977; Scott 1977; Dworkin 1977; and Floud 1982). Recurrent themes in much of this work were the definition of dangerousness, its assessment and prediction, and what to do with people who may be dangerous in the future, but equally may not – in essence a 'rights' or proportionality discussion concerning the level of state intervention in their lives. It is fair to say that many of these points remain very contemporary (see below) although significant strides have been made in the development of a range of risk assessment tools – indeed the government unfolded a new-generation risk assessment tool in June 2006 (Clarke 2006). Although better tools may make decisions more 'defensible' the wider social and political context may instead encourage 'defensive' decisions based less upon rigorous perceptions of risk and more upon contemporary public and political pressures (a point developed further below).

The Butler Committee reported in 1975 following the public furore caused by the discharge from special hospital of the man who became known as the St Albans Poisoner, Graham Young. As a teenager, Young was responsible for the murder of his stepmother and serious illness of his father by poisoning – a process that fascinated him. At the age of 15, Young was committed to a special hospital (Broadmoor) for a period of 15 years. Discharged after eight years as fit for a return to the community, he had during his hospitalisation nurtured and developed his knowledge of poisons, undoubtedly becoming one of the leading specialists in the country. His discharge arrangements entailed him working in a factory that manufactured camera lenses, offering a ready supply of poisonous chemicals. Young poisoned several workers at the factory, fastidiously recording the effect of his chosen poison (thallium) on his victims. He was eventually charged with two counts of murder and two of attempted murder and sentenced to life imprisonment (for a full discussion see Holden 1974, and Bowden 1996). Much of the debate over this case therefore focused upon the decision to agree an earlier discharge date for him than that recommended by the sentencing judge. Central to this release decision was the idea that the patient had been 'cured' and therefore his recovery superseded the element of punishment in his sentence. It is variants of this issue that have recurred with some frequency in subsequent years and is of course central to some of the more notorious cases receiving attention at the start of the twenty-first century (see the discussion of the murders of Sarah Payne and John Monkton below).

The Butler Committee defined dangerousness as a propensity to 'cause serious physical or lasting psychological harm' – a definition that has stood the test of time. Part of the fall-out from their inquiry would be an attempt to improve risk assessment and develop more effective post-release supervision of potentially dangerous offenders. In similar fashion one notorious offender in Scotland (Jimmy Boyle) also triggered a major inquiry and the Scottish Council on Crime reported in 1975. It defined dangerousness as 'the probability that he will inflict serious and irremediable personal injury in the future'. We therefore begin to see the essential qualities of dangerousness: unpredictability (the behaviour may be rare and unusual and therefore difficult to fit into a pattern), a future orientation (will it occur or not?) and criminal behaviour of a very serious or dangerous nature (life threatening or causing severe psychological harm – but potentially conflated with more 'ordinary' offending patterns). Even in this brief description it is not difficult to see that, for everyday criminal justice practice, there are problems. The very uncertainty of prediction poses problems for staff and the rarity of such serious behaviour also ensures that experience in dealing with such people will be limited and perhaps as such more susceptible to external influences.

Shifting the dangerousness ground

Despite the apparent widespread public concern over offenders such as these, little changed in terms of policy towards them since those early debates. In seemingly less threatened times, there was a strong human rights focus in much of the literature noted above and, to a certain extent, this appeared to hold back the strengthened measures that have now become commonplace. However, it was to be the political reaction of the governments referred to earlier that really triggered a sharp turn in the response to potentially dangerous offenders. As already indicated, events in America began to significantly shape those in the UK. In particular it was to be two developments that would provoke sharp change in UK policy and eventually practice. The first was the development of 'three strikes' legislation in America. The intention of this punitive measure was that third-time felons would automatically receive a life sentence, hence the use of the baseball term 'three strikes and you're out'. Unfortunately the legislation failed to hit many of its intended targets as America's prisons, especially the commercially driven Supermax (super maximum security) facilities, filled their cells with many small-scale, but third-time, offenders. The intended target appears to have been serious offenders and it is this risk of inflation of more ordinary crimes into measures aimed at the potentially dangerous that runs throughout much of this period's policies and practice. The American policy was picked up by then Home Secretary Michael Howard, and with the Conservatives in their fourth administration, it became something of a battleground with the Shadow Home Secretary and later Leader of the Opposition Tony Blair. In the end, the UK variant (two strikes in fact) was enshrined in law in the Crime (Sentences) Act of 1997 (a Labour government measure). However, more than the actual measure itself was the tone it had set and the debate became increasingly punitive in philosophy from the mid-1990s onwards.

The second major American development was the release to the public of the details of convicted sex offenders being returned to the community (known as community or sex offender notification). This followed the murder of 7-year old Megan Kanka by a released sex offender. The upshot of this, and other similar incidents, was the creation of mandatory community notification procedures in 1996 by President Bill Clinton. Although formal and routine community notification procedures have not been established in the UK, the issue has remained politically sensitive, the subject of much media interest and seemingly attractive to the general public. In 1998 widespread local opposition occurred following attempts by the Probation Service to accommodate convicted paedophile murderers Robert Oliver and Sidney Cooke in a variety of locations. Aside from not wanting such people in their communities many people began to call for fuller information on released sex offenders. Three other incidents would significantly ratchet up the debate at this time. In July 2000, 8-year-old Sarah Payne went missing while visiting her grandparents in Sussex. She was found dead

17 days later with a convicted (and then registered) sex offender as prime suspect (the sex offenders' register having been established by the Sex Offender Act 1997). Within a month there were a number of serious public disturbances around the country fuelled by a campaign in the *News of the World* newspaper to 'name and shame' sex offenders to try to force the government into introducing community notification. The worst of these occurred at Paulsgrove, Portsmouth (see Williams 2004; Williams and Thompson 2004a, and 2004b; Silverman and Wilson 2002). Finally the calls were renewed, following a quieter period, when Ian Huntley killed Holly Wells and Jessica Chapman in August 2002.

Cases such as these are rare but seep into the public consciousness, fuelling demands to governments for ever-tougher measures. It is in this climate of fear and insecurity that agencies involved in public protection have to work, knowing that each new incident will not only lead to public blame but almost certainly an increase in the punitive nature of their daily working practice. For agencies such as the Probation Service, ostensibly committed to offender rehabilitation, it is clear that their established moral position is likely to be severely compromised by dangerousness issues.

Public protection policy is therefore set in a context of quick responses to tragedy with a constant sense of plugging the loopholes revealed by each new case. For example, in resisting the calls to open up sex offender registers to public notification, the government quickly moved to create sex offender orders (SOOs) in the 1998 Crime and Disorder Act. These orders, to be imposed on known sex offenders 'causing concern' would not only limit movement but also trigger automatic registration – without a new offence having been committed – and included a maximum of a five-year prison sentence for non-compliance. This was a clear attempt to plug the loophole of the 100,000 sex offenders in the community estimated not to be eligible to be included on the register at its inception (Home Office 1997). It was also intended to placate public and media demands for widespread community notification. As such it could be argued that SOOs would constitute additional punishment in terms of the right to free movement and represented a move towards punishing people for who they were (the label they wore) rather than for any contemporary criminal behaviour. This sense of anticipating future harm runs through all measures dealing with potentially dangerous offenders and can include sentencing that exceeds the 'norm' for the instant offence. This process has been described by Garland (2000: 350) as 'penal marking' – and it may well increasingly be for life, ascribing a label that no one is prepared to remove for fear of getting it wrong. In essence, the basic premise of proportionality – that punishment should be proportionate to the seriousness of the crime – disappears when punishment is imposed for *possible* rather than *actual* offences.

Aside from the legislative developments there were also a number of significant and rapid policy shifts throughout this period. The 1990s saw Her Majesty's Inspectorates emerging as significant players in policy formation and two documents written by HM Inspector of Probation (HMIP) were to prove very influential. The first appeared in 1995 and was a thematic inspection of the work of probation officers with dangerous offenders (HMIP 1995). The report, written at a time of heightened public concern with the levels of violence in society, called for the police and probation services to work more closely together. It reported on cultural differences and information blockages but also noted an embryonic collaborative arrangement between the two services with limited protocols or memoranda of understanding on information sharing. The latter were seen as the minimum for future good practice along with public protection emerging as a shared priority for both services.

A second HMIP report (HMIP 1998) on working with sex offenders revealed what was described as significant progress in information flow, joint meetings and shared risk assessment and management. In the area of public protection at least there had been a significant coming together. By the time the Criminal Justice and Court Services Act 2000 formally required that multi-agency public protection arrangements (MAPPA) be established, they were already well underway in much of the country. These arrangements, now widespread and formalised, did, however, have another side to them. The closer working relationships, notably between police and probation staff, did witness something of a cultural shift, perhaps most marked among probation officers. The public protection agenda bore a strong resemblance to the crime control ethos of policing and it was therefore unsurprising to see something of a drift away from the traditional probation position towards the ground associated with policing. In commenting on this phenomena Nash (1999) referred to the creation of a hybrid 'polibation' officer and Kemshall and Maguire (2001) referred to the 'policification' of probation.

However, it is more than a simple case of role overlap and part fusion. For police and probation officers it involves a significant redefinition of roles and although for probation this might represent a cultural shift, for police it actually involves becoming involved in processes that were traditionally outside of its remit. For example, being part of the MAPPA as a responsible authority means that police services are actively engaged in assessing risk and determining the risk management plans for serious and high-risk offenders in the community. This moves them on a stage from 'keeping an eye' on known offenders in the community. The new expectation is that they are as responsible as other community-based agencies in ensuring that risk is minimised in the community. As such the police service routinely deploys staff to work with MAPPA at local and county levels, with staff from constable right through to senior ranks involved in public protection. Indeed, a senior police officer recently gave the author his business card, which indicated he was responsible for 'offender management and public protection'. The police obviously have legal responsibility for the sex offenders register but operate beyond a bureaucratic oversight to become actively involved in home visits to offenders with probation colleagues. Police services have recently begun, in some areas, to appoint analysts to

MAPPA and VISOR (the violent and sex offenders register). The whole public protection agenda has therefore shifted the way in which police and probation services operate, skewing resources and experienced staff to these 'top-end' offenders. However, such deployment is rarely matched by additional funding and there are already indications that resources are overstretched or that other contemporary but possibly short-term initiatives demand a shift in direction. While recognising the importance of public protection, the Chairman of the Police Federation made the following point in respect of the proposals for violent offender orders, that '... they will inevitably result in adding further pressure to an already overstretched criminal justice system. It would be wrong for an overstretched police service to become the babysitter to known dangerous offenders just to appease an overburdened prison service' (*Police Federation* press release, 20 April 2006).

It should also be noted that these developments also now see the Prison Service assuming a different role. For example, it is now the case that prison staff will come out into the community to help in the multi-agency assessment of risk at MAPPA meetings. This is of course a welcome and overdue development in that prison staff have an important perspective to offer on prisoner/offender behaviour. However, just as with police deployments, there may be emerging resource issues arising from these developments.

Dangerous and different?

What emerged therefore was a sense that dangerous offenders were somehow different from other offenders and required special attention, either in the form of sentencing or agency community supervision arrangements. However, to a large extent they may be viewed as a political construct. Little evidence emerged throughout the 1990s and into the early twenty-first century of a significantly worsening problem with dangerous offenders. In other words, numbers were not significantly increasing or there had not been an upsurge in repeat offending by this group. The public, however, had become increasingly aware of them and a vicious circle of fear and a punitive mentality quickly developed. The media had taken the issue to heart and highlighted every failing, thus making it a major political issue. Seizing upon this issue was one of the many areas in which New Labour defeated the Conservatives in 1997, at least in part, by stealing the Tories' law and order clothes. This electoral victory did not, however, witness any reduction in the law and order policies and philosophy of the triumphant Tony Blair – indeed many of their subsequent measures have been very punitive in intent and would not have looked out of place in any Conservative election manifesto. Thus despite attempts to perhaps adopt a more community-based and restorative approach (the famous 'Tough on crime and tough on the causes of crime' slogan), it has been the measures triggered by concerns with dangerousness that have largely set the tone of penal policy since 1997, with considerable knock-on effects throughout the criminal justice process. In reading party political responses to dangerousness issues since the 1990s it is almost impossible to find any attempt to take the heat out of the situation by explaining the rarity of dangerous behaviour. Instead, these political responses have not just fuelled the fires of a punitive public expectation, but developed an expectation of safety that is not possible to meet.

The working context

A series of tragic cases, and the responses to them, has therefore changed the legal, practice and moral context in which probation and other criminal justice staff operate. Risk assessment and risk management dominate this context and, although usually stated as an impossible aim, zero risk often lurks behind public and media attention and expectation. Failure as such is deemed to be unacceptable but should be regarded as inevitable, albeit in rare cases, when dealing with unpredictable and explosive behaviour. An essential part of working in this context has been the development of a range of risk assessment tools, with these increasingly being refined and made user-friendly to a diverse range of agencies. Chapter 10 has detailed some of the development of and debates within the risk assessment agenda. Needless to say it has dominated practice and done much to bring together previously diverse criminal justice agencies.

Risk assessment might therefore be viewed as a unifying mechanism for joined-up working arrangements, but as suggested elsewhere (Nash 2006), it is perhaps important that 'multi'-agency thinking does not become 'mono'-thinking. It is also important that staff do not become over-reliant upon the tools themselves, especially when their professional judgment and perhaps intuition screams a different story to them (see Maden 2007). Professional assessment tools should aid judgment but it is often the case that experience and understanding of human behaviour can make the difference in assessing present and future risk.

It is in this context that the thorny issue of human rights and proportionality occur. As we have noted, the external focus on potentially dangerous offenders is an unforgiving one. The effect of this is to push offender rights somewhat down the agenda. If this has always been the case popularly, it has been less so with probation staff. Yet, such is the public and political interest in dangerousness that professional credibility rests on protecting the public rather than defending the rights of potentially marginalised and excluded offenders. The more serious the offender's past and potential crimes, the less they are deemed to merit a rights consideration. This issue was tackled within the first dangerousness debate (see above) and the influential review by Floud and Young (1981) concluded that it was appropriate to negate the rights of potentially dangerous offenders if, in a 'competing rights' framework, their offending is so (potentially) serious as to shift the balance in favour of potential victims. Implicit in this position is that somehow certain offenders, by dint of their previous and potential behaviour, lose some of the rights expected by ordinary citizens, or indeed by other types of offender, in other words they are distinctly 'different'. This theme has continued and to a certain extent been expanded upon in recent legislative developments. It is perhaps interesting to reflect on how the Probation Service has come to sit so easily with this position. An organisation once fully committed to re-establishing offenders back as full citizens in the community is now very much involved in the virtually permanent exclusion of a (growing) number of *potentially* dangerous offenders. This represents a significant shift away from treatability and restoration towards control and management, with risk reduction an absolute priority. This is of course fine in many ways. Most people would support criminal justice personnel in attempting to manage and reduce risk of serious harm. The problem is that so many offenders are now entering the system that risk will inevitably be overestimated (avoiding blame if something goes wrong) or underestimated (resources being unable to cope with too many potentially dangerous offenders). In simple terms, if we placed offender rights on one side of the scales and the public's right to be protected on the other, in the early twenty-first century they would tip heavily towards the latter. The question is, as asked earlier, has the problem become so much worse in the past 20 years or so to merit this change in the balance?[1] Furthermore, regardless of the answer, is the Probation Service comfortable with the inevitable change in its focus that this shift in balance entails?

Risk has therefore become over-associated with dangerousness. As we know, one of the real problems with actuarially driven tools is that they are based on generalisations across large-scale populations. Yet dangerous offender populations are much smaller and their offending is likely to be individualised and highly situational. Therefore there is a strong chance of predicting reoffending rather than predicting dangerousness – the two are not necessarily always the same. However, in an inquiry (HMIP 2006a) into the murder in London by a released prisoner, the investigators noted that perhaps too much attention had been paid to dynamic (changing) rather than static (actuarial) risk factors. However, even if this advice had been followed, would reconviction predictions actually be about the nature of offending or simply its recurrence? Risk therefore needs to be delineated, e.g. risk of what and when? Many people pose a risk but few pose a risk of potential danger, and it is in this general conflation that perhaps too many offenders end up being included in the process at least if not into risk of serious harm categories. The so-called 'ordinary' criminal may have little in his history to predict future dangerous offending but may commit such a crime. The so-called dangerous offender may commit another crime but of an 'ordinary' nature. Any combination can be constructed and it is evident that previous offending history, so often the basis of prison classification and release decisions, will not of itself predict future dangerousness or non-dangerousness. It is therefore not difficult to see why the job of the Parole Board and others is not at all clear-cut.

This scenario has huge implications for criminal justice practice. In essence it means that more and more offenders enter the system because they are deemed to pose a 'risk', with probation staff encouraged not to take any chances. This risk is often generalised and can be a moving feast as fears and insecurities metamorphose over time and in response to changing situations. A basic equation would indicate that the increased vulnerabilities felt by the population is reflected in the greater number of behaviours thrown into the risky category. Now, it may be the case that through a process of assessment many of these will be thrown out, but in so doing there are huge resource implications for the selection process. The problem is of course that in an anxious public and professional community, there will be a reluctance to downgrade risk in case something goes wrong. The effect therefore is likely to be more people assigned as potentially dangerous whereas they may be more likely to be potential reoffenders – but not necessarily dangerous. Who though will risk downgrading their status? Who would be confident enough to state that risk of future offending may be of 'ordinary' crimes rather than very serious harm?

Processing potentially dangerous offenders

It should be clear by now that potentially dangerous offenders, especially those convicted of sexual crimes, are processed differently to others within the criminal justice process. Increasingly this difference can be identified in sentencing arrangements and, for the purpose of this chapter, the most recent developments will be noted.

Two major pieces of legislation, the 2003 Criminal Justice Act and the 2003 Sexual Offences Act, dominate the way in which potentially dangerous offenders will be dealt with in the near future. Readers will be aware of the public furore in 2006 when in several cases people released from prison had gone on to commit very serious crimes, including murder (see Jewkes, this volume). Part of the disquiet concerned the apparently 'short' sentences people had served for serious crimes and thus their release had been earlier than many felt appropriate (see report by the Chief Inspector of Probation, HMIP 2006a). It is not for us to consider the appropriateness of various sentence lengths; however, it is pertinent to discuss the role of the discretionary life sentence. This measure has long been available for many serious crimes but has not been used as frequently as critics might have wished. This could be due to the life sentence's 'special' status in relation to murder, but it must be said that if imposed for *potential* danger (as well as the seriousness of the instant office) a number of offenders who had committed further serious crimes might not have been free to do so.

In the Crime (Sentences) Act of 1997, an attempt had been made to ensure that judges marked further serious offending by creating mandatory sentences for those who might usually be considered to be in the potentially dangerous category. Thus a range of offences, committed for the second time, would trigger the imposition of an automatic life sentence, commonly known as 'two strikes and you're out', aping and going further than the better known American 'three strikes' legislation (the qualifying offences included among others: manslaughter and soliciting murder, rape or attempted rape, offences of grievous bodily harm and robbery using a firearm). These sentences, however, did not prove popular with judges who found sufficient reasons not to pass them in the numbers the government might have wished. They came in at a time when Labour and Conservative politicians were battling for the hearts and minds of the voters and disappeared when Labour was (relatively) secure in its third term (see Thomas 2004).

This chapter has already indicated the problematic nature of defining dangerousness and, in particular, how this issue can increase or decrease the numbers considered to be eligible for special measures. We have seen that classifications are often politically determined and confused with risk of further offending rather than risk of serious harm. A noticeable trend has been to define dangerousness by offence with the obvious problem that many serious crimes may be committed by people without a history of committing those crimes – but maybe they were people who gave off other signs or indications. Offence categories therefore may be a useful starting point but their limitations need to be recognised. However, the 2003 Criminal Justice Act has taken the offence classification base for dangerousness to new heights. A total of 153 offences now come into this 'potential dangerousness' category – 65 violent offences and 88 sexual offences.

As Thomas (2004: 07) explains, practitioners will need to learn a new language with terms such as 'specified offence', 'specified violent offence', 'specified sexual offence', 'serious offence' and 'relevant offence'. Violent or sexual offences become 'serious' if punishable by a life sentence or imprisonment of ten years or more. In the case of the life sentence eligible cases, if the court is convinced that there is a significant risk of harm to the public, a life sentence *must* be passed. This provision differs from the Crime (Sentences) Act in that the life sentence is not automatic following further offences but is contingent upon a risk of serious harm assessment. This though, as we have seen, remains a bone of contention. Perhaps the interesting new development lies in those offences falling outside of the life sentence qualification that, if they meet the serious harm conditions, must result in a 'sentence for public protection'. These sentences are indeterminate and thus to a certain extent mirror life sentence provisions. With a minimum tariff to be served and release dependent upon the Parole Board, it is likely that more prisoners will serve longer terms than previously. It is also the case that the workload of the Parole Board will increase at a time when its budget is being reduced (see, for example, Johnson 2006).

These measures are clearly aimed at continuing to detain offenders at the end of their sentence in order to prevent serious further offending. In 2006 this had become a very hot political issue and with media and public attention and concern at its height, it is very likely that more people will be detained rather than released at the end of their tariff period. This means that detention continues to rely less upon a full and proper risk assessment and more on political and media pressures at the time. It is difficult to envisage a time in the near future when public feeling will lessen sufficiently for the Parole Board to think about taking more risks with release. One immediate impact of this situation will of course be an increase in the long-term prisoner population[2] and also an undoubted increase in the numbers of prisoners seeking redress for what they might regard as a breach of their human rights based upon inadequate assessments of their risk (PRT 2007).

A flurry of 'scandals' in the spring of 2006 emphasised how quickly these situations can take hold. Alongside the cases reported on by the Chief Inspector of Probation (noted above), a series of other issues hit the Home Office. These focused upon old chestnuts such as not knowing how many illegal asylum seekers were in the country, to a number of revelations of prisoners absconding from open prison conditions or offenders in the community ripping off their electronic tags with impunity. Among these were said to be a number of serious or dangerous offenders (although obviously adjudged of sufficiently low risk to be in open conditions or in the community). The battleground of potential dangerousness was thus becoming more widespread. In short the issues focused upon over-lenient sentencing, inappropriate prison classifications, release which was too early in terms of the seriousness of the offence, a lack of concern with protecting the public and inadequate supervision of those released and back in the community. The paedophile issue also raised its head again after a released sex offender resident in a probation hostel abducted and repeatedly abused a 3-year-old girl in Wales. The furore increased when, despite sentencing the offender to life, the sentencing judge indicated that he could be considered for release in just over five years. This led to another *Sun* newspaper campaign to sack soft judges but has also, more concretely, led the government to move between 60 and 70 paedophiles out of hostels located near to schools. The government has also introduced limited disclosure to parents whereby previous child sex offence convictions will be revealed concerning those who have access to their children. Announced in February 2008 as part of the Home Office Violent Crime Action Plan, it will be piloted in four English counties from June 2008. Add to this the report written by David Rose in the *Observer* (28 May 2006) indicating that serious crime, when measured by police statistics, was much higher than Home Office claims and that prosecutions for these crimes were falling, the picture for any Home Secretary is very grim indeed.

The Home Secretary post has not been a happy one for recent Labour governments and following Charles Clarke's resignation it was John Reid who took up the mantle and has taken up the mantle at the time of writing and walked into a storm over the performance of the Home Office and related criminal justice agencies. It was in this context that he addressed the Parole Board annual lecture on 23 May 2006. His opening comments emphasised the tone of recent events: 'I do not underestimate the difficult – often complex tasks that you face. It can be, quite literally, a matter of life and death.' He went on to develop a theme touched upon above, namely a rebalancing of offender human rights and the community's right to protection. He described the case of Stone (see HMIP report 2006b) as 'tragically, disastrously mistaken' and that an individual offender's rights have to be balanced with those of 60 million people to live free from fear. Reid did acknowledge that 'Predictions of human behaviour, however scientific, can never eliminate risk. But we can and must minimise that risk through high quality risk assessment and management.' Despite his caveat, it is clear that the public mood is not tolerant towards such explanations and, if risk cannot be accurately assessed, then put more people in prison for longer!

Conclusion

Dangerous offenders are not a new phenomenon. However, the public have been made much more aware of their presence in recent years and, perhaps more importantly, how they are dealt with by the criminal justice system. This information has to a certain extent redefined the impression and understanding of these offenders. In other words, their sentences and release arrangements, and perceived problems therein, have in many ways increased the seeming seriousness of their behaviour and the nature of the problem itself[3].

The response to dangerous offenders is increasingly a tough and punitive one, and probably for many people this is the correct approach. Yet this chapter has argued that there may be flaws in this tactic. For example, the at times almost glib application of the label 'dangerous' or high risk has meant that an increasing number of offenders are drawn into the net of severe measures. At the same time, the still rare occurrences of further 'serious' offending by these people is enough to alarm the public, especially when it receives saturation media coverage. Thus there is widespread support for repressive and punitive measures which has forced the government that introduced the Human Rights Act to backtrack quite quickly. The net result is that the criminal justice system is now rapidly becoming full, not only with dangerous prisoners, but also with others caught in an upwardly punitive spiral (Nash 2006: 105). With the most cautious prediction (Home Office 2006b) concerning the prison population estimating its passing the 80,000 mark in the summer of 2008 (which in fact happened in early 2007), the most senior judge in the land called for restraint in the use of custody. Allison (2006) reported the Lord Chief Justice as describing the prison service as 'fatally flawed'. Lord Chief Justice Phillips argued that more space should be freed in the prison system by having more people dealt with by robust sentences in the community. However, as we have noted above, the likelihood is that prison numbers will continue to rise, not only as a result of harsher sentencing, but also because of reduced opportunities for release and higher failures on more stringent parole conditions.

As a result of the increased publicity given to dangerous offenders, decision-making has moved from a secretive to a much more public process. A principle of 'defensible decisions' (based upon sound risk assessment) may give way to 'defensive' decision-making – based upon greater caution with potential public disapproval in mind when matters go wrong. Professional decision-makers are to be much more open to public scrutiny. For example, lay advisors have been appointed to MAPPA through the 2003 Criminal Justice Act and following a pilot in eight areas in 2002. These advisers are meant to bring a community focus to the oversight and management of dangerous offenders and were in part a response to the demands for the community notification of sex offenders (Williams 2004). Pushing this development further, a victim perspective has been introduced into Parole Board hearing. When set alongside a government pilot scheme for victim advocates to be given a voice in sentencing in cases of murder and manslaughter it is very clear that the responses to dangerous offenders has served to open up the criminal justice process in an unprecedented way. It can also be expected that this lay participation could lead to greater caution 'in the public interest' in a series of important decision-making arenas and thereby increase many of the problems identified throughout this chapter.

Discussion questions

1 Does the reality of dangerous offenders merit the resources it requires of a range of criminal justice agencies?
2 Do you think that the departure from proportionality evident in many measures aimed at potentially dangerous offenders is warranted?
3 Working with dangerous offenders through MAPPA has encouraged an increasing multi-agency approach to a range of offender groups. What impact do you think this will have upon the 'traditional' practice of the core agencies (police, probation and prisons)?

Notes

1 For confirmation of this shift in thinking readers need look no further than the government's document entitled *Rebalancing the Criminal Justice System in Favour of the Law Abiding Majority. Cutting Crime, Reducing Reoffending and Protecting the Public* (Home Office 2006a).
2 Anne Owers, the Chief Inspector of Prisons, reported that over 400 indeterminate sentences had been made since legislation had been enacted. She argued

that, '[there is] no national strategy for dealing with these sentences' (*BBC News*, 3 March 2006).

3 For a similar discussion on the social construction of paedophiles and 'vigilantes' see Williams (2004).

Further reading

Kemshall, H. (2003) *Understanding Risk in Criminal Justice*. Buckingham: Open University Press. This text explores the growth of the 'risk business' and its impact upon a range of criminal justice agencies in their policy and practice. The book also offers valuable insights into the development of risk assessment tools and risk management processes as a significant influence on criminal justice policy.

Nash, M. (2006) *Public Protection and the Criminal Justice Process*. Oxford: Oxford University Press. This text builds upon the growth and extension of the public protection industry under Labour governments. It explores the extent to which a range of agencies have been drawn into the agenda and its impact upon core agencies such as the police and probation. It also considers stereotyped constructions of dangerousness and offers 'alternative' sites of danger which tend to be minimised in the current climate.

Nash, M. and Williams, A. (2008) *The Anatomy of Serious Further Offending*. Oxford: Oxford University Press. This text explores what happens when things go wrong in public protection or the processing of cases of serious further offending. It considers the way in which tragedies are handled in a variety of sectors from nuclear industries to health, and asks what lessons can be learned for the criminal justice process.

References

Allison, E. (2006) 'Prison Service fatally flawed says top judge', *The Guardian*, 30 May.

Bottoms, A.E. (1977) 'Reflections on the renaissance of dangerousness', *Howard Journal of Criminal Justice*, 16: 70–96.

Bowden, P. (1996) 'Violence and mental disorder', in N. Walker (ed.), *Dangerous People*. London: Blackstone Press.

Butler Committee (1975) *Report of the Committee on Mentally Abnormal Offenders*, Cmnd 6244. London: HMSO.

Clarke, C. (2006) *Home Secretary Announces New Public Protection Measures*, 20 April. Available at: http://press.homeoffice.gov.uk/press-releases (retrieved 25 May 2006).

Dworkin, R. (1977) *Taking Rights Seriously*. London: Duckworth.

Floud, J. (1982) 'Dangerousness and criminal justice', *British Journal of Criminology*, 22 (3): 213–28.

Floud, J. and Young, W. (1981) *Dangerousness and Criminal Justice*. London: Heinemann.

Garland, D. (2000) 'The culture of high crime societies: some preconditions of recent "law and order" policies', *British Journal of Criminology*, 40 (3): 347–75.

HMIP (1995) *Dealing with Dangerous People: The Probation Service and Public Protection, Report of a Thematic Inspection.* London: HMSO.

HMIP (1998) *Exercising Constant Vigilance: The Role of the Probation Service in Protecting the Public from Sex Offenders, Report of a Thematic Inspection.* London: HMSO.

HMIP (2006a) *An Independent Review of a Serious Further Offence Case: Damien Hanson & Elliot White.* London: Home Office.

HMIP (2006b) *An Independent Review of a Serious Further Offence Case: Anthony Rice.* London: Home Office.

Holden, A. (1974) *The St Albans Poisoner: The Life and Times of Graham Young.* London: Hodder & Stoughton.

Home Office (1997) *Community Protection Order: A Consultation Paper.* London: Home Office.

Home Office (2006a) *Rebalancing the Criminal Justice System in Favour of the Law-abiding Majority. Cutting Crime, Reducing Reoffending and Protecting the Public.* London: Home Office.

Home Office (2006b) *Prison Population Projections 2006–13, England and Wales,* Home Office Statistical Bulletin 11/06. London: Home Office.

Johnson, P. (2006) 'How dangerous men are freed to kill', *The Telegraph,* 24 April. Online at: http://www.telegraph.co.uk/opinion/main.jhtml?xml=/opinion/2006/04/24/do2402.xml (accessed 4 June 2008).

Kemshall, H. and Maguire, M. (2001) 'Public protection, partnership and risk penality. The multi-agency risk management of sexual and violent offenders', *Punishment and Society,* 3 (2): 237–64.

Maden, A. (2007) *Treating Violence: A Guide to Risk Management in Mental Health.* Oxford: Oxford University Press.

Nash, M. (1999) 'Enter the Polibation Officer', *International Journal of Police Science and Management,* 1 (4): 360–8.

Nash, M. (2006) *Public Protection and the Criminal Justice Process.* Oxford: Oxford University Press.

Office for Criminal Justice Reform (2005) *Hearing the Relatives of Murder and Manslaughter Victims: The Government's Plan to Give Bereaved Relatives of Murder and Manslaughter Victims a Say in Criminal Proceedings.* London: Department for Constitutional Affairs.

Police Federation for England and Wales (2006) Press release, 20 April. Online at: http://www.polfed.org/PR_Violent_Offender_Order_Comment_200406.pdf (retrieved 25 September 2006).

Prison Reform Trust (PRT) (2007) *Indefinitely Maybe – How the Indeterminate Sentence for Public Protection Is Unjust and Unsustainable.* London: PRT.

Scott, P. (1977) 'Assessing dangerousness in criminals', *British Journal of Psychiatry,* 131: 127–42.

Scottish Council on Crime (1975) *Crime and the Prevention of Crime.* Edinburgh: HMSO.

Silverman, J. and Wilson, D. (2002) *Innocence Betrayed: Paedophilia, the Media and Society.* Cambridge: Polity Press.

Thomas, D. (2004) 'The Criminal Justice Act 2003: custodial sentences', *Criminal Law Review,* 702–11.

Williams, A. (2004) '"There Ain't No Peds in Paulsgrove". Social Control, Vigilantes and the Misapplication of Moral Panic Theory'. Unpublished PhD thesis, University of Reading.

Williams, A. and Thompson, B. (2004a) 'Vigilance or vigilantes: the Paulsgrove riots and policing paedophiles in the community, Part 1: the long slow fuse', *Police Journal*, 77: 99–119.

Williams, A. and Thompson, B. (2004b) 'Vigilance or vigilantes: the Paulsgrove riots and policing paedophiles in the community, Part 2: the lessons of Paulsgrove', *Police Journal*, 77: 199–205.

Chapter 14

Understanding and engaging with problematic substance use

Julian Buchanan

Introduction

This chapter will introduce the reader to the complex issue of substance use. The term substance use rather than drug use includes all legal substances such as alcohol, tobacco, prescribed substances such as benzodiazepines and anti-depressants, solvents such as aerosols and glue, and the more commonly known illicit substances such as crack cocaine, heroin and cannabis. The knowledge and value base underpinning policy and practice in this area is not without confusion, conflict and contradiction. These tensions will be highlighted throughout the chapter. In keeping with the focus of the book on addressing offending the primary focus of the chapter will be to examine substance use which is more commonly associated with legal consequences to the individual and/or others. The chapter will explore the changing patterns of substance use over recent decades, types of substance use, the legal context, the nature of 'addiction' and the links with crime, before finally exploring what can be done to help problem substance users.

Setting the context

Given the growing anxiety concerning a problematic population who use 'drugs', it is important to put this apparent new phenomenon into context by acknowledging that virtually everyone uses substances to achieve some degree of pleasure. The use of substances for pleasure is not confined to a deviant sub-group. On a daily basis people feel the need to start the day with a shot of caffeine (found in tea, coffee, hot chocolate or Coca Cola). They'll probably repeat this process frequently throughout the day. At regular intervals (perhaps 10 or 20 times a day) tobacco users will want to enjoy a cigarette. After a hard day's work many will enjoy two or three units of alcohol in the form of a glass of red wine, a beer or shot of whisky to help them relax. When trying to understand and engage with problem substance users it is important to acknowledge that virtually everyone is a substance user.

The use of substances for pleasure is recorded throughout our history. The book of Genesis (contained in the Holy Bible) which was written around 1420 BC records Noah drinking alcohol to excess. The Hindu sacred text Atharva Veda written around 1500 BC cites the use of cannabis (bhang). More recently opium (similar to heroin) was once widely legally available and used across the UK. A surprising number of distinguished people used opium including William Gladstone, William Wordsworth, Samuel Taylor Coleridge and William Wilberforce. Taking substances for their desired effect has been enjoyed throughout the ages and will continue in the future. However, in the twentieth century legislation supported heavily by tough law enforcement measures was introduced to outlaw the use of particular substances, while paradoxically allowing other substances such as alcohol and tobacco to be promoted. Paradoxically, some of these legal substances which enjoy the privileged position of being heavily promoted, advertised and widely distributed are arguably inherently more dangerous. This bifurcation process between illegal and legal substances has created a confusing and contradictory reductionist framework. It presents the use of legally approved substances as a social and cultural norm, while in contrast, illegal substances are presented as dangerous and deviant. The portrayal of illegal substances as a powerful evil that threatens our lives and communities is well illustrated by an extract from the Home Office minister referring to new legislation to tackle illegal substance use:

> Drug misuse can ruin individual lives, tear open families and blight whole communities with the menace of dealers ... people who profit in the misery of others ... vicious circle of drugs and crime ... dealers will face harsher sentences where they prey on children ... Drugs are a scourge on the world. (Flint 2005: 7)

There can be no dispute that substance use (legal as well as illegal) can sometimes be dangerous to individuals, families and the wider community, but an emotive focus on illicit substances blurs the issues and oversimplifies the complexities of present-day recreational substance use. It is a grave mistake to adopt a narrow and somewhat blinkered approach to substances by focusing heavily upon illegal substances while overlooking the very serious dangers posed by legal substances such as alcohol and tobacco. However, these legal substances are embedded within western expressions of pleasure. For example, drinking alcohol – often to excess – is seen as a fitting and appropriate way to celebrate a special occasion or achievement. This cultural norm is not without its legal, social and physiological consequences to the individual or society. Over a quarter of the adult population drink above recommended guidelines, causing health, social and personal problems (DoH 2005). The links between alcohol and violence are well established – 44 per cent of all violent crimes are carried out by an offender who was believed to be under the influence of alcohol and in respect of 'stranger violence' this figure rises to 54 per cent (Home Office 2006). Tobacco health-related problems costs the NHS up to £1.7 billion every year (Home Office 1998a), and kills 120,000 people every year (DoH 2003). In comparison, in 2004 the number of all illegal substance-related deaths totalled 1,429 (National Statistics 2006). Substance use, legal and illegal, is a key leisure activity and very much embedded within our society. The widespread use of substances among young people in particular was recognised by the government's Advisory Committee on the Misuse of Drugs (ACMD):

> Among the 6.8 million 16–24-year-olds in the UK, there are an estimated 2.1 million daily smokers, 1.9 million who drink more than twice the recommended daily alcohol limit at least once a week and 1 million who have used another drug in the past month. (ACMD 2006: 6)

The increasing use of illegal substances

Historically there has always been a small but discrete minority of people who used illegal substances. However, the number of illegal users has grown steadily and significantly over the past 30 years. The sharp increase in illegal substance use began in the 1980s with the 'outbreak' of heroin use – a highly addictive substance that is used medically as a very effective painkiller. Unlike the largely middle-class substance users of the 1960s who used substances to enhance social pleasures, the new 1980s users were young, unemployed, single, lived at home in socially deprived areas, and had few or no educational qualifications (Buchanan and Wyke 1987; Parker et al. 1988). These substance users were predominantly working-class youth who lived in areas that were dependent upon heavy industry such as coal, shipping and manufacturing for employment and growth. The young people, who started smoking heroin (chasing the dragon) in the 1980s lived in labour-intensive areas badly affected by economic decline and deindustrialisation. They were unable to find employment and felt discarded by an unsympathetic right-wing government. Unlike the discrete group of middle-class users of the 1960s, these new 1980s users didn't take illegal substances to enhance life but took a painkilling substance (heroin) to escape the realities of life (Buchanan and Wyke 1987). On heroin these users could escape to a 'euphoric oblivion', although with heavy and dependent use this desired effect was rarely achieved, as users quickly became dependent and needed to take heroin primarily to alleviate unpleasant withdrawal symptoms. Home Office statistics of registered 'addicts' illustrate the rapid increase in illegal substance use. In 1980 2,846 people were registered to the Home Office; by 1987 it had risen to over 10,000 (Robertson 1987), and by 1996 over 43,000 were registered (Buchanan and Young 2000a).

The widespread use and availability of heroin has continued since the 1980s to the present day. However, in the 1990s a new wave of illegal substance use emerged that was associated with the rave culture. This wave of illegal use centred upon ecstasy – the dance drug of choice. Unlike the heroin outbreak of the early 1980s the rave scene of the 1990s was based upon the pursuit of pleasure and involved a substance which is not particularly addictive, physically or psychologically. Despite the moral panic rhetoric and introduction of new legislation to curb rave events the scene grew considerably and attracted thousands of mainly students and employed people (Measham et al. 2001). By 1995 8 per cent of 15–16-year-olds reported having tried ecstasy (Miller and Plant 1996). This widespread use of illegal substances for pleasure led some researchers to suggest that illicit substance use had become a normalised adolescent experience (Parker et al. 1998).

By the twenty-first century an estimated 3.1 to 3.7 million people in the UK admitted to having tried an illegal substance (Atha 2004; Condon and Smith 2003). According to the British Crime Survey one in four 16–24-year-olds used an illegal substance in the previous year (Condon and Smith 2003). Another UK survey involving over 10,000 secondary school children found that 23 per cent of 15-year-olds had taken an illegal substance in the previous month, and 38 per cent in the previous year (NatCen 2004). The 'gateway theory' that suggests that people who start using 'soft' drugs such as cannabis will progress to taking hard drugs is somewhat discredited by these statistics. The vast majority of these users will be occasional or recreational users who will not go on to develop a substance use problem. If it could be argued that there was a gateway substance the research would tend to suggest use of tobacco at an early age rather than cannabis as the gateway to more serious problematic substance use (Home Office 2002).

There are now estimated to be between a quarter and half a million problem (illegal) substance users in England and Wales (Godfrey et al. 2002). However, it is important to differentiate between illegal substance use and problematic illegal substance use. Edmunds et al. (1998) estimate that 97 per cent of illegal substance users are occasional or recreational users and only 3 per cent are problem users. The growing number of people using illegal substances means more people will risk being caught up in the criminal justice system. Criminalising large numbers of otherwise law-abiding people raises practical and ethical issues. Between 2002 and 2003 the total number of drug offences in England and Wales rose by 5 per cent to 133,970, and Class A offences (heroin, cocaine, LSD and ecstasy) rose by to 6 per cent (Kumari and Mwenda 2005: 1).

Patterns of substance use

It is difficult to categorise legal and illegal substance use because substance users are not a homogenous group and there are a range of different substances and distinctive groupings. However, three broad categories of substance use can be described: (a) occasional use; (b) recreational use; and (c) problematic use. The occasional user is an ad hoc user and may just experiment or sometimes use the substance if it's offered; the recreational user takes the substance at regular times and places of their choice. They enjoy the desired effect of the substance, don't suffer any particular negative consequences or loss of control, and they don't tend to present any particular harm or risk to others. The problematic user has lost a degree of self-control and takes the substance regularly, probably dependently. Their pattern of substance use negatively impacts physically, psychologically and/ or socially upon the user and probably upon their wider family, friends and community. The vast majority of people use substances (legal and illegal) on a recreational basis without posing risk or harm to others. Problematic substance users tend to use a wide range of different substances depending upon what is available at the time, though heroin, crack cocaine and alcohol tend to be popular choices. It is this group that are more likely to come to the attention of the police, prison and probation services and treatment agencies.

It would seem appropriate for enforcement agencies to concentrate their efforts almost exclusively upon the problematic users of the more dangerous substances. However, the criminal justice system supported by the United Nations 10-year plan 'Towards Drug Free World – We Can Do It!' (Arlacchi 1998), has a broader agenda to eradicate all illegal substance use – regardless of whether it is recreational or problematic. It may seem odd that the vast majority of drug seizures and arrests concern not crack cocaine or heroin but cannabis use. In 2004 70 per cent of all drug seizures related to cannabis with a total of 88 tons of cannabis seized compared to 2.1 tons of heroin, 4.6 tonnes of cocaine and 4.6 tonnes of ecstasy (Mwenda and Kaiza 2006).

The law and recreational substance use

In respect of legal substances the rationale behind the legal status of different substances can be a little difficult to comprehend. The government's Advisory Council on the Misuse Drugs (ACMD 2006) has rightly highlighted the dangers of legal substances and suggested changes. However, at present it is an offence to give alcohol to a child under five years old, but not an offence to give alcohol to a child who is five years old (though it may indeed be considered highly inappropriate or indeed a form of abuse). A 16-year-old can buy and drink beer or cider (but not spirits) in a pub provided they are having a meal. Drinking alcohol and driving a vehicle is allowed provided the alcohol levels remain less than 80 mg of alcohol in every 100 ml of blood. In respect of tobacco it is legal to possess or use tobacco products at any age; however, it is illegal for someone to sell tobacco to children aged under 16 years (the government may increase this to 18 years).

The status of illegal substances is largely contained in the Misuse of Drugs Act 1971 which divides the controlled substances into three categories A, B and C. Class A, the most serious, includes ecstasy, LSD, heroin, cocaine, crack, magic mushrooms and amphetamine (if prepared for injection). The penalties for possession are up to seven years in prison and/or an unlimited fine. The penalties for giving or selling (dealing) a Class A substance to another person are severe – up to life imprisonment and/or an unlimited fine. Class B drugs include amphetamines, methylphenidate (Ritalin) and pholcodine linctus. The penalties for possession are up to five years in prison and/or an unlimited fine. The penalties for dealing are up to 14 years in prison and/or an unlimited fine. Class C drugs include cannabis, tranquillisers (such as ativan, valium), GHB (gamma hydroxybutyrate) and anabolic steroids. The penalties for possession are up to two years in prison and/or an unlimited fine. The penalties for dealing are up to 14 years in prison and/or an unlimited fine. (More information on the legal status and consequences of illegal drugs can be found on the Release website http://www.release.org.uk.)

The current classification of illegal substances is misleading because it doesn't accurately reflect the 'hierarchy of harm' posed by different substances (Police Foundation 2000). Despite the more severe sentencing options Class A substances are not necessarily more harmful than Class B and C substances. For example, it could be argued that ecstasy, a Class A drug, is generally less physically and psychologically addictive and has fewer side effects than tranquillisers, a Class C drug. The lack of consistency and the significant anomalies of the ABC drug classification have led a specialist government committee to conclude that: 'The current classification system is not fit for purpose and should be replaced with a more scientifically based scale of harm, decoupled from penalties for possession and trafficking' (House of Commons Science and Technology Committee 2006: 3).

Given that some substances are illegal and carry severe penalties for distribution it is confusing and perhaps difficult to comprehend that some illegal substances are not intrinsically more dangerous than their legal counterparts. On the contrary it could be argued that some legal substances are considerably more harmful and dangerous than some substances controlled by the Misuse of Drugs Act. For example, the health risks and levels of addiction caused by tobacco could be argued to be greater than the health risks and level of addiction caused by LSD. The graph in Figure 14.1, devised by the government's Advisory Council on the Misuse of Drugs, provides a league table of harms posed by different substances. It is based upon assessments from a group of independent experts that included psychiatrists and specialists working with 'addiction' who used a rating scale that covered physical harm, psychological harm and social harm. Figure 14.1 indicates clearly that the classification of illegal substance under the Misuse of Drugs Act 1971 (which is given at the top of each bar) is not a good indicator of harm. It also illustrates that some legal substances pose

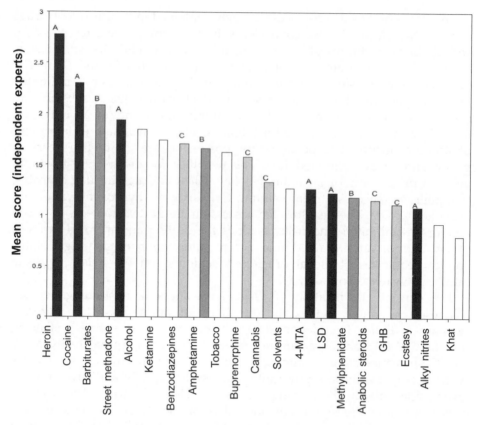

House of Commons Science and Technology Committee 2006: Ev114

Figure 14.1 Independent assessment of harm posed by 20 substances

greater risk than many illegal substances. Interestingly the independent experts rated alcohol as the fifth most dangerous substance.

Further measures to eradicate illegal substance use in the UK have been introduced in the Drugs Act 2005. This Act enables 'drug' testing suspected illegal substance offenders on arrest rather than on charge, and gives provision for any person who tests positive for a Class A substance to be assessed by a drugs specialist. If the person arrested is suspected to have swallowed an illegal substance to avoid detection the Act gives the police powers to remand the person in police custody for up to 192 hours so that the evidence can be recovered. If that person refuses without good cause to consent to an intimate body search, X-ray or ultrasound scan the Act allows the court or jury to draw an adverse inference. A new presumption of intent to supply is introduced where a defendant is found to be in possession of a certain quantity of controlled substances. The Act also amends the 1998 Crime and Disorder Act to introduce a new civil intervention order requiring adults whose anti-social behaviour is believed to be drug related to attend drug counselling as part of an ASBO.

It is clear that both legal and illegal substances can potentially have a devastating impact, although the vast majority of substance users don't experience significant difficulties. Contrary to popular perceptions the use of an illegal substance does not inevitably or generally lead to difficulties or any escalation of substance use. Substances do vary considerably in terms of toxicity, effect, physical dependence, tolerance, psychological dependence and legal status. This factual information is widely available and updated on web sites such as 'Drugscope' and 'Talk to Frank' and will therefore not be detailed here. Some substances are undoubtedly more difficult to control than others, though this depends upon the person and the environment and not just the substance. However, it is important to acknowledge that there are considerable *additional* risks taking a substance that has been made illegal (Buchanan 2005).

Leisure, risks and dangers

Individualism, choice, pleasure, uncertainty and risk are key tenets of postmodern life. The hedonistic pursuit of leisure and pleasure feature widely throughout advertising, and for many young people taking calculated risks with one or more substances is one of many available recreational pleasure choices. The 'drug choice' is one of many other risk choices.

Should I risk using a mobile phone? Should I risk eating genetically modified food? Should I risk going into major debt by going to university? Should I risk this job – is it secure? Can I risk taking out a mortgage? Can I risk starting a family – will the relationship last? Although young people are now widely exposed to illegal substances whether taking illegal substances has become a normalised adolescent activity remains contested (MacDonald and Marsh 2002; Pearson and Shiner 2002). However, it should be acknowledged that there are unprecedented levels of substance use among young people, including new patterns of excessive legal substance use, – 'binge' drinking in particular. As Measham observes, these users engage in calculated and controlled risks:

... to balance the potential pharmacological pleasures with the perceived risks from individual legal and illicit drugs, despite the complexity of poly-drug pharmacology and the limitations of current scientific knowledge on actual risks involved. The user not only pursues a desired state of intoxication, but also attempts to avoid an undesired state. The casualties in the toilets and the embarrassments on the dance floor are a reminder for most legal and illicit drug users of where to draw the line not only because of the financial, health and safety implications but also the lack of cultural credibility of extreme intoxication. This is the rational cost–benefit analysis in recreational drug use. (Measham 2004: 319)

The message regarding substance use is confusing. It is say 'no' to all illegal substances and this is vehemently monitored and enforced by increasingly invasive measures to 'drug' test a wide range of people: prisoners, suspected users on arrest, school children and a growing number of employees. In contrast, the message in relation to alcohol is more tolerant and reasonable – as illustrated by the government's document on alcohol entitled 'Drinking Responsibly' (Home Office 2005). Those working with substance users will need to untangle these mixed messages concerning the different effects, risks and dangers posed by illegal and legal substances. People who regularly use illegal substances tend to be fairly well informed. Any sweeping or ill-informed message regarding the comparable dangers of illegal and legal substances is likely to lead to a loss of credibility and trust between the worker and substance user – a key factor when professionals are trying to assist someone who uses substances in a problematic way. An overemphasis upon illegal substance could also fail to appreciate the very real risks posed by legal substances (JRF 2000).

It is the 3 per cent who use substances in a problematic way that warrant most attention. Problematic use can seriously disrupt family life, cause stress, conflict and disruption (Barnard 2005). Illegal substances in particular can have a damaging affect on the wider community resulting in crime, prostitution, neighbourhood unease and anti-social behaviour (McKeganey et al. 2004). The economic costs for each problematic illegal user are estimated to be in excess of £10,000 per year, while the social costs are in the region of £35,000 per year (Godfrey et al. 2002). These personal, social and economic costs of problematic use have justifiably warranted social/public concern. However, the vast majority of problem users are people who had considerable difficulties before they began taking illegal substances. Problem illegal substance users are disproportionately from poor disadvantaged families and communities, a high percentage have been in care and excluded from education, and have few or no qualifications, limited family support, a poor employment record and a criminal record. The association between problem substance use and social disadvantage/ social exclusion has important policy and practice implications. For example, expecting a recovered long-term problem user to find new routines, hobbies and employment is probably unrealistic if their entire adult life experience has been centred upon illegal substance-related activities. Many problem users have had very limited positive adult life experiences and will need considerable support to engage in mainstream society and achieve social reintegration. For many a 'drug-centred' adult life is all they have ever known: 'The all-consuming drug-centred lifestyle is the only adult existence they have known, and should be seen as an inappropriate solution, rather than the problem' (Buchanan 2004: 398). Unless these underlying problems of social and economic exclusion are addressed the increasingly demanding treatment options tied into the criminal justice system which concentrate upon tackling physical and psychological addiction will only result in expanding a prison population already laden with people who have substance-related problems.

The relationship between problematic use, poverty, crime and social exclusion remain relatively unexplored (Seddon 2000, 2006), though it has long been argued that drug policy and practice should take greater account of structural factors rather than focusing upon addiction and individual choice: 'socio-economic environmental factors, instead of the tendency to stress personal responsibility and genetic predisposition' (MacGregor 1995: 20). While physiological and psychological understandings of substance dependence are important to any appreciation of problematic substance use, seen in isolation they fail to comprehensively appreciate the nature of the problem and overlook important social dimensions. This can sometimes lead to narrow policy and strategy interventions that risk internalising and pathologising dependence by taking little account of important structural factors and underlying social inequalities (Foster 2000; Parker and Egginton 2004; Buchanan 2005).

Problematic illegal users have become further isolated and excluded by the 'war on drugs' which in practice has led to in a 'war on drug users' (Buchanan and Young 2000b). This has resulted in prejudice, discrimination and hostility from individuals, communities and agencies towards problematic illegal users who are an easy group to target – a scapegoat for the ills of the local community. This isolation and discrimination makes the task of rehabilitation and reintegration more difficult and relapse more likely. Recognising the multiple needs and severe difficulties problem users face Kemp and Neale argue:

> A more realistic strategy to help move problem drug users closer to being job ready requires a co-ordinated approach that tackles their dependency and related problems before focusing more closely on employment, education and training schemes … work to help drug users secure or remain settled in suitable accommodation and targeted support (including both medical and psychosocial components) to tackle the physical and mental health problems they commonly experience. (Kemp and Neale 2005: 41)

Exploring the crime connection

The connections between substance use and crime can be understood at three levels: substance defined, substance influenced and substance related.

- *Substance defined*. These are actions involving substances that are specifically mentioned and defined by legislation as criminal, for example possession of heroin, driving with excess alcohol, giving an ecstasy tablet to a friend. Defined crimes are socially constructed; the use of the substance

255

is prohibited by laws which are designed to protect the individual and the wider community from the harms of substance use. These crimes are more easily measured: for example, in 2004 there were 107,360 drug seizures by police and HM Revenue and Customs in England and Wales (Mwenda and Kaiza 2006).

- *Substance influenced*. These are crimes that don't refer to substance use but are committed when 'under the influence' or intoxicated by a substance. Substance-influenced crimes are more difficult to measure in that it requires an assessment that indeed the offender is under the influence of a substance, and secondly that intoxication played some part in the commission of the offence. Examples are criminal damage, assault and murder, committed when the person was under the influence of, say, alcohol, tranquillisers, crack cocaine, etc.

- *Substance related*. These are crimes that are committed that don't refer to substance use, that are not committed while under the influence but are somehow connected, related and/or motivated by substance use, typically a heroin user who steals from a shop in order to fund a heroin habit. These crimes require an assessment that the person is a substance user, and secondly that the crime was in some way related to their substance use habit.

There has been growing attention in the past decade about the connections between illegal substances and crime (Bennett and Holloway 2005). This has led to a considerable and much needed investment in drug treatment, but this has been tied to court orders as part of the wider Drugs Intervention Programme (DIP). The evidence of a clear causal link between illegal substance use and substance-related crime remains unclear. Philip Bean offers three major explanations: (a) substance use leads to crime; (b) crime leads to substance use; (c) substance use and crime have a common aetiology (Bean 2004: 31). It has also been argued that any analysis of problematic substance use and crime must be located within a wider analysis of social inequality, exclusion and discrimination (Bennett and Holloway 2005, Buchanan 2004; Seddon 2006). While the specific links between substance-related and substance-influenced crime are open to debate, there can be little dispute that illegal substance use involves a huge illegal economy which requires a robust and widespread underground business enterprise, policed by a considerable government enforcement effort costing around £20bn per year (Kushlick 2004).

Treatment within the criminal justice system

The present government's strategy for tackling illegal substances was launched in 1998 by the appointment of a US-style 'Drug Tsar' Keith Halliwell who presided over a ten-year drug strategy *Tackling Drugs to Build a Better Britain* (Home Office 1998b). This strategy was later superseded by the Updated Drugs Strategy in 2002 which focused attention on Class A drugs and committed considerable additional resources to tackle illegal substance use. Interestingly the strategy did not include legal substance use. Following devolution for Wales in 2000 the Welsh Assembly refined the original ten-year drug strategy and chose to incorporate alcohol, resulting in *Tackling Substance Misuse in Wales: A Partnership Approach* (National Assembly for Wales 2000). In 2004 the *Alcohol Harm Reduction Strategy for England* was published (Cabinet Office 2004).

The Drug Intervention Programme referred to as *Out of Crime, into Treatment* is a critical part of the strategy for tackling illegal substance use in England and Wales. The strategy has provided significant new money for treatment, but this is locked within the criminal justice system. It introduced coercive measures to 'encourage' problem users to get 'treatment' or face serious court sanctions. The Criminal Justice Act 2003 which came into force in April 2005 introduced a new sentencing framework. In respect of illegal substance use the Act introduces a new drug rehabilitation requirement that requires the offender to have treatment to reduce or eliminate their dependency on/or tendency to take drugs. This requirement also insists that the offender is subject to regular drug testing and regular court reviews. The order can last for a minimum of six months and a maximum of three years. The requirement can be attached to a community order or a suspended sentence order (when the maximum period is fixed at two years). The emphasis given to regular drug testing in these new compulsory treatment regimes tied to criminal justice may create an unrealistic expectation of abstinence and may eschew the focus upon crime reduction. Worryingly, studies in the US indicate relatively poor long-term outcomes for those engaged in coercive treatment (Gossop 2005).

In respect of alcohol users similar legal provisions apply in the alcohol treatment requirement. This can be attached to a community order or sentence order to eliminate or reduce alcohol dependency, although unlike drugs this requirement does not involve alcohol testing or court reviews. Neither the drug rehabilitation order nor the alcohol treatment order specifies what treatment substance users will be given, nor do they specify the pace of change required. Despite this assurance, conflicts will inevitably occur as criminal justice agencies want to see measurable and significant changes occur especially in terms of a reduction or cessation of substance usage and criminal activity. This tension will need to be carefully managed. Treatment needs to be carefully and appropriately matched to individual need and circumstances, while the pace of change will need to be sensitive to what the individual substance user can realistically be expected to achieve, or else they will be 'set up to fail'. Determining appropriate treatment and negotiating a realistic pace of change will depend upon the worker's ability to: give the substance user permission to speak honestly; listen and perceive the world from the substance user's perspective rather than the worker's; accurately assess motivation to change; accurately assess the personal resources of the user; be aware of what services are available; and understand the struggle to change behaviour that is fraught with chronic relapse.

Assessment and interventions

Agencies engaged with substance use will tend to be committed to abstinence and/or harm reduction. To illustrate the different perspectives an abstentionist would argue that a person is only 'cured' when they are completely drug free, whereas a person committed to harm reduction would argue that it is when a person can use substances safely in a controlled manner. The Alcoholics Anonymous (AA 2006) 12-step programme is a good example of an abstentionist model. This approach tends to see substances as possessing an inherent power over the person and sees the substance user as having an illness. This view is not generally shared by those who support harm reduction. The harm reductionists don't see addiction as a disease but as a social, legal, health and behavioural problem that requires a pragmatic and realistic response. A harm reductionist may be content to provide life-long methadone maintenance to a substance user if it is reducing harm. Not surprisingly abstentionist-orientated agencies that embrace an illness model of substance use may struggle to work in partnership with harm reductionist agencies that are willing to provide substitute drugs and clean needles and inform people how to use substances more safely. While rejecting the disease model harm reductionists can support a user's desire for abstinence. However, in practice, despite major philosophical differences these agencies often forge constructive working relationships. While harm reduction is widely accepted as an effective way of engaging with problem substance use the growing use of drug testing as part of court orders may unwittingly promote a drive towards an abstinence-based philosophy that could in the long term prove counterproductive.

The 'cycle of change' is probably the cornerstone to most work with addictive behaviours (for a general discussion of its use see Tallant *et al.* this volume). It was originally developed in the early 1980s to tackle cigarette smoking but has been adapted to good effect to illegal substance use. The cycle of change model (Prochaska *et al.* 1995) has been widely adapted and continues to be used (Goodman 2007). It is a useful assessment tool that helps to identify a person's dependent habitual behaviour within one of six stages:

1 *Pre-contemplation.* The person can't see or won't see that the current pattern of substance use warrants change.
2 *Contemplation.* The person has insight and occasional desire for change but is generally ambivalent.
3 *Preparation.* The person has decided to change and is exploring what to do, when, where and how.
4 *Action.* The person has taken action and is in the process of changing current patterns of behaviour.

5 *Maintenance.* The person has achieved the desired change and has control over their habit.

6 *Relapse.* The person has lost control of their behaviour and returned to their habit.

Identifying more accurately which stage in the cycle of change the person is at enables the worker to engage more appropriately and effectively. For example, if a person is at the pre-contemplation stage then a genuine exploration of the pros and cons of substance use (from the user's point of view, not the worker's) is more likely to have a positive impact than a goal-setting approach based upon becoming drug-free. Indeed encouragement to become drug free could have a counterproductive impact. For example, a pre-contemplator substance user with an outstanding court case may feel pressured to acquiesce with a drug-free agenda. In such cases it could be argued that the worker has set the substance user up to fail. The cycle of change is an assessment tool that usefully identifies what type of intervention may be most effective depending upon what stage the person is at. It encourages engagement with substance users at all stages. The cycle of change suggests relapse should not be seen as failure but an almost inevitable occurrence and a learning process. This is quite different from some abstentionist approaches which see relapse as failure and would suggest the person has to 'hit rock bottom' before they can receive help and be ready to change. Unless the substance user is motivated, properly prepared, supported and fully committed to an appropriately well matched intervention programme, arrangements are likely to founder. Herein lies a dilemma because the range of treatment available under DIP is sometimes limited.

Motivational interviewing (Miller and Rollnick 2002) complements the cycle of change because the approach doesn't seek to manipulate drug users towards a particular outcome. Instead, it attempts to empower the drug user by assisting them to reflect upon their own situation as they perceive it. There is sometimes a misunderstanding that motivational interviewing involves the worker using their energy and enthusiasm to motivate change in the substance user. To the contrary, motivational interviewing involves a non-judgmental, non-directive approach that seeks to facilitate the substance user to review negative and positive aspects of their lives from their own perspective and experience and to reach their own conclusion. This process can help create an inner conflict that stimulates the substance user out of contemplation and into action as they become motivated for the change that they desire (for a general discussion of motivational interviewing see Tallant *et al.* this volume).

Intervention strategies will need to be combined with a commitment to understand and, most importantly, address the underlying causes of problematic substance use (unemployment, poverty and social exclusion) otherwise the person is unlikely to progress. The daily routine involved in managing a heavy substance use habit occupies the user providing routine:

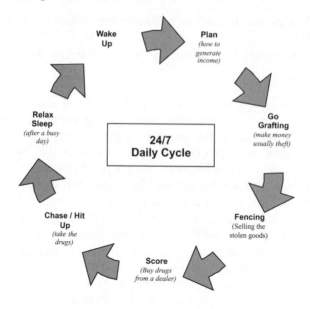

Source: Buchanan (2006b: 56).

Figure 14.2   The 24/7 daily cycle of a problem substance user.

demands, targets, network, highs, lows, rewards, pressures, skills, etc. This routine is represented in Figure 14.2 If this is going to be removed as part of 'treatment' then it is crucial that something is in place that is able to fill the vacuum left behind.

Conclusion

As a society we have an ambiguous relationship with our use of substances for pleasure. Legislation, policy, practice and values are at times contradictory, not evidence based, and therefore communicate confusing messages. Although recreational illegal substance use poses little harm to wider society and limited risk to the individual it remains a serious criminal offence and the acquisition of a criminal record for a drugs offence presents serious social, economic and political difficulties to the individual. The main focus of attention for criminal justice workers will inevitably be centred upon working with problematic illegal substance use. Hostility towards illegal substances has become synonymous with hostility toward illegal substance users making it much harder for those recovering to socially reintegrate. With a growing commitment by the UK government to use the criminal justice system to deliver drug treatment combined with rigorous drug testing and regular reviews, there is a risk that the physical aspects of addiction may be mistakenly over-emphasised. If people are to be helped to recover from long-term substance use problems then it is crucial that sufficient attention must be given to the deep-seated underlying psycho-social and structural problems that are part of the aetiology of most problematic substance use. Unless these precipitating factors are addressed the majority of problematic substance users will, despite intensive drug rehabilitation orders, be ill-equipped and unable to access mainstream society. Relapse and a return to a drug-centred lifestyle then becomes almost inevitable, as illicit problem substance users with few legitimate options and limited social capital are unable to socially reintegrate. Prison then becomes more likely. Shamefully, our overcrowded prisons have become silos to house seriously disadvantaged and damaged problem substance users.

Discussion questions

1 Are the reasons why people take illegal substances any different to the reasons why people take legal substances?
2 To what degree do you think problematic substance is a physical, psychological, legal or social problem?
3 Why do you think there is strong association between illegal substance use and crime?

Further reading

Bennett, T. and Holloway, K. (2005) *Understanding Drugs, Alcohol and Crime*. Maidenhead: Open University Press. An accessible and comprehensive introduction to understanding the relationship between problem substance use and criminal activity.

Goodman, A. (2007) *Social Work with Drug and Substance Misuse*. Exeter: Learning Matters. An easy-to-read, practical and accessible text that examines all aspects of working constructively with problem substance users.

Hughes, R., Lart, R. and Higate, P. (eds) (2006) *Drugs: Policy and Politics*. Maidenhead: Open University Press. This book looks at assessing drug policies and political responses, and locates problem substance use within a wider social policy context.

Robson, P. (2004) *Forbidden Drugs: Understanding Drugs and Why People Take Them*. Oxford: Oxford University Press. This is an authoritative carefully considered examination of substances and their place and use in society.

References

Advisory Council on the Misuse of Drugs (ACMD) (2003) *Hidden Harm: Responding to the Needs of Problem Drug Users*. London: Home Office.

Advisory Council on the Misuse of Drugs (ACMD) (2006) *Pathways to Problems*. London: Home Office.

Alcoholics Anonymous (AA) (2006) *The Big Book Online*. Available at: http://www.aa.org/bigbookonline (accessed 3 June 2008).

Arlacchi, P. (1998) 'Towards a drug-free world by 2008 – we can do it', *UN Chronicle*, Summer. Geneva: United Nations Department of Public Information.

Atha, M.J. (2004) *Taxing the UK Drug Market*. Available online from the Independent Drug Monitoring Unit at: http://www.idmu.co.uk.

Barnard, M. (2005) *Drugs in the Family: The Impact on Parents and Siblings*. York: Joseph Rowntree Foundation.

Bean, P. (2004) *Drugs and Crime*, 2nd edn. Cullompton: Willan.

Bennett, T. and Holloway, K. (2005) *Understanding Drugs, Alcohol and Crime*. Maidenhead: Open University Press.

Buchanan, J. (2004) 'Missing links? Problem drug use and social exclusion', *Probation Journal Special Edition – Rethinking Drugs and Crime*, 51 (4): 387–97.

Buchanan, J. (2005) 'Problem drug use in the 21st century: a social model of intervention', in T. Heinonen and A. Metteri (eds), *Health and Mental Health: Issues Developments and Actions*. Toronto: Scholars Press, pp. 65–84.

Buchanan, J. (2006a) Long-Term Problem Drug Use: Vocational Rehab and Social Reintegration. Conference paper at the 2006 National Drug Treatment Conference published online at: http://www.exchangesupplies.org/conferences/NDTC/2006_NDTC/speakers/julian_buchanan.html.

Buchanan, J. (2006b) 'Understanding problematic drug use: a medical matter or a social issue?', *British Journal of Community Justice*, 4 (2): 47–60.

Buchanan, J. and Wyke, G. (1987) 'Drug Use and Its Implications: A Study of the Sefton Probation Area'. Unpublished report, Merseyside Probation Service, Waterloo.

Buchanan, J. and Young, L. (2000a) 'Examining the relationship between material conditions, long-term problematic drug use and social exclusion: a new strategy for social inclusion', in J. Bradshaw and R. Sainsbury (eds), *Experiencing Poverty*. London: Ashgate Press, pp. 120–43.

Buchanan, J. and Young, L. (2000b) 'The war on drugs – a war on drug users', *Drugs: Education, Prevention Policy*, 7 (4): 409–22.

Cabinet Office (2004) *Alcohol Harm Reduction Strategy for England*. London: HMG Strategy Unit.

Condon, J. and Smith, N. (2003) *Prevalence of Drug Use: Key Findings from the 2002/2003 British Crime Survey*, Home Office Research Findings No. 229. London: Home Office.

Department of Health (DoH) (2003) *Statistics on Smoking*, Statistical Bulletin 2003/21. London: DoH.

Department of Health (DoH) (2005) *The 2004 National Alcohol Needs Assessment for England*, Alcohol Needs Assessment Research Project (ANARP). Available at: http://www.dh.gov.uk/assetRoot/04/12/22/39/04122239.pdf.

Edmunds, M., May, T., Hearnden, I. and Hough, M. (1998) *Arrest Referral: Emerging Lessons from Research*, DPI Paper No. 23. London: Home Office DPI.

Flint, C. (2005) Home Office Minister, quoted in *Drink and Drugs News*, 10 January, p. 7.

Foster, J. (2000) 'Social exclusion crime and drugs', *Drugs Education Prevention and Policy*, 7 (4): 317–30.

Godfrey, C., Eaton, G., McDougall, C. and Culyer, A. (2002) *The Economic and Social Costs of Class A Drug Use in England and Wales, 2000*. London: Home Office.

Goodman, A. (2007) *Social Work with Drug and Substance Misuse*. Exeter: Learning Matters.

Gossop, M. (2005) *Drug Misuse Treatment and Reductions in Crime: Findings from the National Treatment Outcome Research Study (NTORS)*, Research Briefing 8. London: NTA.

Home Office (1998a) *Smoking Kills: A White Paper on Tobacco*, Cm 4177. London: Home Office.

Home Office (1998b) *Tackling Drugs to Build a Better Britain: The Government's 10-Year Strategy for Tackling Drug Misuse*, Cm 3945. London: Stationery Office.

Home Office (2002) *The Classification of Cannabis under the Misuse of Drugs Act 1971*. London: ACMD.

Home Office (2005) *Drinking Responsibly: The Government's Proposals*. London: Home Office.

Home Office (2006) *Crimes and Victims*. London: Home Office. Available at: http://www.homeoffice.gov.uk/crime-victims/reducing-crime/alcohol-related-crime/.

House of Commons Science and Technology Select Committee (2006) *Drug Classification: Making a Hash of It?* 5th report of session 2005–6, HC1031, 31 July. Available at: http://www.publications.parliament.uk/pa/cm200506/cmselect/cmsctech/1031/1031.pdf.

Joseph Rowntree Foundation (JRF) (2000) *Drugs Dilemmas, Choices and the Law*. York: JRF.

Kemp, P. and Neale, J. (2005) 'Employability and problem drug users', *Critical Social Policy*, 25 (1): 28–46.

Kumari, K. and Mwenda, L. (2005) *Drug Offenders in England and Wales 2003*, Home Office Research Findings 256. London: Home Office. Available at: http://www.homeoffice.gov.uk/rds/pdfs05/r256.pdf.

Kushlick, D. (2004) 'The true price of prohibition', *The Guardian*, 6 August.

MacDonald, R. and Marsh, J. (2002) 'Crossing the Rubicon: youth transitions, poverty, drugs and social exclusion', *International Journal of Drug Policy*, 13: 27–38.

McGregor, S. (1995) *Drug Policy, Community and the City*, Occasional Paper, November, Middlesex University.

McKeganey, N., Neale, J., Parkin, S. and Mills, C. (2004) 'Communities and drugs: beyond the rhetoric of community action', *Probation Journal Special Issue: Rethinking Drugs and Crime*, 51 (4): 343–61.

Measham, F. (2004) 'The decline of ecstasy, the rise of "binge" drinking and the persistence of pleasure', *Probation Journal Special Issue: Rethinking Drugs and Crime*, 51 (4): 309–26.

Measham, F., Aldridge, J. and Parker, H. (2001) *Dancing on Drugs*. London: Free Association Press.

Miller, P. and Plant, M. (1996) 'Drinking, smoking and illicit drug use among 15 and 16 year olds in the United Kingdom', *British Medical Journal*, 313: 394–7.

Miller, W.R. and Rollnick, S. (eds) (2002) *Motivational Interviewing: Preparing People for Change*. New York: Guildford Press.

Mwenda, L. and Kaiza, P. (2006) *Seizures of Drugs England and Wales 2004*, Home Office Statistical Bulletin. London: Home Office.

NatCen (National Centre for Social Research and the National Foundation for Educational Research for the Department of Health) (2004) *Drug Use, Smoking and Drinking among Young People in England in 2003*. London: DoH.

National Assembly for Wales (2000) *Tackling Substance Abuse in Wales: A Partnership Approach*. Available at: http://new.wales.gov.uk/topics/housingandcommunity/safety/publications/substancemisusestrategy?lang=en (accessed 3 June 2008).

National Statistics (2006) *Health Statistics Quarterly*, Autumn. Basingstoke: Palgrave.

Parker, H. and Egginton, R. (2004) *Managing Local Heroin–Crack Problems: Hard Lessons about Policing Drug Markets and Treating Problem Users*. Surbiton: Anchor Press.

Parker, H., Bakx, K. and Newcombe, R. (1988) *Living with Heroin*. Buckingham: Open University Press.

Parker, H., Aldridge, J. and Measham, F. (1998) *Illegal Leisure: The Normalisation of Adolescent Drug Use*. London: Routledge.

Pearson, G. and Shiner, M. (2002) 'Rethinking the generation gap: attitudes to illicit drugs among young people and adults', *Journal of Criminology and Criminal Justice*, 2 (1): 71–86.

Police Foundation (2000) *Drugs and the Law: Report of the Independent Inquiry into the Misuse of Drugs Act 1971*. London: Police Foundation.

Prochaska, J., Norcross, J. and DiClemente, C. (1995) *Changing for Good*. New York: Avon Books.

Robertson, R. (1987) *Heroin, Aids and Society*. London: Hodder & Stoughton.

Seddon, T. (2000) 'Explaining the drug–crime link: theoretical, policy and research issues', *Journal Social Policy*, 29 (1): 95–107.

Seddon, T. (2006) 'Drugs, crime and social exclusion', *British Journal of Criminology*, 46: 680–703.

Chapter 15

Delivering accredited programmes – key knowledge and skills for programme staff

Simon Feasey

Introduction

This chapter intends to focus on the underpinning knowledge and understanding that programme tutors need to develop in order to ensure that offenders are enabled to fully engage with the materials specified within accredited programmes. Highly structured programme manuals present a real challenge to practitioners: many offenders have histories of disengagement with traditional learning environments and many also have poor literacy and numeracy skills. In order to make the written exercises accessible tutors need to have a sound awareness of groupwork theory and key skills and approach the task with a degree of reflection that ensures adequate preparation and planning. Although the programmes' approach to group work is relatively specific to offender management, the underpinning principles of effective group work practice have been developed over many decades and remain relevant and pertinent to the roll-out of accredited programmes.

Accredited programmes based on What Works principles were introduced into both the prison and probation services during the 1990s and very swiftly became the central plank of the effective practice movement, securing significant resource allocation and much attention from policy-makers, service managers and academic researchers. Many probation areas completely reorganised their delivery of interventions with offenders to support the rapid integration of accredited programmes as income related performance targets were set by the Home Office. Within a timeframe of less than ten years much interventions work was radically transformed; large numbers of prison and probation staff had been trained in programme delivery and a range of new roles such as programme tutors and programme and treatment managers were developed with prescribed and clearly defined responsibilities.

This chapter does not seek to debate the broader policy issues associated with the development and introduction of accredited programmes; this is undertaken within Chapters 2 and 3 of this volume. Clearly there are divergent views about the overall efficacy and benefits of accredited programmes and the research evidence regarding their impact and effectiveness within England and Wales is in its infancy; early findings can seem contradictory and confusing (Harper and Chitty 2005). Some of this discourse focuses on the theoretical and conceptual frameworks which underpin accredited programmes (Kendall 2004), while other commentators have been more concerned with the implementation and roll-out issues associated with a heavily policy-driven initiative (Kemshall *et al.* 2004).

One of the criticisms of the programmes approach is that they have provided a 'one size fits all' approach to working with offenders, both in terms of their theoretical and conceptual frameworks (generally cognitive-behavioural) and by their failure to recognise the diversity of offenders in terms of age, ethnicity, sexual orientation, intellectual capacity, literacy level, mental and physical heath and impairment, and divergent learning styles. 'Responsivity' was identified as a core What Works principle (McGuire and Priestley 1995) but has tended to be reframed by the expression 'motivation and engagement'. The discussion has focused on the extent to which accredited programmes are constructed and delivered in such a way as to promote the motivation and engagement of offenders. There have been in particular major concerns regarding issues of race and gender (Shaw and Hannah-Moffat 2004).

However, although there remains an ongoing discussion about effectiveness it is nevertheless the case that, within the area of practice, programmes are well established and require the engagement of significant numbers of criminal justice workers. This chapter therefore seeks to identify what needs to be in place to support the effective delivery of accredited programmes. The specific focus is primarily at a practitioner level: what key skills underpin programme delivery; what are the core components essential for achieving programme and treatment integrity; what approaches and strategies are likely to result in greater compliance and completion. Underpinning the themes of the chapter is an understanding that the knowledge, skills, experience and commitment of programme tutors is fundamental to effective delivery and that the relationships between tutors and offenders develop within a group process where knowledge of both groupwork theory and skills are essential. This clearly does not apply to programmes that are delivered on a one-to-one basis, although some of the underpinning skills associated with such programmes closely resemble those that are located within group work.

Before moving into an examination of delivery skills it would be useful to identify what is meant by the term 'accredited programme'. In 1999 the Home Office established the Joint Prison/Probation Accreditation Panel, which subsequently became the Correctional Services Accreditation Panel (CSAP), as a key part of its developing What Works initiative. One of the primary purposes of the panel, which consists of a range of appointed independent experts and nominated representatives from key agencies, is to ensure that newly developed programmes of intervention with offenders are based on sound and evidence-based principles, thereby maximising the likelihood of impacting positively on reconviction rates for programme completers. The CSAP annual report 2006–7 provides a useful summary of their understanding of programme effectiveness:

> The 'What Works' evidence, based on meta-analytic reviews of large numbers of varied offender treatment programmes evaluated on differing bases, suggests that defined and structured programmes using particularly, but not exclusively, cognitive-behavioural techniques can significantly reduce expected re-offending. The meta-analytic reviews do not suggest that there is any single, outstanding approach that is by itself guaranteed to work as a means of reducing re-offending but broadly, the principles associated with effective interventions include:
>
> • Effective risk management
> • Targeting offending behaviour
> • Addressing the specific factors linked with offenders' offending
> • Relevance to offenders' learning styles
> • Promoting community reintegration
> • Maintaining quality and integrity of programme delivery.
>   (CSAP 2006–7)

(Annex B of the annual report includes a full list of programmes that have achieved accredited status.)

The remainder of this chapter will look primarily at issues associated with maintaining the quality and integrity of programme delivery.

Programme and treatment integrity

The concept of maintaining integrity within programme implementation and delivery was referred to by James McGuire as one of the six key What Works principles in 1995 (McGuire 1995) and in the same publication Clive Hollin writes:

> It is now clear that that the most effective programmes, in terms of reducing recidivism, have high treatment integrity; they are carried out by trained practitioners, and the treatment initiators are involved in all the operational phases of the programme. In other words, effective programmes with high treatment integrity are characterized by sound management, tight design and skilled practitioners. (Hollin 1995: 96)

In this chapter programme identity (PI) is defined as an all encompassing concept that includes the overall management of a programme. This would include the effective selection of offenders; the proper training of staff who are involved with the programme; the allocation of sufficient time and resources to support effective delivery; the availability of appropriate premises and infrastructure; the integration of pre- and post-programme work by offender managers; the maintenance of proper monitoring and evaluation of programme processes; and ongoing audit and inspection.

Treatment integrity (TI) is more specifically concerned with what actually happens within the programme sessions: are the tutors delivering the programme as designed, using a skilled and motivational approach that results in most participants remaining fully engaged? Hollin (1995) identifies potential threats to TI and classifies these as follows:

- *Programme drift* – in which over a period of time the programme's original aims begin to change. For example, a programme based on a cognitive-behavioural model might move toward a person-centred approach.

- *Programme reversal* – in which programme staff seek to impose their own theoretical approach that undermines the programme's conceptual framework. So a drugs programme that was originally designed to promote a harm reduction approach begins to shift toward a drug prevention model as a result of the tutor's own perspectives. The process may be deliberate or unconscious but the outcome can be similar. For example, generic offending behaviour programmes adopt a cognitive-behavioural approach. The exercises are designed to fit into this framework but could be tweaked to accommodate others. One of the key concepts within the cognitive-behavioural approach is that to understand a problem situation you have to focus on the thoughts, feelings and behaviour of the individual; the external environment impacts on these internal processes but the focus is on the interaction between the individual and the environment, not the external factors in themselves. If a tutor had an approach that was underpinned by a view that offending was primarily associated with external factors this could result in a mode of delivery that took the focus away from the functioning of the individual offender and his or her responsibility for their own behaviour.

- *Programme non-compliance* – in which, for a number of reasons, staff decide to exclude certain parts of the programme, introduce new exercises and gradually the nature of individual sessions are significantly altered. Sometimes it is clear when non-compliance is an issue; tutors might run out of time and not complete a session, for example. However it can also be the case that tutors often develop 'favourite' and 'least favourite' exercises; some exercises seem usually to go well, others appear more difficult. It can be tempting to focus and spend time on the apparently more accessible and popular parts of the programme and avoid the more difficult parts. Additionally the tutor might think that they have better ways of achieving the session objectives and use their own material at the expense of the manual.

The argument is that if tutors undermine the integrity of delivery by any of these three approaches, the overall effectiveness of the programme will be seriously undermined. However, there is an interesting discussion around the concept of programme non-compliance which relates to the extent to which tutors should feel constrained by the range and type of exercises that are detailed within programme sessions. One approach would maintain that the tutors should remain very faithful to the content described by the programme manual and that any deviation potentially undermines the achievement of the session outcomes. Alternatively there is an opinion that supports the idea of trained and experienced tutors having a degree of flexibility and autonomy in introducing alternative exercises and approaches when it is felt that this would provide a more effective means of achieving the outcomes for that particular session. So, for example, this view would enable a tutor to change the context of a prescribed activity to suit the particular profile of group members.

The debate around non-compliance and flexibility within delivery reflects a broader discussion concerning levels of offender engagement and participation with programme material. In therapeutic terms it is well established that learning and change is more likely to take place within an environment in which participants are fully engaged, alert and responsive to the inputs of the tutors (Hopkinson and Rex 2003). If the materials prescribed within a specific manual do not promote the required levels of engagement, there is an argument for replacing them with alternative approaches that will. So, for example, a programme that is heavily dependent on written exercises could benefit from the introduction of greater role play as an alternative mechanism for achieving improved engagement and outcomes.

The key issue here is that it is possible to avoid drift, reversal and non-compliance but nevertheless experience a group of participants who are unmotivated, disengaged and clearly not benefiting from attendance. This therefore suggests that there is a fourth critical threat to treatment integrity which can be called:

- *Programme non-engagement* – which occurs when the materials are delivered in such a way as to diminish the engagement of the offenders resulting in boredom, disinterest and reduced motivation. There is little point remaining faithful to the manual if no one is listening! If this fourth element were introduced as part of TI it would expect tutors to work at making the session interesting and lively while abiding by the other three requirements of TI.

The following section will discuss what approaches are likely to enhance the active involvement of participants within the group process and thereby reduce the risk of developing programme non-engagement.

Promoting effective offender engagement with programmes

Much of the work undertaken within programmes is located within highly structured groups and it is therefore essential that programme tutors have a reasonable grasp of some basic groupwork theory that will equip them to manage the range of issues and challenges that routinely arise within groupwork approaches. This might appear self-evident but during the early roll-out of accredited programmes, a view developed that they did not constitute group work but were primarily concerned with skills training within a teaching environment. The argument was that as the groups were not designed to be 'therapeutic' there was minimal group process and the focus had to be almost exclusively on delivering the content. In 2001 Kevin Gorman commented:

> Moreover, programme integrity – which requires that effective programmes of intervention should be adequately resourced and implemented by staff appropriately trained in the underlying theoretical perspective – is often reduced to a mechanistic process of transforming the so-called principles of 'What Works' into 'one-size-fits-all' interventions. These demand that the obedient delivery of programme content, and the monitoring thereof, take precedence over proper resourcing or understanding. (Gorman 2001)

Such an approach appears to misrepresent commonly understood paradigms about both how groups operate and how people learn. Within accredited group programmes offenders typically come together with a common purpose in a highly structured environment over a period of a number of weeks; they therefore constitute a structured, purposeful and discreet group who will interact with each other and with programme tutors. The nature of this interaction will impact on how individuals perform within the group and also how the group performs as a single entity. Although the nature of the group programme is primarily content rather than process led, the manner by which individuals engage with the content will be significantly determined by the developing relationships between group members. Of particular significance will be the contribution of the tutors to the development of the group as the particular nature of the group is 'directive' or leader oriented. Douglas states:

> Groups which benefit from a directive leadership are usually those where the actual resources of the group members are of secondary importance to those exercised by the group leadership. Such groups are those in which the understanding and knowledge of the leadership is essential in guiding the group members, explaining, offering information to which the group members had no previous access, revealing the consequences of particular behaviour patterns ... and in general applying knowledge on a wider more substantial scale to

the kinds of predicaments and problems possessed by the group's members. (Douglas 2000: 5)

Given that offenders and tutors are engaging in a groupwork process it is critical that tutors are able to draw on an understanding of groupwork theory to inform their approaches to managing and directing the group. There are of course many theoretical approaches to understanding how groups work, develop and interact. However, one very useful, relatively straightforward and frequently referred to theoretical approach has been developed by Tuckman (1965) and Tuckman and Jensen (1977) and this will be drawn upon to highlight the key developmental stages that an accredited programme will experience during its lifetime.

Tuckman adopted a linear analysis of group development that sought to explain how a group changes from its initial inception to its final parting. Within this model he identified five discreet stages: forming, storming, norming, peforming and adjourning.

How groups work

Group forming

Group forming occurs when members of the group are initially introduced to each other for the first time. Individual participants will generally be anxious and seeking other people with whom they may feel some affinity. This initial stage of group development is characterised by:

- much dependence on the tutors;
- an apparent willingness to conform;
- a reluctance to participate and engage in discussion;
- high levels of uncertainty/anxiety.

The group is prone to be dominated by an extrovert individual who may make a bid for leadership. It is important that tutors recognise the high levels of anxiety within the group and prevent individual members adopting an early dominant and demanding role. In order to assist the group to come together more effectively tutors should aim to:

- facilitate introductions and help members to join together;
- explain the purpose of the group – 'why we are here';
- negotiate and agree a group contract;
- explain and discuss the group programme and methods;
- begin to establish a group culture.

The initial meeting of the group will provide an opportunity for participants to observe the approach of the tutors who will need to demonstrate empathy and warmth, while encouraging individual participation using structure exercises in pairs, small groups and whole-group discussion. Critically tutors will be modelling the pro-social behaviours (Trotter 1996, 1999) that will be expected of group members.

Group storming

Group storming occurs at the point when members start to assert themselves and conflict can arise as individuals attempt to establish power and control within the group. This stage of development is characterised by:

- resistance to the group and resentment of the power of the tutors;
- challenges to the validity and purpose of the group – 'I'm only here because the court sent me';
- a recognition that unrealistic high expectations will not be met and a subsequent depressed feeling;
- anxiety about loss of individual significance in which personal needs have to be compromised;
- a belief that the group will not be able to assist them.

Group storming can be difficult to manage as it can appear that the entire group is resistant and unwilling to engage positively. In order to assist the group to move on from the storming phase, tutors should:

- set up simple achievable activities which are unthreatening to involve all members in group activity;
- provide positive feedback and create a culture of successful completion of tasks;
- control individual members if they test the limits;
- maintain an appropriate balance between confrontation and support, avoiding any polarisation of these two approaches.

Tutors may be tempted to be over-rigid and controlling during this phase of development and this can be counterproductive. Instead there is an opportunity for the tutor to challenge storming behaviours and offer a model of operating which uncovers, explores and resolves group concerns. This will involve a number of skills to be practised by the tutor, e.g. self-disclosure of feelings; reflecting back observations of what is happening; remaining assertive but not becoming aggressive or confrontational; listening and receiving feedback; encouraging members to consider alternative behaviours; and reframing negative and undermining attitudes and behaviours. The intention is to mediate conflict and work towards participants taking ownership of the group and committing themselves to working cooperatively.

Group norming

Group norming occurs at the point at which group members reach a degree of reconciliation and cohesion. Individuals, having 'found their position' in the group, may look for ways of coming together and seek a common identity. Some of the feelings of belongingness come from the experience of working through the conflicts of the previous stage to an understanding of each other. Consequently each member may feel he or she has a role in the group and appreciate the role that each other plays. Individuals are more likely to want to know how others think and feel about things and are more likely to ask for feedback from the group as well as listen to the feedback received. This stage of development is characterised by:

- participants appearing committed to the collaborative nature of the group programme;
- a higher level of engagement and contribution to group activities;
- participants needing less directive leadership from tutors and being given some responsibility for group activities;
- a recognition that the group is starting to work together more effectively.

The norming stage enables participants to settle into established patterns of behaviour which feel relatively safe and comfortable. However, tutors must still provide effective leadership although there are also opportunities to move increasingly to a more facilitative role as group members demonstrate the potential to assume some responsibilities within the group. In order to support the norming stage of development tutors should:

- identify opportunities to enable participants to take greater responsibility;
- reinforce the progress of the group by offering positive feedback;
- provide the group with some degree of choice over group activities and tasks;
- encourage greater reflection on learning and model this by looking back over how the group has developed and how it will continue to progress.

It is important to understand that movement from one group stage to another is neither automatic nor consistent and it is equally possible for groups to regress to an earlier stage of development. The timeframes are also very variable – it is difficult to predict how long it will take a group to reach the norming phase. The key learning is to recognise the symptoms of stage development and then respond accordingly.

Group performing

Group performing occurs at the point at which the group achieves a level of performance and effectiveness such that the group leaders are no longer required and can withdraw, leaving the group members to continue alone. This stage is clearly not achieved within accredited programmes. An example of a performing group would be when a community development worker sets up a community group and is able to withdraw after six months to let the group manage itself. It is probably not a good idea to let a probation group, undertaking an accredited programme, manage itself!

Group adjourning

Group adjourning occurs at the point at which the group is disbanded. Tutors need to realise that this may be a positive or negative experience for the group generally and for individual participants. Individual offenders who do not complete may experience feelings of failure which are compounded by previous negative memories of earlier problems within education/training. When programmes end either for individuals or groups, tutors should:

- reinforce positive feelings of achievement by providing certificates and introducing some degree of ceremony and celebration;
- recognise that leaving the group may impact negatively on some participants and consider future support mechanisms;
- ensure that arrangements are in place for post-programme work to consolidate the learning and understanding achieved.

Recognising the stages of group development enables tutors to plan and structure their approaches to group leadership accordingly. By responding to obstacles and barriers in the most effective manner, groups are likely to progress and compliance and completion rates improve. This last point is particularly significant given the growing body of research evidence that suggests that programme completion is a critical factor in reducing reconviction. Within some recent evaluations of accredited programmes the most heavily reconvicted group were non-completers who were more likely to go back before the courts than a matched comparison group who were not offered the programme intervention (Hedderman and Hearnden 2000).

Key skills in groupwork delivery

However, recognising group difficulties does not necessarily guarantee that the tutor will have the necessary skills to address them appropriately and it is also important to acquire the range of techniques that effective tutors rely on within group programme delivery. Many of these skills are generic in that they underpin all effective work with offenders across a range of settings. Core skills such as pro-social modelling (PSM) (Trotter

1996, 1999) and motivational interviewing (MI) (Miller and Rollnick 2002) are discussed elsewhere in this book (Tallant *et al.*, Buchanan) and will not be described again here. The broad point is that programme work clearly provides invaluable opportunities to adopt PSM approaches. The tutor has an audience and her or his responses to individual offenders are witnessed and interpreted by the entire group. Both one-to-one and group programmes require tutors to adopt the four underpinning principles of PSM: to be responsive; to be active; to model pro-social attitudes and behaviours; and to maintain legitimacy. One aspect specific to groupwork delivery is the nature of the relationship between the two programme tutors. Here is an opportunity to model an equal, mutually supportive relationship in which tasks are shared and responsibilities accepted and in which consistency of approach is maintained throughout the programme. However in order to ensure that the co-working relationship does work effectively some careful preparation and planning must be undertaken.

While it is accepted that PSM is critical to the effective delivery of accredited programmes there is more debate concerning the contribution that MI can make within a group setting. MI had traditionally operated within individual casework when a practitioner engages in a structured dialogue with an individual, drawing on a range of techniques that are designed to encourage the client to make self-motivational statements about change. There is much research evidence regarding the positive impact of MI within one-to-one work (Burke *et al.* 2002) but there are doubts about how it can be applied within a groupwork setting '... the transfer of motivational interviewing into a group format seems anything but straightforward. Group-based approaches have been implemented by people quite experienced with individual approaches and thus far have yielded disappointing results' (Miller and Rollnick 2002: 390).

Of course MI has much to offer offender managers who undertake pre- and post-programme work and programmes that are delivered one-to-one but its application within groupwork is clearly problematic. MI demands prolonged dialogue between individuals and generally this should be avoided within groups; it is likely to result in resentment from other group members. However, it may well be that some of the principles of MI do provide a very useful basis for group engagement. In the experience of this author, expressing empathy, developing discrepancy, avoiding argumentation, rolling with resistance, avoiding labelling, promoting individual responsibility and supporting self-efficacy can all be achieved within a groupwork setting. This may not constitute the rigorous application of MI but nevertheless a framework for group engagement can usefully be applied.

The co-working relationship

The relationship between the two co-tutors underpins effective group programme work and ideally time should be set aside before engaging with the group to identify how the co-working relationship will be managed. In this pre-group discussion tutors should think about the following:

- *Power dynamics.* Programme tutors are modelling a relationship to the rest of the group; if there is seen to be an imbalance of power this will be picked up by group members and will be interpreted. Issues of gender and ethnicity are particularly important as power imbalance can reinforce negative stereotypes.

- *Values.* Tutors need to recognise and discuss their own values base and accommodate differences as much as possible. It cannot be assumed that co-tutors share common beliefs; divergence of views located around what constitutes pro- and anti-social behaviours and attitudes should be avoided and recognising potential areas of disagreement can enable more effective engagement with group members.

- *Splitting.* If group participants perceive that the tutors are working in a conflictual manner they are likely to try and undermine their authority by driving a wedge between them. Tutors need to be alert and prepare for attempts by the group to create a split between them. Tutors should never criticise or contradict co-tutors within the group; differences should be resolved in private and a united front presented at all times.

- *Language.* Tutors should agree strategies for addressing abusive/oppressive/discriminatory language and behaviour, who is going to respond, when the co-tutor will intervene, what the response will consist of. Pre-planning responses avoids contradictory and undermining approaches.

- *Styles.* Different natural tutor styles need acknowledging and working with; one tutor may be extrovert and confident, the other introvert and less experienced; one may be skilled at managing group process issues, the other better at delivering content. Tutors should work to their strengths and try and ensure that different styles are complementary.

- *Support.* Tutors need to plan how they will support each other in the group. There may be occasions when a tutor is not sure how to respond to a particular situation that arises. The co-tutor needs to be able to recognise this and intervene appropriately in a manner that does not draw attention to the situation.

- *Feedback.* Tutors need to ensure that they have a framework for mutual feedback which should also involve a third person/supervisor/consultant. It can be difficult sometimes to address problems in the co-working relationship without a third person being involved.

- *Practicalities.* Tutors need to pre-plan who is taking responsibility for which parts of the session, how handovers are managed and what pacing and timing constraints need to be considered.

It is never possible to predict precisely what may happen in a dynamic group situation and inevitably there will be occasions when tutors are required to think on their feet and respond accordingly. However, by careful planning and preparation it is possible to develop greater confidence and skills in managing the unexpected, thereby ensuring a more productive and engaging groupwork experience.

Leadership within accredited programme delivery

Although we often refer to tutors as facilitators there is no doubt that within the context of accredited programmes they are also expected and required to undertake a significant leadership role, particularly during the early stages of group forming. Some understanding of the different conceptual models of leadership is therefore helpful in assisting tutors to develop effective leadership skills. Effective leadership is not necessarily a skill or quality that is routinely developed among criminal justice practitioners but within a groupwork situation it can hardly be avoided.

John Adair (1996) has usefully identified that effective leadership requires the management of three distinct variables which include group process, individual needs and group task. Within accredited programmes the group task is determined by the programme manual and achieving the desired outcomes depends on tutors managing both the individual needs of offenders and also the changing relationships and dynamics within the group. In leading/facilitating a group the tutors need to keep an eye on the task they are setting out to achieve (programme content); the process of engagement within the group (how is the group as a whole managing); and the individual offenders within the group (whether they are experiencing particular problems, etc.).

An understanding of groupwork theory and skills will assist with this but consideration must also be given to the specific nature of the relationship between the tutors and the other participants. It is likely that by instinct individuals will have preferred approaches to tutoring: some may prefer a more relaxed approach with the use of humour to reduce anxiety and promote open discussion and communication; others may veer toward a more formal and controlled approach which keeps group members to task. Usually the particular context and purpose of groups determine how group facilitators should approach their role. A community group designed to promote self-empowerment and community development might require a particularly facilitative group leader who seeks to gradually reduce the significance of the leadership role. On the other hand, a therapeutic group seeking to develop participants' efficacy and self-esteem would naturally benefit from a leadership style that focuses particularly on individual need and process rather than content.

The literature on leadership styles is extensive but a particularly useful source is provided by Kurt Lewin *et al.* (1939) who undertook research with classes of school children that identified three primary leadership styles which will now be discussed.

Democratic/participative leadership

The democratic approach to leadership within groups enables consultation and discussion to take place before decisions are made. This allows group members to express their views but does not guarantee that these feelings will be acted upon. This style is an ideal method of leadership within accredited programmes as the group is more likely to contribute to the decision-making process and thereby promote a sense of ownership of the group's planned outcomes and purpose. However, given the nature of accredited problems it is important to be clear about what is negotiable and which decisions rest solely with the programme tutors. There are a lot of 'givens' in programme work and it is not helpful to give the impression that group members have more power to influence the process that they do in reality. However, small negotiations can occur which can model a democratic exchange. Lewin *et al.*'s (1939) research concluded that the democratic approach provided the most effective leadership style.

Authoritarian/autocratic leadership

The authoritarian approach would expect the tutors to determine, on their own, the decisions within the group; information is passed on to the group rather than options being discussed openly. This is a style that might be preferred by very large groups in which an autocratic leader can speed up a decision-making process. This can be important when issues such as the group's physical safety are involved and might be expected to predominate within military conflicts, for example. However, within accredited programmes this is not an appropriate model and is obviously at odds with the principles of both PSM and MI. An over-controlling and autocratic approach from tutors is likely to result in non-participation, withdrawal, resentment and reduced learning. Lewin *et al.* (1939) concluded that this approach promoted the greatest level of discontent among participants.

Delegative/laissez-faire leadership

This approach expects leaders to offer little or no guidance to group members who then have a large degree of control over decision-making. While this style can be effective in situations where group members are highly qualified in an area of expertise, it often leads to poorly defined roles and a lack of motivation. Tutors adopting this approach would expect participants to take on responsibility for aspects of programme delivery. This works best when a well functioning group, i.e. one that may be in a performing phase, is working towards a well defined task. This method is exceptionally difficult if more than a handful of group members are present and is often used within sub-groups to perform specific sub-tasks. This approach is clearly not generally appropriate for accredited programmes. Lewin *et al.*'s (1939) research indicated that this approach had the least productive outcomes for participants.

Impact of leadership style

It is useful to consider how these different leadership styles could impact within an accredited programme and in order to do so some thought will be given to a key initial group task: setting ground rules. Most effective group work begins with a process which seeks to establish clarity about the rules within which the group will seek to operate. This is of course important in ensuring that participants feel safe, that behavioural and attitudinal difficulties can be addressed, that there is legitimacy, consistency and accountability within decision-making and that fairness and equity are established as an underpinning principle. At the onset of group forming, developing ground rules provides an invaluable mechanism for promoting group members' participation and engagement and can assist in moving toward the stage of norming. One option in terms of setting ground rules is for tutors to have established these prior to the group session, introduce them as a fait accompli and explain to the participants their rationale and justification. This would reflect a largely authoritarian approach to leading this session and is less likely to result in group members feeling committed to and bound by the rules set. An approach based on a laissez-faire style would ask the group to set their own ground rules, with potentially highly inappropriate consequences given the legal context of accredited programmes. Below is suggested an alternative strategy, based on a democratic leadership style, which is likely to enable group cohesion and ensure a greater commitment to appropriate ground rules:

- Tutors explain to the group the legal context of their attendance and recognise that certain requirements are non-negotiable and do not allow for discussion or discretion.
- Tutors open a discussion within the group focusing on why groups require rules to perform well.
- Within this discussion tutors ensure that members consider what is meant by 'treating people with respect', enabling individual participants to express their own views and opinions.
- Tutors record the key features of the respect agenda concentrating on respect for diversity and what constitutes acceptable means of communication, language and behaviour.
- Tutors lead the discussion into debate around issues of timekeeping and attendance with a view to agreeing baselines that are both acceptable to the group and compatible with programme requirements.

- Tutors lead a discussion about what group members expect from each other and how this can be achieved.

Such an approach might be relatively time-consuming and potentially problematic; consensus is not necessarily achieved. However the process is likely to strengthen group identity and ensure that the resulting ground rules have real meaning.

Dealing with difficulties within accredited programme delivery

It is inevitable that even with proper planning and preparation, difficulties in delivering programmes will emerge. Within any group, individuals have the capacity to be disruptive, fail to participate and undermine the group's progress; within accredited programmes these problems can be exacerbated by the involuntary nature of the group and low levels of motivation to complete the programme. The arena is potentially relatively hostile and difficult to manage.

Within this context it is also likely that during the course of the group's development, individuals will assume the characteristics of specific roles that research tells us are frequently problematic. It is recognised that certain roles can create particular difficulties challenges for group facilitators and leaders. These include:

- *The scapegoat.* When one group member becomes isolated and is identified as representing a range of negative characteristics that other group members do not acknowledge in themselves and other group members. The scapegoat can be blamed for the poor performance or disruption or other negative characteristics of the group. Often a person who has difficulties with being assertive, with low confidence and low self-esteem is at risk of being made a scapegoat.

- *The monopoliser.* When a participant cannot or will not stop contributing with the result that other group members become irritated and start to feel excluded. It is encouraging at the stage of group forming if a member is actively contributing and the tutor will often reinforce this by giving positive feedback. If the member is a potential monopoliser this could exacerbate the problem.

- *The silent member.* When a group member never makes a verbal contribution. He or she might appear to be listening and concentrating but does not respond to the prompts that you might use to encourage active participation. The difficulty is in understanding what lies beneath this silence and adopting a strategy that does not make things worse. Doing nothing is probably not an option as a silent member impacts on the other group members frequently in a negative and destructive way. Silence can be a very powerful dynamic within a group.

- *The disrupter*. When a participant will often be constantly challenging the ground rules and will seek to make it difficult for the tutor to remain focused on the objectives of the session. Often he or she might seek to form alliances with other group members and attempt to take control and power away from the tutors via attention seeking and obstructive behaviour.

- *The clown*. When a group member takes on the role of the group clown which is a form of disruptive and attention-seeking behaviour. Good humour within a group can be a very positive dynamic but when one individual attempts to joke excessively other members will be disinclined to take the group seriously.

So what are some of the strategies that you might make use of to address the problematic roles and behaviours described above? Drawing on the knowledge and experience of some of the key authors (Douglas 2000; Brown and Caddick 1993; Preston-Shoot 1987) it is possible to outline a number of strategies that can be helpfully employed.

Doing nothing immediately

Often it is advisable not to leap in straightaway unless the behaviour requires an immediate response. Waiting until the end of the session has a number of advantages: the problem behaviour might stop, the noisy person may say less, the quiet one more. You will also have an opportunity to check out how other members are reacting to the behaviour. If the behaviour remains problematic you have an opportunity to discuss with your co-worker the most appropriate means of addressing the issue.

It is not suggested that tutors wait until a break if there is a major challenge to the ground rules such as a racist remark. This needs addressing immediately and tutors should already have developed a strategy to deal with such an issue prior to the group session.

Indirect responses

An indirect response seeks to effect a change in behaviour in a way that does not refer directly to it or the person concerned: working in pairs might encourage a silent member; the tutor's use of body language and physical movement in the group room can 'close people down' or 'open them up'; using different methods of feedback such as 'going round the circle' rather than asking for volunteers can even out the balance of contributions. There are many other indirect responses to think about.

Direct implicit responses

This approach expects the tutor to address the issue in a way that does not draw attention to the specific individual who is presenting a problem behaviour – he or she is not singled out as a consequence of the response. So, for example, if one member was constantly being the first to answer questions and was monopolising the discussion the tutor would introduce a system for taking turns without referring to the issue. Similarly, if one member has not contributed throughout a session the tutor could start the next one with a general reminder about agreed expectations of active participation without referring to any existing specific concerns.

Direct explicit responses

1 Speak directly to the individual.
2 Speak directly to the rest of the group.
3 Address the group as a whole.

This approach to addressing a problematic member needs to be utilised with care. The first option of speaking directly to the individual within the group obviously runs the risk of creating a confrontational situation that might take some time to manage, thereby losing time needed to complete the session objectives. In addition singling the individual out can have the impact of splitting the person off from the group thereby creating greater difficulties. Moreover, if the individual is acting up in an attention-seeking way, focusing directly on him or her might be exactly what they want. If the tutor decides to deal with the problem behaviour directly there needs to be clarity of purpose and a clear strategy. Obviously the circumstances tend to dictate the response: it might be very destructive to single out a silent member but quite appropriate to directly challenge a disrupter.

Another option is to speak directly to the group whereby the tutor seeks to involve other participants in thinking about how the group should respond to the issue. If, for example, one member (Jane) was monopolising the tutor could say to the other members of the group: 'You seem to be letting Jane do all the work. We'd like to hear what you've all got to say.' This is often a helpful approach but again it runs the risk of splitting Jane from the group.

The third explicit response is to raise the issue with the whole group including the problem member with a view to agreeing a way forward that is acceptable to all. This can work but can be very time-consuming as everyone will need to be given an opportunity to express their views and other hidden agendas might emerge. This can prove to be a high-risk strategy.

Contact outside the group

This can be a legitimate tactic particularly in a group which is primarily focused on content rather than process. Tutors decide that a quiet private word with the individual might well address the issue; this might be a sensitive way of discussing with a silent member any problems they may be experiencing.

Whole-group problems

In addition to the problems caused by individuals there is also the possibility of coming across whole-group problems which can include group non-participation, group resistance, group hostility and group deviance. The most difficult scenario to address is when the group collectively resists and refuses to engage constructively with the tutors or the material. The first thing to consider is whether the resistance is in fact being fuelled by a particular individual or a small clique within the larger group. If so it is worth thinking about dealing with them using the strategies above. If two individuals are together adversely impacting on the behaviour of others then focus on them and not the others. Alternatively discuss with the others why they are allowing themselves to be manipulated.

However, it might be necessary to call a temporary halt to proceedings and set some time aside to revisit the purpose of the group and the original contract. If so this needs to be undertaken in a time limited session as this will affect the achievement of programme integrity. In addition, if the group thinks that it can avoid the session materials by acting up then they may be tempted to do the same again. If tutors find that they frequently have to renegotiate ground rules it is likely that the group are manipulating the tutors.

Conclusion

The introduction and development of accredited programmes within criminal justice practice has been a critical and underpinning element within the emergence of What Works. It is apparent that there remains much debate and discussion about the efficacy of the roll-out of programmes within the managerial focus and context of offender management and what has become increasingly evident is the necessity to ensure that programme work sits alongside other key interventions in a joined up and cohesive model of delivery. Accredited programmes cannot stand alone and do not provide a simplistic panacea to the problem of reducing reconviction rates. The evidence base for their impact is still in its relative infancy and further primary research is required to provide a more developed and secure understanding of their real value.

However, this chapter has provided a framework for ensuring that the delivery of programmes is consistent with some of the well-established knowledge and understanding about working most effectively with offenders in groups and has started from the premise that the programme experience is dynamic and driven by the interactions between group members. While the programmes are inevitably content-focused, it is only by tutors having a sound understanding of process issues that the content can be made accessible and engaging to participants. Associated with process awareness are a range of applied skills that can assist group facilitators and leaders to maximise the likelihood of individual and group learning. Delivering accredited programmes well is one of the most challenging and demanding areas of offender management. However, when the group experience is constructive and participants are being challenged constructively by their peers, opportunities for attitudinal and behavioural change are considerable. Offenders who successfully complete well delivered programmes, frequently express their surprise at the positive impact of the experience and the extent to which it has started to change their thinking.

The skills and experience of programme tutors will be crucial to the outcomes for offenders and appropriate training and support is necessarily required. However, there has now developed a greater awareness of the need to create dynamic and engaging environments for offenders. An extract from a short piece written by James McGuire in 2004 sums up rather well one of the key messages that needs to be fully integrated into practice:

> The interpersonal skills of programme staff are vital as they strive to make ideas and methods usable by a wide range of offenders. There is potentially enormous flexibility in how this can be achieved in any given session, even within a single exercise. Practitioners are allowed, indeed encouraged, to use their initiative and creativity in making innovations in exercises and materials: for example by employing the most relevant or local examples relating to points covered in the programme. (McGuire 2004)

Developing a group experience which supports the motivation and engagement of diverse offenders is critical to the future success of accredited programmes.

Discussion questions

1 What do you think are the most effective ways of ensuring that the delivery style within a programme meets the learning needs of diverse offenders?
2 What do you think are the key areas to discuss and negotiate with your co-tutor before you start session one of an accredited programme? What would you do if you have difficulty in achieving consensus during this discussion?
3 To what extent do you think that it is possible to draw on the principles and processes of motivational interviewing within the delivery of accredited programmes?

Further reading.

Brown, A. and Caddick, B. (1993) *Groupwork with Offenders*. London: Whiting & Birch. This text has a more offender focus and therefore is particularly useful when considering the statutory and enforced nature of accredited programmes. It does, however, pre-date the emergence of the What Works initiative.

Douglas, T. (1993) *A Theory of Groupwork Practice.* Basingstoke: Palgrave Macmillan. A useful introduction to theory and practice. Tom Douglas has written a number of accessible texts; his style is transparent and he links the discussion to real world examples.

Mistry, T. and Brown, A. (1997) *Race and Groupwork.* London: Whiting & Birch. This is one of the few texts which has a particular focus on issues of diversity and relates well to the offender management context. Again, there are a range of practice examples discussed.

Preston-Shoot, M. (2007) *Effective Groupwork.* Basingstoke: Palgrave Macmillan. This text relates rather more to a social work tradition and thereby provides a useful alternative perspective to the offender-specific examples above.

References

Adair, J. (1996) *Effective Leadership.* London: Pan.

Brown, A. and Caddick, B. (1993) *Groupwork with Offenders.* London: Whiting & Birch.

Burke, B.L., Vassilev, G., Kantchelov, A. and Zweben, A. (2002) 'Motivational interviewing with couples', in W.R. Millar and S. Rollnick (eds), *Motivational Interviewing: Preparing People for Change.* New York: Guilford Press.

CSAP (2007) *Annual Report 2006–7.* London: NOMS.

Douglas, T. (2000) *Basic Groupwork.* London: Routledge.

Gorman, K. (2001) 'Cognitive behaviourism and the Holy Grail: the quest for a universal means of managing offender risk', *Probation Journal*, 48 (1): 3–9.

Harper, G. and Chitty, C. (2005) *The Impact of Corrections on Re-offending: A Review of 'What Works'*, Home Office Research Study No. 291. London: Home Office Research, Development and Statistics Directorate.

Hedderman, C. and Hearnden, I. (2000) 'The missing link: effective enforcement and effective supervision', *Probation Journal*, 47 (2): 126–8.

Hollin, C.R. (1995) 'The meaning and implications of "programme integrity"', in J. McGuire (ed.), *What Works: Reducing Reoffending.* Chichester: Wiley.

Hopkinson, J. and Rex, S. (2003) 'Essential skills in working with offenders', in W.H. Chui and M. Nellis (eds), *Moving Probation Forward: Evidence, Arguments and Practice.* London: Pearson Longman.

Kemshall, H., Holt, P., Bailey, R. and Boswell, G. (2004) 'Beyond programmes: organizational and cultural issues in the implementation of What Works', in G. Mair (ed.), *What Matters in Probation.* Cullompton: Willan.

Kendall, K. (2004) 'Dangerous thinking: a critical history of correctional cognitive behaviouralism', in G. Mair (ed.), *What Matters in Probation.* Cullompton: Willan.

Lewin, K., Lippit, R. and White, R.K. (1939) 'Patterns of aggressive behavior in experimentally created social climates', *Journal of Social Psychology*, 10: 271–301.

McGuire, J. (2004) 'Think First Treatment Integrity', *What Works News*, Issue 18.

McGuire, J. (ed.) (1995) *What Works: Reducing Reoffending: Guidelines from Research and Practice.* Chichester: John Wiley.

McGuire, J. and Priestley, P. (1995) 'Reviewing "What Works": past, present and future', in J. McGuire (ed.), *What Works: Reducing Reoffending.* Chichester: Wiley.

Miller, W.R. and Rollnick, S. (2002) *Motivational Interviewing: Preparing People to Change Addictive Behaviour*. New York: Guilford Press.

Preston-Shoot, M. (1987) *Effective Groupwork*. Hampshire: Macmillan.

Preston-Shoot, M. (2007) *Effective Groupwork*. Basingstoke: Palgrave Macmillan.

Shaw, M. and Hannah-Moffat, K. (2004) 'How cognitive skills forgot about gender and diversity', in G. Mair (ed.), *What Matters in Probation*. Cullompton: Willan.

Trotter, C. (1996) 'The impact of different supervision practices in community corrections: causes for optimism', *Australian and New Zealand Journal of Criminology*, 29: 29–46.

Trotter, C. (1999) *Working with Involuntary Clients: A Guide to Practice*. London: Sage.

Tuckman, B.W. (1965) 'Developmental sequence in small groups', *Psychological Bulletin*, 63: 384–99.

Tuckman, B.W. and Jensen, M.A.C. (1977) 'Stages of small-group development revisited', *Group and Organization Management*, 2 (4): 419–27.

Chapter 16

Life after prison

Paul Senior

This chapter explores the changing measures for the support and surveillance of offenders during and after release from custody. By setting it in a historical context this chapter draws out the elements of continuity in the needs ex-prisoners have and in the continuity of various policy responses. We have witnessed three step changes in provision in the last 20 years. Firstly, the official response has moved towards compulsory licensing post-release which potentially reaches across the entire prison population with the advent of the Criminal Justice Act 2003. Secondly, an emphasis on What Works has sought to focus on internal processes of cognitive behavioural change in the individual offender as a necessary though not sufficient condition of reform and rehabilitation. Thirdly, the organisational arrangements for the delivery of resettlement services has been refashioned following the modernisation impulses of government, the Carter Report (2003) and subsequent legislation concerning the development of the National Offender Management Service. However, throughout the history of resettlement one element has remained constant. The delivery of support services, whether mentoring, education, training and employment, accommodation advice, drug and alcohol support or other services, reoccurs as a necessary condition for successful reintegration. The deliverers of such services may be changing but whatever the step changes in policy the importance of needs-based support to successful outcomes remains central.

Introduction

There is a long history of support for people leaving prison. Such histories are well documented (Crow 2006) and need not be repeated here. Motivation for helping in the early years of the twentieth century often stemmed from religious and philanthropic motives, helping those seen as 'less fortunate' make a successful return to society. Services for offenders in prison targeted those who demonstrated an inclination for reformation and penance. The 'saving of souls' (McWilliams 1983) was a key mission statement. This has continued into the modern day with many faith groups and voluntary organisations visiting prisons to offer support, mentoring and counselling. It is unpaid voluntary work in the truest sense which is there for prisoners if they wish to take up the offer. As the modern Probation Service developed and as services for supporting the welfare needs of prisoners transferred to that service in 1962 a more professionally driven approach to after-care developed. It became known in the 1960s and 1970s as voluntary after-care (VAC) and under Probation Rules it was a duty of the probation officer to provide such care. Caseloads were controlled by a mixture of natural wastage – many people did not want to contact probation – and by focusing help on immediate resettlement problems – accommodation, education and training, employment, health and benefits advice, etc. Some control was exerted by officer inertia too. Probation officers would visit prisoners and offer support by visits and letters sometimes utilising probation volunteers – as indeed I started my probation career as one such volunteer in the early 1970s. Contact would be made with families to ensure they were coping with the absence of a key family member and sometimes links would be made to some of the ad hoc services mentioned above. Sometimes this became a specialist function in after-care teams (Goodman 2007) but often VAC was just part of the caseload. It never carried the same attention as statutory community-based work resulting from probation orders and then, latterly, community service orders. Nor did the allocation of time match the importance of statutory after-care work that was a feature of work with young offenders and, from 1968, with the introduction of parole and then lifers work, adults too. VAC was, nevertheless, at the heart of the probation mission to 'advise, assist and befriend', but as that mission began to be superseded in the 1980s it was statutory after-care which took precedence. This was reflected in the low priority accorded to VAC in the 1984 Statement of National Objectives and Priorities:

> Sufficient resources should be allocated to throughcare to enable the Service's statutory obligations to be discharged ... Beyond that, social work for offenders released from custody, though important in itself, can only command the priority which is consistent with the main objective implementing non-custodial measures for offenders who might otherwise receive custodial sentences. (Home Office 1984)

With the control and surveillance function relatively muted in the 1970s and early 1980s it is instructive to recall that the motivation for the introduction of parole was rehabilitative, not a concern with risk management. It recognised that the pains of imprisonment itself (Sykes 1958) were such that assistance in resettlement was vital to effective rehabilitation. Although parole was only to be recommended if there was a platform for reform and risk of reoffending was low, in fact parole was often more likely to be granted in cases where the offender had been convicted of serious but few offences than in cases of the multi-offending background of the petty persistent offender. Thus those who arguably led more chaotic and difficult lives and experienced numerous short-term prison sentences were rarely subject to statutory after-care and their needs became increasingly sidelined as VAC went down the priority listing. The most advanced expression of this programmatic response for statutory licences was the very impressively organised and staged reporting for lifers who were carefully managed on their return to society (Senior 1998). However, rational deliberative judgments guiding a lifer's release back into the community were not based entirely on readiness for rehabilitation as political decisions determined the ever rising tariff for minimum periods in prison for lifers. From Leon Brittain in 1983 onwards to the present day, this has continuously spiralled for lifers, political and public acceptability for release often superseding risk assessments in the Parole Board, with the late Myra Hindley being the starkest example of this inequitable and double jeopardy process.

By the turn of the century statutory after-care, or more correctly supervision, was the focus for the probation service with VAC just a memory in the minds of longer-serving probation officers or an aspiration for the voluntary sector in projects designed to support offenders on release (Maguire *et al.* 2000).

What is resettlement?

Terminology for describing work in the transition from prison to community has been changing. The notion of 'after-care', which had its heyday following the Morrison Committee in 1962 when after-care responsibilities were taken over by the Probation Service, carried with it connotations of social work help and assistance and a tendency to channel the focus on the process post-release. In the 1980s 'through-care' became more prevalent as the defining term seeking to exemplify a concern for reintegration of offenders and exemplifying a process starting at the point of sentence to prison, through the prison experience and in community provision afterwards (Maguire and Raynor 1997; Her Majesty's Inspectorates of Prison and Probation 2001). This increasingly became badged as 'resettlement' which remains a currently used term though the latest phrase, 'end-to-end offender management', also seeks to describe that through-care focus. Resettlement is sometimes considered a misnomer describing a process which assumes offenders previously had a settled role in their community whereas the impact of exclusionary policies often create a rootlessness among offenders which challenges the notion of *re*settlement. In Europe reinsertion is the preferred term and in the USA re-entry is more commonly used. Reintegration and rehabilitation are also used interchangeably in the same context.

Collectively the terms used seek to acknowledge firstly that imprisonment is a dislocation from the community. Its exclusionary intention takes people away from their normal surroundings for which care needs taking in the process of (re)establishing people in society. Secondly, as so powerfully demonstrated by the Social Exclusion Unit Report in 2002, whatever the public protection dimensions involved in returning people to communities, successful resettlement will be more likely to occur if the basic needs of an offender are met. No one element necessarily dominates this agenda although it is arguable that without sustainable accommodation and employment resettlement success is significantly reduced. The complexity of the relationship between *needs*, *risk* and *public safety* means that successful resettlement is a daunting target and on average 60 per cent fail to achieve that transition if measured solely in terms of reoffending over a two-year period.

Fundamental to the process of effective reintegration is resolving the often uneasy relationship which exists between risk and need. The statutory services, notably prison, probation and the police, are increasingly exercised by the political imperatives of public protection and ensuring that the management of offenders upon release, particularly where there is a high risk of harm and of reoffending, drives their practices. This is reflected in large-scale risk assessment processes, cautious decision-making, arbitrary increases in sentence tariffs to incapacitate risky offenders for longer, risk registers, community notification, public protection panels, electronic surveillance, supervised accommodation, stringent monitoring requirements and information to victims. This panoply of surveillance measures signals the move in statutory services from care to control. This is reflected in the changing directives of National Standards since their inception in 1992, now demanding a process of increasing intensification of supervision, accelerated measures for breach and a corresponding decrease in the importance of managing need. If this is to be the key statutory focus of offender management in the future then it cannot be assumed that assessing and responding to need is no longer necessary or is not relevant to public protection and risk management. Nor can it be assumed that this process is entirely containable within the statutory correctional services. Resettlement strategies and practices must balance risk, need and treatment within a responsibilised community, making sure that reintegration is possible by an attitude where communities and its key agencies of social responsibility – health, education, community safety – engage in that rehabilitative process.

Balanced provision

This chapter argues that there are three dimensions to good resettlement practice which, if developed in a balanced and complementary manner, can help to reduce reoffending, reduce risk to the public and victims and enable individuals to develop productive functioning lifestyles. This is a concern for communities as much as it is for criminal justice agencies. Resettlement directly implies settling back into communities which may be hostile to their reintegration. Such a goal may take a number of steps for individuals to achieve including half-way houses and hostels, rehabilitation services, risk management via MAPPAs, drugs intervention programmes (DIPs) and prolific and other priority offender (PPO) schemes, but such steps cannot be productively managed unless the 'wall of exclusion', identified by Buchanan (2005) in relation to problematic drug users but applicable in differing degrees by all resettling individuals, is positively breached. Buchanan (2005) notes how treatment services can support detoxification and achieve clinical rehabilitation effectively but failure to deal with the social isolation and exclusion experienced by drug users means that relapse is likely. Resettlement takes more than commitment from the individuals involved to treatment and to change; it demands that communities find ways of re-engaging such alienated individuals and removing the barriers to that achievement. Figure 16.1 illustrates this process and places the responsibility on all of us to open doors – whether it is housing landlords reducing restrictions to re-entering the house market, employers opening their minds and revising their attitudes towards employment of ex-offenders and communities creating a social milieu which welcomes those seeking to change and reform. In a responsibilised community it requires individuals caught up in the system themselves also to support this process, and some of the recent developments in peer-led solutions to education, employment and training offers some positive avenues to follow (see O'Keeffe *et al.* 2007).

Crucial to a balanced portfolio of services is *flexibility, availability* and *diversity* of provision. *Flexibility* seeks to avoid the risk of assuming that all individuals need the same service or outcome. The research on desistance (Farrall 2002, 2004; Farrall and Calverley 2005; Maruna 2000; McNeill 2005;

Community

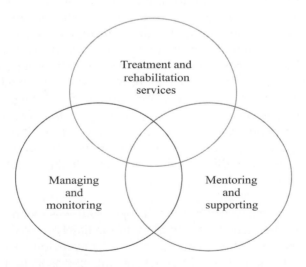

Figure 16.1 The three pillars of resettlement.

McCulloch and McNeill, this volume) shows that individuals leave criminal activity for a variety of reasons and in a myriad of different circumstances. The needs of individuals leaving prison vary enormously and what might work for one group of male adult offenders may not work for another group, or for women, young people or black and minority ethnic (BME) groups. If services cannot respond sensitively to the needs of individuals it risks an ineffective and ultimately self-defeating and costly provision. This can particularly apply in relation to treatment services. The early optimism of offending behaviour programmes has undergone some radical rethink as programme integrity can undermine other goals (Mair 2004). However, flexibility is dependent on availability of services. Too often provision is unavailable for specialist needs or the capacity to enter one support programme is undermined by the non-existence of other services. Seeking employment, a goal associated with successful resettlement, cannot realistically be attempted without accommodation needs being first met, for example.

Availability of services can no longer be guaranteed by a single agency. The diversity of skills and practices needed to respond to the complex demands of people re-entering society from custody cannot be provided by one agency alone. If we take seriously the need for community re-engagement as a successful parameter for effective resettlement we also need to recognise that a mixed economy of providers is demanded. The growth of services provided by the voluntary and community sector, particularly in prison but increasingly in the community, is now recognised as an essential adjunct to resettlement. As discussed above the move towards a primarily surveillance role of the statutory services has left a gap in the voluntary and community sector (VCS) provision of support and treatment services. In addition the VCS has a long history of specialist provision in focused areas of practice such as work with sex offenders, drug and alcohol services, employment, training and education (ETE) provision, mental health services and so on. The huge investment in mentoring offenders during and immediately after release has been delivered in the main by VCS organisations. Although the research evidence is sparse about the impact of mentoring on reducing reoffending, it is clearly evident that if individuals are enabled to access the services they need through the close support mentoring offers they have at least not failed at the first hurdle (Clancy *et al.* 2006). Indeed the short journey from prison to provision or reporting centres in probation or police is often replete with a plethora of temptations and diversions which is compounded when the individual does not have the basic skills to access the services they need:

A major frustration expressed by many project staff was the inadequacy of support for offenders in the period immediately following their release when they are often tempted to revert to previous drug using and criminal behaviour. Gaps in provision for ex-prisoners and long waiting lists were noted, typically where help was needed in securing accommodation, financial support or drug treatment. (Raynor 2004)

Diversity of provision to focus on the needs of particular groups and individuals has always been hard to deliver across every area. The focus in What Works programmes on programme integrity has reduced the opportunity for programmes to be customised to different groups. Much of the literature in the 1980s and 1990s about group work has been ignored in the construction of these programmes. The end result can mean programmes which fail to address the concerns of particular groups, who then feel alienated from the official processes. Here the VCS has always provided more tailored services but in the policy context of today this is not always seen as helpful. To use housing as an example, the provision of housing advice in prisons to support residents has been seen as an essential component of resettlement. Local services designed to respond to particular groups such as BME groups or women or young people are typically small, locally based and precariously funded organisations. Their very responsiveness, characteristic of the VCS (Senior *et al.* 2005), is also their own vulnerability. As prisons have looked to regional provision for housing advice across a range of prisons, larger organisations such as Shelter and Nacro are likely to win contracts and the smaller groups become disenfranchised to the loss of the particular groups they serve. Cost-effectiveness of provision may put at risk diversity of provision (see Cole, this volume).

The three pillars of resettlement

This chapter argues that a successful resettlement process must balance what is termed here as the 'three pillars of resettlement': these are managing and monitoring; treatment and rehabilitation; and mentoring and support. There is a real risk that one element dominating provision will lead to a breakdown in effective service outcomes (Raikes 2002). Raikes, using a propeller analogy, argued that if one element began to dominate practices and policies the resultant imbalance would be self-defeating. This will only become manifest when problems occur in the future. What seems increasingly accepted from the evidence-base is that the three elements combined remain essential to effective delivery even if the agencies delivering any one of these services changes over time. Organisational coordination of services remains a key task and thus organisational issues will be further discussed towards the end of the chapter.

Managing and monitoring

The political agenda in a risk society has created a culture of surveillance as one pillar of any process of resettlement. Sometimes it can feel as if this is the only pillar to which the political agenda responds, but it is argued here that such a singular policy imperative would be at best ineffective and at worst deeply counterproductive. The behaviour of individuals alienated from communities is not likely to be affected positively in a climate which only views them as individual dots on a computer and chastised for any breach of the protocol of release. This, however, is not a rejection of the need to manage and monitor offenders on release but rather to see it alongside the other pillars discussed below. We need to be clear about the purpose underlying managing and monitoring. We need to manage and monitor such offenders upon release for three interrelated purposes – those of surveillance to support risk control, enabling access and attracting resources.

Surveillance has shifted the relationship between public and private spaces in late modernity where the capacity to record and monitor movement has increased through technological advances and political demand. Early objections to electronic surveillance based on technological inefficiency have now been dismissed as those problems have been overcome (Nellis 2004). The search for the ultimate surveillance tool continues with global positioning systems using satellites being explored to enhance the reach of monitoring. For many offenders the reality is less intrusive and involves reporting to a probation officer/offender manager within a schedule determined by National Standards with rigidly enforced breach arrangements. This is a demanding requirement in its own right but potentially creates a stable starting point for contact as a first base for other services. However, for many, reporting remains the only key service and is treated as a necessary evil to remain in the community rather than the beginning of productive engagement in resettlement. Home detention curfews have been the clearest example of surveillance-only provision, the concern of which is to ensure that the requirements are not breached, not that there is any positive responses to release which might reduce the likelihood of reoffending. Further such monitoring can be appropriately achieved, ticking all the boxes contained in reporting protocols, and still people will offend.

It is important that there is a realism about what can be achieved by such supervision if it is not to degenerate into such high-level community surveillance that freedom of movement and liberty become meaningless concepts. Flexibility based on risk assessments will ensure that only those who warrant high levels of surveillance receive it. We have seen more productive approaches taken in the MAPPAs and PPO projects where levels of risk direct the degree of surveillance demanded. The ubiquitous demand for public protection can hide the fact that unless we have total surveillance over all released offenders there will be situations in which ex-offenders will not be under surveillance. If complementary work has been undertaken with such people then this will have contributed to altered thinking and produce potential desistance from further criminal activity. Given the high levels of reoffending associated with release from prison, on average still around 60 per cent within two years of release, then we can realistically expect some reoffending to occur. Short of house arrest and electronic implants we have to find ways of enabling ex-offenders to feel empowered to move beyond their offending patterns and into new and productive lifestyles. Recognising reoffending can occur thus must be incorporated as part of the developing process of change and further support to reduce the amount, severity and frequency of reoffending. Thus even managing and monitoring has to have rehabilitation goals, not simply be the object of surveillance. We shall return to this below.

Managing offenders is also about ensuring that they can *access the services* they need to support change and rehabilitation. Reporting to an offender manager is about ensuring that they are linked into the services they require, not simply or only because there is a need to report. Indeed, the use of excessive breaching protocols can inhibit the very process of access which good reporting practices were meant to facilitate. This aspect of managing and monitoring offenders is crucial to any successful reduction in reoffending. Often failure to attend treatment services is not the result of wilful action on the part of an offender, though it can be a factor too. Regular reporting allows an administrative check on progress, and judicious offender management will help oil the wheels connecting the offender to other services. It can be expected that the chaotic nature of many offenders' daily lives makes it hard for them to routinely keep their appointments. Contact can drive further contact provided the offender manager takes their brokerage role seriously.

Increasingly too, *resources* are targeted on identified offenders on statutory orders only. The provision of services for voluntary after-care, such a marker of resettlement in the 1960s, 1970s and early 1980s, will not return. Those offenders targeted as needing most support because of their high risk of reoffending or their high risk of harm will attract the most resources for help and surveillance. It is the key job of managing those services to ensure that such resources are accessed at the right time to support rehabilitation. In addition those who are less likely to tick the boxes for high levels of surveillance may still need high levels of support. This duty may no longer rest with the probation officer but modern resettlement practices still require the provision of support services to those released under no licence whatsoever. It is to those services that we will return below.

Treatment and rehabilitation services

Late modernity has not, as was once feared by practitioners and signalled by research, abandoned the notion of rehabilitation. Despite the signalling of the death of the ideal in the 1970s – though always overstated if deeply influential – the 'nothing works' mantra has given way to a 'What Works' strap line which has been accompanied by the increasing acceptance of evidence-based practices mainly focused around cognitive-behavioural therapies and much influenced by the work of Canadian researchers (for example, in relation to resettlement, see Fabiano and Porporino 2002). This resurgence of rehabilitation has been well documented (Underdown 1998; Chapman and Hough 1998) and well resourced in England and Wales, though early results show somewhat stubbornly that evidence-based practitioners are not as successful as the most evangelical supporters felt they would be (Mair 2004). This should not over-concern reflective practitioners. Policy-makers, somewhat in haste, abandoned the question mark around 'What Works', applying positivistic optimism that the ultimate solution had been found. The question mark is instructive and important for practitioners. The shifts in thinking such cognitive-behavioural therapy (CBT) programmes engender have to be set in a context where learning is mediated through the stresses and strains of living. It is the very chaotic nature of offenders' lives which militate against neat solutions. Training for professional practice emphasises the need for reflexivity in considering how offenders can move on and desist from offending and there is much still to be learnt about What Works(?). As Maruna notes in the desistance research: 'Whereas active offenders ... seemed to have little vision of what the future might hold, desisting interviewees had a plan and were optimistic that they could make it work' (Maruna 2000).

However, there is no doubt that the state of treatment services is now much more advanced than even 20 years ago. Both inside prisons and on release in the community there are a range of programmes which seek to impact on the thinking patterns and behaviour of offenders in general and in particular areas such as anger management, drug counselling, sex offender programmes, domestic violence and alcohol education, to name just a few. Indeed a specific programme for resettlement is now available in prisons: the For-a-Change Programme which helps prisoners' awareness of gaps between what prisoners aspire to be and their current situation/behaviour.

Where other factors can be controlled – attendance, consistency of delivery, programme integrity, cultural sensitivity, appropriate learning styles – there is evidence of success. Positive effects of good work in prison (including the FOR programme) are dependent on good continuity of services after release. Realism should drive this work and the current emphasis on end-to-end offender management is a recognition of the need to co-ordinate and manage access to treatment programmes if they are to be successful. Learning can take place on a programme but unless it is part of a well-constructed motivational model of care then in isolation it is unlikely to be sustainable.

Mentoring and support services

The research involved in the Social Exclusion Unit Report (2002) brought attention to the huge range of social and personal difficulties resettling offenders need to deal with if they are to make a successful re-entry to the community. Examples from accommodation or from employment and training show how their resolution will be vital to the wider prospects of desistance from reoffending. When you extend this to issues of health and mental health, drugs and alcohol abuse, violence, fractured familial and personal relationships, the stigma and isolation of a prison sentence, hostile communities and so on, it illustrates that the task of effective rehabilitation and reintegration is not an easy or self-evident one. The last ten years have seen clarity emerge over what is required, though no commitment of resources or joined-up practices has been universally developed. Paul Cavadino makes the point succinctly:

> The facts speak for themselves. Research shows that prisoners released with a job are half as likely to reoffend as unemployed ex-prisoners. Getting released prisoners into stable accommodation cuts their likelihood of reoffending by one fifth. Prisoners who have had education in literacy and numeracy reoffend at one-third of the rate of those who have not. Prisoners released without family support are up to six times more likely to reoffend than those without it. Drug addicted ex-prisoners who take part in treatment programmes reoffend at one-fifth of the rate of those who do not. In short, improving prisoners' resettlement can play a vital part in cutting crime. (Nacro 2000)

There have been good examples of positive resettlement practices both at a strategic (Senior 2003) and at a practice level (see the Re-Connect Project in Home Office 2004). The parameters of support can be subsumed under the following key points:

- This is a multi-agency and inter-agency task *and* responsibility.
- Generating and sustaining motivation is vital to the maintenance of the processes of change.
- It is the responsibility of all individuals, groups and communities, not just the criminal justice service agencies – partnership has to be meaningfully addressed.
- Community reintegration of offenders should drive community safety partnership agendas, not the exclusionary 'nuts and bolts' approach which can predominate.
- Polices need to be predicated on reducing the stigma and prejudice which bedevils the efforts of individuals to find a place back into society.
- Ex-offenders can have a key role in supporting their peers' resettlement.
- Offender managers need to ensure support is delivered through a coordinated approach to case management and referral.

This is not a new concept. The notion of preparing offenders to return to the community is a long-standing and stubbornly recurrent theme in resettlement practice. We know that the risks of rearrest, reconviction and reincarceration remain high. The risks to public safety remain high and therefore supportive structures of intervention and support are vital if crime is to be reduced and, ultimately, there are to be fewer victims of crime. Supervision services and support, to be most effective, should be aligned to the period of time when likelihood of reoffending is greatest. This is the first few days and then the first few weeks following release. Front-loading supervision and support services focuses on the highest risk period. This gives a primacy to effective partnerships in delivering that support and to the coordination of services which can be sustainable over a prolonged period of time.

There is an important caveat here. Just as I argued above that monitoring and managing should not be seen as an isolated goal, nor should the provision of support. It is the combination of services working together with the whole person which has most chance of success. The desistance literature notes that dealing with social problems may be an important element in preparing an offender for a changed lifestyle, but it is not just an end in itself. Without altering thinking and attitudes or creating a motivational atmosphere for change no amount of support alone will be successful. It is perfectly possible to become a well-housed, financially sound, healthy, employed person and still offend. However, the inability to resolve such issues will make motivation for change that much more difficult and sustaining change will only be built on the support a stable lifestyle can bring (McNeill 2005).

At the heart of support services is the concept of mentoring, and peer mentoring in particular. Though under-researched and theorised in the offender world it has become the modernised version of 'advise, assist and befriend' delivered by a myriad of public and voluntary sector agencies and is at the heart of good resettlement processes. The social glue which mentoring assists ensures continuity of care and control is possible. One project (O'Keeffe *et al.* 2007) illustrated how peer mentoring and support helped keep women on board when resettling from custody. This element of involvement from offenders themselves as the peer mentors was significant in this process.

Resettling organisational relationships

The seamlessness at the heart of positive resettlement practices through the decades has foundered on the failure of the correctional services – most notably prison and probation services – to work in a coordinated and integrated manner. Solutions in some countries have resulted in a merger of the two organisations (e.g. Sweden) and this was threatened in England and Wales. In the end the Carter Report 2003, endorsed by the government upon its release, set the blueprint for change in this jurisdiction:

> Building on the significant improvements in delivery over the last seven years, a new approach is needed to focus on the management of offenders.
>
> • Prison and probation need to be focused on the management of offenders throughout the whole of their sentence, driven by information on what works to reduce re-offending.

- Effectiveness and value for money can be further improved through greater use of competition from private and voluntary providers.

This means

- The establishment of a National Offender Management Service – restructuring the Prison and Probation Services – with a single Chief Executive accountable to Ministers for punishing offenders and reducing re-offending.
- Within the new Service there should be one person – the National Offender Manager – who is responsible for reducing re-offending – supported by Regional Offender Managers. They would supervise offenders and commission custody places, fine collection and interventions – whether in the public, private or voluntary sector. (Carter 2003: 43)

No history of the National Offender Management Service has yet been written as its birth and growth have been stunted and remoulded by the constant changes in the Home Office (now Ministry of Justice) and by Probation and Prison Service resistance and opposition: even though the Offender Management Act has reached the statute books the precise workings of the new arrangements are still unfolding. This is not the place to recount these developments but its relevance to the development of effective resettlement services needs to be addressed. This will cover three dimensions:

- the practical impact of the Offender Management Model on resettlement;
- the impact of commissioning;
- the mixed economy of provision.

Offender Management Model

The neat rationality of the OMM (NOMS 2007) offers an organisational matrix for order in offender supervision. However, at the root of the model is whether services to offenders are given entirely on the basis of risk rather than need. In this situation the more needs-based elements of resettlement could easily slip down the priority level if attending to such needs are not deemed to be connected to criminogenic issues or problems. The potential mismatch between resourcing of the offender management services and key resettlement needs may well continue the neglect of such services since 1984. This is particularly central to the treatment of AUR (automatic unconditional release) prisoners who currently are released without formal supervision, a situation Custody Plus was designed to resolve, but which has now been seemingly permanently abandoned on the legislative agenda. Short-term prisoners, both male and female, have high reconviction rates with 30 per cent back in prison within two years. A high proportion have major social and personal problems and multiple needs, often exacerbated by continued incarceration where jobs, accommodation and relationships are fractured and stigma and prejudice heightens rejection and nourishes low morale (Lewis *et al.* 2003).

The model itself is merely a model of case management and can be administered as a mechanistic response to the problems of coordination across agency boundaries. It is not the first time that planned interventions/ responses have been attempted for resettlement practices. The doomed history of 'sentence planning' in the 1990s should caution us about optimism over delivering coordinated services. The offender manager is being given the licence to transcend agency boundaries to link together services of offender supervision, case administration and key worker roles in interventions. The model strives to deliver across the range of services required by an individual offender. The OMM at least offers an organisational arrangement which fits with findings about what is needed in the positive management of an offender. It offers a structured process enabling continuity, referral to holistic provisions and a personal relationship (much neglected in recent years but now re-emerging as a central concept underpinning successful interventions), and is based on a model of change which is designed to be responsive, participatory, motivational, and a pro-social model in execution. This model, however, is not needs-driven but risk-driven. The priority an offender manager will give to allocating resources is based on the risk assessments undertaken. In this situation the danger is that the complementary services highlighted above as the third pillar of resettlement at best get shunted to voluntary services and at worse disappear altogether. Good holistic offender management must ensure such an approach is not allowed to develop.

The impact of commissioning

One of the key intentions of developing NOMS was to create a distinction between providers and purchasers of services. The creation of regional structures with a Regional Offender Manager was to be the vehicle for such commissioning to take place and in an environment of competition euphemistically called contestability. While this model has suffered from planning blight and institutional and political resistance and uncertainties, the basic principle of commissioning (and contestability) has stubbornly remained. The intention to have local as well as regional commissioning may be a recipe for an inconsistency in approach which might be negatively reflected in the effective development of resettlement services. On the other hand, the more crime reduction is seen as a local issue the more engagement through community safety partnerships (CSPs) may bring attention to the responsibilities of local people and organisations for providing a positive return to the community where those sent to custody originated. This offers a more inclusive approach to policy and practice in resettlement. Thus commissioning of services for resettlement which are coordinated locally need to engage all welfare agencies, not just be seen as the province of offender-oriented services. It probably falls to CSPs to provide needs-based services to those offenders not deemed higher risk, but for whom the reality of the revolving door of prison remains acute.

The mixed economy of provision

The moves to commissioning have been developed in an environment of contestability whereby the provision of services can be provided by a range of public, private or voluntary organisations. There is a real danger that NOMS can end up with different forms of fragmentation rather than greater integration as was envisaged by its architects. Prisons and probation remain, offender management and intervention are separated and interventions could be supplied by any combination of public, private and voluntary sector providers. NOMS is not a required feature for the principle of joining up and it is as much a recognition of the properties of successful partnership in resettlement as any organisational realignment which will produce improved resettlement outcomes. Partnership in delivery, given the potential plethora of agencies involved in the resettlement process, has to be a central starting point for organisational success in resettlement. The competition at the heart of contestability and therefore commissioning and the encouragement of a mixed economy can undermine those principles. Partnership is, in many ways, a contested concept and its history in this field is no less chequered than across other welfare services. We know that probation's aspiration to partnership was more often a recipe for purchaser–provider relationships than genuine partnership. Likewise the Prison Service has commissioned many services from the voluntary sector in the past 15 years or so, but the same lack of a level playing field emerges from research (Senior 2005).

Concluding thoughts

The current organisational milieu and the state of knowledge and research offer a blueprint, at least on paper, for success. However, the capacity of agencies to deliver on this agenda is fraught with difficulties. There may be insufficient staff skills to deliver this agenda effectively. The moves towards adequate learning and development for all practitioners remain stalled by political indecision and need to be sector-wide to touch the myriad of agencies involved in resettlement. Within probation particularly, the context of organisational upheaval, including moves to trust status, and low staff morale make survival the predominant response rather than wholesale engagement. Modernisation of the criminal justice sector has produced over-bureaucratic responses and conflicts between utilising evidence-based practices and the political demands of a penal populist climate (Senior *et al.* 2007).

The issues raised in this chapter concerning coordination and communication between agencies, both personal and IT-based, remain in chaos with restricted access to OASys, poor information exchange protocols between agencies (Senior 2005) and the demise of C-NOMIS, the latest in a series of IT disasters which beset the criminal justice field. Funding is uncertain and the offenders most at risk of losing support and services are those released after less than 12 months incarceration – just the population for whom coordinated efforts would work best. Offender managers have the model to deliver holistic casework but a chronic overload of offenders, each with too many conditions that need policing, may reduce the more innovative relational work. It is still evident that attitudes to ex-prisoners from non-criminal justice service agencies remain problematic, and without the engagement of communities resettlement becomes an aspiration with little chance of meaningful achievement. Finally, can a coordinated approach drawing on the best of research in desistance and interventions actually reduce reoffending, and, if not, how long will the political resolve be sustained to support agency workers?

Life after prison may remain the most challenging of prospects for the *most needy* ex-prisoners who fall outside the services currently available for the *most risky*.

Discussion questions

1 How far should local authorities and local organisations play an active part in developing and supporting resettlement services?
2 Does the Offender Management Model enable resettlement to be genuinely 'through the prison gate'?
3 Resettlement as a term is so contested it lacks useful meaning. What would describe better the processes of support and supervision for the sentenced prisoner during custody and post-release?

Further reading

Clancy, A., Hudson, K., Maguire, M., Peake, R., Raynor, P. and Vanstone, M. (2006) *Getting Out and Staying Out: Results of the Prisoner Resettlement Pathfinders*. Bristol: Policy Press. There is little British-based research into resettlement and this offers a good overview of the most recent work.
Crow, I. (2006) *Resettling Prisoners: A Review*. University of Sheffield/NOMS. A good literature review which acts as an essential starting point for further investigation.
Maruna, S. and Immarigeon, R. (eds) (2004) *After Crime and Punishment: Pathways to Offender Reintegration*. Cullompton: Willan. This collection of papers reviews the increasing potential for desistance theories to offer models for resettlement practice.

Senior, P. Crowther-Dowey, C. and Long, M. (2007) *Understanding Modernisation In Criminal Justice.* Open University Press. All practice developments are hemmed in by modernisation of government departments and agencies. The framework developed here offers a conceptual underpinning which can help describe and unpack the resettlement process.

Social Exclusion Unit (2002) *Reducing Re-offending by Ex-Prisoners.* London: Office of the Deputy Prime Minister. This government report shows unequivocally the importance of needs-based assessments and support for resettling prisoners.

Hucklesby, A. and Hagley-Dickinson, L. (2007) *Prisoner Resettlement: Policy and Practice.* Cullompton: Willan. Provides a review and analysis of resettlement policy and practice in England and Wales in the early part of the twenty-first century.

References

Buchanan, J. (2005) 'Problem drug use in the 21st century: a social model of intervention', in T. Heinonen and A. Metteri (eds), *Social Work in Health and Mental Health: Issues, Developments and Actions.* Toronto: Canadian Scholars Press.

Carter, P. (2003) *Managing Offenders, Reducing Crime: A New Approach.* London: Home Office.

Chapman, T. and Hough, M. (1998) *Evidence Based Practice: A Guide to Effective Practice.* London: Home Office.

Clancy, A., Hudson, K., Maguire, M., Peake, R., Raynor, P. and Vanstone, M. (2006) *Getting Out and Staying Out: Results of the Prisoner Resettlement Pathfinders.* Bristol: Policy Press.

Crow, I. (2006) *Resettling Prisoners: A Review.* University of Sheffield/NOMS.

Fabiano, E. and Porporino, F. (2002) *Focus on Resettlement – A Change.* Canada: T3 Associates.

Farrall, S. (2002) *Rethinking What Works with Offenders.* Cullompton: Willan.

Farrall, S. (2004) 'Social capital and offender re-integration: making probation desistance focused', in S. Maruna and R. Immarigeon (eds), *After Crime and Punishment: Pathways to Offender Reintegration.* Cullompton: Willan.

Farrall, S. and Calverley, A. (2005) *Understanding Desistance from Crime: New Theoretical Directions in Resettlement and Rehabilitation.* Milton Keynes: Open University Press.

Goodman, A. (2007) '289 Borough High Street, the After Care and Resettlement Unit (ACU) in the Inner London Probation Service 1965–1990', *British Journal of Community Justice,* 5: 2.

Her Majesty's Inspectorates of Prison and Probation (2001) *Through the Prison Gate: A Joint Thematic Review.* London: Home Office.

Home Office (1984) *Probation Service in England and Wales. Statement of National Objectives and Priorities.* London: Home Office.

Home Office (2004) *Reducing Re-Offending: National Action Plan.* London: Home Office.

Lewis, S., Maguire, M., Raynor, P., Vanstone, M., and Vennard, J. (2003) *The Resettlement of Short-Term Prisoners: An Evaluation of Seven Pathfinder Programmes,* Research Findings 200. London: Home Office.

Maguire, M. and Raynor, P. (1997) 'The revival of throughcare: rhetoric and reality in automatic conditional release', *British Journal of Criminology*, 37: 1–14.

Maguire, M., Raynor, P., Vanstone, M. and Kynch, J. (2000) 'Voluntary after-care and the Probation Service: a case of diminishing responsibility', *Howard Journal of Criminal Justice*, 39: 234–48.

Maguire, M. and Raynor, P. (2006) 'How the resettlement of prisoners promotes desistance from crime: or does it?', *Criminology and Criminal Justice*, 6 (1): 17–36.

Mair, G. (ed.) (2004) *What Matters in Probation*. Cullompton: Willan.

Maruna, S. (2000) *Making Good*. Washington, DC: American Psychological Association.

Maruna, S. and Immarigeon, R. (eds) (2004) *After Crime and Punishment: Pathways to Offender Reintegration*. Cullompton: Willan.

McNeill, F. (2005) 'Towards a desistance paradigm for probation practice', *Criminal Justice*, Special Issue.

McWilliams, W. (1983) 'The Mission to the English Police Courts 1876–1936', *Howard Journal of Criminal Justice*, 232: 129–47.

Nacro (2000) *The Forgotten Majority: the Resettlement of Short Term Prisoners*. London: Nacro.

Nellis, M. (2004) '"I know where you live!": electronic monitoring and penal policy in England and Wales 1999–2003', *British Journal of Community Justice*, 2: 3.

NOMS (2007) *The NOMS Offender Management Model. Version 2*. London: National Offender Management Service.

O'Keeffe, C., Senior, P. and Monti-Holland, V. (2007) 'Barriers to employment, training and education in prison and beyond: a peer-led solution', in R. Sheehan (ed.), *What Works with Women Offenders: A Cross-national Dialogue*. Cullompton: Willan.

Raikes, S. (2002) 'A model for community safety and community justice', *British Journal of Community Justice*, 1: 1.

Raynor, P. (2004) 'The Probation Service "Pathfinders": finding the path and losing the way?', *Criminal Justice*, 4 (3): 309–25.

Raynor, P. and Maguire, M. (2005) 'End-to-end or end in tears? Prospects for the effectiveness of the National Offender Management Model', in M. Hough, R. Allen and U. Padel (eds), *Reshaping Probation and Prisons: The National Offender Management Service and Probation Work*. Bristol: Policy Press.

Senior, P. (1998) *Working with Lifers: A Workbook for Probation Staff*. London: Home Office Probation Unit.

Senior, P. (2003) *Pathways to Resettlement: A Strategy Document for Yorkshire and the Humber*. SHU Press.

Senior, P. with Feasey, S. and Meadows, L. (2005) *Enhancing the Role of the Voluntary and Community Sector: A Case Study of the Yorkshire and Humber Region*, NOMS Report.

Senior, P., Crowther-Dowey, C. and Long, M. (2007) *Understanding Modernisation in Criminal Justice*. Open University Press.

Social Exclusion Unit (2002) *Reducing Re-offending by Ex-Prisoners*. London: Office of the Deputy Prime Minister.

Sykes, G.M. (1958) *The Society of Captives*. Princeton, NJ: Princeton University Press.

Underdown, A. (1998) *Strategies for Effective Offender Supervision*. London: Home Office.

Chapter 17

Victims

Brian Williams and Hannah Goodman Chong

Those who work primarily with offenders, in the probation, youth offending and prison services, have increasingly had to pay attention to the needs and rights of victims in the period since the publication of the first Victim's Charter in 1990. This chapter begins by briefly discussing the current legislative and policy framework which requires the staff of these agencies to do such work, before moving on to review some current policy debates, consider the skills and techniques needed by practitioners to do this work effectively, and finally look at some broader issues about how and why certain interventions are used and their limitations and potential dangers.

The current legislative framework

Most of the legislation concerning the work of statutory criminal justice agencies with victims of crime is relatively recent. The Victim's Charters of 1990 and 1996 had no statutory force, although Home Office Circulars were issued from 1994 once it became clear how inconsistently the original charter was being implemented (see Williams 1999a).

Legal reforms implemented from 1999 under the Youth Justice and Criminal Evidence Act (YJCEA) passed that year introduced the concept of the 'vulnerable or intimidated witness' and required that Crown Courts provide 'special measures' for such witnesses. Other criminal justice agencies have an important role in identifying the people judges should consider providing with such special measures (which include the opportunity to give evidence by video link, the possibility that judges and barristers might remove their wigs and gowns to create a less formidable atmosphere in court, and so on). Apart from the measures identified in the Act, it also led to the construction of many new court buildings with separate waiting areas so that witnesses no longer had to wait for their cases to be called alongside defendants and their associates (see Williams 2005).

With the introduction of the 1998 Criminal Justice Act, a version of restorative justice became available to the victims of (initially) young offenders in England and Wales. Although the new arrangements had a number of limitations, they provided a place for victims at the table where penalties and treatments to be meted out to many young offenders were decided and increased the opportunities for victims to choose whether or not to be involved in such decision-making (Williams 2005). The 1999 YJCEA extended these arrangements to cover all but the most serious and the most trivial young offenders and their victims, by creating youth offender panels and referral orders. Restorative justice became a possibility for adult offenders and their victims in some areas under the Criminal Justice Act 2003, which created conditional cautions (Home Office 2004a). These allow the police to caution adult offenders subject to conditions aimed at ensuring their rehabilitation and the making of restoration – but their implementation so far appears to be patchy. While the government professes to be committed to the introduction of restorative justice in respect of adult offenders and their victims, it has been tentative, to date, about implementing this commitment fully (Home Office 2004b, 2005a). This means that there is an inconsistency, with the victims of young offenders receiving services and information which are not routinely provided when the perpetrators are adults.

The Domestic Violence, Crime and Victims Act 2004 was hailed as the biggest shake-up of domestic violence laws for thirty years (Hitchings 2005). It introduced the Code of Practice for Victims of Crime, a Victims' Commissioner and domestic violence homicide reviews. The 2004 Act has also been praised as a positive development because it 'emphasises domestic violence as a crime, with strengthening of protection orders and prosecution of breaches, and has made common assault an arrestable offence' (Hester 2005a: 79). This is important because (Hester 2005b: 449) describes this as moving domestic violence from a 'private to a public issue'.

The code of practice sets out minimum requirements for all the statutory criminal justice agencies, and has the force of law under the 2004 Act. It provides a route for victims to complain to the parliamentary ombudsman if issues they raise are not dealt with satisfactorily at a local level. It also sets up a new Victims' Commissioner, a victims' 'champion'.

The Code of Practice for agencies working with victims of crime placed statutory duties on a variety of agencies for the first time, including the police, the Probation Service, the Crown Prosecution Service and Witness Care Units. Under the code certain actions must be carried out for either the direct victim and a parent or guardian if they are aged under 17, or one of their representatives where the victim has been killed or incapacitated. For example, the code included timescales within which agencies were required to pass information on to victims. The police must notify vulnerable or intimidated victims within one day if someone is arrested and must notify all victims within five days. Witness Care Units have been set requirements around assessing the needs of witnesses and communicating with them with regard to court dates and verdicts.

The service to victims of serious crimes introduced under the Victim's Charter included the Probation Service providing those victims who wished to receive it information about the progress of their case and of the offender concerned. This was put on a statutory footing (having initially been, in effect, discretionary on the part of probation) under the 2000 Criminal Justice and Court Services Act, which also widened victims' entitlement to such contact. Thus, since 2000, the victims of all sexual and violent offences by an adult offender sentenced to 12 months or more in prison have the right to the victim contact service (see Spalek 2005, and Home Office 2001). The details of how it is provided were tightened up under the Code of Practice for Victims of Crime which came into force in 2006. The Domestic Violence, Crime and Victims Act 2004 extends this to include for the first time victims whose offenders are mentally disordered, giving them the same rights to a service from probation staff as those victims whose offenders are not mentally disordered.

Other secondary legislation relevant to victims of crime includes the arrangements for Victim Personal Statements to be taken by police officers, introduced in 2001. This system is discussed in greater detail later in the chapter; it involves the police taking an additional statement from victims in which they are invited to explain the impact of an offence on them for the information of criminal justice agencies making decisions about the handling of the case (Home Office 2006a).

The current policy debate

Much of the literature, especially material emanating from official sources, tends to refer to Victim Support as if it was the only organisation offering support to victims. It is an effective and successful organisation, but it does not have a monopoly of such work, nor can it meet the needs of all victims of crime. It receives the great majority of its funding from the Home Office and, while this need not prevent it from criticising government policy, prudence dictates that it does not routinely bite the hand that feeds it. There is, indeed, a danger that Victim Support may be co-opted by the officials it has cultivated over the years (see Rock 2004). It is therefore important to bear in mind that other organisations, while perhaps less congenial to officialdom, have an important role to play; these include Refuge and Rape Crisis. They do routinely criticise government policy and they tend to be underfunded and overstretched.

This reflects the fact that there are types of crime which do not always receive appropriate attention when work with victims is under discussion. While the position has changed to some extent in recent years, organisations working with domestic violence (which affects children as well as the direct victims) and sexual violence remain relatively marginalised and they are not as closely involved in policy debates at the national level as Victim Support. Other types of crime are also sometimes neglected – hate crimes, including those motivated by racism, Islamophobia and homophobia, spring to mind. The neglect, exploitation and abuse of people living in institutions also fail to be addressed in many analyses of victimisation. Health and safety transgressions and other types of corporate crime are often completely omitted from discussions of criminal victimisation, although each incident may have many victims who suffer severely from the act or omission concerned. Similarly, exploitative organised crime with 'invisible' victims, such as trafficking in people and the illegal exploitation of cheap labour from other countries, fails to receive the attention it deserves (see Rawlinson 2005; Spalek 2005; Tombs 2005; Williams 2005).

These omissions apart, the current state of debate about victims of crime in the UK is a cause of some concern to those who are interested in seeing an improvement in the ways in which victims are treated. While there have been many beneficial changes made since 1990 (and particularly since 1997), political rhetoric appears to have taken a dangerous turn. Victims as a group are almost always spoken of in opposition to offenders; improved rights for victims, it is implied, have an inevitable cost in terms of defendants' rights. Thus politicians speak of a 'justice gap' (the perceived gap between the number of defendants charged with offences and the number subsequently convicted) and of 're-balancing' justice. There are many reasons for the justice gap, only one of which is that some of these defendants are in fact innocent of the offences they were charged with. Also, rebalancing justice as between victims and defendants presupposes the need to play out a 'zero sum game' in which victims can only gain if the other party loses. This is rhetorically neat but logically unsatisfying. There are many ways in which victims' experience of the criminal justice system can be improved without affecting the treatment of offenders at all. This has been discussed at length elsewhere (Jackson 2004; Spencer 2004; Williams 2005) and need only be noted here.

Another concern is that improvements in criminal justice procedures, practices and legislation which affect victims are increasingly seen by politicians and criminal justice agency managers in terms of their potential for improving public confidence in criminal justice. While it is undoubtedly important that criminal justice should be seen as legitimate by the population at large and that victims in particular should perceive its operation as fair, consistent and just, there is a danger in treating public confidence as the main aim when making changes to the system. Victims deserve respectful, courteous, efficient and empowering treatment in their own right, not only as part of a programme of improving public confidence in the system. Unless these values are embodied in any change programme, there is a danger that changes will be made to satisfy perceived public opinion rather than to make the system fairer and less gratuitously revictimising for victims.

Driven by the desire to appease the media and appeal to voters, politicians have tended to introduce eye-catching initiatives 'for' victims without any attempt to discover what might be genuinely beneficial for them. This has not always been the case: for example, the Code of Practice for Victims of Crime introduced under the 2004 Domestic Violence, Crime and Victims Act reflects the real needs of victims as revealed by a wide range of research (see, for example, Maguire and Kynch 2000; Tapley 2005). However, some attempts to legislate 'for' victims have been botched, and others have been little more than gimmicks. Examples include the Victim Personal Statement scheme introduced in 2001 despite an evaluation of a pilot project having strongly advised against extending it nationally and, arguably, the more recent pilot scheme providing murder victims' families with legal representation in the Crown Court.

The current move to require the prison and probation services to embrace privatisation more wholeheartedly includes an expectation that the victim contact work currently undertaken by the Probation Service will be 'market tested' and 'be delivered by providers who have demonstrated that they are best placed to provide these services' (Home Office 2006b: 11) by 2011. Even though at the time of publication of the 'contestability prospectus' document in which this proposal appeared the necessary legal changes had yet to be made, the Home Secretary's introduction to this paper made it clear that 'we are requiring local probation areas, on a voluntary basis [sic], to double and then double again the proportion of services they contract out' (Home Office 2006b: 2). Victim contact work was one of only a small number of services singled out in the paper as possible candidates for competitive tendering exercises, and it seems likely that a system with which victims are currently highly satisfied (Williams 2005) will in many areas be contracted out. Ideological commitments sometimes override victims' interests, it seems. While it is difficult to speculate about the likely long-term impact of the introduction of the National Offender Management Service and contestability on victim services, it seems clear that there will be a period of considerable confusion in at least some areas while victim contact services are reorganised and put out to tender.

Relevant skills and techniques of practitioners

The literature on victims' needs and on their satisfaction or otherwise with existing services gives a number of indications of the skills and techniques required by criminal justice practitioners if they are to work successfully with victims of crime (Nettleton *et al.* 1997; Williams 1999a, 1999b; Maguire and Kynch 2000). Victims wish to be treated with respect, preferably to be believed and to be provided with services in a dignified, non-discriminatory way. They want, most of all, to be kept informed of the progress of their cases and given reasons for decisions made by professionals. In many respects, their rights to have these expectations met have increased significantly in recent years, as noted above; however, it is important that the relevant professionals are properly trained to deliver the requirements of (for example) the Code of Practice for Victims. Meeting deadlines and providing information in a timely way are important, but understanding why this matters to victims is often equally important.

Ideally, all staff coming into contact with victims of crime should receive at least basic victim awareness training, sensitising them to victims' individual and sometimes idiosyncratic responses to victimisation and to the common reactions to particular types of offence. This training should include some coverage of the symptoms of post-traumatic stress so that the abnormal reactions of a small minority of victims can be appropriately dealt with (normally by referral to those qualified to offer appropriate professional treatment). Staff should be aware that common reactions to victimisation may include 'denial, shock, humiliation, and shame … nightmares … withdrawal from social life …' (Williams 2007: 324).

People working directly with victims on a regular basis need rather more preparatory training than this. Basic training for criminal justice professionals such as police and probation officers has begun to change in order to reflect this need, but this has been a slow process and qualifying training curricula still do not always include even basic attention to victims' issues. It is important to build upon existing skills and to demystify the task of working with victims. Youth offending team members, probation officers, police officers and to a lesser extent prosecutors and other lawyers do have transferable skills; reminding them of this can make appropriate in-service training seem less daunting.

The needs commonly expressed by victims (described in the first paragraph of this section) give pointers towards the kind of issues which ought to be addressed during in-service training on victim work. Staff should be helped to work on their interviewing skills and consider how these might need to be adapted when working with victims; they need to know the relevant law and standards, including the relevance of the Code of Practice in their setting; they should gain understanding of the place of victims and witnesses within the criminal justice system. Some awareness of the agencies to which victims can be referred in the local area should be gained from such training, as well as sources of information for those wishing to explore the issues further and some 'practice wisdom' – the 'dos and don'ts' developed by experienced staff. Staff should be empathetic and treat victims with respect. Where victims are not treated in this way, this can lead to secondary victimisation, which refers to 'the various additional adverse material and emotional consequences that a victim may experience at the hands of all those responsible for responding to an offence' (Dignan 2005: 199).

This list suggests that a mixture of styles of training delivery is likely to be required. Some of the material can be covered using traditional didactic 'chalk and talk' methods, while experiential learning including role-play is likely to cover other issues more effectively (and the use of professional actors has been particularly effective in large settings such as national conferences). Small-group discussion is most likely to provide opportunities for sharing existing experiences and exploring the ways in which staff skills in working with (for example) offenders are transferable to victim work. Supporting materials can be provided in relation to factual information such as legislation, further reading, the Code of Practice and local contacts.

Experience in the police, probation and youth justice services suggests that the skills needed to work effectively with offenders are indeed transferable to victim work (Williams 1999b). Empathy and respect may come to the fore when working with victims, but effective interpersonal relationships have always been required to work successfully towards change with offenders (Nellis 2005; Burnett and McNeill 2005). What does *not* work with victims (or indeed with offenders) is a purely bureaucratic approach. Victims want to receive and give information and they expect their representations to have some impact upon decisions. In many cases they prefer to engage with an individual representative of the criminal justice system, such as a family liaison officer or a victim contact officer, with whom they have developed some rapport and for whom they feel respect (Nettleton *et al.* 1997; Tapley 2005; Williams 2005). The development of victim services with a view to improving the quality of the evidence victims give in court is based on a rather limited view which fails to take account of the potential benefits of treating victims better for its own sake (or at least for the sake of improving their confidence in the system).

Robinson and Stroshine (2005, n.p.) wrote that 'Advocates have long cautioned that women's experiences with a criminal justice system that is insensitive to their needs and wishes may negatively impact their involvement with and future use of the system, and that 'Police activities that indicate a greater degree of investigative effort, such as completing a crime report or making an arrest, are positively correlated with victim satisfaction with the police'. Greater emotional support, information and explanations for what is happening throughout the criminal justice system may therefore have a great impact on victims' experiences of the process.

Theoretical and conceptual issues

While the standards introduced by the Code of Practice are important, their impact may not be as great as the government had wished because many of the duties are similar to those already recommended by the Victim's Charter, albeit that not all of these were on a statutory basis previously. Other requirements that were present in the draft indicative edition of the code published in March 2005 included the requirement for Victim Support to contact victims of crime within two working days and to offer a national telephone support line. This was missing from the final version leaving victims without a statutory right to contact from voluntary agencies.

The effect of having no statutory duties placed on services within the voluntary sector means that the level of wider support may differ according to location and funding. Hester (2005: 80) argues that

> Generally, research indicates that criminal justice interventions are unlikely to be effective on their own, and are most effective when carried out in a context of wider support and advocacy for those victimised.

This may limit the extent to which victims of domestic violence are enabled to participate in the criminal justice system.

Overall, the requirements of the code, if met, would lead to improved information flow to victims, leading to victims having more awareness of the progress of their case through the criminal justice system and any implications of decisions made or sentences passed. This is important because 'Some research suggests that victims who are satisfied with the police are more likely to cooperate in the prosecution of their cases ... They may also be more likely to seek criminal justice interventions in incidents of future violence ...' (Robinson and Stroshine 2005: n.p).

The question therefore is: to what extent will these requirements be met? The targets set for many agencies are relatively strict, and are considered by many to be 'stretch targets', never intended to be met immediately. Other initiatives that were introduced previously have been announced alongside funding for their creation, such as Witness Care Units. In reality, however, the funding has not always been sufficient to provide the staff required to undertake the tasks assigned to them. Funding may also be time limited, allowing services to be set up but then the expectation is that these services will be kept running through the use of mainstream funding, which is often already overstretched.

Reasons for change

The reasons for these changes being introduced could also be questioned. The Office for Criminal Justice Reform released a document entitled *Increasing Victims' and Witnesses' Satisfaction with the Criminal Justice System* which offers two possible motivations within its summary. The document claims that these changes are needed because 'it is the right thing to do' but also to rebalance the system away from offenders in favour of victims and witnesses. There is a third, less altruistic, motivation, namely concern about the 'justice gap' discussed earlier.

Doak, however, sees these changes as consistent with victims being seen as 'consumers of the criminal justice system' (2005: 295). This could be an oversimplification of the matter though as victims have little choice about becoming users of the system. Victims are often unaware of the criminal justice process that they may go through and therefore information and communication become very important to them. Victims are often left feeling particularly let down when these needs are not met.

Doak goes on to discuss whether victims should be granted the right to participate in criminal proceedings and, if so, what form this might take. He argues that:

If, as most theorists state, the main function of the criminal justice system ought to be the punishment of the guilty and acquittal of the innocent, questions need to be addressed concerning the proper place of the 'private' interests of a third party. (2005: 295)

This has led to the development of methods to allow victims to participate only after a guilty verdict has been reached.

Victim awareness work with offenders

The recognition of the importance of victims of crime within the criminal justice system has extended past the traditional support agencies. Staff in organisations such as probation are now expected to think about the effects a crime has had on victims while writing pre-sentence reports and parole reports. Specifically in relation to probation officers, there are also national standards on the requirement to cover the impact upon victims of offences discussed in pre-sentence reports (Home Office 2005b: para. SS2.9), although in practice probation staff preparing reports do not always have sufficient information to do this as thoroughly as they might wish (see Dominey 2002).

Victim awareness has also become an important aspect of the cognitive behavioural programmes that are offered by probation areas. While there is no accredited course which comprises solely of victim awareness, this is an element of many perpetrator programmes. Bowen *et al.* (2002: 225) wrote that with regard to domestic violence:

The core assumptions of programmes should include emphasising: that the offender is responsible for his behaviour; that violence is a choice of behaviour that is functional and intentional; to challenge minimisation, denial, victim blaming and those attitudes and beliefs that condone their behaviour; to challenge men's expectations of power and control over women and that the focus should be on men as perpetrators rather than victims.

Hester (2005b) argues that developments around criminalisation of domestic violence owe much to the Duluth project in the USA. The Duluth project began as a community project working with male perpetrators of domestic violence (Crime Reduction website 2004), but very much based upon a feminist model which saw offenders as abusers of male power over women, and so it is interesting that work with offenders has led to higher levels of awareness of victims' needs.

Domestic violence perpetrators will often minimise the amount of harm they have caused when discussing their offences. This is also true of racially motivated offenders. Court (2003) wrote about his experiences of trying to work with racially motivated offenders who on the whole rejected the label of being 'racist'. He stated that their accounts of the offence often blamed the victim, included the belief that offenders were acting in their own defence – and they failed to mention racist elements. Court worked to present them with the victim's view of what had taken place, and to discuss the discrepancies. He argued that:

> This form of offending is also characterized by an absence of victim empathy or awareness, especially immediately after conviction, when an offender frequently expresses hostility towards their victim. I have found it more effective not to approach discussion of the offence early in the programme as the minimization of the incident and anger towards the victim impedes any sincere or meaningful revisiting of the incident. (2003: 56)

Court concluded that:

> Until the probation service and the youth offending teams develop the skills and confidence to explore racial hostility, in particular where the victim rather than the court alone have identified it, assessments of risk of harm to the public can only be partial at best, and at worst dangerously misleading. (2003: 58)

Conclusion

Recent legislation has been introduced with the aim of improving the experiences of victims of crime, including the Youth Justice and Criminal Evidence Act of 1999 and the Domestic Violence, Crime and Victims Act of 2004. There have been changes in practice introduced by the Code of Practice for Victims of Crime and there will be implications because of this for criminal justice agencies in terms of demanding timescales and increased demands on staff needed to bring these about. While these changes have been introduced in order to bring about much needed improvements in the service provided to victims, gaps remain, including services for the victims who find it hard to be seen and treated as such. There are also dangers inherent in the current debates which place the needs of victims and offenders at opposite ends of a balance, as if increasing one would decrease the other. The chapter goes on to highlight why it is so vitally important that staff are adequately trained to work with victims of crime, bearing in mind the needs that they may be faced with, the services and gaps in service provision which victims may experience, and the important victim awareness work that can only be carried out with offenders if staff are sufficiently aware of victim issues.

Discussion questions

1 To what extent are the skills used in working with offenders transferable to victim work? Is specialist training and the establishment of specialist units to engage with victims preferable to generic working across offender and victim work in (for example) the police and youth offending services?
2 Is the growth of restorative justice approaches likely to be beneficial to, and welcomed by, victims of crime?
3 What needs do victim personal statements meet, where the scheme is working well?

Further reading

Spalek, B. (2005) *Crime Victims*. Basingstoke: Palgrave; Williams, B. (2005) *Victims of Crime and Community Justice*. London: Jessica Kingsley. Up-to-date accounts of many of the issues discussed in this chapter, at greater length than it has been possible to provide here.
Winstone, J. and Pakes, F. (eds) (2005) *Community Justice*. Cullompton: Willan. Discussions of specific issues.

References

Bowen, E., Brown, L. and Gilchrist, E. (2002) 'Evaluating probation-based offender programmes for domestic violence perpetrators: a pro-feminist approach', *Howard Journal*, 41 (3): 221–36.
Burnett, R. and McNeill, F. (2005) 'The place of the officer–offender relationship in assisting offenders to desist from crime', *Probation Journal*, 52 (3): 221–42.
Court, D. (2003) 'Direct work with racially motivated offenders', *Probation Journal*, 50 (1): 52–8.
CPS (n.d.) *Narrowing the Justice Gap*. Available at: http://www.cps.gov.uk/publications/prosecution/justicegap.html (accessed 5 September 2006).
Crime Reduction website (2004) *Domestic Violence*. Available online at: http://www.crimereduction.gov.uk/domesticviolence43.htm (accessed 18 September 2006).
Criminal Justice System (2005) *Victims' Code of Practice: Consultation*. Available online at: http://www.cjsonline.gov.uk/downloads/application/pdf/Victims%20Code%20of%20Practice%20Consultation.pdf (accessed 5 September 2006).
Dignan, J. (2005) *Understanding Victims and Restorative Justice*. Maidenhead: Open University Press.
Doak, J. (2005) 'Victims' rights in criminal trials: prospects for participation', *Journal of Law and Society*, 32 (2): 294–316.
Dominey, J. (2002) 'Addressing victim issues in pre-sentence reports', in B. Williams (ed.), *Reparation and Victim-Focused Social Work*, Research Highlights 42. London: Jessica Kingsley.

Hester, M. (2005a) 'Making it through the criminal justice system: attrition and domestic violence', *Social Policy and Society*, 5 (1): 79–90.

Hester, M. (2005b) 'Transnational influences on domestic violence policy and action', *Social Policy and Society*, 4 (4): 447–56.

Hitchings, E. (2005) 'A consequence of blurring the boundaries – less choice for the victims of domestic violence', *Social Policy and Society*, 5 (1): 91–101.

Home Office (2001) *Further Guidance on the National Probation Service's Work with Victims of Serious Crimes*, Probation Circular 61/2001. London: Home Office.

Home Office (2004a) *Conditional Cautioning: Criminal Justice Act 2003, sections 22–27, Code of Practice and Associated Annexes*. London: Home Office. Available online at: http://www.homeoffice.gov.uk/documents/cond-caution-cop?view=Binary (accessed 24 August 2006).

Home Office (2004b) *Restorative Justice: The Government's Strategy – Responses to Consultation*. London: Home Office. Available online at: http://www.homeoffice. gov.uk/documents/rj-consult-replies.pdf?view=Binary (accessed 24 August 2006).

Home Office (2005a) *Restorative Justice: Helping to Meet Local Needs. A Guide for Local Criminal Justice Boards and Agencies*. London: Home Office Communications Directorate.

Home Office (2005b) *National Standards for the Supervision of Offenders in the Community 2005*, Annex A to Probation Circular 15/2005. London: Home Office. Available online at: http://www.probation.homeoffice.gov.uk/files/pdf/PC15%202005.pdf (accessed 25 August 2006).

Home Office (2006a) *Making a Victim Personal Statement*, leaflet. Available online at: http://www.homeoffice.gov.uk/documents/victimstate.pdf?view=Binary (accessed 24 August 2006).

Home Office (2006b) *Improving Prison and Probation Services: Public Value Partnerships*. London: Home Office NOMS. Available online at: http://www.noms.homeoffice. gov.uk/downloads/imroving-prison-and-probation-services.pdf.

Jackson, J. (2004) 'Puttting victims at the heart of the criminal justice system: the gap between rhetoric and reality', in E. Cape (ed.), *Reconcilable Rights? Analysing the Tension between Victims and Defendants*. London: Legal Action Group.

Maguire, M. and Kynch, J. (2000) *Public Perceptions and Victims' Experiences of Victim Support: Findings from the 1998 British Crime Survey*. London: Home Office RDSD.

National Probation and Prison Service (2003) *Driving Delivery: A Strategic Framework for Psychological Services in Prisons and Probation*. London: Applied Psychology Group.

National Probation Directorate (2002) *The Treatment and Risk Management of Sexual Offenders in Custody and the Community*. London: NPD.

Nellis, M. (2005) 'Dim prospects: humanistic values and the fate of community justice', in J. Winstone and F. Pakes (eds), *Community Justice*. Cullompton: Willan.

Nettleton, H., Walklate, S. and Williams, B. (1997) *Probation Training with the Victim in Mind: Partnership, Values and Organisation*. Keele: Keele University Press.

Office for Criminal Justice Reform (2004) *Increasing Victims' and Witnesses' Satisfaction with the Criminal Justice System*. London: Home Office.

Rawlinson, P. (2005) 'Understanding organised crime', in C. Hale, K. Hayward, A. Wahidin and E. Wincup (eds), *Criminology*. Oxford: Oxford University Press.

Robinson, A.L. and Stroshine, M.S. (2005) 'The importance of expectation fulfilment on domestic violence victims' satisfaction with the police in the UK', *Policing: An International Journal of Police Strategies and Management*, 28 (2): 301–20.

Rock, P. (2004) *Constructing Victims' Rights: The Home Office, New Labour and Victims*. Oxford: Oxford University Press.

Spalek, B. (2005) *Crime Victims: Theory, Policy and Practice*. Basingstoke: Palgrave Macmillan.

Spencer, J. (2004) 'Criminal procedure: the rights of the victim, versus the rights of the defendant', in E. Cape (ed.), *Reconcilable Rights? Analysing the Tension between Victims and Defendants*. London: Legal Action Group.

Tapley, J. (2005) 'Improving confidence in criminal justice', in J. Winstone and F. Pakes (eds), *Community Justice*. Cullompton: Willan.

Tombs, S. (2005) 'Corporate crime', in C. Hale, K. Hayward, A. Wahidin and E. Wincup (eds), *Criminology*. Oxford: Oxford University Press.

Williams, B. (1999a) *Working with Victims of Crime: Policies, Politics and Practice*. London: Jessica Kingsley.

Williams, B. (1999b) 'Initial education and training for work with victims of crime', *Social Work Education*, 18 (3): 287–96.

Williams, B. (2005) *Victims of Crime and Community Justice*. London: Jessica Kingsley.

Williams, B. (2007) 'Victims', in R. Canton and D. Hancock (eds), *Dictionary of Probation and Offender Management*. Cullompton: Willan.

Chapter 18

Working with mentally disordered offenders

Rob Canton

Alec is 28 years old. He has several convictions recorded against him for offences of dishonesty and violence. Four years ago, he was convicted of threatening to kill a probation officer – a threat that was expressed in rage and was not repeated, but was still seen as a substantial and serious risk which caused considerable alarm and distress. He has more than once lost his temper with reception staff at the probation office when he has felt that they were talking about him – as indeed they might well have been, either to inform the supervising probation officer of his arrival at the office or because his demeanour and appearance are so intimidating. He is extremely aggressive and demanding at interview. He complains of sleeplessness and anxiety and looks for signs of hostility towards him or plotting against him. On one visit, he asked for a cup of coffee; the next day he returned and accused the probation officer of having put something in his coffee which had made him feel agitated and distressed, bringing a sleepless night.

He lives on his own and has been systematically destroying his flat. He has ripped wiring from the walls and smashed radiators. Having torn out the gas fire, he tried to generate heat by putting a cigarette lighter flame directly to the gas pipe and was fortunate not to have hurt himself badly. He punches the walls in rage and frustration, busting his knuckles and turning anger into acts of self-harm. Sometimes he head-butts the wall and splits his forehead. The impression he makes on everyone who works with him is a deeply disquieting combination of high risk of violence to others and profound distress and need.

All the chapters in this book consider the many challenges and dimensions of working with offending behaviour, the legal, policy and institutional framework and the distinctive skills, knowledge and values required to work with offenders. This contribution also discusses mental disorder, which has its own frameworks affirming ideals of care, treatment and support – priorities that, at least potentially, might sit uncomfortably with the discourse, policies and practices of crime and punishment. Nor is it just a question of trying to reconcile the institutions and practices of two discrete policy domains: their convergence around the problems of working with *mentally disordered offenders*, as we shall see, gives rise to distinct challenges of its own. It might, for example, be thought that the designation *mentally disordered offender* should call for complementary endeavours from criminal justice and mental health agencies and there are no doubt circumstances in which this ideal is attained. On the other hand, it can lead to rejection and neglect, at the uneasy interface between two institutional domains with their different priorities, policies and theoretical understandings.

Problems of definition and prevalence

It is conventional to begin discussion by remarking upon the difficulty of defining *mental disorder*, although the implications of these difficulties for policy and practice are not always taken seriously enough. Definitions remain, as a Dr Good put it more than a century ago, 'so narrow as to set at liberty half the patients at Bethlem or the Bicêtre ... or so loose and capacious as to give a strait waistcoat to half the world' (Clare 1980: 14). To seek to define *mentally disordered offenders* adds an additional layer of complexity. Insisting that consideration should not be confined to those who are *disordered* under the criteria of the Mental Health Act – and thus preferring the term *disturbed* – NACRO's influential Mental Health Advisory Committee proposed:

> Those offenders who may be acutely or chronically mentally ill; those with neuroses, behavioural and/or personality disorders; those with learning difficulties; some who, as a function of alcohol and/or substance misuse, have a mental health problem; and any who are suspected of falling into one or other of these groups. It also includes those offenders where a degree of mental disturbance is recognised even though that may not be severe enough to bring it within the criteria laid down by the Mental Health Act 1983. It also applies to those offenders who, even though they do not fall easily within this definition – for example, some sex offenders and some abnormally aggressive offenders – may benefit from psychological treatments. (NACRO 1998)

While this definition is much closer to the concerns of those who work with offenders, it is arguably too inclusive. For example, now that the What Works initiative has identified cognitive-behavioural treatment as the preferred intervention for most offenders, it is no longer easy to see who is *excluded* by this definition. It is not at all clear that policy or practice guidance could be framed on the basis of such a definition (Canton 2002).

319

Indeed, it is at least arguable that it is impossible to construct a serviceable definition that demarcates a group whose members have enough in common with one another to be considered *as a group* or are sufficiently different from many others who fall outwith the definition.

Part of the difficulty is that there are lay, psychiatric and legal vocabularies of mental disorder that overlap but do not completely coincide. Negotiations take place every day in police stations, offices and courts about whether or not an individual ought to be designated as a mentally disordered offender. This is not just a clinical assessment: an attribution of mental disorder usually has legal and clinical implications, with consequential claims on resources, giving individuals and organisations reasons for applying (or resisting) that designation. Definitional dispute in the literature reflects and reproduces these difficulties.

Such problems are not 'merely definitional'. One immediate consequence is that it becomes impossible to assess the numbers of mentally disordered offenders (how, without definition, is it to be determined who is included in the count?). No less seriously, policy is likely to be flawed through uncertainty – or even substantial and principled disagreement – about the scope of its application. In particular, policy stumbles through a failure to recognise the diversity of mental distress. It will be suggested, for example, that these uncertainties are in large degree responsible for the limited success of the policy of diversion (Grounds 1991).

The term *mentally disordered offender* may not even be reserved for those whose offending is in some way causally associated with their mental condition. Mental health legislation – notably Part Three of the Mental Health Act 1983 – applies to defendants and offenders who are assessed as disordered irrespective of any putative association between this condition and their offending.

Since the term is used so erratically and contestably, any attempt to construct a descriptive definition (the term is used like this) is forlorn. Stipulative definitions (let's use the term in this way) are variably useful in advancing discussion. In this chapter, a *mentally disordered offender* (or defendant) will be a suspect, defendant or offender (including those in prison or under criminal justice supervision in the community) who is or may be mentally disordered. *Mental disorder* must be taken to encompass a range of distress and predicaments, including schizophrenia, stress, anxiety states, personality disorders, mild learning disabilities and autism – from the distress that arises from extreme and disabling forms of entirely familiar human experiences to the qualitatively different experiences of psychosis. It may already be apparent that it is doubtful that anything useful can be said in general terms about such a diverse range of conditions and experiences.

This analysis calls into question the possibility of determining numbers of mentally disordered offenders (Badger *et al.* 1999; Mullen 2002a). What can be said with some confidence, however, is that the incidence of mental disorder among defendants and offenders is much greater than in the general population. This is well established for prison populations (Singleton *et al.*

1998) and seems also to be true for people in approved probation premises (Nadkarni *et al.* 2000; Hatfield *et al.* 2004). Attempts to assess the incidence among offenders on probation and other community agency caseloads have come up with widely varying estimates. Vaughan *et al.* (2000) identified 7.5 per cent of the probation caseload in the surveyed geographical area as mentally disordered (of whom only about one-fifth were under formal psychiatric supervision). A Napo review asked probation staff in nearly half the probation areas in England and Wales and found that '27% of offenders on [probation] caseloads were defined by probation staff as having a mental disorder' (Napo 2003).

The extremes of Alec's feelings, words and behaviour take him outside the normal range, even among violent offenders. Should he be understood to be, in some sense, *mentally disordered*? If so, what practical difference would this characterisation make to addressing his offending behaviour and supervising him in the community? Does an attribution of mental disorder require a different approach to the assessment of the risks he presents? Does it raise a special entitlement to *care*? (What kind of care?) Does it call for a different mode of enforcement? (How is compliance to be gained?) If mentally disordered, does it follow that he is in some sense less responsible for (can't help) his bad behaviour? And should he therefore be considered to be less deserving of punishment? Ought he be referred to another agency? What might reasonably be expected of another agency? What might be the nature of any mental disorder and might it be responsive to *treatment* of some kind? What kind? Is his sense that people are against him *delusional* – or a realistic interpretation of the suspicion and unease that he elicits from almost everyone? Does his daily experience of avoidance and rejection by others lend systematic reinforcement to his suspicious mindset?

The legal and policy context: doubts about diversion

For much of the past twenty years, *diversion* has been at the centre of policy – the idea that mentally disordered offenders should be identified as soon as possible and then 'diverted' from criminal justice proceedings into health care (for an instructive review of this policy, see Prins (2005: 51ff.)). There can be little doubt that some diversion schemes – in police stations and Courts – have averted unnecessary and oppressive prosecutions in many cases (Cavadino 1999; Geelan *et al.* 2000). At the same time, the policy, its rationale, feasibility and consequences have been called into question (Grounds 1991; Prins 1992, 2005; Canton 2002). In particular, it is increasingly clear that diversion can make only a small – though certainly significant – contribution to the management and treatment of (some) mentally disordered offenders.

There may be consensus (though even this cannot be assumed) that people with a psychosis should be diverted from prosecution, but it is much less clear that offenders with stress, anxiety or depression should be dealt with outside of the criminal justice system. Moreover, now that some diagnoses are so expansive that *by definition* (Prins 1999) many – probably a majority – of prisoners have one or more personality disorders (Singleton *et al.* 1998; Canton 2002), proponents of the diversion of mentally disordered offenders seem to be committed to arguing that *most* people in prison ought not be there. There is surely no agreement that prison is in principle the wrong place for offenders with an anti-social personality disorder or that they ought not be prosecuted. At least part of the reason why diversion has been described as 'an aspiration with a long history of failure' is that it over-generalises and 'fails to take into account the heterogeneity of psychiatric conditions and clinical needs' (Grounds 1991: 38).

While James and colleagues (2002) discovered that the clinical outcome for those 'diverted' from a criminal justice process into *hospital* was at least 'acceptable' in 86 per cent of cases (and usually better than acceptable), fewer than 25 per cent were diverted into hospital. The more common experience is referral to outpatient services or to a community mental health team and Shaw and colleagues (2001) found that, among those so referred, fewer than one-third attended even a first appointment.

Green *et al.* (2005) followed up a number of people who had been assessed by a criminal justice mental health team, also interviewing some of the service users themselves. At the time of the original assessment, among this cohort substance misuse problems were much more common (71 per cent) than severe mental illness (20 per cent). The great majority were outside statutory mental health service referral criteria and so did not qualify for formal treatment. The conclusion of the study, supported by the accounts of the service users themselves, was that the assessment service brought 'few demonstrable advantages' (2005: 589) to the majority in terms of housing, employment or subsequent reoffending.

For those who have not been diverted before sentence, there are some particular measures available to Courts under the Mental Health Act 1983 Part Three. These provisions and their deployment are well discussed elsewhere (especially Stone 2003; Prins 2005). Here it is important to emphasise that the numbers of offenders dealt with under these distinctive measures are small: in 2004, 657 unrestricted (s. 37 (1) (3)) and 288 restricted patients (s. 37 with s. 41) were admitted to hospital (Ly and Foster 2005).

The great majority of mentally disordered offenders, then, are dealt with by quite the same range of sentencing measures as other defendants and may therefore be expected to be found among those on community orders, prisoners and people paying fines. The idea that diversion constitutes 'the solution' to the problem of responding to offending by mentally disordered people is implausible. The implication is that, at all points in the criminal justice system, workers in the community and criminal justice sector will encounter them and need to develop skills and knowledge in their work with them.

Policy and the dominance of risk

While mental health and crime are the responsibilities of different government departments and may be expected to have distinct policy trajectories, there has in recent years been convergence around the theme of *risk*. Risk dominates contemporary criminal justice policy (Garland 2001) and has become increasingly influential in shaping the government's approach to mental health (Busfield 2002; Laurance 2003; Canton 2005).

Reforming the Mental Health Act begins '... The vast majority of these people [*sc.* those with mental health problems] pose no threat to others and, in many cases, are among the most vulnerable in society. But in a minority of cases, people with mental health problems may pose a serious threat to the safety of others.' (Department of Health/Home Office 2000: 1). The paper goes on to develop specific policy in relation to those with a dangerous severe personality disorder (DSPD) and deploys a number of assumptions (often implicit) that have been generally influential on policy development. These include the ideas:

- that in an uncertain number of cases those with mental illness pose a significant risk of harm to others;
- that their mental ill health is the cause of the risk they present;
- that such people should be identified as soon as possible so that treatment may be made available to them;
- that such treatment should normally be compulsory (because informal or voluntary treatment affords insufficient public protection).

The paper sets out options in response to these concerns, including the possibility of indeterminate periods of detention for those assessed as DSPD. This preoccupation with the risk of violence to others troubles many mental health practitioners. Mullen makes the point eloquently:

Surely it is obvious that the chances of a mentally disordered person acting violently should be carefully evaluated and every step taken to prevent such a consequence. It is, perhaps, not quite as obvious that a central, if not the primary, responsibility of a mental health professional is to the wider community rather than their patient. It is not entirely obvious how a responsibility to predict risk is to be discharged. It is certainly not obvious how a clinician should act if they do suspect their patient is more probable to act violently. And finally, it is far from obvious that we should allow concerns about the risk which some of our patients may present to others to become a major determinant of our approach to all our patients. (Mullen 2002b: xv)

Others have argued that this concern with risk is sometimes self-defeating (Munro and Rumgay 2000; Rumgay and Munro 2001) and may not be the best way to enhance public protection. Laurance (2003) suggests that the emphasis on coercion and the quality of the patient experience drives people away from mental health services – a suggestion that receives some confirmation from a few respondents in Green et al.'s (2005) survey. Canton, (2005) accordingly urges a closer connection between risk management policy and strategies for securing compliance.

These debates – around the (perceived) tension between the priority of public safety and, on the other hand, the human rights of patients and their therapeutic needs – largely account for the 'labyrinthine progress' of government plans to amend the Mental Health Act 1983 (Peay 2007: 523). While the amending legislation will no doubt attempt to strike a balance, there are several reasons to feel concern about what this could entail for mentally disordered offenders. There is a clear trend towards understanding offenders in terms of their personality disorder – particularly anti-social personality disorder, a category that has shown itself to be inclusive and expansive (as witness its fivefold increase in the prison population in less than a decade) (Canton 2002). As the DSPD programme shows, there is at least the potential to set aside due process safeguards once a psychiatric diagnosis has been made. The combination of these policy trends must be disquieting.

It is to the foundation assumption of much of this policy, however – the connections between mental ill health and crime – that we next turn.

Correlations, causes and effects

A year ago, Alec was seen by a psychiatrist and assessed as having an *anti-social personality disorder*. This is defined (in International Classification of Diseases (ICD) – 10:

F60.2 Dissocial (Antisocial) Personality Disorder
Personality disorder, usually coming to attention because of a gross disparity between behaviour and the prevailing social norms, and characterized by at least 3 of the following:

(a) callous unconcern for the feelings of others;
(b) gross and persistent attitude of irresponsibility and disregard for social norms, rules and obligations;
(c) incapacity to maintain enduring relationships, though having no difficulty in establishing them;
(d) very low tolerance to frustration and a low threshold for discharge of aggression, including violence;
(e) incapacity to experience guilt and to profit from experience, particularly punishment;

(f) marked proneness to blame others, or to offer plausible rationalizations, for the behaviour that has brought the patient into conflict with society.

The report said that Alec's condition might amount to psychopathy within the meaning of the legislation but, since it could not be said that there was treatment available that was 'likely to alleviate or prevent a deterioration for his condition' (MHA 1983, s. 37(2)(a)(i)), he could not be given a hospital order. He was made subject to a Community Rehabilitation Order.

To what extent does the diagnosis *explain* Alec's dispositions and conduct? Or does it merely describe them? (Are there other ways of understanding him?) Is Alec less deserving of punishment because of this ascribed disorder? Should Alec be 'diverted'? (Where to and what would be the likely upshot?) If there is no available medical treatment likely to ameliorate his condition, what type of intervention is called for?

There is some evidence to suggest that certain kinds of mental disturbance do make offending – especially violent offending – more likely, although this increased risk is not associated with most kinds of mental disorder (Blumenthal and Lavender 2001; Busfield 2002). Hodgins concludes that 'Persons who develop major mental disorders are more likely than persons with no mental disorders to be convicted of criminal offences' (Hodgins 2004: 220). Blumenthal and Lavender cautiously propose that some 'symptom profiles' – especially violent thoughts and delusions, threat/control override symptoms (feelings of being dominated by some outside force) – might lead to violence. It is these symptom profiles – more than the diagnostic label itself – that are indicators of risk (Blumenthal and Lavender 2001: 60).

At the same time, it seems that criminal predictors generally 'outperform' diagnostic ones – that the risk factors for mentally disordered offenders are substantially the same as for other offenders. A meta-analysis by Bonta and colleagues demonstrated that, both for general and violent forms of recidivism, 'Clinical or psychopathological variables were either unrelated to recidivism or negatively related' (Bonta *et al.* 1998: 139). Indeed, the presence of mental illness indicated less recidivism.

Mullen found that 'In considering associations between mental health variables and future violent and offending behaviours the best established variables are certain diagnoses and the presence of substance abuse, with combinations of the two generating far and away the strongest associations.' He concluded that, in the long term prediction of the risk of violence, mental health variables 'pale into insignificance when they are placed alongside traditional criminological variables like gender, age, past history of offending, and social class' (Mullen 2002a: 297).

A complication in these discussions is that, wherever offenders are found to be mentally disordered, it is assumed that the disorder is in some way causally responsible for their misbehaviour. This is a persistent motif in the history of madness. All speech and conduct come to be scrutinised through the lens of a madness once ascribed and an attribution of mental disorder commonly closes down any further inquiry into motivation (Canton 1995). This is true even when (as in the case of Alec) it is not at all clear that the ascribed mental disorder *explains* the misbehaviour or (again as in Alec's case) is amenable to treatment. While correlations between mental disorder and offending are unreflectively taken to be causal associations, in reality people who are mentally disordered act for just the same repertoire of reasons as everyone else.

Moore wisely remarks that 'It is not sufficient to ask whether the client suffers from a mental illness ... most of the actions of a mentally ill person are a result of non-illness factors' (Moore 1996: 41). Mental illness, she adds, can contribute to an explanation of offending in different ways – as a sufficient, necessary or significant part of the motivational drive or as a disinhibiting factor. Such distinctions are important because unless psychiatric and criminogenic factors are carefully disentangled, stability or improvement in a psychiatric condition could mislead a risk assessor into overlooking an increase in the level of risk (Skeem and Mulvey 2002). Conversely, where the mental illness *is* causally influential, early identification of symptoms and 'falling out of care' may be singularly important (Moore 1996; Prins 1999).

If significant correlations could be established between offending and mental ill health, there would be three possibilities:

1 Mental disorder causes crime.
2 Crime (and its consequences) cause mental disorder.
3 A third factor is causally related to them both.

All three possibilities should be taken seriously. The first is the subject of an extensive literature (see Blumenthal and Lavender 2001; Mullen 2002a; Hodgins 2004; Prins 2005 and the many references there cited). The second is a neglected possibility and the third opens up intractable and contested questions about the origins of mental disturbance.

A *medical model* tends to dominate both the literature and policy in relation to mentally disordered offending (an accessible introduction to 'models' is Tyrer and Steinberg 1998). Very roughly, this assumes that aberrations in the biochemistry of the brain underlie most forms of mental disorder and this seems to call for drug therapies to 'heal the illness'.

A different model, however, emphasises the *social* origins of mental distress. Read and Haslam (2004) demonstrate that this model – 'bad things happen and can drive you crazy' – is much more consonant with lay understandings of mental distress. It also has a potential to explain the greater incidence of some types of mental disorder among women, people from some minority ethnic groups, the poor and the oppressed (Read 2004).

A sophisticated and influential attempt to measure the impact of 'bad things' is to be found in the work of George Brown and colleagues which was the basis for the Life Events and Difficulties Schedule (LEDS) (Brown and Harris 1989). Stressful and distressing experiences – or, more precisely, the personal meaning and significance ascribed to these events – can be shown to be associated with mental ill health. The extent to which LEDs *cause* mental disorder or rather *precipitate* or trigger disorder in those who are biogenetically vulnerable is unclear. However that may be, even the most uncompromising proponents of a medical model of mental disorder acknowledge that social factors make a significant difference to the onset, development and treatment of a range of mental disorders and to prospects of recovery. Leff (2001) demonstrates convincingly, for example, that a significant amelioration of the environment, especially in the quality of personal relationships, is at least as effective as medication in guarding against relapse in depression and schizophrenia.

It can now be seen how crime and its consequences might 'cause' mental disorder. Lifestyles associated with high levels of offending typically bring their perpetrators considerable anxiety and stress. The offences themselves, the fears and realities of detection and punishment can bring enormous stress as well as undermining those factors that stabilise and nurture mental health – not least (though not only) supportive relationships. Offending and its consequences – conspicuously (though again not only) imprisonment – result in social exclusion, disaffection, the destruction of opportunities and relationships – all factors associated with mental ill health.

The point is well made by Keyes:

> The 'mentally disordered offenders' we have encountered have carried enormous burdens of social and psychological deprivation. These are lives of material and spiritual poverty – lonely, disenfranchised, angry … It's not the whole picture, of course, but I cannot accept that these powerful factors are not intimately connected to the 'mental distress' in which much offending behaviour takes place. (Keyes 1995: 3)

For these people, plainly, there is a dynamic relationship between their mental disorder and their offending that is distorted by an assumed simple, linear cause–effect relationship like that in Figure 18.1.

A more plausible model would be like that shown in Figure 18.2 (where *social exclusion* denotes social isolation, the closure of opportunities and lack of availability of networks, relationships and opportunities that conduce to

crime

Figure 18.1 Simple linear cause–effect model of the relationship between mental disorder and offending.

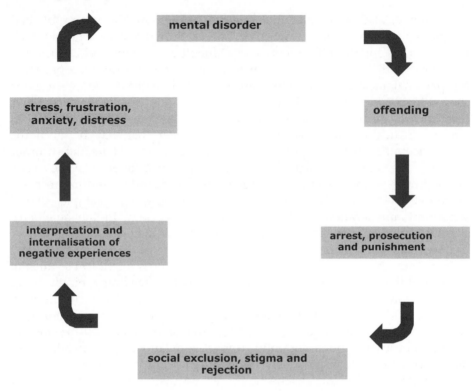

Figure 18.2 More plausible model of relationship between mental disorder and offending.

desistance and to mental well-being). Thus understood, social exclusion seems to be associated with (cause and effect of) both crime and mental disorder.

Bentall shows how 'life events and symptoms exacerbate each other in an escalating spiral of psychopathology' (2003: 433) and offending can be an aspect of this escalation. It may well be impossible to claim a causal priority or to track a sequence of cause and effect: this dynamic understanding of the relationship between offending and mental disorder points to a possibility of intervention at different points and, most likely, to a multi-modal intervention of which psychiatry and medication are just one component.

If the philosophy of diversion implies that medical treatment is the proper response to offending by those who are mentally disordered, the foregoing analysis suggests that criminal justice sector workers can be actively involved in the 'treatment' of mental illness. In helping people to manage their criminogenic needs – through the provision of services and by helping them to improve their social skills and problem-solving – criminal justice workers are addressing many of the factors that exacerbate mental vulnerability and are accordingly contributing to the treatment of mental illness.

'Dual diagnosis'

> Over time it became clear that Alec was misusing substances, probably methamphetamine, and also self-medicating his anxiety and unhappiness with alcohol. He was seen by a drugs worker who said that she found it very difficult to assess his use or his motivation to manage it. She was concerned about his mental state and felt that a psychiatric assessment would be more relevant to him. Until some progress was made here, it would be difficult to engage with Alec in addressing his substance use.
>
> The psychiatric unit was initially reluctant to see Alec. When he was eventually seen, it was felt that there was nothing much to add to the earlier assessment of anti-social personality disorder. The view was expressed that unless his substance use was addressed things were only likely to get worse.

Substance misuse is commonly a contributory factor to the escalation of mental disturbance, offending and social exclusion. As we have seen above, substance misuse was a much more common characteristic of the 'diverted' cohort followed up by Green *et al.* (2005) than was severe mental illness. Mullen (2002a see above p. 325) suggests that substance misuse is much more strongly correlated with violent offending than any other mental health variable (see also MacArthur Research Network, n.d.).

Dual diagnosis – the coincidence of more than one type of mental disorder or of a mental disorder with substance misuse – is not a single clinical condition, but may be implicated in a wide constellation of needs and behaviours. Such an assessment should enable individuals to have access to services that meet their complex needs, but in practice it can become the occasion for their rejection. In this respect, it is not unlike the term *mentally disordered offenders* – 'the people nobody owns' (Webb and Harris 1999).

People who are mentally disturbed are at least as likely as anyone else to misuse substances – and often more so (Watkins *et al.* 2001). While misuse of certain substances can produce signs of mental illness, no less can mental distress lead to substance misuse – for example through self-medication. Again, conjecture about causal priority is likely to be unprofitable. Neither problem can be understood without an appreciation of the other: it is precisely the interaction that exacerbates the distress and the risk. And again the implication is that therapeutic intervention should address both the substance misuse and the mental distress in a complementary multi-disciplinary endeavour.

On referring

It has been argued here that much of the literature (and most of the policy) concerning mentally disordered offenders has been grounded on a misleading and oversimplified understanding of mental disturbance, crime and the relationship between them. Once the diversity of mental distress is acknowledged – and its complex origins and development in biogenetic, psychological and social experiences are appreciated – the strategy of diversion becomes increasingly inadequate and the need for a multi-modal and multi-disciplinary strategy becomes apparent (Canton 2002).

Rather than asking how an offender manager or other criminal justice practitioner can identify the characteristics of mental illness or disorder – since psychiatric diagnosis is never the responsibility of criminal justice personnel – the better questions, perhaps, are about the occasions for and mechanisms of *referral*. Table 18.1 summarises some of the more salient questions. Some of these questions are explored further below.

Table 18.1 Salient questions for referral

What?	In what circumstances should referral to a mental health service be considered? What is it about this person that raises the question of mental disturbance? How far should the community justice practitioner go in exploring (say) a delusional state?
Who?	Who is the best person to refer to? The GP? A community agency? A community mental health team? (and who in that team?) A special forensic service?
When?	Is this a matter for urgent referral? Should referral take place now or (say) after the release of a serving prisoner?
Where?	Where might an assessment take place? For example, is the person likely to keep an outpatient appointment? Or (in another case) could a representative of the mental health team visit the prison?
Why?	Why is a referral being made? What is the purpose? What does the referring worker hope will follow? Are there any drawbacks to making the referral?
How?	What are the precise mechanisms of the referral? How is this possibility to be put to the person? To their family? To the court?

In what circumstances should referral to a mental health service be considered?

Criminal justice personnel are variably confident in their abilities to recognise mental disorder. It is, perhaps, likely that more florid manifestations of disorder will be detected, but states of depression or anxiety may be less apparent. It is said that even general practitioners miss one-third of cases of depression (Leff 2001: 31) and that reliable assessment is even more uncertain for patients from minority ethnic groups (National Institute for Mental Health 2003). It should also be remembered that anger, confusion, fear, anxiety and despondency are usual and entirely familiar responses to many of the situations in which defendants and offenders find themselves and the point at which it is appropriate to interpret these reactions as manifestations of mental disturbance is often not easy to determine.

Table 18.2 lists some of the circumstances in which the involvement of mental health services should be considered. It must be emphasised that none of these features is necessarily an indication of mental disorder. Nor does their absence conclusively rule it out. At the same time, it must be helpful if everyone involved is aware of the grounds for referral. It bears repeating that it is not within the competence or authority of a criminal justice practitioner to attempt diagnosis.

To whom should referral be made and how?

Practice here too is likely to be variable and will depend on local arrangements. As well as formal mental health services, a number of voluntary and independent sector agencies have developed considerable expertise and, in particular, can sometimes offer immediate advice and support. Primary care support may be accessible and appropriate, although this is a pathway to health care that seems less available to some groups. For example, there is evidence that 'there are significant and sustained differences between the white majority and minority ethnic groups in experience of mental health services and the outcome of such service interventions' (National Institute for Mental Health 2003: 10) and this report goes on to express concerns about the adequacy of primary mental health support to people from minority ethnic groups.

In some areas, community justice agencies may have established service-level agreements, protocols or more informal understandings that enable direct referral to a community mental health team. Forensic teams are especially experienced in working with those whose clinical conditions are diagnosed imprecisely, which Blackburn (1993) sees as characteristic of mentally disordered offenders. Nor should it be forgotten that while there are procedures and protocols to be observed, mental health teams typically include social workers and psychologists as well as psychiatrists to whom referral may be made.

While there is no doubt a need for improved training in mental health work in the community justice sector, skills and knowledge can only flourish in a coherent and appropriately resourced organisational context. Unless there is negotiation about the circumstances in which referral should be made – for example, regular meetings in which agencies exchange experiences about the adequacy and relevance of each other's practice – there will be misunderstandings and frustrations that are unlikely to be affected by enhanced training.

The legal and organisational frameworks within which inter-agency work may take place are conveniently set out in Department of Health (2005). The Care Programme Approach is of particular importance here (Department of Health 1999) in offering a systematic but flexible framework for referral, assessment and inter-agency cooperation.

Table 18.2 Circumstances for the involvement of mental health services

Hallucination	Perceptions for which there is no external stimulus – for example *hearing voices* (the person's thoughts spoken aloud to them, voices referring to the person as in a commentary, often critical or abusive), although any of the senses may be affected.	These are among the 'first rank' symptoms of schizophrenia, but all of them may have other origins – for example substance misuse – or significance. Some types of hallucination are common and even prized in some settings (Rack 1982; Leff 2001). Determining a delusion is complex, especially
Delusion	'False' beliefs, often tenaciously held, which are out of keeping with the person's culture or subculture.	when practitioner and patient do not share a culture or language. Age and class differences can also complicate.
Thought broadcasting	The sense that one's thoughts are directly accessible to others.	Passivity phenomena may be a rhetorical or figurative way of articulating helplessness.
Thought withdrawal or insertion	The sense that one's thoughts are being taken away or put there by someone else or an external influence.	
Passivity of behaviour	The sense that one's actions are not one's own, but in some sense determined by another agency.	
Bizarre offence	Where 'no reason' can be found for the offence, where the behaviour does not 'add up' and seems unclear – perhaps even to the offender.	Remember that sensitive discussion and interpretation can bring understanding to that which is initially puzzling.
Extreme and volatile emotion	Extreme and/or fast mood swings – highs as well as lows.	These may be signs of affective disorders (disorders of emotion).
Emotional emptiness	Anhedonia (finding no satisfaction in things that normally bring pleasure); helplessness; problems of motivation.	
Changes in sleep patterns or energy levels		
Marked change	The feeling by someone who knows them well that the person has changed, is 'not her/himself'.	
Self-harming		

The 'psychiatric probation order' must also not be overlooked. This provision – now a *mental health treatment requirement* (Criminal Justice Act 2003, s. 207) – is not used frequently and has been in long-term (numerical) decline since the early 1970s (Clark *et al.* 2002). Remarking that it has been used so 'infrequently and ineffectively', Clark and colleagues call for its wider adoption. Support for the increased use of this measure, however, has been muted in the Probation Service. At the same time, Davies's attempt to identify conditions conducive to successful practice has wider application for an understanding of good inter-agency work (see Table 18.3).

Although a full reappraisal of the opportunities and shortcomings of community orders with a mental health treatment requirement would be a valuable exercise, it may in practice prove difficult to reinvigorate a declining measure that may not have the confidence of the courts or the Probation Service. Arguably, where liaison between probation and psychiatric services is well-established, the measure is unnecessary and may even be intrusive, while where liaison is poor, the arrangement is unlikely to work in any case.

Table 18.3 Conditions conducive to successful practice

Contributing to success	Contributing to failure
Good assessments	Generally the opposite of those
Understanding of respective roles and responsibilities	contributing to success
	Inappropriate orders
Good liaison and record-keeping	Conflicting recommendations
Clear risk-management procedures	Complex personality problems
Access to appropriate resources	Lack of understanding about
Removal from a chaotic lifestyle	breach criteria
Vigorous proactive work by the probation officer	

Source: Davies (2002: 185).

Why refer?

What is the purpose of referral? Those making a referral need to be clear not only about the grounds for their referral, but about what they can reasonably expect to follow. If the referral is successful (to the extent that contact is established between the individual and mental health services), some form of assessment will take place. The conclusion may be that mental disorder is not a significant factor and this in itself may be a useful thing to establish. A formal diagnosis may or may not be made; treatment may or may not be effectively forthcoming; treatment may or may not make a difference to the concerns that occasioned the referral. In short, the position may well remain much as it was before referral.

In some circumstances, even if there is no continuing direct contact between the individual and the psychiatric services, mental health practitioners may offer indirect support through advice and consultancy to the community justice worker. Some years ago a forensic consultant in a large health authority went so far as to say that 'The most effective role for any forensic psychiatrist is as adviser to his local probation service', adding: 'It cannot be stressed too heavily how important it is for probation officers to see themselves as part of their regional forensic psychiatric service' (Higgins 1991: 178).

Referral should never be seen as an opportunity to pass responsibility to another organisation, but rather as an occasion to reconfigure networks of intervention and support. For a case manager this implies a clarity about role and role boundary, about communication and, above all, about how to help the individual at the centre to make sense of this network of support.

Alec's probation officer contacted the psychiatric services again. This time, while acknowledging that he had before been assessed as having a personality disorder, she pointed to a number of indications which she felt *may* be associated with the onset of a depressive illness. She told them about an increase in his self-harming behaviour, his seriously disturbed patterns of sleep, loss of appetite and frequent expressions of worthlessness. She explained that her continuing responsibility of working with Alec would be significantly supported by assessment and by any treatment that may result. Alec was seen and treatment offered. A further assessment of his substance use took place and, as motivation and self-confidence began to increase slightly, his use of drink and drugs began to decrease.

There was no continuing direct involvement from the psychiatric services, but the probation officer was encouraged to feel able to contact a community psychiatric nurse who knew Alec and to discuss changes of circumstances or behaviour and their possible psychiatric implications. This level of support, while a relatively modest commitment by the health services, was invaluable to the probation officer.

Alec was still difficult to work with, of course, but the officer's patience and determination began to win some trust. She made it clear that aggression and threat were unacceptable, but, acknowledging his frustrations and unhappiness, she showed that she was resolved to continue to offer him help to avoid offending. She also insisted on his compliance with the formal requirements of his supervision, but administered this sensibly and with an emphasis on compliance rather than on threat of breach. While breach proceedings had to be initiated, she attended the court and argued forcefully – in Alec's presence – that she was convinced that community supervision should continue. This consistency of concern for him was new to Alec.

Working with mentally disordered people in a community justice context

Discrimination often originates in the exaggeration of difference. It is assumed, for example, that specialised health care provision is needed for mentally disordered offenders, whereas the great majority of people so designated can be cared for in mainstream health care settings (NACRO 1998). In the same way, the core professional skills of community justice workers – skills of engagement, motivation, case management, assessment, planning, intervention and evaluation – are, for the most part, quite as relevant and appropriate for mentally disordered offenders. It is necessary, to be sure, to attend to what is distinctive and special about each individual (Cherry 2005), but again this is generally true and not peculiar to people who are mentally disturbed. It is not the case that mentally ill people are so 'alien', remote or inaccessible that they are unreachable and can only be worked with by mental health professionals.

Yet denial of difference can also lead to unfairness. Are there, then, special skills, knowledge or values required to work with people who are mentally disordered? There is some specialised *knowledge* that is required. Good practice here calls for sufficient knowledge of the relevant legal provisions, of the way in which health professionals understand and respond to mental distress, of the availability and appropriateness of sources of support. But the *values* that guide practice are surely no different from the values that should find expression in all community justice work.

But are there any distinctive *skills* or personal qualities required to work with mentally disordered offenders? Even to put the question is to expose its shortcomings and its neglect of the diversity of mental distress. There are, nevertheless, some broad considerations that can be put forward here.

First, workers need to be aware of their own reactions to the mental distress of others. Some of these responses will be shaped by an individual's biography. For example, someone with a personal experience of depression may bring greater understanding and empathy to their work with a depressed person – or (and/or) might also themselves experience greater anxiety or distress because of memories evoked. Again, since there are numerous stereotypes of 'madness', most of them negative (Scheff 1984; Porter 2002), there is a cultural legacy of suspicion and unease with mental distress that has an abiding influence and can bring an awkwardness or unkindness to working with people who are mentally disturbed. Practitioners need to be aware of their own reactions and manage these in ways that do not compromise the integrity of their practice or lead to inappropriate or unfair treatment. This possibility – that unacknowledged attitudes can lead to unfair or otherwise inappropriate practice – is an entirely familiar precept in working with all aspects of diversity.

Workers need to be able to work with and through uncertainty and not be overwhelmed by it. Many of these uncertainties are characteristic of general community justice practice, but in addition there is often a diagnostic uncertainty and doubts, for example, about the implications of an expressed delusion or intrusive thought. Many of the questions posed about the subject of our case study have no clear answer and yet there is plainly work to be done with Alec.

Clarity of role is more than ever important. If inter-agency work is to thrive, all involved need a clear understanding of their responsibilities in the collective endeavour and what those involved can reasonably expect of each other. Not least, the offender-patient will need to have this explained, clarified and reviewed. As well as having a sufficient understanding of these roles, all need to be clear about 'the rules' – for instance, expectations about information exchange and confidentiality. A corollary is each agency's acceptance of its responsibility to its staff. Workers are entitled to good quality support and supervision here which might include both consultancy in difficult cases and the mutual accountability that recognises both the case worker's particular contribution and the duties of the agency.

Careful, active listening is essential. People's words must always be taken seriously. For example, many people who harm others or themselves often tell someone that they are going to do so. This can be so hard to hear that it is just shut out. If someone says that they are thinking of harming themselves or others, the worker should encourage them to say more about this. These are painful and frightening thoughts and if a worker shows they may not be discussed, they will not go away, just become even more secret and powerful. Responding to a threat is not the same as giving into it. And at the same time as taking words seriously, the worker must remain sensitive to context, to the 'whole message' and recognise that words may need to be interpreted.

Delusions and hallucination

It is not to be assumed that someone is deluded just because a worker has difficulty in understanding them or in seeing things their way. They may have a way of expressing themselves that is unfamiliar or they may be struggling to make sense of something that is very painful or confusing. There are particular challenges when this is overlaid with cultural difference or distance between worker and offender-patient (for example, Rack 1982).

A worker should not collude with hallucinations and delusions, but ought not deny their reality: in a significant sense, they are very real to the person concerned. If a client trusts a worker enough to talk about (say) their 'voices', they do not want to be simply dismissed, but at the same time there should be no pretence that the worker can hear them. Similarly, it is unwise to try to share in someone's delusions. On the contrary, the worker can be an *anchor to reality* through clear and patient communication. Honesty, straightforwardness and clarity are more than usually important.

Depression

Depression can feed on itself and can almost be infectious – in the sense that spending time with a very depressed person can make one feel low oneself. Workers need to be aware of this and to use colleagues to 'debrief'. It can be valuable for depressed people to express their feelings and accept them and helpers should not discourage this. It is easy to reassure, but often inappropriate. People commonly feel ashamed of depression, thinking they should be able to cope, and premature reassurance can make things worse.

What can help is spending time with someone, listening to them, allowing them to express and accept their feelings, respecting them and showing them they are people of worth. (Counselling may be a specialised skill, but everyone involved must strive to show this individual respect and concern.) Some people are helped by being reminded that these feelings will pass, that it won't always feel like this, that their depression is something that can be managed. The core community justice value of *belief in the possibility of personal change* is a guiding principle here.

The central insight of cognitive behaviourism is the dynamic interrelationship between feelings, thoughts and behaviour (McGuire 2000). This is a reminder that change can be effected by alterations in behaviour and thinking: depressed people can become preoccupied with their feelings, but – rather than waiting until the feelings are more positive – it can be more helpful to try to help people to *achieve* or to vary patterns of thinking and this in itself can lead to better feelings.

At the same time, people who are depressed often find it very hard to motivate themselves to act. A worker may assume that missed appointments, for example, are a sign of indifference or recalcitrance and become frustrated. Sometimes this non-compliance can be associated with depression – to which threat of breach is unlikely to be the most effective response. The task of a community justice worker is to create opportunities for change and, if people do not avail themselves of such opportunities, this does not mean that their concern and effort were not worthwhile or that the attempt should not be made again.

Personality disorder

For present purposes, personality disorder may not be the most useful description: it is much better to concentrate on the particular characteristics and behaviours of the person. People may be trying, demanding, unfair, suspicious or aggressive – most of us are at least some of the time – and we have all developed ways of responding to this. Community justice professionals have to balance acceptance and understanding with an attempt to promote change. Workers too are entitled to respect and have their own needs. Nor is it helpful for (say) Alec to be allowed to behave so inconsiderately.

Among the relevant skills here is *pro-social modelling* (Trotter 1999; Cherry 2005). Alec's experience is that most people he deals with want him to go away and a persistent attempt to show concern, courtesy and respect may in time elicit better behaviour from him. (It is very hard to show respect when one has little experience of receiving it.) The difficulties of bringing this about must not be underestimated and there is no doubt scope for specialised intervention – perhaps in seeking to remould the schemas through which Alec interprets his experiences (McGuire 2000) – but everyone has a role in trying to show him the boundaries of acceptable behaviour.

Conclusions

It has been argued that a simplistic and unrealistic understanding of the relationship between mental disturbance and offending has vitiated policy and its implementation. The idea that there is a straightforward causal association between mental disturbance and offending fails to recognise the diversity of mental distress and the many ways in which it can be implicated in offending. Policy has been further distorted by an excessive emphasis on the risks posed to others by mentally disturbed people. This preoccupation can even be actively self-defeating: insistence on coercion and compulsion can lead to a disaffection, suspicion and avoidance of health care by those who, both for their own well-being and for the protection of the public, are most in need of it (Canton 2005).

Medical intervention has a critical contribution to make in many cases, but cannot be seen as a complete response to the many challenges of working with offenders who are mentally disturbed. An appreciation of the social influences on mental distress makes it possible to recognise the ways in which community justice workers can make a difference.

Often, what is required to work with mentally disordered offenders in the community justice sector is a diligent, patient and confident application of familiar helping skills. There is also a need to be able to recognise when it is appropriate to seek support from elsewhere, but, as we have seen, in the great majority of cases, successful referral leads to the involvement of others in a collective endeavour rather than a 'taking away' of the person or problem.

Community justice agencies have to find ways of making their services relevant and accessible to people who are mentally disordered and not continue to avow that they lack the necessary expertise. The fact that they are not the competent authority to 'treat' is not to the point: they ought to find ways of making the same range of services available even so. Many criminogenic needs, as we have seen, are dynamically associated with psychological distress and sensitive attention to addressing these needs is in itself an invaluable form of 'treatment'. Community justice practice – not least the management of risk – will be most effective when it responds to mental disturbance as an aspect of diversity and as a challenge to provide accessible service and ceases to see mental distress as 'other', alien and the responsibility of someone else.

Discussion questions

1 Does anti-social personality disorder *explain* persistent bad behaviour – or does it just describe it in a particular way? Since psychologists and psychiatrists hold different views about the extent to which some personality disorders respond to treatment, is the diagnosis helpful in any way?
2 Is there a tension between public safety and the human rights and treatment needs of mentally disordered offenders? (Try to think of specific examples and to propose solutions.)
3 Should people with mental disorders be sentenced differently from other defendants? Why, or why not? If so, what should be the differences?

Further reading

Buchanan, A. (ed.) (2002) *Care of the Mentally Disordered Offender in the Community*. Oxford: Oxford University Press. A collection containing several insightful papers.

Leff, J. (2001) *The Unbalanced Mind*. London: Phoenix; Bentall, R. (2003) *Madness Explained*. London: Allen Lane. Correctives to the dominance of a medical/biochemical understanding of mental disorder.

Peay, J. (2007) 'Mentally disordered offenders, mental health, and crime', in M. Maguire, R. Morgan and R. Reiner (eds), *The Oxford Handbook of Criminology*, 4th edn. Oxford: Oxford University Press. A sound general introduction.

Porter, R. (2001) *Madness: A Brief History*. Oxford: Oxford University Press. A concise and authoritative historical introduction to the many ways in which madness has been understood and misunderstood by various societies at different times.

Prins, H. (2005) *Offenders, Deviants or Patients*, 3rd edn. London: Routledge. An excellent text for all aspects of working with mentally disordered offenders.

Prins, H. (1999) *Will They Do It Again? Risk Assessment and Management in Criminal Justice and Psychiatry*. London: Routledge. Another valuable text.

Those wanting to track the long and confusing passage of the statute that will supersede the Mental Health Act 1983 should start at http://www.dh.gov.uk/PolicyAndGuidance/HealthAndSocialCareTopics/MentalHealth/fs/en.

Among the best websites is the Internet Mental Health Website http://www.mentalhealth.com/ which gives access to European (ICD-10) and American (DSM-IV) definitions of disorders. The Institute of Mental Health Act Practitioners http://www.imhap.org.uk/ is a very rich resource. The MIND website http://www.mind.org.uk/index.htm and the Revolving Doors site http://www.revolving-doors.org.uk/ are also highly recommended.

References

Badger, D., Nursten, J., Williams, P. and Woodward, M. (1999) *Systematic Review of the International Literature on the Epidemiology of Mentally Disordered Offenders CRD Report 15*. Executive Summary available online at: http://www.york.ac.uk/inst/crd/report15.htm (accessed June 2007).

Bentall, R. (2003) *Madness Explained: Psychosis and Human Nature*. London: Allen Lane.

Blackburn, R. (1993) *The Psychology of Criminal Conduct: Theory, Research and Practice*. Chichester: John Wiley.

Blumenthal, S. and Lavender, T. (2001) *Violence and Mental Disorder: A Critical Aid to the Assessment and Management of Risk*. London: Jessica Kingsley.

Bonta, J., Hanson, K. and Law, M. (1998) 'The prediction of criminal and violent recidivism among mentally disordered offenders: a meta-analysis', *Psychological Bulletin*, 123 (2): 123–42.

Brown, G. and Harris, T. (eds) (1989) *Life Events and Illness*. London: Unwin Hyman.

Busfield, J. (2002) 'Psychiatric disorder and individual violence: imagined death, risk and mental health policy', in A. Buchanan (ed.), *Care of the Mentally Disordered Offender in the Community*. Oxford: Oxford University Press.

Canton, R. (1995) 'Mental disorder, justice and censure', in D. Ward and M. Lacey (eds), *Probation: Working for Justice*, 1st edn. London: Whiting & Birch.

Canton, R. (2002) 'Rights, probation and mentally disturbed offenders', in D. Ward, J. Scott and M. Lacey (eds), *Probation: Working for Justice*, 2nd edn. Oxford: Oxford University Press.

Canton, R. (2005) 'Risk assessment and compliance in probation and mental health practice', in B. Littlechild and D. Fearns (eds), *Mental Disorder and Criminal Justice: Policy, Provision and Practice*. Lyme Regis: Russell House.

Cavadino, P. (1999) 'Diverting mentally disordered offenders from custody', in D. Webb and R. Harris (eds), (1999) *Mentally Disorder Offenders: Managing People Nobody Owns*. London: Routledge.

Cherry, S. (2005) *Transforming Behaviour: Pro-social Modelling in Practice*. Cullompton: Willan.

Clare, A. (1980) *Psychiatry in Dissent: Controversial Issues in Thought and Practice*, 2nd edn. London: Routledge.

Clark, T., Kenney-Herbert, J. and Humphreys, M. (2002) 'Community rehabilitation orders with additional requirements of psychiatric treatment', *Advances in Psychiatric Treatment*, 8: 281–90.

Davies, S. (2002) 'Compulsory treatment in the community', *Advances in Psychiatric Treatment*, 8: 180–8.

Department of Health (1999) *Effective Care Co-ordination in Mental Health Services: Modernising the Care Programme Approach: A Policy Booklet*. Available online at: http://www.dh.gov.uk/PublicationsAndStatistics/Publications/PublicationsPolicyAndGuidance/PublicationsPolicyAndGuidanceArticle/fs/en?CONTENT_ID=4009221&chk=k0eztB (accessed June 2007).

Department of Health (2005) *Offender Mental Health Care Pathway*. Available online at: http://www.dh.gov.uk/PublicationsAndStatistics/Publications/PublicationsPolicyAndGuidance/PublicationsPolicyAndGuidanceArticle/fs/en?CONTENT_ID=4102231&chk=P2de%2Bt (accessed June 2007).

Department of Health/Home Office (2000) *Reforming the Mental Health Act: Part II: High Risk Patients*, Cm 5016–II. Available online at: http://www.archive.official-documents.co.uk/document/cm50/5016-ii/5016ii.htm (accessed June 2007).

Garland, D. (2001) *The Culture of Control: Crime and Social Order in Contemporary Society*. Oxford: Oxford University Press.

Geelan, S. *et al.* (2000) 'A bail and probation hostel for mentally disordered defendants', *Journal of Forensic Psychiatry*, 11 (1): 93–104.

Green, G., Smith, R. and South, N. (2005) 'Court-based psychiatric assessment: case for an integrated diversionary and public health role', *Journal of Forensic Psychiatry*, 16 (3): 577–91.

Grounds, A. (1991) 'The mentally disordered offender in the criminal process: some research and policy questions', in K. Herbst and J. Gunn (eds), *The Mentally Disordered Offender*. Oxford: Butterworth-Heinemann in association with Mental Health Foundation.

Hatfield, B., Ryan, T., Pickering, L., Burroughs, H. and Crofts, R. (2004) 'The mental health of residents of approved premises in the Greater Manchester Probation Area: a cohort study', *Probation Journal*, 51: 101–15.

Higgins, J. (1991) 'The mentally disordered offender in the community', in K. Herbst and J. Gunn (eds), *The Mentally Disordered Offender*. Oxford: Butterworth-Heinemann in association with Mental Health Foundation.

Hodgins, S. (2004) 'Offenders with major mental disorders', in C. Hollin (ed.), *The Essential Handbook of Offender Assessment and Treatment*. Chichester: Wiley.

James, D., Farnham, F., Moorey, H., Lloyd, H., Hill, K., Blizard, R. and Barnes, T. (2002) *Outcome of Psychiatric Admission through the Courts*, RDS Occasional Paper No. 79. London: Home Office. Available online at: http://www.homeoffice.gov.uk/rds/pdfs2/occ79outcome.pdf (accessed June 2007).

Keyes, S. (1995) 'Revolving doors: eggs, empathy and Erewhon', *Criminal Justice Matters*, 21: 3–4.

Laurance, J. (2003) *Pure Madness: How Fear Drives the Mental Health System*. London: Routledge.

Leff, J. (2001) *The Unbalanced Mind*. London: Phoenix.

Ly, L. and Foster, S. (2005) *Statistics of Mentally Disordered Offenders 2004: England and Wales*, Home Office Statistical Bulletin 22/05. London: Home Office.

MacArthur Research Network (n.d.) *The MacArthur Community Violence Study*. Available online at: http://macarthur.virginia.edu/violence.html (accessed June 2007).

McGuire, J. (2000) *Cognitive-Behavioural Approaches: An Introduction to Theory and Research*. London: Home Office. Available online at: http://inspectorates.homeoffice.gov.uk/hmiprobation/docs/cogbeh1.pdf (accessed June 2007).

Moore, B. (1996) *Risk Assessment: A Practitioner's Guide to Predicting Harmful Behaviour*. London: Whiting & Birch.

Mullen, P. (2002a) 'Serious mental disorder and offending behaviours', in J. McGuire (ed.), *Offender Rehabilitation and Treatment: Effective Programmes and Policies to Reduce Re-Offending*. Chichester: John Wiley.

Mullen, P. (2002b) 'Introduction', in A. Buchanan (ed.), *Care of the Mentally Disordered Offender in the Community*. Oxford: Oxford University Press.

Munro, E. and Rumgay, J. (2000) 'Role of risk assessment in reducing homicides by people with mental illness', *British Journal of Psychiatry*, 176: 116–20.

NACRO (1998) *Rights and Risks: Mentally Disturbed Offenders and Public Protection*, Report by NACRO's Mental Health Advisory Committee. London: NACRO.

Nadkarni, R., Chipchase, B. and Fraser, K. (2000) 'Partnership with probation hostels: a step forward in community forensic psychiatry', *Psychiatric Bulletin*, 24: 222–4.

Napo (2003) *Mentally Disordered Offenders: A Briefing*. London: Napo.

National Institute for Mental Health (2003) *Inside Outside: Improving Mental Health Services for Black and Minority Ethnic Communities in England*. Available online at: http://www.dh.gov.uk/PolicyAndGuidance/HealthAndSocialCareTopics/MentalHealth/MentalHealthArticle/fs/en?CONTENT_ID=4002020&chk=PFFceH (accessed June 2007).

Peay, J. (2007) 'Mentally disordered offenders, mental health, and crime', in M. Maguire, R. Morgan and R. Reiner (eds), *The Oxford Handbook of Criminology*, 4th edn. Oxford: Oxford University Press.

Porter, R. (1987) *A Social History of Madness: Stories of the Insane*. London: Weidenfeld & Nicholson.

Porter, R. (2002) *Madness: A Brief History*. Oxford: Oxford University Press.

Prins, H. (1992) 'The diversion of the mentally disordered: some problems for criminal justice, penology and health care', *Journal of Forensic Psychiatry*, 3 (2): 431–43.

Prins, H. (1999) *Will They Do It Again? Risk Assessment and Management in Criminal Justice and Psychiatry*. London: Routledge.

Prins, H. (2005) *Offenders, Deviants or Patients*, 3rd edn. London: Routledge.

Rack, P. (1982) *Race, Culture, and Mental Disorder*. London: Tavistock.

Read, J. (2004) 'Poverty, ethnicity and gender', in J. Read, L. Mosher and R. Bentall (eds), *Models of Madness: Psychological, Social and Biological Approaches to Schizophrenia*. London: Routledge.

Read, J. and Haslam, N. (2004) 'Public opinion: bad things happen and can drive you crazy', in J. Read, L. Mosher and R. Bentall (eds), *Models of Madness: Psychological, Social and Biological Approaches to Schizophrenia*. London: Routledge.

Rumgay, J. and Munro, E. (2001) 'The lion's den: professional defences in the treatment of dangerous patients', *Journal of Forensic Psychiatry*, 12 (2): 357–78.

Scheff, T. (1984) *Being Mentally Ill: A Sociological Theory*, 2nd edn. New York: Aldine.

Shaw, J., Tomenson, B., Creed, F. and Perry, A. (2001) 'Loss of contact with psychiatric services in people diverted from the criminal justice system', *Journal of Forensic Psychiatry*, 12 (1): 203–10.

Singleton, N., Meltzer, H. and Gatward, R. (1998) *Psychiatric Morbidity among Prisoners: Summary Report*. London: Government Statistical Service. Available online at: http://www.statistics.gov.uk/downloads/theme_health/Prisoners_PsycMorb.pdf (accessed June 2007).

Skeem, J. and Mulvey, E. (2002) 'Assessing the risk of violence posed by mentally disordered offenders being treated in the community', in A. Buchanan (ed.), *Care of the Mentally Disordered Offender in the Community*. Oxford: Oxford University Press.

Stone, N. (2003) *A Companion Guide to Mentally Disordered Offenders*, 2nd edn. Crayford: Shaw & Sons.

Trotter, C. (1999) *Working with Involuntary Clients: A Guide to Practice*. London: Sage.

Tyrer, P. and Steinberg, D. (1998) *Models for Mental Disorder: Conceptual Models in Psychiatry*, 3rd edn. Chichester: John Wiley.

Vaughan, P., Pullen, N. and Kelly, M. (2000) 'Services for mentally disordered offenders in community psychiatric teams', *Journal of Forensic Psychiatry*, 11 (3): 571–86.

Watkins, T., Lewellen, A. and Barrett, M. (2001) *Dual Diagnosis: An Integrated Approach to Treatment*. London: Sage.

Webb, D. and Harris, R. (eds) (1999) *Mentally Disordered Offenders: Managing People Nobody Owns*. London: Routledge.

Chapter 19

Working with perpetrators and victims of domestic violence

Mark Rivett and Alyson Rees

Introduction

In this chapter, we will both provide details of the current context in which work with perpetrators of domestic violence occurs and explore the predominant approaches to this work. Because work with perpetrators cannot be a distinct activity which does not have a relationship to victims and survivors of domestic violence, we will also outline how perpetrator work fits into a coordinated community approach to domestic violence. This particular discussion will be set within the context of public policy and current practice with both offenders and victims.

Definitions and prevalence of domestic violence

Clearly it is crucial at the outset to have an understanding of what is meant by the term 'domestic violence' and it is also important to recognise the ubiquity of such violence. Domestic violence/abuse can take a variety of forms from emotional and financial to physical. In many services the terms 'abuse' and 'violence' are used interchangeably because it is recognised that for violence to occur there must be other forms of non-violent abuse present. It is also acknowledged that too strong an emphasis on the term 'violence' tends to underemphasise the significance of non-'violent' abuse upon family members. Accordingly, throughout this chapter we will sometimes use either term.

There are two commonly accepted definitions of domestic abuse/violence and these come from two distinct agencies. Walby and Allen (2004) define it as:

> Any violence between current or former partners in an intimate relationship, wherever, or whenever the violence occurs. The violence may include physical, sexual, emotional or financial abuse. (2004: 2)

The Women's Aid Federation, however, adopts the following definition:

> Domestic violence [*is*] physical, sexual, psychological or financial violence
> that takes place within an intimate or family-type relationship and that
> forms a pattern of coercive and controlling behaviour. (2006: 1)

There is one significant difference in these definitions which will have
relevance to our later discussion about work with perpetrators of domestic
violence. The Women's Aid Federation definition implies that abuse has a
purpose (*control*) while the Home Office definition does not.

Public awareness of domestic violence has increased greatly over the past
two decades. There is a vast quantity of international research and policy
literature which chronicles the extent of domestic violence worldwide
(for example, Mullender 1997; UNICEF 2000). It is widely acknowledged
that the vast majority of domestic violence is perpetrated by men against
women (Walby and Allen 2004). Such violence is characterised by clear
gender asymmetry, especially so in terms of men's violence being more
frequent, more physically damaging and more likely to be part of a pattern
of controlling behaviours. Women's violence to men, on the other hand,
tends to be retaliatory or defensive (Mooney 2000).

In the UK, a variety of sources demonstrate that domestic violence and
abuse are very widespread and prolific. A community survey of women in
London reported that:

- More than one in two women had been in psychologically abusive
  relationships their lives.
- One in four women had been in a psychologically abusive relationship in
  the past year.
- One in three women had suffered physical and sexual abuse requiring
  medical attention.
- One in nine women had suffered physical and sexual abuse requiring
  medical attention in the past year. (Mooney 2000)

A more traditional way of measuring the rate of domestic violence is within
the British Crime Survey. In 2001 this included a detailed self-completion
questionnaire designed to ascertain the most accurate estimates of the extent
and nature of domestic violence, sexual assault and stalking in England and
Wales. This method of survey is likely to be more effective in eliciting a
'true' estimate because it is completed by the individual and did not involve
stressful one-to-one interviews. The Survey included a representative sample
of 22,463 women and men aged 16–59. It concluded that:

> There were an estimated 129 million incidents of domestic violence
> (non sexual threats or force) against women and 2.5 million against
> men in England and Wales in the year prior to the interview. (Walby
> and Allen 2004: vi)

The nature and severity of the abuse, however, was very different for women victims. Women were overwhelmingly the most heavily abused group:

> Among people subject to four or more incidents of domestic violence from the perpetrator, of the worst incidents (since age 16), 89% were women. (Walby and Allen 2004: vii)

Moreover, most of the reported violence was:

> concentrated in ... a minority, largely women, [who] suffer multiple attacks, severe injuries, experience more than one form of inter-personal violence and serious disruption to their lives. (Walby and Allen 2004: v)

All researchers also note that incidence figures of domestic violence recorded by *any* method are *underestimates* because, as it involves intimate details of people's relationship lives, abuse within this context is less likely to be reported. Kaufman *et al.* (1990) estimated that at least 93 per cent of cases were not reported. Similarly, Dobash and Dobash (1979) estimated that only 2 per cent of domestic violence incidents were reported to the police. If incidence recorded by criminal justice agencies is considered historically, the police have traditionally preferred not to log domestic violence as a crime, thus also leading to underestimates (Buzawa and Buzawa 2003). This resistance to intervention and recognition of domestic violence was not unique to the police force. McKie (2005) comments that:

> Many agencies and professionals are fearful of scrutiny of their practices, especially if these might be considered to promote frequent intervention into family life. (McKie 2005: 65)

This therefore made domestic violence an under-recognised problem and an actively neglected one.

The magnitude and severity of male on female violence has lead some to conclude that male-dominated societies set the scene and legitimise male violence (Hearn and Whitehead 2006). Therefore to address this behaviour we need to 'treat society as well as reform individual abusers' (Gondolf and Russell 1986: 163). This view is supported by studies that explore male attitudes to violence upon women. The *Young People's Attitudes towards Violence Survey* (Burton *et al.* 1998) found that one in two young men considered hitting a woman or forcing her to have sex to be acceptable in at least one of the identified circumstances (1998: 1). In another survey in North London only 37 per cent of men said they would not use violence against a woman (Mooney 2000). Moreover, it is clear that while some forms of men's violence to women are less frequent, others are common, and in that sense routine (Hearn and Whitehead 2006). It is argued by many that fundamental beliefs about men being 'better' than women underlie and excuse the behaviour of male perpetrators. This analysis therefore leads onto the assumption that to change a perpetrator from being an abusive person, his beliefs about women, his sense of entitlement over women and his wish to control women, all must be challenged and changed. This view, as we shall explore later, underpins the predominant form of treatment available for perpetrators and is well summarised by the creators of this model:

> Men are culturally prepared for their role of master of the home even though they must often physically enforce the 'right' to exercise this role. They are socialized to be dominant and women to be subordinate. (Pence and Paymar 1993: 5)

Social responses to domestic violence

Despite the severity and ubiquity of domestic violence in the UK, it was not until the 1970s that there was a growing recognition that it constituted a social and individual problem that society should address. The initial response to domestic violence was the refuge movement which functioned as a way of protecting women and children from abuse. In 1971 the first official refuge was set up for women and children in the UK. Out of this grew the Women's Aid Federation in 1972 and, from this beginning, refuges were established in all major cities and urban communities. However, this movement remained isolated in many ways: relying on unstable funding and having to employ staff on uncertain contracts. For many activists in this movement, it continued to feel as if real resources were not being dedicated to dealing with domestic violence and a real change possibly only occurred in the UK in the late 1990s when the Labour government began to commit increasing resources to ending domestic violence and supporting survivors. Hearn and Whitehead (2006) noticed this change:

> The creation of specialist courts, policies and practices may signal a sea change in the authorities' recognition of the scale and scope of men's violence to known women and increase the level of intervention into such violence. Such initiatives may indicate a growing recognition of gendered imbalances of power between men and women. (Hearn and Whitehead 2006: 52)

There were a number of reasons for this 'sea change'. One was the recognition that domestic violence actually cost significant amounts of money to various welfare agencies including the criminal justice system (Robinson 2005). For instance, the police realised that 25 per cent of all recorded crime was domestic violence (Home Office 1999). Further, significant numbers of these (albeit under-reported) assaults were *repeat* assaults: in other words appropriate action earlier may have prevented the new assault. The Crown Prosecution Service also noted that large numbers of complainants in domestic violence cases withdrew their complaints (Home Office 1999). Again, a view emerged that better management of these cases would lead to better convictions and safer victims.

A second reason for the sea change in policy has been the support of politicians both in the devolved governments (Scotland, Wales and London) and in the national government. In the last ten years there has been a raft of policy guidance and legal change that has affected domestic violence services. These are summarised in Table 19.1.

Table 19.1 Legislative developments with regard to domestic violence

1974	This year saw one of the first signs of public recognition with the Home Affair Select Committee publishing a report on domestic violence.
1976	The Domestic and Violence and Matrimonial Proceedings Act enabled married women to obtain injunctions through the County Court. (This has now been superseded by the Family Law Act 1996.)
1978	The Domestic Proceedings and Magistrates Court Act enabled married women to apply for orders through the magistrates' court (now superseded by the Family Law Act 1996).
1987	The Metropolitan Police Force advised all officers to use their powers of arrest and treat domestic violence as a criminal offence.
1988	The Criminal Justice Act, s. 23, allowed written evidence to be accepted where a victim of violence refuses to give evidence in court out of fear.
1989	Children Act puts the interests of the child first in any proceedings.
1989	Working with male perpetrators began to develop in the UK with the CHANGE project (Central Region of Scotland), closely followed by Lothian Domestic Violence Probation Project. These projects drew on research about American projects such as Duluth, where it was found that the criminalisation of domestic abuse is the single most effective treatment.
1990	Home Office Circular 60/90 gave advice to the whole of the police service. As a result many forces set up domestic abuse units and joined multi-agency fora as they developed.
1990	The Victims Charter (updated in 1996) made the Probation Service responsible for liaison with the victims of offenders sentenced to life imprisonment or families of the victims.
1997	Part IV of the Family Law Act 1996 made available non-molestation orders and occupation rights in the home to 'associated persons'.
1997	Implementation of Protection from Harassment Act which makes it a criminal offence to behave in a way a person knows, or ought to know, causes someone else harassment, fear or violence.
1999	Publication of a national government strategy *Living Without Fear: An Integrated Approach to Tackling Violence against Women*.

Table 19.1 continued

2000	Implemented 1 April 2001, Criminal Justice and Court Services Act, s. 67, placed a statutory duty on police and probation to establish local multi-agency public protection arrangements to manage the risk posed by serious sexual and violent offences. Section 67 placed a statutory duty on police and probation to consult and notify victims about the release arrangements for all sexual and violent offenders sentenced to imprisonment for 12 months or more.
2003	In June, publication of consultation document *Safety and Justice: The Government's Proposals on Domestic Violence*. The document focused on three key strands of prevention, protection and justice, and support.
2003	In December, publication of *Summary of Response to Safety and Justice: The Government's Proposals on Domestic Violence*. This was accompanied by the publication and introduction into Parliament of the Domestic Violence, Crime and Victims Bill.
2004	In November, the Domestic Violence, Crime and Victims Act receives Royal Assent (provisions to be implemented 2005/6). The Act represents the biggest piece of legislation on domestic abuse in thirty years.
2005	In October, implementation of s.11 of the Children Act 2004 placing a statutory duty on key persons and bodies to make arrangements to ensure that in discharging their functions they have regard to the need to safeguard and promote the welfare of children.

Source: Home Office Circular Issue 1.0, June 2006, EPIC website.

There is a last reason why this sea change has occurred: possibly for the first time since the scale of domestic violence was uncovered, a way of intervening has been promulgated which has practical and enforceable mechanisms for effecting change. It is within this 'coordinated community response' that treatment for perpetrating men has fitted.

Domestic violence services within a coordinated community response

In particular, in the city of Duluth, USA, it was recognised that to change social attitudes to domestic violence, firstly all criminal justice agencies had to 'take domestic violence seriously' so that offenders knew they would be held accountable for their actions (Shepard and Pence 1999). Secondly, this emphasis must be supported by a view that it was all agencies' (and communities') responsibility to act to keep the safety of women and children paramount. This required a coordination of criminal justice with child protection services. It also led to a better coordination of police, prosecution and probation agencies and these with non-governmental service providers (Buzawa and Buzawa 2003). It also led to an 'integrated' system for responding to domestic violence. Karan *et al.* (1999) suggested that the following elements were essential for such a system:

- interagency collaboration;
- comprehensive victim advocacy;
- effective pre-arrest procedures;
- effective post-arrest procedures;
- multi-agency intake;
- integrated case recording;
- effective prosecution and defence;
- effective treatment programmes;
- monitoring and judicial review.

In addition, as this model was adopted in Duluth, an independent monitoring entity, the DAIP (Domestic Abuse Intervention Program), was established, as financially independent from the criminal justice system. This allowed the DAIP to function as a referral and monitoring agency for perpetrators who had been mandated by the court to attend education groups.

In the UK, the establishment of a coordinated community response to domestic abuse has been lead by the Crime and Disorder Reduction Partnerships (CDRPs). These were established in 1998 and have been given a central role at the local level to ensure delivery of appropriate and effective services to the victims of domestic violence and to hold perpetrators accountable for their actions (Madoc-Jones 2005). The Home Office Report on Domestic Violence and Crime Reduction Partnerships (Home Office 2004) identifies that CDRPs are working with a range of partner agencies but that the range varies from area to area. Thus despite rhetoric, in only just over half of the cases (55 per cent) were domestic violence forums consulting with a CDRP: joined-up working clearly continues to be an aspiration that is difficult to implement.

Other initiatives have, however, also had an impact on domestic abuse provision which has promoted a coordinated community response. For instance, Hester and Westmorland (2004) examined how a number of 'one-stop-shop' projects were being able to create an integrated response. But this study also demonstrated that this task often ran into problems when multiple agencies needed to work together. These initiatives have begun to provide evidence for how a coordinated community response might be adapted to suit UK contexts. We will now outline an example of these before turning to UK perpetrator programmes.

An example of an integrated 'one-stop shop'

The Cardiff Women's Safety Unit (WSU) was set up in 2001, taking the first referral on 10 December 2001. This is an example of a successful and integrated community response to domestic violence:

The unit provides a central point of access for women and their children experiencing domestic violence or known perpetrator rape in the Cardiff area. While the overriding aim of the WSU is to help victims gain safety, the WSU team also provides advice, advocacy, specialist counselling services, legal services, housing services, refuge provision, target hardening and collects evidence. (Robinson 2005: 5)

The unit employs a range of project workers. For instance, there is a police officer, a seconded nurse (with connections to Accident and Emergency services) and a number of independent domestic violence advocates (IDVAs) based within the project. The unit has solicitors offering free consultations on a fortnightly rotational basis; these are from firms that are signed up to a Best Practice Agreement in relation to domestic violence. The unit offers training to a wide range of professionals across the region and has particularly focused on health. It has acted as a catalyst in transforming the police response to domestic violence. Now there is a positive arrest policy in Cardiff and a response based on keeping the victim safe which originated in Killingbeck (Hanmer and Griffiths 2000). This includes a range of measures such as the use of 'target hardening' activities (securing the home of the victim), 'occurrence markers' (to speed up police response to a call out) and 'drive by' (regular police contact).

The WSU also has a strong presence in the court system. It has helped to initiate a fast-track court where domestic violence cases are flagged up during the pre-trial review. The WSU has trained the magistrates and prosecutors that sit in this court. Advocates from the unit accompany the women victims to the court. Evaluations have shown that these interventions have increased not only prosecutions but also women's confidence that they will be protected by these agencies (Robinson 2005).

The WSU also demonstrates, and has trail-blazed, many of the innovations that have been introduced to the criminal justice system to increase victim safety across the whole of England and Wales. For instance, Multi-Agency Risk Assessment Conferences (MARACs) were first developed in Cardiff. These were an intervention to reduce the re-assault (or revictimisation) rates in the city. They are meetings attended by all relevant agencies who meet to plan how they are going to intervene to prevent further assaults on high-risk victims. Robinson (2004) describes these meetings as follows:

In Cardiff, about thirty victims per month are being identified as very high risk. MARACs have been running monthly ... They are attended by members of many agencies, including police, probation, local authority, health, housing, refuge and WSU. The circumstances of very high risk victims and their children are discussed and plans are created to help promote their safety. An initial evaluation of the MARAC was recently completed with results indicating that the majority of victims (about 6 in 10) had not been revictimised since the MARAC. (Robinson 2004: 29)

Robinson (2006) showed that 'MARACs produced a positive, measurable impact in victims' lives and, therefore, are an important innovation in the area of a coordinated community responses to domestic violence' (2006: 784).

The other major innovation that has been developed by the WSU is that of the fast-track domestic violence court mentioned above. Specialist Domestic Violence Courts (SDVCs) have operated in parts of the USA and Canada for twenty years, but the first specialist court in Britain (at Leeds) was established only in 1999. The intention of such courts is to concentrate expertise in the prosecution of domestic violence offences in a court which has access to advocacy for the victims, contact with services to treat the offender, and a quicker response to the crime (as the longer it takes to get a case to court the less likely safety will be achieved) (Cook *et al.* 2004: 5). The core components for SDVCs (Sacks 2002) are summarised in Table 19.2.

Table 19.2   Core components for SDVCs

- *Access to advocacy services*. Advocates act as a 'liaison, buffer and contact' between the victim and the court, a source of referrals to other services and, with consent, a conduit of information to the court.

- *Coordination of partners*. This was accomplished with regular meetings and joint training.

- *Victim and child friendly court*. Security at the court should be reviewed and if necessary improved, building on best practice (e.g. separate waiting areas, childcare facilities, security guards trained in domestic violence).

- *Specialist personnel*. Specialist domestic violence training for all magistrates/ judges, court administrators, prosecutors and other key personnel.

- *Even-handed treatment*. Both parties should be adequately represented and the court's tone should indicate that domestic violence is being treated seriously.

- *Integrated information systems*. Systems and protocols in place for sharing and accessing information, to connect the court with community-based service providers and ensure compliance with orders.

- *Evaluation and accountability*. Plans for evaluation (and the systems to carry it out) should be in place from the outset.

- *Protocols for risk assessment*. All agencies should gather information on factors known to increase risk to facilitate risk assessment.

- *Ongoing training*. Training should be on a continuous rolling basis and be joint training (to increase each agency's understanding of each other's roles).

- *Compliance monitoring*. Through submission of reports to the court or regular review hearings, defendants' compliance with court orders should be monitored.

- *Sentencing*. Should be consistent and promote accountability from domestic violence offenders.

Cook *et al.* (2004) evaluated five such courts running in Cardiff, Derby, Leeds, West London and Wolverhampton. This evaluation was particularly focused on assessing the 'added value' of such courts in terms of reducing retractions, increasing prosecutions and increasing victim safety. Their results indicated that some of these aims were met but that there remained major issues in inter-agency working. They comment that:

> Reflecting on our research, it is apparent that the governance of criminal justice gives rise to conflicting goals for differing agencies engaged with domestic violence cases; for example the government's (and the criminal justice agencies whose targets it sets) 'Narrowing the Justice Gap' means speeding up cases, although this may have adverse consequences for some victims who need extra time for support. Similarly, 'Bringing Perpetrators to Justice' may not be what all domestic violence victims want and may also place them at greater risk of repeat victimisation, especially given the perceived 'leniency' of current sentencing practices (which focus mainly on financial penalties). (Cook *et al.* 2004: 22)

Interestingly, Robinson and Cook (2006) later commented that there is a risk that criminal justice interventions continue to view victims as 'statistics' and 'cases' rather than as people (2006: 209).

We have outlined some of the crucial changes to the criminal justice response and the gradual acceptance of a coordinated community response to domestic violence with reference to a beacon 'one-stop shop' service. We will now return to the active treatment of the perpetrators of domestic violence.

Perpetrator programmes

Perpetrator programmes have variously been described as originating within the anti-sexist men's movement (Stoltenberg 1990, 1993; Pease 1997, 2000) and from within the women's refuge movement (LaViolette 2001). The impetus from these sources was clearly different but ultimately these differences led to a unity of purpose.

Anti-sexist men's groups wanted to make an impact on the general attitudes of men towards women and saw the development of groups for perpetrators of domestic violence as a way to achieve this goal. This impetus has continued in the vibrant success of the White Ribbon Campaign which is a global campaign by men against domestic violence (see http:// www. whiteribbon.com). The impetus from the women's refuge movement was in some senses more practical: they wanted to ensure that the serial abusers with whom their clients had relationships were held to account for their abusive behaviour. These separate influences have been reflected in the history of perpetrator programmes.

The early programmes had a preference for a therapeutic approach with abusers and had little connection to the criminal justice or refuge system (Dutton and Sonkin 2003). However, as the influence of feminist-informed approaches to domestic violence began to grow with policies such as 'pro-arrest' being trailed in the United States, a more critical approach began to affect perpetrator programmes. There then began an integration of the two streams of influence outlined above and a number of 'pro-feminist' programmes began to emerge which used some of the therapeutic methods of intervention that had become common in the anti-sexist men's movement tradition.

Two dominant programmes then emerged in the USA during the 1980s and 1990s: the Boston Emerge (Adams 2000) and the Duluth (Pence and Paymar 1993) programmes. Both of these have accurately been described as pro-feminist, cognitive-behavioural programmes. These approaches are pro-feminist because they assume that underlying men's abuse of women is a sense of *entitlement* that men share in patriarchal society. This is well summarised by Pence and Paymar (1993) in the earlier quote.

This model also advocated against the use of anger management methods with perpetrators of domestic abuse because anger management was not their problem (Gondolf and Russell 1986). Largely because the Duluth programme of Pence and Paymar (1993) was so well described and also because it fitted into the *coordinated community response* to domestic violence (Shepard and Pence 1999), it was this programme that became the 'benchmark' for other programmes.

On a policy level this development of perpetrator programmes had some significant consequences. Firstly, at least within the United States in the 1990s, the criminal justice system began funding and researching programmes. Secondly, this system as well as the refuge movement began to expect 'standards' of treatment from the providers of perpetrator programmes. This led to a process where perpetrator programmes had to meet a set of standards set often by state legislatures. These standards often included requirements about the programme philosophy, about the length of the programme, about the professional qualifications of the programme facilitators, and about the connection of the programme to 'systems of protection', e.g. child protection, refuge and criminal justice agencies (Gelles 2001). The last consequence was inevitably the decline of 'voluntary' and 'therapeutic' programmes.

Before we develop a more in depth description of the Duluth programme and outline its influence upon perpetrator work in the UK, it is important to note that we would be wrong to assume that all 'voluntary' or 'therapeutic' programmes have been lost. Indeed, in the USA there have been increasingly vocal calls for the lessons of therapeutic work to be rediscovered in the field of domestic violence (Geffner and Rosenbaum 2001). Moreover, there have been a number of important contributions to perpetrator work from 'therapeutic' sources. Jenkins' (1990) *Invitations to Responsibility*, for instance has had a high impact on perpetrator work in Australia while more recently authors have described the use of solution-focused approaches (Lee *et al.* 2003) and individualised cognitive-behavioural approaches (Murphy and Eckhardt 2005) to domestic violence perpetrator work. In the UK there are also significant examples of programmes that have been influenced by the therapeutic tradition (Rivett and Rees 2004; Rees and Rivett 2005).

The 'Duluth' programme and the Integrated Domestic Abuse Programme

In this section we wish to describe the Duluth programme with the intention of leading into a description of the predominant intervention programme used in criminal justice within the UK: the Integrated Domestic Abuse Programme (IDAP). The Duluth programme is a 26-week 'open' rolling group format which means that a man can join the group at any time and complete the 26 weeks. The primary teaching tool of the programme is the Power and Control Wheel (see Figure 19.1).

The programme is divided into three-week 'sections'. Each 'section' shares a theme which is one aspect of the Power and Control Wheel. Thus the first week is typically spent defining the theme of the section, such as 'What is intimidation?' This will often be taught with a concentration on an example of intimidating behaviour that might be demonstrated in a video clip. The 'Duluth' programme assumes that men learn by a process of watching, analysing and then applying it to themselves. This has been termed an 'outside-in' approach (Featherstone *et al.* 2007). The second teaching technique is the 'control log' which is a record of the control tactics that a man in the group uses in the week between sessions. In the second week therefore these behaviours will be focused on with the emphasis upon how the behaviour increases a man's power over his partner. In the last week on the theme, alternative behaviours are practised in role plays and skills sessions. This demonstrates that the Power and Control Wheel requires the Equality Wheel (Figure 19.2) as a balance and the behaviours described on it are seen as 'ideals' to aim for.

The 'Duluth' programme is described as an 'education' model of treatment. Indeed the original designers of the model employed the famous educationalist Paulo Friere (1972) to help them create a programme which encouraged men to feel motivated in changing their behaviour. It is also relevant to note that because the culture of services in the USA is more therapeutic, therapeutic skills, as such, are rarely mentioned in these programmes. Yet many practitioners who work for perpetrator programmes in the USA will have trained in one form of therapeutic intervention or another (Rosenbaum and Leisring 2001).

In the UK, the Duluth programme has become the hegemonic form of intervention within the criminal justice system when working with men who perpetrate domestic abuse upon their partners. It has become the predominant model adopted by Respect (2004), a collection of agencies who

355

Figure 19.1 The Power and Control Wheel
Reproduced with permission of the Domestic Abuse Intervention Project.

work with male perpetrators of domestic violence. This grouping has been meeting since the early 1990s as a pressure group and learning forum for practitioners. 'Duluth' has been adapted and adopted into what has been named the Integrated Domestic Abuse Programme (or IDAP). All areas of the Probation Service are expected to implement a programme for domestic abuse perpetrators and such programmes have become the object of audit procedures. The IDAP manual says that:

> IDAP is designed as a programme that will target domestic violence-supportive core belief systems and change abusive behaviours towards partners. (2005: 22)

It is therefore clearly cognitive-behavioural in its orientation:

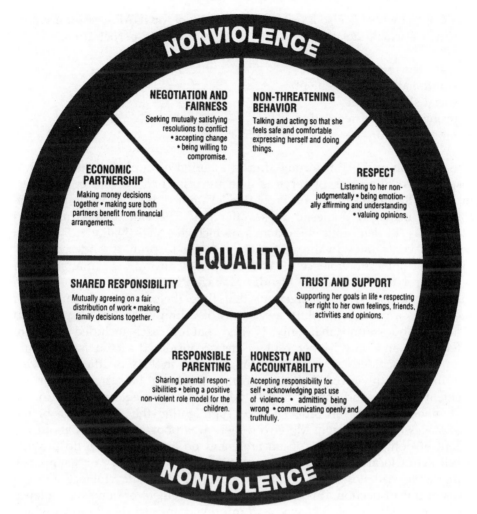

Figure 19.2 The Equality Wheel.
Reproduced with permission of the Domestic Abuse Intervention Project.

> IDAP is designed to challenge participants' pattern of thinking and rationalisations that underpins and maintains their violent and abusive behaviour. Belief systems are elicited, explored and challenged and particular attention is paid to looking at their origination and implications of their beliefs. (2005: 37)

The IDAP Manual provides a thorough review of the research around the 'causes' of domestic violence and it describes a series of possible 'typologies' of abusive men. Yet it also states clearly that the underlying philosophy of the programme is one in which 'battering is construed as an intentional act used to gain some form of power and control over the partner, (IDAP 2005: 38). This is an echo of the 'Duluth' programme philosophy. Thus the Power and Control wheel is also a primary teaching tool for IDAP. The programme is aimed at changing five key areas of functioning for perpetrators:

- distorted thinking
- emotional mismanagement
- social skills deficits
- problems in self-regulation
- motivation for change. (IDAP 2005: 42)

The adoption of IDAP has come during a period of unprecedented political inspection of the work of services that are tasked to prevent crime. Thus in 2004 HM Inspectorate of Probation examined how probation officers routinely managed domestic abuse offenders. The aim of this inspection (2004) was 'to determine the extent to which the NPS (National Probation Service) contributes to the reduction of harm to primary and secondary victims of domestic violence'. It was conducted during the initial stages of setting up NOMS (National Offender Manager Service) and included seven probation areas. What emerged at that time (before the introduction of IDAP) was a profound lack of awareness of victim safety within probation practice. They found that only 19 per cent of cases included a victim safety plan and only 34 per cent of cases considered victim issues. Only four cases included work with victims by victim liaison officers (VLOs). The inspection reviewed domestic violence cases that had triggered serious incident reviews and found that 84 per cent of incidents occurred in the first nine months of an order/licence, highlighting the significance of the first stages of supervision. Moreover, there was poor information about the extent of domestic violence in an area, and no areas were able to provide a full list of local domestic violence support units (statutory or voluntary). Three areas had no specific protocols covering domestic violence. On the basis of this inspection, it is clear that the management of domestic violence offenders needed to be reviewed and improved and the IDAP model which was designed to include partner (victim) support was meant to do this. Before IDAP was adopted it was piloted by the National Probation Service in four areas. One of the four pilot areas was North Devon, which had been chosen as there was already a community programme called 'Repair' running for perpetrators, an experienced women's support service run by Women's Aid, plus a multi-agency review panel and a well supported multi-agency approach (Wolf-Light 2006). North Devon was thus an ideal location as it had the foundations of a coordinated community response as advocated by the Duluth model.

Limitations of Duluth/IDAP

It is important to note that there have been a number of criticisms of the Duluth/IDAP approach which have come from a range of authors and practitioners. Some have argued that a strict 'manualised' approach limits the ability of a programme to engage the heterogeneity of abusers in changing their thoughts and behaviours (Rees and Rivett 2005). Others have commented about the strict programme integrity which is required in IDAP. It is claimed that this does not allow for responsiveness to the individual offender's needs or indeed the needs of that specific group. 'Responsivity' is something which has been neglected with regard to the perpetrator in the criminal justice process and with regard specifically to the domestic violence perpetrator and group (Rees and Rivett 2005). This was noted during the pilot in North Devon by Wolf-Light (2006):

> One further tension that had been felt throughout was the difficulty of working with process within such a structured programme. In fact process seemed to be completely ignored in the structure as laid out in the manual. (Wolf-Light 2006: 6)

Mankowski *et al.* (2002) in the USA have argued that there has been 'collateral' damage in adopting the 'power and control' thesis of domestic violence. They suggest that this 'damage' lays in limiting the ability to engage some men whose lives are experienced as powerless and out of control. As referred to earlier, many contemporary mental health clinicians also argue that this model fails to account for the individual psychological difficulties of many abusive men and will therefore fail to give them the treatment necessary for them to cease the abuse (Dutton 1995). Indeed, Gadd (2004) believes that programmes such as IDAP and Duluth have been introduced as a result of 'political processes' rather than evidence that they work (2004: 189). Again, on the other side of the Atlantic, Gelles (2001) has declared that it is too soon to determine which programmes should be 'standardised' because it is still unclear which programmes 'work' for which men in which circumstances. We will now therefore consider the research evidence on exactly this question.

The evidence base for perpetrator programmes

In a short chapter it is impossible to cover in a thorough manner the evidence base for perpetrator programmes. What we can do is highlight useful findings. But we should also note the complexity of researching the outcomes of such treatments. There are methodological problems about the measurement of outcome, the appropriate follow-up period and the ethics of comparing different treatment approaches in a random control trial (Buzawa and Buzawa 2003: 232). These complexities are made more difficult given the transient nature of the population of abusing men and the inconsistent monitoring methods employed by most criminal justice systems. However, we can report on a number of reasonable studies and two good meta-analyses of outcomes.

Two UK quasi-experimental studies (Dobash *et al.* 2000; Burton *et al.* 1998) concluded that programmes did prevent recidivism. But the sample sizes were small: 51 and 36 respectively. Two meta-analyses have provided less convincing results. Babcock and La Taillade (2000) and Babcock *et al.* (2004) found 'small effects' in perpetrator treatment programmes. Interestingly, they also noted that Duluth-style programmes were no better at preventing further abuse than were 'couples therapy' or 'psycho-educational' approaches. On the other hand Gondolf (2002) compared the outcomes for four different programmes and concluded that they had a significant effect on men's future abusive behaviour. Further, he concluded that his results demonstrated a 'programme effect', i.e. that the programme had an influence on behaviour long after it ended. Thus at 30 months after a programme, 80 per cent of the men had been 'violence free' for the previous year. This rose to 90 per cent being violence free in the last year after 48 months (a substantial follow-up period). In a similar conclusion to Babcock *et al.* (2004), Gondolf reported that programme length, programme philosophy and programme method ('cognitive' or 'process orientated') was not greatly significant in terms of outcome. Only one researcher has studied why these different programme philosophies might influence outcome. Garfield (2006) compared outcomes, programme approaches and styles of group intervention across three separate perpetrator programmes. She concluded that 'outcomes' were better for the programmes that sought to actively engage perpetrators in their own change and used the therapeutic alliance between group member and facilitator to achieve this. She believed that this might cause risk to increase when 'contained' groups ended. But she also demonstrated that the manualised, IDAP intervention had less ability to engage men and give them a sense of involvement than the other more 'therapeutic' programmes. She states that:

> Facilitation quality and duration intersect; you need both in good measure, to begin to effect desired change in men in group. (2006: 21)

It would therefore seem that although one model of perpetrator intervention is seen as central to working with domestic abuse offenders, there is enough evidence to suggest that this model may need to be 'softened' in practice and may indeed be challenged in the coming years. Essentially the therapeutic route of perpetrator programmes may be returning with a different perspective (Rivett 2006). This view, however, needs to be put within the context of the hegemony of the Duluth model which is now being replicated in centrally set standards such as those designed by Respect (2004).

Conclusion

This chapter has described the context of work with perpetrators of domestic violence and it has outlined the predominant model of that work. It has sought to place such work within the context of a coordinated community response to domestic violence. The chapter has also shown that although there are clear 'good practice' guidelines in this area of practice, these are by no means undisputed. We have shown that although the evolution of approaches to perpetrator work has largely reached a consensus of what should be done, the evidence that this approach works better than others, or that it suits all perpetrators, is still uncertain. We have shown that the evidence that such interventions make women and children safer is rather more clear. We have also established that perpetrator work within the UK is becoming more and more connected to a coordinated community response to domestic violence. But we have also highlighted that controversy remains 'part of the territory' in perpetrator work. As programmes for perpetrators expand both within and outside the criminal justice system, it therefore becomes more crucial that research continues to assess the most effective approaches with different groups of men.

Acknowledgements

The authors are grateful for permission from the Domestic Abuse Intervention Project 202 East Superior Street, Duluth, Minnestota 55802 (http://www.duluth-model.org) to reproduce the Power and Control and Equality Wheels.

Discussion questions

1 What are the causes of domestic violence and how are the various theories about these causes translated into proposals to reduce it?
2 What kind of approach to working with abusive men is most supported by the criminal justice agencies?
3 How can work with men who perpetrate domestic violence be more fully integrated into a coordinated community response?

Further reading

Featherstone, B., Rivett, M. and Scourfield, J. (2007) *Working with Men in Health and Social Care*. London: Sage. An excellent summary to orientate practitioners to working with men generally and with abusive men in particular.

Gondolf, E. (2002) *Batterer Intervention Systems*. Thousand Oaks, CA: Sage. The best summary of effectiveness evidence for perpetrator programmes.

Hanmer, J. and Itzin, C. (2000) *Home Truths about Domestic Violence*. London: Routledge. A thorough review of the coordinated community response in the UK.

Jukes, A. (1999) *Men Who Batter Women*. London: Routledge. A book that approaches work with perpetrators from a therapeutic perspective.

Pence, E. and Paymar, M. (1993) *Education Groups for Men Who Batter*. New York: Springer. The original and best source for the 'Duluth' programme: a feminist cognitive-behavioural approach to work with perpetrators.

Taylor-Browne, J. (ed.) (2001) *What Works in Reducing Domestic Violence?* London: Whiting & Birch. Another thorough review of the use of various intervention strategies for reducing domestic violence.

References

Adams, D. (2000) 'The Emerge program', in J. Hanmer and C. Itzin (eds), *Home Truths about Domestic Violence*. London: Routledge, pp. 323–39.

Babcock, J. and La Taillade, J. (2000) 'Evaluating interventions for men who batter', in J. Vincent and E. Jouriles (eds), *Domestic Violence: Guidelines for Research Informed Practice*. London: Jessica Kingsley.

Babcock, J., Green, C. and Robie, C. (2004) 'Does batterers' treatment work? A meta-analytic review of domestic violence treatment', *Clinical Psychology Review*, 23: 1023–53.

Burton, S. and Kitzinger, J. (with Kelly, L. and Regan, L.) (1998) *Young People's Attitudes towards Violence, Sex and Relationships*. Edinburgh: Zero Tolerance.

Burton, S., Regan, L. and Kelly, L. (1998) *Supporting Women and Challenging Men*. Bristol: Policy Press.

Buzawa, E. and Buzawa., C. (2003) *Domestic Violence: The Criminal Justice Response*, 3rd edn. Thousand Oaks, CA: Sage.

Cluey, E. (2005) 'Effective supervision of domestic violence cases', *Probation Journal*, 52: 190–1.

Cook, D., Burton, M. and Robinson, A. (2004) *Enhancing Safety and Justice: The Role of Specialist Domestic Violence Courts in England and Wales*. Paper to the British Society of Criminology Conference, University of Portsmouth, 6–9 July.

Dobash, R. and Dobash, P. (1979) *Violence against Wives*. London: Paramount.

Dobash, R., Dobash, P., Cavanagh, K. and Lewis, R. (2000) *Changing Violent Men*. London: Sage.

Dutton, D. (1995) *The Batterer: A Psychological Profile*. New York: Basic Books.

Dutton, D. and Sonkin, D. (2003) 'Perspectives on the treatment of intimate violence', in D. Dutton and D. Sonkin (eds), *Intimate Violence: Contemporary Treatment Innovations*. New York: Haworth Press.

Featherstone, B., Rivett, M. and Scourfield, J. (2007) *Working with Men in Health and Social Care*. London: Sage.

Friere, P. (1972) *Pedagogy of the Oppressed*. Harmondsworth: Penguin.

Gadd, D. (2004) 'Evidence led or policy led evidence? Cognitive-behavioural programmes for men who are violent towards women', *Criminal Justice*, 4: 173–97.

Garfield, S. (2006) 'Minding the Gap: The Therapeutic Alliance in Domestic Abuse Intervention Groups'. Unpublished PhD thesis, UCL.

Geffner, R. and Rosenbaum, A. (2001) 'Domestic violence offenders: treatment and intervention standards', in R. Geffner and A. Rosenbaum (eds), *Domestic Violence Offenders: Current Interventions, Research, and Implications for Policies and Standards*. New York: Haworth Press.

Gelles, R. (2001) 'Standards for men who batter? Not yet', in R. Geffner and A. Rosenbaum (eds), *Domestic Violence Offenders: Current Interventions, Research, and Implications for Policies and Standards*. New York: Haworth Press.

Gondolf, E. (2002) *Batterer Intervention Systems*. Thousand Oaks, CA: Sage.

Gondolf, E. and Russell, D. (1986) 'The case against anger control treatment programs for batterers', *Response*, 9: 2–5.

Hanmer, J. and Griffiths, S. (2000) 'Policing repeated domestic violence by men', in J. Hanmer and C. Itzin (eds), *Home Truths about Domestic Violence*. London: Routledge, pp. 323–39.

Hearn, J. and Whitehead, A. (2006) 'Collateral damage: men's "domestic" violence to women seen through men's relations with men', *Probation Journal*, 53 (1): 38–56.

Hester, M. and Westmorland, N. (2004) *Tackling Domestic Violence: Effective Interventions and Approaches*, Home Office Research Study No. 290. London: Home Office.

Home Office (1999) *Living Without Fear*. London: Cabinet Office.

Home Office (2004) *Domestic Violence and Crime and Disorder Reduction Partnerships: Findings from a Self-Completion Questionnaire*. Online report at: http:/www.homeoffice.gov.uk/rds/pdfsolr5604.pdf.

Jenkins, A. (1990) *Invitations to Responsibility*. Adelaide: Dulwich Centre.

Karan, A., Keilitz, S. and Denard, S. (1999) 'Domestic violence courts: what are they and how should we manage them?', *Juvenile and Family Court Journal*, 71: 75–86.

Kaufman, M., Kantor, G. and Strauss, M. (1990) 'Response of victims and the police to assaults on wives', in M. Strauss and R. Gelles (eds), *Physical Violence in American Families: Risk Factors and Adaptations to Violence in 8,145 Families*. New Brunswick, NJ: Transaction Books, pp. 473–86.

LaViolette, A. (2001) 'Batterers' treatment: observations from the trenches', in R. Geffner and A. Rosenbaum (eds), *Domestic Violence Offenders: Current Interventions, Research, and Implications for Policies and Standards*. New York: Haworth Press.

Lee, M., Sebold, J. and Uken, A. (2003) *Solution Focused Treatment of Domestic Violence Offenders*. New York: Oxford University Press.

McKie, L. (2005) *Families, Violence and Social Change*. Maidenhead: Open University Press.

Madoc-Jones, I. (2005) 'Research and reports: tackling domestic violence', *Probation Journal*, 53: 442–3.

Mankowski, E., Haaken, J. and Silvergleid, C. (2002) 'Collateral damage: an analysis of the achievements and unintended consequences of batterer intervention programs and discourse', *Journal of Family Violence*, 17: 167–84.

Mooney, J. (2000) 'Revealing the hidden figure of domestic violence', in J. Hanmer and C. Itzin (eds), *Home Truths about Domestic Violence*. London: Routledge, pp. 24–43.

Mullender, A. (1997) *Rethinking Domestic Violence: The Social Work and Probation Response*. London: Routledge.

Murphy, C. and Eckhardt, C. (2005) *Treating the Abusive Partner*. New York: Guilford Press.

Pease, B. (1997) *Men and Sexual Politics*. Adelaide: Dulwich Centre Publications.

Pease, B. (2000) *Recreating Men: Postmodern Masculinity Politics*. London: Sage.

Pease, R., Pringle, K. *et al.* (eds) (2001) *A Man's World: Changing Men's Practices in a Globalised World*. London: Zed, pp. 21–37.

Pence, E. and Paymar, M. (1993) *Education Groups for Men Who Batter*. New York: Springer.

Probation Service (2006) *Integrated Domestic Abuse Programme Manual*. London: Home Office.

Rees, A. and Rivett, M. (2005) '"Let a hundred flowers bloom, let a hundred schools of thought contend": towards a variety in programmes for perpetrators of domestic violence', *Probation Journal*, 52: 277–88.

Respect (2004) *Statement of Principles and Minimum Standards of Practice for Domestic Violence Perpetrator Programmes and Associated Women's Services*. London: Respect.

Rivett, M. (2006) 'Editorial: treatment for perpetrators of domestic violence: controversy in policy and practice', *Criminal Behaviour and Mental Health*, 16: 205–10.

Rivett, M. and Rees, A. (2004) 'Dancing on a razor's edge: systemic group work with batterers', *Journal of Family Therapy*, 26: 142–62.

Robinson, A. (2004) *Domestic Violence MARACs for Very High Victims in Cardiff: A Process and Outcome Evaluation*. School of Social Sciences, Cardiff University.

Robinson, A. (2005) *The Cardiff Women's Safety Unit: Understanding the Costs and Consequences of Domestic Violence*. Cardiff: Cardiff University.

Robinson, A. (2006) '"Reducing repeat victimisation among high-risk victims of domestic violence": the benefits of a coordinated community response in Cardiff, Wales', *Violence against Women*, 12 (8): 761–88.

Robinson, A. and Cook, D. (2006) 'Understanding victim retraction in cases of domestic violence: specialist courts, government policy, and victim-centred justice', *Contemporary Justice Review*, 9: 189–213.

Rosenbaum, A. and Leisring, P. (2001) 'Group intervention programmes for batterers', in R. Geffner and A. Rosenbaum (eds), *Domestic Violence Offenders: Current Interventions, Research, and Implications for Policies and Standards*. New York: Haworth Press.

Sacks, E. (2002) *Creating a Domestic Violence Court: Guidelines and Best Practice*. London: Family Violence Prevention Fund.

Shepard, M. and Pence, E. (1999) *Co-ordinating Community Responses to Domestic Violence: Lessons from Duluth and Beyond*. Thousand Oaks: Sage.

Stoltenberg, J. (1990) *Refusing to Be a Man*. New York: Meridian.

Stoltenberg, J. (1993) *The End of Manhood*. London: UCL Press.

UNICEF (2000) *Domestic Violence against Women and Girls*, Innocenti Digest No. 6. Florence: UNICEF.

Walby, S. (2004) *The Cost of Domestic Violence*. London: Women and Equality Unit.

Walby, S. and Allen, J. (2004) *Domestic Violence, Sexual Assault and Stalking: Findings from the British Crime Survey*, Home Office Research Study No. 276. London: Home Office.

Wolf-Light, P. (2006) 'Duluth Program: examined and amended', *Respect Newsletter*, Spring, pp. 3–15.

Women's Aid Federation (2006) *Women's Aid Response to: Overarching Principles: Domestic Violence – Consultation Guideline*. Available online at: http://www.womensaid.org.uk.

Part 4

Values

Chapter 20

'Values talk' in the criminal justice system

Elizabeth Lancaster

Introduction

Values discussions can be notoriously complex and concepts difficult to grasp. The aim of this chapter therefore is to offer a simple introduction to 'values talk' in the criminal justice system and begins by investigating the 'values' statements made by different organisations within the criminal justice system as a way of grounding the discussion in the precise guidance given to practitioners in various organisations. An interpretation of this material is offered by adapting a framework of analysis from the social work literature which suggests that there are three levels at which discussion of values occurs. This framework is not context-specific and is a useful aid for understanding the different levels at which 'values' discussions take place in the criminal justice system.

This framework highlights the need to include broader social theory discourses in any discussion of values and to think beyond the confines of the behaviour between worker and service user. However careful a worker may be about exploring, developing and incorporating their personal/professional/organisational value base into their daily practice, there is an overall criminal justice context which influences, both explicitly and implicitly, the way these employees are able to practise. In conclusion I suggest that a more holistic approach to 'values talk' in the criminal justice system would benefit practitioners and that the different levels of 'values talk' are recognised and openly explored.

Values in the criminal justice system – who says what

When reviewing statements made about values by the various elements which make up the criminal justice system one discovers a fair amount of semantic confusion which can mislead the unwary practitioner seeking guidance for their practice. The confusion arises because the label 'values' is attached to a range of statements, extending from those covering how practitioners work on an individual or collective basis, through to what appear to be organisational aims and objectives. Can 'we treat everyone with respect' and 'we deliver for the public' (http://www.homeoffice.gov.uk/about-us/purpose-and-aims) really both be called values?

A general dictionary definition of values is, for example: *'values-* (in pl.) moral principles, standards, etc.' (Kirkpatrick 1983). A social science definition is more expansive: 'Relatively general cultural prescriptions of what is right, moral and desirable. Values provide the broad foundations for specific normative regulation of social interaction' (http://www.britac.ac.uk/portal). Both these definitions imply that values can be rather large ideas, something general, abstract or even universal – a belief in justice, for example, or equality. These general prescriptions do not in themselves offer much guidance about how they are translated into practice. This guidance is often found in the form of rules of behaviour; such rules are properly termed 'ethics'. Thus values are 'abstract and general notions of what is good and bad' and ethics are regular practices supported by 'conceptions of normatively required action' (Clark 2000: 37). Values summarise abstract ideas, ethics are more concerned with practical application and often find some expression in professional codes of conduct.

In exploring the statements made about values in the various elements of the criminal justice system I will make reference to the following organisations: the Home Office, Skills for Justice, the National Offender Management Service and the police. The intention here is to review the guidance given about what is 'right, moral and desirable'. These organisations are the key statutory organisations of the criminal justice system and the documents have been chosen after an Internet search of the relevant sites. These appear to be the only accessible 'values' or 'principles' statements issued by these organisations. Moreover, none of them include the word 'ethics' or a derivative of it, even though some of the statements could easily be described as rules of behaviour and thus more properly called ethics. The police force does have a separate Code of Professional Standards which offers guidance as to how its values may be represented in practice (http://www.homeoffice.gov.uk/about-us/haveyoursay/). The full text of each values statement is contained in an appendix to this chapter; key passages are reproduced below.

The Home Office provides a succinct statement:

The values we developed in consultation with our staff and stakeholders underpin how we will achieve our objectives and guide our behaviour:

- we deliver for the public;
- we are professional and innovative;
- we work openly and collaboratively;
- we treat everyone with respect. (http://www.homeoffice.gov.uk/about us/purpose-and-aims)

Skills for Justice, which has overarching responsibility to make sure that all those who work in the justice sector have the right skills for the job, lists the following in a document entitled *Total Equality Scheme*:

Our values

- Demonstrating integrity
- Living diversity
- Actively working with others
- Striving for excellence
- Communicating effectively. (http://www.skillsforjustice.com/websitefiles/Total_Equality_Scheme.pdf)

Each heading is followed by a brief paragraph of expansion (see appendix).

The National Offender Management Service does not provide a single statement; rather the two elements of this structure, the National Probation Service (NPS) and the Prison Service, refer to their separate statements of values. The NPS relies on a statement drawn up some years ago:

Valuing NPS staff and partnership colleagues – seeing them as the organisation's greatest asset.
Victim awareness and empathy are central.
Law enforcement, taking positive steps to ensure compliance but, where this fails, acting swiftly to instigate breach or recall proceedings.
Rehabilitation of offenders, working positively to achieve their restoration.
Empiricism, basing all offender and victim practice on the evidence of 'What Works' – also applying the same principles to the design and reconstruction of the Service.
Continuous improvement, always pursuing excellence.
Openness and transparency in all aspects of service delivery and in the internal workings of the NPS.
Responding and learning to work positively with difference in order to value and achieve diversity.
Problem solving as a way of resolving conflict and 'doing business'.
Partnership, using a highly collaborative approach to add value to the capacity of the NPS to achieve its expected outcomes.
Better Quality Services so that the public receive effective services at the best price.

(National Probation Service 2001: 8)

The Prison Service in its Statement of Purpose includes under the heading 'Our Principles':

In carrying out our work we:

- Work in close partnership with our commissioners and others in the Criminal Justice System to achieve common objectives
- Obtain best value form the resources available using research to ensure effective correctional practice
- Promote diversity, equality of opportunity and combat unlawful discrimination, and
- Ensure our staff have the right leadership, organisation, support and preparation to carry out their work effectively.

(Prison Service 2008)

The *Common Values for the Police Service of England and Wales: A Message from the Home Secretary* issued in 2007 states under the heading 'Values' (other headings being 'Your Mission', 'Accountability', 'Serving locally, protecting nationally', 'Continuous improvement'):

Every police officer and member of police staff must be animated by the sense of service to the public and policing must always be rooted in our shared, core values. As Home Secretary I will expect the service to show: fairness and impartiality, integrity, freedom from corruption, respect for liberty and compassion. It must be free from racism, serve all communities equally, and be committed to our individual protection and our common well-being.

This listing above is perhaps a little tedious. However, it illustrates the point that values statements, or statements of principles, in reality do include rather general and abstract statements relating not only to how workers might relate to offenders, colleagues and other professionals, but also broadly to what the organisation's aims and objectives might be.

Leaving to one side for the moment further comment on the range of issues addressed under the heading values or principles, I want to pause to consider the similarities and differences in the above statements. All these organisations generally make strong statements around three themes in their values statements: relationships with service users and others; the way the organisation conducts itself in broad terms; and relationships with other organisations. For simplicity, referencing of these statements is to the extracts contained in the appendix to this chapter: (A) refers to the Home Office, (B) Skills for Justice, (C) Probation, (D) Prison Service and (E) the Police Force.

The first theme concerns relationships with service users and others: 'we treat everyone with respect' (A); 'living diversity' (B); 'Responding and learning to work positively with difference in order to value and achieve diversity' (C); 'Promote diversity, equality of opportunity and combat unlawful discrimination' (D). The Home Secretary wanted a police service which is 'Trusted and respected everywhere' (E). Respect, equality and diversity are key words in any attempt to describe the development of the discussion around worker–client relationships over the last four decades, and this vocabulary is much more recognisable as the language of values than words such as 'excellence' (B, C), or 'transparency' (C), for example. Formerly, much of the discussion around values in the criminal justice system was contained within the discussion of generic social work values, and there is a hefty literature on this subject (see Banks, 2001, for a summary). The distinctiveness of values in the criminal justice system, and specifically the probation context, has been continuously debated, with Nellis a key figure in proposing a separate set of values for the probation context (Nellis 1995; Nellis and Gelsthorpe 2003). Recently Gelsthorpe has discussed the possibilities of human rights providing the value base for the Probation Service (Gelsthorpe 2007).

Politically, a line was drawn across this connection with social work by the removal of probation training from social work training in 1995. Furthermore in my experience new entrants to the Probation Service, while finding some echoes for their own practice within what they perceive to be social work values (though these, of course, are also subject to discussion, development and revision) nevertheless view their practice context to be sufficiently removed from social work to require its own set of values.

It is intriguing, therefore, to observe the longevity of the word 'respect', as within the academic literature referred to above this is viewed as a 'traditional' social work value. The Home Office and the police both use the word; Skills for Justice in its statement 'Vision, Mission and Behaviours' includes 'Treat others with respect and kindness' as one of ten 'common behaviours' (http://www.skillsforjustice.com/template01.asp?PageID=105). The NPS statement of values avoids the word, and I would suggest this is intentional as a way of countering any suggestion that the organisation could not quite divorce itself from its social work past. Indeed, the statement makes use of the word 'value' on a couple of occasions (e.g. 'valuing NPS staff') where 'respect' might have conveyed more meaning. However, respect, in spite of the Probation Service's coyness, persists as a value within the broader criminal justice system and I will make more comment below on the longevity of this traditional social work concept.

The second theme identified in the values statements refers to the way the specific organisation conducts itself. Thus 'we deliver for the public', 'we are professional and innovative' (A); 'demonstrating integrity' and 'striving for excellence' (B); 'continuous improvement always pursuing excellence', 'Openness and transparency in all aspects of service delivery and in the internal workings of the NPS', 'Better Quality Services so that the public receive effective services at the best price' (C); 'Obtain best values from the resources available' (D); 'serve all communities equally' and 'Accountable and public facing' (E). These statements say very little about the context of the criminal justice system and could be taken from the 'vision' or 'mission statement' of any number of public sector organisations. A reason for this is that this vocabulary is a reflection of the managerialist agenda of both the Conservative and New Labour governments of the 1980s and 1990s. Both governments sought a reorganisation of the public sector by such strategies as increasing accountability, developing consistency in service delivery, target setting, performance indicators, offering 'value for money' and increasing the centralisation of policy-making (Nellis and Gelsthorpe 2003: 238–9; Beaumont 1995: 47–70). The criminal justice system is simply one structure among many in this scenario.

The third theme is relationships with other organisations, and these are invariably described in partnership terms: 'we work openly and collaboratively' (A); 'Actively working with others' (B); ' Valuing NPS staff and partnership colleagues – seeing them as the organisation's greatest asset', 'Partnership, using a highly collaborative approach to add value to the capacity of the NPS to achieve its expected outcomes' (C); 'work in close partnership with our commissioners and others in the Criminal Justice System to achieve common objectives' (D); 'Collaborative, working in partnership with other forces and authorities and with other partners' (E). The emphasis on partnership has been a key development in the criminal justice sector since the Criminal Justice Act 1991 and while the meaning of the term partnership is open to some interpretation, the context above suggests an understanding of partnership as 'system efficiency' (Rumgay 2003: 201), a means of replacing fragmentation with some kind of system integration.

Finally, probation statements make reference to the rehabilitation of offenders, law enforcement and breach, and victim awareness as values when working with all service users. The Home Secretary's statement in 'Drawing on these core values', looks to 'the delivery of neighbourhood policing'. These are specifically about the working context of probation staff and the police and reflect the view that the practice content is important when considering what values should guide practitioners.

A framework for understanding 'values talk'

The above section has scrutinised the statements made by key organisations in the criminal justice system. From this it can be seen that there is a similarity of approach and of language when discussing values. Some of this appears at odds with the original definition of values as general principles and clearly drifts into the specifics of organisational comportment. Some sense can be made of this by adopting the view that values can operate at several levels. Dalrymple and Burke, for example, draw a distinction between ultimate values, intermediate values and instrumental values, i.e. abstract values, values which are more explicit to a desired end state and values as modes of conduct (which might more correctly be termed ethics). This is promising as a starting point, but this framework is not then sufficiently interrogated to make it meaningful in practice (Dalrymple and Burke 1995: 41). Nellis and Gelsthorpe refer to 'primary and secondary (derivative) values' without expansion (Nellis and Gelsthorpe 2003). Within the literature on social work values, Stephen Shardlow (2002) offers a framework for understanding the scope of 'values talk' and I would suggest that this can readily, and fruitfully, be transposed to the criminal justice area.

Shardlow offers three interpretations of the scope of values discussions, a 'restricted description', a 'mid-range description' and a 'broad definition'. The 'restricted description' focuses on workers' behaviour with clients. The 'mid-range description' would add (to paraphrase for the criminal justice context) the nature of criminal justice intervention as a professional activity, the function of the criminal justice system in society, the interface between criminal justice and the law, the characteristics of criminal justice organisations and their influence on the behaviour of individual workers. The 'broad definition' could further add the construction of criminal justice intervention as a social activity, the relationship of criminal justice to religious belief systems and the nature and form of knowledge in the criminal justice context (Shardlow 2002: 31).

The narrow interpretation of values – the focus on the worker–client relationship – is easy to trace in the community justice context. Criminal justice organisations all refer to relationships with service users and as already noted some are not embarrassed about using the vocabulary of 'respect'. This focus on the worker–client relationship tends to place the responsibility for delivering 'respect' – or whatever else is deemed 'right, moral and desirable' on the actual practitioner (see Cole, this volume for a discussion of this in relation to assessment tools and ethnicity).

Shardlow's mid-range interpretation of values – the nature of criminal justice intervention as a professional activity, the characteristics of criminal justice organisations – can be found in texts on values from the 1990s (Williams 1995; Vass 1996). In the statements from criminal justice organisations given above, the second and third themes – the way the organisation conducts itself and relationships with other organisations suggest a mid-range interpretation of values. It is also possible to determine from the statements some implicit comment about other 'mid-range' activities: the function of the criminal justice system in society and the nature of criminal justice intervention. Thus the shift towards public protection noted above is reflected in the value 'Paramountcy of public protection particularly where there are specific, known victims of violent and sexually violent crimes' (C). The nature of criminal justice intervention can be found in 'Rehabilitation of offenders, working positively to achieve their restoration' (C). Both of these values are from the National Probation Service's list; nothing relating to this mid-range level of discussion is found in the specific values statements of other organisations. However, the Home Office and the Prison Service, in addition to their 'values', both offer a list of 'objectives' intended to 'protect the public', and make it clear that this is a central function of the criminal justice system (A, D).

The broad definition of values – the construction of criminal justice intervention as a social activity, the relationship of criminal justice to religious belief systems and the nature and form of knowledge in the criminal justice context – is the most difficult to discern in the material above. Both the NPS and the Prison Service make reference to empiricism or research, and while this touches upon the nature of knowledge in the criminal justice context there is no particular debate about this knowledge. Indeed the probation statement takes for granted the centrality of the 'What Works' literature in shaping interventions with offenders. Comment and interpretation of this broader context can be found in the wider academic literature on penal practice, and this will be discussed in more detail below.

In summary, in applying this explanatory framework of three levels of discussion about values to the statements offered by the statutory criminal justice agencies, some of the statements which on first reading appear as organisational aims, on closer consideration help us understand something of what the organisation believes its role to be – a mid-range understanding of the scope of 'values talk'. I would not, however, wish to appear too charitable in my interpretation of the chosen values statements: some of these are clearly little more than organisational rhetoric and their translation into something tangible to guide workers in their practice is not an easy task. The Home Office's assertion that 'we deliver for the public' serves to illustrate this, and the Probation Service's 'Continuous improvement, always pursuing excellence' is little better.

A little theory

Turning now to comment upon the theoretical influences on these values statements there are three strands I want to consider: Kantian influences, utilitarian tendencies and anti-oppressive practice debates. The values statements above contain plenty of comment about worker–client relationships. In theoretical terms much of the discussion about individual worker–client relationships is inextricably bound up with Kantian ethics. Kantian ethics are sometimes known as deontology or theory of duty, and the key principles are: the importance of the individual as a rational, self-determining being; that an individual is worthy of respect and is uniquely valuable, even if they behave in a morally unacceptable way; the importance of following one's duty, for example telling the truth, even if this is likely to have a bad outcome (Clark 2000: 71–2). In summary, a Kantian approach tends to emphasise the individual, a worker–client relationship based on 'respect' and the 'rightness' of an action as distinct from its outcome. The Home Office and the police still use the word 'respect', while the Prison Service, in a statement headed 'Race and Diversity', refers to 'the wider decency agenda' (http://www.hmprisonservice.gov. uk/abouttheservice/raceanddiversity/) and in the Statement of Purpose to treating prisoners 'decently' (D). While a full definition of this concept is missing, the context suggests it bears more than a passing similarity to 'respect'.

Critiques of Kantian values bases suggest that the individual focus of this approach does not take sufficient account of structural issues which influence a person's life chances and choices. However, I think this is an unnecessary limitation of how to interpret and apply 'respect' in a twenty-first century context. The critique of individuality is more to do with the individualistic focus of criminal justice/social work intervention at the time the word became prominent in debates about the nature of the worker–client relationship in the 1960s rather than with the concept itself. I will return to this point later.

The major shift in the orientation of criminal justice intervention since the early 1990s has been the move away from a Kantian approach which focuses on intervention with an individual offender within a rehabilitative ethos, to a much more broadly based conception of protecting the public in which the idea of individual rights is overshadowed by the more pressing imperative of the public good. This echoes a key utilitarian principle that the right action is the one which produces the greatest balance of good over evil (the principle of utility) (Clark 2000: 72–3). Traces of a utilitarian approach to criminal justice can be found in the statements made by the key criminal justice organisations, for example: 'we deliver for the public' (A); and 'Paramountcy of public protection particularly where there are specific, known victims of violent and sexually violent crimes' (C).

However, Hudson observes of utilitarianism that it 'does not offer adequate protection of each individual citizen against encroachments in the name of the good of society as a whole, or of the majority'. In the criminal justice context this means that 'the rights of offenders to proportionate punishment cannot be guaranteed against the good of crime prevention in the wider society' (Hudson 2003, xi). The shift from proportionate punishment, i.e. what an offender has done in the past, to punishment based on the risk of what someone may do in the future is commented upon elsewhere in this volume (see contributions by Nash and Philips in Part 2 of this volume). Here it is sufficient to note the shift in focus from the offender to the public and the introduction of a utilitarian strand to the values of the criminal justice system.

A third element warrants comment and that is the influence on values statements of the anti-oppressive practice debates which emerged in the 1970s, as without exception the values statements of the various criminal justice agencies include words such as diversity and equality (though not usually oppression or anti-oppressive).

Briefly put, anti-oppressive debates helped identify issues of class, race and gender as key determinants in the characteristics of offenders. Strictly speaking debates around class emerged in the 1970s, with debates about 'radical' practice taking place in advance of the focus on race and gender which generated the broader anti-oppressive approach. The intention was to place individuals in their social context and give proper regard to societal structures that restricted the choices and the life opportunities of individuals. Such structures caused groups of people to be discriminated against on the basis of particular characteristics they held in common. Awareness of discrimination was extended to other 'categories' of people, particularly in regard to sexuality, disability and age, though the dominant themes in the criminal justice system were race and gender. It was a commonplace then for values statements in the probation and social work arena to include reference to societal oppression and call for practice to be anti-oppressive (for example, CCETSW 1991).

Turning to current values statements in the criminal justice system, all organisations use the moderate language of equality, diversity and discrimination rather than the more structurally focused language of oppression or anti-oppression. This is done in generalist terms, thus: 'Living diversity. We will value everyone for their contribution and actions, irrespective of personal differences, and promote inclusiveness and equal access to opportunities, challenging any form of discrimination' (B), and 'Promote diversity, equality of opportunity and combat unlawful discrimination' (D).

However, none of these texts make an explicit reference to structural issues forming the backdrop to how individuals should be treated in a face-to-face context and I return to this below.

The big picture

It is at this point that we should consider in more detail the third level of discussion about values – the broad definition – which considers the nature of criminal justice intervention as a social activity. Not surprisingly, there is no explicit comment in these values statements about this. Instead, we need to look elsewhere, to the broader discourses around penality and the values implicit in these.

Discussion of trends in penality clearly forms a substantial body of literature and it falls outside the remit of this chapter to explore this in detail. However, Nellis has helpfully outlined three 'distinct and competing' discourses in this literature: 'punitive-repressive', 'surveillant-managerial' and 'humanistic-rehabilitative' (Nellis 2005: 44). These are briefly summarised to help interpret the 'big picture' of 'values talk' in the criminal justice system.

The first of these discourses, punitive-repressive, tends to have 'no belief that offenders are reformable, merely that they can be frightened (deterred) into law-abidingness or have their spirits broken, in or out of prison'. The second, surveillant-managerial, 'focuses primarily on the assessment and amelioration of certain pre-specified risks, mirroring the "actuarialism" of the insurance industry'. The third, humanistic-rehabilitative, offers 'a belief that criminality can be educated or counselled out of individual offenders, especially if certain kinds of practical help with employment, accommodation, addiction and family relationships are also offered' (Nellis 2005: 44–6). Nellis argues that current criminal justice policy follows a surveillant-managerial course, with a backdrop of rhetoric about society's approach to criminal behaviour which uses the language of the 'punitive-repressive' discourse. His conclusion, therefore, is that humanistic values – rehabilitation, belief in change, restorative justice, citizenship, human rights – are overshadowed by the retributive and regulatory approaches which are apparent in contemporary policy and practice.

This is a persuasive argument for the context of criminal justice practice in western and English speaking countries, and the introduction of policy and practice within a managerial-surveillant discourse has consequences for practitioners with humanistic values. Nellis suggests that in the Probation Service many such practitioners have switched allegiance to this managerial-surveillant discourse believing this to be the only effective challenge to the encroachments of 'populist punitivism' of the punitive-repressive discourse. In my own experience, probation officers of a certain age and professional history of practice within the humanistic tradition have taken early retirement rather than accommodate their practice to the changing probation ethos.

The retention of respect

Mission and vision statements, objectives and purpose, principles and values, discourses on penality: Shardlow's framework suggests a way in which these can all be recognised as 'values talk'. Thus a value such as 'respect' is not competing with a value such as 'rehabilitation' or 'restorative justice' but rather refers to a different level of interpretation of what we understand as values. Debating respect is not to deny or disregard these broader discourses. Rather there is an overarching context of how we construct criminal justice intervention as a social activity within which we form the nature of criminal justice intervention and the function of the criminal justice system within which practitioners relate to individuals: 'values talk' has a legitimacy at all these levels.

In the review of values statements above it could be seen that all criminal justice organisations are trying to communicate something about the nature of the worker–client relationship, whether the language is of equality, respect or decency. The form of expression used tries to embody something about being non-judgmental – perhaps even that good Kantian principle of accepting the person while not condoning the behaviour – and I would argue for the retention of 'respect' as the shorthand for encapsulating the nature of the worker–client relationship. Some readers may find this anachronistic, or think that the word suggests an association with social work which is now incompatible, though 'respect' clearly has a resonance with the statutory agencies quoted above. Moreover, victims of crime referred to in the chapter by Williams and Goodman elsewhere in this volume state that they wish to be treated with respect, practitioners are enjoined to treat offenders with respect and be 'respectful' (Tallant *et al.*, this volume), and respecting each other forms a basic rule of conduct for group members in accredited programmes (Feasey, this volume). 'Respect' even has a place in the street vernacular of showing 'nuff respect' and of not 'dissing' anyone. Finally it is the chosen word for the government's initiative around anti-social behaviour, the Respect Action Plan, which aims 'to build a modern culture of respect', with 40 Respect Areas chosen, and possibly the ultimate twenty-first century accolade, a web address – http://www.respect.gov.uk.

There is clearly a risk in all this of the word being used carelessly. In the criminal justice context I offer the following guidance: respect is not an antiquated concept, for as the historical and practice context changes the knowledge base which underpins what we understand by 'respect' changes and develops. Thus 'respect' in the twenty-first century is underpinned by an awareness of the social context of offenders in a way that 'respect' in the 1960s was not. The importance of anti-oppressive debates of the 1970s to the early 1990s was to uncover knowledge and develop awareness of the different treatment of particular groups in society. While this analysis ground to a halt under the weight of an increasing number of 'isms' (racism, sexism, disablism, ageism), and has been replaced by a gentler sounding critique around diversity and difference, awareness of structural issues does not simply evaporate. Practitioners and educators do not stop knowing what they know about oppression and anti-oppressive practice. Police officers, prison officers, probation officers, substance misuse counsellors, all have more awareness of these structural issues than their counterparts of 40 years ago. Treating offenders (or clients) with 'respect' is informed by an awareness of the structural as well as the individual factors which lead to offending. 'Respect' conveys something about the quality of the relationship between offender and criminal justice worker and in a context where so much of this relationship is recorded in quantitative terms – was the interview conducted within a given time frame, was the offender seen the 'right' number of times – we need something to remind us about the quality of worker client relationships, not least because of the importance of these relationships in the outcome effects of accredited programmes in the probation context (McGuire 2005: 274–5).

Conclusion

This chapter has examined the values statements of several organisations in the criminal justice system as the starting point for a discussion of 'values talk'. Strong statements around three themes were identified: relationships with service users, the way the organisation conducts itself in broad terms and relationships with other organisations. While some of these statements may appear more like organisational aims rather than 'values' in the general sense of the word, one way of making sense of these statements as 'values' is to adopt a framework proposed by Shardlow in the social work context. The scope of 'values talk' can be narrow, or a mid-range definition applied, or a broad definition, addressing among other issues the worker–client relationship, organisational aims and the nature of criminal justice intervention as a social activity. The explicit statements made by criminal justice agencies about values fall within Shardlow's narrow and mid-range definitions. However, the values implicit in penal discourses form part of the broader definition offered above.

There is an extent to which 'values talk' in or about the criminal justice system has focused either on worker–client relationships or on the larger themes of penal discourse. However, these different interpretations of values are not competing, they are different levels of discussion about the same issue and paying attention to one area should not be seen as dismissing or avoiding the concerns of the other level of discussion. A holistic understanding of 'values talk' in the criminal justice system would help integrate these levels and uncover areas for consideration. For example: does a focus on the worker–client relationship divert practitioners' attention from the big picture of trends in penality? If practitioners are encouraged to view anti-oppressive/anti-discriminatory/'respectful' practice as their individual responsibility do they then fail to recognise the organisational constraints that limit their ability to practice in this way? Is a demonstration of respect within an organisational aim of public protection different to a demonstration of respect within the aim of rehabilitation? Consideration of how different levels of 'values talk' can be integrated may enable the development of a value base for the criminal justice system which encompasses both practice and context.

Discussion questions

1 How useful as a guide to practice is the values statement of your particular organisation?
2 How does awareness of the 'big picture' discourses affect daily practice in the criminal justice system?
3 Does the term 'respect' have any validity when working with offenders in the criminal justice system of the twenty-first century?

Further reading

Nellis, M. (2005) 'Dim prospects: humanistic values and the fate of community justice', in J. Winstone and F. Pakes (eds), *Community Justice: Issues for Probation and Criminal Justice*. Cullompton: Willan. This is an excellent discussion of the trends in penality and of the competing discourses in the literature.

Shardlow, S. (2002) 'Values, ethics and social work', in R. Adams, L. Dominelli and M. Payne (eds) *Social Work: Themes, Issues and Critical Debates*. Basingstoke: Palgrave. This chapter provides the framework for part of the discussion above.

Appendix

The full text of statements relating to values made by key organisations in the criminal justice sector cannot be reproduced here for copyright reasons. However, extracts of the most relevant sections are given below.

(A) Home Office

Our values

The values we developed in consultation with our staff and stakeholders underpin how we will achieve our objectives, and guide our everyday behaviour:

- we deliver for the public
- we are professional and innovative
- we work openly and collaboratively
- we treat everyone with respect.

(http://www.homeoffice.gov.uk/about-us/purpose-and-aims

(B) Skills for Justice

Total Equality Scheme – Managing Inclusion

Our values

- **Demonstrating integrity**
  We will conduct our business in a consistent, open and transparent manner and use our time, money and resources wisely. We will do what we say we are going to do, when we say we are going to do it.

- **Living diversity**
  We will value everyone for their contribution and actions, irrespective of personal differences, and promote inclusiveness and equal access to opportunities, challenging any form of discrimination.

- **Actively working with others**
  We will each understand how our individual contribution helps the organisation meet its aims and actively work in collaboration with others to achieve these aims. We will strive to build a world-class team in which every member feels valued and supported.

- **Striving for excellence**
  We will continually review the way we work in order to deliver the highest quality performance in everything we do. We will consult,

encourage feedback and aim to provide services that meet or exceed the levels that are expected of us.

- **Communicating effectively**
  We will listen to the values and opinions of others and be aware that people have different levels of knowledge relating to our work. We will aim to communicate in a way that is understandable and meaningful to everyone. We will recognise that effective and timely communication is integral to becoming the successful organisation we want to be.

(http://www.skillsforjustice.com/websitefiles/
Total_Equality_Scheme.pdf

(C) Probation Service

At the time of writing, nothing has superseded the statement contained in the five-year strategy document entitled *A New Choreography* (NPS 2001):

A New Choreography

Valuing NPS staff and partnership colleagues – seeing them as the organisation's greatest asset.

Victim awareness and empathy are central.

Law enforcement, taking positive steps to ensure compliance but, where this fails, acting swiftly to instigate breach or recall proceedings.

Rehabilitation of offenders, working positively to achieve their restoration.

Empiricism, basing all offender and victim practice on the evidence of 'What Works' – also applying the same principles to the design and reconstruction of the Service.

Continuous improvement, always pursuing excellence.

Openness and transparency in all aspects of service delivery and in the internal workings of the NPS.

Responding and learning to work positively with difference in order to value and achieve diversity.

Problem solving as a way of resolving conflict and 'doing business'.

Partnership, using a highly collaborative approach to add value to the capacity of the NPS to achieve its expected outcomes.

Better Quality Services so that the public receive effective services at the best price.

(National Probation Service for England and Wales 2001: 8)

(D) Prison Service

Statement of Purpose

Her Majesty's Prison Service serves the public by keeping in custody those committed by the courts. Our duty is to look after them with humanity and help them lead
law-abiding and useful lives in custody and after release.

Our Vision

- To provide the very best prison services so that we are the provider of choice
- To work towards this vision by securing the following key objectives.

Objectives

To protect the public and provide what commissioners want to purchase by:

- Holding prisoners securely
- Reducing the risk of prisoners re-offending
- Providing safe and well-ordered establishments in which we treat prisoners humanely, decently and lawfully.

In securing these objectives we adhere to the following principles:

Our Principles

In carrying out our work we:

- Work in close partnership with our commissioners and others in the Criminal Justice System to achieve common objectives
- Obtain best value from the resources available using research to ensure effective correctional practice
- Promote diversity, equality of opportunity and combat unlawful discrimination, and
- Ensure our staff have the right leadership, organisation, support and preparation to carry out their work effectively.
                    (http://www.hmprisonservice.gov.uk/abouttheservice/
                                              statementofpurpose/

(E) Police

Common Values for the Police Service of England and Wales

Values

Every police officer and member of police staff must be animated by the sense of service to the public and policing must always be rooted in our shared, core values. As Home Secretary I will expect the service to show:

Fairness and impartiality, integrity, freedom from corruption, respect for liberty and compassion. It must be free from racism, serve all communities equally, and be committed to our individual protection and our common well-being.

Serving locally, protecting nationally

Drawing on these core values, I want a police service which is:

- **Trusted and respected everywhere: which serves locally and protects nationally.** Trust is the bedrock of policing and the police act with the consent of citizens and communities. Trust drives effective policing and, in turn, generates respect.

- **Accountable and public facing.** Many police operations will be out of the public view, but the delivery of neighbourhood policing must be driven by public need and expectations.

- **Collaborative, working in partnership with other forces and authorities and with other partners.** Jointly many things can be achieved that cannot be achieved alone. More and more, the need to work with other forces and agencies to identify and solve problems will come to the fore in order to tackle the local and national challenges we face.

The public is constantly indebted to the police for their service, which can include sacrifices and real courage. We must continue to attract dedicated and talented individuals to fulfil this mission.

(http://police.homeoffice.gov.uk/publications/
police-reform/policing-values-letter)

References

Adams, R., Dominelli, L. and Payne, M. (eds) (2002) *Social Work: Themes, Issues and Critical Debates*, 2nd edn. Basingstoke: Palgrave.

Banks, S. (2001) *Ethics and Values in Social Work*, 2nd edn. Basingstoke: Palgrave.

Beaumont, B. (1995) 'Managerialism and the Probation Service', in B. Williams (ed.), *Probation Values*. Birmingham: Venture Press, pp. 47–74.

Central Council for Education and Training in Social Work (1991) *Rules Requirements for the Diploma in Social Work*, CCETSW Paper 30, 2nd edn. London: Central Council for Education and Training in Social Work.

Chui, W.H. and Nellis, M. (eds) (2003) *Moving Probation Forward*. Harlow: Pearson Longman.

Clark, C.L. (2000) *Social Work Ethics*. Basingstoke: Macmillan.

Dalrymple, J. and Burke, B. (1995) *Anti-oppressive Practice: Social Care and the Law*. Buckingham: Open University Press.

Gelsthorpe, L. (2007) 'Probation values and human rights', in L. Gelsthorpe and R. Morgan (eds), *Handbook of Probation*. Cullompton: Willan.

Gelsthorpe, L. and Morgan, R. (eds) (2007) *Handbook of Probation*. Cullompton: Willan.

Hudson, B. (2003) *Justice in the Risk Society*. London: Sage.

Kirkpatrick, E.M. (ed.) (1983) *Chambers 20th Century Dictionary*. Edinburgh: Chambers.

McGuire, J. (2005) 'Is research working? Revisiting the research and effective practice agenda', in J. Winstone and F. Pakes (eds), *Community Justice: Issues for Probation and Criminal Justice*. Cullompton: Willan, pp. 257–82.

National Probation Service for England and Wales (2001) *A New Choreography: An Integrated Strategy for the National Probation Service for England and Wales – Strategic Framework 2001–2004*. London: Home Office.

Nellis, M. (1995) 'Probation values for the 1990s', *Howard Journal*, 34: 19–44.

Nellis, M. (2005) 'Dim prospects: humanistic values and the fate of community justice', in J. Winstone and F. Pakes (eds), *Community Justice: Issues for Probation and Criminal Justice*. Cullompton: Willan.

Nellis, M. and Gelsthorpe, L. (2003) 'Human rights and the probation values debate', in W.H. Chui and M. Nellis (eds), *Moving Probation Forward*. Harlow: Pearson Longman, pp. 227–44.

Prison Service (2008) http://www.hmprisonservice.gov.uk/abouttheservice/statementofpurpose/2008.

Rumgay, J. (2003) 'Partnerships in the probation service', in W.H. Chui and M. Nellis (eds), *Moving Probation Forward*. Harlow: Pearson Longman, pp. 195–213.

Shardlow, S. (2002) 'Values, ethics and social work', in R. Adams, L. Dominelli and M. Payne (eds), *Social Work: Themes, Issues and Critical Debates*. Basingstoke: Palgrave.

Vass, A.A. (ed.) (1996) *Social Work Competences*. London: Sage.

Williams, B. (ed.) (1995) *Probation Values*. Birmingham: Venture Press.

Winstone, J. and Pakes, F. (eds) (2005) *Community Justice: Issues for Probation and Criminal Justice*. Cullompton: Willan.

Websites

http://police.homeoffice.gov.uk/news-and-publications/publication/police-reform/policing-values

http://www.britac.ac.uk/portal

http://www.hmprisonservice.gov.uk

http://www.hmprisonservice.gov.uk/abouttheservice/raceanddiversity/

http://www.hmprisonservice.gov.uk/abouttheservice/statementofpurpose/

http://www.homeoffice.gov.uk/about-us/purpose-and-aims

http://www.homeoffice.gov.uk/documents/police-code-consultation

http://www.respect.gov.uk

http://www.skillsforjustice.com/websitefiles/Total_Equality_Scheme.pdf

http://www.skillsforjustice.com/template01.asp?PageID=105

Chapter 21

Working with female offenders

Clare Beckett

Introduction

It is unusual, in the twenty-first century, for women to be considered a minority group. The lessons of feminism over the last 150 years have reminded us that women are half the population and should be represented alongside men. This realisation has come late to criminology. Writings about women criminals were very rare before the 1960s, and the main schools of criminological thought have had, and perhaps still have, little or nothing to say about women offenders. The statistical evidence is that women are a minority within the criminal justice system. That in itself is an interesting phenomenon, but it has resulted in silence about women's particular relationship with law and order rather than in interrogation of women as a specific group. Exceptions have been those women whose 'crimes' catch the eye, like the small number of women who attack or kill husbands. Media coverage encourages us to see these women as individual wrongdoers. Silence about the location of women to offending has meant that services developed in mainstream organisations like probation do not usually address women as a category. This 'gender blind' approach can promote equality, but can also obscure particular practices that advantage or disadvantage women. Alongside mainstream services specific, usually voluntary, agencies have developed to promote and meet the needs of women.

In this chapter I intend to question ways in which women can be seen as having specific requirements from service providers, and to look at what some of those specifics might be. I begin by looking at ways in which women, and by extension women's offending, are explained in a theoretical perspective. That in itself does not help us to understand the position of women and their relationship with the criminal justice system. In the second part of this chapter I have drawn together available statistical and demographical information about women's offences and available responses. The information in those sections informs the final part of the chapter, a discussion about the institutional and personal responses made by and required from criminal justice agencies and practitioners.

'Women's needs'

Historically, men and women perform different roles in day-to-day life, and different behaviour is expected. For example, there has been huge controversy over the depiction of girls and boys in children's reading. Children's books frequently portray girls as acted upon rather than active. Girls are represented as sweet, naive, conforming and dependent, while boys are typically described as strong, adventurous, independent and capable. Often, girl characters achieve their goals because others help them, whereas boys do so because they demonstrate ingenuity and/or perseverance. There are various accounts of this process: as early as 1978 Anne Marie Wolpe discussed the ideas, while a more up-to-date and specific analysis can be found in Swann (1992). Changes in law and social requirements have meant that traditional gender divisions, where women's primary identification is in the home, have become blurred. It is no longer acceptable or fashionable to say women do different things from men without explanation. For instance, women often play as big a part in providing family income as their male partners. This social change has been accompanied by a change in how women are seen, or more accurately in how gender differences are explained. It is still not true to say that women and men as groups hold equal positions or power in society, as Sue Lees' (1996, 1997) interrogation of rape and criminal justice shows.

Assuming women have different attributes, abilities, behaviours, even 'natures' from men minimises differences between women. Not only does it obscure different abilities in individual women, it also minimises intersections of difference like race, class or ability. The policy and practice implications of this kind of global view of woman are difficult to maintain, leading as they do to questions like 'How is this woman the same as any other woman client?', or 'How can diversity be filtered by skin colour or cultural background?' However, the assumptions run deep, both in practice and theory.

Those assumptions of different attributes are connected to different ways of seeing the reasons behind gender difference. Those theoretical ways of understanding women and men have a long history, and influence thinking today. Beliefs rooted in theoretical ideas about gender difference are a very powerful force in creating the reality of policy and practice. I will start by looking at explanations based in theories of 'nature', and continue by looking at explanations based in theories of 'nurture', because historically this is the way that accounts have developed. This approach can appear more clear-cut and logical than the development of ideas has been, but it does form a coherent narrative for the purpose of interrogating the development of ideas about women and their connection to offending.

Women's nature

The idea that women are 'naturally' different from men is rooted in different physical attributes and possibly different physical roles. Difference in expectation and position becomes conflated with ideas about physical differences between men and women. Women are often (but not always, and in some geographical areas not usually) smaller and less obviously muscled than men. (For a full comparison between men and women see Nicholson 1993). The primary role that women play in conceiving and bearing babies is seen as tailoring their wishes and expectations. So, biological difference is seen as extending past physical difference to inform the way women feel or behave. Because women bear children, they are also seen to have an attribute to care for those children, and this attribute of caring becomes the defining part of 'being a woman'.

Gender difference becomes a clear two-part category, with men occupying one position and women very clearly occupying another. Some of these attributes can be traced below.

Men	Women
Strong	Weak
Dominant	Subordinate
Active	Passive

So, to be a woman is to have in your biology and therefore in your 'nature' those attributes of behaviour that belong to women.

There has been an avalanche of argument against this deterministic image of being a woman, not only in the last century. (A clear overview of the 'nature/nurture' debate can be found in Oakley (1972)). It is a difficult image to shake off, both for women and for men. Images of dependent and caring women surround us from media outlets, and being caring is a good thing to be. (Similarly, men are surrounded by images of power and dominance.) The implications are far reaching and include differentials in employment, pay and social position. It is easier for individual women to move away from these assumptions – by, for instance, refusing a passive role in their own lives, than for the category of 'woman' to lose this biological image.

It is not surprising that early criminological theorists described women as being defined by their physical and sexual make-up. As Heidensohn says, in her overview of criminologists Lombroso and Ferrero, Thomas and Pollak:

Women, in this view, are determined by their biology and their physiology. Their hormones, their reproductive role, inexorably determine their emotionality, unreliability, childishness, deviousness. (Heidensohn 1996: 112)

These attributes defined not only understanding of why women committed offences, but also what offences they committed. So, for instance, the crime of prostitution could be seen as linked to 'unwomanly' sexuality and become the crime of choice for a particular woman.

It is a weak explanation for offending in the twenty-first century. Most obviously, if women's nature renders them likely to offend through passivity or unreliability, why do such a small proportion of modern women offend? However, it is not dead. I will argue that assumptions about woman's nature inform current responses by the criminal justice system and its representatives, even if biology is no longer simply presented as a reason for offending.

Women's nurture

An alternative set of explanations for gender differences takes social and economic structures as the starting place. Women and men are seen as acting differently because they receive different lessons about what is perceived of and expected from them. This does not mean that any simple picture of teaching is used, just that men and women see and become skilled at adapting to expectations based in gender. Anne Oakley (1981) interrogates subtle ways in which baby boys and girls are welcomed, handled and talked about. Her point is that from the moment of birth children enter a gendered world, where reactions are tailored by perceptions of difference.

Feminist analysis has used the idea of learned difference to underpin critiques of social structures where gender difference becomes gender inequality. Sylvia Walby (1990), among others, identifies key social agencies in which a power difference between men and women is enshrined. In her analyses, a patriarchal society creates and reinforces gendered differences in order to maintain power. Of course, structural inequality is a reality in twenty-first century life. In 2003, 50.9 per cent of men were of working age, but only 27.6 per cent of women in the British population were in full-time employment (Payne 2006: 87). Figures for all economic indicators show a similar differential. This is not a simple picture of men holding power over women, but a more nuanced analysis where the institutions of society are seen as maintaining pre-eminence by reinforcing gendered patterns of inequality.

This analysis moves explanations of women as offenders away from a model based on individual pathology. Here, women's offences are seen as in some way a reaction to the social institutions that limit them. Offences of stealing or deception could thus be linked to institutionalised poverty or sexism. Like explanations rooted in women's nature, however, this does not begin to explain why so many women subject to the same social forces do not offend.

Feminist explanations

The growth of feminist analysis in the social sciences during the 1960s and 1970s has had a considerable influence on our understanding of women and the criminal justice system. In particular, Carol Smart's (1977) work has been axiomatic in founding new feminist research.[1] Two major contributions have been to offer a general critique of stereotypical images of women summed up in the 'nature or nurture' debate, and to identify ways in which assumptions have framed discussion of and policy towards women and criminal justice.

There has been an avalanche of comment on general stereotypical images of women from different feminist perspectives, too extensive to reference adequately here. Perhaps the most relevant work has been to introduce a stratified critique of women where gendered inequality in access to employment, wealth and property disproportionately excludes women. (There are several up-to-date presentations of gendered inequality: particularly useful are Braham and Janes 2002: ch. 3, or Payne 2006: ch. 3. An approach rooted in feminist analysis is given by Lorber 2007). While explanations for this exclusion echo explanations for gender difference in any other arena, the extent of inequality makes such assumptions seem inadequate.

The contribution of feminism to understanding the relationship between offending women and the criminal justice system has been less well documented. It is not always possible to identify where a particular idea has come from, or where general critiques have become accepted to the point where they become applied to criminal justice without specific iteration. (Heidensohn 1996, offers, an overview of feminism and criminology.) It is possible to identify three themes:

- Women and men are defined by assumptions about their role and behaviour. Assumptions affect ways in which people look, behave and react. Being 'female' or being 'male' means taking a particular place in the social world. Not taking that place leaves the individual open to being seen as a breaker of 'norms' or rules. Women are expected to be passive, non-violent and caring. Women who do not conform to these stereotypes are open to criminalisation because they break gender expectations. Therefore women who commit violent offences may be seen as criminal even if their actual offence, on some objective scale, is less serious than that of a man. A woman may be arrested for shouting when a man would not, for instance. Women's relationship with the criminal justice system is complicated by a view that women who offend against the law also offend against their stereotypical image.

- Because of images of normality, and because explanations of women's behaviour are rooted in a 'nature/nurture' debate, women who offend are seen as 'mad' or 'sad'. 'Mad' explanations pathologise women who offend in some way – she must have been 'crazy' to behave like that. 'Sad' explanations assume that women offend because of economic exclusion or because of personal inability.

• Assumptions about gender and stereotypical behaviour affect offenders, practitioners and judges alike.

The combination of these three themes contributes to any understanding of women and the criminal justice system, both in theory and in practice. As you can see in the following section, they inform interrogation of women's offences and punishments.

Who are 'offending women' and what are their offences?

The Home Office has been required to collect and publish statistics on women since 1991, under the provisions of s. 95 of the Criminal Justice Act 1991. Unless otherwise stated, all figures used in this section are drawn from *Statistics on Women and the Criminal Justice System* (Home Office 2003).

One obvious statistic is that proportionately fewer women than men offend. In 2002, only 19 per cent of known offenders were women, and this proportion has held true for most of the twentieth century. It is not clear why this should be so. Home Office research (Home Office 2004b) has investigated similarities and differences in risk factors for offending (measured by convictions) for brothers and sisters in a longitudinal study. In that study, 44 per cent of brothers had convictions for criminal offences, compared to only 12 per cent of sisters. In general, the most important risk factors to indicate early onset (before 17 years of age) offending were similar for brothers and sisters and included low family income, high delinquency rates among peers and offending among other family members. The study indicates that different parenting methods may influence boys or girls to offend, but does not draw clear conclusions.

There are differences in age between male and female 'known offenders'. Both groups seem to grow out of petty crime, but the peak age of offending for girls is reported as 15, while for boys it is 19. This is slightly different from the ages identified in Home Office Findings 196, which shows sisters offending between 19.9 years and 24.3 years, while brothers' major offences are committed between 18.5 and 25.1 years. The difference may be related to differences in conditions between the 1970s, where research on brothers and sisters was undertaken, and findings from 2003. It may also reflect growth in the numbers of women in the population during the relevant periods: in 2006, there are around 1.8 million more women aged 14–59 in the population than were counted in the 1970s. The percentage of these women aged between 10 and 14 has fallen, while those aged between 15 and 20, or those most usually represented in criminal justice figures, has risen. This proportionate rise reflects social trends during the last twenty years. However, the conflict in the figures has not yet been researched or explained, adding to the gaps in our knowledge of women offenders.

It could be that women commit different crimes from men. Home Office Findings 196 seems to support this, with the following comparisons between offences:

- Burglary comprised 20 per cent of brothers' offences but only 6 per cent of sisters' offences.
- Theft of vehicles comprised 13 per cent of brothers' offences but only 4 per cent of sisters' offences.
- Shoplifting comprised 28 per cent of sisters' offences but only 6 per cent of brothers' offences.
- Deception comprised 27 per cent of sisters' offences, and 12 per cent of brothers'.

That research also indicates that brothers committed more offences than sisters.

Perhaps women are sentenced differently from men for similar crimes. Figures for 2002 show that women are more likely than men to be discharged or given a community sentence for indictable offences and are less likely to be fined or sentenced to custody. Women sentenced to custody receive shorter sentences on average than men. In 2002, women accounted for 14 per cent of those starting orders under supervision by the Probation Service. The most common community sentence for women was a community rehabilitation order, while for men it was a community punishment order. (These orders were replaced by provisions made under the Criminal Justice Act 2003.) 'Theft and handling' was the most common offence for women given a community sentence whereas for men summary offences were most common.

There is a great deal of information available for those women sentenced to custody. Between 2001 and 2002 the percentage of women in custody increased by 15 per cent, while the percentage of men in custody increased by only 6 per cent. This increase is not explained by increases of women in the general population. Above average increases can be seen for burglary (up 49 per cent), robbery (up 24 per cent), and offences of violence against the person (up 21 per cent). There were reductions in the female sentenced population for fraud and forgery (down 6 per cent). The increase in drugs offences of 17 per cent was similar to the overall increase in the female sentenced population (15 per cent), but this does not necessarily mean that one increase explains another. Indeed, only 439 women were imprisoned for 'production, supply and possession with intent to supply a class A controlled drug' in 2002.

There are other anomalies between women and men in prison, both in terms of the general population and of specific ways of relating to custody. Predictably perhaps, women prisoners are less likely than the general population to be in a stable relationship but more likely to have child-care responsibilities, and an estimated 20 per cent of women in prison have experienced some time in care. In contrast to the small numbers of women imprisoned for drug offences, 47 per cent of women reported using crack cocaine and 57 per cent heroin in the year before coming to prison, compared to 28 per cent and 35 percent in males respectively. In *Between Ourselves – Prison Governors* (BBC 4, 9.30 p.m., 8 August 2006) a prison governess estimated that 70–80 per cent of women admitted to prison needed a detoxification programme on entry. Drug use may be connected to the fact that female prisoners have a higher rate of offending against prison discipline than men. Also, however, 15 per cent of women had been committed to mental hospital at some time previously. Educational attainment of women in prison is significantly lower than that of the general population but is slightly higher than that of male prisoners. It is not surprising that a 2001 resettlement survey revealed that only 18 per cent of women had employment or a training course arranged for their release compared with 30 per cent of adult males. While women committed to prison reflect a small proportion of women offenders within the criminal justice system, courts have been using custody more frequently for women over the last few years even though the nature and seriousness of their offending has not, on the whole, been getting worse. For example, magistrates' courts used custody three times more frequently for women in 2002 compared to 1994. The evidence suggests that courts are imposing more severe sentences on women for less serious offences. There has also been an increase in women serving longer sentences for drug importation and so we have seen a sharp rise in the number of female foreign nationals in prison – 20 per cent of the female prison population are foreign nationals and 68 per cent of these are sentenced to four years or more (including life).

Women are also represented in alternatives to custody. Women offenders starting community sentences or pre- or post-release supervision by the Probation Service in 2002 numbered 23,400. They accounted for 14 per cent of all persons starting such supervision. The proportion of female offenders starting a community punishment order (CPO) has risen steadily from 6 per cent in 1992 to 12 per cent in 2002. There is a similar trend in the proportion of females starting community punishment and rehabilitation orders (CPRO) (10 per cent in 2002). For community rehabilitation orders (CRO) the figure rose gradually between 1993 and 2000, but stabilised at around 21 per cent in each of the years 2001 and 2002. Female offenders on community sentences are more likely to receive a CRO than any other type of order (60 per cent receive CROs, 30 per cent CPOs and 8 per cent CPROs in 2002) whereas male offenders are more likely to receive a CPO (43 per cent). (Again, these orders have been replaced under the provisions of the Criminal Justice Act 2003.)

Responses to women offending

The above statistics do not show a clear picture of women as a category with specific offences and specific needs, but there is some evidence that there are differences between men and women in the type of offence committed. Certainly the figures above would support Frances Heidensohn's (1989) view that overall women commit less serious offences than men. Sandra Walklate (2001: 5) agrees that women are represented in every category of offence, but looks more closely at some categories. She points out that in more serious crimes and in particular offences of violence and murder women are underrepresented:

> If we take a look at the more serious crimes we find, for example, that in the case of murder, the sex crime ratio is at its most clearly defined. Murder is predominantly a male activity. Men constitute the majority of the perpetrators and the majority of the victims of murder. (Walklate 2001: 5)

She then argues that, where women do commit the offence of murder, their motivation tends to be connected to violent relationships with a male partner. In this paradigm, women are presented as committing fewer offences, committing different offences and having different motivations for offences.

It is difficult to carry this picture of women as a specific category of offender into an investigation of sentencing policy. Arguments that women are treated either more leniently or more harshly than men in the criminal justice system are found in academic texts and in popular representations of women who offend. Frances Heidensohn (2000) summarises research into sentencing, and argues that there is evidence to support both standpoints. The arguments here echo the three themes identified previously, where the way in which women's behaviour is theorised affects ways in which behaviour is judged and sentenced.

It is easy to see how both poles of this argument can be linked to images of women's 'nature' or their 'nurture'. In this way, explanations of women's offending are linked to stereotypes of behaviour that fit images of a category 'woman'. These assumptions can also be seen in policy responses, and possibly in personal responses to offending women. Perhaps they can be summed up by saying that women offenders are seen as mad, or bad, or sad, and that their offending is then seen as coming from one of those three categories. This picture could be demonstrated by thinking of, for example, Myra Hindley portrayed as 'mad', a survivor of domestic abuse as 'sad', or a prostitute as 'bad'.

The policy response

Gender is at the forefront of current government policy. The Equality Act 2006 creates a duty on public authorities to promote equality of opportunity between women and men and prohibits sex discrimination and harassment in the exercise of public functions. In 2007, this duty was reinforced by the creation of a Commission for Equality. However, there are only two specific mentions of women offenders in the 2005–6 National Probation Service business plan, both concerned with providing suitable premises for women in custody. The Department for Constitutional Affairs Strategy 2004–2009 does not mention women offenders (or offenders at all, for that matter). It does, however, support an increase in the appointment of women to the judicial benches.

Silence on any foreseeable issues about the relationship between women and criminal justice does not reflect the active engagement with women in other areas. Gender equality is an open and discussed issue in education or employment, and women's rights to equal treatment have been enshrined in law since the Equal Pay Act 1970 and the Sex Discrimination Act 1975. It is easy to make this issue humorous by stating the obvious – that women should have an equal right to offend. The evidence in this chapter indicates that women's relationship to offending is different from men's. Therefore commitment to supporting diversity would argue at least a discussion of the needs of women in the criminal justice system. That this has not yet begun can be illustrated by the most common risk assessment tool, OASys. The research and development process of this tool revolved around male, white offenders.

Silence about diversity is particularly loud when the focus of investigation is widened to include changes in law and policy that are not specifically directed at women. For instance, the government's commitment to parenting orders is an initiative designed to support the family and citizenship. A parent/carer who receives a parenting order will be required to attend counselling or guidance sessions. They may also have conditions imposed on them such as attending their child's school, ensuring their child does not visit a particular place unsupervised or ensuring their child is at home at particular times. A failure to fulfil the conditions can be treated as a criminal offence and the parent/carer can be prosecuted. Given the relative numbers of male and female single parents it is more than likely that more women than men will be subject to potential criminalisation through breach of these orders. The Sexual Offences Act 2003 extended the definition of prostitution to include male prostitutes, but it is an offence for someone who is a common prostitute to solicit or loiter in a public place for the purposes of prostitution. The penalty is a £500 fine for the first offence, and £1,000 for further offences (Street Offences Act 1959, s.1 Before this offence applies, it is necessary to prove that the individual is a common prostitute, that is regularly operates as a prostitute. This is done by administering two or more cautions for prostitution. This brief administrative process provides an opportunity to give an individual details of available appropriate support. It is highly likely that the process will be used to identify more women, whose pattern of prostitution is to be available on the street, than men, whose sexual activity is more likely to take place in clubs or other enclosed spaces.

Current government policy about women offenders is inconsistent. Some facets are positive. For instance, in 2004 the Home Office published an action plan intended to link efforts across agencies to reduce women's offending (Home Office 2004a). In 2004 the Treasury promised funds to pilot radical new initiatives for this group (HM Treasury 2004). This was followed through by the announcement in March 2005 of two new pilot community centres as alternatives to custody for women offenders. Concern over treatment of women in prison has resulted in two new privately run prisons for women opening, in June 2004 and March 2005, and in the dismantling of the Prison Service's separate line management for women's prisons. The *women's prison population rose by more than 400 between January and July 2005.*

The Criminal Justice Act 2003 revised systems of punishing offenders. Since April 2005 there has been a single, generic community order with a range of requirements available to sentencers. The changes are intended to make transparent community measures to reduce offending. The policy intention is to make a visible statement of intent about the purpose of non-custodial sentences. Stress on control, rehabilitation, education and reparation are all designed to allay public fears that non-custodial sentences are lenient. The legislation assumes that requirements will be delivered without reference to gender. This gender-blind approach has meant that the evidence of women's different needs and offending patterns has not been included in the policy debate. At the time of writing statistical evidence has not been made available, but it is likely that the new powers will affect women and men differently. For instance, 'unpaid work' orders may be disproportionately difficult for women to meet because of their differential position in the workforce. Specified activities may be less useful to women, with their slightly higher average level of educational attainment. The position of women on training programmes to change behaviour may be difficult. More importantly perhaps, current probation programmes have been developed around a model of white heterosexual masculinity. This may not be adequate when addressing women.

Some custodial sentences have also changed. In part, this is a response to rising prison populations coupled with rising public fear of crime. Of these, perhaps the most hopeful for women is the introduction of 'a new sentence of intermittent custody, which will help some offenders to stay in employment while serving their sentence' (Blunkett 2004). Trialled at Moreton Hall women's prison during 2005, intermittent custody allows an offender to serve their 'prison time' non-consecutively. For instance, if a woman offender had childcare available at weekends she would be able to serve her prison time then. Of course, this initiative is most useful to women as carers. It does not address other issues of women's offending. As I complete this chapter, this initiative has been discontinued.

Other custodial initiatives in the 2003 Act are designed to allay public fears about the risk offenders present. The focus is on offenders serving long sentences or imprisoned for violent or sexual offences. Women form a very small part of this constituency of offender. The anticipated outcome of the extension and transparency of community sentences and the focus on long-term prison sentences is to increase the use of community orders to enhance flexibility and commitment to rehabilitation. Custody should be reserved for the dangerous, persistent and more serious offenders. Shifting low-level offenders away from custody has been an underlying aim of probation, sometimes more explicitly than at others.

In sum, current criminal justice policy appears to be following a 'gender blind' path, where commitment to supporting equality and providing for diversity is not carried through into positive action for women offenders. Stress on family policies has a considerable effect on women but these effects are not acknowledged, perhaps ironically because for many years women have argued against the limitations of recognition only through their caring role. Stress on reduction of risk in sentencing policy disguises the extent of women's offending because women are seldom clearly and obviously a risk to the general public through violent or sexual offences. Particularly, the spectrum of drug-related offences that has swelled the prison population of ethnic minority women is not a current policy issue in the same way as, for instance, returning asylum seekers is a priority. However, policy that clearly delineates between offences carrying a custodial sentence and offences carrying a community sentence on the basis of seriousness does benefit women. Since the majority of female offenders commit crimes of petty theft or deception, they will benefit from non-custodial treatment.

The individual response

Regardless of policy intention, women's experience of the criminal justice system will be tailored by the individuals whom she sees as representing her sentence and supervision. Here, every reaction made to an individual woman will be shaped by the practice and assumptions of individuals. For instance, under the 2003 Act, judges and magistrates are able to choose which requirements to add to a community order, depending on the seriousness of the offence and the potential risk of harm the offender poses. While good practice does give guidelines for both seriousness and risk, interpretation is subjective. Subjective judgments may reflect stereotypical images of women. Perhaps reactions to women through sentencing can reflect a 'demonised' or a 'pathologised' paradigm: demonised, in the sense introduced by Heidensohn (1989), that women who offend are not only offending against the law but also against their gender 'norm'; pathologised in the sense that women who offend must be sick or mentally ill. A risk assessment process will usually be carried out before sentencing and a report prepared for the judge by the Probation Service. Probation service personnel may also have a subjective view of women, and this may be evident in risk assessment. While tools, like OASys or OGRS (Offender Group Reconviction Score) are designed to help avoid individual reaction, they are created to represent a majority population and arguably reflect an image of a male and white offender.

The Probation Service publishes three objectives for gender equality (NPS 2003):

1 To ensure that NPS policy and strategy is compatible with the aims and objectives of the Home Office.
2 To promote greater use of community sentences for women where they are appropriate.
3 To promote effective service delivery to women offenders.

All these aims will work towards more women becoming subject to supervision within the criminal justice system. Effective supervision and requirements for equal treatment mean that practice and practitioners will be expected to take into account women offenders. The question in the last part of this chapter is to what extent women should be treated or managed in ways that reflect gendered difference.

Conclusion – 'managing' women offenders

Managing women offenders relies on institutional and individual practices interweaving and supporting each other. Institutions are able to include policies and practices that enable women, carried out by individual practitioners. I have concentrated on three key areas where understanding 'women' may inform practice.

The first and arguably most axiomatic of these is directly linked to ideas about what a 'woman' is. Ideas about gendered behaviour can lead to disproportionate reaction when those ideas are breached. In this way, a woman with a violent offence, or one who does not look, dress or behave as expected, may receive inappropriate supervision.

Autobiographical accounts and some feminist writers explore the ways in which 'womanly' behaviour is policed and 'unwomanly' behaviour is punished. (Examples showing the development of these ideas include Sharpe 1976; Brownmiller 1984; Weitz 1998.) On the other hand, it may be easy for an officer to relate to and choose appropriate methods for a person who they feel able to relate to: an offender who behaves like 'one of the girls' or in a recognisably feminine way. (Officers who themselves feel uncomfortable with gendered behaviours, and have other ways of expressing themselves, may also find themselves misunderstood by offenders and by colleagues.) To use an example from my own practice, an offender with a very good chance of gaining a privilege was refused this by a tribunal. When I asked why, the tribunal chair told me, 'She swore at us – no self-respecting woman swears.' While this example may seem extreme, it is a concrete example of more subtle difficulties caused by ideas of gendered difference and happened within the last ten years.

The most obvious example of gendered assumptions is the idea that catering for women is always linked to provision for children. Often, the timing or geography or actual arrangement of interventions for women is based upon their needs as primary carers for children (and of the elderly and disabled, though this is less common and less obvious). It would clearly be inappropriate to make provision for women that did not recognise this need. However, meeting this need alone is insufficient. It is self-evident that not all women have children, and that children are not the universal leveller between diverse women. Assuming that a childless and economically active woman would be better served in a group of women with children, than in a group of men may be inappropriate. However, it may be difficult for her to be accepted into the male group. It could be equally inappropriate to assume that women from different religious, class or cultural backgrounds will use and benefit from provision that is set up primarily to meet the need for childcare. This is not to reiterate the usual mantra that all offenders are different and should be treated according to their needs: it is to point out that simply organising around children does not in itself answer any question about supervising women.

This is not to ignore the second of these principles: that supervision of women also involves recognising their specific location within the social order. This recognition goes further than the observation that women are more often excluded from economic activity by virtue of their gender and are more often responsible for children than are men. Women are more often subject to violence in their everyday lives; they are less able to travel alone or at specific times of day or to specific places; they may have absorbed or react to messages about appropriate behaviour, including passivity and shyness. Cultural and kinship networks can make some actions and behaviours, inoffensive in themselves, impossible for women. All of these factors should inform the organisation and provision of supervision and intervention with women offenders. Sylvia Walby's (1990) argument that social institutions uphold patriarchy is a useful tool for understanding potential influences on the ways in which women comply with or resist supervision. Again, this analysis has implications for personal behaviour. It is difficult for offenders and practitioners to detach themselves from institutional forms of power. So, the relationship between offender and supervisor, and supervisor and colleagues, will reflect gendered expectations of role. Gendered expectations of role include expectations of power, but are mediated by other diversities like class, colour or age. Expectations of role, in a largely heterosexual society, include some interplay of sexualised behaviour. Again drawing on my practice, a detective inspector of the police explained that it was much easier for him to establish compliance from junior women officers if he employed a friendly approach and used a small amount of 'banter'. Both he and his colleagues were comfortable with his behaviour, and I would stress that there was no question of complaint against him. Yet, in his eyes and in mine as observer, the interchanges relied on an expectation of 'men' and 'women' that included the possibility of sexual attraction. I would argue that many relationships follow this model and rely on this method of relating. This interchange, in its turn, relies on gendered expectations of role and of power. However, it works – perhaps because it is an expected and familiar pattern. Awareness of the potential to relate in this way will help to minimise problems caused by overstressing gendered division.

Thirdly, I would argue that supervision and intervention for women offenders should always attempt to enable women to make choices and take power within their own particular environment. Traditional stereotypes of women minimise their ability to take action for themselves, and stress dependency and compliance. While I do not advocate non-compliance, passivity may encourage women to continue harmful or offending behaviour. Women officers can be role models to demonstrate independent and 'strong' female behaviour: male officers should be aware of the potential for gendered behaviours to recreate power differentials.

Finally, in this chapter I have described the background to traditional views and stereotypes of women. I have interrogated and described both the actual pattern of women's offending and ways in which the criminal justice system uses traditional reactions to work with women differentially to men. I have considered particular principles for work with women. I would also like to point out that ways of intervening successfully with women have not been researched and established. The current tools for offender management have been developed within a generic 'gender blind' model. Until we have overall investigation into the specific requirements of women – a 'what works' with female offenders – good intervention will rely to a large extent on individual officers and services, and good practice will remain isolated and unknown.

Acknowledgements

I would like to thank Cris Dewey for the original outline from which this chapter was drawn, and Elizabeth Wrighton for helpful comments and up-to-date practice information.

Questions for discussion

1 Why do women offend?
2 How could different ideas about 'women' change how women's needs are seen?
3 How could the criminal justice system begin to meet women's needs?

Further reading

Heimer, K. and Kruttschnitt, C. (2006) *Gender and Crime: Patterns of Victimization and Offending*. New York: New York University Press. Continues the arguments in the chapter about types of women's offences.

Lombroso, C. and Ferrero, G. (2004) *Criminal Woman, the Prostitute, and the Normal Woman*, trans. and with a new intro. N.H. Rafter and M. Gibson. Durham, NC: Duke University Press. Gives a detailed analysis of 'nature' arguments for women's offending.

Morash, M. (2006) *Understanding Gender, Crime, and Justice*. London: Sage. A comprehensive and detailed overview of theoretical concepts.

Sheehan, R., McIvor, G. and Trotter, C. (2007) *What Works with Women Offenders*. Cullompton: Willan. An updating of current practice to include recent research about women.

Note

1 Here, feminism is used in the sense suggested by Frances Heidensohn (1996: 145) as:
   * intending to make women visible;
   * on, by and for women;
   * employing 'non-sexist' methodologies.
   * research should be useful to the women's movement.

References

Blunkett, D. (2004) *Reducing Crime, Changing Lives: The Governments' Plans for Transforming the Management of Offenders*. London: Home Office.

Braham, P. and Janes, L. (2002) *Social Differences and Divisions*. Oxford: Blackwell and the Open University.

Brown, J. and Heidensohn, F. (2000) *Gender and Policing: Comparative Perspectives*. Basingstoke: Macmillan.

Browne, A. (1987) *When Battered Women Kill*. New York: Macmillan.

Brownmiller, S. (1984) *Femininity*. London: Hamish Hamilton.

Department of Constitutional Affairs (2004) *Delivering Justice, Rights and Democracy: DCA Strategy 2004–2009*. London: DCA. Available at: http://www.dca.gov.uk/dept/strategy/index.htm.

Heidensohn, F. (1989) *Crime and Society*. Basingstoke: Macmillan Education.

Heidensohn, F. (1996) *Women and Crime*, 2nd edn. London: Macmillan.

Heidensohn, F. (2000) *Sexual Politics and Social Control*. Milton Keynes: Open University Press.

HM Treasury (2004) *Spending Review: New Public Spending Plans 2005–2008*. London: Treasury.

Home Office (2003) *Statistics on Women and the Criminal Justice System: A Home Office publication under Section 95 of the Criminal Justice Act 1991*. London: Home Office. Available at: http://www.homeoffice.gov.uk/rds/pdfs2/s95women03.pdf.

Home Office (2004a) *Women's Offending Reduction Programme Action Plan*. London: Home Office.

Home Office (2004b) *Gender Differences in Risk Factors for Offending*, Home Office Research Findings 196. London: Home Office Research, Development and Statistics Directorate. Available at: http://www.homeoffice.gov.uk/rds/pdfs2/r196.pdf.

Lees, S. (1996) *Carnal Knowledge: Rape on Trial*. London: Hamish Hamilton.

Lees, S. (1997) *Ruling Passions: Sexual Violence, Reputation and the Law*. Buckingham: Open University Press.

Lorber, J. (2005) *Gender Inequality: Feminist Theories and Politics*, 3rd edn. Los Angeles: Roxbury.

Lorber, J. (2007) *Gender Inequality: Feminist Theories and Politics*. Oxford: Oxford University Press.

Nicholson, J. (1993) *Men and Women, How Different Are They?*, 2nd edn. Oxford: Oxford University Press.

National Probation Service (2003) *The Heart of the Dance: A Diversity Strategy for the National Probation Service for England and Wales 2002–2006*. London: Home Office.

National Probation Service (2005) *National Probation Service for England and Wales Business Plan 2005–6*. London: National Probation Directorate. Available at: http://www.probation2000.com/documents/NPD_Businessplan0506.pdf.

Oakley, A. (1972) *Sex, Gender and Society*. London: Maurice Temple Smith.

Oakley, A. (1981) *Subject Women*. London and New York: Fontana/Pantheon.

Payne, G. (2006) *Social Divisions*, 2nd edn. Basingstoke: Palgrave Macmillan.

Sharpe, S. (1976) *'Just Like a Girl' : How Girls Learn to Be Women*. Harmondsworth: Penguin.

Smart, C. (1977) *Women, Crime and Criminology – A Feminist Critique*. London: Routledge & Kegan Paul.

Swann, J. (1992) *Girls, Boys, and Language*. Oxford: Blackwell.

Walby, S. (1990) *Theorising Patriarchy*. Oxford: Basil Blackwell.

Walklate, S. (2001) *Gender, Crime and Criminal Justice*. Cullompton: Willan.

Weitz, R. (1998) *The Politics of Women's Bodies: Sexuality, Appearance, and Behaviour*. New York and Oxford: Oxford University Press.

Wolpe, A.-M. (1978) *Some Processes in Sexist Education*. London: Women's Research and Resources Centre Publications.

Chapter 22

Working with ethnic diversity

Bankole Cole

Introduction

Available research evidence indicates that minority ethnic people in the UK are disproportionately represented in the crime figures and are more likely to be treated less favourably than their white counterparts in the criminal justice system. The evidence suggests that criminal justice decisions are sometimes influenced by racist stereotypes and prejudice (see Cook and Hudson 1993; Bowling and Phillips 2002). In addition, there is now a growing concern about discriminatory practice and unfair treatment of minority ethnic offenders post-sentence, for example in prisons, young offender institutions or while on community punishments (see, for example, Calverley *et al.* 2004).

This chapter considers how ethnic diversity is addressed in offender management. It will examine what evidence there is of a true understanding of 'race' issues in the current approaches to the assessment of criminogenic risks and needs. The chapter also explores whether the current approaches to working with minority ethnic offenders truly address the causes of black and minority ethnic offenders' offending behaviour. Discussions in the chapter will be centred on the following issues:

- the capacity of assessment tools to predict the criminogenic risks and needs of offenders from minority ethnic backgrounds;
- how well work with minority ethnic offenders is tailored to meet the needs and circumstances of minority ethnic offenders;
- the competence of practitioners working with offenders from minority ethnic backgrounds;
- the limitations of offender programmes in addressing the offending behaviour of minority ethnic offenders.

Since the Macpherson Report (1999) and the publication of the Race Relations Amendments Act 2000 there has been a considerable political move in the UK to address diversity issues in criminal justice. Current

New Labour criminal justice policies highlight the need for transparency and accountability in criminal justice in order to ensure that discriminatory practices are eliminated in the delivery of services to minority ethnic people. Examples include the introduction of effective monitoring through impact assessment of criminal justice activities and the setting up of public service agreement (PSA) targets on race in the criminal justice system (see, for example, Criminal Justice System 2005; National Probation Service 2003; HM Prison Service 2006). In addition, training in ethnic diversity has been introduced for criminal justice practitioners and it is expected that lessons learnt from such training are translated into effective practice.

This chapter argues that whereas significant changes are, indeed, taking place within the criminal justice system to address ethnic diversity in the treatment of offenders, work with minority ethnic offenders is still largely influenced by generalised concepts of 'risk' and 'needs'. Criminal justice interventions are not yet adequately responding to 'race' issues because a fundamental factor in minority ethnic offending – racism – is yet to be fully acknowledged in the assessment of minority ethnic offenders' offending behaviour and in the work done with these offenders. Assessment tools currently used by probation and prison officers significantly ignore racism as a criminogenic risk factor for minority ethnic people. While ethnic diversity is specified as an important issue in the delivery of offender programmes and in offender management generally, there is not much clarity on how this is to be achieved. At the level of professional practice, much is left to personal development and structured professional judgment (SPJ).

Rule usage and ethnic diversity

> Rules may be followed or not, they may or may not be complete, they may or may not be exact, definition may or may not have its own logic. Parsons suggests that rules *can* be followed, and provides us with units in which rules *might* be followed, but we are without a description of the way rules *are* followed. (McHugh 1968, cited in Carlen 1976: 3)

Organisational behaviour essentially involves the use of rules. In *Magistrates Justice*, Pat Carlen (1976) demonstrated how both abstract rules (legal and administrative rules) and situational rules (rules that people apply when they want to get things done or justify an action taken in the context of the abstract rules) can be manipulated to facilitate an appearance that justice is being done. Carlen described how, in the context of the routine operation of magistrates' courts, rule-governed behaviour is shaped by the nature of the abstract rules being applied, the competence and performance of the rule users themselves and the "accounting" procedures that they invoke as they 'antecedently, situationally and ex post facto attribute normative meaning to their actions' (Carlen 1976: 5).

Criminal justice practitioners are essentially workers who define their situation and justify their actions in terms of the official abstract rules that they are meant to apply. In this chapter, I define the abstract rules as all laws, administrative guidelines, assessment tools (for example OASys) and manuals that are used in post-sentence work with offenders both in prison and in the community. Whereas the rules identify ethnic diversity as an issue in offender management, there is no research evidence of how the rules are followed in practice. Evidence suggests that much is left to knowledge gained from training and experience. 'Experience' provides 'prior' knowledge upon which future decisions are based. According to Peter McHugh in *Defining the Situation* (1968):

> The term 'prior' ... suggests that nothing much happens in the situation itself ... [The practitioner] comes to know he is in [the situation] automatically rather than having to decide he is in it, ... his prior attitudes and conceptions, his predispositions, are mechanically triggered into play. (McHugh 1968: 61)

The value of 'experience' in working with ethnic diversity is stressed in the following advice given by the Suffolk Probation Area to its staff:

> There are no easy answers ... effective practice depends on workers' ability to think for themselves, drawing on their knowledge, values, skills and experience. That is what needs to be developed if anti-racist practice is to become a reality. It can only be achieved if the thinking and values dimension is prioritised rather than taken for granted or relegated to second place ... As workers we need to acquire and maintain awareness of our own cultural biases, values, feelings and attitudes and be prepared to continually review and challenge these. We need to check ourselves for conscious and unconscious prejudice and stereotyping to ensure this does not distort our practice. We need to develop our knowledge regarding the nature and impact of racism and oppression through reading, consulting research findings and, above all, listening to the minority ethnic offenders we supervise. (Suffolk Probation Area 2002: 3–4)

This statement recognises the importance of 'race' awareness in offender management but sees this as something that is the responsibility of the individual practitioner; that is, something for personal practice. It is a position that does not question the rules being applied but points to the need for practitioners to 'account' for their actions by reference to 'knowledge', 'experience' and 'personal development'. Because the rules are accepted, probation and prison officers are more likely to look for discriminatory practice or even racism in their own actions, not in the rules that they are applying.

It is not surprising therefore that the discussion of 'race' or ethnicity in criminal justice post-sentence has focused much more on the discriminatory attitudes of prison and probation officers and how institutional practices and environments discriminate against minority ethnic offenders (for example, Muslim offenders in prison) than on the inadequacy of the rules being applied in addressing ethnic diversity issues. Whereas much literature exists on rule usage and discriminatory practice in criminal justice, from stop and search up to the point of sentence, not enough attention has been given to rule usage and 'race' issues post-sentence.

In this chapter, it is argued that the assessment tools used to determine the appropriate intervention (the abstract rules) and the interventions themselves do not fully address minority ethnic people's offending behaviour because the significant impact that 'racism' has on minority ethnic people's reoffending is yet to be fully acknowledged in these processes.

Ethnic diversity and reoffending

Working with ethnic diversity implies having a definite understanding of what offending behaviour means in terms of ethnicity or 'race'. But there is no definite definition of 'offending behaviour'. It is a 'label' that is often imposed where a person displays a pattern of offending that raises a cause for concern about his or her future conduct. It is not a term that one expects would normally be used for a first offender, however serious the offence. The label does not only define the offender's lawbreaking behaviour but also assumes that the offender is the type who will most likely be in trouble again or reoffend, if the initial causes of offending are not addressed. In other words, the label presupposes that the offending is routine, not unusual and that there are fundamental reasons for this. Underlying the definition of offending behaviour, therefore, are, presumably, assumptions or theoretical perspectives about why people are likely to reoffend. One of the main aims of offender behaviour work is to reduce the risk of reoffending. Addressing offending behaviour in relation to ethnicity, therefore, centralises the questions of whether minority ethnic people's reoffending can be explained differently compared with that of the majority white population; if this is the case, should interventions be tailored to meet this difference and, if so, how should this be done? The central question here is: in terms of general reoffending, why do minority ethnic people reoffend?

Whereas it is acknowledged that minority ethnic offending can result from disproportionate exposure to prejudice, discrimination and social exclusion compounded by their 'race' (for example, the fact that minority ethnic offenders are more likely to experience criminogenic factors such as exclusion from school, unemployment, poverty and living in crime-infested areas), the popular official response has been that so would 'anybody' who shared the same experiences (see Bradshaw *et al.* 2004). Thus discriminatory treatment in society as a result of 'race' (racism) is recognised but not fully acknowledged as a factor in minority ethnic people's offending. Minority ethnic offenders are often seen as people who share similar characteristics with most people in society who frequently offend. However, if it is accepted that the reasons for offending are often those that also trigger reoffending, then it is important to research how the common experience of racism affects minority ethnic people's reoffending.

More importantly, the question needs to be asked whether in the process of addressing the offending behaviour of minority ethnic offenders, some emphasis should be placed on the effect of racism as a criminogenic factor, in addition to other general, individual or personal reasons for reoffending, irrespective of ethnicity. The position of this chapter is that the effect of racism should be prioritised in the debate about minority ethnic people's reoffending because the risk of reoffending is high where one is confronted by racism even after the completion of a sentence (see Calverley *et al.* 2004; Cole and Wardak 2006).

Racialising criminogenic risks

Factors that can trigger reoffending are often discussed under two headings: criminogenic risk factors and criminogenic needs factors (see Philips, this volume). Criminogenic risk factors, on the one hand, are the characteristics of an offender that indicate a probability that the offender may offend again or cause future harm to others or themselves. Criminogenic risk factors are regarded as permanent, static or unlikely to change over time. Often included are: offence history, type of offence, previous convictions, age at first conviction, breaches and pattern of offending. Since the introduction of National Standards in 1992, it has become mandatory for pre-sentence reports to contain a section on criminogenic risks.[1] Criminogenic need factors, on the other hand, are the circumstances of the offender, lifestyle, personal attitudes or behaviour that increase the likelihood of reoffending. Often referred to as 'dynamic' factors, they are believed to be susceptible to change in the sense that a positive change to them could reduce the chances of reoffending. Often included are: lack of education or training, unemployment, homelessness, peer pressure, illicit drug or alcohol misuse, relationship problems, poverty, emotional well-being or mental health problems, temperament, low self-esteem and attitude to others or towards offending. But not all 'needs' are criminogenic. In their definition of the 'needs principle' Andrews and Bonta (1998) drew attention to the need to distinguish between two types of 'needs' – criminogenic and non-criminogenic needs. Criminogenic needs are attributes of an offender that are directly linked with offending and which, if addressed, decrease the probability of reoffending. Non-criminogenic needs are also attributes of an offender that are dynamic but not necessarily associated with offending; therefore addressing them may not decrease the probability of recidivism (cf. Hannah-Moffat 2005: 39). The dilemma in post-sentence intervention lies in distinguishing between the 'needs' that are directly linked to offending and therefore in need of attention and those that are not. As Aubrey and

Hough (1997: 3, cited in Hannah-Moffat 2005: 39) simply put it: 'Should a probation officer try to address an offender's poverty or poor housing if these are unrelated to the probationer's offending?' Criminogenic risks and needs are often treated as interconnected but they are assessed separately in the process of predicting reoffending.

There have been some debates over whether criminogenic risk factors are the same for all offenders, irrespective of ethnicity. In her discussion of risk assessment of Canadian aboriginal offenders, Tanya Rugge (2006) concluded that research to date indicates that the majority of criminogenic risk factors are the same for both aboriginal and non-aboriginal offenders. She added that:

> Research has also found that some of the more widely-recognized risk assessment instruments, such as the Statistical Information on Recidivism (SIR) scale ... and the Level of Service Inventory – Revised [LSI-R] ... are equally valid and predict recidivism equally well for male Aboriginal offenders, even though they were designed [and] based on a non-Aboriginal population. (Rugge 2006: i)

In addition, Rugge (2006) argued that the injustices that have been committed against many Aboriginal people and which have resulted in disadvantages (presumably also in offending) should not play a role in risk assessment. According to her, 'the goal of risk prediction is to predict not explain' (Rugge 2006: iv).

This position is counteracted by a growing body of sound arguments on the need for culturally-specific and gender-specific risk factors. Simon has argued (1987, 1988, 1994, cited in Hannah-Moffat 1999) that definitions and interpretations of what constitute 'risks' are contingent upon specific cultural, political and moral evaluations of behaviours and events. This is echoed in Baker and Simon (2002, cited in Hannah-Moffat 2005: 38) where it is argued that what is a risk differs across time and space, not according to an objective scientific process, but rather according to the logic and influence of institutions. Hannah-Moffat concluded that the concept of risk is indeed 'ambiguous, fractured and flexible' (Hannah-Moffat 1999: 71).

With regard to gender, Shaw and Hannah-Moffat (2000, 2004) have argued that risk assessment tools do undermine gender differences as they are often validated on white male adult and young offender populations. It has been argued that many of the factors that predict risk for men are invalid for women (Farr 2000, cited in Shaw and Hannah-Moffat 2000: 166). In the UK, Hedderman (2004) assessed the available evidence and concluded that programmes which focus on male criminogenic factors are unlikely to be as effective in reducing reconviction among female offenders as they are for men. Canada has recognised the need to develop 'gender-sensitive' or 'women-specific' assessment tools which adequately reflect the experiences of women and respond to the gender-specific causes of women's crimes. This is a step in the right direction in the sense that it acknowledges the fact that female offenders have a different range or types of problems that contribute to their criminal behaviour than do men (see Hannah-Moffat 1999; Shaw and Hannah-Moffat 2000). In the UK, risk assessment tools are also 'gendered' in the sense that some risk assessment tools are classified as not applicable to women. These are mainly assessment tools used for assessing sexual violence (see Risk Management Authority Scotland 2006).

No such recognition exists for ethnicity in risk assessment in the UK. As Hudson and Bramhall (2005) noted, there is a 'lack of attention to race in risk studies and to risk in race studies' (2005: 723). This is unlike other countries with similar diverse ethnic populations. For example, in Australia, research has shown that a risk assessment instrument developed specifically for indigenous offenders can be more accurate than instruments that were developed to assess the risk of general recidivism (Allan and Dawson 2004). Similarly, in Canada, it has been suggested that risk instruments should take account of the life experiences of black and minority people, for example their colonial history and experiences of racism and discrimination (see Shaw and Hannah-Moffat 2000). Anne Worrall has argued that instruments and methods developed for the 'general population' are not necessarily appropriate for all cultures and indigenous groups (see Worrall 2000). The assessment of criminogenic risk factors for minority ethnic offenders must prioritise factors that affect their offending and reoffending as a distinct offender category.

The position of this chapter is that criminogenic risk factors are not the same for all ethnic groups. Risk assessment instruments must acknowledge ethnic diversity. This means that life experiences that are peculiar to minority ethnic offenders because of their ethnicity or 'race' and known to be specifically related to their offending must be acknowledged in the assessment of their risk of reoffending. The current approach to criminogenic risk assessment is far too rigid. If a particular situation explains a behaviour then it also predicts that behaviour. The experience of racism explains and predicts minority ethnic people's offending and reoffending. In this regard it is important that the experience of racism is acknowledged as a criminogenic risk factor for minority ethnic people and included in the list of criminogenic risk factors for such offenders.

Racism as a criminogenic risk factor for minority ethnic people can be viewed at two levels: first, at the level of the fact that minority ethnic people are more likely to be at risk of being victims of racially motivated crime (see Gill and Marshall 1993; Dixon 2002, cited in Smith 2006); secondly, at the level of the fact that racism is, sadly, a static and permanent condition in the life experiences of minority ethnic people. Both arguments have implications for 'race' issues in addressing offending behaviour. On the one hand, it is relevant in terms of the 'treatment' of the racist (presumably white) offender whose racist behaviour needs challenging in the process of addressing his or her offending behaviour and, on the other, in terms of the minority ethnic offender whose chances of not reoffending are narrowed by the continuous experience of racism in the wider society, after the completion of sentence. This may not be a new argument but it needs to be emphasised. The fact that racism does not disappear after the completion of sentence means that it cannot be ignored in the understanding of minority ethnic people's risk of reoffending. In spite of this fact, racism is yet to be recognised as a variable in criminogenic risk assessment tools in the UK.

The Offender Assessment System (OASys) is the main standardised assessment tool used by probation and prison officers in the UK to assess criminogenic risks and needs of offenders (that is, the risk of reoffending). OASys is classified as a tool for general application (Risk Management Authority Scotland 2006).[2] It is scored and is also based on structured professional judgment. SPJ means that some of the decisions in OASys are based on 'the training and experience of assessors to evaluate factors being assessed' (Risk Management Authority Scotland 2006: 81).

Over a hundred sections and subsections exist in the OASys forms but not a single one relates to how the offender's own experience of racism or racial discrimination may have contributed to their offending or reoffending, despite the fact that studies in the UK have shown that the most frequent form of explanation offered to account for offending by black offenders, for example, is racism (Denney 1992: ch. 2; Calverley et al. 2004; see also Bhui 1999: 173, where the author categorised racism and discrimination among what he called the external precursors of offending). As far back as 1989, Green had raised the issue, in relation to probation service practice, of how the racist context in which the offending behaviour of Black and minority ethnic people took place is ignored in the report to the courts and in criminal justice response to their offending behaviour (cf. Gelsthorpe 2006). Because the rules do not stipulate that the ethnicity of the offender matters in the assessment of risks of re-offending, then much depends on SPJ with regard to how ethnicity is to be taken into consideration in such an assessment.

Studies on risk assessments indicate that minority ethnic offenders are, however, assessed differently. In a study of risk assessments by probation officers, Hudson and Bramhall (2005) found that pre-sentence reports on Asian offenders tended to be 'thinner'. They found that Asian offenders are more likely than their white counterparts to be recorded as reckless/ irresponsible, and more likely to deny responsibility for the offence and have mental problems (Hudson and Bramhall 2005: 729). The authors noted that 'distancing language' was used in the pre-sentence reports of Asian offenders whereas the language in the pre-sentence reports of their white counterparts revealed that a process of negotiation had taken place and a mutually accepted position reached. The fact that failure or refusal to accept responsibility for an offence may be due to the offender's belief that the offence was racially provoked was not acknowledged by the report writers. The result was that the Asian offender's offending behaviour is more likely to be linked to lifestyle and personality factors in which case they are less likely to be recommended for community supervision than their white counterparts (Hudson and Bramhall 2005: 731). Furthermore, the authors noted that while for white offenders, employment, family and associates were problems of absence, for Asian offenders, they were problems of presence (Hudson and Bramhall 2005: 731). The authors showed how the same boxes can be ticked for different reasons and how the problems associated with offending are linked to popular stereotypes. The authors concluded:

> The Asian offender's criminality is less likely than the white offender to be constituted as due to adverse circumstances, but is seen as arising from his own character: he may be less dangerous than his white counterpart, but he is certainly constructed as more blameworthy. Moreover, his family and his community are implicated in this blameworthiness. (Hudson and Bramhall 2005: 732)

The above assessments are obviously racist and they stem from the fact that much is left to SPJ in risk assessment. In a situation like this, practitioners with prejudices can satisfy themselves with impunity, knowing that their professional judgments will most likely not be questioned.

There is already an established position that assessment tools are not adequate in measuring risks. The attempt here is not simply to argue for or against risk assessments. Of that, much has already been written. The argument is that the variables upon which risk of future offending is based exclude a fundamental variable for minority ethnic offenders – the experience of racism in society. The argument in support of the current 'standardised' approach to risk assessment is that it eliminates subjectivity and reduces bias and prejudice, and that the method is apparently morally neutral and 'scientific' (see Douglas 1992). The reality proves otherwise. As Hudson and Bramhall (2005: 738) argued, risk is the contemporary language of stigma. The current approach 'places greater emphasis on individual pathology than on contextual and institutional factors in explaining events and behaviour' (Shaw and Hannah Moffat 2000: 169).

Of course, 'race' or ethnicity is not a predictor of offending behaviour but it is relevant where racism is added to the causes of offending behaviour. However, it may be argued that if racism is added to minority ethnic offenders' risk factors, it may, on the one hand, increase their risk scores. On the other hand, it may highlight the need to take ethnic diversity seriously in the planning of interventions. There is also the issue of what a risk assessment instrument for minority ethnic offenders should look like and whether a risk assessment tool developed for minority ethnic people could be used for all minority offenders, irrespective of the differences between the groups. Moreover, there are issues around whether this assessment should translate into similar intervention programmes or distinctions should be made between specific sub-groups. This chapter's position is that the acknowledgment of racism as a risk factor for minority ethnic offenders should lead to a more sympathetic attitude towards minority ethnic offending and how their offending behaviour is dealt with.

Ethnic diversity and criminogenic needs

Offender behaviour work is mainly about addressing criminogenic needs. It is therefore necessary, in the context of ethnic diversity, to ask what part the ethnicity of the offender should play in the assessment of needs. The evidence in the UK suggests that a person's ethnicity is not normally taken into consideration in needs assessment (see Calverley *et al.* 2004). In OASys, ethnicity and gender are to be regarded as factors that are not 'implicitly criminogenic' (Howard *et al.* 2006: 3). In OASys, criminogenic needs are defined, generally, in terms of the thoughts, behaviour and circumstances leading up to the offence and the offender's motivation to address their offending behaviour.

OASys is used for all offenders irrespective of ethnicity or gender. This is unlike other countries where there are specific criminogenic needs assessment tools for minority ethnic offenders. In New Zealand, for example, the Māori Culture Related Needs Assessment (MaCRNs) is an assessment tool used to assess the criminogenic needs of Māori offenders in relation to their offence. The MaCRNs is meant to identify cultural factors that may, if addressed, encourage the offender to address their criminogenic needs. The MaCRNs is the cultural component of the generic assessment tool used for all offenders who have a higher risk of reconviction and imprisonment, the Criminogenic Needs Inventory (CNI). The CNI operates on the same principle as the OASys – it is designed to identify the criminogenic (or crime-producing) needs of the offender by exploring the thoughts and behaviour leading up to the offence, and assesses the offender's motivation to address that offending behaviour. In addition, the MaCRN explores whether an obvious cultural dimension exists to the offender's criminogenic behaviour. This cultural dimension may be represented by a lack of connection with, misunderstanding about or negative perception of traditional concepts, values and beliefs. The MaCRNs assessment is aimed to better target Māori specific rehabilitation resources by identifying those Māori offenders for whom an improved understanding of Māori cultural concepts, values and beliefs may be of most benefit. It rests on the belief that understanding cultural dimensions, or cultural needs may explain the offending behaviour of some Māori and, if addressed by the right cultural intervention, may increase the offender's motivation to address their criminogenic behaviour and reduce the risk of reoffending (cf. State Services Commission, New Zealand 2005).

OASys also expects that practitioners take 'cultural' issues into consideration when assessing or working with offenders. The OASys Manual enjoins probation and prison officers to take into account cultural diversity issues that may affect the assessment when interviewing offenders, gathering and evaluating offence-related information or making a decision on placement (Home Office 2001: 22). In particular, practitioners are expected to be aware of offenders' attitudes or behaviour that may have been influenced or can be explained by culture, for example in the offending-related categories of relationships, lifestyle and associates, and emotional well-being (Home Office 2001: chs. 3 and 6). In addition, with regard to placements, the Manual asks practitioners to be aware of religious or cultural issues that may place limitations on suitability and availability for community punishment, electronic monitoring and programmes (Home Office 2001: 113). Moreover, practitioners are expected to take account of traditions within the offender's community when making an assessment (Home Office 2001: 67). But, most importantly, the Manual stated that scoring in this regard should be based on the assessor's analysis of the situation (Home Office 2001: 67).

Whereas the above OASys provisions could be taken to imply that OASys does recognise the need to consider 'cultural' factors when making decisions on criminogenic needs and placements, in reality OASys is quite vague on how this to be done. The result is that much is left, again, to SPJ and situational rules. In fact, the main bulk of OASys questions require SPJ. In a recent Home Office study of black and Asian offenders on probation, Calverley *et al.* (2004) found that black and Asian offenders with lower criminogenic needs were placed on similar orders as their white counterparts with higher criminogenic needs. Where the abstract rules are vague or unclear, discriminatory practice is encouraged.

Ethnic diversity and the delivery of offender programmes

There have been long-standing concerns about the 'relevance' of offender programmes to the offending behaviour of black and minority ethnic offenders. The debates have been around the differential delivery of services and how the 'effective practice' principle is being applied to such offenders (see Williams 2006). McGuire (2002) has argued that offender interventions should attempt to accommodate variations in ethnicity and focus on the adaptation of materials to meet the needs and cultural differences of offenders. However, in the light of the diverse nature of the minority ethnic population in the UK offender population, the question could be asked as to how much emphasis should be placed on the differences between the sub-groups? Ideally, an approach to offending behaviour that truly respects ethnic diversity cannot be seen to be relevant to one ethnic sub-group and not another.

Ethnic diversity in programme delivery is often discussed in terms of two concepts: accessibility and responsivity. Accessibility implies making sure that mainstream accredited programmes are equally accessible to minority ethnic offenders and are acceptable and effective in use with this group of offenders. Responsivity refers to the delivery of programmes or interventions in a manner that is compatible with each offender's ability, style of learning and intervention needs.

Accessibility

Accessibility implies ensuring that all offenders, irrespective of their ethnicity, should be given the choice and opportunity to access programmes or services that are suited to them. This position is emphasised in the Probation Service policy document, *A New Choreography: An Integrated Strategy for the National Probation Service for England and Wales*, as follows:

> Inclusiveness, equality and fairness ... No one should be excluded from ... our services because of gender, race, ethnicity, religious beliefs, disability or sexual orientation. (National Probation Service and Home Office Communications Directorate 2001: 2–3)

However, the selection criteria for mainstream accredited programmes are not determined by 'race', ethnicity or gender but by the criminogenic needs of offenders and their suitability for particular programmes, and programme integrity is defined in terms of how the programme is equally effective with all suitable offenders regardless of background. The 'concept' of accessibility simply implies that certain offenders are better placed in certain groups for work with them to be most effective. With regard to minority ethnic offenders, accessibility is often approached in two ways. Firstly, minority ethnic offenders are given the choice of participation in single- or mixed-'race' groups and efforts are made to ensure that staff who handle these groups are adequately trained in diversity issues or skilled in working with offenders from culturally diverse backgrounds and/or are of similar ethnic origins as the offenders themselves (see National Probation Service and HM Prison Service 2002; HMI Probation 2006; Calverley *et al.* 2004). Secondly, minority ethnic offenders are given the opportunity or choice to access programmes designed specifically for minority ethnic offenders. In a Home Office review of programmes for black and Asian offenders on probation, Powis and Walmsley (2002) identified 13 programmes that had been developed in ten probation services specifically to target black and Asian offenders, five of which were running at the time of their study, the remainder being no longer offered to offenders. Four distinct types of programme were identified:

1 Black empowerment programmes
2 Black empowerment within general offending programmes
3 Black empowerment and reintegration programmes
4 Offence-specific programmes (for example, Asian drink driving programme; Asian domestic violence programme). (Cf. Powis and Walmsley 2002: iv)

What is strategic is the revelation that even though these programmes were based on a range of theoretical models, they all used cognitive-behavioural approaches. In addition, most of them were available only to men (Powis

413

and Walmsley 2002; see also Hedderman 2004). Moreover, only a very few probation areas have these programmes although this is not a problem as offenders could attend the programmes in neighbouring probation areas. It should be noted that the Prison Service does not run offender behaviour programmes for minority ethnic offenders. All the nine offender behaviour programmes currently run by Her Majesty's Prisons are mainstream offender behaviour programmes delivered to all prisoners irrespective of ethnicity. This is a significant error considering the fact that black and minority ethnic people are more likely to be sent to prison for their crimes (Cook and Hudson 1993; Bowling and Phillips 2002; Ministry of Justice 2007).

There is still lack of clarity about how ethnicity is to be dealt with in the delivery of programmes. Durrance and Williams (2003: 211) talked about programme materials which 'might better engage Black and Asian offenders and others who may find it difficult to relate to more established problem-solving approaches'. Williams (2006) further argued, in relation to probation, that there is little that the Probation Service can do to change the social environments within which offenders live. Therefore the only way that the Probation Service can help minority ethnic offenders is to 'assist them through the exploration of self-identity and self-conceptualisation to change their views about the choices available within those environments' (Williams 2006: 149). Powis and Walmsley's review (2002) indicates some considerable support for the 'empowerment' approach to the delivery of programmes to black offenders but the central theme in the 'empowerment' approach is that:

> The individual must ... be provided with an opportunity to identify strategies for coping with events that influence his/her lifestyle but for which he/she does not have ultimate control for change. (Duff 2002: 10, cited in Williams 2006: 151)

It is doubtful whether these perceptions truly address the needs and circumstances of minority ethnic offenders. A term like 'empowerment' is politically sexy as it implies increasing strength and building confidence, but as the following observation from a Joseph Rowntree Foundation study of mentoring of disaffected young people based on an empowerment model showed, there is still some confusion about what it means in practice:

> While project staff ... talked of role models and of increasing self-esteem and of empowering young people, there was no clear sense of how the young people were expected to change. (Shiner et al. 2004: 48)

Other countries have also experimented with providing programmes that are designed specifically for minority ethnic offenders, especially those incarcerated in prisons, and with much success. In Canada, for example, there are culturally based programmes and services for Inuit and Métis offenders in correctional institutions. Culturally based programmes are programmes which are culturally responsive to or specifically targeted at the specific cultural characteristics, needs and home environment of minority ethnic offenders. Research findings in Canada indicate that such programmes are more beneficial for minority ethnic offenders in reducing reoffending than mainstream offender programmes (Trevethan *et al.* 2003, 2004; Moore *et al.* 2004). Similarly, in New Zealand, an evaluation of culturally based programmes for Māori offenders shows that 'Māori offenders who have discovered or re-connected with their culture have improved pro-social behaviour and are more motivated to address the underlying causes of their offending' (State Services Commission, New Zealand 2005: 2).

It is unclear whether this implies that programmes which 'revive' cultural values are more likely to be successful in reducing reoffending. In New Zealand, the conclusion reached was that there was insufficient evidence to show that culturally based programmes on their own were effective in changing offending behaviours. More success was achieved where culturally based programmes were used to complement proven mainstream treatment processes (State Services Commission New Zealand 2005). Moreover, in another Canadian study, Dell and Boe (2000) warned against over-emphasising the ethnicity element in the provision of services. Such an attempt assumes that similarities between individuals 'arise more from racial experience than from shared common life histories' (Dell and Boe 2000: iii). Dell and Boe continued:

> Criminological research that forefronts offender race may also need to account for individual life histories, acknowledging potential similarities across racial groupings. Individuals differ due to their racialized experiences but they also resemble one another due to common life experiences. The overall implication is that caution must be exercised in focusing research exclusively on race. With the current trend in research focusing on cultural heterogeneity, the lack of attention to similarity across racial categories may result in overlooking or minimizing elements of individual shared life histories that may contribute to understanding and identifying criminogenic factors (risk and needs). (Dell and Boe 2004: iv)

Dell and Boe (2004) are simply alerting practitioners to the need to balance both the racial and individual (general) factors in offender management. However, there is the tendency, in practice, to overemphasise the 'similarities across racial categories' and undermine the 'racialized experiences'. Dell and Boe have simply emphasised the confusion that still exists over how ethnicity diversity is to be addressed in offender management.

Responsivity

The responsivity principle refers to the delivery of offender interventions in a manner that is compatible with each offender's criminogenic needs, individual or personal characteristics, abilities and learning styles, within an environment that is conducive to effective learning (see Andrews and Bonta 1998). In other words, responsivity factors are those characteristics of an offender and the intervention environment that could either interfere with or facilitate engagement with the offender or affect the successful delivery of offender programmes. The concept is based on a recognition of the fact that offender characteristics and programme environment are important in offender management.

The responsivity principle is usually discussed under two headings: general and specific responsivity (Andrews and Hoge 1995). On the one hand, general responsivity is about 'what works' best with offenders. The most common approach to general responsivity is the adoption of cognitive-behavioural methods in the delivery of correctional programmes. This approach is thought to be the best suited for addressing the factors that underlie criminal behaviour such as anxiety, low self-esteem, interpersonal and cognitive immaturity, psychopathy, inadequate problem-solving skills and low verbal intelligence. Intervention should address the risk of reoffending by targeting these criminogenic needs. It should also focus on skills building and social learning. The programme should, preferably, be located in the offender's natural setting and be delivered in such a way as to motivate the offender to participate and provide optimal conditions for learning. Specific responsivity, on the other hand, relates to the need for programmes to be delivered in ways that match the personal characteristics of individual offenders. Characteristics associated with specific responsivity include: race, gender, age, social background, life experiences, disability and learning style (see Kennedy 1999; Crime and Justice Institute 2006). According to Dana (1993, cited in Crime and Justice Institute 2006: 15), failure to address specific responsivity factors may contribute to inaccurate assessment of the motivation or readiness of individuals referred to treatment, not to mention inaccurate assessment of criminogenic needs.

Responsivity is also discussed under the headings of 'internal' and 'external' responsivity. On the one hand, internal responsivity refers to the offence and offender characteristics discussed above. External responsivity, on the other hand, refers to the characteristics of programme settings and of the practitioners or service providers themselves – their training, attitudes, behaviour and perceptions – that may hinder or facilitate learning or engagement with the offender (Kennedy 1999). In other words, external responsivity relates to the provision of the optimal conditions or environment under which offenders are motivated and willing to learn. The concept recognises the fact that certain offenders may perform better in certain treatment settings, or certain staff members may be better able to work with certain offenders than other staff members (see Sperber 2003).

Available research evidence in the USA suggests that general offender populations respond differentially to various correctional environments and that personality type (of both treatment providers and clients) could affect treatment outcome. Research in the USA and Canada has shown that correctional treatment programmes that match offenders to treatment modalities based on the responsivity principles are more successful than those that treat offenders as if they are all alike. Research in those countries has also shown that when offenders are matched to treatment based on their individual characteristics, they perform better and that programmes that address responsivity issues have better outcomes for clients or service users (see Sperber 2003 for a review of these research findings).

Furthermore, in the USA, there are classification instruments that could be used to categorise offenders according to the principles of responsivity. An example is the Jesness Inventory. This assessment tool could be used to guide practitioners in their efforts to individualise treatment by matching the offender to treatment setting, style and staff, thereby providing a more effective treatment for the offenders. Sperber (2003) argued that programmes that assess responsivity with standardised reliable and valid assessment tools can better match clients to therapist and setting characteristics, thereby improving treatment outcomes.

Although OASys recognises the need to take cultural and individual characteristics into consideration while assessing criminogenic needs and in sentence planning generally, it is not strictly a responsivity classification assessment tool. However, offender programmes in the UK are mostly based on the principles of general responsivity, supported by the 'What Works' agenda. Specific responsivity is also addressed in policy documents and programme manuals and is highlighted as an important element of effective professional practice in professional training manuals. For example, the Diversity Review Report on Cognitive Skills Programmes (National Probation Service and HM Prison Service 2002) recommended that diversity reviews should be considered for all accredited programmes and that responsivity and diversity should be an integral part of programme design and delivery.

With regard to specific responsivity, two approaches appear to be commonly used – but only by the Probation Service, in the attempt to achieve specific responsivity in relation to minority ethnic offenders on offender programmes. First, is the validation of mainstream accredited programmes for minority ethnic offenders. A good example is the Think First Black and Asian Offender Programme (TFBAO) run by the Greater Manchester Probation Area. The aim of this programme is to offer black and Asian offenders the opportunity to undertake offence-focused group work from their own perspective. The second approach is the use of cultural examples during the delivery of mainstream offender programmes to mixed groups, for example in the form of role-plays. Practitioners who deliver these programmes are trained (see De Montfort University 2006), but there is still a query over how knowledge gained from training is translated into effective practice. In a Skills for Justice report it is noted that:

In HMI Probation's report, *A Joint Inspection of Community Penalties 2005*, it was found that many staff from different agencies have received training in valuing diversity or anti-discrimination. However, staff are not yet able to relate the generic training received to specific situations which might occur during the enforcement of community penalties. This is coupled with a lack of organisational guidance about such matters. (Skills for Justice 2007: 413)

However, studies have continued to show that minority ethnic offenders perform better in particular programme settings, and especially where the programmes are delivered by people who understand them as a distinct category of offenders and are, preferably, from the same ethnic background as themselves (see Calverley *et al.* 2004; 2006).

NOMS, ethnic diversity and the voluntary and community sector

The passing of the Offender Management Act 2007 implies that more services for offenders may be contracted out to the voluntary and community sector. The value of this sector to offender management is acknowledged in NOMS' newly formed 'faith, voluntary and community alliance structure'. In this set-up, faith groups and voluntary and community organisations are regarded as valuable partners in the tasks of tackling offender behaviour, addressing criminogenic needs and providing services geared to reducing reoffending both in the community and in prisons (see Home Office 2005b, 2006). The voluntary sector has long been a valuable arm in the provision of grass roots services that meet the needs of particular offender populations. They have provided specialist services often geared towards specific criminogenic needs such as drug treatment, employment and mentoring schemes targeted at offenders in particular communities.

However, while the law expects equal participation of the voluntary and community sector in offender management, it is clear that the introduction of the criteria of commissioning and contestability into the relationship with NOMS implies that strategic 'barriers' have been set against this relationship. Experience in the business sector has shown that commissioning and contestability do not favour small organisations. Large organisations and those who can provide 'broad' services in a 'cost-effective' manner because they already have the experience and structures in place to deliver to government 'contracts' are more likely to be successful in bidding for funding than smaller organisations, no matter how relevant or innovative the ideas of the smaller organisations might be. There is no such thing as a fair and transparent market, competitive neutrality or a 'level playing field'. It is all market-driven politics (cf. Leys 2003). Favoured organisations are more likely to be national while local organisations are either taken over or squeezed out. Organisations that are focused exclusively on providing for black and minority ethnic offenders' criminogenic needs are most likely to be local and small. They cannot compete with larger organisations who claim to be able to provide for 'all types' of offenders. In larger organisations, minority ethnic offenders are simply numbers; even in organisations where they are in the majority, they are more likely to be treated as their white counterparts who are in the minority. Commissioning involves 'deciding what services are needed and in what form, and contracting for their delivery' (Home Office 2005c). This means that organisations have to work to 'contracts' imposed by NOMS over which they have no power. Terms such as a long history or experience of working with offenders will be used to marginalise smaller organisations that are attempting to address issues relating, perhaps specifically, to minority ethnic groups and their offending behaviour and are located within minority ethnic communities but do not have a history of offender work behind them. So, services will eventually be transferred to a handful of large organisations – 'the same old crowd'. The result is that valuable services necessary in addressing offending behaviour that are contracted out, such as basic skills education, employment schemes and drug rehabilitation and treatment, are more likely not to be contracted out with specific interest in ethnic diversity but according to the economic criteria of cost-effectiveness or cost-benefits.

Voluntary and community organisations that are rooted in the community are more likely to understand the 'local' offender population better than national organisations which may have a presence in the local community but are trying to apply a strategy devised at a regional or national level. Work with minority ethnic offenders is more likely to be tailored to meet their needs and circumstances if delivered by organisations that are set up by and rooted in minority ethnic communities and staffed by people from the same ethnic background as the offender population that they deal with. The emphasis here is that the initiative for who delivers offender programmes should come from the local community, not the state.

Conclusion

The offender management approach introduced by NOMS implies that services are individualised and 'capable of adapting to the diverse needs, risks and circumstances of individual offenders' (NOMS 2006: 12). Ethnic diversity is referred to extensively in policy documents of both NOMS and its constituent criminal justice agencies. This, no doubt, is the result of the recommendations of the Macpherson Report and the passing of the Race Relations (Amendment) Act 2000. The probation and prison establishments both have race equality and anti-racist policies in place to ensure the elimination of unlawful discrimination and guarantee equal treatment of all offenders, clients and service users, irrespective of 'race'. These include carrying out an impact assessment of action plans and ethnic monitoring of staff, offenders and victims (see, for example, Home Office 2004, 2005a), providing staff training in race awareness and cultural diversity, and having mechanisms in place to ensure transparency, accountability and the minimisation of discriminatory practices so that services provided are seen to be fair by offenders of all ethnic groups.

However, NOMS appears to have taken over the role of the prime initiator of change and a top-down approach seems have taken root in the delivery of initiatives and ideas. This is a common side effect of centralisation. In the process of NOMS taking shape, Bhui (2006: 171) has argued that 'there is a danger that some critical areas of knowledge and practice will fail to develop' and that 'anti-racist practice is proving to be one of those areas'. Unless the drive to provide a fair and anti-racist service comes from within the constituent organisations themselves and is flexible and strong enough to resist political pressures, criminal justice initiatives for offenders will continue to be driven by the government's definitions of reality. In the current climate of performance culture, the strength to oppose the government's directives is quite low.

In a nutshell, there is ample development on the policy front but this is yet to be fully translated into effective practice. The discretionary power of professionals is not challenged. The abstract rules do not specifically respect ethnic diversity. We are left with practitioners who define their situation in terms of 'experience', situational rules and SPJ. We are yet to know whether training in ethnic diversity adequately prepares practitioners for dealing with diversity issues when working with offenders of minority ethnic backgrounds. There appears to be some confusion over how to address the criminogenic needs of minority ethnic offenders and how they should be viewed as offenders. While there is support for specific responsivity, its application in the delivery of programmes to minority ethnic offenders is yet to be evaluated. There is a strong need to look again at staffing. The research evidence that the employment of more black and minority ethnic staff is important to the effective delivery of programmes to minority ethnic offenders should not be ignored. However, this is not simply about numbers; it is about how minority ethnic staff are utilised at various levels of decision-making where ethnic diversity issues are being debated and relevant policies formulated. Offender programmes must address the root causes of minority ethnic offenders' reoffending. Even though shared common life histories are important in assessing criminogenic needs, the starting point for minority ethnic offenders should be the recognition of racism as a criminogenic risk factor.

Working with ethnicity in offender management cannot really begin unless and until the differences between ethnic groups in terms of their differential risk of reoffending is recognised. If racism is not adequately targeted as a major factor resulting in the offending behaviour of minority ethnic offenders then it means that the criminal justice system is not ready to deal with the disproportionate offending of black and minority ethnic people. Why wouldn't the disproportionate representation of minority ethnic people in crime continue if a major cause of their offending is not recognised by those who claim to be addressing their offending behaviour?

While a lot is being done to create a non-discriminatory environment and promote non-discriminatory practices, the intervention tools and approaches are yet to fully reflect the needs and circumstances of minority ethnic offenders. Creating a non-discriminatory environment and addressing ethnic diversity issues are not entirely the same.

Discussion questions

1 Should ethnicity be important in the assessment of criminogenic risks? What would be the implication for sentence planning?
2 How would you deal with a situation where an offender insists that his or her offending behaviour is due to racism in society? Would you consider this a barrier to successful engagement with the offender?
3 Is there a solid case for culturally based programmes for minority ethnic offenders on supervision and in prison? Give reasons for your answer.

Further reading

Bowling, B. and Phillips, C. (2002) *Racism, Crime and Justice*. London: Longman. This book provides an excellent background on issues of race and racism within the criminal justice system
Denney, D. (1992) *Racism and Anti-Racism in Probation*. London: Routledge. This is a classic text. Although written on probation, the book highlights issues that are relevant to other agencies.
Hannah-Moffat, K. (2005) 'Criminogenic needs and the transformative risk subject', *Punishment and Society*, 7 (1): 29–51. This is an excellent paper on the relationship between 'risks' and 'needs'. It provides a sound theoretical perspective to this controversial area of offender management, relevant also to issues of ethnic diversity.
Lewis, S. *et al.* (2006) *Race and Probation*. Cullompton: Willan. This is the most recent and up-to-date collection on race issues. It focuses on probation but also covers wider areas and issues on working with ethnic diversity.

Notes

1 Criminogenic risk is discussed in this chapter in the context of the risk of future offending in the general sense, not in terms of the risk of future harm (RoH).
2 OAsys was not validated in Scotland and was partially validated in the UK. It is used throughout the National Offender Management Service in England and Wales.

References

Allan, A. and Dawson, D. (2004) *Assessment of the Risk of Reoffending by Indigenous Male Violent and Sexual Offenders*, Criminology Research Council Trends and

Issues in Crime and Criminal Justice No. 28. Canberra: Australian Government/ Australian Institute of Criminology.

Andrews, D. and Bonta, J. (1998) *Psychology of Criminal Conduct*. Cincinnati, OH: Andersen.

Andrews, D. and Hoge, R.D. (1995) 'The psychology of criminal conduct and principles of effective prevention and rehabilitation', *Forum on Corrections Research*, 7 (1): 12–14.

Aubrey, R. and Hough, M. (1997) *Assessing Offenders' Needs: Assessment Scales for the Probation Service*. London: Home Office.

Baker, T. and Simon, J. (2002) *Embracing Risk: The Changing Culture of Insurance and Responsibility*. Chicago: University of Chicago Press.

Bhui, H.S. (1999) 'Race, racism and risk assessment: linking theory to practice with black mentally disordered offenders', *Probation Journal*, 46 (3): 171–81.

Bhui, H.S. (2006) 'Anti-racist practice in NOMS: reconciling managerialist and professional realities', *Howard Journal*, 45 (2): 171–90.

Bowling, B. and Phillips, C. (2002) *Racism, Crime and Justice*. London: Longman.

Bradshaw, J., Kemp, P., Baldwin, S. and Rowe, A. (2004) *The Drivers of Social Exclusion: A Review of the Literature for the Social Exclusion Unit*. York: Social Policy Research Unit, University of York.

Calverley, A., Cole, B., Kaur, G., Lewis, S., Raynor, P., Sadeghi, S., Smith, D., Vanstone, M. and Wardak, A. (2004) *Black and Asian Offenders on Probation*, Home Office Research Study No. 277. London: Home Office.

Calverley, A., Cole, B., Kaur, G., Lewis, S., Raynor, P., Sadeghi, S., Smith, D., Vanstone, M. and Wardak, A. (2006) 'Black and Asian probationers: implications of the Home Office study', *Probation Journal*, 53 (1): 24–37.

Carlen, P. (1976) *Magistrates Justice*. London: Martin Robertson.

Cole, B. and Wardak, A. (2006) 'Black and Asian men on probation: social exclusion, discrimination and experiences of criminal justice', in S. Lewis, P. Raynor, D. Smith and A. Wardak (eds), *Race and Probation*. Cullompton: Willan.

Cook, D. and Hudson, B. (eds) (1993) *Racism and Criminology*. London: Sage.

Crime and Justice Institute (2006) *Evidence-Based Practices: A Framework for Sentencing Policy*. Boston: Crime and Justice Institute.

Criminal Justice System (2005) *Fairness and Equality in the CJS. Toolkit to Help Local Criminal Justice Boards Increase the Confidence of the Black and Minority Ethnic (BME) Community They Service*. London: Home Office.

Dana, R. (1993) *Multicultural Assessment Perspectives for Professional Psychology*. Boston, MA: Allyn & Bacon.

De Montfort University (2006) *Valuing Diversity Workbook*. Leicester: De Montfort University.

Dell, C.A. and Boe, R. (2000) *An Examination of Aboriginal and Caucasian Women Offender Risk and Needs Factors*. Ottawa: Research Branch, Correctional Services of Canada.

Denney, D. (1992) *Racism and Anti-Racism in Probation*. London: Routledge.

Dixon, L. (2002) 'Tackling racist offending: a generalised or targeted approach', *Probation Journal*, 49 (3): 205–16.

Douglas, M. (1992) *Risk and Blame: Essays in Cultural Theory*. London: Routledge.

Duff, D. (2002) *A Programme for Change and Rehabilitation: Black Self-Development Groupwork Manual*. London: LPA.

Durrance, P. and Williams, P. (2003) 'Broadening the agenda around what works for black and Asian offenders', *Probation Journal*, 50 (3): 211–24.

Farr, K.A. (2000) 'Classification for female inmates: moving forward', *Crime and Delinquency*, 46 (1): 3–17.

Gelsthorpe, L. (2006) 'The experiences of female minority ethnic offenders: the other "other"', in S. Lewis, P. Raynor, D. Smith and A. Wardak (eds), *Race and Probation*. Cullompton: Willan.

Gill, A. and Marshall, T. (1993) 'Working with racist offenders: an anti-racist response', *Probation Journal*, 40 (2): 54–9.

Green, R. (1989) 'Probation and the black offender', *New Community*, 16 (1): 81–91.

Hannah-Moffat, K. (1999) 'Moral agent or actuarial subject: risk and Canadian women's imprisonment', *Theoretical Criminology*, 3 (1): 71–94.

Hannah-Moffat, K. (2005) 'Criminogenic needs and the transformative risk subject', *Punishment and Society*, 7 (1) 29–51.

Hedderman, C. (2004) 'The "criminogenic" needs of women offenders', in G. McIvor (ed.), *Women Who Offend*. London: Jessica Kingsley.

HM Prison Service (2006) *The Prison Service Associate Race Equality Scheme. Annual Report 2005–2006*. London: Home Office.

HMI Probation (2006) *Offender Management Inspection Criteria (OMIC) March 2006*. London: Home Office.

Home Office (2001) *Offender Assessment System OASys User Manual*. London: Home Office.

Home Office (2004) *Race and Ethnic Monitoring – Achieving Quality Data and Effective Implementation of 2001 16+1 Census Categorisation*, Probation Circular 60/2004. London: Home Office.

Home Office (2005a) *The Race Equality Duty and the Statutory Three Year Review*, Probation Circular 21/2005. London: Home Office.

Home Office (2005b) *The Role of the Voluntary and Community Sector in Service Delivery: A Cross Cutting Review*. London: Home Office.

Home Office (2005c) *Reducing Re-offending, Cutting Crime: Improving Offender Management*, Press Release, 20 October. London: Home Office.

Home Office (2006) *NOMS: Improving Prison and Probation Services: Public Value Partnerships*. London: Home Office.

Hood, R. (1992) *Race and Sentencing*. Oxford: Clarendon Press.

Howard, P., Clark, D. and Garnham, N. (2006) *An Evaluation of the Offender Assessment System (OASys) in Three Pilots 1999–2001*. London: Home Office.

Hudson, B. and Bramhall, G. (2005) 'Constructions of "Asianness" in risk assessments by probation officers', *British Journal of Criminology*, 45: 721–40.

Kennedy, S. (1999) 'Responsivity: the other classification principle', *Corrections Today*, 61 (1): 48–51.

Leys, C. (2003) *Market Driven Politics: Neoliberal Democracy and the Public Interest*. London: Verso.

McGuire, J. (2002) 'Integrating findings from research reviews', in J. McGuire (ed.), *Offender Rehabilitation and Treatment: Effective Programmes and Policies to Reduce Reoffending*. Chichester: Wiley.

McHugh, P. (1968) *Defining the Situation: The Organisation of Meaning in Social Interaction*. Indianapolis, IN: Bobbs-Merrill.

Macpherson, W. (1999) *The Stephen Lawrence Inquiry: Report of an Inquiry by Sir William Macpherson of Cluny*, Cm 4262-1. London: Home Office.

Ministry of Justice (2007) *Statistics on Race and the Criminal Justice System – 2006*. London: Ministry of Justice.

Moore, J., Trevethan, S. and Conley, J. (2004) *Program and Service Needs of Federally Incarcerated Métis Offenders in Saskatchewan*. Ottawa: Correctional Services of Canada, Research Branch.

National Offender Management Service (NOMS) (2006) *The NOMS Offender Management Model*. London: Home Office.

National Probation Service (2003) *The Heart of the Dance: A Diversity Strategy for the National Probation Service for England and Wales 2002–2006*. London: Home Office.

National Probation Service and HM Prison Service (2002) *Offending Behaviour Programmes: Diversity Review Report on Cognitive Skills Programmes*. London: Home Office.

National Probation Service and Home Office Communication Directorate (2001) *A New Choreography: An Integrated Strategy for the National Probation Service for England and Wales*. London: Home Office.

Powis, B. and Walmsley, R.K. (2002) *Programmes for Black and Asian Offenders on Probation: Lessons for Developing Practice*, Home Office Research Study No. 250. London: Home Office.

Risk Management Authority Scotland (2006) *Risk Management Tools Evaluation Directory*. Paisley: Risk Management Authority Scotland.

Rugge, T. (2006) *Risk Assessment of Male Aboriginal Offenders: A 2006 Perspective*. Canada: Public Safety and Emergency Preparedness.

Shaw, M. and Hannah-Moffat, K. (2000) 'Gender, diversity and risk assessment in Canadian corrections', *Probation Journal*, 47: 163–72.

Shaw, M. and Hannah-Moffat, K. (2004) 'How cognitive skills forgot about gender and diversity', in G. Mair (ed.), *What Matters in Probation*. Cullompton: Willan.

Shiner, M., Young, T., Newburn, T. and Groben, S. (2004) *Mentoring Disaffected Young People: An Evaluation of Mentoring Plus*. York: Joseph Rowntree Foundation.

Simon, J. (1987) 'The emergence of a risk society: insurance, law and the state', *Socialist Review*, 95 (1): 93–108.

Simon, J. (1988) 'The ideological effects of actuarial practices', *Law and Society Review*, 22 (4): 771–800.

Simon, J. (1994) 'In the place of the parent: risk management and the government of campus life', *Social and Legal Studies*, 3 (3): 15–45.

Skills for Justice (2007) *Sector Skills Agreement: An Assessment of Justice Sector Education and Training Provision. England and Wales*. Sheffield: Skills for Justice.

Smith, D. (2006) 'What might work with racially motivated offenders?', in S. Lewis, P. Raynor, D. Smith and A. Wardack (eds), *Race and Probation*. Cullompton: Willan.

Sperber, K.G. (2003) *Potential Applications of an Existing Offender Typology to Child Molesting Behaviours*. PhD dissertation, Division of Criminal Justice, University of Cincinnati.

State Services Commission, New Zealand (2005) *Briefing Papers and Report – Review of Targeted Policies and Programmes (1) Corrections: Briefing Paper to Minister on Eight Programmes*. Wellington: State Services Commission. See: http://www.ssc.govt.nz/display/home.asp.

Suffolk Probation Area (2002) *Working with Minority Ethnic Offenders: Policy and Practice*. Ipswich: Suffolk Probation Area.

Trevethan, S., Moore, J. and Thorpe, M. (2003) *The Needs of Métis Offenders in Federal Correctional Facilities in British Columbia*. Ottawa: Correctional Services of Canada, Research Branch.

Trevethan, S., Moore, J., Naqitarvik, L., Watson, A. and Saunders, D. (2004) *The Needs of Inuit Offenders in Federal Correctional Facilities*. Ottawa: Correctional Services of Canada, Research Branch.

Williams, P. (2006) 'Designing and delivering programmes for minority ethnic offenders', in S. Lewis, P. Raynor, D. Smith and A. Wardak (eds), *Race and Probation*. Cullompton: Willan.

Worrall, A. (2000) 'What works at One Arm Point? A study in the transportation of a penal concept', *Probation Journal*, 47: 243–9.

Chapter 23

Discrimination and the poor: using incentives and privileges as a framework for anti-discriminatory practice

Simon Green

Introduction: discriminating against the majority

Poor people make up the overwhelming majority of offenders in the criminal justice system (Prison Reform Trust 2007; Social Exclusion Unit 2002). This is troubling. Either poor people commit more crime or poor people are more likely to be convicted. Either of these perspectives can be understood in terms of discrimination. There is a wealth of material which has attempted to demonstrate that poor people commit more crime, poor people are more likely to have their behaviour criminalised and poor people are more like to be convicted for their crimes. Why then are poor people the forgotten people of anti-discriminatory practice? What, if anything, should be done to address this?

In recent years, ideologies of welfare and redistribution have been swept away and replaced with new governing philosophies about inclusion and responsibility. Poor people, intrinsically bound-up with the value commitments of the welfare tradition, have been one of the main casualties of this transformation. By disentangling poor people from this ideological malaise and realigning them with a new value base, namely the anti-discriminatory principle of fairness, it becomes possible to consider how poor people are treated within the criminal justice system without recourse to traditional welfare or redistribution debates. Instead, Eysenck's (1969) article on technologies of consent will be used to argue that the incentives and earned privileges scheme in the prison setting should be extended into the community where it can be proactively used to address both reoffending and discrimination from within a broad community justice framework.

Discriminating against poor people: an ideologically infused minefield

Poor people is a term not often used by politicians, policy-makers or academics. Instead, terms like social exclusion, socio-economic circumstances and structural conditions are routinely used to talk about poor people. These terms have particular political meanings (see below) which construct debates around poor people in particular ways. This often amounts to talking about poor people without referring to them. Talking – or writing – about poor people even feels a little taboo, something that evokes a sensation of awkwardness or mild anxiety when publicly expressed.

Yet poor people is a descriptive phrase based upon a relative judgment of social, cultural and economic wealth. This implies nothing about whether the existence of poor people is good or bad, or how we might go about reducing the number of poor people. These would be ideological or normative positions that are largely out of vogue in the current political and criminal justice climate. In fact the most plausible explanation for why poor people have fallen off the edge of the anti-discriminatory map is precisely because they have always been talked about in terms of wider political ideologies. Apart from the wholesale transformation of social and economic conditions, this language leaves little conceptual space to consider how practical steps can be taken to alleviate discrimination against the poor. Yet poor people exist and, as will be shown, are discriminated against in the criminal justice system. Hence the only normative claim in this discussion is that discrimination is bad and should be avoided wherever possible. This would seem to be a position entirely consonant with the current political and criminal justice climate.

As Cavadino and Dignan (2007) have noted, there are no regular official statistics which look at social class or occupation in relation to crime and criminal justice. However, in 2002 the Social Exclusion Unit produced a report which explored the characteristics of the prison population in comparison to the general population. A brief overview of this research shows that 67 per cent of the prison population were unemployed prior to conviction compared to a national rate of 5 per cent, 48 per cent of prisoners had a reading age of below 11 (compared to 21–23 per cent), 65 per cent had a numeracy age below 11 (compared to 23 per cent), 27 per cent had been in care as a child (compared to 2 per cent) and 72 per cent of male prisoners had suffered from two or more mental disorders (compared to 0.5 per cent). Other characteristics around schooling, drug-use and drinking go on to demonstrate similarly large differences. It is obviously difficult to extrapolate these findings to those offenders serving their sentence in the community or who are given fines or cautions but it is certainly indicative of the widely held conviction that the offending population is a poor population. For example, the Social Exclusion Unit website states: 'Crime is also disproportionately committed by people from socially excluded backgrounds' (http://www.socialexclusionunit.gov.org). Hale (2005) and Reiner (2007) also provide summaries of recent research which looks at the relationship between economic inequalities and the crime rate.

Irrespective of whether there is an over-representation of poor people in the offending population or whether there is a relationship between economic conditions and the crime rate these are not, in themselves, indicators of discrimination. Nonetheless, when considered next to the extensive research into discrimination within the criminal justice system the case becomes compelling in the extreme. There is an extensive literature on the sociology of the law which explores the way in which the legal framework is constructed and in whose interests (e.g. Chambliss and Mankoff 1976; Hall *et al.* 1978; Quinney 1969, 1973, 1977). While heavily influenced by Marxist teachings these readings dispel the myth that the law is either neutral or independent from wider social, economic and political forces. Research into the treatment of corporate and white-collar crime clearly demonstrates a process that rarely resorts to criminal proceedings or holds individuals to account (Sutherland 1949; Croall 1992; Punch 1996; Slapper and Tombs 1999). In other words, the criminal law focuses disproportionately on the activities and behaviour of the poorest in society and the criminal justice apparatus criminalises poor people and the spaces they inhabit far more readily than their more affluent equivalents. In public spaces Norris and Armstrong (1999) and McCahill (2002) have shown how those operating surveillance technologies tend to focus disproportionately on the demonstrably poor (among others). Reiner's (2002) review of policing clearly demonstrates that the police see poor people as 'police property' and are more heavily policed and frequently arrested as a result. Further research shows that middle-class young people are far more likely to get off with a caution than working-class boys (Bennett 1979; Phillips and Brown 1998). Later on in the system, poor people are discriminated against with regard to their housing and employment status for both bail decisions (Hucklesby 2002) and sentencing decisions (Cavadino and Dignan 2007).

This is a necessarily brief overview of the different stages of discrimination within the criminal justice system and is intended as no more than a reminder that poor people are discriminated against. Given the weight of this literature and the number of poor people in the offending population it becomes difficult to understand why the gaze of anti-discriminatory policies and practices pays so little attention to this group. Given the general commitment to diversity, difference and anti-discriminatory practice, this is an anomalous trend which is in need of exploration.

Poor people in context: from the welfare state to social exclusion

Understanding the nature of the current political and criminal justice climate is essential if meaningful practice and policy suggestions are to be made. Until Margaret Thatcher came to office in 1979 there was a broad political consensus that the state should provide a minimum level of welfare to ensure certain social and economic rights for all its citizens. Thatcher's governments began a gradual process which politically debunked and socially reconstructed the meaning of welfare and the basis on which it is provided. The gradual but eventual consequence of this transformation culminated in the formation of New Labour's Social Exclusion Unit. New

Labour's articulation of social exclusion formalised a shift away from redistributive welfare to moral and integrationist discourses.

This transformation is considered by Levitas (1998) and Young and Matthews (2003). Levitas (1998) highlights an important shift in New Labour's thinking regarding social exclusion. Levitas (1998) points to three different discourses on social exclusion: a redistributionist discourse (RED), a moral underclass discourse (MUD) and a social integrationist discourse (SID). Essentially, Levitas (1998) argues that New Labour has shifted from the redistributionist discourse to a confused meshing of the moral underclass and social integrationist discourse. According to Levitas (1998) all three of these discourses prioritise paid work as the major component of social integration, but differ in terms of what the excluded are deemed to be lacking. In RED, they have no money, in MUD they have no morals and in SID they have no work. She goes on to argue that both SID and MUD are more narrowly defined than RED with regards to what constitutes social exclusion. In SID it is largely economic exclusion, while in MUD it is cultural.

This blurring of both MUD and SID is further demonstrated by Young and Matthews (2003) who suggest that New Labour's approach to tackling social exclusion is based on three interrelated strategies: 'the *prevention* of social exclusion, the *reintegration* of the excluded, and the delivery of *basic minimum standards*' (Young and Matthews 2003: 10, emphasis in original). Young and Matthews (2003) go on to agree with Levitas (1998) that these strategies represent a fundamental shift in New Labour's approach to social exclusion, from redistributionist to integrationist policies. This, they argue, divorces structural debates about inequality and material conditions from the causes of social exclusion, choosing instead to focus on the need to tackle the 'excluded people's handicapping characteristics' (Young and Matthews 2003: 18) rather than focus on the ways in which individuals and groups are excluded.

This approach sidelines economic inequalities and their structural causes when seeking to explain social problems, and reinforces the notion that the excluded are a 'group of people outcast, spatially cut off from the rest of society, with perhaps different values and motivations' (Young and Matthews 2003: 17). As Young and Matthews (2003) argue, this approach focuses attention on a socially, economically and culturally excluded group who are cut off from mainstream society. In accordance with Levitas (1998) this begins to concentrate attention on the characteristics of the poor rather than the structural conditions in society. Inequalities across the rest of the society are ignored and the socially excluded become increasingly presented as a definite group, distinctively different from the rest of society.

New Labour's rhetoric of responsibility and its moralising on family and civic behaviour shares much in common with the communitarianism of Etzioni (1995). As Crawford (1996) has commented, it is Etzioni's (1995) political 'vision' that New Labour has latched onto. For Etzioni (1995) it is the decline of community that is responsible for the decline of public morality. As such he sees the revaluation of families and schools as the fundamental community institutions that can lead to the regeneration of public morality and the civil society.

Thus social exclusion uncouples structural conditions from explanations of people's life circumstances. Instead it is the characteristics of the poor which are the focus of social exclusion. Immorality and unemployment in the form of apathy and laziness are the cause of social exclusion:

> This exclusion from the labour market was the exclusion from civil society: an underclass left stranded by the needs of capital on housing estates either in the inner-city, or on its periphery, those who because of illiteracy, family pathology, or general disorganization were excluded from citizenship, whose spatial vistas were those of constant disorder and threat, and who were the recipients of stigma from the wider world of respectable citizens. The welfare 'scroungers', the immigrants, the junkies and the crack heads: the demons of modern society. (Young 2002: 465)

This means that policies which seek to address social exclusion focus not on addressing social or economic conditions but on what is wrong with the attitudes and behaviour of people. How can they be helped to change? What can be done to them if they do not accept this help? Nowhere is this more evident than in the criminal justice system. Cognitive-behavioural programmes (Feasey, this volume) or motivational interviewing (Tallant *et al.* this volume) clearly demonstrate the importance of personal responsibility when working with offenders. Poor people are off the anti-discriminatory agenda because the structural conditions which lead to someone being poor are no longer the issue.

Political economy and poor people: advanced liberalism and the 'respect' agenda

One of the main explanations for why poor people have slipped off the social and political agenda is tied to political economy. Political economy is a much confused term (Reiner 2007) that has dual meanings which are sometimes used ambiguously. In the postwar period political economy has been used in reference to the economic model: the principles by which the economy is governed. Yet the original use of political economy is located in the work of eighteenth- and early nineteenth-century moral philosophers such as Adam Smith (1776) and Karl Marx (1976). In their original conception political economy is to do with the ordering and structure of society. It is therefore interesting to look at the way in which the structure of society, or its political economy, has changed and the impact this has had on the way poor people are thought about.

Over the last decade or so, New Labour has repeatedly talked of the need to balance individual rights with responsibilities. This emphasis is apparent within both their general policy framework and their criminal justice rhetoric. For example, the 2001 Labour manifesto states:

> We all know the sort of Britain we want to live in – a Britain where we can walk the streets safely and know our children are safe. We have a ten-year vision: a new social contract where everyone has a stake based on equal rights, where they pay their dues by exercising responsibility in return, and where local communities shape their own futures. (p. 31)

The implication of this is that a lack of responsibility is somehow to blame for society's ills. In his pamphlet, *The Third Way, New Politics for the New Century,* Blair (1998) reiterates this theme calling for the need to create a strong civil society based on a balance of rights and responsibilities. More recently this perspective has morphed into the 'respect' agenda (see Respect Task Force 2006) which focuses on the lack of respect in society and in particular its young people. This loss of respect is intrinsically linked to crime and anti-social behaviour and is therefore tackled by working with parents, schools, communities and individuals to encourage more respect in society.

Underlining New Labour's respect agenda is Anthony Gidden's (1998, 2000) development of 'The Third Way'. His influential texts concern themselves with the political, economic and social challenges of contemporary society. Within them Giddens (1998, 2000) details the 'death of socialism' in the light of the neo-liberal domination of the Thatcher/Reagan administrations. As a result of the impact of these New Right ideologies the traditional left had to modernise in an effort to respond to both electoral pressures and a shift in the political landscape. Giddens (1998) views 'The Third Way' as the basis from which social democracy can be renewed. Within this context, Giddens refers to the need to reinvest in the civil society, a society where there are 'no rights without responsibilities' (p. 65). Underpinning this assertion is the belief that 'The Third Way' requires 'a new social contract, appropriate to an age where globalisation and individualism go hand in hand. The new contract stresses both the rights and responsibilities of citizens. People should not only take from the wider community, but give back to it too' (Giddens 2000: 165).

This statement provides the bedrock of New Labour's normative commitment to community and civil society. This commitment is underpinned by strategies of responsibilisation (Garland 1996, 2001) and community participation in crime control. The growth of restorative practices and parenting orders are examples of such strategies. These are complemented by an approach to community safety that vigorously endorses a zero-tolerance stance on anti-social and disorderly behaviour (McLauglin 2002). This approach is premised upon engendering parental responsibility for juvenile delinquency. New Labour's early years are a catalogue of moralising statements, strongly reflecting a commitment to the family as the vehicle for civic renewal. This reflects an ideological agenda concerned with developing strong communities via the social institution of the family. For example:

> I have no doubt that the breakdown of law and order is intimately linked with the break up of a strong sense of community. And the break up of community in turn is, to a crucial degree, consequent on the breakdown of family life. If we want anything more than a superficial discussion of crime and its causes, we cannot ignore the importance of the family. (Blair 1993, in Mandelson and Liddle 1996: 48)

> The family is the bedrock of a decent, civilised society. But it is under enormous strain. Divorce and separation have increased, lone parenthood has risen and child poverty has worsened. The reasons for this may be varied, but the impact is clear: 'more instability, more crime, greater pressure on housing and social benefits'. (Secretary of State for Social Security and Minister for Welfare Reform, Frank Field 1998: 13)

Alongside New Labour's rights and responsibilities mantra, advanced liberalism and governmentality represent a growing discourse on how government exercises power in contemporary society (Stenson 1993, 2000, 2001; Rose and Miller 1992; Rose 1996). Advanced liberalism has been defined by Rose (2000) as:

> a widespread recasting of the role of the state, and the argument that national governments should no longer aspire to be the guarantor and ultimate provider of security: instead the state should be a partner, animator, and facilitator for a variety of independent agents and powers, and should exercise only limited powers on its own, steering and regulating rather than rowing and providing. (Rose 2000: 323–4)

Stenson (2001) summarises advanced liberalism as a move away from the notion that the state should provide top-down bureaucratic government to one where increasingly informal and interconnected networks of control exist. Rather than the state providing for its citizenry, people are expected to provide for themselves. Yet this self-government is not conducted in a vacuum but in a regulated environment where policy still determines the boundaries for activities.

Advanced liberalism is therefore a strategy of governing. It is not a political philosophy in the sense that it outlines a notion of what constitutes the 'good' society, neither is it a simple reiteration of the neo-liberal assertion that the role of the state should remain as minimal as possible (Rose 1993). Instead, it denotes government at a distance (Miller and Rose 1990; Garland 1997; Dean 1999) where:

> Advanced liberal government entails the adoption of a range of devices that seek to recreate the distance between the decisions of formal political institutions and other social actors, and to act upon these actors in new ways, through shaping and utilizing their freedom. (Rose 1993: 295)

This conception resonates strongly with Foucault's (1982, 1991) notion of governmentality which provides Rose (1993, 1996, 2000) with an analytical tool to consider advanced liberalism.

Foucault's (1982) discussion of governmentality is presented as a revised concept of power in which he attempts to sidestep the long-standing criticism that he neglects the role of the state and his tendency to overemphasise citizens as 'docile bodies' rather than active subjects (Garland 1997). Governmentality is thus construed by Foucault (1982) as the process by which active choices by individuals are the mechanism by which power is exercised. Therefore, government creates individuals who will exercise their choices in line with governmental priorities. In other words to govern is to 'shape' the way in which individuals exercise their choices: 'To govern, in this sense, is to structure the possible field of action of others' (Foucault 1982: 221). Within this analysis Foucault (1982) locates a range of governmental authorities who have responsibility for regulating people's conduct. These include the family, medicine, psychiatry, education and employers. As Garland (1997) states, this means that traditional boundaries between state and civil society or between public and private become blurred. The business of governing is thus diverted through those 'social bodies' that have responsibilities for providing modern forms of 'pastoral' care (Foucault 1982). To this list of governmental authorities community has been added by Rose (1996).

Rose (1996) argues that in recent years most advanced industrial societies have witnessed a transformation of their welfare systems:

> One sees the privatization of public utilities and welfare functions, the marketization of health services, social insurance and pension schemes, educational reforms to introduce competition between schools and colleges, the introduction of new forms of management into the civil service modelled upon an image of methods in the private sector, new contractual relations between agencies and service providers and between professionals and clients, a new emphasis on the personal responsibilities of individuals, their families and their communities for their own future well-being and upon their own obligations to take active steps to secure this. (Rose 1996: 327-8)

For Rose (1996) this represents the end of social government in the sense that its aims should be the national provision of collective welfare. The welfare agenda was criticised for its cost, injustices and burdens. Too much power was centralised in the hands of the welfare system and its agents. Instead, a libertarian consensus emerged which focused on the rights and empowerment of 'active citizens' which led to a fundamental shift in the locus of responsibility. No longer is civic responsibility to be understood in terms of an obligation between the state and its citizens; rather it is each person's responsibility to behave respectfully towards others and access existing resources on their own initiative.

This change in political economy provides a powerful explanation for why poor people are rarely considered in anti-discriminatory practice. Whether it is New Labour's third way or Foucault's governmentality, the role of the state has been shifted away from the redistributive goals of the welfare system thus liberating government from having to take responsibility for inequalities. Social exclusion now plugs this gap and, as has been discussed, is not based on a redistributive ethic but an integrationist one. This fits snugly with advanced liberalism and its focus on responsibility, opportunity and active citizenship. Armed with this knowledge it becomes possible to think about addressing the discrimination of poor people in the criminal justice system. Within the current climate policy or practice initiatives need to fit within these wider political conditions to be given much credence.

Anti-discriminatory practice in an oppressive regime

How might practitioners avoid compounding discriminatory processes that lead to the criminalisation of so many poor people? When practitioners work within an inherently discriminatory and oppressive regime what can be done to alleviate these negative processes? As Thompson (1992) so succinctly puts it:

> There is no middle ground; intervention either adds to oppression (or at least condones it) or goes some small way towards easing or breaking such oppression. In this respect, the political slogan, 'If you're not part of the solution, you must be part of the problem' is particularly accurate. An awareness of the socio-political context is necessary in order to prevent becoming (or remaining) part of the problem. (Thompson 1992: 169–70)

For Thompson (1992, 2006) practice is not undertaken in a vacuum; it exists as part of a wider system which can both discriminate and oppress certain sections of the population. This is well established when considering anti-discriminatory practice in relation to ethnicity, gender, disability, sexuality, age and religion. Thompson (2006) goes on to state:

A clear danger, therefore, is to fail to take account of the class dimension – the socioeconomic circumstances which (a) underpin and magnify other forms of oppression and (b) act as a major source of oppression in their own right. The danger, therefore, is one of going from a situation (for example in the 1970s) where class was seen as the primary, if not only, dimension of oppression to a situation in which it is barely considered at all. (Thompson 2006: 179)

Hence, ignoring poor people will only exaggerate the levels of discrimination against them. As has already been discussed the political climate is one which no longer accepts direct responsibility for addressing socio-economic conditions. Yet this climate has emerged out of political and ideological shifts which have sought to escape the entrenched politics of state versus free market economics. These shifts have little to do with discrimination which remains firmly on the political and ideological agenda and therefore demands that poor people are given the same considerations as other disadvantaged groups.

To ensure that anti-discriminatory practice is delivered for poor people requires an ongoing commitment to think about the ways in which discrimination has, and can, occur through personal assumptions and institutional practices. As a consequence of changes in the political economy there is a very real danger that poor people are inadvertently being discriminated against as they have slipped off the agenda as an identifiable social group to be considered alongside other disadvantaged groups like black people or young people. This problem is even further exacerbated within the criminal justice context as the very language of 'diversity' and 'difference' (see, for example, Home Office 2003) focuses attention on those people and groups who are outside of the majority. As has been shown, poor people constitute the majority of offenders and are therefore more easily overlooked when using words like these as guiding lights.

The main way that discrimination against poor people can be minimised by practitioners is to make sure that awareness about the forms of discrimination which have traditionally led to the over-representation of poor people in the criminal justice system remains on the agenda and in the minds of practitioners. Anti-discriminatory practice has its roots in human rights and it is now a widely held moral and legal prerogative to be treated fairly and equitably with others (see Gelsthorpe 2007, for an interesting discussion of this). Awareness of the discrimination against a particular group encourages personal reflection about assumptions and bias we all make all of the time. These cannot be eradicated, but they can be controlled. Regardless of whether it is the way someone dresses, their accent or their neighbourhood, practitioners should always be guarded against largely inadvertent and unintentional negative judgements which may disadvantage an individual or group.

435

The technology of consent: extending privileges and incentives into the community

Alongside these practice-based concerns lies the policy context which can also be used to address issues of anti-discriminatory practice. Making policy suggestions that are likely to be taken seriously by policymakers requires that any such suggestions are compatible with the current political climate. As has already been discussed part of the reason poor people have been ignored in recent years is that discussion of them has nearly always been underpinned by a normative claim regarding wider ideological concerns about creating the 'good society' (such as the redistribution of wealth or a reduction in poverty). Hence, in the current climate, any policy suggestion for addressing discrimination against poor people must also pay attention to, and be compatible with, current practice, wider policy, public opinion and political direction.

In 1969 Hans Eysenck published a short article in *New Scientist* called 'The Technology of Consent'. In the introduction to this article Eysenck makes a somewhat prophetic comment that:

> As individuals and nations become ever more closely bound together by the web of civilisation, the social maverick becomes less and less tolerable. The author foresees that the techniques of experimental psychology will be increasingly used in the future to 'save these brands from the fire', and eventually to inculcate the whole of society with a suitable 'responsible' attitude. (Eysenck 1969: 688)

Eysenck's (1969) article goes on to explore the ways in which psychologists can control behaviour through classical behavioural conditioning, or the use of positive and negative reinforcements. This he refers to as the technology of consent: the ability to 'engineer a social consent which will make people behave in a socially adapted, law-abiding fashion' (Eysenck 1969: 688). This resonates strongly with both governmentality and cognitive-behavioural group work for offenders. However, Taylor *et al.* (1973) lambasted Eysenck, among others, for his positivist methodology and assumptions. Taylor *et al.* (1973) argue that positivism reduces human beings to passive actors and is a reductionist and oversimplified epistemology for understanding them, and also fails to appreciate its own value-base or limitations as a methodology. This critique is both a powerful and now a widely held perspective in the social sciences and humanities. Yet, if the epistemological and normative complaints about Eysenck's overstated argument are put to one-side there are two points in Eysenck's article which are perhaps worth salvaging. These are that quite a lot is known about how to control people's behaviour and that positive reinforcement (rewards) are a more effective way of achieving behavioural change than negative reinforcement (punishment).

Within the custodial setting there is a system of incentives and earned privileges designed to encourage good and responsible behaviour, hard work, constructive activity and discipline (Liebling *et al*. 1995). The scheme operates at three levels: basic, standard and advanced. The prisoner's behaviour determines progress through the levels and each level effectively provides more earned privileges. The range of privileges include earning private money, community visits, wearing own clothes, in-cell TV, more prison visits and getting better prison jobs. Yet there is no equivalent system in the community setting. Apart from the remote chance of an early discharge most offenders serving, or continuing, their sentence in the community either comply with the conditions of their sentence or are sent back to court and possibly to prison. Thus the threat of beginning 'breach' proceedings and sending an offender to prison is overwhelmingly the main way in which compliance with a sentence is enforced. As a result the Probation Service, and those voluntary and community sector partners who also work with offenders, have very little outside of pro-social 'praise' to encourage offenders to comply with the conditions of their sentence or licence. The range of different strategies designed to reduce reoffending (i.e. housing, education and employment support) are considered part of a wider sentence plan and are therefore requirements or components rather than earned privileges. Consequently, it becomes difficult to demonstrate to offenders the positive advantages of complying with their sentence, even though a huge amount of interventions are focused primarily on achieving offender motivation to change (see Tallant *et al*. and Madoc-Jones in this volume).

A system of incentives and earned privileges that constructed the types of supports available in the community for offenders as something to be earned could help reduce reoffending, improve the completion rates on programmes and encourage long-term goal-setting by offenders. It also adds an intermediate layer of potential sanctions which might positively benefit the current pressure on the prison population. A system of incentives and privileges also allows for the removal of privileges if behaviour deteriorates, meaning that there is another tier of sanctions available before an offender is 'breached' and sent back to prison. Hence, incentives and privileges should be considered as part of a wider sentencing plan which would be periodically reviewed and would fit with the wider goals of enforcement, public protection and rehabilitation. This could build upon, and link in with, the current prison scheme so that already earned privileges could be translated into the community setting. This would encourage continuity between custody and the community and fits well within the organisational framework of the National Offender Management Service (NOMS).

The exact nature of privileges in the community would have to be adapted from those in custody to reflect the different conditions. Yet there are already a number of schemes, both in the UK and overseas, which use incentives and privileges to achieve behavioural change. For example, in the UK there are schemes for improving diet, exercise and school attendance (Trouton *et al*. 2005). Of particular interest in this context is the use of incentives and privileges to address anti-social behaviour in young people. According to Trouton *et al.* (2005), there are 12 of these schemes running across the UK. Most of these schemes operate on a points-based system, similar to a loyalty card for a supermarket. Points are awarded at various rates for completion of different activities. These points can then be exchanged for immediate rewards such as money-off coupons, access to leisure centres, restaurant meals and so on. Other relevant forms of incentives include employment schemes for offenders which can include training, work experience, mentoring and eventually employment (see, for example, Gill 1997; Sarno *et al.* 1999). The government has even published a Green Paper based around incentives to work for offenders (Department for Education and Skills 2005). In the youth justice system successful compliance by a young offender with a referral order can lead to the offence being 'spent' early which can improve employability and reduce social stigma. Further, the option of early discharge still remains and could also be considered as part of a wider incentives and privileges scheme.

When considering the use of incentives and privileges in the community there are a number of important factors to be taken into account, particularly in relation to the appropriateness of privileges. Appropriateness needs to be thought about in terms of the offender and their offending history and in terms of the wider political and public attitude. It would clearly be hugely inappropriate to consider a sex offender for any privilege that brought them into contact with children. Similarly, it would be politically untenable to offer privileges that resembled rewards that would be considered widely desirable, such as games consoles, holidays abroad and so forth. Yet privileges still need to be desirable to offenders or they become meaningless. If the privileges formed part of a wider sentencing plan which built on and reinforced other pro-social interventions such as cognitive-behavioural group work and which were discussed and agreed with the offender, privileges could be both highly motivational and highly compatible with many other types of interventions which encourage goal-setting and a 'stake in conformity' (Hirschi 1969). These long-term privileges might include access to a desirable work experience placement, better housing or early discharge. These long-term privileges or goals would need to be matched by short-term privileges. Eysenck argues that 'an action followed by a small but immediate gratification will tend to be repeated' (1969: 689). Hence some short-term privileges are required to reinforce the desirable behaviour. Such privileges must also fit with the appropriateness criteria outlined above. Within the framework of a points-based scheme there is no reason why offenders could not undertake additional or extra civic-minded activities to earn more points. Thus this sort of scheme would also fit well within the 'no rights without responsibilities' ethos outlined earlier.

In terms of Eysenck's (1969) article or this discussion of incentives and privileges the focus is predominantly upon encouraging sentence compliance and behavioural change. While these are deemed socially desirable goals they are basically about social control. Incentives and privileges may well fit well with advanced liberalism, governmentality and communitarianism but how does this scheme help to address discrimination against poor people? It would seem that incentives and privileges can do nothing to avoid discriminatory processes at most stages of the criminal justice process. Discrimination will already have taken place. Yet an incentives and privileges scheme in the community can work to address some of the wider economic and social pressures which lead to the repeated criminalisation of poor people. This is achieved by ensuring that the incentives and privileges available are developed with the wider themes of reintegration, community cohesion, civic obligation and social and economic improvements in mind. Further, if rolled out in such a way as to promote offender reintegration, incentives and privileges could help counteract negative perceptions of offenders that lead to discriminatory attitudes.

Within this context the community justice initiatives currently running in North Liverpool and Salford offer a good model for rolling out an incentives and privileges scheme with offenders. The now well-established North Liverpool community justice centre is based around bringing together in one building a residing judge, probation, youth justice, police, addictions workers, employment and housing support agencies, legal and financial advice and victims services (see http://www.communityjustice.gov.uk). This model is based on a scheme run in New York designed to actively involve the community and respond to local problems (Berman and Mansky 2005). Within a collaborative, community-based centre like North Liverpool there is no reason why incentives and privileges could not also expand the range of local partners to include the private and sectors not-for-profit alongside the statutory, voluntary and community. Whether it is through local business crime prevention needs, public–private partnerships or employment and leisure schemes, the private sector could be a powerful ally in helping develop incentives and privileges in this context. With the government's focus on community cohesion, incentives and privileges under the mantle of community justice could be an important way of helping offenders to improve their social and economic circumstances.

Incentives and privileges are not a new scheme and neither are they only used exclusively in the prison setting. Extending incentives into the community is an effective way of enhancing the delivery of justice and reducing discriminatory forces. For this to be possible certain key principles need to be enshrined in the scheme. Incentives and privileges should therefore be:

- both short and long-term;
- desirable to the offender;
- clearly and fairly explained and awarded (a points system);
- continued-over from privileges earned in custody;
- delivered and administered in partnership;
- contingent upon the offender's behaviour (therefore also removable);
- hierarchical in nature (to encourage motivation and goal-setting);
- part of an ongoing sentence plan discussed with the offender;

- anti-criminal and pro-social in nature;
- appropriate to the offender's history and risk category;
- politically and publically acceptable (in terms of the privileges available);
- designed to reduce reoffending;
- designed to enhance reintegration and community cohesion.

This is quite a long list of principles reflecting a concern to ensure that an incentives and privileges scheme does not become a topic of tabloid denunciation or appropriated by a misguided attempt to revitalise ideological battles about welfare and redistribution. For incentives and privileges to work it must be based on a dual concern to reduce reoffending and build anti-discriminatory arrangements into work with offenders. With this in mind there a range of direct and indirect benefits which are worth outlining. Incentives and privileges can:

- reduce reoffending through positive reinforcement;
- reduce reoffending by reinforcing other interventions with offenders;
- reduce reoffending by providing social and economic support;
- reduce the prison population (removal of privileges rather than breach);
- encourage personal responsibility and pro-social attitudes in society;
- build partnership between agencies involved in scheme;
- introduce the business sector into the delivery of privileges;
- build community cohesion through community justice initiatives;
- build anti-discriminatory practices into sentence plans;
- challenge discriminatory attitudes and practices about offenders;
- raise awareness of discrimination against poor people in the criminal justice system.

Conclusion: addressing discrimination and reducing reoffending

This chapter began by asserting that poor people had fallen off the anti-discriminatory radar. The reasons for this seem tied to wider changes in the social and political foundations of society. In particular welfare and redistribution values appear to have been replaced with a new set of moral values about personal and civic responsibility. At a political level the fate of poor people has been heavily intertwined with welfare and redistribution values and as these have fallen out of favour so poor people have increasingly fallen off the agenda. Part of the challenge in this discussion has been to try and disentangle poor people from this value base so they can be reclaimed within an anti-discriminatory context.

At a practice level one of the main obstacles to anti-discriminatory practice is the failure to acknowledge that poor people, constituting the majority of offenders, are a group which are subjected to discrimination.

At the policy level an incentives and privileges scheme should be extended to offenders in the community. This scheme seems compatible with current political and criminal justice dynamics and fits well within community justice initiatives like those in Liverpool and Salford. If handled carefully incentives and privileges can help offenders improve their own social and economic conditions, simultaneously making amends for their earlier discrimination in the criminal justice system and providing them with the means to escape the conditions that led to it. It also reduces reoffending.

Discussion questions

1 What do you think the principles of justice are?
2 Can anti-discriminatory practice ever compensate for bias and oppression in the criminal justice system?
3 Are incentives and privileges just another social control mechanism or can they reduce discrimination? Are these two goals inherently opposed?

Further reading

Berman, G. and Mansky, A. (2005) 'Community justice centres: a US–UK exchange', *British Journal of Community Justice*, 3 (3): 5–14. A good overview of the community justice centres in New York and Liverpool. These centres provide an interesting model for both partnership and community collaboration which is well worth exploring.

Garland, D. (1997) 'Governmentality and the problem of crime: Foucault, criminology, sociology', *Theoretical Criminology*, 1 (2). This is a very good overview of governmentality as applied to crime and criminology. Foucault can be quite inaccessible and Garland has been very successful at bringing Foucault's ideas to a larger audience.

Levitas, R. (1998) *The Inclusive Society? Social Exclusion and New Labour.* Basingstoke: Palgrave Macmillan. An excellent companion to Young's text (below). More informed by social policy, Levitas unpicks the direction and hidden values of Tony Blair's government.

Thompson, N. (2006) *Anti-discriminatory Practice*, 4th edn. Basingstoke: Palgrave Macmillan. This is the definitive text on anti-discriminatory practice and is mandatory reading for social work students and probation trainees. Chapters 1 and 8 are of most relevance to the discussion in this chapter.

Young, J. (1999) *The Exclusive Society.* London: Sage: An insightful analysis of social exclusion and the conditions of contemporary society in which poor people are shunned and excluded.

References

Bennett, T. (1979) 'The social distribution of criminal labels', *British Journal of Criminology*, 19: 134–45.

Berman, G. and Mansky, A. (2005) 'Community justice centres: a US–UK exchange', *British Journal of Community Justice*, 3 (3): 5–14.

Blair T. (1993) Extract from speech, in P. Mandelson and R. Liddle (1996) *The Blair Revolution: Can New Labour Deliver?* London: Faber & Faber.

Blair, T. (1998) *The Third Way, New Politics for the New Century*, pamphlet no. 588. London: Fabian Society.

Cavadino, M. and Dignan, J. (2007) *The Penal System: An Introduction*, 4th edn. London: Sage.

Chambliss, W.J. and Mankoff, M. (1976) *Whose Law? What Order?* London: John Wiley & Sons.

Croall, H. (1992) *White Collar Crime.* Buckingham: Open University Press.

Dean, M. (1999) *Governmentality: Power and Rule in Modern Society.* London: Sage.

Department for Education and Skills (2005) *Reducing Reoffending through Skills and Employment*, Green Paper, Cmn 6702. London: Department for Education and Skills.

Etzioni, A. (1995) *The Spirit of Community: Rights, Responsibilities and the Communitarian Agenda.* London: Fontana.

Eysenck, H. (1969) 'The technology of consent', *New Scientist*, 26 June, pp. 688–90.

Foucault, M. (1982) 'The subject and power', in H.L. Dreyfus and P. Rabinow (eds), *Michel Foucault*, 2nd edn. Chicago: Chicago University Press.

Foucault, M. (1991) 'Governmentality', in G. Burchell, C. Gordon and P. Miller (eds), *The Foucault Effect: Studies in Governmentality.* London: Harvester.

Garland, D. (1996) 'The limits of the sovereign state: strategies of crime control in contemporary society', *British Journal of Criminology*, 36 (4): 445–71.

Garland, D. (1997) 'Governmentality and the problem of crime: Foucault, criminology, sociology', *Theoretical Criminology*, 1 (2): 173–214.

Garland, D. (2001) *The Culture of Control.* Oxford: Oxford University Press.

Gelsthorpe, L. (2007) 'Probation values and human rights', in L. Gelsthorpe and R. Morgan (eds), *Handbook of Probation.* Cullompton: Willan.

Giddens, A. (1998) *The Third Way: The Renewal of Social Democracy.* Cambridge: Polity Press.

Giddens, A. (2000) *The Third Way and Its Critics.* Cambridge: Polity Press.

Gill, M. (1997) 'Employing ex-offenders: a risk or an opportunity', *Howard Journal*, 36 (4): 337–51.

Hale, C. (2005) 'Economic marginalisation, social exclusion and crime', in C. Hale, K. Hayward and E. Wincup (eds), *Criminology.* Oxford: Oxford University Press.

Hall, S., Critcher, C., Jefferson, T., Clarke, J. and Roberts, B. (1978) *Policing the Crisis: Mugging, the State and Law and Order.* London: Macmillan.

Hirschi, T. (1969) *The Causes of Delinquency.* California: University of California Press.

Home Office (2003) *The Heart of the Dance: A Diversity Strategy for the National Probation Service for England and Wales 2002–2006.* London: NPS.

Hucklesby, A. (2002) 'Bail in criminal cases', in M. McConville and G. Wilson (eds), *The Handbook of the Criminal Justice Process.* Oxford: Oxford University Press.

Labour Party (2001) *Ambitions for Britain.* Manifesto.

Levitas, R. (1998) *The Inclusive Society? Social Exclusion and New Labour.* Basingstoke: Macmillan.

Liebling, A., Muir, G., Rose, G. and Bottoms, A. (1995) *Incentives and Earned Privileges for Prisoners – An Evaluation*, London: Home Office Research Findings No. 87. London: Home Office.

Marx, K. (1976) *Capital: A Critique of Political Economy*, Volume One. Harmondsworth: Penguin.

McCahill, M. (2002) *The Surveillance Web: The Rise of Visual Surveillance in an English City*. Cullompton: Willan.

McLaughlin, E. (2002) 'The crisis of the social and the political materialisation of community safety', in G. Hughes, E. McLaughlin and J. Muncie (eds), *Crime Prevention and Community Safety: New Directions*. London: Sage.

Miller, P. and Rose, N. (1990) 'Governing economic life', *Economy and Society*, 19 (1): 1–31.

Norris, C. and Armstrong, G. (1999) *The Maximum Surveillance Society: The Rise of CCTV*. Oxford: Berg.

Phillips, C. and Brown, D. (1998) *Entry into the Criminal Justice System: A Survey of Police Arrests and Their Outcomes*, Home Office Research Study No. 185. London: Home Office.

Prison Reform Trust (2007) *Bromley Briefings Prison Factfile*. London: Prison Reform Trust.

Punch, M. (1996) *Dirty Business: Exploring Corporate Misconduct Analysis and Cases*. London: Sage.

Quinney, R. (ed.) (1969) *Crime and Justice in Society*. Boston: Little, Brown.

Quinney, R. (1973) *Critique of Legal Order: Crime Control in Capitalist Society*. Boston: Little, Brown.

Quinney, R. (1977) *Class, State and Crime*. London: Longman.

Reiner, R. (2002) *The Politics of the Police*. Oxford: Oxford University Press.

Reiner, R. (2007) 'Political economy, crime and criminal justice', in M. Maguire, R. Morgan and R. Reiner (eds), *The Oxford Handbook of Criminology*, 4th edn. Oxford: Oxford University Press.

Respect Task Force (2006) *Respect Action Plan*. London: Home Office.

Rose, N. (1993) 'Government, authority and expertise in advanced liberalism', *Economy and Society*, 22 (3): 283–99.

Rose, N. (1996) 'The death of the social? Re-configuring the territory of government', *Economy and Society*, 25 (3): 327–56.

Rose, N. (2000) 'Government and control', *British Journal of Criminology*, 40 (2): 321–39.

Rose, N. and Miller, P. (1992) 'Political power beyond the state: problematics of government', *British Journal of Sociology*, 43 (2): 172–205.

Sarno, A., Hough, M., Nee, C. and Herrington, V. (1999) *Probation Employment Schemes in Inner London and Surrey – An Evaluation*, Home Office Research Findings No. 89. London: Home Office.

Secretary of State for Social Security and Minister for Welfare Reform (1998) *New Ambitions for our Country: A New Contract for Welfare*, Cm 3805. London: Stationery Office.

Slapper, G. and Tombs, S. (1999) *Corporate Crime*. London: Longman.

Smith, A. (1776) *An Inquiry into the Nature and Causes of the Wealth of Nations*. London: Routledge.

Social Exclusion Unit (2002) *Reducing Reoffending by Ex-Prisoners*. London: Office of the Deputy Prime Minister.

Stenson, K. (1993) 'Community policing as a governmental technology', *Economy and Society*, 22 (3): 373–89.

Stenson, K. (2000) 'Crime control, social policy and liberalism', in G. Lewis, S. Gewirtz and J. Clarke (eds), *Rethinking Social Policy*. London: Sage.

Stenson, K. (2001) 'The new politics of crime control', in K. Stenson and R.R. Sullivan (eds), *Crime, Risk and Justice: The Politics of Crime Control in Liberal Democracies*. Cullompton: Willan.

Sutherland, E.H. (1949) *White Collar Crime*. London: Holt, Rinehart & Winstone.

Taylor, I., Walton, P. and Young, J. (1973) *The New Criminology: For a Social Theory of Deviance*. London: Routledge.

Thompson, N. (1992) *Existentialism and Social Work*. Aldershot: Avebury.

Thompson, N. (2006) *Anti-discriminatory Practice*, 4th edn. Basingstoke: Palgrave Macmillan.

Trouton, A., Kavanagh, J., Oakley, A., Harden, A. and Powell, C. (2005) *A Summary of Ongoing Activity in the Use of Incentives schemes to Encourage Positive Behaviour in Young People*. London: EPPI Centre, Social Science Research Unit, Institute of Education, University of London.

Young, J. (2002) 'Crime and social exclusion', in M. Maguire, R. Morgan and R. Reiner (eds), *The Oxford Handbook of Criminology*, 3rd edn. Oxford: Oxford University Press.

Young, J. and Matthews, R. (2003) 'New Labour, crime control and social exclusion', in R. Matthews and J. Young (eds), *The New Politics of Crime and Punishment*. Cullompton: Willan.

Conclusion

A time of fear and excitement

Simon Green, Elizabeth Lancaster
and Simon Feasey

The premise of this book

The idea for this book was originally conceived in the autumn of 2005. Back then the three of us were responsible for managing the academic side of the diploma in probation training (DipPS) across Yorkshire and Humberside. At that time the future direction of probation training was unclear (and remains so at this time of writing) and we began to think about what might emerge from the organisational changes planned under the National Offender Management Service (NOMS). What became clear to us was that whatever training arrangement emerged there was very little published work about the skills and practices we were teaching on a daily basis. With the possibility that probation training might be taken away from higher education we felt that an important pool of knowledge and experience might be lost and it would be a good idea to bring this knowledge and experience together in a single volume.

Thus the idea behind this book was to try and bring together practitioners, academics and practice-trainers to write about and discuss the context, skills and values involved in working with offenders – a multi-agency book if you like. We have been less successful than we would have hoped, and liked, at recruiting people currently in practice, but at least half of the contributors in this edited collection either do, or have, worked in practice. Our aim was to create a comprehensive collection which would mainly focus on skills, while paying due attention to the context and values of work with offenders. Within the DipPS there are three core learning outcomes that govern the direction in which training takes place. Broadly speaking, these are:

- the integration of research and practice;
- personal reflection about learning and practice;
- awareness of diversity and anti-discriminatory practices.

It is our conviction that the combination of these three learning outcomes creates the framework for best practice when working with offenders. Hence, the chapters in this book are designed to bring together critical debates, real practice issues and awareness of moral and ethical dilemmas.

It should also be noted that this is not a book about the probation service. There are many good books about probation on the market and they will enlighten readers about the wider political and organisational debates in probation (e.g. Gelsthorpe and Morgan 2007; Ward *et al.* 2002; Mair 2004). Neither is this a book just for probation trainees. This is a book about working with offenders. It is for anyone interested in this area and we have striven, as far as possible, to keep the focus of the book on generic skills and issues rather than tie the focus to a particular organisation. With the growth of multi-agency and partnership work and with the likelihood that the private sector will become more and more involved in work with offenders this book is designed to provide a skills-based discussion of practice which will be relevant and applicable across all the different sectors and irrespective of organisation.

We have chosen to conclude with four key themes that emerge out of the chapters in this book and which have implications for how we address offending behaviour. These themes represent unresolved tensions that will help determine the future direction of work with offenders. Some of these tensions have caused anger, frustration and fear among practitioners and academics. While we share some of these concerns we are also cautiously excited about both the pace of change and its potential for improving current practice. Many changes still remain unfinished and the future direction of work with offenders hangs very much in the balance. But at least it isn't boring.

The criminal justice marketplace

Words like contestability and commissioning haunt those who work with offenders. Economic competition for service destabilises work with offenders and undermines the public service values that focus on the needs of individuals and society, replacing them with profit-margins and corporate image. The government's continuing ambition to bring together the public and the private sector affects all areas of public service and it is increasingly clear that work with offenders will be no exception. Problems with the privatisation of prisons do not help alleviate these anxieties and the expansion of this open market into the community could both jeopardise good working practices and undermine the legitimacy and authority of criminal justice. In addition to this, there are substantial issues for the voluntary and community sector in responding to the agenda of contestability and the commissioning of services clearly needs to be predicated on effective practice and proven delivery rather than just best value or crude cost-driven criteria.

While it would be naive in the extreme to ignore the dangers inherent in creating a mixed market in the criminal justice system, it need not be the case that the private sector spells doom for working with offenders in the community. Introducing the private sector could be used to help provide social and economic opportunities that are so far unavailable to offenders. Similarly, non-share distributing business models like cooperatives, community interest companies (CICs) and not-for-profit organisations could help bridge the gap between public and private sector values. Involving the private sector in the delivery of interventions represents both practical and political dangers which need to be thought through very carefully, yet there are also opportunities worth exploring.

The future of training

This book is partly aimed at the training needs of those who work with offenders. With the future of probation training still hanging in the balance and with the training opportunities for those working in the community and voluntary sectors still developing there remain important structural and practical questions about training which could impact significantly upon the success of other strategies. The separation of interventions work from case management in probation and its growing reliance upon its own risk assessment tools and accredited programmes creates a closed shop which could inhibit the development of multi-agency work and create barriers with other organisations.

Good training underpins good practice. Training arrangements are often thought about in territorial terms specific to the needs of particular organisations. Yet as we have tried to demonstrate in this text, skills are often generic and although they may be employed within different contexts and according to different organisational needs they can be learnt and shared cooperatively. Hence, a far-sighted training programme might provide a core of training available to many organisations which could help build both understanding and cooperation between organisations. Specialist or in-house training could then supplement this generic training. Instead of probation training, social work training or youth work training there would be engagement skills training, risk assessment training and interventions training. Training instils organisational cultures which can create barriers and exclude some groups. Both the voluntary and community sector would benefit from access to this level of skills training and while there would inevitably be financial and structural constraints this style of training could provide a fertile source of new and imaginative collaborations that help break down organisational barriers.

Managerialism and other values

Within this text there is a concern about the pervasive influence of managerialism. The audit culture, its key performance indicators, cost-effectiveness and evidence-led practice permeate nearly all areas of criminal justice and new directions and future strategies are increasingly considered in terms of their ability to meet management criteria. These criteria are often seen as contrary to the values of public service and the rehabilitative ethic. Managerialism has therefore become the embodiment of risk assessment, enforcement and control, while professional autonomy and public service represent rehabilitation and care.

For many practitioners and academics managerialism represents the antithesis of all that public service once meant. Either overtly or implicitly many discussions of work with offenders adopt this perspective. This polarisation of perspectives can inhibit innovation and create tensions between old and new working cultures. Managerialism creates accountability for public money and can be an active aid to good practice. While the invasive gaze of managerialism might well be both an insult and a threat to professionalism it can also be harnessed to determine levels of risk and inform sentences and interventions with offenders. Hence managerialism can also provide the basis for defensible decision-making in an increasingly emotive and litigious environment.

To ensure good practice requires practitioners to constantly reflect on their work and consider it, and themselves, in reference to wider ideas and developments. Without this, practice becomes inward and myopic. Managerialism can be an inhibitor to initiatives that resist measurement or are costly, but it can also help prevent squandering, poor practice and inertia. Managerialism is not, and should not, be the value-base itself and it is a mistake to think of it as such. Instead, managerialism is better thought of as a tool and guide for making cogent arguments for getting new ideas adopted.

Partners or competitors?

Partnership between agencies and the growing market in the criminal justice system suggest yet a further tension. How can there be partnership between organisations competing for resources? The answer to this is that funding is increasingly contingent upon partnership, and while agencies might compete for resources, they will need to work together to demonstrate their value for money and justify their necessity. To operate in isolation has become a dangerous strategy that invites questions about usefulness which can jeopardise continued funding.

As local authorities become more involved in the commissioning of services decisions about priorities will begin to shape the agendas of local and regional services. Local authorities are therefore becoming the vehicle by which funding priorities are decided. Examples such as the North Liverpool community justice centre demonstrate that these arrangements can work effectively. If so, the future will see a greater range of consortiums and conglomerates bidding together to provide combined services across an entire area. Thus partnership and the market are not opposing forces but evolving dialogues which will encourage organisations to find new ways to work together or face extinction.

And finally a note of optimism

Addressing offending behaviour is currently undertaken in a climate of rapid change in which the future direction of working with offenders remains unclear. Change can be frightening, it can be exhausting and it can be confusing. Recent years have seen unprecedented levels of change in the criminal justice sector. New legislation, new policies and incessant reorganisation have become commonplace and there is no real reason to expect this to stop any time soon. This does not sound very optimistic but for all the fear and anxiety caused by change it can also be motivating, innovative and, most of all, exciting. Whether change is viewed as frightening or exciting depends to a large extend on how it is responded to.

For too long addressing offending behaviour has been trapped between a care and control discourse that has dominated the process of change and how people have responded to it. This discourse either directly or implicitly filters into most debates about working with offenders. Yet it is a stifling debate between two polarised factions that seem more intent on defeating each other than generating new ways of thinking. Change can help liberate us from this quandary. We believe some of the chapters in this text start to do that by providing new perspectives and approaches for thinking and talking about addressing offending behaviour. Our hope, therefore, is that not only will this book provide a very useful resource about the context, practice and values of addressing offending behaviour, but that it can also play a part in helping to set the agenda for the future.

References

Gelsthorpe, L. and Morgan, R. (2007) *Handbook of Probation*. Cullompton: Willan.
Mair, G. (2004) *What Matters in Probation*. Cullompton: Willan.
Ward, D., Scott, J. and Lacey, M. (2002) *Probation: Working for Justice*, 2nd edn. Oxford: Oxford University Press.

Appendix

Useful websites

Alcohol Concern
www.alcoholconcern.org.uk/servlets/home
Barnardo's
www.barnardos.org.uk/
Centre for Crime and Justice Studies
www.crimeandjustice.org.uk
Citizens Advice
www.citizensadvice.org.uk/
Clinks
www.clinks.org/(S(aln43t45huexiyiw2m5cgxab))/index.aspx
Cognitive Centre Foundation UK
www.cognitivecentre.com/prosocial_programmes.htm
Community Justice Portal
cjp.org.uk/servlet/PageServer
Community Safety
www.homeoffice.gov.uk/crime-victims/reducing-crime/community-safety/
Criminal Justice System On-line
www.cjsonline.org/index.html
Crimlinks.com
www.crimlinks.com/
Department for Constitutional Affairs
www.dca.gov.uk/
Domestic Violence
www.homeoffice.gov.uk/crime-victims/reducing-crime/domestic-violence/
  and www.duluth-model.org
Home Office
www.homeoffice.gov.uk/
Howard League for Penal Reform
www.howardleague.org/
Learning and Skills Council
www.lsc.gov.uk/

Mind (National Association for Mental Health)
www.mind.org.uk/
Ministry of Justice
www.justice.gov.uk/
Ministry of Justice Inspectorates
inspectorates.justice.gov.uk/
Motivational Interviewing
www.motivationalinterview.org/
National Archives
www.nationalarchives.gov.uk/
National Association for the Care and Resettlement of Offenders
www.nacro.org.uk/
National Offender Management Service
www.noms.homeoffice.gov.uk/
National Probation Directorate
www.probation.homeoffice.gov.uk/output/Page1.asp
National Statistics
www.statistics.gov.uk/
National Treatment Agency
www.nta.nhs.uk/
Police Reform
police.homeoffice.gov.uk/police-reform/
Police Service
www.police.uk/
Prison Reform Trust
www.prisonreformtrust.org.uk/
Prison Service
www.hmprisonservice.gov.uk/
Radical practice
www.radical.org.uk/barefoot/
Restorative Justice Consortium
www.restorativejustice.org.uk/
Shelter
england.shelter.org.uk/home/index.cfm
Skills for Justice
www.skillsforjustice.com/default.asp?PageID=1
Social Exclusion Unit
www.cabinetoffice.gov.uk/social_exclusion_task_force.aspx
Solution Focused Therapy
www.brieftherapy.org.uk/
SOVA (Supporting Others through Volunteer Action)
www.sova.org.uk/
Victim Support
www.victimsupport.org.uk/
Youth Justice Board
www.yjb.gov.uk/en-gb/

Index